1 MONTH OF FREE READING

at

www.ForgottenBooks.com

By purchasing this book you are eligible for one month membership to ForgottenBooks.com, giving you unlimited access to our entire collection of over 1,000,000 titles via our web site and mobile apps.

To claim your free month visit:

www.forgottenbooks.com/free912864

* Offer is valid for 45 days from date of purchase. Terms and conditions apply.

ISBN 978-0-265-93935-2
PIBN 10912864

This book is a reproduction of an important historical work. Forgotten Books uses state-of-the-art technology to digitally reconstruct the work, preserving the original format whilst repairing imperfections present in the aged copy. In rare cases, an imperfection in the original, such as a blemish or missing page, may be replicated in our edition. We do, however, repair the vast majority of imperfections successfully; any imperfections that remain are intentionally left to preserve the state of such historical works.

Forgotten Books is a registered trademark of FB &c Ltd.
Copyright © 2018 FB &c Ltd.
FB &c Ltd, Dalton House, 60 Windsor Avenue, London, SW19 2RR.
Company number 08720141. Registered in England and Wales.

For support please visit www.forgottenbooks.com

THE
Publications
OF
The Harleian Society.

ESTABLISHED A.D. MDCCCLXIX.

Volume LVII.

FOR THE YEAR MDCCCCVIII.

The Four Visitations of Berkshire,

1532, 1566, 1623, 1665-6.

Vol. II.

ADDITIONAL PEDIGREES AND NOTES.

EDITED BY

W. HARRY RYLANDS, F.S.A.

LONDON:
1908.

Introduction.

IN the first place I must refer to some necessary corrections to the first Volume:—

Pages 5 and 22, add a ? to the words "alias Lyons," under the Arms of Chocke. I think the writer of the addition on page 22, from the Caius Coll. MS., "Witheridge alias Lyons," refers more to the Arms than to the name of the family. In the grant of a Crest (page 106) the Arms are simply attributed to Witherige by Robert Cooke, and Lyons is not mentioned. Perhaps until some other evidence is produced we may conclude that, as the Arms of Witherige were according to the Patent "Argent, a Chevron sables betweene thre Lyons cowshant gules," the Arms of Lyons may have been "Argent, a chevron between three lions couchant Gules." There is nothing "coward" about the lions; and the piece of glass illustrated by Mr. Paul* must, one would think from the colours, have referred to the family of Lyons, and not to that of Chocke.

Page 10, for "Newborough," it may be necessary to substitute "Merebrooke."

Page 11, the charges in the Arms of Fraye are, as is usual, tricked as "bee-hives;" they should be "fig frays."

Page 44, More of Cookham, add the Christian names [William] Berkeley, [John] Byrde.

Page 55, Tyghall. The third John Tyghall was the son of [Robert].

Page 223, Hugh Hene married [Catherine] da. of [Anthony] Bickerstaffe.

* See an interesting Paper on The Arms of Lyons of Long Ashton, Somerset, by Roland W. Paul, F.S.A., in the Proceedings of the Clifton Antiq. Club, 1904-1908, vol. vi., 1908, pp. 208—215.

INTRODUCTION.

Page 244, Lyford of Hurley, after Speprue add [*Sheprue*].

Page 273, in the pedigree of Rich of Sonning the italics in brackets, "Sir, K^t Alderman," should be struck out. They were added, as the Townsend MS. included these words in the running text. Reference may be made to "Some account of the Lord Mayors and Sheriffs of the City of London, 1601 to 1625," compiled by G. E. Cokayne, London, 1897, p. 83 *n.*, where the confusion so often found between the two men named William Cokayne is fully cleared up. I am indebted to the writer of this book for the correction.

The present Volume contains nearly all the flotsam and jetsam gathered during the time the four Visitations of Berkshire were under consideration.

With the exception of the List of those summoned to attend Ashmole and deliver their Arms and Pedigrees, I have again arranged the various Pedigrees and Notes in alphabetical order for convenience of reference. The Table of Contents shews at once the description of the different items.

The copies of the Grants of Arms preserved in MS. Ashmole 858, fol. 189, etc., being those exhibited to him at the Visitation made in 1665-6, have been supplemented from MSS. in the College of Arms, and other MS. Books of Grants in private collections.

In the Introduction to Vol. I. there were printed some letters referring to the obstructions put in Ashmole's way in following the usual custom, that a Herald going on Visitation could obtain copies of the earlier Visitations of the county he was about to visit. It is certain that he obtained a copy of that made in 1623, which he himself transcribed, the signatures to the Pedigrees being imitated. This is preserved in MS. Ashmole 852, pp. 235 to 385, and was the text used for the copy printed in Vol. I.

In the same Volume (MS. Ashmole 852) is another set of Pedigrees, some of which will be found printed in the present Volume. Mr. W. H. Black, in his catalogue of the Ashmole MSS., describes Part I. of MS. Ashmole 852 as "Pedigrees taken at sundry Visitations of Berkshire reduced into one Alphabetical Series by Elias Ashmole, Windsor Herald."

INTRODUCTION.

They occupy pages 1 to 202, and of this portion of the Volume Mr. Black remarks that they "seem to have been written later than the following MS. [*i.e.*, the copy of the Visitation of 1623], which is bound up with it."

The Pedigrees are, many of them, taken from the Visitation of 1566, but there are some additional ones, and these I have printed in the present volume. Unfortunately their origin is not even suggested.

Without having had any opportunity of comparing them, I think that the first part of MS. Ashmole 852 is a copy of either Vincent's or Philipott's Berkshire collections, probably the latter, and that Ashmole, finding the official copy of the 1566 Visitation was not sufficiently complete, chose the MS. of one, or it may be of both, or made a combination of or selection from the works of the other two Heralds.

Some, at least, of these additional Pedigrees appear to have been copied from the original papers, thrown out for one reason or another, at the time the office copy was made; others seem to have been compiled in order to fill the blanks between the Pedigrees entered at different Visitations, and thus shew the continuous existence of the family.

In the present Volume will be found transcripts of the original copies, signed by the head of each family, of at least eighteen Pedigrees, prepared for the Visitation made in 1665-6, and thrown out by Ashmole, principally because certain fees of entry could not be obtained. The reason is stated in many instances on the Pedigrees themselves, "fee unpaid," etc., having been added.

It is thus clear that a Visitation was not an official record of the Gentry of a County, but comprised only the Pedigrees of those who were prepared to pay the Fees of Entry.

Of course it is impossible to say that these thrown-out Pedigrees, now found in MS. Rawlinson, D. 865, are all that were so treated, and indeed if the list of those summoned to appear at the Visitation is studied it will be found that in a number of cases there is no explanation given why the Pedigrees were not recorded.

It is almost needless to point out that these eighteen Pedigrees, having been received and written out by the Herald, and signed by the head of each family,* are of equal value with those entered in the Visitation Book of 1665-6, as the mere fact of the non-payment of the fees cannot,

---

* They were "entered" in the first instance; see the letters, pp. 91 and 178.

of course, in any way depreciate the quality of the information they contain.

A somewhat similar instance is referred to by the late Dr. Jackson Howard in his edition of the Visitation of London made in 1568 (p. 13). " The Pedigree of White, prepared in 1568, but not entered in the vellum Visitation-book, G. 10, at the College of Arms, appears in F. 1 " [the original papers from which it was compiled] " at fol. 318."

Some few Pedigrees have also been added from the Harleian MSS., the number being given in every instance.

The text I have called the Smith MS. is a copy made, I believe, by Samuel Stebbing, Somerset Herald, about the year 1708. The full title of the book is, "The Visitation of Berkshire made in Anno 1566 By William Harvey al's Clarenceux King of Armes, Transcripta et Augmentata p' Will^{mum} Smith al's Rougedragon Anno 1600."

The Tricks of Arms are in every case copies of the original drawings, and every addition made by myself is in italics, within square brackets.

When the volumes containing copies of all the inscriptions in the Churches of Berkshire, visited by Ashmole, are issued, it will be possible to increase the Armorial of the County, and to add some dates and other information to the fleshless skeletons of the Visitations.

In some instances the series of interesting letters received by Ashmole during the time of his. Visitation, as also some Arms and Pedigrees, seemed to require a little addition, and if it be considered that I have now and then gone beyond my tether I would plead the words of so great an authority as Sir William Dugdale: "I am as willing to confine my selfe to ye circuite of this Shire as he or any man can be to desire it; but they y^t understand what belongs to these things cannot but know that now and then a little light at a remote distance will helpe much."

My thanks are due to my friend Everard Green, Esq., F.S.A., Rouge Dragon, for his kindly interest in my efforts to gather in the flotsam and jetsam of Berkshire contained in the present Volume.

W. HARRY RYLANDS.

Contents.

	PAGE
Disclaimers at the Visitation, 1623	1
Disclaimers at the Visitation, 1665-6	2-4
Justices of the Peace, 1665	4-5
High Constables and Bailiffs, 1665	5
Mayors of Towns, 1665	v
The Corporation of Newbury, 1665	6
The Corporation of New.Windsor, 1665	6-7
The Corporation of Maidenhead, 1665	7
The Corporation of Reading, 1665	ɩ
The Corporation of Wallingford, 1665	o
Warrants; to whom delivered, 1665	8
Places where Ashmole sat during the Visitation, 1665	8-9
List of Householders in Berkshire, 1665-66	9-47
ALBERY of Wokingham. Patent, 1590	48
ALDRIDGE of Old Windsor, for the Visitation, 1665-6	48
ALDRIDGE of Charlton, near Wantage, for the Visitation, 1665-6	49
ALDWORTH of Aldworth. Exemplification of Arms, 1623	49
ALDWORTH of Reading and Wargrave, ? for the Visitation, 1623	50
AMORE	51
ANGEL of Binfield. Letter.	51
ANGEL of Binfield. Visitation of Surrey, 1662-68	51
ARMORER. Patent of Augmentation, 1662	52-53
ATMORE of Bray.	53-54
AVELYNE of Frogmore	54-55
BABHAM of Cookham. Visitation of Bucks, 1634	56
BACKHOUSE. Patent of Arms, 1574	57
BACKHOUSE. Patent of Arms, 1579	58

CONTENTS.

	PAGE
BAKER. Patent of Arms, 1579	59
BAKER. Patent of Arms, 1573	60
BAKER of New Windsor. Patent of Arms, 1655	61
BALL of Barkham. Visitation of London, 1633-5	62
BAMFIELD. Patent of Arms, 1604	63
BARKER of Newbury. Original Paper, Visitation, 1665-6	63-64
BARKER of Sunning. Pedigree, 1619 (?)	64
BARNES of Bray, for the Visitation, 1665-6	65
BARNES of Bray. Letter, 1666	65
BARON of Reading. Arms	66
BASKERVYLE of Bayworth and Sunningwell. Orig. Paper, Visitation, 1665-6	66
BEISLEY of Abingdon. Letter, ? 1665	67
BELL of Lawrence Waltham. Arms	67
BELLAMY. Patent of Arms, 1571	68
BELLINGHAM of Finchamsted. Visitation of Wilts, 1565	69
BESSELLS of Besselsleigh	69-70
BLAGRAVE	70-71
BLAGRAVE. Visitation of London, 1687—1700	72-73
BLAKE of Reading. Letter, 1665	73
BOND of Bray	74
BOSTOCK	74-79
BOULSTRODE of Upton (? co. Bucks)	79-80
BRADLEY of Wokingham. Visitation of Yorkshire, 1665	80-81
BRAHAM of New Windsor. Patent of Arms, 1646	81-82
BRAYBROOKE of Bright Waltham	82
BRAYBROOKE of Bright Waltham. Visitation of Oxford, 1634	83
BRIGHTWELL of Padworth, for the Visitation, 1665-6	84
BRINCKHURST of Bisham. Visitation of Bucks, 1634	84-85
BROWNE alias MOSES of Wokingham. Visitation of London, 1633-5	85
BULLOCK of Arborfield	86
BURLEY of Wokingham. Visitation of Surrey, 1623	86
BURREN of Reading. Visitation of London, 1687—1700	87
CALCOTT or CALDECOTT of Abingdon. Visitation of Leicestershire, 1682-3	87-88
CALCOTT of Abingdon. Arms	89

CONTENTS.

	PAGE
CALTON of Milton, for the Visitation of 1665-6	90
CALTON of Milton. Letter, 1665	91
CASTELLION of Benham Valence	91-92
CASTELLION of Benham Valence. Draft of Patents, 1563	94-95
CASTELLION of Benham Valence. Draft of Patent, 1597	96-97
CATCHER of Binfield. Visitation of London, 1633-5	97
CATER of Letcombe Regis. Patent of Arms, 1559	98-99
CHAMPION of Reading	99-102
CHENEY of Woodhey	102-105
CHOKE of Avington. Patent of Arms, 1576	106-107
CHOCK of Avington. Note of a Charter	107
CLARKE of Ardington	108
CLAVILE	109
COLLINS of Betterton. Letter, 1666	109-110
COLLINS of Betterton. Patent of Arms, 1672	110
CURTEYS of Enborne. Patent of Arms, 1559	111
DALBY of Reading. Original Paper for the Visitation, 1665-6	111-112
DANCASTLE of Wellhouse. Patent of Arms, 1586	112
DAY of Windsor. Patent of Arms, 1582	113
DEANE of Wallingford. Visitation of Hampshire, 1622—34	114
DENTON of Witham. Visitation of Oxfordshire, 1574-5	115-116
DRAPER of Sunninghill. Letter, 1665	117
DRAPER. Visitation of London, 1634-5	117
DRAPER, Thomas. Funeral Certificate, 1631	118
DRAPER of Stroud Green. Patent of Arms, 1612	118-119
DRAPER of Sunninghill	119
DRAPER of Sunninghill. Arms	120
EDMANDS of Inkpen, for the Visitation, 1665-6	120
ENGLEFIELD of Englefield. Letter, 1664 (1665)	121
ENGLEFIELD of Englefield	121-124
ESSEX of Lamborne	124-125
EVERARD. Patent of Arms	126

CONTENTS.

	PAGE
FERRERS of Cookham. Visitation of London, 1633-5.	126
FETIPLACE of Buckland. Original Paper for the Visitation, 1665-6	127
FETTIPLACE of Lambourne. Original Paper for the Visitation, 1665-6	127-128
FLEGG of Bray. Note of Arms	128
FULLER or FULWAR of Chamberhouse	128-130
GARDINER of White Waltham. Note of Arms	131
GARRARD of Newbury, for the Visitation, 1665-6	131
GAULTON of Ashampsted. Note of Arms	131
GEFFE or JEFFE of Enborne. Patent of Arms, 1579	132
GOODYER of New Windsor. Patent of Arms, 1579	132
GOSSON of Binfield. Letter, 1666	133
GOSSON of Binfield. Patent of Arms, 1608	133
GYLES of Windsor	134
GWYNNE of Windsor. Visitation of London, 1633-5	134-135
HALLSTED of Sonning. Visitation of London, 1633-5	135-136
HALSTEDD of Sonning. Patent of Arms, 1628	136
HANSON of Blewbury. Visitation of London, 1664	137
HARECOURT of Witham	138
HARRIS of New Windsor	138-139
HARISON of Beech Hill. Letter, 1665	139
HARRISON of Hurst	140
HARRISON of Reading. Visitation of London, 1633-5	141
HATT of Leckampsted. Visitation of London, 1633-5	142
HAYES of Windsor. Patent of Arms, 1661	143
HAYNES of Reading. Patent of Arms, 1578	144
HENN or HENE of Winkfield. Patent of Arms, 1642	145
HERBERT of Arborfield. Letter, 1664 (1665)	146
HILL. Patent of Arms, 1618	146
HOBY of Bisham. Letters, 1665-6-7	147-149
HOBY of Bisham. Patent of Arms, 1570	149-150
HOBY of Bisham. Draft of a Grant of Arms, 1664	150-151
HOBY of Bisham. Grant of Arms, 1664	151-152
HOLLOWAY of Sunningwell. Letter, 1665	152

CONTENTS.

xiii

	PAGE
HOLLOWAY of Sunningwell. Visitation of Oxford, 1634	153
HOPER of Sonning, for the Visitation, 1665-6	154
HORDE of Shilton. Visitation of Oxfordshire, 1634	155
HUNGERFORD of Buscott. Original Paper for the Visitation, 1665-6	156
HYDE of South Denchworth. Patent of Crest, 1600	156-157
HYDE, ATTE HYDE of Denchworth	157
HYDE of Kingston Lisle. Letter, 1664 (1665)	158
HYDE of Pangborn. Letter, 1665	158
HYDE of Wallingford. Visitation of London, 1633-5	159
JOANES of Welford	159
JUSTICE of Reading. Patents of Arms, 1551, 1574	160
KETE or KEATE of Hagborne, Lockinge, etc.	160-162
KEATE of Hagborne. Visitation of London, 1633-5	162-163
KEATE of Cholsey. Letter, 1664 (1665)	163
KEMBLE. Patent of Arms, 1602	164
KENT of Avington, for the Visitation, 1665-6	164-165
KIRTON. Note about the Arms	165
KNIGHT of Reading. Letter, 1665	166
KNIGHT of Ruscombe. Note about Arms	166
LANGLEY. Visitation of Yorkshire, 1666	167
LANGTON of Staneswick. Note about Crest	167
LAWRENCE of Chilton, for the Visitation of 1665-6	168
LEDER. Note about Arms	168
LENTHALL of Bessels Leigh, for the Visitation, 1665-6	169
LENTHALL of Besselsleigh	169-171
LOVEDAY	171
LOVEDEN of Loveden. Patent of Arms (? 1589)	172
LYFORD of Hurley. Original Papers for the Visitation, 1665-6	172-174
LYTCOTT. Visitation of London, 1687—1700	174-176
LYTELL of Bray. Note about the Arms	177
MARSHALL of Blewbury. Note about the Arms	177
MARYETT of Remenham. Patent of Arms, 1586	177-178

CONTENTS.

	PAGE
MAYOTT of Abingdon. Letter, 1665	178
MICHELL of Old Windsor. Patent of Arms, 1581	179
MILLS of Knightington. Patent of Arms, 1588	180
MORLAND of Sulhamstead. Visitation of London, 1687—1700	180-181
NEVILL of Billingbere	181
NEWBURY of Wolfines. Visitation of Worcestershire, 1682-3	182
NEWMAN. Patent of Arms, 1664	183-184
NORRIS of Fyfield and Yattenden. ? Visitation, 1566	184-186
ORPWOOD of Abingdon	186-187
ORPWOOD of Apleford, for the Visitation, 1665-6	187
PACKER of Donington, for the Visitation, 1665-6	187-188
PALMER of Wokingham	188-190
PALMER of Wokingham. Patent of Arms, 1665	190-191
PARRY of Hampstead Marshall	191
PAUL of Bray	191-192
PAUL. Patent of Arms, 1660	192-193
PECK of Remenham. Visitation of London, 1633-5	193
PERROT of Fyfield	193-194
PHELIPES of Hurst. Note about Arms	194
PHIPPS of Reading, for the Visitation, 1665-6	195
PICTON of Wyvill Court	195
PLEYDELL of Shrivenham. Original Paper, Visitation, 1665-6	196
POCOCK of Chieveley	196-197
POCOCK. Patent of Arms, 1761	197
POCOCKE of Childrey. Letter, 1664 (1665)	198
POWLE. Patent of Arms, 1569	198-199
POYNANT. Patent of Arms, 1508	199-200
PUSEY of Pusey. Original Paper for the Visitation, 1665-6	200-201
QUARLES. Patent of Arms, 1577	201-202
READE of Barton. Patent of Arms, 1597	202
READE of Pumney, for the Visitation, 1665-6	202-203

CONTENTS.

	PAGE
READE of Barton	203-205
REYNALDS. Note about the Arms	205
RYDER of Newbury. Patent of Arms, 1662	205-206
SAMBOURNE of Aston Tirrold. Letter, 1664 (1665)	206
SAMPSON of Binfield	207
SCOWLES of Charlton. Patent of Arms, 1613	208
SMITH of Abingdon. Visitation of London, 1633-5	208-209
SMITH of Abingdon. Visitation of London, 1687—1700	209-210
SMITH of Bray. Visitation of Middlesex, 1663	210-211
SMITH of Cookham and Bray. Visitation of London, 1664	211
SMITH of Bray. Patent of Arms, 1654	212
SMITH of Old Windsor. Letter, 1665	213
SMITH of Old Windsor. Patent of Arms, 1671	213
SNOWBALL of Old Windsor. Visitation of Northamptonshire, 1564	214
SOUTHBY of Careswell. Patent of Arms, 1631	214
STAFFORD of Bradfield	215
STAMPE of Moulsford. Patent of Arms, 1586 (?)	216
STONHOUSE of Radley. Letter, 1665	216
STONHOUSE of Radley	217
STONHOUSE of Radley, for the Visitation, 1665-6	217
STONHOUSE of Radley. Patent of Arms, 1556	218
SYMS or SIMS. Patent of Arms, 1591	218
THOROLD of Binfield, for the Visitation, 1665-6	219
THORNE of Sonning. Visitation of Surrey, 1572	219
TOUCHET of Southcott. Letter, 1665	220
TRUMBALL of East Hampstead. Patent of Arms, 1662	220-221
UNTON of Wadley	221-222
WAKE of Windsor. Visitation of Bucks, 1634	223
WATTYS. Patent of Arms, 1503	223
WELLESBORNE of Hanney	224
WHITE of Wokingham. Letter	225

CONTENTS.

	PAGE
WHITLOCK of Wokingham. Letter, 1664 (1665)	225
WHITLOCK of Wokingham. Visitation of Surrey, 1662—1668 . .	225-226
WHITLOCK of Wokingham. Visitation of London, 1633—1635 . . .	226
WHITLOCK of Wokingham. Visitation of Buckingham, 1634 . .	226-227
WICKHAM of Abingdon. Affidavit, 1635	228
WILKINSON of Laurence Waltham. Original Note for the Visitation, 1665-6	228-229
WILLIAMS of Burfield. Note about the Arms	229
WILMOTT of Letcombe Regis. Patent of Arms, 1627	230-231
WINCH of Fifield. Letter about Arms, 1667	231
WINCHCOMBE of Newbury. Patent of Arms, 1549	232-233
WINCHCOMBE of Newbury	233
WINTERSELL of Sutton. Visitation of Wiltshire, 1565	234
YATE of Buckland. Note about Arms	234
YONGE of Basildon. Patent of Arms, ? 1607	235
YONGE. Crest	235
YONG of Basildon and Wittenham. Note about Arms	235

...mina et Arma Equitum Auratorum de Com Berks, qui cum ...ardo Primo Rege, Stipendia merebant in Scotia, et alibi.

S.r T. Coudrey	S.r Rob. Archard	S.r Ric. Jockeram	S.r Rob: Grindlesham
S.r John De la River	S.r John De la Hoest	S.r John Leyham	S.r Philip Martell Baron 33. Edw. 1.
S.r Roger Englefeild	S.r Wm. Videlou	S.r John Beche	S.r Ric. Windsor
	S.r John Foxley.		

Visitations of Berkshire.

DISCLAIMERS AT THE VISITATION MADE IN THE YEAR 1623.

[*MS. Ashmole 852, f. 385.*]

Wee whose names are here vnder subscribed do disclaime to beare Armes, or to vse the title of Squire or Gentleman; and doe promise from henceforth not to take vpon vs the title of Squire or Gentleman any more.

Francis Hurlock.
Robert Philipson.
Will: Fynmore.
Rich: Kys [*Keys of Benham?*].

Disclaimed at Abingdon, Berks.

[*Charles*] Tucker of Abingdon Esquire. no proofe of his Armes.
Hugh Keate of Hagborne no gent:
.... Tutball of Chelsewell.
Robert Philips of Comner.
William Lane of the same.
.... Hurlock of Kennington.
Thomas Shury of Marcham.
Thomas Stevens of Steventon.
William Fynmore of Witenham longa.
Thomas Wilcocks disct [*? of the same*].
Nath: Hagthorne of Cookham.
John Page Disct [*? of the same*].
Thomas Quatermaine disct [*? of the same*].
Rich: Powning disct [*? of the same*].
Rich: Sawcer als Cisu of Reading [*al's Sesdio*].
John Williams disclaimed at Burfield.
Rich: Cyes of Benham [*? Ayes or Eyes*].
Richard Whyte disclaimed, of Hurst.
James Winch of Purley.
Richard Pottinger of Burfield.
Vincent Goddard.
Reynold Brooke.
Michaell Woodyer of Cookham.
Thomas Turner.
Thomas Godfrey of Maidenhead.
Thomas Castle of Est Hendred.
John Keate of Locking.
Rich: Booth of Sparsholt.
Tho: Dolman.
Rich: Keyes of Benham.
George Goddard of Brimpton.

DISCLAIMERS AT THE VISITATION MADE IN THE YEARS 1665-1666.

[*MS. Ashmole 851.*]

Wee whose Names are herevnder written, being duly summoned by Elias Ashmole Esqr Windsor Herald at Armes Deputy & Marshall to Sr Edward Bysshe Knight Clarenceux King of Armes, in his Visitacōn of the County of Berke : aswell for the approving & iustifying our bearing of Armes, as the taking vpon vs the Names & Titles of Esquires or Gentlemen : and not being able to shew any good proofe or right to either of those Titles ; nor knowing of any Armes belonging to vs, do hereby disclaime all such Attributes & Armes ; And doe promise henceforth to forbeare to make vse of either, vntill such tyme as we can by lawfull authority do the same.

William Markham of Reading.
Thomas Martin of Ockingham.
The marke of O O Edmund Verney of Ockingham.
Thomas Miller of Wokingham.
William Mills of Reading.
Ralph Reddall of Whitley.
William Cooke of Wallingford.
Thomas Norton of Wallingford.
Richard Kirby of Wallingford.
Moses Slade of the same.
John Rusden of Wallingford.
John Leaver of Brightwell.
William Leaver of Brightwell.
The marke N of Thomas Leaver of Brightwell.
The Marke R of Ralph Whistler of Brightwell.
The marke of W of William Leaver of North-Morton.
Clement Stiles of South-Morton.
Christopher Alnewick of Aston Terold.
The marke of U Edward Sawyer of Dudcott.
Thomas Buckridge of Basseldon.
Robert Sayer of Coscutt.
Jonathan Sayer of East-Hagborne.
Robert Hyde of East-Hagborne Jū.
Richard Blake of Dudcott.
W[*illiam*] Garnam of Catmere.   Memorand. that Mr Garnam hath
William Price of Farnborough.   entred his descent in this Visi-
John Head of West Ildsley.   tacōn, since he disclaimed.
John Allin of Basledon.
John Pocock of East-Ilsly.
The marke I of John Allen of Compton.
Richard Pottinger of Compton.
Thomas Basset of Wallingford.
Robert Jennings of Dudcott.
Joseph Pearse of South-Hinksey.
Walter Whightwick of Appleton.
The marke *J* of John Lane of Appleton.
John Knapp of Swinford.
John Finmore of Abbingdon, for my father
William Finmore of North-Hinksey and for my selfe.
Henry Ranckell of Botly, for my father
Peter Ranckell of Botly & for my selfe.
Francis Shury of Marcham.

DISCLAIMERS 1665-6.

Thomas Ring of Comner [*Wring written by another hand*].
Edward Cleue of Wotton.
Peter Stephens of Appleton.
Robert Payne of Abbingdon.
Laurence Farr of Farringdon.
John Loder of Stanford.
John Loder of Shellingford, the son of the aforesaid John Loder.
Thomas Warwick of litle Farringdon.
Alexander Tavie [*Tanne: Tame*] of Sparsholt.
Thomas White of Aishbury.
John Cox of Ardington.
John Doe of East Lockinge.
Francis Pearce of East Lockinge.
Thomas Saunders of Hardwell.
John Cole of the parish of Ashbury.
John Collins of Betterton.   Memorand that after this disclaimer he entred his descent.
Jeremy Hand of Newbury.
John Curr of Kintbury Eaton.
Thomas Cheney of Shaborne cum Bagshott.
William Smith of the same.
Richard Fanner of Newbury.
John Edmunds of the Parish of Inkpen.
Richard Pocock of Chiuely.
Adam Head of Letcombe Basset.
William Meere of Enboren.
Thomas Causlade of Newbery.
Richard Mathew of Hampsted Norris.
Giles Spicer of Leckhampsted.
Richard Hall of Leckhampsted.
Henry Blagrave of Leckhampsted.
Giles Blagrave of Brightwalton.
John Stroude of West-Shefford.
Arthur Wollgar of Bucklebury.
John Pocock of Woolly.
John Saunders of Chadleworth.
William Young of Whatcombe.
Timothy Lucas of Hungerford.
Adam Blandy of Letcombe Basset.
John Blandy of Inglewood.
John Watts of Wood-Spene.
William Pearce of Newbery.
Francis Coxhead of Newbery.
John Merriman of Newbery.
George Cawslade of Newbery.
Clement Marlow of Reading.
James Maynard of Reading.
Humfry Mason of Reading.
William Wilder of Reading.
Thomas Aylioyn of Reading.
George Sanders of Sulhampsted Banister.
Henry Sharpe of Reading.
John Silverwood of Reading.
Symon Beckley of Fifield in Bray.
Edmund Paxton of Fifield aforesaid.
James Seaward of Fifield in Bray.
Robert [*? Richard*] Powney of Hawthorne in Bray.
Richard Taylour of Hurley.

NOTES : VISITATION 1665-6.

John Aunger of Hurley.
Samuel Winder of Bray.
Henry Bolstrode of Warfeild.
Thomas Barker of Easthampsted.
George Knap of Chilton.
Thomas Stratton of Shrevenham.
Thomas Pearce of Knighton.
Robert Hide the elder of Harwell.
Robert Southby of Borton.
Lawrence Whistler of Moulsford.
John Peck of Abinton.
Gregory Geering of South-Denchworth.
John Phelp[s] of Shinfield.
The marke M of Moses Maynard of Winhurst in Hurst.
Thomas Langford of West Shafford.
Thomas Richards of Shinfield.
William Louch of Marlstone.
Edward Jennings of Harwell.
James Jennings of Long Wittnam.
William Grove of Grove.
Roger Knight of Childrey.
Henry Webb of Kintbery-Amsbury.
Thomas Kent of Avington.
Thomas Powell of Thatcham.
Francis Powell of the same.
William Stroud of Ruscombe.
Angell Bell of Wokingham.
John Harding of Ashbery.

[*MS. Rawl. D. 865, fol. 34ᵇ.*]

JUSTICES OF PEACE. [*1665.*]

K⁺ of yᵉ shire	John Lovelace Esqʳ *Lᵈ Lovelace son.*	
	Hen: Moore Barᵗ *Farley.*	
B. of Abingdon	Ger: Stonehouse Barᵗ.	
	Geor: Pratt Barᵗ.	
	Cæsar Coldclough Barᵗ.	
	Tho: Drap Barᵗ.	
	Tho: Rich Barᵗ.	
B. for Windsor	Rich: Braham Kᵗ & Barᵗ.	
Kᵗ of yᵉ shier	Rich: Powle Kᵗ of yᵉ Bath.	
	Ed: Sayer Kᵗ.	
	Wᵐ Armorer Kᵗ.	
	Robᵗ Pye Kᵗ.	
B. for Redᵍ	Tho: Doleman Kᵗ.	
	Jo: Fettiplace Kᵗ *Childrey.*	
	Jo: Davis Kᵗ.	
	W: Backhouse Bar.	
	Humfry Hyde Esqʳ *Kᵉston.*	Esqʳ.
	Rich: Nevill *Billingbeare*	,,
	Perigrin Hobby *Bysham*	,,
	Wᵐ Barker *Sunning*	..
	Rich: Harrison *Hurst*	
	Hen: Barker Clerke of yᵉ Crowne	,,
Burg: p Reddᵍ	Rich: Aldworth *Ruscombe*	

JUSTICES, ETC. 1665-6.

Burg: p Redd* Wm Trumball *Esthampsted* Esqr.
            Wm Hinton   ,,
            Jo: Harrison *Beck hill*
            Geo: Purefoy *Wadley*
            Jo: Sowthby *Carswell*
B. p Wallingford Robt Packer *Denington*
            Anth: Barker *Sunning*
            Tho: Fettiplace
            Jo: Elwes *Barton*
            Jo: Blagrove *of Southcott*
            Edw: Hobbey *q' if Perigrins son ?*   ,,
            Wm James *Denford*
            Charles Fettiplace
            Tho: Garrard *of Cheping*
            Roger Drap
            Hen: Porter *Clewer*
            Tho: Holt *Abbington*
            Tho: Sanders *of Mungill in Oxon*   ,,
            Ed: Dalby *Red*^{*s*}
            Fr: Pigott *of Marcham*
            Ed: Keate *of Lockinge*
            John Allen *Strelley*
            Wm Nelson *Chadleworth*
            Wm Dormer
            Rich: Palmer *of Ockingham*   ,,

[*The additions in italics are in red ink in the original.*]

BERKS. [1665.]

[*MSS. Rawl. D.* 1480, *fol.* 17, *and D.* 865, *fol.* 35.]

The Names of the Hundreds.	High Constables.		Bayliffe.
⎧ Sonning	Wm Meller	Jo: Turner	.... Breach.
⎪ Charleton	Tho: Symons	Jo: Hollier	....
⎨ Moreton	Robt Pope	Peter Edlyn	Gregory Acres.
⎩ Compton	Jo: Pocock	Wm Binte	Rich: Smith.
⎧ Horiner	Jos: Pearce	Ric: Barely	Will: Pullen.
⎩ Oke	Tho: Nevil	Hen: Peade	Rich: Alder.
⎧ Farringdon	Fr: Knapp	Wm Greene	Will: Hall.
⎩ Ganfield	Moses Couldrey		Robt Clement.
⎧ Wanting	Sam: Bathurst	Jo: Collins	Robt Clement.
⎨ Shrivenham	Jo: Bedford	Ric: Joyner	Robt Mills.
⎩ Lamborne	John Seamour		Will: Tarrant.
⎧ Kintbury	Jos: Sare	Ric: Vtkins	Paule Wheeler.
⎪ Faire Cross	Wm Hedges	Ferd: Clerke	Paule Wheeler.
⎨ Reading	Jo: Hawkins	Edw: Strowde ⎫	Will: Fellow.
⎩ Theale	Fr: Parfitt	Wm Wingfield ⎭	
⎧ Beynhurst	Wm Grove	Tho: Rowland	
⎪ Wargrove	John Grove		Tho: Seyward.
⎨ Bray	Math: Petifer	Fr: Larkin	.... Singleton.
⎪ Ripplesmore	Jo: Cotrill	Wm Russell	
⎩ Cookham	John Ray	John West	.... Singleton.

NOTES: VISITATION 1665-6.

MAIORS OF TOWNES 1664 [1664-5].

Reading	Tho: Kenton.
Windsor	W^m: Galland.
Newbury	John Munday.
Abbingdon	Jonathan Howe.
Wallingford	Francis Day.

[*MS. Rawl. D. 1480, fol. 18.*]

THE CORPORAC'ON OF NEWBURY. [1665.]

John Mundy gent. Major.
Lord Craven Baron of Hamsted Marshal high Steward.
Robert Garrard Deputy Steward.
George Cowslade ⎫
Gabriell Cox ⎥
Philip Weston ⎬ Aldermen.
John Giles ⎭
q. John Edmonde.
Robert Garrard.
Thomas Cowslade.
John Rider.
Richard Pocock.
,, William Godwin.
,, Thomas Wilson.
James Watte.
Will: Pearse.
Joseph Pinfall.
John Hedges.
Will: Smart.
Rich: Shaw.
Rich: Young.
Thomas Hawker.
,, Robert Hide.
Levy Smith.
Joseph Garrard.
Abraham Stockwell.
Thomas Aden.
Jonas Narraway.

[*MS. Rawl. D. 1480, fol. 18ᵇ.*]

THE CORPORAC'ON OF NEW WINDSOR. [1665.]

William Galland Maior.
John Visc: Mordant Baron of Riegate Vic: Aveland Constable of the honer & Castle of Windsor, High Steward.
Francis Ridley vnder steward & Towne Clearke.

Richard Church \
Samuell Mihill
Rich: Nash
Will: Poole
Henry Choone } Aldermen.
George Say
John Randall
Will: Row
Tho: Merwyn /
John Church } Benchers.
John Nash
Thom: Mansfield } Bailiffe.
Will: Carey

THE CORPORAC'ON OF MAIDENHEAD. [1665.]

Richard Baker Warden.
Nevill Kidwell } Bridgmasters.
James Spratley
Thomas Staples Esqr Steward.
Rich: Robinson.
John Cherry señ.
Will: Silvester.
Tho: Russell.
John Cherry iuñ.
Robt West.
Rich: Cherry.
John Cowley.

[*MS. Rawl. D. 1480, f. 33^b.*]

CORPORAC'ON OF REDING. [1665.]

Thomas Kenton Maior
Edward Dalby Esqr Steward
William Braxton señ *Disclaimes* \
George Thorne *Disclames*
Tho: Seakes
Robt Creede *Disclaimes*
James Winch
Edw: Johnson } Aldermen.
Tho: Cotes
Will: Braxton Jun. *Disclaimes*
Robert Terrold
Mich: Reading *Disclaimes*
Tho: Tilliard *Disclaimes* /
Rich: Fellowes

[*Additions in the original in red ink are in italics.*]

CORPORAC'ON OF WALLINGFORD. [1665.]

Francis Day Maior.
Earle of Berks high Steward.
Anthony Barker Recorder.
William Loder señ ⎫
Thomas Eldridge ⎪
William Lane ⎬ Aldermen.
Anthony Leaver ⎪
Richard Skinner ⎭

[*MS. Rawl. D. 865, fol. 36.*]

WARRANTS: TO WHOM DELIU'ED. [1665.]

[*Words in italics have been written in red ink in the original.*]

Windsor Towne . . .	to the Maior of Windsor.
Wallingford Towne . .	to the Maior of Wallingford.
Riplesmere Hund. . .	to the high Constables.
Wargrove hund. . . .	to the high Constable.
Theale hund. . . .	to the *high Constables.*
Sonning hund. . . .	to the *Bailif.*
Charleton hund. . .	to the *Bailiff of Suning.*
Moreton hund. . . .	to the *Bailiff.*
Compton hund. . . .	to the *Bailiff.*
Hormer hund. . . .	to the *Bailiff.*
Oke hund.	to the *Bailiff.*
Farringdon hund. . .	to the *Bailiff of Shrivenham.*
Ganfield hund. . . .	to the *Bail[i]ff of Hormer.*
Towne of Abbingdon .	to the *Bailiff.*
Wanting hund. . . .	to the *Bailiff.*
Shrivenham hund. . .	to the *Bailiff.*
Lamborne hund. . .	to the *high Constable.*
Kintbury hund. . .	to the ⎫ *Bailiff.*
Fairecross hund. . .	to the ⎭
Reads hund. . . .	to the *Bailiff.*
Beynhurst hund. . .	to the ⎫
Bray hund.	to the ⎬ *Bailiff of Suning.*
Cookham hund. . . .	to the ⎭
Readinge Towne . .	to the *Maior.*
Newbury Towne . .	to *Paule Wheeler.*

[*MS. Rawl. D. 1480, fol. 17b.*]

BERKS. AN° 166$\frac{4}{5}$.*

	The names of the Hundreds.	The Place of Sitting.	The Day of the Weeke.	The Day of the Moneth.
1	⎧ Sunning Charleton & ⎫ Towne of Reading & ⎨ Okingham ⎭	⎫ Reading at the signe ⎬ of the Beare ⎭	Saterday	11th March.
2	⎧ Moreton & ⎨ Compton ⎩	⎫ Wallingford at the ⎬ signe of the Eliphant ⎭	Tuesday	14: March.

[* *1665, Feb. 17, Sir Edward Bish sealed his Deputation to me for visiting Berkshire. Mar. 11, I began to make my Visitation of Berkshire at Reading (Ashmole's Diary).*]

DISCLAIMERS 1665-6.

	The names of the Hundreds.	The Place of Sitting.	The Day of the Weeke.	The Day of the Moneth.
3	Hormer Oke & Towne of Abbingdon	Abbingdon at Mr Edward Harte being the New Inn	Thursday	16. March.
4	Farringdon & Ganfield	Farringdon at the Crowne	Saterday	18. March.
5	Wanting Shrivenham & Lamborne	Wantage at the signe of the Beare	Tuesday	21. March
6	Kintbury Faire Cross & Newbery Towne	Newbury at the signe of the Mairemaid	Thursday	23. March.
7	Reading & Theale	Reading at ye Vpp Ship	Saterday	25. March.
8	Beynhurst Wargrove & Cookham.	Maydenhead at the signe of the Beare	Tuesday	28. March.
9	Ripplesmore Bray & Burrough of New Windsor	Windsor at the Three Tunns	Thursday	30. March.

LIST OF BERKSHIRE HOUSEHOLDERS AS ARRANGED FOR THE VISITATION OF 1665—1666.

The following list I have compiled from :—

1. MS. Rawlinson D. 865, folios 8—29^b, called in the catalogue a list of all the persons summoned to appear at the visitation in the years 1665—1666. This forms the basis of the following list.
2. Folios 38—42 of the same MS., headed, Non-appearances vpon the first Summons ; these names are marked in the following list, " No App."
3. Folios 44—46, Adiournment for entry till Easter Tearme 1665.
4. Folios 47—48^b, headed, Gent. sumoned to Reding Assises 166⅘.
5. MS. Rawlinson D. 1480, folios 19 to 33^b. Another list, in Ashmole's handwriting. It is a list compiled from the others, after weeding out all those (?) who did not come within the scope of the Visitation.

Each list has a number of notes and corrections written by Ashmole, as well as the names of persons added by him from time to time. All these additions are here printed in italics.

List No. 1 is printed in ordinary type. It is no doubt the list furnished to Ashmole at the commencement of the Visitation, and from a note by him, after Bradfield, " 247 Harthes," it may be assumed that it contains a fairly accurate list of the principal hearths in Berkshire in the year 1665, more or less completed by Ashmole's additions.

A number of the names are marked with lines and crosses, +, × ; these I have left out, as they seem to follow no exact rule.

No reliance whatever can be placed on the title *Gent.*, so often occurring in MS. No. 1. Many of the names so distinguished drop out before the compilation of the final list No. 5, without having any information attached to them, as mort, gone away, disclaimed, and the like. *They are here marked* " *Not in Rawl. D.* 1480."

Any notes not in the main text are printed in square brackets.

VOL. II.

NOTES : VISITATION 1665-6.

[*MS. Rawl. D. 865, fol. 8—42.*]

COM: BERKS. HUNDRED OF HORMER.

ABINGDON.

Francis Carliel [*crossed out*].
Thomas Philips [*crossed out*].
William Chaney [*Not in Rawl. D.* 1480].
. . . . Fountaine [*crossed out*].
Ambrose Deakins [*Not in Rawl. D.* 1480].
John Prince [*crossed out*].
Wm Wells [*Not in Rawl. D.* 1480].
James Curtin geñ [*gen. crossed out*] *respit till Easter Tearme, a Burges.*
Thomas Sparkes [*gen. crossed out. Not in Rawl. D.* 1480].
Thomas Broughton [*Not in Rawl. D.* 1480].
John Mayott geñ [*gen. crossed out*] *Intr. fee vnp^d.*
Constantine Barnard [*crossed out*].
Tho: Holt Esqr *adj^d till Easter Tearme* 1665. *Intr.*
Tho: Hucotts [*Not in Rawl. D.* 1480].
John Billingsley [*Not in Rawl. D.* 1480].
John Finmore *adj^d till Easter Tearme* 1665. *Disclaimed, neu'theless respit till East' T.*
Rich: West [*Not in Rawl. D.* 1480].
Will: Forster [*Not in Rawl. D.* 1480].
Alexander Beasley gen: [*gen. crossed out*] *entred Gratis as being a decayed gent. & so certified by the Maior & diu'rs of the principall Burgesses.*
Tobias Garbrand al's Harkes D^r of Phisick *Disclaimed.*
John Hanson *app'ed but would not enter.*
Hen: Meales sen: [*Not in Rawl. D.* 1480].
Jonathan Hawes (*Howes*). *Maior adj^d till Easter Tearme* 1665.
John Mayott gen: [*crossed out, see above*].
Wm Holliday [*crossed out*].
Thomas Bottendon [*Not in Rawl. D.* 1480].
Tho: Trapham [*crossed out*].
Edmond Franklyn, Major [*crossed out*].
Francis Payne [*crossed out*] *respit till Easter Tearme, a Burges.*
Peter Hasler [*Not in Rawl. D.* 1480].
Capt: John Peck Disclaimed.
John Dew gen: [*crossed out*].
Tho: Southby gen: *respite till Mich'as Tearme* 1665 [*gen' crossed out*] *entr. in Ganfield Hund. at Stanford.*
Wm Bostock gen: [*gen. crossed out*] *entred gratis vpon certif' of his losses for the King & p'sent pou'ty.*
Wm Willmot *adj^d till Easter Tearme* 1665 [*& 1666 ?*].
Simon Hawkins [*Not in Rawl. D.* 1480].
Robert Payne gen: *Disclaimes.*
Wm Stevenson [*Not in Rawl. D.* 1480].
Rich: Ely [*Not in Rawl. D.* 1480].
Jonas Badcock [*Not in Rawl. D.* 1480].
George Bayly [*Not in Rawl. D.* 1480].
John Fletcher [*Not in Rawl. D.* 1480].
Robert Mayott gen: [*crossed out*].
Will: Fox [*Not in Rawl. D.* 1480].
Charles Tucker [*gen' erased*] *Intr.*
Will: Weston [*crossed out*] *respit till Easter Tearme, a Burges.*

LIST OF THOSE SUMMONED TO APPEAR.   11

HUNDRED OF HORMER.

SHIPPON.

Jo: Thatcher
Charles Sherwood
Edw: Weston
Tho: North.
} [*Not in Rawl. D.* 1480].

KENNINGTON.

George Coxiter gen: *mort.*
George Cornish Clerke [*Not in Rawl. D.* 1480].
John Smith gen: *dwells at Oxford, his fath' was Maior of Oxford & a Burgess of p'liam' for Oxford in the beginning of the long p'liam'.*
John Bunce [*Not in Rawl. D.* 1480].
Will: Bostock gen: [*crossed out*] *lives in Abbington.*

THRUP.

Thomas Hart gen: [*Not in Rawl. D.* 1480].
Alexander Reade gen: *of Pumney. is now at London, his fath' was young' B' to S' Th: Reade of Barton neere Abbingdon. Entr but voyd.*
John Wichelow [*Not in Rawl. D.* 1480].

SUNNINGWELL.

Haniball Baskervile Esq' *Entr.*
Charles Holloway Serjant at Law *adj'd till Easter Tearme* 1665.
[*Walter*] Jones D' of Divinity *one of the Prebends of Westm' war' left w'th his Tennant.*
John Stevenson *Disclaimes by Haniball Baskervill Esq'.*
Christopher Blower gen: *an Ator. his elder B' Robert dwells at Hurst, respit till Easter Tearme if his B' doth not enter for him.*

NORCOTT.

John Yateman geñ *an Ator. adj'd till Easter Tearme* 1665, *will app'e in London next Tearme.*
Will: Porter geñ *Receiv' of the Hearth money adj'd till Easter Tearme* 1665, *will app'e in London next Tearme. Ator.*

RADLEY.

S' George Stonehouse Barr' *Justice of Peace, will send y' fee to Wantage, but did not.*
John Herbert Clerke [*Not in Rawl. D.* 1480].
Henry Avery [*Not in Rawl. D.* 1480].
Tho: Price gen: *one of y' Yeomen of the Guard.*

SANDFORD.

John Thatcher *vide Shippon.*

BESSELSLEIGH.

John Lenthall Esq' *Intr. fee vnp'.*

GRAMPOLE.

James Heron gen: *Intr. dwells in Oxford, warr' left w'th his Tenant*
Francis Tomlins *Disclaimes.*
Will: Croswell [*Not in Rawl. D.* 1480].
Tho: Lapworth [*Not in Rawl. D.* 1480].
Robert Greenaway [*Not in Rawl. D.* 1480].

HUNDRED OF HORMER.

CUMNER.

Will: Phillipson gen: [*gen. crossed out*] *hath let his estate & is gon into Oxf. shire.*
John Langford Clerke [*Not in Rawl. D.* 1480].
Rich: Stibbs [*Not in Rawl. D.* 1480].
Hen: Hutt [*Not in Rawl. D.* 1480].
John Willis [*Not in Rawl. D.* 1480].
Wm Bond sen̄ [*Not in Rawl. D.* 1480].
Mrs Lane [*crossed out*].

SWINFORD IN CUMNER.

John Knapp gen: *Disclaimed.*

CHAWLEY IN CUMNER.

Francis Peacock gen̄ }
John Peacock gen̄ } *Entry made.*
Wm Godfrey [*Not in Rawl. D.* 1480].

WIGHTHAM.

The Earle of Lindsey
Anthony Hodges *Clerke*
Edmond Greene
Tho: Willgoose. } [*Not in Rawl. D.* 1480].

SEA COURT.

Richard Leaving gen: *sick, he was warned by . . . . lyes bedrid.* [*crossed out*].
Wm Cantwell gen̄ *he was sent to by the Const: to app^r at Wantage: but did not app's* [*crossed out*].

WOTTON.

John Hyde of *Blagrave* house *a Grocer at the 3 flower de luces in the old change.*
Rich: [*Hide*] *Sadler to the Duke of Yorke both Grandchildren to Sr Rich: Hide of Blagrove, descended of a 3^d son of Hide of Denchworth.*
Edward Cleve gen̄ *Disclaimed.*
Will Busfield gen̄ [*No App.*].
Will Vinar }
Edward Boswell } [*Not in Rawl. D.* 1480].

CULHAM.

Mrs. . . . . Berry [*Bury*] [*crossed out*] *Oxfordshire.*

WHITLEY.

Edward Dudson gen: *Intr.*
William Bradley }
John Glover } [*Not in Rawl. D.* 1480].

STROUDE.

Francis Stany }
Henry Taylour } [*Not in Rawl. D.* 1480].

LIST OF THOSE SUMMONED TO APPEAR.

HUNDRED OF HORMER.

HILL END.

Will: Cheney } [*Not in Rawl. D.* 1480].
John Spene }
Wm Davies *dwells at Woodstock.*
John Bullock } [*Not in Rawl. D.* 1480].
George Noble }

SOUTH HINKSEY.

Will: Thomas [*Not in Rawl. D.* 1480].
Joseph Pierce *one of the high Constable[s]* *Disclaimes*
Thomas Gardiner } [*Not in Rawl. D.* 1480].
John Willps Jun: }

NORTH HINKSEY.

Henry Ruffin [*Not in Rawl. D.* 1480].
Kath: Greenaway widd: [*crossed out*].
Wm Finmore *Disclaimes.*

BOTLEY.

Edward Panton [*Not in Rawl. D.* 1480].
Peter Ranckle *Disclaimes.*
Tho: Wright [*Not in Rawl. D.* 1480].

CHELSWELL.

Thomas Norton [*crossed out*].
Paule Norton, [*No App:*] *a Butcher.*

MORETON HUNDRED.

HARWELL.

John Sayer Clerke [*Not in Rawl. D.* 1480].
John Harwell [*crossed out*].
John Loder Esq. *lives at Balsam p'ke neere Kintbury.*
Robert Loder sen [*Not in Rawl. D.* 1480].
Will: Chancellor [*Not in Rawl. D.* 1480].
John Fortie [*Not in Rawl. D.* 1480].
Edward Jennings sen gen: *M^r of Arts.* [*No App.*]
Thomas Norton [*Not in Rawl. D.* 1480].
John Jennings.
Robert Hide sen' *Disclaimed, father to Rob't Hyde of Est-Hagborne.*

DUDCOTT.

Robert Bristow Clerke [*crossed out*] *mort.*
Rob't Lydall gen: *Intr.*
John Dew gen *vide Hatford in Ganf: h:*
Edward Sawyer *Disclaimes.*

MORTON HUNDRED, DUDCOTT.

Richard Blake *Disclaimes.*
Robt Jennings Jun'. *son of Edw: Jen: of Harwell. Disclames.*
Peter Ayleffe [*Not in Rawl. D.* 1480].
Tho: Harward [*Not in Rawl. D.* 1480].

EAST HAGBORNE.

Robert Sayer of Coscott *Disclaimes.*
George Keate geñ *served & was at Abingdon 7 July but did not appr; his father Hugh disclaimed* 1623.
Tho: Humfries [*Not in Rawl. D.* 1480].
Jonathan Sayer *Disclaimes.*
John Chesington [*Not in Rawl. D.* 1480].
Robt Hyde Jun. *Disclaimes.*
Henry Boseley ⎫
Henry Bunce ⎬ [*Not in Rawl. D.* 1480].
Samuell Fox ⎪
Rich: Armstrong ⎭

WEST HAGBORNE.

Rich: Cressell [*Not in Rawl. D.* 1480].
Robt Hyde señ [? *Disclaimed under Harwell*] [*crossed out*].
John Tirrold [*Not in Rawl. D.* 1480].
Rich: Andrewes alias Taylour [*Not in Rawl. D.* 1480].

NORTH MORETON.

Edmund Platt [*Not in Rawl. D.* 1480].
John Gregory Jun: [*Not in Rawl. D.* 1480].
Wm Leaver *Disclaimes.*
John Mayne ⎫
Hen: Slade ⎬ [*Not in Rawl. D.* 1480].
John Kerfoote ⎭

SOUTH MORETON.

.... Bredon Clerke *Disclaimes.*
Henry Punt [*Pount*] geñ: *Entr.*
Tho: Curtis [*Not in Rawl. D.* 1480].
Lawrence Lewenden ⎫
Wm Payne ⎪
Tho: Field ⎬ [*Not in Rawl. D.* 1480].
Hen: Corderay ⎪
John Whichelow ⎪
Jacob Bennet ⎭
Clement Styles *Disclaimes.*

BRIGHTWELL.

Ralph Whistler *Disclames.*
Will: Leaver *Tho: his son app'ed & disclaimed.*
Anthony Leaver *mort, his son Will: ap'ed & disclaimed.*
John Leaver *Disclaimes.*
Rich: Goodday ⎫
Christopher Webster ⎪
John Wilkins ⎬ [*Not in Rawl. D.* 1480].
Ralph Sherwood ⎪
Rich: Collins, Making Court house ⎭

LIST OF THOSE SUMMONED TO APPEAR. 15

MORTON HUNDRED.

CLAPCOTT & PRYORY.

John Ford [*Not in Rawl. D.* 1480].
.... Mullens Esqr [*crossed out*].

SATWELL.

.... Whistler widdow
Roger Grigson } [*Not in Rawl. D.* 1480].
.... Malorough widdow

BASELDEN.

George Fane Esqr   *mort, his son K^t of ye Bath.*
John Edling
Isaack Mathew } [*Not in Rawl. D.* 1480].
Tho: Heredge
Henry Allen   *mort. warr^t left at the house.*
John Allen   *Disclaimes.*
Tho: Buckeridge   *Disclaimes.*

STREATLEY.

John Allen Esqr   *Justice of ye peace, Intr.*
George Philipson   *has an estate in Wiltshire where his fath^r dwells & will enter there.*
Robert Hulet Clerke   [*Not in Rawl. D.* 1480].
Anthony Harvey   [*Not in Rawl. D.* 1480].
John Eyston, Intr.

ASHAMSTEAD.

.... Singleton Clerke   [*Not in Rawl. D.* 1480].
Will: Elmes.

MOULESFORD.

Anthony Libb Esqr   *lives at Hardwick in Com' Ox.*
John Havell   [*Not in Rawl. D.* 1480].
John Whistler   *mort. sum'ons left at the house, his sons name is Laurence.*
Laurence Whistler, *Disclaimed.*
.... Samborne   [*crossed out*].

ASTON TIRROLD.

Henry Samborne Esqr   *app'd, but being he is entred in the last Visit, & not married, & consequently no addicc'on to the family I dismist him.*
Edward Bellenger   *Clerke, he is at London.*
Christopher Artwick   *Disclaimes.* [*Christopher Alnewick, disclaimed.*]

ASTON VPTHORPP.

Leonard Slade
John White } [*Not in Rawl. D.* 1480].
Nich: Kerfoote
Rich: Tirrold

MORTON HUNDRED.

WALLINGFORD TOWNE.

William Loder *sen', dwells at Howbery in Com' Ox'n.*
Tho: Richardson   [*Not in Rawl. D.* 1480].
John Rusden *Disclaimes.*
Francis Day gen: *Maior, Grandchild to Dr Day B^p of Winch: & Deane of Windsor.*
John Vernon *sick.*
Rich: Payne gen: [*crossed out*].
Rich: Seamour   *adj^d till Easter Tearme* 1665.
Tho: Ely [*crossed out*] *mort.*
Rich: Carter   [*Not in Rawl. D.* 1480].
James Anslow   [*Not in Rawl. D.* 1480].
Anthony Leaver   *alderman. Borough Constable of Wallingford.*
Stoner Crowch   *Borough Constable of Wallingford an Ator. app'd but can make no proofe of armes.*
Rich: White   [*Not in Rawl. D.* 1480].
Robt Pearson   *mort.*
Will Elliott, at the Elephant   [*Not in Rawl. D.* 1480].
Tho: Norton gen: *Disclames.*
Will: Lane gen: [*crossed out*].
Rich: Kirby geñ: *Discl'.*
Peter Enewright   [*Not in Rawl. D.* 1480].
Moses Slade geñ   *an Attor. Disclaimes.*
Thomas Basset gen: *Disclaimes.*
Will: Cooke   *Disclaimes.*
John Gregory gen: *adj^d till Easter Tearme* 1665. *at London.*
Will: Loader señ geñ.   [*Not in Rawl. D.* 1480, *see above*].
Tho: Eldridge geñ.
.... Ireland gen: *Schoolm^r*   [*Not in Rawl. D.* 1480].
George Castle D^r of Phisick   [*No App:*] *son to Dr Castell late of Westm'.*
Thomas Byshop   [*Not in Rawl. D.* 1480].
Rich: Skinner.   [*No App:*] *Alderman.*
Josiah Lane D^r of Phisick adj^d till Easter Tearme 1665.

CASTLE OF WALLINGFORD.

John Freeman gen: *a Pensioner to the K^g Entr.*
Edward Cowslip geñ.
Henry Knapp geñ   [*crossed out*] *removed to Oxford.*

OCK HUNDRED.

DRAYTON.

Isaack Horsford   [*Not in Rawl. D.* 1480].
Robert Tirrold señ   [*Not in Rawl. D.* 1480].
Sr John Southcote L^d of the Mann^r: he lives in Surrey or Essex.

STEVENTON.

Rich: Smalbone   *Intr.*
John Smalbone   *Intr.*
Alice Stevens widdow   [*crossed out*].
Tho: Doe   [*Not in Rawl. D.* 1480].
Hen: Smalbone geñ   *will app' at Wantage wth his B^r Jo: Smalbone Jo: Entred there or both.*

LIST OF THOSE SUMMONED TO APPEAR.   17

OCK HUNDRED.

MILTON.

Paul Calton Esqr   *Intr. fee vnp^d.*
George Hyne Clerke   *Disclaimes.*
Francis Yateman gen.   *an Attor.*   [*Not in Rawl. D.* 1480].
Robert Stone   [*Not in Rawl. D.* 1480].

SUTTON [COURTNEY].

Thomas Wollascott geñ   *Intr.*
John Quelch   [*Not in Rawl. D.* 1480].
John Fewin   [*Not in Rawl. D.* 1480].
Will: Bartlet   *No app: sumoned.*
John Curtis   [*Not in Rawl. D.* 1480].
Tho: Justice   [*Not in Rawl. D.* 1480].

SUTTON WICK [*No entry*].

APLEFORD.

Tho: Reade gent   *Intr.*
Thomas Orpwood, Entred but refused to pay fees.
Jane Whichelow widdow   [*Not in Rawl. D.* 1480].

LONG WITTNAM.

Bryan Holland Clerke   [*Not in Rawl. D.* 1480].
James Jennings   *his son will app' at Bradfield 11 July instant, but did not. Will app' at London wth Mr Hart or Mr Mallet.*

LITLE WITTNAM.

Edmund Dunch Esqr   *Intr. will send to London next Tearme.*

KINGSTON BAGPUZE.

Thomas Latten Esqr   *Entr.*
Rich: Castle
Hen: Wibbley
Tho: Carwood   } [*Not in Rawl. D.* 1480].
Tho: Tuckwell

FIFIELD.

Charles White geñ   [*crossed out*] *mort. but hath a son, his widdow married Judge Mallet's son.*
Kath: Evans Widdow   [*Not in Rawl. D.* 1480].
Hen: Hodgeson.
Michael Mallet Esqr   Intr. for himself & his nephew, Charles White, will app' also for young Mr Rich: Aldworth.
Richard Aldworth, an Infant, cannot find him related [*to*] *any of that family entred a^o* 1623.   [*Not in Rawl. D.* 1480.]

MARCHAM.

Francis Piggot Esqr.   *Justice of ye Peace   Int.*
John Reade Clerke   *Intr. Gratis. Respit is given till Easter Tearme to p'uve his armes.*

VOL. II.   D

OCK HUNDRED, MARCHAM.

    Francis Shewrey geñ *Disclaimes.*
    John [or] Francis Wrigglesworth geñ [*No app.*] *Will: Wriglesworth notice left wth his wife.*
    Thomas Horsley [*Not in Rawl. D.* 1480].
    John Hawkins sen'. [*Not in Rawl. D.* 1480].
    John Bowles an Attor. *adj^d till Easter Tearme* 1665. *will app' at London next Tearme.*

APPLETON.

Robt Southby gen: *Intr.*
Walter Wightwick geñ *Disclames.*
Jacob Stevens geñ [*Not in Rawl. D.* 1480].
John Lane geñ *Disclaimed.*
Peter Stevens *Disclaimes.*
Rich: Dodwell [*Not in Rawl. D.* 1480].
Rich: Sellwood [*Not in Rawl. D.* 1480].

TUBNEY.

Henry Langley *D^r in Divinity.*
Robt Southby gen [*crossed out*] *vide Appleton.*
Sr *Tho: Aston.*

LYFORD.

John Yate geñ. *adjourned till Easter Tearme* 1665. *will app' at London next Tearme, being not well now.*
Johan Ashcombe widdow [*crossed out*] *hath 2 sons who live in Lyford.*
John Ashcombe *Intr.*

FRILFORD.

John Bowlis [*crossed out.*]
Will: Howard ⎫
James Tubb ⎬ [*Not in Rawl. D.* 1480.]
Hen: Peade ⎭

GOOSEY.

Will: Nelson Esqr. *lives at Chaddleworth by Newbury, in Kintbury hund.*
Griffin Mathew [*Not in Rawl. D.* 1480].

EAST HANNEY.

Thomas Collins [*Not in Rawl. D.* 1480].

DRAYCOT MO[O]RE.

John Hissey [*Not in Rawl. D.* 1480].
Peter Yeate geñ *lives at Stanlake in Com' Ox:*

GARFORD.

Rich: Badcock [*crossed out*].
Tho: Howard [*Not in Rawl. D.* 1480].
John Peck [*Not in Rawl. D.* 1480].

WANTING HUNDRED.
Wanting Towne.

William Masmore \
Samuell Saxon \
Anthony Webb \
Thomas Hurdman } [*Not in Rawl. D.* 1480]. \
Tho: Wells \
Tho: Farmer \
Rich: West \
George Champion geñ *an Ator. Intr.* \
Rich: Pettifer *Disclaimes.* \
Augustine Cooke [*Not in Rawl. D.* 1480]. \
Rich: Brookes geñ *Intr.* \
Robt: Alden geñ [*crossed out*].

Pryors Hold in Wanting.

Francis Slade Clerke *Disclaimes.* \
Laurence Castle [*No App.*]. \
Thomas Aldworth gen: *Entr.*

Grove.

William Grove geñ [*No App.*]. \
Tho: Winterborne señ [*Not in Rawl. D.* 1480].

Charlton.

Sʳ George Wilmot Knᵗ: *Intr.* \
Tho: Aldridge geñ *fee vnpᵈ.* \
John Jennings [*Not in Rawl. D.* 1480]. \
Samuell Bathurst geñ [*crossed out*] *high Constable, Intr.* \
Will: Barr [*Not in Rawl. D.* 1480]. \
John Peacock of Wooley [*crossed out*].

Childrey.

Sʳ: John Fettiplace *Knt. Justice of Peace, he dwells at Swinbroke in Com' Oxon'.* \
Edw: Pocock *Dʳ in Divinity, adjᵈ till Easter Tearme* 1665. \
Roger Knight geñt. *adjourᵈ till Easter Tearme* 1665. *Summoned to Reading Assises* 166⅔. *Not at home. will app' next Tearme & enter.* \
Will: Bunce [*Not in Rawl. D.* 1480]. \
James Fisher gen. *Intr. gratis.*

Sparsholt.

Rich: Edmondson Clerke *Disclaimes.* \
Henry Grove. \
Alexander Tanne [*Not in Rawl. D.* 1480]. \
Edmund Wiseman [*crossed out*].

Denchworth.

Gregory Gearing (*Gery*) *No App. Summoned to Reading Assises* 166⅔. *Disclaimed.* \
John Keate Clerke [*Not in Rawl. D.* 1480].

East Hanney.

Henry Dew [*crossed out*] *mort.*

WANTING HUNDRED.

WEST HANNEY.

Anthony Ayleworth sen: geñ } *Entr.*
Andrew Ayleworth
Peter Adams Clerke [*Not in Rawl. D.* 1480].
Will: Yeate gen: $\frac{B^r}{Son.}$ of John Yate of Lyford.
Edward Bowlis. [*Not in Rawl. D.* 1480].
Tho: Dunsdon [*Not in Rawl. D.* 1480].

ARDINGTON.

John Clarke Esqr [*crossed out*].
Bennet Hobbs Esqr *Intr.*
John Clarke, Clerke, Intr.
John Sherwood gen: *Intr.*
Rich: Hobbs gen: *Vncle to Bennet Hobbs.*
Marke Zigher [*Not in Rawl. D.* 1480].
Eliz: Berwick widdow [*Not in Rawl. D.* 1480].
Wm Clarke gen: *No App. q' if he y^t Mr Edw: Keate has tooke order for.*
John Cox gen: *Disclaimes.*

EAST LOCKING, BETTERTON & WEST GINGE.

Edward Keate Esqr. *Just: Intr.*
.... Page D^r in Divinity [*crossed out in Rawl. D.* 1480].
John Collins *Disclaimes afterwards Entred.*
John Doe gen *Disclaimes.*
John Pomfrey [*Not in Rawl. D.* 1480].
Edward Hyde. *Disclamed.*

EAST GINGE.

Tho: Reynolds [*Not in Rawl. D.* 1480].

WEST LOCKING.

James George [*Not in Rawl. D.* 1480].

WEST HENDRED.

Edmund Wiseman Esqr *was son of Sr Charles Wiseman of Sparsholts Court.*
Tho: Wight Clerke [*Not in Rawl. D.* 1480].

EAST HENDRED.

Will: Eyston Esqr *Int.*
John Sherwood geñ *Int:*
Tho: Butler geñ. *adjourn^d till Easter Tearme* 1665. *will app'e at London next Tearme & gaine a Certif: from Coll: Butler y^t he is of his familey.*
Robt Norris Clerke [*No App.*].

GANFIELD HUNDRED.

STANFORD.

Tho: Coxe geñ. *dwells in Wiltshire.*
John Loder *Disclaimes.*
Giles Bingley Clerke.
John Moulder [*Not in Rawl. D.* 1480].
Thomas Southby, Intr.

LIST OF THOSE SUMMONED TO APPEAR. 21

GANFIELD HUNDRED.
BUCKLAND.

Sʳ Charles Yeate Barrᵗ *Intr.*
Joseph Wright Clerke [*Not in Rawl. D.* 1480].
Lawrence Ambrose [*Not in Rawl. D.* 1480].
Henry Warneford geñ *Intr.*

SHELLINGFORD.

Roḃt Packer Esqʳ [*No App.*] *Just: & p'liamᵗ man for Wallingford.*
Rich: Clayton Clerke. *adjournᵈ till Easter Tearme* 1665.
John Loder. [*crossed out*] *son to Jo: Loder of Stanford, Disclaimed.*

HATTFORD.

Francis Hathaway Clerke [*Not in Rawl. D.* 1480].
Tho: Palmer geñ *Intr.*
Will: Jordan geñ *lives in Hatton gardens.* [*crossed out*].
Edward Balla [*Not in Rawl. D.* 1480].
John Deacon [*Not in Rawl. D.* 1480].
John Dew. *Adjournᵈ till Easter Tearme* 1665. *will app' by Mʳ Hart.*

CARSWELL.

John Southby Esqʳ *Just: Intr.*

PUSEY.

John Dunch Esqʳ *Intr.*
Mary Pusey widdow *her son is young: this family hathe Kanutes Horne.*
Intr. for her son fee vnpᵈ.

CHARNEY.

John Dunch Esqʳ [*crossed out, see under Pusey*].
John Woodbridge [*Not in Rawl. D.* 1480].

LONGWORTH.

Peter Ingram Clerke [*Not in Rawl. D.* 1480].
Ann Marten *wife to Coll: Martin.* *q' if her sons name be Henry.*
Henry Marten, *son to Coll: Martin attainted of high Treason.*
John Jones ⎫
Thomas Tuckwell ⎪
Rich: Goodall ⎬ [*Not in Rawl. D.* 1480].
Anthony Burch ⎪
Will: Day ⎭

DUXFORD.

John Fettiplace, *Sʳ Ch: Yate will send his descent & to be entr: gratis at*
Sʳ Charles Certif. of his Pou'ty.

HINTON.

Joseph Hill Clerke *Disclames.*
Charles Nott geñ *gon thence.*
John Southby [*Not in Rawl. D.* 1480].

FARRINGDON HUNDRED.

FARRINGDON TOWNE.

Sr Robert Pye Knight   *Just: Intr.*
Barthol: Yeates geñ   *Intr.*
Tho: Blagraue geñ   *an Attor.*   [*No App:*]   *at London.*
Crane Rivers   [*crossed out*]   *mort.*
Solomon Symonds   [*Not in Rawl. D.* 1480].

PARTE OF GREAT FARRINGDON.

Tho: Fowler Clerke   [*crossed out*].
John Payne clerke, Disclaimes.
John Turner   [*crossed out*]   *mort.*
.... Shepard Widdow   [*Not in Rawl. D.* 1480].
Gabriell Tucker   *Entr*[*ed*].
.... Arden widdow ⎫
Tho: Barley   ⎪
Philip Collier   ⎬   [*Not in Rawl. D.* 1480].
Rich: Worthien   ⎭

HOSPITALL LIB'TY IN FARRENDON.

Will: Odey   [*crossed out*]   *respite till next Tearme.*
Alexander Taim, *Taine* [*No App.*] *dwells at Sparsholt.   warrant d'd to his B^r will app' at Wantage, but did not.*

LITLE COXWELL.

William Bryant   *Disclamed.*

GREATE COXWELL.

Mary Fettiplace widd.
Francis Morrice geñ   *Intr. gratis.   vpon Mr Justice Southbys request & certif: of his poverty.*
Will: Day   [*Not in Rawl. D.* 1480].

ENGLISHAM.

Walter Legatt.
Will: King.
Alex. Cleve   [*No App.*]   *dwells at Blunsdon in Wilts.*

SHILTON.

Tho: Horde Esqr   *dwells at Cote in Com' Ox. & will ent' there.*
Will: Baggs señ   *mort.   Fr: Knapp married his Daughter & is farmer Wilders wifes B^rs son.*
Francis Grove Clerke   *will app' at Wantage.   2^d som'ons d'd to his B^r*   [*Not in Rawl. D.* 1480].
Anthony Turfory   [*No App:*]   *The Constable served his B^r Thomas.*

LANGFORD.

Rich: Broderwick geñ   *Intr.*
Mary Copley widdow ⎫
Philip Clerke   ⎪
Rich: Howes   ⎬   [*Not in Rawl. D.* 1480].
Rich: Arnold   ⎭
Walter Bush   ⎫ [*in list of Non appearances*
Thomas Stevens ⎭   *and crossed out there.*]

FARRINGDON HUNDRED.
LITLE FARRINGDON.
Thomas Warwick *Disclaimes.*

BARRINGTON.
Reynold Bray Esqr [*No App:*] *served. one halfe of his house in Glouc. the oth^r in Berks. served to app' 7 July* [16]65, *at Abingdon but did not.*
Will: Harris Clerke [*Not in Rawl. D.* 1480].

COMPTON HUNDRED.
ALDWORTH.
John Whistler [*No App:*] *will app' at next Read^g Assises & then giue an acc^t of the Armes belongs to him, & wch are vpon the M^{ot} of John Whistler Recorder of Oxford in Haseley Church in Com' Ox: whose fath^r & this Jo: Whistlers Grandfath^r were brothers. As also vpon the M^{ot} of Ellen & Margets Mo^{ts} his sisters in Goring. respit till next assises at Read^g discharged there.*
Samuell Woodward Clerke [*Not in Rawl. D.* 1480].
Rich Skermer. [*No App.*] *respit till next assises at Read^g discharged then.*

EAST ILDSLEY.
Francis Hildesley geñ *Int. dwells at litle Stoke in Oxfordsh.*
John Pocock *Disclames, L^d of the mannor of Est Hildsley.*
Will: [Pocock] *mort.* [*crossed out*].
John Dolman ⎫
Lawrence Piper ⎬ [*Not in Rawl. D.* 1480].
Robt Hignill ⎭

WEST ILDSLEY.
John James Clerke *ejected & gon, & Dr Falham in his roome.*
John Head of Hodcott *Disclames having 500^l p' ann'.*
Dr Fulham, *Prebend of Windsor.*
John Smith [*Not in Rawl. D.* 1480].

COMPTON.
Rich: Pottinger *Disclames.*
John Alleñ señ *Disclames.*

EAST COMPTON.
Rich: Hazell Clerke ⎫
Tho: Holmes. ⎭ [*Not in Rawl. D.* 1480].

FARNEBAROW & CATMERE.
Will: Garnam gen: *Disclaimes, he afterwards entred.*
Barth: Price *Rector. Disclaimes will search for his Descent.*
Will: Price *Disclaimes.*

CHILTON.
Tho: Lawrence Clerke *Intr.*
Edward Head [*Not in Rawl. D.* 1480].
Geo: Knapp *Disclaimed.*
Tho: Pomfrey ⎫
John North ⎭ [*Not in Rawl. D.* 1480].

LAMBORNE HUNDRED.
CHEPING LAMBORNE.

Tho: Garrard Esqr: *Just: Entr:*
Tho: Mashing ⎫
Henry Dawtry ⎬ [*Not in Rawl. D.* 1480].
Rob̈t: North ⎪
John Farmer ⎭

VPP LAMBORNE.

Charles Fettiplace Esqr *Just: Intr:*
John Kemble gen: *Intr.*
.... Southby gen [*Not in Rawl. D.* 1480].
Will: Wilmot Esqr *Sr Geo: Wilmots son & heire.*
.... Payne geñ [*Not in Rawl. D.* 1480].

BOCKHAMPTON IN LAMBORNE.

John Smalbone geñ *Entr. his B^r Hen: of Steventon will app' wth him.*
Eliz: Garrard widd. *of Rog' Garrard, hath a son lives here.*
Roger Garrard [*list of No App.*] *Entr wth his B^r Philip Garrard of Hadley in Lamborne.*

BLAGRAVE IN LAMBORNE.

Tho: Seymor geñ *Entr. respit for p'fe of Armes till ye Tearme & then to confer wth Mr Carrant.*
Eliz: Seymour widd. [*Not in Rawl. D.* 1480].

HADLEY IN LAMBORNE.

John Eyston geñ Int^r q' if not the same of Streatly.
Philip Garrard gent. *Intr.*
Charles Garrard [*in list of Non App.*] *B^r to Mr Garard of Lamborne.*

ISBURY.

John Gifford geñ *he dwells in London.* [*Not in Rawl. D.* 1480.]
Giles Spicer [*Not in Rawl. D.* 1480].

EAST GARSTON.

Dame Eliz: More widd *to Sr Hen: More & Moth' to Sr Hen: Moore of Fawley.* [*Not in Rawl. D.* 1480].
Adam Battin *Entr. further tyme given to p'ue Coat vizt: till next Assises & now* [17 *July* [16]65] *will send his B^r to me to consider of a Grant of Armes.*
John Lord [*Not in Rawl. D.* 1480].
Tho: Seymor. *mort.* [*crossed out*].

SHRIVENHAM HUNDRED.
IDSON [IDSTONE].

Tho: Pearce ⎫ *of Knighton* [*list of Non App:*] *mort.* [*crossed out*].
Fr: Pearce ⎬ broth^{rs}
            ⎭ *Disclaimed.*

LIST OF THOSE SUMMONED TO APPEAR. 25

SHRIVENHAM HUNDRED.

ASHBURY.

S‍ʳ George Browne [*crossed out*] *he dwells at West Shefford in Kintb: h:*
John Cole gen: *Disclames.*
John Harding geñ *Disclaimes by l're vnder his hand.*
Antho: Weekes geñ *dwells not here.*
Tho: Whyte geñ *Disclaimes.*
John Ferebe Clerke. *Disclaimes.*

SHRIVENHAM.

Major John Wildman Esq‍ʳ [*Not in Rawl. D.* 1480].
Oliver Pleydell Esq‍ʳ [*No App:*] *Summoned to Reading Assises* 166⅔.
   [" Esq " *crossed out*].
Will: Langton Esq‍ʳ *Intr.*
Jane Stratton widd. *she hath a son lives w*ᵗʰ *her. Thomas Stratton Disclaimes.*
Tho: Bunce Clerke *Disclames.*
John Ridley gen: *An Attor.* [*crossed out in list of Non App:*]
Charles Blagrave [*Not in Rawl. D.* 1480].
Tho: Clearke [*Not in Rawl. D.* 1480].

BUSCOTT.

Walter Hungerford *D*ʳ *in Divinity. Intr.*
George Smith gen: *Intr.*
Edward } Loveday *Intr.*
Christop
Edmund Gregory *Intr.*

ODSON.

William Phillipps [*Not in Rawl. D.* 1480].

BECKETT.

Major John Wildman Esq‍ʳ [*Not in Rawl. D.* 1480].

WATCHFIELD.

Rich: Franklyn }
Tho: Joyner   } [*Not in Rawl. D.* 1480].

COLSHILL.

S‍ʳ George Pratt Barr‍ᵗ *Intr.*
Edward Redford [*crossed out*] *mort.*
John Cox   }
John Hinkley Clerke } [*Not in Rawl. D.* 1480].

BOURTON.

Tho Hinton Esq‍ʳ *Intr.*
Mary Langton Widd. *2 sonns* [*crossed out*].
Hen: Hodges geñ *dwells at Warnborow in Com' Wilts. but hath an estate at Bourton.*
Robt Southby geñ *Disclaimd. Doth assume the title of Gent. but disclaimed.*

WADLEY, LITLEWORTH & THRUPP.

George Purefoy Esq‍ʳ *Intr.*
John *Vines, Steward to M*ʳ *Purefoy* [*crossed out*].
Will: Mayland [*Not in Rawl. D.* 1480].

VOL. II.

NOTES: VISITATION 1665-6.

SHRIVENHAM HUNDRED.

COMPTON, KNIGHTON & HARDWELL.

John Wildman Esqr *Major* [*Not in Rawl. D.* 1480].
Edw: Hillary Clerke [*Not in Rawl. D.* 1480].
Tho: Saūders *Disclames.*
Tho: Pearce of Knighton, Disclames.

KINGSTON [LISLE] & FAWLER.

Humfrey Hyde Esqr *Entr.*
Alexander Fettiplace. Adiourned till Easter Tearme 1665. *Entr but not p^d will app'e next Tearme at London to pay his fee.*

VFFINGTON.

Anthony Fairbeard [*Not in Rawl. D.* 1480].

WOOLSTON.

John Saunders geñ *Intr.*
John Stoakes geñ *a Major in the K^s Army & dwells now at White Knights neere Read^g & maried Mr Anthony Englefield's daughter.*
Gregory Geringe [*Not in Rawl. D.* 1480].

BALKING.

John Tubb [*Not in Rawl. D.* 1480].
Edward Davies [*Not in Rawl. D.* 1480].

FERNHAM.

Tho: Fettiplace Esqr *Just. Intr.*
Edmund Fettiplace Esqr formerly of Bessells Leigh, wilbe at the Assises at Abingdon 7 *July* [16]65. *Summoned to Reading Assises* 166⅘, *Constable made noe retorne, nor no app'ance.*

LONGCOTT.

Tho: Hinton *a poore man* [*No app. ? crossed out*].

EATON HASTINGS.

Edward Cox geñ *Entr.*
John Tinder [*Not in Rawl. D.* 1480].

KINTBURY EAGLE HUNDRED.

WEST SHEFFORD.

Sr George Browne Kn^t of the Bath [*No App.*].
Joseph Nixon Clerke.
Will: Baker [*Not in Rawl. D.* 1480].
Will: Falbrooke [*Not in Rawl. D.* 1480].
John Stroud [*or Strand*] *Disclaimes.*

EAST SHEFFORD.

Tho: Smith [*Not in Rawl. D.* 1480].
John Blagrave. *adjourn^d till Easter Tearme* 1665. *Sumoned to Reding Assises* 166⅘. *Excused by Sr Bolste Whelocks l're. he is B^r to the Minister of Purley.*
Thomas Langford. [*No App.*] *Sumoned to Reding Assises* 166⅘. *Disclaimed.*

LIST OF THOSE SUMMONED TO APPEAR. 27

KINTBURY EAGLE HUNDRED.

CHADLEWORTH & WOLLEY.

Will: Nelson Esqr *Just: Entr.*
Tho: Blagraue Clerke. *he dwells at Purley neere Reading* [*Not in Rawl. D.* 1480].
Tho: Saunders & *Disclaimes.*
John [*Saunders*] *Disclames.*
John Pocock of Woolley *& of Poffley. Disclaimes.*
Mr Reeves *dwells out of the County.*
Gabriell Pile B^r *to Sr Seamor Pile. Int:*

NORTH & SOUTH FAWLEY CUM WHATCOMBE.

Sr Henry Moore Barr^t *Just: Entr:*
Will: Young of Whatcombe geñ *Disclaimes.*
Tho: Moore geñ *son to Sr Franc: Moore s'jant at Law & vncle to Sr H. Moore Bart: liues in Norff.*

LETCOMBE REGIS.

Alex: Fettiplace juñ geñ [*No App.*] *Sumoned to Reding Assises* 166⅘. *unmar.* [*name crossed out.*] [*in Rawl. D.* 1480.]
Francis Wallington. [*Not in Rawl. D.* 1480.]
Timothy Stevens Clerke. [*crossed out, see below.*]
Edward Farmer Clerke *Disclaimes.*
Adam Head. [*crossed out, see below.*]
Hen: Burdet geñ *mort. sine prole.*
John Blandy. [*crossed out.*]
[*Thomas*] *Goodlake Intr.*

LETCOMBE BASSET.

Eliz: Blandy widdow *she hath a son there, Adam, Disclamed.*
Margaret Hobbs widd. [*Not in Rawl. D.* 1480.]
Timothy Stevens Clerke, M^r of Arts. *adjourn^d till Easter Tearme* 1665: *respit till Trin' Tearme* [1666].
Adam Head *Disclaimes.*

EAST CHALOW.

John Tull. *Entr.*

WEST CHALOW.

Francis Piggot geñ *eldest son to Ralph B^r to Alban Pigot of Marcham.*

ENBORNE.

Hen: Greetham Clerke *Disclamed.*
Will: Mayres. *Disclaimed.*
John Edmonds. *Disclaimed.*

HAMSTED MARSHALL.

Wm Childley Clerke [*crossed out*].
M^r .... Day Clerke. [*crossed out.*]
Tho: George ⎫
Tho: Glass　　⎬ [*Not in Rawl. D.* 1480].
Tho: Smith　 ⎪
John Wise　　⎭
Luke Latham [*No App.*] *Now in North'tonsh.*

KINTBURY EAGLE HUNDRED.

WEST WOODHEY.

[Sarah] Ruddyerd widd. *she hath a son called Beniamin. Entr.*
John Osborne Clerke. *adjourn⁴ till Easter Tearme 1665, will send to his B' Edw: at the Rose neere Holborne Conduit & giue me his answ: next Trin. Tearme.*
Tho: Osborne [*Not in Rawl. D.* 1480].

KINTBURY EATON.

Dame Anne Darrell widd. [*crossed out*].
John Elwes Esq' Just: *Entr: M' Munday of Newbury will see it p⁴.*
Will: James Esq' Just. *Entr M' Mundy of D'⁰ Comons will pay y' fee.*
John Blandy gen'. [*crossed out*] *respit. till Trin' Tearme. aft' disclaimed.*
Danyell Haynes. *Entr.*
Tho: Whitwick Clerke.
Ferdinando Gunter. *Intr. Md: to inquire of him how M' Gunter of Read⁸ is related to his family.*
John Curr. *Disclaimes.*
John Loder [*crossed out*].

KINTBURY AMSBURY.

Daniel Haynes geñ [*Not in Rawl. D.* 1480, *see above*].
Tho: Barret geñ *adjourn⁴ till Easter Tearme 1665. mistaken for Banet & so not served* [*with sumons to Reding Assises 166⅘*] *M' Lother* [*Loder*] *of Balston p'ke will bring his desc' to London, & therefore respite till next Easter Tearme.*
Barth: Tipping geñ *Intr.*
Tho: Lovelock [*Not in Rawl. D.* 1480].
.... Petty widdow [*Not in Rawl. D.* 1480].
Hen: Webb geñ [*No Att⁰⁸*] *Sumoned to Reding Assises 166⅘. Excused his coming by M' Gunter of Kintbury: to send vp his Armes & descent next Tearme by M' Munday.*
Rich: Butcher [*Not in Rawl. D.* 1480].
John Waterman geñ *Sumoned to Reding Assises 166⅘. Intr.*
John Curr geñ [*crossed out, see Kintbury Eaton*].
Francis Young geñ [No Att.] *Sumoned to Reding Assises 166⅘. Excused by S' John Elwaies.*

AVINGTON.

Francis Chokk Esq' *Entr.*
Tho: Kent geñ *Intr. will pay 23 Mar: but did not. M' Maior of Newbury & M' Sand'⁸ can p'ue his p'mise.*
James Anderton Clerke, the same of Boxford in Faircross hund.

BALSOM P[AR]KE.

John Loder Esq' [*Esq' crossed out*] *Intr.*

INCKPEN.

Tho: Brickenden Esq' *Intr.*
Antho: Ettrick [*or Ellrick*] gen: *dwells in Dorset shire.*
Will: Gough Clerke *adjourn⁴ till Easter Tearme 1665. respite of Entry till Trin Tearme next.*
Jasper Scholes gen: *dwells at Erleston in Hants.*
Margaret Heron widd. *she hath a son* [*crossed out*].

LIST OF THOSE SUMMONED TO APPEAR. 29

KINTBURY EAGLE HUNDRED.

SHAWBORNE CUM BAGSHOTT.

Tho: Cheney *Disclaimes his elder B*^{rs} *son dwells at Wever neere Marlborow*
Will: Smith *Disclaimes.*
John Munday gen̄ [*No App.*] *Sumoned to Reding Assises* 166¾.
Rich: Clifford gen̄ *Intr.*
Jethro Tull *Intr. fee rec^d* 15 *June & will make entry next Tearme will app'e
    at London next Tearme, of Bagsholt in the p'ish of Shawborne.*
Will: Lapetch [*crossed out*].
Rob't Burdet, *dwells in y^t p't of Shawburne wch is in Wilts.*

HUNGERFORD CUM MEMBRIS.

James Herbert Esqr [*No App.*] *B^r to the E: of Pembr: q' if children?
    Sumoned to Reding Assises* 166¾. [*name crossed out.*]
Will: Dyer [*Not in Rawl. D.* 1480].
Edward Mills gent: *an Attorn'. mort.*
Timothy Lucas *Disclamed.*

HIDEN & EDINGTON.

Tho: Goddard & } *respit till next Tearme &*
John Goddard } *expect an acc^t by Jethro Tull.*
Roger Beckington. [*Not in Rawl. D.* 1480].

SANDENFEE.

John Clarke Clerke [*crossed out*].
.... Curr.

LEVERTON CUM COAKEWOOD.

Edward Peareman *dwells at Est Woodhay in Hants.*

CHURCH SPEENE.

Rich: Watts [*crossed out*].
Eliz: Castilian widd. [*Not in Rawl. D.* 1480.]
Fr: Atkinson Clerke *Disclaimes.*

BEENHAM & WESTBROOKE.

Will: Dennington Esqr *Beenham Valence* [*No App.*] [*crossed out*].
Rich: Hill [*Not in Rawl. D.* 1480].
Robert Garrard Esqr [*crossed out*] *he dwells at Newbury.*

FAIRE CROSS HUNDRED.

NEWBERRY TOWNE.

Rich: Farnnour [*Fanner*] *Disclaimes.*
Rich: Yonng
John Hedges
Geo: Kirby
Paul Wheeler   } [*Not in Rawl. D.* 1480].
Jeremy Chadsey
Samuel Clarkson
Joseph Pinfall
Jo: Seely sen̄ & iun̄.

FAIRE CROSS HUNDRED, NEWBERRY TOWNE.

Gabriell Cox geñ *adjourn^d till Easter Tearme* 1665 *an Attor. of ye K^s B.*
Beniamin Woodbridge Clerke [*Not in Rawl. D.* 1480].
Tho: Pearce [*Not in Rawl. D.* 1480].
Geo: Cowslade *Discld.*
Nath: Collins [*Not in Rawl. D.* 1480].
Robt Garrard Esqr & [*Esqr crossed out*] *Intr.*
Joseph [*Garrard*] *Intr.*
Philip Weston geñ. *adjourn^d till Easter Tearme* 1665. *will appeare at London. Steward* [*of Newbury ?*].
Hugh Barker D^r of Phisick *Intr.*
Will: Goodwyn geñ. *an Attor.* [No App.]
Will: Smart [*Not in Rawl. D.* 1480].
Rich Pocock geñ *an Attor. refers to Dr Pocock.*
John Munday gen: *Maior of Newbury Intr.*
Will Goldborne [*Not in Rawl. D.* 1480].
John Snow señ. [*Not in Rawl. D.* 1480].
John Edmands geñ *Disclaimed after entry* 500^l [*p. an. ?*].
Dame Margaret Woodward of Sandleford [*crossed out*].
Mary White of the same widd ⎫
Nich: Cloudes ⎬ [*Not in Rawl. D.* 1480].
Henry Linch ⎭
John Merryman geñ *Disclaimed.*
Joseph Sawyer (*Sayer*) *Clerke. Disclaimes.*
Dr Walter James. [No App.] *D^r of Phisick. B^r to Wm James of Denford.*
Geo: Carwarden gen'. adjourn^d till Easter Tearme 1665.
John Rider. *adjourn^d till Easter Tearme* 1665. *respit till I can speake wth Mr Ryd^r Sr E. W. Cler'* [sic] *whose Brother he is.*
Francis Coxhead. Disclaimes.
Tho: Cowslade Disclaimed.
John Kingsmill Esqr [*No App^r*].
Jeremiah Hand Disclaimes.
Wm Pearce Disclaimes.
Thom: Wilson. Mr Munday will bring vp ye fee next Tear'.

GREENHAM.

Sr Cæsar Coclough Barr^t *Just:* [No App.] *Sumoned to Reding Assises* 166⅔ *In Ireland now at London* [1666].
Sr St John Moore Kn^t. [No App.] *sumoned to Reding Assises* 166⅘. *went away from Reding & entred not.*
John Howes geñ *Intr.*
Roger Knight Esqr [*crossed out*].

HAMSTED NORRIS.

.... Moore Clearke [*Not in Rawl. D.* 1480].
Rich: Mathew *Disclaimed.*

YATENDON.

Joseph Sayer Clerke [*Joseph struck out*] *Disclaimes.*
Thomas Clarke *Disclaime*[*s*].

FRILSHAM.

Edward Paty [*Not in Rawl. D.* 1480].

STANFORD DINGLEY.

Samuell Smith Clerke [*Not in Rawl. D.* 1480].
Ferdinando Clerke geñ *Disclaime*[*s*].
Tho: Lyford geñ *yonger B^r to Tho: Lyford of Hurley in Beynhurst hund.*

FAIRE CROSS HUNDRED.

MARLSTON.

John Whightwick Esqr *Intr.*
Wm Elkes Clerke *adjourn^{d} till Easter Tearme* 1665. *respit till Trinity Tearme* [? 1666].
Will Louch [*in list of Non App^{ces}*] *Sumoned to Reding Assises* 166$\frac{5}{6}$. *Disclamed.*

MIDGHAM.

Rich: Garrard gent. *Intr.*

BRIMPTON.

John Loveday gent. *Intr. Adjourn^{d} till Easter Tearme* 1665. *Sumoned to Reding Assises* 166$\frac{5}{6}$. *Intr. will app' at London & make out his Armes. sent excuse by Mr Worrall of Basing because now sick & will come & app' to me at Lond. next Tearme. He obtayned a respite till next Trin. Tearme.*
Alexander Chokk geñ [*crossed out*] *dwells at Aldermaston.*

WAZING.

Tho: Worrall Clerke *Disclaimes.*

BRIGHT WALTON.

Gyles Blagrave *Disclames.*
Zachery Pocock *Clerke. Disclaimes.*

SPEENHAMLAND.

Rich: Cox [*Not in Rawl. D.* 1480].
Jane Cantrell widd. [*crossed out.*]
Tho: Stampe gent. *Entr.*
Rich: Bramley [*Not in Rawl. D.* 1480].
Tho: Grinfield [*Not in Rawl. D.* 1480].
Francis Atfield. [No App.] *Sumoned to Reding Assises* 166$\frac{5}{6}$.

BOXFORD.

Rich: Jones Esqr [*crossed out*].
James Anderton Clerke *adjourn^{d} till Easter Tearme* 1665. *respit of Entry till next Tearme. is Trustee for Mrs Jones of Welford.*
Coll: .... Hatt. [No App.] *Discharged before at Newbury.*

BEEDEN.

Will: Broad Clerke [*Not in Rawl. D.* 1480].

CHEIVELY.

Rich: Pocock geñ & Giles [*Giles left out*] *Rich. Disclaim'd* 500 p' *ann.*
Rich: Nixon Clerke.

WINTERBORNE.

James Bisset. [*Not in Rawl. D.* 1480.]

SHAW.

Sr Tho: Dolman Kn^{t} *Just: Intr.*
Hen: Pierce Clerke [*Not in Rawl. D.* 1480]
Francis Doncastell geñ *Will confer with Mr Doncastle of the Welhouse about his Armes & retorne an acc^{t} next Tear'e.*
Robt Pleydell [No App.] *Sumoned to Reding Assises* 166$\frac{5}{6}$.

FAIRE CROSS HUNDRED.

DONNINGTON.

Will: Packer gent   *Entr. but refused to pay his ffee.*

WELFORD, EASTON & WESTON.

Rich: Jones Esqr *mort. hath Mary a daught^r whose moth^r lives at Welford. Mrs Jones of Welford for her daughter Mary, dwells in Hants. Intr.*
Fr: Mundy D^r in Divinity   *adjourned till Easter Tearme 1665. Mr Mundy will enter for him next Tearme.*
Will: Howes *of Elton* geñ *Brother to M^r Jo. Howes of Greenham.* [*No App.*] *Sumoned to Reding Assises* 1664/5.
.... *Elton.* [*Not in Rawl. D. 1480.*]

PEASMORE.

Bryan Alder Clerke   *Disclaimes.*
Adam Hatt }
Tho: Savory } [*Not in Rawl. D. 1480*].

WOODSPEENE CUM BAGNOR.

John Parker geñ   *serves the Duke of Buck.*
Randolph Brookes geñ   *dwells at Barfield.*
..... Sherwood widd.   [*Not in Rawl. D. 1480*].
John & Henry Watts   *Disclamed.*

LACKHAMPSTED.

Rich: Hatt   *Disclaimed.*
Gyles Spicer   *Disclaimed.*
Hen: Blagrave   *Disclaimed.*

WELHOUSE, ELING & BOTTOMSTED IN HAMPSTED NORRIS P'ISH.

John Dancastle geñ   [*No App.*]   *Sumoned to Reading Assises* 1664/5 *his fath^r who dwells at Binfield hath Entred. Is from home, in Hampshire, & will retorne a month hence. Intr.*
Francis Kidgell   *Disclaimes.*

READING HUNDRED.

READING TOWNE.

Edward Langford geñ   *Chirurgeon   Disclaimes.*
Anthony Melward   [*Not in Rawl. D. 1480*].
Tho: Singleton schoolem^r *will informe himselfe of his family.*
Sr Will: Armourer K^t *Just.*
Tho: Shirley geñ   [*Not in Rawl. D. 1480*].
David Webb geñ   [*Not in Rawl. D. 1480*].
Edward Dalby Esqr *Recorder of Redding.   Just.   Intr.   gratis.*
Nich: Pottinger geñ   [*crossed out*].
Clement Marlow gent   *Discl^r.*
James Maynard   *Disclaimes.*
Tho: Curtis   [*Not in Rawl. D. 1480*].

LIST OF THOSE SUMMONED TO APPEAR.

READING HUNDRED.

[*Parish of*] S^T LAURENCE [*in Reading*].

Nich: Johnson   [*Not in Rawl. D.* 1480].
Charles Calverley   [*No App.*]   *son to Hugh Calv'ly of Laur: Waltham.* [*Not in Rawl. D.* 1480].
John Mills   [*Not in Rawl. D.* 1480].
John Cowdray   [*Not in Rawl. D.* 1480].
Tho: Stampe gen   [*Not in Rawl. D.* 1480].
Sr Tho: Clargis Knight & Barr^t.
Tho: Trevor gent   [*Not in Rawl. D.* 1480].
Fr: Hungerford D^r in Phisick   [*No App.*].
Austin Maltis [*Malthus*] *adjourn^d till Easter Tearme* 1665. *M^r of Arts of Magdalen Hall in Oxon'. will app. next Tearme.*
Anthony Medcalfe Phisitian   [*Not in Rawl. D.* 1480].
Rich: Johnson gent.   [*Not in Rawl. D.* 1480].
Walter Knight gent   *adjourn^d till Easter Tearme* 1665. *will app' in London next Tearme.*
Edward Johnston gent.
.... Johnson widdow   [*crossed out*].
Soloman Barnard } [*Not in Rawl. D.* 1480].
Henry Paine }
.... *Mewes D^r in Divinity.* [*No App.*]
Rich: Haynes   [*crossed out*].
Giles Pocock } [*Not in Rawl. D.* 1480].
Tho: Mose }

ST. MARIES [*Parish in Reading*].

Dame Lettice Vachell widd   [*crossed out*].
Joell Stevens gen   [*crossed out*].
Chr: Fowler Clerke   [*crossed out*].
Jo: Harison   *adjourn^d till Easter Tearme* 1665. *respite till Lady Day* [1666].
Wm Wilder [*Wilmer*]   [*No App.*]   *adjourn^d till Easter Tearme* 1665. *Sumoned to Reding Assises* 166⅔. *Discl^r.*
Tho: Blower   *Intr.*
Fr: Barnard   *of the Beare*   [*Not in Rawl. D.* 1480].
Rich: Brookes.
John Bowler }
John Edkins } [*Not in Rawl. D.* 1480].
Griffin Eldridge }
Will: Markham }
Philip Nye.   [*No App.*]
John Paice   [*Not in Rawl. D.* 1480].
.... Elles gent   [*crossed out*].
Geo: Thorne gent   *Disclaimes.*
Captaine .... Armstrong   [*crossed out*].
Thom Calvert gent.   *adjourn^d till Easter Tearme* 1665. *subfarmer of the Excise, will app'e next Tear'e.*
Samuell Jemett.   [*No App.*]   L. *adjourn^d till Easter Tearme* 1665. *Sumoned to Reding Assises* 166⅔. *respite till Lady Day* [1666].
Fr: Phipps.   *Intr. gratis.*   [*Intr. crossed out.*]
Tho: Harison.   [*No app.*]   L. *adjourn^d till Easter Tearme* 1665.
Leonard Welbeck.   *Entred gratis for his good services in the K^{rs} Army, & p'sent pou'ty.*
Tho: Blany.   *Intr.*
Will: Tatnall   *Disclaimes.*
Rob't Squibb.   *Entr.*

READING HUNDRED.

[Parish of] S^T GYLES [in Reading].

Rich: Milson   [*Not in Rawl. D.* 1480].
Will: Brackston   *Disclames.*
Martin Hobbs   [*Not in Rawl. D.* 1480].
Wm Kenrick gen   [*Not in Rawl. D.* 1480. *See below*].
Rob't Terrill.
Tho: Warner   [*Not in Rawl. D.* 1480].
John Blake   [*No App.*] *L. adjourn^d till Easter Tearme*, 1665. *respite till Lady day. vide l'ram G. Lloyd.*
Humefry Moore   [*Not in Rawl. D.* 1480].
John Kenton   [*Not in Rawl. D.* 1480].
Thomas Kenton Maior   *adjourn^d till Easter Tearme* 1665. *Sumoned to Reding Assises* 166⅔ *respit this warr^t till I come to Read^r. Respit till Easter Tearme* [? 1666.]
Tho: Seakes   *adjourn^d till Easter Tearme* 1665 [*& again* 1666 ?].
[Nicholas] Gunter.   *Intr.*
Will: Wilmer.   *L. will app' againe at Lady Day.*

WHITLEY in the pish of St Gyles REDING.

Ralph Reddit   [*crossed out*]   *Disclaimed.*
Will: Claydon   [*crossed out*].
William Kendrick   Intr.
Rich Howse.   Intr.

TYLEHURST.

Simon Lowth Clerke   *will i'forme himself of his family.*
Henry *Zinzan* [*alias Alexander*] Esqr   *Intr.   vnpd.*
John Curtis   [*Not in Rawl. D.* 1480].
Will: Browne señ   [*Not in Rawl. D.* 1480].
John Wilder   [*crossed out*].
John Bowyer   [*Not in Rawl. D.* 1480. *See Theale*].
Rich: Wilder   [*Not in Rawl. D.* 1480. *See Theale*].
Walter Blagraue.   [*No App.*] *Sumoned to Reding Assises* 166⅔. *John Curtis of Tylehurst high Constable made noe retorne, nor noe app'ance of anyone.*

THEALE TITHING.

John Bowyer }
Rich: Wilder }   [*Not in Rawl. D.* 1480].

PANGBORNE.

Sr John Davys Knight   *Just: Entr.*
Ambrose Staveley Clerke.
John Justice   [*Not in Rawl. D.* 1480].

CHOULSEY.

Richard Samborne geñ   *Intr: rec^d* 10^s *will send ye rest to Jo: Haynes.*
John Whithilowe   [*No App.*].
.... Comyn geñ.
John Keate Esqr.   [*No App.*] 80 *yeares old, & no son.*
.... Sawyer geñ   [*Not in Rawl. D.* 1480].
Beniamin James   [*Not in Rawl. D.* 1480].

LIST OF THOSE SUMMONED TO APPEAR. 35

READING HUNDRED.
BUCKLEBURY.

Tho: Coward Clerke.
.... Inglefield [? *S*ʳ *Thomas Englefield K*ᵗ] *Sumoned to Reding Assises* 166⅘. [*entered under Reading Town. "lyes at Leonard Welbecks."*]
John *Elston* [*Eyston*] geñ *Int. a Maior in y*ᵉ *K*ˢ *Army. B*ʳ *to W*ᵐ *Eston of Est Henreth, who hath entred & dwells at Streatley. Entred of Streatley in Compt. hund: will app' at London next Easter Tearme* [16]66.
Arthur Woulger geñ *Disclaimes.*

THATCHAM.

Henry Wicker [*Not in Rawl. D.* 1480].
Barth: Mortimer [*Not in Rawl. D.* 1480].
.... Waller [*crossed out*].
Widdow Faukner for her son Sumoned to Reding Assises 166⅘.
*M*ʳ *Francis Perkins. adjourn*ᵈ *till Easter Tearme* 1665. *Ator: respite till next Tearme* [1666] *has no child? & aged.*
Robert Smeaton. *Intr.*
John Hassall. *Sumoned to Reding Assises* 166⅘. *Intr.*
Sir Tho: Lee *dwells at Chamb'house.*

ABSTREETE TYTHING.

Tho: Narraway. [*Not in Rawl. D.* 1480.]

COLDRAKE.

John Hawkins [*Not in Rawl. D.* 1480].

Mᴿ GODDARDES TYTHING [*blank*].

EARLE OF WORCESTᴱˢ TYTHING.

*S*ʳ Dowse Fuller of Chamberhouse *Knight.* [*No App.*] *Sumoned to Reding Assises* 166⅘. *married S*ʳ *Tho: Allens only dau: of London.*

HENWICK TYTHING.

James Cox [*Not in Rawl. D.* 1480].
Tho: & Fr: Powell *Tho:* [*No App.*] *Sumoned to Reding Assises* 166⅘.
Fr: [*No App.*]. *Sumoned to Reding Assises* 166⅘.

PARSONAGE TYTHING.

John Winchcombe Esqʳ *dwells neere S*ᵗ *James & will enter there, by M*ʳ *Rob't Garrard of Newbury.*
Robt Smeaton *Intr. will not faile to app' next Tearme at Lond: & enter there M*ʳ *Hutch is his friend.*
Barth: Springet.

BEENHAM.

Constantine Skinner Esqʳ [*crossed out*] *dwells in Tidm*ʳ*sh.*
Richard Perkins geñ *is sick. a batchelor. hath a B*ʳ *in London Aprentice to M*ʳ *Jerman a Chirurgeon next the bl*ᵉ *Swan in Holborne.*
Rich: Hildesley geñ [*crossed out*].
Norris Goldier [*Not in Rawl. D.* 1480].
Thomas Aldridge. Disclaimes.

BLEWBURY.

Tho: Justice & Edw: *Thomas.* [*No App.*]

EAST HENDRED [*blank*].

READING HUNDRED.

GREASLY HAMLET.

Ann James widd. *to Wm James of Denford in Kintb. Hund.* [*Not in Rawl. D.* 1480].

BEACH HILL.

Sr Henry Winchcombe *Bar^t Intr.*
John Harison Esqr *Entr. Just: adjourn^d till Easter Tearme* 1665 *will enter next Tearme at London.*
Charles Evans geñ *adjourn^d till Easter Tearme* 1665. *Steward to Sr Hen: Winchcombe & will app' next Tearme at London.*
Arthur Maynwaring, Esq. Intr. gratis.

THEALE HUNDRED.

SULLAM.

Will: Lawrence Clerke [*crossed out*].
Francis Hyde Esqr. [*No App.*] *Sumoned to Reding Assises* 166⅔.
Rob̄t Mason gent. [*No App.*] *Sumoned to Reding Assises* 166⅔. *? not well.*
Rich: Lybb gen [*crossed out*].

TIDMARSH.

Constantine Skinner Esqr *Sumoned to Reding Assises* 166⅔ *he is now at London will enter next Tearme at London. Mort.*
Rich: Wright Clerke [*crossed out*].
.... Leveston Esqr *his residence is at Lond:*

WOLLHAMPTON.

Martin Wollascott Esqr *Entr.*
Edw: Paris Clerke.
John Blanch [*Not in Rawl. D.* 1480].
Stephen Malthus. [*No App.*] *Sumoned to Reding Assises* 166⅔ *but did not app'e.*

ENGLEFIELD.

Henry Englefield Esqr *is at London & B^r to Anth: Inglefield of Early in Charleton hund who entred wth him yet p^d but one fee.*
Humfry Drake Clerke [*crossed out*].
Mary Potinger widd. [*crossed out.*]

BRADFIELD.

Rich: Bayly D^r: in Divinity [*Not in Rawl. D.* 1480].
George Wharton [*Not in Rawl. D.* 1480].
Eliz: Harison widd. [*Not in Rawl. D.* 1480].
John Harrison. [*No App.*] *sum'oned.*
Charles Stafford Esqr *Intr. gratis.*
John Pordage D^r: *Intr: rec^d* 17^s 6^d *of Fr. Pord:*
Hen: Brayton geñ [*Not in Rawl. D.* 1480].
Will: Wingfield geñ [*No App.*] *Sumoned to Reding Assises* 166⅔.
Tho: Browne [*Not in Rawl. D.* 1480].

SOUTHCOTT.

Dame Rose Blagrave widd. [*crossed out.*]
Mervin Tutchet Esqr [*No App.*] *Sumoned to Reding Assises* 166⅔ *he will app'e before the Lds. Con^s when I shall sumon him.*
Alex: Blagrave Esqr *Intr.*

THEALE HUNDRED.

ALDERMASTON.

Sr Humfrey Forster Bar^t *Intr.*
Edward Lovelock at Roundwood house   [*crossed out*].
Tho: Henwood   [*crossed out*].
.... Garret geñ   [*crossed out*].
.... Whistler geñ.
.... *Forster Bar^t* [*Not in Rawl. D.* 1480. *See above*].
Alexander Chokk, gen' 2^d son to S^r Fr: Chock.

PURLEY.

Tho: Blagrave Clerke.   [*No App.*]

PADWORTH.

Samuell Brightwell Esqr [*No App.*]   *Sumoned to Reding Assises* 166$\frac{2}{5}$.   *Entr refers p'fe & fee to London. he is a Barester of Lincolnes Inn. his son a Barester.*   [*Entr. crossed out.*]

HARTLEY DUMMER.

Peter Noyes gent [*gent. crossed out*]   *Intr.*
Barthol: Smith geñ   [*crossed out*].
Christopher Palmer   [*Not in Rawl. D.* 1480].

STRATFIELD MORTIMER.

Henry Lord Pawlet   [*Not in Rawl. D.* 1480].
Alex: Staples Esqr *adjourn^d till Easter Tearme* 1665.   *will enter at London at ye Temple.*
John Harrison Esqr *son to Mr Harison of Beech hill.*
John Coop̄   [*Not in Rawl. D.* 1480].
Daniell Whyte   [*Not in Rawl. D.* 1480].
Robt Vintner Clerke.
Tho: Headland   [*Not in Rawl. D.* 1480].
Joel Stevens   [*Not in Rawl. D.* 1480].

WORKFIELD.

Charles Pearce geñ   *Intr.*   [*gen. crossed out*].

UFFTON.

Francis Perkins Esqr *Intr.*
Martin Good Clerke   [*Not in Rawl. D.* 1480].
William Blunt of Feldhouse.   [*No App.*]   *Sumoned to Reding Assises* 166$\frac{2}{5}$.   *sewer to y^e Q: & no Issue.*

SULLAMSTED BANISTER.

James Fayrer Clerke   *Discl'.*
Charles Pearce gen: [*crossed out*]   *dwells at Wookefield in y^e hund & hath entr.*
George Sanders   *Discl'.*
Read Whittacre   [*Not in Rawl. D.* 1480].
Rich: Higgs sen: [*Not in Rawl. D.* 1480].

BURFIELD.

.... Dancer Clerke   [*Not in Rawl. D.* 1480].
Will: Brookes (*Brockes*)   [*No App.*]   [*crossed out*].
Rich: Pottinger geñ   *Intr.*

NOTES: VISITATION 1665-6.

THEALE HUNDRED, BURFIELD.

 Daniell Goddard [*No App.*] *sumoned to Reding Assises* 166⅚. *If he makes not p'fe of Armes next Tearme then disclaime him. younger B^r to Vincent Goddard. p'tends to Arms.*
 John Richards [*Not in Rawl. D.* 1480].
 Rich: Brewer [*Not in Rawl. D.* 1480].
 James Mathewes *of the Hill house. Sumoned to Reding Assises* 166⅚ *a Barrester.*

SUNNING HUNDRED.
OCKINGHAM TOWNE.

Tho: Martin geñ *Disclaimes.*
Anthony Spire geñ [*crossed out*] *broth^r to Rich: Spire of Wargrave & entred by him.*
John Sampson geñ [*No App.*]. *at the Kings head.*
John Gooding geñ.
Edward Cotton Esqr *Entr.* [*Esqr crossed out*] *has an Estate in Devonsh: & a Sojourner here.*
Hen: Montague geñ [*No App.*] *Sumoned to Reding Assises* 166⅚.
Edmund Verney geñ *Disclames.*
Angell Bell geñ *Disclames by l're vnder his hand.*
Rich: Smith [*Not in Rawl. D.* 1480].
Pearce Planer [*Not in Rawl. D.* 1480].
Tho: Miller gent: *Disclames.*
Capt. Henry Barker gent: *of Hurst. Intr.*
.... Bradley.
Humfrey Cantrell. *Intr.*
Humfry Broughton. *Intr.*
John White *Entr: son & heir of Sr Rich: White of Warnborow in Hants. Respited for app'ance till Lady Day at the vpp' ship in Red^g.*

WOKINGHAM P'ISH.

Humfrey Cantrell gent: [*crossed out, see above*].
Will: Marlow [*crossed out*].
Robt Whitlock gent: *he dwells in London. entred 3 yeare since at Clapham in Surrey.*
Hen Staverton geñ [*No App.*] *of Tangleys. Sumoned to Reding Assises* 166⅔.
John Cottrell [*Not in Rawl. D.* 1480].
Rich: Palmer Esqr *Justice of Peace. Entr. of the Office of Pleas in Lincolnes Inn.*
Wm Yeldesley (*Hildesley*) *Intr. will app' againe at Red^g at Lady day,* 17^s 6^d.
James Rouse.
John Plan[n]er. *a Brewer in Lond: but hath an Estate in Ockingham.*

ARBORFIELD.

Geo: Hodges gent: [*gent. crossed out*] [*No App.*] *Sumoned to Reding Assises* 166⅚. *dwells now at Shinfield.*
Edward Herbert Esqr *vide l're: son to Sr Arnold Herbert, a gent.-Pensioner.*
Alex: Stokes Clerke.
John Booth geñ. *Intr. dwells at Barkham.*
William Standen Esqr [*No App.*] *dwells at Beconsfield.*

LIST OF THOSE SUMMONED TO APPEAR. 39

SUNNING HUNDRED.

NEWLAND.

Rich: Webb [*Not in Rawl. D.* 1480].

SUNNING.

Sr Tho: Rich Barr^t *Intr.*
William Barker Esqr *Just*[*ice*]   *Intr.*
Anthony Barker Esqr *Just.*
Geo: Blagrave gen &   *of Bulmarsh. Intr.*
John *Blagrave of Suthcot.* [*Not in Rawl. D.* 1480.]
William Offley D^r of Law.   *Intr.*
Samuel Rayner Clerke   [*crossed out*].
Nath: Hopp[er] gent.   *Intr. but no fee p^d.*
Hugh Ferriman geñ.   [*Not in Rawl. D.* 1480].
Laurence Halsted.   Sumoned to Reding Assises 166⅔, *at London.*

WINERSH IN HURST.

Hugh Champion gent. }
.... Edwards widd.   }   [*Not in Rawl. D.* 1480].
Moses Maynard. [*No App.*] *sumoned to Reding Assises* 166⅔. *Disclaimed, an Estate of* 100^l *p' ann'.*
Robert Blower, Hurst. [*No App.*] *sumoned to Reding Asises* 166⅔ *dwells in Wiltshire.*

RUSCOMBE.

Will: Stroud geñ   *Just. of peace & Sheriff in Cromwells tyme.* [*No app.*] *sumoned to Reding Assises* 166⅔. *very sick. q. if his house doe not stand in Wilts.*
Richard Bigg, of Haynes hill.   Sumoned to Assises at Reding 166⅔. *Intr.*
Rich: *Aldworth Esqr Just: his house stands in Wiltshire but in Ruscombe p'ish.   Intr.*

SINSHAM GREENE *in Hurst p'ish.*

.... Smith. *Sumoned to Reding Assises* 166⅔. *who married the Lady North.*

SANDHURST.

Rich: Lodge geñ   *Discl'. respit of Entry vpon Mr Gallants request but Disclames.*
Rich: Geale &   [*No app.*] *Sumoned to Reding Assises* 166⅔.
Sam: *Geale*   }
Rich: Bankes   }
Abraham Spooner }   [*Not in Rawl. D.* 1480].
Tho: Dicy   }

HURST.

Robert Blower   broth^r to Christo: Blower of Sunningwell in Horm' hund. a Barester.   dwells in Wiltshire.

BEYNHURST HUNDRED.

HURLEY.

John Lord Lovelace   [*Not in Rawl. D.* 1480].
Francis Lovelace Esqr B^r to ye Ld Lovelace   dwells at Kilham with Mr Rich: Lovelace at Wargrave.
John Anger gent   *Disclames.*
Tho: Lyford geñ   *Intr: elder B^r to Jo: Lyford of Stanford Dingley.*

BEYNHURST HUNDRED, HURLEY.

John Micklen [*Not in Rawl. D.* 1480].
Robt. Fenn of Hallplace Esqr *An Alderman of London.*
Tho: Martin geñ [*No App.*].
Rich: Taylor geñ *Disclaimes.*
John Tyle geñ [*No App.*].

REMNHAM.

Sr Edward Partridge Kn^t.
John Salter geñ *Intr.*
Mathew Reade ⎫
Nath: Wade   ⎬ [*Not in Rawl. D.* 1480].
Alex. Barnard ⎭

BISHAM.

Peregrine Hobby Esqr *Just.* [*No App.*]

SHATSBROKE.

Sr Rich: Powle Kn^t of the Bath. *Just. Intr.*
Geo: Welden geñ *Intr. heirs of ye family of Welden of Shottesbroke.*
Hen: Boult [*Not in Rawl. D.* 1480].

BERRY IN P'OCHIA WHITE WALTON.

Sr Paule Neale Kn^t ⎫
Thomas Grove   ⎬ [*Not in Rawl. D.* 1480].
John Weston geñ [*No App.*] *Imployd by Sr Edmund Savage to collect the Kings Rents.*
. . . . Harding Clerke [*Not in Rawl. D.* 1480].
Tho: Hawes [*Not in Rawl. D.* 1480].

HEYWOOD in the same p'ish.

Sr Edmund Sawyer Kn^t [*Not in Rawl. D.* 1480].

LIBERTY of FINS (*Feens*) in the same p'ish.

John Whitfield Esqr [*crossed out*] *he lives in Maidenhead.*
Robert Wade for Fines [*Not in Rawl. D.* 1480].

CHARLETON HUNDRED.

WISTLEY IN HURST.

Rich: Harison Esqr *Just: Intr.*
William Clarke geñ *Disclaimes by his wife.*
Tho: Bagley geñ *adjourn^d till Easter Tearme* 1665. *Respit of app'ance to Lady day & East: Tearme.*
Geo: Coles [*No App.*] *Sumoned to Reding Assises* 166⅔. *dwells in Wiltsh: brother to Mr John Cole of Liss in Hampshire.*
Will: Button [*Not in Rawl. D.* 1480].
Rich: Palmer *Disclaimes.*

BARKHAM.

Alex: Stokes Clerke [*crossed out*] *he dwells in Arberfield.*
John Stroughill gent: *Entr.*
John Booths gen *Sumoned to Reding Assises* 166⅔ *Intr: now of Arberfield in Sun^e hund.*
Rich: James geñ [*No App.*] [*crossed out*].

LIST OF THOSE SUMMONED TO APPEAR. 41

CHARLETON HUNDRED.

FINCHAMSTED.

George Tettershall Esqr [*No App.*] *Sumoned to Reding Assises* 166⅔ *Intr.*
Tho: Bright Clerke.
Peter Sparke geñ. *Intr.*
Willm Reeves geñ [*No App.*].
John Morry (*Marry*) gent. [*No App.*]
Martyn Eyston (*Elston*) [*No App.*] *Sumoned to Reding Assises* 166⅔.
Samuel Banister. [*No App.*] *sumoned to Reding Assises* 166⅔ *one of the Exa'iers in Chancery.*

SHINFIELD.

Eustace Hooby geñ [*crossed out*] *mort.* [*Not in Rawl. D.* 1480].
Rich: Hyde geñ [*No App.*] *Sumoned to Reding Assises* 166⅔. *Intr. will give satisf: in his Armes next Tearme, saith he is desc: from Hyde of Norbury. not of the family of Hyde of K^eston* [*Lisle, Co: Berks*].
John Phelps *Sumoned to Reding Assises* 166⅔ *Disclamed.*
Will: Osborne geñ *Examiner in Chancery.*
Gilbert Garrard geñ *Intr.*
Tho: Richards. *Sumoned to Reding Assises* 166⅔ *Disclaimed.*
Edmund Ansley (*Anslow*) [*No App.*] *Sumoned to Reding Assises* 166⅔ *dwells in Wiltsh:* [*Not in Rawl. D.* 1480].
Samuel Woodcock } [*No App.*] *Sumoned to Reding Assises* 166⅔. *M^r*
[Samuel Richards] } *Anslow for Samuell Richards, mistaken for Woodcock. Mr Anslow is* [*h*]*is* [*Samuel Woodcock's*] *guardian.*
[*Peter*] Noyes of Trunkwall [*Trunkwood*] *Intr.*
.... Hooke [*crossed out*] *mort. he was eldest son to Hooke of Hooke in Com' Hants.*

SWALLOWFIELD.

Sr Will: Backhouse Bar^t *Just: high Sheriff. Int: Gratis.*

EARLEY.

Anthony Englefield Esqr *Intr.*
John Hyde geñ [*No App.*] 3^d B^r *to Hyde of Kingston, & refers to his entry.*
John Stampe geñ *dwells at Caversham.*
Rich Loader geñ [*crossed out*].
Sr John Fettiplace [*crossed out*] *lives at Childrey.*
John Stokes. [*No App.*] *son in law to Mr Anth: Englefield, & of Woolston in Shriv: hund: Sumoned to Reding Assises* 166⅔. *Christian name mistaken & y^tfore will not app^r: Excused by Mr Englefield of White K^{ts} Junior whose daught^r he marr.*

WARGROVE HUNDRED.

WARFIELD.

Will: Hughson Clerke [*Not in Rawl. D.* 1480].
Stephen Ferry (*Terry*) *Clerke.*
Simon Ager [*No App.*] *Serjant of ye Poultry. Sumoned to Reding Assises* 166⅔.
Will Finch
John Boult } [*Not in Rawl. D.* 1480].
Will: Bodkin

WARGROVE HUNDRED, WARFIELD.

John Marden geñ. *adjourn^d till Easter Tearme* 1665. *Sumoned to Reding Assises* 166⅔. *will app' & enter at London.*
Emanuel Hatch. [*No App.*] *now in Herefordsh:* ⎫
Lovell Young. [*No App.*] ⎪
Robert Dawkes [*No App.*] *Citizen* ⎬ *direcc'ons given to the Const.*
Hugh Read [*Rod*] [*No App.*] *Coroner.* ⎪ *to warne them to London.*
Henry Bulstred. [*No App.*] *Disclaimes* ⎭

WARGRAVE.

Rich: Lovelace Esqr *Just:* [*No App.*] *dwells at Hurley in Beynurst hund:*
Francis Lovelace Esqr [*No App.*] *Sumoned to Reding Assises* 166⅔. *B^r to the Ld Lovelace.* [*Not in Rawl. D.* 1480.]
Will: Smith ⎫
John Grove ⎬ [*Not in Rawl. D.* 1480].
Fr: Barnard ⎭
Rich: Spier geñ *Intr.*
Nathan Rogers geñ *Intr.*
Robt Mundy [*Not in Rawl. D.* 1480].

LAWRENCE WALTHAM.

Rich: Nevill Esqr *Just. Entr.*
Hugh Coverley geñ *belongs to the Ewery & his son Charles is a lynin drap' at Read^s.*
Sr Tho: Foote Kn^t *he dwells in London.* [*Not in Rawl. D.* 1480.]
Thomas Cotten [*Not in Rawl. D.* 1480].
Robt Styles [*Not in Rawl. D.* 1480].
Thomas Wilkinson Clerke. Intr. Gratis.

COOKEHAM HUNDRED.

SUNNINGHILL.

Sr Tho: Drap Barr^t *Just: adjourn^d till Easter Tearme* 1665. *will app' at London by Mr Leigh.*
Thomas Hancock geñ [*No App.*].
.... Richards geñ ⎫
.... Sawyer Clerke ⎬ [*Not in Rawl. D.* 1480].
Rich: Humfry ⎭

BINFIELD.

Robt Gosson Esqr *Adjourn^d till Easter Tearme* 1665. *his son Angell entred in Surrey, but noth^s of Gossons Da: Sumoned to Reding Assises* 166⅔. *Mort.*
Robt Lee Esqr *Intr. fee will be p^d at London.*
Will: Angell Esqr *Sumoned to Reding Assises* 166⅔. [*Name crossed out.*] *Entred in Surrey wth S^r Ed: Bysshe & marr: the sole da: to Rob: Gosson of Binfield but no menc'on there of his match.*
Will: Lee geñ *Intr.*
John Doncastle [*No App.*] *Sumoned to Reding Assises* 166⅔. *he dwells at Binfield but his son dwells at Welhouse. Intr.*
Tho: Bullock *adjourn^d till Easter Tearme* 1665. *frend to Fr: Phipps. Entred but refused to subscribe to it, but will app' at Lond.*

LIST OF THOSE SUMMONED TO APPEAR.

COOKEHAM HUNDRED, BINFIELD.

 John Pocock   [*No App.*].
 Rich: West   [*Not in Rawl. D.* 1480].
 Samuell Nelson.   [*No App.*] *dwells about Heckfield.*
 Will: Clarke Clerke.
 Robt Humes geñ   [*No App.*]. *dwells in London.*
 Gabriell Young geñ   [*No App.*].
 Hen: Lord Sterling.   [*No App.*] *Sumoned to Reding Assises* 166⅔ *he maried Mr Lees Daught: of Binfield* [*crossed out in Rawl. D.* 1480].
 John Fenwick.   [*No App.*] *Sumoned to Reding Assises* 166⅔. *Prisoner in Read^g being a Quaker.*
 Will Thorald.   [*No App.*] *Sumoned to Reding Assises* 166⅔. *Intr. son to Mr Wm Thorold heretofore of Arborfield. marr: Mr Doncasters Da: of Binfield.*

MAYDENHEAD.

 John Hoare   }   [*Not in Rawl. D.* 1480].
 Robt Bennet }
 Edw: Pouten   [*Not in Rawl. D.* 1480].
 Richard Robinson.   *Entr.*
 Nevill Kidwell   *app'd but can make out nothing. will app' next Tearme & Enter, search in Surrey. his fath^r & Grandf: dwelt at Kingston he now receives* 40^l *p' ann' a penc'on as a footman to the King.*
 William Cherry (*Cheny*) *Ator.* [*No App.*] [*See under Maidenhead in Bray Parish*, p. 44.]

COOKHAM.

 Fr: Crawley Clerke   [*Not in Rawl. D.* 1480].
 John Smith   [*Not in Rawl. D.* 1480].
 John Ferrers geñ.   *Intr.*
 John Dodson   [*Not in Rawl. D.* 1480].
 Rich: Woodyerre (*Woodier*) geñ *an Ator. adjourn^d till Easter Tearme* 1665. *Sumoned to Reding Assises* 166⅔. *will enter next Tearme.*
 Anth: Turbervile Esqr.   *Intr. of Coyte in Glamorganshire.*
 Will: Weldon geñ   *Intr.*
 Roger Barnes geñ   *serv^t to Mr Turbervile.*
 Will: Winch geñ.
 Nichol: Brice geñ—voyd   [*No App.*] *Sumoned to Reding Assises* 166⅔.
 .... Kidwell geñ—voyd   }   [*Not in Rawl. D.* 1480].
 .... Plumer geñ—voyd }

BRAY HUNDRED.

BRAY TOWNE.

 John Forrest   [*Not in Rawl. D.* 1480].
 Ralph Day geñ   [*No App.*] *Sumoned to Reding Assises* 166⅔. *he would disclame by ye high Court.*
 Rich: Winch geñ   [*No App.*] *Sumoned to Reding Assises* 166⅔ *many here of y^t christ: name, therefore knew not wch to serve.*
 Robert Marten   [*No App.*] *Sumoned to Reding Assises* 166⅔. *a Tanner.*
 John Peneman   [*Not in Rawl. D.* 1480].

BRAY HUNDRED.

CRESWELL in BRAY pish.

Peregrine Wilcox geñ. *Entr.*
Rich: Barnes geñ. *Adjourn⁴ till Easter Tearme 1665. Sumoned to Reding Assises 166⅔. Entr. will bring his Armes & fee to my Chamb'. in the Temple.*
Christop: Towes geñ [*No App.*] *A Baker at Shoelane end ou' ag⁴ y⁵ Salutac'on Tau'ne in Holborne.*
Mathew Petifer [*Not in Rawl. D.* 1480].
Samuel Wender. *Disclaimes.*

HOLY PORT in BRAY pish.

Thomas Kemball [*Not in Rawl. D.* 1480].

EAST OCKELEY in BRAY pish.

Rich: Franklyn geñ *he dwells at Colbrook.* [*Not in Rawl. D.* 1480.]
Rich: Powney geñ *Discl'.*
Simon Page geñ *Entr.*
Will: Kirby [*Not in Rawl. D.* 1480].
Robert Salter *B⁵ to Jo: Salter of Remnham in Beynhurst H. & entred by him.*

FIFIELD in BRAY pish.

Simon Winch geñ *Entr.*
Simon Beckley geñ & *Disclames.*
Humf. [*Beckley*] *son to Simon & entred wth him.*
Robt Curtis geñ *an Ator.* [*No App.*] *dwells in Lincolnes Inne Fields neere the Plow Stables.*
James Seaward geñ *Disclaimes.*
Will: Hockley [*Not in Rawl. D.* 1480].

STRAND in BRAY pish.

Edward Fulbam D⁵ in Divinity. *one of the Prebends of Windsor.*
Tho: Page *B⁵ to Simon Page of Est Okley in Bray.*
.... Rugman widd [*Not in Rawl. D.* 1480].

TUTCHIN in BRAY pish.

Henry Parteridge gen: [*No App.*] *Citizen of London.*
John Boylett geñ [*No App.*].
Will: Lyford [*Not in Rawl. D.* 1480].

WALTER OCKELEY in BRAY pish.

.... Johnson widdow [*Not in Rawl. D.* 1480].

BRAY-WICK.

John Whitfield Esq⁵ [*crossed out, see below*].
Tho: Wingrove [*crossed out*].
Tho: Micklam [*Not in Rawl. D.* 1480].

LIST OF THOSE SUMMONED TO APPEAR.

BRAY HUNDRED.

MAYDENHEAD in BRAY pish.

John Whitfield Esqr *adjourn^d till Easter Tearme* 1665. *Sumoned to Reding Assises* 166⅔. *Mr Turbervill saith he will enter at London.*

Will: Silvester
.... Harmor
.... Wintershell } [*Not in Rawl. D.* 1480].
.... Wigmore
Simon Hicks

Mr *Will. Cherry (Cheny) an Ator. in Brick Co^{rt} midle Temple. Sumoned to Reding Assises* 166⅔. [*name crossed out.*]
Mr *Tho: Staples. son to Mr Alex: Staples of Stratfield Mortimer.*
M^r .... *Turbevile.* [*crossed out.*] [*See under Cookham,* p. 43.]

RIPLESMEERE [HUNDRED].

OLD WINDSOR.

Richard Cooke. adjourn^d till Easter Tearme 1665. *Sumoned to Reding Assises* 166⅔. [*name crossed out.*] *will app^r next Tearme in London.*
Thomas Smith at the Mañor Lodge
John Barrey Esqr } [*Not in Rawl. D.* 1480].
.... Southwood gen:
Will: Powell. [*No App.*] *Sumoned to Reding Assises* 166⅔ [*name crossed out*]. [*in List Rawl. D.* 1480].
Will: Smith geñ   Mr *James Smiths elder B^r.*
John Powney geñ [*No App.*] *dwells at ye Mewes, & one of ye purveyors.*
Humf: Mitchell [*Not in Rawl. D.* 1480].
Franc: Levar [*No App.*] *Sumoned to Reding Assises* 166⅔ [*name crossed out*].
James Smith geñ *of the midle Temple. has entred wth Sr Edw: Byssh. he did not.*
Dr Gyles [*crossed out*] *mort.* [*Not in Rawl D.* 1480].
.... Weldon. [*No App.*] *son of Geo: Weldon of Cookham menc'oned in the last visitac'on Sumoned to Reding Assises* 166⅔ [*name crossed out*].
.... Christmas. [*No App.*] *Sumoned to Reding Assises* 166⅔ [*name crossed out*].
Robert Aldridge *Sumoned to Reding Assises* 166⅔. [*name crossed out*] *Intr. but fee vnpd.*

CLEWER.

Joseph Tyler geñ *Intr.*
Will: Flood geñ [*crossed out*].
Hen: Proctor Esqr *Just:* [*No App.*].
Alex: Hayes geñ [*No App.*] *Sumoned to Reding Assises* 166⅔. [*name crossed out.*]
Fr: Powlton geñ [*crossed out*].
John Brice.

RIPLESMEERE HUNDRED.

East Hamsted.

Will: Trumbull Esqr *adjourn^{d} till Easter Tearme* 1665 *Entr.*
John Brice Clerke [*Not in Rawl. D.* 1480].
Simon Wilkes [*crossed out*].
Tho: Barker (*Baker*). [*No App.*] *Sumoned to Reding Assises* $166\frac{5}{6}$. *Disclaimed at Windsor.*
John Gibeon geñ [*crossed out*].
Rich: Bagley geñ [*No App.*] *Sumoned to Reding Assises* $166\frac{5}{6}$ *vpon Mr Baglyes request suspended till next Tearme.*
John Culvar.
Francis Broughton. Entred by his B^{r} Humfry B: of Ockingham.

Winkfield.

Sr Hen: Henn Kn^{t} *& Bar^{t}. Entr.*
John Hercy Esqr *adjourn^{d} till Easter Tearme* 1665. *Entr.*
Jeremy Terrent Clerke *Parson of Clewer.*
Rich: Lock. [*Not in Rawl. D.* 1480.]
John Hill at Simley Rayles (*Singley Rayles*) [*No Att.*] *Sumoned to Reding Assises* $166\frac{5}{6}$. *Int^{r}.*
Samuell Winder geñ *dwells at Bray.*
Simon Page geñ *dwells at Bray.*
Andrew Mylam [*Not in Rawl. D.* 1480].
Oliver Pretty geñ.
Barth Mountague geñ—voyde [*Not in Rawl. D.* 1480].
Francis Harris.

Dedworths.

Will: Bowles gent. *he dwells in Clerkenwell.*
Tho: Hayes geñ [*crossed out*].
Rich: Winch geñ [*No App.*] *Sumoned to Reding Assises* $166\frac{5}{6}$. *will enter at London.*

New Windsor Towne.

Daniell Quarterman *at y^{e} Garter. adjourn^{d} till Easter Tearme* 1665.
Tho: Mansfield *Drap^{r}.* [*No App.*]
Geo: Lay geñ.
Will: Poole geñ *Baker.*
Will: Carey geñ *Taylor.*
John Nash geñ *Brewer.*
Rich: May Esqr [*No App.*] *of the Midle Temple, & dwells in Sussex.*
Major Fincher [*No App.*] *Sumoned to Reding Assises* $166\frac{5}{6}$ [*name crossed out*]. [*In Rawl. D.* 1480.]
Samuell Onley. Intr.
George Downes. Intr.
Richard Webb. [*No App.*]
Thom: Westhrop. Ator. Intr.
Fr: Ridley. Register to the Deane &c. Steward. Adj^{d} till Easter Tearme 1665. *will enter at London.*
John Blew. [*No App.*]
Rich: Nash [*Not in Rawl. D.* 1480].
Will: Tayleur Esqr *Intr.*
John Denham D^{r} of Phisick [*crossed out*]

LIST OF THOSE SUMMONED TO APPEAR. 47

RIPLESMEERE HUNDRED, NEW WINDSOR TOWNE.

    Capt: Nathaniel Harris   [*No App.*].
    George Starkey Esq'   [*No App.*]   *Sumoned to Reding Assises* 166⅘   [*name crossed out*].   [*In Rawl. D.* 1480.]
    Peter Comeñ Marques &c.   [*? crossed out*].
    John Woodson geñ   *an Ator. Intr.*
    Johan Sunnibanks   [*name crossed out*]   *mort.*
    Tho: Cox.   *a Chorurgeon.*   [*No App.*]
    Tho: Holford   [*Not in Rawl. D.* 1480].
    Capt: Edw: Rauisburrow—void   [*crossed out*]   *dwells at Staines.*
    John Bennet   [*Not in Rawl. D.* 1480].
    Christoph: Whitchcock geñ   [*crossed out*]   *mort.*
    Alex: Baker geñ   *Intr.*
    Andrew Plumpton geñ   *Intr.*
    Will: Franklyn D' of Phisick   *adjourn^d till Easter Tearme* 1665.   *will Enter at London.*
    Timothy Eman   *Intr.*
    John Plummer   *Esq' Intr.*
    Rich: Fishbourne geñ   *Intr.*
    Rob: Harris geñ   *adjourn^d till Easter Tearme* 1665.   *Sumoned to Reding Assises* 166⅘.   [*name crossed out.*]   *will enter at London next Tearme.*
    George Pennington   [*Not in Rawl. D.* 1480].
    William Baker Esq'   *Intr.*
    John Finch Esq'   [*crossed out*]   *dwells at Langley in Com' Buck.*
    S': Rich: Braham K^t & Bar^t *Just. Entr.*
    James Haylor of Cranbourne   [*Not in Rawl. D.* 1480].
    John Woodson geñ   [*Not in Rawl. D.* 1480].
    Will: Bowles   [*crossed out*].
    M' Richard Baley   [*No App.*].
    M' Charles Whiteaker adjourn^d till Easter Tearme 1665.   *will enter at London.*
    Leonard Bennet Esq'. Intr.
    M' Bankes   [*No App.*].
    Richard Spencer   [*No App.*].
    Edmund Wilson   [*No App.*].
    John Topham Esquire.   S'jant at Armes   *his elder B' is of Graies Inn. & he will enter in London.*
    Tho: Vachell Esquire.   *Intr.*
    John Baker.   [*crossed out.*]
    Hargill Baron.   *Clearke of ye Signet. Intr.*
    George Litleton. an Ensigne in W: [*? Windsor*].
    Samuell Hales. Intr.
    Barthol'. Mountague. respit.   [*See under Winkfield,* p. 46.]

Albery, of Wokingham.

[*MS. Books of Grants: and Harl. MS. 1532, and Add. MS. 4961, p. 94ᵇ.*]

Patent of Arms by Robert Cooke Clarenceux to Thomas Albery of Wokingham in com̃ Berks. 15⁇0.

[*Argent*] a Cross ing^d between 4 Stock Doves B.

CREST: On a Wreath a Stock Dove B. in his Beaque a Sprig v^t fflowered Gules.

Aldridge, of Old Windsor.

[*MS. Rawl. D. 865, f. 91.*]

[*In Ashmole's handwriting, marked* fee vnp^d. *For the Visitation* 1665-6: *not included.*]

[*No arms given.*]

Robert Aldridge of Woodlande in Com̃ Bucke.=

Robert Aldridge of Old Windsor=Mary da: to .... Baldwyn of Wilsons in Com̃ Berke. | Greene in Com̃ Bucke.

3. Samuell Aldridge.
2. John mar: Hanna da: to John Lever of Old Windsor.
1. Robert son & heire æt. 35 annorum 30 Mar: 1665. =Eliz: da: to John Grove of West Wickham [*Wycombe*] in Com̃ Bucke.
Mary wife to Humfry Beckley of Bray in Com̃ Berke.

1. Robert.   2. John.   3. Thomas.   1. Elizabeth.   2. Mary.

SAMUEL ALDRIDGE for my [*orig.*]
father ROBERT ALDRIDGE,

OF BERKSHIRE.   49

Aldridge, of Charlton, near Wantage.

[*MS. Rawl. D. 865, f. 88ᵇ.*]

[*In Ashmole's handwriting, marked* vnpaid. *For the Visitation of* 1665-66: *not included.*]

[*No arms given.*]

Henry Aldridge of Detford=Anne da: to .... Blake of Walsingham
in Com̃ Kent.   in Com̃ Norff.

1. Ralph   2. Thomas Aldridge of=Katherine the da: of .... Bateman of Tot-
Aldridge   Charlton neere Wanting neux Co‘t [*Tottenham Court*] in Com̃ Midd.
ob: s: æt: 55 ann: 21 Mar: relict of John Clarke of Ardington in Com̃
prole.   1664.   Berke Esqʳ.

Elizabeth.

THO: ALDRIDGE. [*orig.*]

Aldworth, of Aldworth.

[*MS. Ashmole 840, p. 379.*]

[*In Ashmole's handwriting. See Vol. I., p. 155.*]

ALDWORTH impaling PARSONS.

Visum cognitum et in Collegio Heraldorum tempore visitacionis Comitatus Berchieræ Anno 1623, relatum vna cum stirpe et propagacione Ricardi Aldworthe ex antiquâ familiâ de Aldworth oriundi cuius auita sedis erat apud Aldworth in prefato comitatu Berchiæræ.

Attestor hoc
Jo: Philpott
Rouge Dragon
Deputatus Clar-
enceux Regis
Annorum.

[*The colours of the field* (Argent) *and the bears' heads and crosses-crosslet* (Gules) *are marked on the original trick.*]

Aldworth, of Reading and Wargrave.

[*MS. Ashmole 852*, p. 2.]

[*Additions from Townsend MS.*]

John Aldworth of Reading in Com: Berks Merchant=[*Alice?*].

Margaret da. & heire of=Richard Aldworth of London, *d*: 13=Anne da. of Richard May *of* London first wife. Thomas Deane of Reading in Com: Berks 2ᵈ wife. | May 1623 æt. 66 burᵈ at St. Mary Aldermanbury.

Margaret wife of George Willmott of Letcombe in Com: Berks. | Thomas. — William. | Richard Aldworth of Wargrave=Amy, da. of Thomas Persons of great Milton in Com: Oxon. in Com: Berks 1623, *ob*: 15 *March* 1638, burᵈ at Rushcombe, only son by 1ˢᵗ wife.

Thomas second sonne. | Robert third sonne. | Richard Aldworth eldest sonne. | Henry 4ᵗʰ sonne. | John 5 *o.s.p.* | George 6. — *William* 7. | Anne d. *unm:*

[*See Aldworth of Ruscombe* (*Visit.* 1665-6), *Vol. I.*, p. 155.]

Amore.

[*MS. Ashmole 852*, pp. 8 and 9.]

[*No Arms tricked.*]

William Amore=....

Henry Amore=[Joane] da. of .... Phillips   Richard Amore=Christian da: of ....
[*Harl. MS.* 1153].

Nicholas Amore=Maude da: of Thomas Bereff.   Joane [*John Harl. MS.* 1153.]   William.   Ellenor.

Agnes.   Elizabeth.   Margaret.

.... da. & heire=John Amore=Margaret d: of John Hayte.   Thomas Amore=Joane da: of ....
of Kendall.

John Amore=.... da: of Wm Bradley.   Elizabeth Amore=William Vantare.

Maude.   John Amore.   Margaret.   W^m, Cecill, Jo[hn], Florence [*Flower*], Eliz. Maud, Jane. [*Harl. MS.* 1153.]

Angell, of Binfield.

[*MS. Rawl. D.*, 865, fol. 143.]

Sir
    I am the sonne and heire of John Angell esq^r of Crowhurst in Surrey, who hath entered mee and my marriage with himselfe with Sir Edward Bish. I shall not need therefore to repeate it. Sir, this all frō him who am
                Your humble seruant
                      Williā Angell.

From Binfield
this 30th of March
  1665.
[*Addressed*]   For Elias Ashmole esq^r at the
three Tunns in Winsore these.

[*Red wax seal bearing two angels kneeling with one knee on two hearts, and each supporting a crown with one hand.*]

Ashmole's notes in the lists are: *Entered in Surrey wth S^r Ed: Bysshe & marr. the sole da: to Rob: Gosson of Binfield but no mention there of his match.*

The following is the pedigree, and it contains the match referred to:—

Visitation of Surrey, 1662—1668, *from MS. College of Arms, D.* 15, *fol.* 106.

Thomas Angell of Peakirk=.... da: of .... Herbye of
in Com. North^{ton} g^t. | Glynne in Com. North^{ton}.

```
                                    ▲
                                    |
William Angell of London Ar: Serjt of═Joane da: of .... Povey of
His Maties Achatery.                  | London gt.
```

```
John Angell of Crowhurst in Com. Surry Ar: one of═Elizabeth da: of Sr Robert
ye Pensioners in Ordinary to King James and King │ Edolfe of Hinxsill in Com.
Charles 1662.                                    │ Kent Knt.
```

3. Robert.	5. Justinian.	1. Mary mar:	2. Thomazine mar:	3. Frances.
—	—	Jo: Hardward	Rich: Marriott of	
4. James.	6. Thomas.	Ar:	London gt.	

```
John Angell 2d sonne mar.....    William Angell of═Elizabeth da: and heire of
da: of .... Mellish of Sandersted Bingfield in Com. │ Rich: Gosson of Bingfield
in Surry.                         Berks eldest sonne.│ Ar:
         ═
         |                                          |
   John.  Elizabeth.                        William.  Elizabeth.
                                                     JOHN ANGELL.
```

Armorer.

Grant of Augmentation to the Arms of Sir William Armorer. MS. Coll. of Arms, Misc. Grant, vol. vi., 111b.

Sr William Armourer Knt. Justice of the Peace for Berkshire was summoned to appear, and his name is given in the list under Reading Town in Ashmole's final List. No pedigree was entered.

Harl. MS. 5819, fol. 51, gives the crest, A gauntlet bendwise proper grasping the shaft of a broken tilting lance, Or, with the motto, Phanaticorum Malleus.

The Arms and Crest are tricked in the margin of a copy of this Grant in MS. Ashm. 858, p. 226, and from this the crest has been added.

Sir Edward Walker Kt Garter .... whereas our Soveriigne Lord King Charles II. taking into his princely consideration and very well remembering the [many] great & eminent services done unto him and his late Royal Father King Charles of Ever blessed memory by many of their loyall subjects from the beginning of the unhappy Depedions [*Divisions*] in all his Majts domeneons [*sic*] untill the time of his Maj^{ts} most happy Restaurations [*sic*] and being desireous to testifie unto posterity by sume markes & characters of honour ye Vallewe & esteeme hee hath of ye persons who have wth Courage Constancy & fidelity p^{r}formed ye same to wch Int. his Maj^{ty} hath ther upon bin gratiously pleased to Authorize mee to give grant & assign unto such persons or any of them such augmentations out of sume of his Royall badges as may be properly born for ye hono^r of them & there posterity and wheare as Sr William Armorer K^t hath for a long time served King James, King Charles ye first of Ever blessed memorie & his Maj^{ty} y^t now is in ye condetion of Equeery and is at p'sent first Enquerie [*sic*] of ye great horse stable as alsoe during the last wars wth great Curage, Constancy and fidelity adhered to his Maj^{tys} Just intrests as Major & afterwards Lieutenant Colonell of horse wheare in he Received dives wound followed ye fortune of his Maj^{ty} in his Low Condition beyond the seas & had ye happiness to returne wth him into England and wheare as ye said Sr William Armorer beareth for ye paternall Coate of his family Gules a chevron between three Armed Arames [*sic*] argent. Know yee theirefore that I the said Sr Edward Walker K^t Garter .... by the perticulor power and Authority given unto Mee by his Maj^{ty} to that purpose doe heare by Authorize him the said Sr William Armorer to omitt Leave out the Chevron in his Coate Armour and in the Roome and Stead there of do give grant and Assigne unto him [by way of Augmentation] A Lyon passant gardant or, as hereafter more Lively is depicted wch Augmentac͞on the said Sr William Armorer & the Heyres and Descendants of his body Lawfully begotton for ever [bearing their due and proper differences] may & shall Lawfully use beare & sett forth together wth his paternall Coate of Armes as hereafter is depected at all tymes & upon all occations wthout the lett or interuption of any person whatsoever. In witness wheare of I have Heare Unto Subscribed my name & affixed the Seale of my office the Eaight day of July in the 14th Yeare of the raigne of our Soveraigne Lord King Charles the Second By the grace of God King of England, Scotland France And Ireland Defender of the faith, etc., annoq Dom^i 1662.

[*Signed*]   EDW : WALKER.

[EVERARD GREEN,
    Rouge Dragon, 1908.]

Atmore, of Bray.

[*Harl. MS. 1532, fol. 141.*]

No arms tricked. In the Visitations of Oxfordshire, Harl. Soc., Vol. V., p. 189, the arms are given as : Or, a chevron Gules between three martlets Sable.

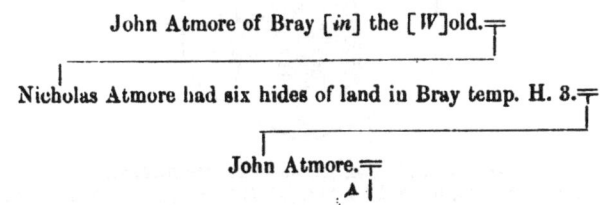

NOTES: VISITATIONS

A

| Nicholas Atmore. =| 2. Thomas Atmore had 4 Children ob. s.p. | Will Atmore of = Cookham *of Braye in the woulde. Harl. Soc., V., p. 189.* | 3. John Atmore. | Joane vx. Scott. | maud vx. W^m mountes. = |

John Atmore m. Jennett d. of Cheyney.

Willm. Mountes psonn of overton in Com. Southton.   John Mountes.

| Ellinor vx. .... Clobbert. = | Isabell vx. John Edyngton. | William Atmore had 6 Children dyed within age. | 2. John Atmore had 4 Children dyed within age. | Mathew Atmore. = |

John Clobbert.

Maud vx. .... Sothwick.

| Stephen Atmore a monk in Reding. | Joane vx. John borne. | Alice vx. John Thorne. | Maud vx. Thom. pury *servant to Kinge Henery the 4th (Harl. Soc., V., 189).* = |

Elizabeth *first wyffe sister* = John Purye of Camberhouse = Isabell *second wyffe* d. of
of Sr John Sysley Knight. | *in Com. Oxonie [Berks].* | .... Wawns of Beverley.

Mariery Pury, *died without issu.*

William Danvers of Chamberhouse by = Anne d. and heire
[right of] his wife [son of John Danvers of Cowthrop, co. Oxon.]. | of John Purye [living in 1517].

(*See Harl. Soc., Vol. V., p. 189.*)

𝔄belyne, of 𝔉rogmore.

[*MS. Ashmole 852, pp. 6 and 7.*]

CREST.—*A lion's head erased Argent, holding in its mouth a broken sword, blade silver, the hilt downwards Or.* (*Add. MS.* 14,283, *fol.* 72^b, 73; *Harl. MS.* 1582, p. 15^b, *etc.*)

OF BERKSHIRE.

Henry [de] Wyke=Sybell, da: and heire of Henry Twyford.

Hugh Avelyne of New=Julyan [da' to Henry de Weke of Werttesdon in right of
Windsore 27: Edw: 3th | Sibill his wi: da' et heire of Hen: Twyford (Harl. MS.
[1353]. | 1153, fol. 31)].

Robert Avelyne 18 Ric:=Agnes, da: of Tho: Shurt-   Robert=Anne, da: of John
secundi [1394, ar: of | ley [Sturteley (Harl. MS.   Dun- | Lorymer [over
New Windsor (Harl: | 1153). Over "Tho.," Ash-   ridge. | "Anne" Ashmole
MS. 1153)]. | mole has written "Rob."]. | has written "Agnes."

John Avelyne 9:=Vrsulah, da: and   John=Eliz. da: John=Christian
H: 5: [1421] & | heire of Robert   Dunridge | of ...   Lory- | da: to
14 H: 6 [1435] | Bitterley of   of Lon- | Staffer-   mer. | William
[of New Windsor | Wokingham [co.   don. | ton. | Siggen-
(Harl. MS. | Berks]. | ham.
1153)].

Robert Avelyne of=Mary da: of John Dunridge   Thomas Lorymer=....
Windsore. | [of London].

Thomas Avelyne of Lorymer [of Frogmore=Agnes da: of Thomas
(Harl. MS. 1153)]. | Lorymer.

Thomas Norreis=*Lettice.*

Edward Norreys marid Alice   *Henry Stauerton 2 sonn:*=*Senton [Lenton]*
da' and h: of John Fowller.   *mar' the da: of Brown of* | *of ye North partes*
                                               Egham. | *1: husb.*

John Norreis mar: Mary da coh: of henry
Staverton of Bray (Harl. MS. 1153).

Christopher Avelyne*=Joyce, da: to John Norris of Fyfield [co. Berks].

Edward Avelyne of Frogmorton=Edith da: of Edward Welden of Philberds [*manor*
in Berkshire [over "morton" | *in Bray co. Berks et of Isabella da' of .... Beke*
Ashmole has written "mere"]. | *of Whit-knights (Harl. MS. 1153).*

Richard Avelyne.   Elizabeth.   John Avelyne.   Isabell.

* *The site of the Priory of Wallingford (with the Prior's house) was granted in 1547 to John Norris, and he conveyed the Priory estate on the 27th of August 1553 to Christopher Avelyn and Jocosa his wife. ("Hist. of Wallingford," by J. K. Hedges, vol. ii., pp. 356—358.)*

Babham, of Cookham.

*From Le Neve's Copy of the Visitation of Buckingham taken 1634, fol. 19.
Arms granted by Sir Christopher Barker, Garter, temp. Henry VIII. [i.e., between 1536 and 1547].
Harl. MS. 1532, fol. 139, gives a trick of these Arms and the Crest of John Babham of Cookham.*
CREST.—*A demi man full faced proper, wreathed about the head with a knot gules, his right hand extended holding a hawk's lure sable, lined or.*

John Babham* of Cookehā com Berksh. =[*Eleanor* 7th] da: of [*John*] Cheney [*Esq.*] of [*Drayton Beauchamp*] in [*com: Bucks*]. [*He died* 1 *July* 1535. *Miscel. G. et H.*, ii., p. 134.]

    Hen Babham of Weston Turuile Com Buck: = Joane da: of .... Ardway of Beconsfeild [*co: Buck*].

        Richard Babham of Weston Turuile liuing 1634. = Joyce da: of Wm Lake of Trenge in Com Hart.

Joyce mar: to Edmond Brudnell of Stoke Mandeuile Esqr [*co: Buck*].

Hen: Babham Son & h: now liueing 1634. = Eliz: da: Edmond Brudnell of Stoke Mandeuille Esqr [*co. Buck:*].

---

* *In the Journal of the Berks Arch. Soc., vol. iii., p. 81, is an abstract of the Will of John Babham of Aston Clinton, co. Bucks, and Cookham, dated the 15th of April 2 Ed. VI. [1548]. It mentions Hellyn his first wife and Dorathee his present wife; also (Ibid., p. 100) the Will of Thomas Babham, Citizen and Grocer of London, [and of Cookham], dated the 11th of October [? 1490].*

Backhouse.

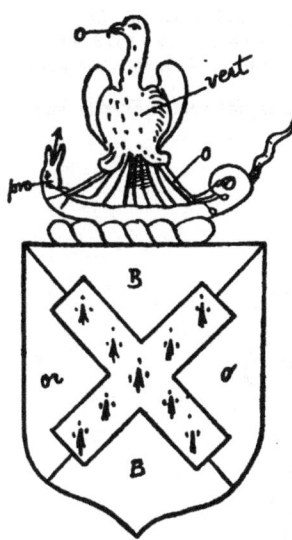

Confirmation of Arms and Grant of a Crest to Nicholas Backhouse of London by Robert Cooke, Clarenceux, dated the 27th of March 1574. (MS. Ashmole 858, pp. 185, 186.)

To all and singuler as well Nobles and Gentills as others to whome these presents shall cõme be sene red or vnderstand Robert Cooke Esquier alias Clarencieulx principall hereault and Kinge of Armes of the South East and Weast partes of this Realme of England from the River of Trent Sowthwardes sendith greeting in our Lord God everlastinge. Wheras Nicholas Backhowse of London Grocer son of Thomas Backhowse of Whitrige in ye Countie of Cumberland whose auncestors longe tyme past did come out of Lancashere where they were of worshipfull degree & did beare these tokens of honor as by searche in myne Office, and vieue of other auncient evidencis I finde set forth on this manner, Geroundy of fower golde & asur a Salter humetie ermyns, and where as well for proofe of their estate at that tyme as for shew of their degree wherein they lived there are yet divers parcells of Lands and other auncient monuments of their name in the said County of Lancastre yet remayninge, which least tyme should weare out being none of accompt of the said howse or name lefte now dwelling in the saide Shire, I the said Clarencieulx King of Armes by due deliberacoñ had and sufficient proofe made for ye confirmacõn of the trewth thereof doe by these presents ratify approve and confirme the said Armes or Ensignes of honor to belong and of right to appertaine to the said house or name of Backhowse whereof the said Nicholas Backhowse is lineally descended, for the further increase of which the said ensignes of honor vppon good & iust consideracoñ me movinge thereto at ye request of the said Nicholas Backhowse by vertue of power and auctority comitted to me by Lr̃es Patents vnder the greate Seale of England have assigned given & granted vnto the said Nicholas Backhowse of London Grocer as is afores^d: & to his issue and posteritie for ever to their said Armes this Creast or Cogniscance thus blased as followeth, on a torse golde & asur a close egle vert beaked & legged golde on a Serpent prop as more playnly apperith depicted in this Margent, which armes Creast or Cogniscance and every parte and parcell thereof I the said Clarencieulx Kinge of Armes do ratifie and confirme give and graunt vnto ye said Nicholas Backhowse & to his issue & posterity for ever & that they ye same shall have holde vse beare enioy & shew forth with their due differencis at all tymes & for ever hereafter at their liberty & pleasure without impediment let or interupcõn of any person or persons, In witnes whereof I the said Clarencieulx Kinge of Armes have set herevnto my hand & Seale of Office the xxvij^th day of March Anno Dñi 1574 & in the sixtenth yere of the raigne of our Soveraigne Lady Quene Elizabeth &c.

Robt Cook Alias Clarencieulx
Roy Darmes.

Backhouse.

Exemplification of Arms and Crest to Nicholas Backhouse of London, by Sir Gilbert Dethick, Knight Garter, dated the 27th of February 1579 (1579-80).
MS. Ashm: 858, *p.* 187. *In the copy MS. Ashm:* 840, *p.* 405, *the date 27th of February is altered to the 26th.*
The Arms quartered, Gules, a saltire Or, a label of five points Ermine, may be intended for Clyderow.

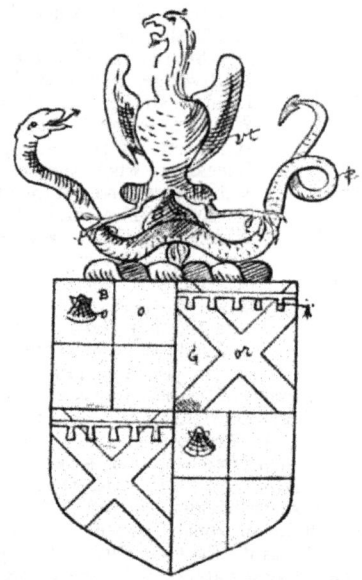

Theis are the Armes & Crest of Nicholas Backhouse Citizen & Alderman of London son of Thomas Backhouse of Whitrigge in the County of Cumberland Gent: & of Ellen the daughter & heire of Richard Parkyns of Holme in the said County of Cumberland gent: Which Armes are found out confirmed Quartered & allowed by me Sr Gilbert Dethick Knt: alias Garter principall King of Armes as wittnes my Recorde. In wittnes whereof I have herevnto set my hand & Seales as by vertue of myne Office the 27th day of Febr: Ano: Dñi 1579, & ano 22: Eliz: Regine.

Per me G. DETHICK alias Garter
principall King of Armes.

𝔅𝔞𝔨𝔢𝔯.

Patent of Arms and Crest to George Baker of London by Robert Cooke, Clarenceux, dated 1 *April* 1579. *MS. Ashm.* 858, p. 198. *Another copy is MS. Ashm.* 840, p. 403.

Omnibus et singulis tam nobilibus et generosis quam alijs quibuscunque Christi ffidelibus ad quos presentes Litteræ pervenerint Robertus Cooke armiger alias Clarencieulx summus Heraldus et Rex Armorum australis orientalis et occidentalis istius regni Angliæ partium a Trenta Fluvio Austrum Versus, salutem in Domino sempiternam, Cum hactenus semper ab ipsis mundi primordijs hominum præclarorum facinora strenue et fortiter ab ipsis gesta varijs multisque monumentis orbi terrarum innotuerint quamque inter ceteros precipuum et maxime vsitatum extiterit insignia quæ Arma decimus in Scutis gestatio, Quæ virtutis et gloriæ bellicæ argumenta sunt, varieque pro hominum meritis et dignitate tribui solent. Qui quidem mos sicut initio prudenter cæpit vsurpari quo magis ad virtutem capessendam animi hominum accenderentur, ita a posteris observatus est et adhuc viget vt qui per virtutem ad rei publicæ imolumentum honestæ vitæ splendore conspicui sunt, dum in rerum pulcherimarum et vtilium accione versantur tum ipsi dum vivunt honorem percipiant, tum evndem ad posteros suos perpetuo successuros transmittant. Hinc est quod Georgius Baker de London generosus me Clarencieulx Regem Armorum rogatum habuit, provt equum est veritatis testimonium prebere, vt in ejus gratiam ex analibus nostri Officij Majorum suorum Insignia qualiacunque ipsi tulerunt ei significarem publicè lucideque adscriberem. Ego quidem claro gratificari cupiens antiquam ejus familiam inveni, Quamobrem ne temporis injuria seu alia quevis occasio nove inquisicionis denuo prebeatur Clipei sui Insignia in hunc modum vt hic in margine depingitur explanavi, A majoribus suis dirivata, ex auctoritate mea meo Officio per Literas Regias annexa atque concessa sub sigillo vt sequuntur magno Angliæ publice et ornata remitto rata etiam facio et confirmata eidem Georgio Baker generoso, ejusque posteritati vtenda gerenda et in clipeis scutisve aut quovis militari ornamento corporisque tegumento provt libitum fuerit absque omni omnium impedimento et questione in contrarium. In cuius rei Testimonium ego prenominatus Clarencieulx Rex Armorum has literas fieri feci patentes quibus Sigillum Officij mei affigi feci datas primo die Aprilis Anno Domini 1579 et anno regni Dominæ nostræ Elizabethæ Dei gratia Angliæ Franciæ et Hiberniæ Reginæ fidei Defensoris &c. vicesimo primo.

           Rob' Cooke alias Clarencieulx
             Roy D' armes.

Baker.

See Visit. Lond., 1634-5, i., 39.
Exemplification of Arms and Grant of a Crest to George Baker of London by Robert Cooke, Clarenceux, dated 10th of May 1573, *15th Eliz.* (*MS. Ashm.* 858, p. 196. *Another copy, MS. Ashm.* 840, p. 424.)

To all and singular aswell Nobles and Gentills as others to whome these p'sents shall come Robert Cooke Esquier alias Clarencieulx principall Herehault & Kinge of Armes of the South East and Weast partes of this Realme of England from the River of Trent Southwards sendeth greeting in our Lord God everlasting, Whereas aunciently from the beginning the valiant & vertuous actes of worthie persons have ben comended to the world with Sondry monuments remembrancs of their good deserts Emongst the which the cheifest and most vsuall hath ben the bearing of signes in Shields called Armes, which are evident demonstracons of prowes and valour diversly distributed according to the Qualities & deserts of the psons, wch Order as it was most prudently devised in the beginning to stirre & kindle the heartes of men to the imitacon of vertue & noblenesse : Even so hath the same ben and yet is continually observed to thende that such as have don comendable service to their Prince or Contry eather in warr or peace may both receave due honor in their Lives and also derive the same Successively to their posterity forever Emongest which Nomber George Baker of London Gentilman Sonne of Christophfer Baker of Tenderden Sonne of John Baker of the same place, sonne of Symond Baker of Feversham in the Countie of Kent Gentleman being one of the bearars of these Tokens of honor as the Recordes of my Office do perfectly approue Nevertheles he not mynding to prejudice any of his blood or name hath required me the said Clarencieulx Kinge of Armes to sett foorth and allow vnto him his auncient Armes with such difference in bearing & such Creast therevnto as may be pper vnto him & meete to be borne by his posteritie for ever, In consideration whereof I the said Clarencieulx Kinge of Armes (by power & aucthoritie vnto my Office annexed and graunted by letters Patents vnder the great seale of England) do ratifie confirme & allow vnto & for the said George Baker Gentilman the Armes & Creast hereafter following That is to saye, golde a greyhound Currant in fesse betwen two barres sables And to the Creast vpon a Healme on a wreath golde & sables a Cocatrice ermyns, membred gules manteled gules dobled silver as more playnly appearith depicted in the margent, To have and holde the said Armes and Creast vnto & for the said George Baker Gentilman and to his posteritie and to all the Posteritie of Christofer Baker his Father with their due differencs and he and they the same to vse beare and shew forth in shilde Coat armour or otherwise at his and their Liberty and pleasure withont impediment lett or interupcon of any pson or psones. In witnes wherof I the saide Clarencieulx Kinge of Armes have sett herevnto my hande, & seale of Office the xth Day [of] May A° Domini 1573 :* and in the fifteenth yeare of the raigne of oure Soveraigne Lady Quene Elizabeth &c.

Rob^r Cooke alias Clarencieulx
Roy D'armes.

ex^d.

* *This date, originally written* 1578, *has been corrected in pencil to* 1573, *which agrees with the other copy of the same Patent* (*MS. Ashm.* 840, p. 424).

Baker, of New Windsor.

Patent of Arms and Crest to William Baker of New Windsor by Edward Bysshe, Garter, dated 14 July 1655. MS. Ashm. 585, pp. 206-7. Another copy, MS. Ashm. 840, p. 404. No trick of Arms in either.

The Trick of Arms here given is from a similar copy in MS., Coll. of Arms, Miscell. Grants, ii., 87.

To all and singuler vnto whom theise presents shall come Edward Byssh Esquire Garter principall King of Armes of Englishmen sendeth greeting. Whereas it hath ben an auntient custome, and to this day is continued that all estates and degrees have byn and are knowne each from other, by sundry markes, as Signes called Armes, being no otherwise then owtward demonstracons and remembrances of the inward worth of the bearers atcheived either by their Valour in the ffeild in tyme of warre or by their Virtuous endeavours in the Comon Wealth in tyme of peace, And forasmuch as Wm Baker of New Windsor in the County of Berks Esquire hath desired me to assigne vnto him such Armes as he may lawfully beare know ye therefore that I have assigned vnto him the Armes hereafter menconed viz: Argent on a Fesse betweene three Trefoyles azure as many swanns necks erased of the first beaked gules and for a Creast on a Helmet and wreath of his colours a Swanns neck erazed argent collered azure, holding in his beake gules a Trefoyle of the second mantled gules doubled Argent as in the Margent more lively is depicted, which Armes and Creast and every pt thereof I the sayd Edward Byssh Garter principall King of Armes of English men by power and authority of mine Office to me comitted vnder the great Seale of England doe by these presents assigne give and grant vnto the aforesaid Wm Baker and to his heires to be by them and every of them borne with their due differences according to the Lawes of Armes for ever. In witnesse whereof I have vnto theise presents, affixed the Seale of my Office & subscribed my name dated in the Office of Armes, the fourteenth day of July, in the Yeare of our Lord God, 1655.

          E: BYSSHE Garter principall
          King of Armes of English men.

Ball, of Barkham.

Visitation of London, 1634-5, I., 40, *Harl. Soc.*, Vol. XV.

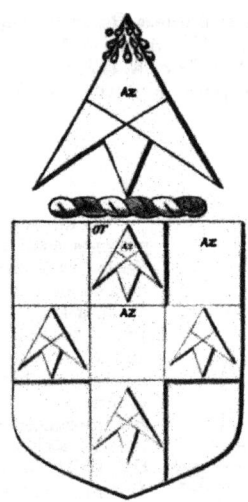

William Ball of Barkham com. Berks died aº 1480.

Robert Ball of Barkham com. Berks died aº 1548.

William Ball sonne & heyre unto whom he gave his personall estate and dwelt at Wokingham [*co: Berks*] died aº 1550.

Edward Ball second sonn vnto whom his father gave all his lands.

.... da. of .... Haynes of Fincharmted [*Finchampsted*] com. Berks. = John Ball sonne & heyre died aº 1599. = Agnes da. of Richard Holloway of Barkham.

1. Agnes. Joane.
2. Blanch.

1. William. Elizabeth.
2. Richard. Joane.

John Ball died 1628. = Elizabeth da. of Thomas Webb of Ruscombe com. Berks.

Robert. Rachel.
Thomas.

William Ball of Lincolnes Inn and one of the 4 Atourneys of the office of Pleas in the Exchequer Court liuing Aº 1634. = Als da. of Richard Waltham of London merchant.

2. Thomas.
3. George.
4. Richard.
5. Samuel.

1. Rachel.
2. Elizabeth.
3. Suzan.

4. Als.
5. Dorethy.
6. Mary.

WILL. BALL.

OF BERKSHIRE.

Bamfield.

Trick from Camden's Grants, i. 2b, ii. 2b.

Bark[shire] Bamfeilde, by William Camden. Or on a bend G: 3: mullets: perced on ye sinister pt. of ye Eschothen an annulet S.: Crest A lion's head Eraced Sa Crowned: G: on ye Neck an annulet or. (MS. Book of Grants.)

These Arms and Crest were confirmed, 18 May 1604, *to Robert Bamfield or Barnfield of Edgmond, co. Salop, a kinsman of Sir Amyas Barnfeld of Poultemore, co. Devon.* "Guillim," 1724, p. 102. (*Visit. Shropshire,* i., 84, *Harl. Soc.,* Vol. XXVIII.)

Barker, of Newbury.

MS. Rawl. D. 865, *fol.* 64. *Not in Ashmole's hand. Original paper. The original of the pedigree in Ashmole's handwriting, printed* vol. i., pp. 165-6, *signed by John Rider for Dir Barker, is MS. Rawl. D.* 865, *fol.* 79.

[No Arms tricked.]

William Barker of Staaksley Father to

Sr Christopher Barker Garter King at Armes Son and Heire [*a note by this entry, sub Hen° 8°*].

By this marryage we claime kindred to William of Wickhā The Founder of New Colledge in Oxford and Winchester Colledge.

Richard 2d son.

Robert Barker of Culworth in the County of Northamptō 3d son. He marryed Marie Daughter to William Danvers wch was Brother to Sr John Davers, Grandfather to Henerie the last Erle of Danby.

Robert Barker of Greate Horwood in the County of Bucks.

By this match I inherit ye 3d part of Crokers Estate in Battisford.

Hugh Barker of Newberry in the Countie of Berks Dr of Physick. Marryed to Joan the Daughter of Edward Goddard of Woodhay Com: South: Esqr But by Her Mother coheire to John Croker of Battisford in the County of Gloster Esqr.

The Armes are Argent 3 Beares heads errased gules, mussled Or, 3 Tortures in cheefe. wch is my claime, from Robert my Grandfather, the brother of Sr Christopher with distinction.

Mr Rider

I desier y^u to Attend m^r Ashmole, and to giue him this accompt of my claime; and that Enterie be made accordingly. P^rsent my service to Him; I am sorry my buisinesse is such that I can not waite vpon Him.

HUGH BARKER [*orig.*].

Mart: 22. 1664.

Barker of Sunning.

[*No Arms given.*]   *MS. Ashmole* 852, p. 11.

.... Barker of Wokingham [*co: Berks*]⊤....

William Barker of Wokingham=Anne da: and Coheire of Wm Burghley.

William Barker of Wokingham.	=Anne da: of Throgmorton of Caughton.	John Barker of Wokingham.	=Kath: da: to Edw: Martin of Shinfield [*co: Berks*].	Ambross Barker 2^d son had 19 children.	=Margaret da: to Thomas Carter.

| Wm Stafferton 6: son to Ralph Stafferton of Warfield [*co: Berks*]. | =Anne da: & heire. | =.... Bridon 1st husband. | | Thomas Barker of Chignall in Essex. | |

William Barker of Sunning in Co: Berks.	=Anne, da: of Laurence Stroughton.	*Anthony* 2nd *son.*	John Barker of Hurst. [*See Barker of Hurst,* Vol. I., pp. 164-5.]	=Frances da: of Henry Mandefeld of Taplow, *Bucks.*

| William dyed young. | Richard Barker 5 sonn. | =Mary da: of John Litcott of Swallowfield in Co: Berks. | Sr Anthony Barker of Sunning second son [*see Barker of Sunning,* Vol. I., p. 163]. | =Jane da: to Edw: Elvington of Bichall [?*Beech Hall*] in Essex a^o 1610. | Tho: Barker 4 son. | =Mary da: of .... Saunders. |

| | Wm Barker 20 yeares olde 1619. | Mary. | | Wm Barker. | .... second sonne. | Anne. |

| Henry Barker 2^d sonne 20: yeares olde, | Nathan^ll 3^d sonne 19 yeares olde. — Anthony 4: son. | William Barker eldest sonne 21 yeares old a^o 1619. | Lawrence 5 sonn. | Francis. — Jane. | Lettice. — Anne. |

OF BERKSHIRE. 65

Barnes, of Bray.

MS. Rawl. D. 865, f. 81. No Arms. In Ashmole's handwriting. For the Visitation 1665-6, not included, marked respit of fee till the Tearme.

Bray hund.

Joseph Barnes of Walderne = Eliz: da: to .... Spencer of
in Com Sussex. | Penshurst in Com Kant.

Joseph Barnes of Good- = Eliz: da: to John Holt of Stone   Eliz: wife to John Cant
hurst in Kent. | in the Isle of Oxney in Kent.   of Walderne in Com Sussex.

Richard Barnes of Bray in Com Berke = Hanna da: to John Bostock
æt: 46 annorum 28 Mar. 1665. | of Eatonbridge in Com Kant.

1. Joseph son & heire æt: 20 = Jane da: to ....   2. Richard.   Hanna.
Annorum 20 Mar. 1664.   Williams of ....

RICHARD BARNES. [*Original.*]

Barnes, of Bray.

MS. Rawl. D. 865, fol. 229, Draft of Letter.

Mr Barnes

You promised when I entred yor descent at Maidenhead, to giue me satisfaccoñ touching yor right to the bearing of Armes. It is now aboue a Yeare since, & hithertoo I haue heard nothing from you, & therefore I hereby giue you notice that in case you doe not (sometyme the next Tearme) come or send to my chamber in the Midle Temple, & there make proof of yor Armes I must in pursuance of his Maties Com & duty of my place ranke you among the number of those who haue no right to Armes, & proclaime you to be such a one at the next Assises to be held for the County of Berkȩ.

[*E. ASHMOLE, Windsor Herald.*]

v. 6. 6. Ju 4.

Richard Barnes of Creswell, in Bray Parish, was first adjourned, then his pedigree was entered. In the final List, Ashmole has written, Int. will bring his Armes & fee to my Chamb' in the Temple.
His name is not in the List of Disclaimers.

Baron, of Reading.

(Called also BARREY and BARREBY.)

Gules a chevron Azure [*Argent?*] between three garbs or, William Baron a gentleman of Berkshire, was one of those who bore arms from their ancestors (see "Fuller's Worthies"), and whose names were returned for the defence of the Kingdom *temp.* Henry VI.*

In E.D.N. 13 (Coll. of Arms) and at the subsequent Visitations of Staffordshire 1614 and 1663 it is blazoned, Or, a chevron Azure between three garbs gules.

Possibly the true blazon should be, Gules, a chevron counter componée Argent and Azure between three garbs or, which is given in Glover's Ordinary, as the coat of "Baron *temp.* Edw. IV."

("Visitation of Staffordshire," 1583, W. Salt. Soc., vol. iii., p. 152, notes by H. S. Grazebrook.)

Baskerville, of Bayworth and Sunningwell.

MS. Ashm. 836, p. 683. *Original paper sent in for the Visitation,* 1665-6.

Berks. Hanybal Baskerville of Bayworth in the said County esq^r offereth to Elias Ashmole esq^r Windsor-Herauld att Armes his descent as followeth.

Sr James Baskerville kn^t heire geñall of the howse of Eardesley married Sybill the daughter of Walter Devereux Ld Ferrers of Chartley by whome he had
  1. Sr Walter Baskerville kn^t.
  2. John Baskerville esq^r &
  3. Phillip Baskerville.

John Baskerville by his wife Alice the daughter and heire of John Bridges of Hereford had

Henry married to Anne the daughter of John Rufford esq^r whoe begatt
  1. Sr Thomas Baskerville kn^t Cheife comaunder of the English in Picardy vnder the French King, and
  2. Nicholas Baskerville esq^r a Captayne many yeares in the Lowe Countryes and dyed att Flushing, and
  3. John Baskerville whoe dyed alsoe in the Low Countryes and
  4. Arnold Baskerville whoe dyed in West India.

Sr Thomas Baskerville marryed Mary the daughter of Sr Thomas Throgmorton kn^t by whom he had

Hanyball Baskerville esq^r whoe marryed Mary Baskerville the wydow of John Morgan esq^r and daughter of the aforesaid Nicholas Baskerville by whom he had
  1. Thomas.
  2. Henry.   and Gertrude and
  3. Nicholas.   Constance.
  4. William.
  5. Robert.
  6. George.

---

* *Fuller's "Worthies," ed. by John Nichols,* vol. i. *William Baron, Ar.* (p. 96). *Johannis Baron of Wytenham* (p. 97).

Beisley, of Abingdon.

MS. Rawl. D. 865, fol. 141.

S^r

Our Antient Family came out of Glocester sheire at a Towne Cald Beisley Neere Glouc̄ for one of our Name did find it out there of late yeares, And all our Antient deeds doe expresse as much. Once againe lett me intreate yo^w to remember me, & yo^w will Euer Engage S^r

Y^r friend & Servt
ALEXANDER BEISLEY.

No address, endorsement, or seal. The Arms and pedigree were entered, see Vol. I., p. 172.

Abstracts of two Wills are printed in the Journal of the Berks Arch. Soc.: Hugh Byseley, dated 20 September 1415 (Vol. III., p. 172); Thomas Byseleye of Abendon, dated 9 June 1553 (Vol. III., p. 201); Hugh "To be bur^d in the par. ch. of All Saints of Byseley."

Bell, of Lawrence Waltham.

Ashm. MS. 852, p. 13, *gives a different Arms and Crest from those found in the Visitation made in 1623 (Vol. I., p. 69). It agrees with Harl. MS. 6173, in leaving out the three estoiles.*

Bellamp.

Exemplification of Arms and Grant of a Crest to Thomas Belamy of Datchett, co. Bucks, by Robert Cooke, Clarenceux, dated the 17 of September 1571 (quartered by Blagrave, see Vol. I., pp. 173, 174). MS. Ashm. 840, pp. 395, 396, and 858, p. 199.

1. BELLAMY. 2. BOYS.
3. GOODLACK. 4. NYX.

To all and singular as well nobles and Gentlemen as others to whome these presents shall come Robert Cooke Esquier alias Clarencieulx principall herehault and Kinge of Armes of the Sowth Est and West partes of this Realme of England from the River of Trent Southwardes sendeth greetinge. That wheras aunciently from the beginninge the valiaunt & vertuous actes of worthy psons have ben cōmended to the Worlde with sondry monum'ˢ and remembrances of their good deserts Emongest the which the cheefest & most vsuall hath ben the bearinge of signes in shildes called Armes which are evident demonstracōns of prowes & voloir, to yᵉ ende that such as by their vertues do shew foorth to the advancem' of the cōmon weale the shine of their good life & conversacōn in daily practise of things worthy & cōmendable maye therefore both receave due honor in their lives and also derive the same successively to their posterity after them. And beinge required of Thomas Belamy of Dackliett in the Countie of Buckingham Esquier seconde sonne to Wᵐ Belamy of Harrow on the Hill in the Countie of Midelsex Esquier sone & heire of Richard Belamy of Harrow aforesaid Esquier to make search in the Registers and Recordes of my Office for the aunciente Armes belonginge vnto that name & familie wherof he is descendid Wherevpon I have at his request made serche accordingly so that findinge the said Armes lawfully vnto him descendid I coulde not without his greate preiudice assigne vnto him any other then those which are vnto him descendid from his auncestors. That is to saye quarterly in the firste for Belamy vert on a bend cotized golde thre cressents gules in the second for Boys silver two Barres a Canton gules a Baston in Bende sables in the thirde for Goodlack p fesse asur and golde a Lion rampant counterchanged in the fourth for Nyx golde a cheveron betwen thre Leopards hedds gules And for that I finde no Creast vnto the same as commonly vnto all auncient Armes there belongeth none I have geven vnto him by way of Encrease for his Creaste or Cognisance vppon his Healme on a wreath golde & vert kneling on a Mownt vert a woodwist or wildeman in his proper cooller yelding vp his Clubbe golde manteled gules dowbled silver as more playnly apperith depicted in this Margent. The which Armes & Creaste & every parte & pcell therof I the said Clarencieulx Kinge of Armes (by power and aucthoritie to my Office annexed & graunted by Letters Patents vnder the greate seale of Englande) do ratifie confirme & allowe vnto the saide Thomas Belamy and to all his Britherne with their due differences and they the same to vse beare and shew in shilde Cotearmour or otherwais at his and their libertie and pleasure, and to the posteritie of either of them without impediment let or interupoōn of any

OF BERKSHIRE.

pson or psons. In witnes whereof I the said Clarencieulx Kinge of Armes have set herevnto my hande & seale of Office the sevententh daye of Septembre in the yere of oure Lord God a Thowsand five hundreth seventy & one, & in the thirtenth yere of the reigne of oure Sovereigne Lady Elizabeth by the Grace of God Quene of England France & Ireland defendor of the faith &c:

ex^d.

ROB^T COOKE alias Clarencieulx
Roy Darmes.

Bellingham, of Finchamsted, co. Berks.

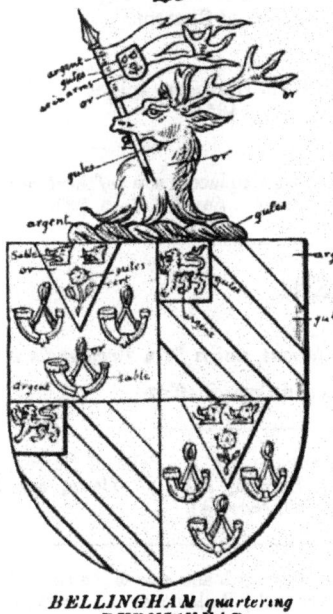

BELLINGHAM quartering
BURNISHEAD.

Coll. of Arms, G. 8, fol. 51^b; Visitation of Wilts, 1565.

John Bellingham of .... in the countie of Kendall Esquire brother to Sr Roger Bellingham of Burneside in com̃ Kendall Knighte maryed .... doughter off [*Robert Tunstall* (*Visit. Westmoreland*, 1615)] and by her had yssue John Bellingham his eldiste sonne and heire.

John Bellingham of ffinchhamsted in com̃ Berk Esquire eldiste Sonne and heire to John Bellingham aforsaide Esquire maried Jone doughter of.... Wakeman and wydowe of .... Aldem of Gylforde in com̃ Sotherye Esquire and by her hath yssue, Henrye Bellingham his eldiste sonne and heire.

Henrye Bellingham of Orston St. George in com̃ Wiltes Esquire eldiste sonne and heire to John Bellingham aforsaide maryed Dorothe doughter of .... Lewkenor of Buckingham in com̃ Sussex esquire.

EVERARD GREEN Rouge Dragon,
Heralds' College, 19 Aug. 1907.

Bessells, of Besselsleigh.

Harl. MS. 1139, folios 113^b to 115. Part of the pedigree of Fettiplace, etc.

Willm̃ de Buckland=....

| Avis da. & coheire ma. John de Bovill. | Joane da. & coheire ma. Rob̃t de fferrarijs. | William de=Maude da. & coheire Averingis. | of Wm de Buckland. |

John de Averingis.=

Elizabeth da. & heire of Jo: de Averingis=Mathew de Besells.

NOTES: VISITATIONS

▲

Geoffrey Bessells=Elleno^r da. of W^m damsell.

Sr Thomas Bessells K^t 1 son=Katherine da: & heire of Jo: de Leygh son of W^m son of Thomas.

Peeter Bessells=Marierie da. of . . . . Hawes.

Thomas Bessells 1 son=. . . . da: of Clement.

Willm Bessells=Alice da. of Sr Rich. Harecourt knight 1 son & heire. [*of the Bath* 26 *May* 1465].

Elizabeth da & heire of Wm Bessells=Richard Fettiplace 2 son [*of East Shefford* of Bessells leigh [*in co: Berks*]. *in co: Berks. See Vol. I.*, p. 28].

Blagrave.

[*No Arms tricked.*] *MS. Ashmole* 852, p. 21.
Additions: [ ] *square brackets from Visitations, italics from Townsend's MS.*

Ralph Blagrave of Vtoxer in Com: Staff:=

[*1*] Richard= Blagrave.

[*2*] Robert Blagrave=Anne da: to . . . . Pyke of Surrey, gent. of London 2^d sonne [*? and of Reading*]. [*? Thomas Pike of Ilford, co: Essex (Visit. Surrey)*].

Thomas Blagrave Esqr M^r of the Queenes Maties=Joane da: & heire to Wm Revells. ob: 18: June 1590: buried at Clarkenwell Bellame & . . . . coheire to neere London. . . . . Wrytt.

John Blagrove son=Joane da: of . . . . Mary vx: Wm Lodg son and heire to and heire 1590. Bodenham in Com: Sr Tho: Lodg of London. Glouc. [*Added by Ashmole.*]

[*Ashmole has added here (in error) Anthony, who married the da: of Thomas Dolman of Shaw, co. Berks.*]

1 John [*Lodge*]. Anne [*Lodge*]. Honor [*Lodge*].
2 Blagrave [*Lodge*]. Mary [*Lodge*].

John Blagrave of Bulnash=Anne da: to Sr Anthony=Elizabeth da: of . . . . Ock-
Co^rt in Sunning in Com: Hungerford of Downe ham 2^d w. I. 9, 139, m^d at
Berks 1566. Amney in Com: Glouces- St Mary's Reading 1568.
▲ ter. B

OF BERKSHIRE. 71

A | B |

[4] Alexander [Blagrave of Southcot]=[Margaret da: to ....] Dorothy [unmar^d 1566.]
[See Blagrave of Southcott, Vol. I., p. 174, and the pedigree from the Visit. of London 1687—1700.]

1. Anthony [Blagrave of Bulmarsh in Com: Berks] marr. [Jane] da: of [Sr John] Borlacy [of Bockmore in Com: Buck].

2. John [Blagrave a famous Mathematician].

Dorothy.

[3] Edward [Blagrave].

[Jane]=[Edward Blagrave].

Sr John Blagrave [of Southcoat] K^t bur. at St Mary's, Reading 11 June 1655 [mar: Magdalen] da: of Tho: [Coteel] de London.

Anthony Blagrave [of Bulmarsh, Esquire] 2 Son mar: [Dorothy] da: of Tho: Dolman [of Shaw Esquire].

Jane marr: to [John] Blacknall of Abingdon [Vol.I., p. 71].

Anne wife to Richard Libb of Hardwick in Com: Ox.

Mary wife to [Sir Charles] Wiseman [of Steventon Kn^t].

1. Susan.
2. Mary.

Anthony [see Visit. 1665-6, Vol. I., p. 173].

[With other children Jone marr: to William Nelson of Chaddleworth, in Berkshire Visit. Oxon. 1634, p. 279.]

Elizabeth da: of .... Cheyney 1st wife. = Elizabeth da: of .... Goddard of Wilts 2^d wife. Richard Blagrave. = Anne, da: of Thomas Mason of Northwood I. of Wight. 3^d w. Thomas s.p. — Oliver.

Edward Blagrave =.... da: of .... Drew.

Cheyney Blagrave =.... Martha.

Edward Blagrave. Drew Blagrave. Thomas Blagrave. Alice.

1. Thomas Blagrave gent. of the Chapel Royal 1672. = Margaret da: of Thomas Clarvox of Parson's Green, Middx.

2. Robert.
3. John.

4. Anthony [mar.] ....

5. Allan. =

Richard B[lagrave] of Norwich, 1672.

Mary.

Blagrave.

Visitation of London, 1687—1700. K. 9, fol. 28-29, Coll. of Arms.

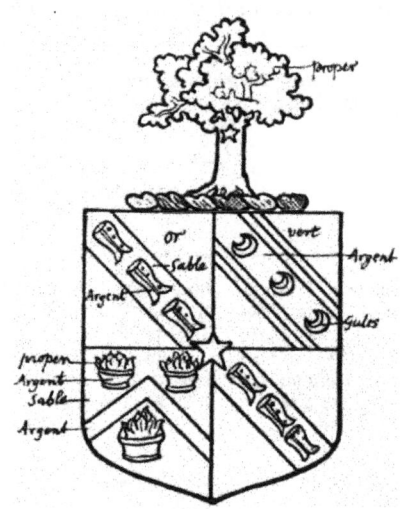

1. BLAGRAVE. 2. BELLAMY. 3. WRYTT. q'.

[*The quartered coats do not belong to this branch of the family.*]

Alexander Blagrave of Southcot in Coṁ Berks=Margaret.

4. Daniel Blagrave of Southcot in Cō Berks married and left issue severall children but he was Attainted for yᵉ murder of K. Ch. I.	5. Joseph Blagrave of Reading married and had issue. — Anne wife of Thomas Brightwell of Padworth in Coṁ Berks.	.... wife of .... Symons. — .... wife of Rob: Dolman Cit: & Stationer of London.	Judith marr. to .... Constantine. — Other daūrs.

1. John Blagrave of Southcot aforesd married Frances daur of Tho. Gregory of Bentley in Coṁ Hants.	2. Walter Blagrave second son married but has now no issue except 2 daūrs.	3. Richard Blagrave=Margaret Citizen and Haberdasher of London, obijt aᵒ 1650 vel circa æt. circa 56.	daughter of George Miller of Swallowfield in Coṁ Berks.

Alexander Blagrave now of Southcot aᵒ D. 1687.	1. Daniel dyed young.	2. Nathaniel dyed young.	3. Joshua dyed young.	4. Jeremiah died unmarried. A

OF BERKSHIRE.   73

| 5. Obadiah = Blagrave Citizen & Stationer of London ætat 45 añ 1687 hath as yet no issue. | Elizabeth daūr of Wm Sondly of Driffeild in Com̄ Glouc. her 1st husband was John Jones of London Bookseller & her 2^d husband was Edward Crofts Citizen and Stationer of London. | 6. Zephaniah died an infant.

1. Susannah married to Richard Smith Citiz: and Silk Throwster of London afterwards to Robt. Taylor Clothworker of Lond : | 2. Ruth marr: to John Swinburne of London afterwards to Robert Fleming Cit : and Weaver of London.

3. Elizabeth died unmarried. |

[*Signed*] OBADIAH BLAGRAVE.

Blake, of Reading.

MS. Rawl. D., 865, *fol*. 137.

S^r

   The bearer hereof John Blake Clothier & Burgess of Reading is ye most honest & discreet Townsman this place affoords Who being sum̄ond before you I thought my self obliged to give this Testimony of him wthout his request but according to ye duty wch I ow to Justice & Friendship.

   Pray S^r excuse my boldnes & let me ever remain in ye number of

S^r
Yo^r most devoted serv^{ts}
WILL¹ LLOYD.

[*Addressed*]   For my most Hon^d Friend Elias
   Ashmole Esq; these.

The red wax seal is damaged; it appears to bear a maunche in a shield. The Crest cannot be made out with certainty.

[*John Blake of the Parish of St. Giles, Reading, is in the Summons List; he did not appear, and had a respite till Lady Day* (1666). *His name is entered in the final list, but he did not enter his pedigree, and he is not in the list of Disclaimers. John Blake was Mayor of Reading in* 1671 *and* 1688.]

VOL. II.

𝔅onđ, of 𝔅ray.

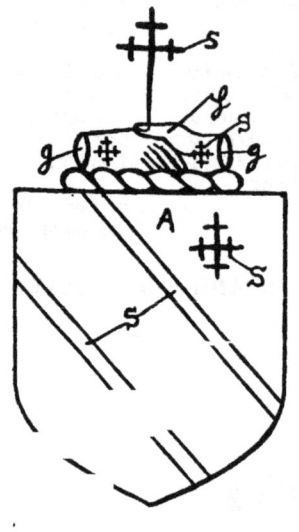

Harl. MS. 1532, *fol.* 146. *See another copy, Harl. Soc.,* Vol. XLIII., p. 63; *combined Visitations of Surrey, collected by Richard Mundy.*

His descent wth Armes & Creast I coppied out of a noate of S^r william dethick knight als Garter being of his owne hand wrighting & Tricking, & what is written in Red I have perffected.

[*The MS. is in the handwriting of Richard Mundy; his additions are here given in italics.*]

```
                          .... Bond.⊤
          ┌─────────────────────┴─────────────────────┐
William Bond Clarke=                    .... Bond descended⊤
of the greene Cloth                     ffrom Bonds Castell
vide Surrey.                            in Northumberland.
                                                 │
                          John Bond of Thorpe=Joane d. of ....
                          in Com. Surrey.     Clarke of Egham.
                                                 │
Elizabeth d. of Richard power of=John Bond of=Allice d. of Thomas Wheeler of
Com. Buck by Anne the d. of      Bray in Com. darking in Com. Surrey widdow
henery Gray sonn of the earle    Berks.       of Simon loggins of Stauerton
of Kent.                                      Com. Berks.
       ┌────────┬──────────┬──────────┐          ┌──────────┐
   mabell.  John Bond.  Rod[g]er ?  dorathe.   James.    Thomas.
```

𝔅ostock.

Smith's copy of the 1566 Visitation.

Sr Osmer de Bostock anno 1066.⊤
|
Hugh Bostock.⊤
|
Richard Bostock.⊤
|
Roger Bostock.⊤
▲

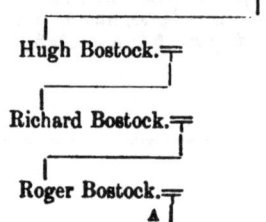

OF BERKSHIRE.

▲
Sr Gilbert Bostock.=

Ranulph de Bostock=Margaret daūr and heir to Warren de Vernon, Baron of Shipbroke.

Sr Warren Bostock=Hawise Sister and Coheir to Randulph 3d Earl of Chester and Lincoln, widow of Robert de Quinci Earl of Lincoln.

Sr Ralph als Sr Henry Bostock=Eleanor daūr and heir to .... Poole of Cheshire.

Sr William Bostock=Elizabeth daūr to Hugh Lord Audley.

Sr Edward Bostock.=

Sr Adam Bostock was knighted by King Edw: I. at the Conquest of Scotland.	Sr Adam Bostock. =....daūr of .... Brereton of Brereton.	
Sr William Bostock was knighted at the Conquest of France by King Edw: 3.	Sr William Bostock. =....daūr and heir to Sr Richard Winnington.	
Sr Adam Bostock was knighted at the Battle of Nazaret in Spain by the Black Prince.	Sr Adam Bostock of Bostock. =Margery daūr and heir to John Whetnall als Kingsley.	Ralph Bostock of Moulton.
Sr Adam Bostock was knighted by King Richd 2, and after at his own House King Hen. 4 gave him the Antelop to his Crest. *See next page.*]	Sr Adam Bostock. =Jenet daūr to Sr Henry Bradshaw.	David Bostock of Churton.
Sr Ralph Bostock was knighted at the Battle of Agincourt by King Hen: 5.	Sr Ralph Bostock. =Isabel daūr and heir to William Lawton.	Henry. Hugh.
The Battle of Blore Heath was in the time of Henry the 6th King of England.	Sr Adam Bostock Knt slain at Blore heath anno 1459. =Elizabeth daūr and heir to Hugh Venables Baron of Kinderton.	Hugh Bostock sans Issue.

From this point the Smith MS. agrees with the Ashm. MS., except that it is not so complete.

Bostock.

MS. Ashmole 852, pp. 22-23.

1. BOSTOCK *quartering* BOSTOCK.
2. VERNON.
3. MALBANK.
4. RANDOLPH BLUNDEVILLE.
5. HUGH LUPUS.
6. HUGH KEVELIOC.
7. HOLLAND.
8. WINNINGTON.
9. WETTENHALL *alias* KINGSLEY.
10. WETTENHALL.
11. LAWTON.
12. MALPAS.
13. MALPAS.
14. STRANGE.
15. VENABLES.
16. VERNON.
17. MOBBERLEY.
18. DEL HEATH.*

Sʳ Adam Bostock of Bostock in Com : = Eliz : da : & heire to Hugh
Palatinat : Cestr : slaine at Blore heath Venables Baron of Kinder-
field anno 1459. ton.

▲

* *Ashmole has written against this quartering, 3 Heathcocks.*

OF BERKSHIRE. 77

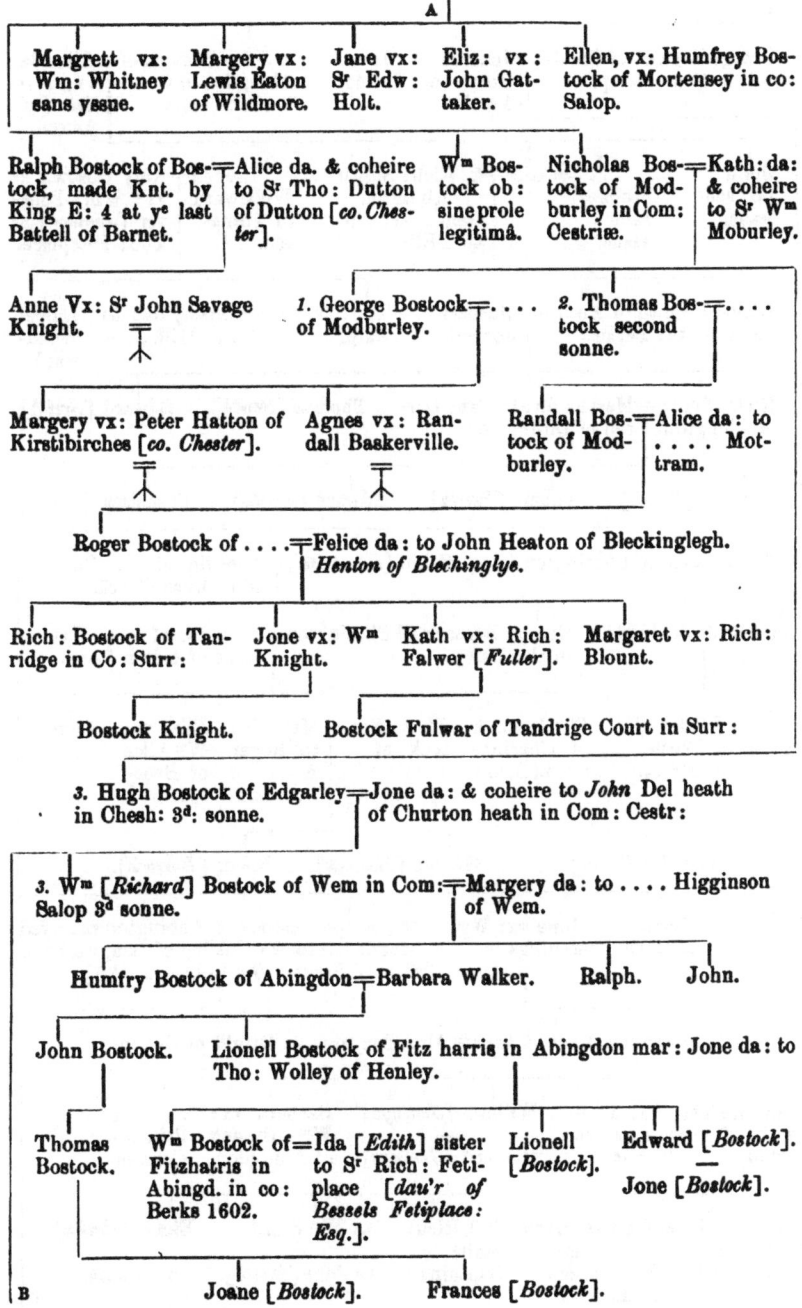

A

Margrett vx: Wm: Whitney sans yssue. | Margery vx: Lewis Eaton of Wildmore. | Jane vx: Sr Edw: Holt. | Eliz: vx: John Gattaker. | Ellen, vx: Humfrey Bostock of Mortensey in co: Salop.

Ralph Bostock of Bostock, made Knt. by King E: 4 at ye last Battell of Barnet. =T= Alice da. & coheire to Sr Tho: Dutton of Dutton [co. Chester]. | Wm Bostock ob: sine prole legitimâ. | Nicholas Bostock of Modburley in Com: Cestriæ. =T= Kath: da: & coheire to Sr Wm Moburley.

Anne Vx: Sr John Savage Knight. =T= | 1. George Bostock =T= .... of Modburley. | 2. Thomas Bostock second sonne. =T= ....

Margery vx: Peter Hatton of Kirstibirches [co. Chester]. =T= | Agnes vx: Randall Baskerville. =T= | Randall Bostock of Modburley. =T= Alice da: to .... Mottram.

Roger Bostock of .... =T= Felice da: to John Heaton of Bleckinglegh. *Henton of Blechinglye.*

Rich: Bostock of Tanridge in Co: Surr: | Jone vx: Wm Knight. | Kath vx: Rich: Falwer [*Fuller*]. | Margaret vx: Rich: Blount.

Bostock Knight. | Bostock Fulwar of Tandrige Court in Surr:

3. Hugh Bostock of Edgarley =T= Jone da: & coheire to *John* Del heath in Chesh: 3d: sonne. | of Churton heath in Com: Cestr:

3. Wm [*Richard*] Bostock of Wem in Com: =T= Margery da: to .... Higginson Salop 3d sonne. | of Wem.

Humfry Bostock of Abingdon =T= Barbara Walker. | Ralph. | John.

John Bostock. | Lionell Bostock of Fitz harris in Abingdon mar: Jone da: to Tho: Wolley of Henley.

Thomas Bostock. | Wm Bostock of Fitzhatris in Abingd. in co: Berks 1602. = Ida [*Edith*] sister to Sr Rich: Fetiplace [*dau'r of Bessels Fetiplace: Esq.*]. | Lionell [*Bostock*]. | Edward [*Bostock*]. Jone [*Bostock*].

B | Joane [*Bostock*]. | Frances [*Bostock*].

NOTES: VISITATIONS

[B]

1. George Bostock of Childs-=Jone da: to John   *2.* John Bostock of=Alice da:
Arcoll in Com: Salop. | Horne of Childs   Abingdon in Com: | to .... re-
                          Arcoll.   Berks 2ᵈ sonn. | lict [*of*]
                                                                  Aston.

John   .... =Alice=2. Rich: Smith   Lionell=Amy Bostock 2ᵈ
ob: sans   Holmes   of Abington   Woodward vx: Wᵐ: Fene-
issue.   sans   Gent: Vsh: to   of Abing- ver [*Jenivor*] 3ᵈ
              yssue.   Qu: Eliz: ton.   Tho: Feteplace.

Richard Smith of Abing-=Barbara   Tho: Wood-=Dorothy da: to   Lionell
don in Com: Berks.   Jodrell.   ward.   .... Hill.   Wood-
                                                               ward.

Richᵈ Smith=Martha da: to Paul Dar-   Thomas [*Smith*].   Edward [*Smith*].
of Abington. | rell of Lillingston.

Richard [*Smith*].   Thom: [*Smith*].   Edward [*Smith*].   Francisca [*Smith*].

Wᵐ Bostock of Cherington in co: Salop [*eldest son*]=Anne da: of .... Good-
                                                     all of Lilshull grā.

Tho: Bostock eldest   George Bostock of Cherington=Amy da: of .... Wix-
son.   in Co: Salop.   stede of Heath Lane.

Margret [*Bostock*]   Wᵐ Bostock   Thos: Bos-=Mary da: Eliz: vx: Anne.
vx: Edm: Foster   of Chering-   tock of   to Roger   Wᵐ Allen
of Watling street.   ton in Salop. Lond: 2ᵈ   Abdy of   of Broc-
                                    sonne.   London.   ton.

Isabell [*Foster*].   George [*Bostock*].   Roger [*Bostock*].

George.   Roger   Jone vx: Wᵐ   [*3.*] Ralph Bostock of Abbington married
          aClarke.   Jenings.   Maude da: to Wᵐ Gosling of Longworth in
                                    Com: [*Berks. See* Vol. I., p. 178].

Tho: Jenings 1 *son & heire*=Alice da: to .... Bright of Collen.

Joane ux: Tho: 1. Tho-   William [*Jenings*].   Barbara vx: .... vx: ....
Smith of Ab-   mas [*Jen-*   —   Wᵐ Branch   Stilman, 2 ....
ingdon.   *ings*].   Richard [*Jenings*]. of Abingdon. Cokswell.

Sʳ Tho: Smith=Frances da: to [*2.*] Rich: [*3.*] Wᵐ Smith.   Elenor [*Smith*].
Kᵗ Clarke of Wᵐ Bruges   Smith a   —
the Councell. Lᵈ Shandes   Captaine.   [*4.*] John [*Smith*]. Alice *Smith*.
              [*Chandos*].

C

OF BERKSHIRE. 79

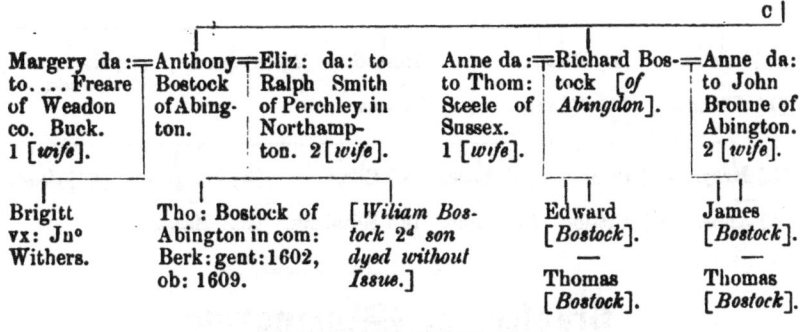

Margery da: to .... Freare of Weadon co. Buck. 1 [wife]. =Anthony Bostock of Abington. =Eliz: da: to Ralph Smith of Perchley.in Northampton. 2 [wife]. Anne da: to Thom: Steele of Sussex. 1 [wife]. =Richard Bostock [of Abingdon]. =Anne da: to John Brouue of Abington. 2 [wife].

Brigitt vx: Jnº Withers. Tho: Bostock of Abington in com: Berk: gent: 1602, ob: 1609. [William Bostock 2ᵈ son dyed without Issue.] Edward [Bostock]. Thomas [Bostock]. James [Bostock]. Thomas [Bostock].

Boulstrode, of Upton.

MS. Ashmole 852, p. 31. No Arms given.

John Boulstrode of Vpton in Com: Berks [? co. Bucks]=Agnes.

John Boulstrode=Margaret da: of Hugh Mountforth of Sᵗ Peter's Chalmfant [*Chalfont St. Peter's, co: Bucks*].

Robert Boulstrode=Agnes da: of .... Sampson of Hughley [*co: Bucks*] [*of Hurley, Ashm: Berks*, iii. 310].

Richard*=Margaret da: & heire of Thomas Knyffe. second son. John Boulstrode of Vpton in Com: Berks [? co: Bucks]. Robert dyed an infant. Alice vxor Will: Wodwell.

Agnes wife of Will: Brudenell. William Boulstrode=Agnes da: of William Norris of Bray [*co: Berks*].

Edward Brudenell of Agmundesham in Com: Bucks. Vide. 4. Edmond. 5. Thomas. 6. Roger. [7. Henry.] 8. George.

[1.] Richard Boulstrode of Vpton married 20: April 33 H. 6 [*1455*]. =Alice da: & heire of [*Richᵈ*] Swift [*Snyff*] [*Richard Kniffe of Chaluey temp: K. H. 6ᵗʰ Visit. Bucks 1634*] Cosen and heire of Nicholas Clopton [*Clopton of langley*]. 2. Rob: Boulstrode [*mar:*] Margaret da: of John Abrahall of Hitchingfield in Co: Hereford. 3. Willᵐ Boulstrode of London [*A Draper of London, Ashm: Berks*, iii., 310] marryed Jane da: of Edward Strangles of London.

* *The pedigree printed by the editor of Ashmole's Antiq: of Berks omits this Richard, and appears to make his daughter "Agnes, widow of William Brudenell," the wife of his brother John.*

| A |
| [2.]* John. [4.] Robert. [6.] Edmond. [8.] Richard. [1.] Richard Boulstrode.
| [3.] Thomas. [5.] Edward. [7.] Thomas.

[1.] Mary. [3.] Bridgit. [5.] Alice. [7.] Ellen. [9.] Margery. [6 ?] Joane.
[2.] Anne. [4.] Lettice. [6.] Anne. [8.] Elizabeth. [10.] Margaret.

Bradley, of Wokingham.

Visitation of York, 1665. *MS. College of Arms*, *C.* 40, p. 18. (*See Surtees Soc.*, vol. xxxvi., p. 8.)

He referreth himselfe to the Visitation of Berkshire for proofe of these Armes but nothing there to be found.

Osgodcrosse Wapentake, Pontefract 7 *Aug.* 1665.

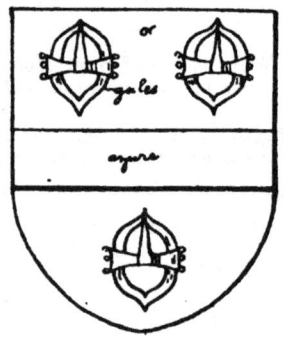

John Bradley of .... in Com. Ebor. an Ensigne in=.... King Henry the eights Army upon his expeditiō to Bulloigne in France.

2. Henry Bradley of Oke-=Barbara daughter of Wal- | 1. Richard. ⎫
ingham in Com. Berks, | ter Lane of Reding in | —   ⎬ died without issue.
died in aº 1645. | Com. Berks. | 3. Abell.   ⎭

1. John Bradley of=Susan, daughter | 2. Thomas Bradley Dr in=Frances daugh-
Miles near Oking- | of John Feilder | Divinity and Chaplein to | ter unto John
ham in Berkshire. | of .... in com. | K. Charles the 1st now | Lord Savile of
                  | South^ton. | Præbend in the Cathedrall| Pomfret in com.
Henry Bradley of Richmund in Surry. | Church of Yorke and Rec- | Eborum.
                                    | tor of Ackworth in Com. |
                                    | Ebor: æt. 67 an. 7º Aug. |
                                    | aº 1665.   A |

* *The numbering of all these children is from Ashm: Berks.,* iii. 310.

OF BERKSHIRE.

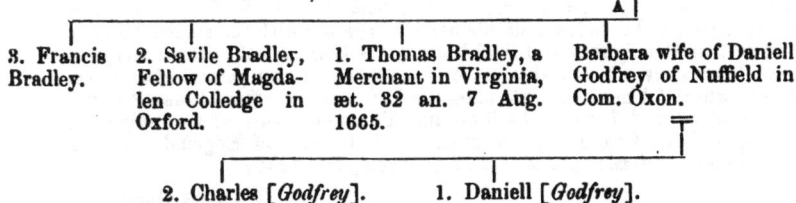

| 3. Francis Bradley. | 2. Savile Bradley, Fellow of Magdalen Colledge in Oxford. | 1. Thomas Bradley, a Merchant in Virginia, æt. 32 an. 7 Aug. 1665. | Barbara wife of Daniell Godfrey of Nuffield in Com. Oxon. |

2. Charles [*Godfrey*].   1. Daniell [*Godfrey*].

Certifyed by Dr THOMAS BRADLEY.

I hereby certify that the above is correctly copied from the Records (C. 40, p. 13^b) in the Heralds' College.
Witness my hand this 26th day of June 1907.

EVERARD GREEN,
Rouge Dragon.

Braham, of New Windsor.

Exemplification of Arms and Grant of a Crest to Sir Richard Braham, Knight, by Sir Edward Walker, Knight, Garter, dated the 10th of June 1646. MS. Ashm. 858, pp. 191-2.

To all and singuler vnto whome these presents shall come Sr Edward Walker Knight Garter principall King of Armes of Englishmen sendeth greeting whereas it is most agreeable to Justice & reason, that those persons, whoe have excelled in wisedome, or eminent Service to their Prince and Country in the tyme of peace or in valour & military experience in the tyme of warr should have due rewards for such their worthy & valiant accōns, amongst which the cheifest and most principall have beene the bearing of signes & Tokens in sheilds commonly called Armes, which are diversly distributed according to the worthinesse of the persons meriting the Same, and as it was prudently devised at first, to stir vp and enflame the hearts of men to doe Acts of honour & virtue so it is still continued to the end that such may receive due honour in their lives and leave the same to their posterity, And where as Sr Richard Braham Knight hath faithfully served his Matie ever since the beginning of these tymes of Distracōon and vniversall Rebellion, so as it is most fitt that he should receive some addition of honour to the auncient Armes belonging to that family, Knowe ye therefore that I the said Sr Edward Walker Knight Garter principall King of Armes of Englishmen by the power & authority annexed vnto my office of Garter by the Statutes of the most Noble Order of the Garter & confirmed vnto me by his Maties Letters Patents, vnder the great seale of England Doe hereby give grant and assigne vnto him the said Sr Richard Braham Knight the Creast hereafter mentioned vizt Fower Feathers erected, sable in a Ducall Crowne or, which Creast the said Sr Richard Braham K^{nt} and the severall descendants of his body & together with the aunceint Armes belonging to that Family may and shall lawfully vse beare & sett forth att all tymes and vpon all occasions, without the lett or interupc͞on of any person whatsoever. In wittnesse whereof I have herevnto subscribed my name & affixed the seale of my Office this Tenth day of June in the Two and Twentieth yeare of the Reigne of our Soveraigne Lord Charles by the grace of God King of England Scotland Fraunce & Ireland Defender of the ffaith &c: Annoq͞ Dm̄ 1646:

Ex   EDW. WALKER Garter.

𝕭𝖗𝖆𝖞𝖇𝖗𝖔𝖔𝖐𝖊, 𝖔𝖋 𝕭𝖗𝖎𝖌𝖍𝖙 𝖂𝖆𝖑𝖙𝖔𝖓.
MS. Ashmole 852, p. 20.

p Roger Machado al̄s Clarenc: 7°: Mar: 1504 (*added by Ashmole*).

James Braybrooke of Suff., Esquire = Margery da: to .... Woodof the Privy Chamber K^g Henry cock of Shinfield in Com: 7th [*Visit*. 1532]. Berks [*Visit*. 1532].

Tho: Braybrooke of Abingdon = Kath: da: to W^m   Eliz: vx: Henry Brounker of in Co: Berks Esqr [*Visit*. 1532]. Barker [*Visit*. [*Mellisham, Harl. MS.* 1532] 1532]. Wiltshier [*Visit*. 1532].

W^m eldest   James Bray- = Martha da: to John   Jane vx: Margaret vx: .... son dyed   brooke of   Yate of Lyford in   Tho: Bas- Andrewes of Sutton sans yssue   Brightwalton Com: Berks, widow   sett Docto^r [& 2^{dy} John Fetty- [*Visit*.   in Com: Berks to Humfry Cheney   of Phisick. *place of Sparsholt*]. 1532].   Esquire.   gent.

OF BERKSHIRE. 83

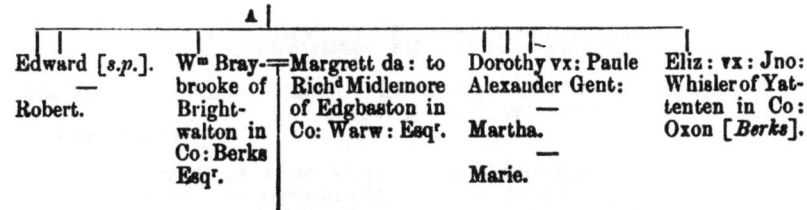

Edward [s.p.].	Wᵐ Bray-=Margrett da: to	Dorothy vx: Paule	Eliz: vx: Jno:
Robert.	brooke of Richᵈ Midlemore	Alexauder Gent:	Whisler of Yat-
	Bright- of Edgbaston in	—	tenten in Co:
	walton in Co: Warw: Esqʳ.	Martha.	Oxon [Berks].
	Co: Berks		
	Esqʳ.	Marie.	

Richard [*Braybrooke only son*].

Braybrooke, of Bright Waltham.

Visitation of Oxford, 1634.   *MS. College of Arms, C.* 29, p. 131.

James Braybrooke of Bright=Martha daur: of [*John*] Yates of Lyford in
Waltham in Com: Berks.   Com: Berks widow of [*Humfrey*] Cheyney.

Martha wife of	Jo Whistler=Elizabeth	Wᵐ Bray-=Margaret daur. of	Robt
Otho Garr of	of Gate- Bray-	broke eld- Ric: Midlemore of	2 son
Grenham in	hampton in broke.	est sonne. Edgvaston in Com.	s.p.
Com. Berks.	Com. Oxon.	Warwick.	

Katharine da: of Wᵐ Ayston=Richard Braybroke=Christian da: of Barton Fawrer
[*Eyston*] of Catmere in Com.   of Malston in Com.   of South Stoke in Com. Oxon.
Berks 2 wife.   Berks.

Lucie.   1. Margaret.   2. Mary.

[*Signed*]   RICHᴰ BRAYBROOKE.

Brightwell, of Padworth.

Prepared for the Visitation, 1665-6. In Ashmole's handwriting, not included. MS. Rawl. D. 865, fol. 83. No Arms: marked fee vnp[d].

Theald Hund.

Thomas Brightwell of Padworth in Com Berk(æt. 86 annorum 25 Mar. 1665. =Anne da: to Alexander Blagrave of Southcot in Com Berk(.

Henry Meux of Norton in Hertf. 2[d] husband. =Anne=Rich: Cleaver of Norton in Com Hertf. first husb[d]. | Samuel of Brightwell of Lincolnes Inne son & heire æt: 34 ann.=Susanna da. to Joshua Loftus of London Goldsmith.

Loftus son & heire æt: 4 annorum 25 Mar: 1665.   2. Thomas.   A   Mary.

SAMUELL BRIGHTWELL. [*Original.*]

Brinckhurst, of Bisham.

Le Neve's copy of the Visitation of Bucks, 1634, fol. 50.

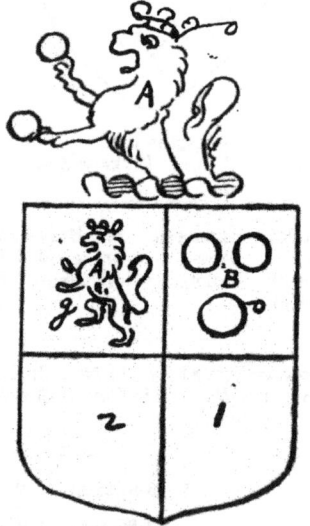

BRINCKHURST quartering ....

John Brinkhurst of Bisham in Com Berks: Marchant of *the* Staple.=Da: of Adam Greay.

A

OF BERKSHIRE.

John Brinckhurst eldest Son: to Eossney [*Tresuror*] of ye English house in Garmany in the time of Charles ye 5th he mar. to his 1st wife Eliz: Blundell & 2ly to Jane Woodford he died without issue & is buried at Bysham.	Rich: Brinckhurst of Bysham 3d son.	= Mary da: of Willm Newberry of Malpas Com Northampton.	Robt: Brinckhurst merchant in London obijt in Garmany.
Mary da: of John Hanford of Wollashall in Com Worcester.	= John Brinckhurst of ye Moore in great Marlow Com Buck. mar: Eliz: da: of ffrancis Poulton of Burton Com Buck: first wife.	= Mary da: of Jo Finch [*of*] Grouechur [*? Grovehurst*] in Ken [*Kent*] 2d wife.	Rupert Brinckhurst of Germany mar[*chant*] 1588.
Charles 2d. — George 3d.	John Brinckhurst eldest son liueing 1623, 13 ye: et Amplius [*sic, ? 1634*].	Charles S.p. — Susan. — Mary.	John, died in Germany S:P:

Browne alias Moses, of Wokingham.

Visitation of London, 1633-4, *Harl. Soc.*, Vol. XV., p. 115.

Faringdon Without.

Richard Browne als =
Moses of Ockingham
in com. Berks.

John Browne als Moses of = Anne da. of John Beard
Ockingham and of London. | of Ockingham.

John Browne.	Richard Browne als Moses of London Woodmonger 1634.	= Bridget daughter of Robert Brian of Henley on Thames com. Oxon.

1. Richard Browne eldest son and heire apparent.   2. John.   Anne.

RICHARD BROWNE.

Bullock, of Arborfield.

Harl. MS. 1532, p. 27ᵇ. *The following descents have been added before Thomas Bullock, who married Alice Yeading.*

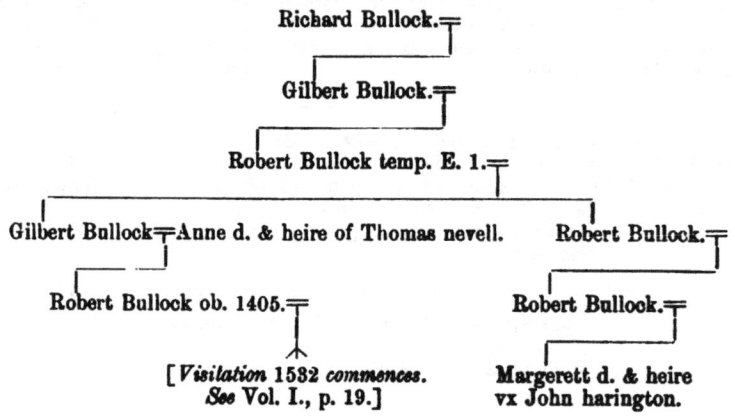

[*Visitation* 1532 *commences.* *See* Vol. I., p. 19.]

Burley, of Wokingham.

Harl. MS. 1139, p. 93, *part of the pedigree of Lydcott, from the Visitation of Surrey,* 1623.

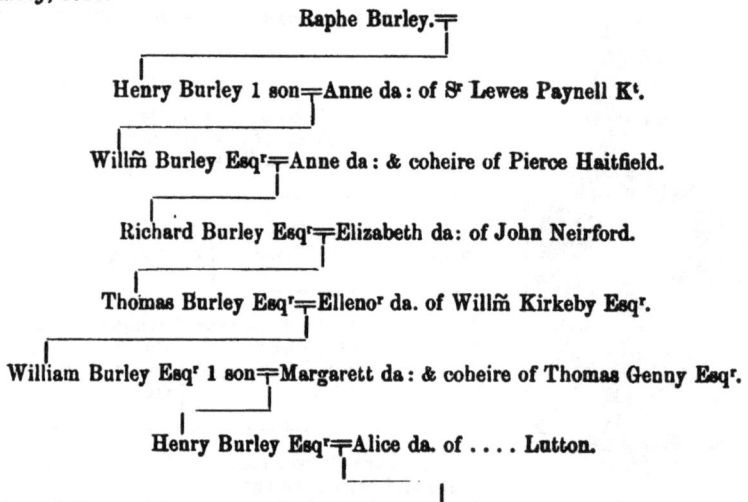

Burren, of Reading.

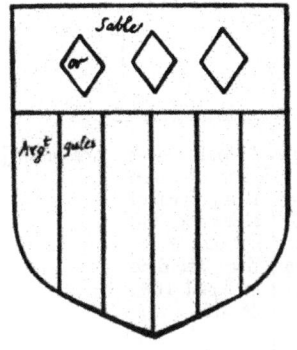

Visitation of London, 1687—1700, MS. College of Arms, K. 9, fol. 202.

Mr Burren referred to Berkeshire but nothing to be found, the Arms from an Escocheon at the Funeral of Mrs Burren his Wife by Russell the Undertaker.

Richard Burren of Reading in Com̃ Berks. obt circa añ 1655 ætat. . . . .

Avice wife of Anthony Philp of London mercht.

Richard Burren born at Reading in Com̃ Berks. was a Mercht in London obt circa añ 1656 ætat. 40 annoȓ. =Mary dar of Anthony Biddolph of London Merchant.

. . . . died a Maid.

Richard died young.

Anthony Burren Citizen and Mercht of London ætat. 35 añ 1687. =Anne dar of . . . . Cleaver of Norton in Com̃ Hertford obt 6° Junij A° 1684.

Mary widow of Thomas Spencer of London Linnen Draper.

Anne only child died an Infant.

[*Signed*] ANTHO: BURREN.

Calcott or Caldecott, of Abingdon.

Visitation of Leicestershire, 1682-3, K. 2, pp. 120, 121, Heralds' College. There is no pedigree of this family in the Visitation of Rutland, 1618-19, Her. Coll., C. 14. The additions below are from Vincent, 132, folio 87, which contains the pedigree as far as the marriage and issue of Agnes Howes. I think Thomas Calcott, or Caldecott, was of Caldecott, near Abingdon.

No Arms exhibited.

Thomas Calcott of . . . . near Abington in Com. Berks.=

Thomas Calcott of . . . . in Com. Berks.=

NOTES: VISITATIONS

Thomas Calcott of Pessmore in Com. Berks. [*fil. 1.*] === John Calcott of Chis-lington [*et Ipston*] in Com. Oxon. === [*Johanna*].

William Calcott.

1. John Calcott died without issue [*fil: et hæres*]. === Agnes daur of Richard House [*Howes*] of [*West*] Wickham in Com. Bucks [*per .... filiam .... Belson de Brill*] first wife. === 2. Thomas Calcott of Barrow and Whitwell in Com. Rutl^d died at Catthorp in Com. Leic. a^o 1648, ætatis 80, having been for years in Comission of the Peace for ye Co: of Leicest^r. === Abigail eldest daur of John Huggeford of Henwood Hall in Com. Warr: Esq: she died in April 1681 2^d wife. === [*Johanna*.]

3. Dorothy ætat 5 [6] ann 1620 now living unmarr: a^o 1682. — 2. Anne æt. 6 [8] ann: 1620, wife of Marmaduke Claver of Oving near Alesbury in Com: Bucks. — 1. Mary ætat 13 ann 1620 died unmarried. — Edward died an infant.

Thomas Calcot als Caldecot of Catthorp in Com. Leic: Esq: High Shiriff of Leicestersh a^o 1665, and one of His Maties Justices of the Peace in the s^d County having been in comission ever since his Ma^ts happy Restoration, æt. 52, an: 1682. === Mary 2^d daur of Alexander Prescot of Thoby in Com. Leic: Esq: she died in August 1681. — 1. Eliz: wife of Theophilus Aylmer of London great grandson of .... Aylmer B^t of London. — 2. Mary now living unmarr^d 1682. — 3. Abigail wife of Christoph^r Bradgate of Wibtoft in Com:Warr. and Lutterworth in Com: Leic:

Charles & Abigal died young. — 6. Henry æt. 12 ann. 1682. — 5. William æt. 17 an. 1682. — 4. Walter Caldecot æt. circa 18 ann. 1682. — 3. George Caldecot of London Mercer æt. 22 anno 1682.

2. Alexander Caldecot æt. circa 23 an. 1682. — 1. Thomas Caldecot now living at Northampton ætatis circa 25 an. 1682. === Matilda daur of .... Evans of Northampton. — 1. Mary. — 2. Isabella. — 3. Elizabeth.

[*Signed*] THO: CALDECOTT.

OF BERKSHIRE.

These are to certifie whom it may concerne That I Randolph Caldecott of Caldicott in Chesshire now of Bishopton in the County of Wilts D^r of Divinity aged 80^tie have often heard & faithfully beleive that Tho: Caldecott of Cattharpe in the County of Leic: Esq: is descended from our fores^d family.

In witness whereof I have hereunto sett my hand & seale this 14th of September 1682.

[*Signed*] RANDOLPH CALDECOTT.

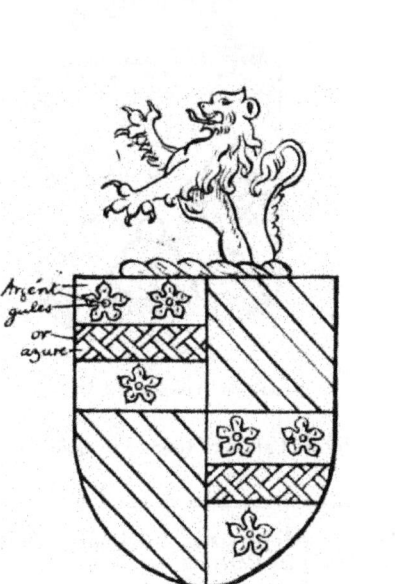

[*No colours are tricked for the second and third quarter, or for the Crest. Argent, three bends sable,* CALCOTT (*Harl. MS.* 1558, *fol.* 10). *The Crest, a demi lion rampant Gules, charged on the shoulder with a cinquefoil Argent* (*Burke*). *The Arms and Crest are those given on the seal.*]

I hereby certify that the above is correctly copied from the Records (Vol. K. 2, pp. 120, 121), in the Heralds' College. Witness my hand this 26th day of June 1907.

EVERARD GREEN,
Rouge Dragon.

Calton, of Milton.

MS. Rawl. D. 865, fol. 85, in Ashmole's handwriting. Prepared for the Visitation 1665-66; not included. Marked not p^d. No Arms.

Ocke hund.

Arms from Ashmole MS. 852, p. 32.

Robert Calton of Goring in Com̃ Oxon:=

Robert Calton of Goring=Joyce sister to Sr Dudley Carleton. æt: 72 an: 16 Mar. 1664.

Mary wife to Sr Thomas Neale of Warneford in Com̃ Hante.

Jane da: to=Paul Calton=Susanna da: to Charles Balam of .... in the Isle of Ely 2^d wife.
Sr John Miller of Bridde neere Dorchester first wife.
of Milton in Com̃ Berke Esquire æt: 32, an: 16 Mar. 1664.

1. Joyce wife to George Brett of Hatherley in Com̃ Glouc:
2. Bridget wife to John Machin of Bensington in Com̃ Ox:

3. Mary wife to Edw: Hungerford of Windredg in Com̃ Glouc.

Paul son & heire æt: 1 an: 16 Mar. 1664.   Susanna.

PAUL CALTON. [*Original.*]

OF BERKSHIRE.

Calton, of Milton.

MS. Rawl. D. 865, fol. 220. Draft of Letter.

Sr

Mr Hart of Abingdon tould me yt you pmised to send me the Fee for entring yor descent & Armes, the next morning after I had made yor Entry, wch though I expected yet heard nothing from you, either then or since, & therefore after so long tyme cannot but put you in minde thereof, & also to desire youle please to send it to the sd Mr Hart at the new Inn at Abingdon, for he hath direction to retorne it vp to me, & for wch I shall rem̃

Yor humble servt
E. A[SHMOLE] W[INDSOR] H[ERALD].

Midle Temple. 6 May [16]65.

To PAULE CALTON Esqr at Melton in Berke.

Castellion, of Benham Valence.

CASTILLION *quartering* COMPAIGNE.

Ashmole MS. 852, fol. 42, 43.

Peter Castelion of Thurin in Piomont in Italy.
┬
│
├─────────────────────────────┬─────────────────────────────┐
John Baptist Castellion of Benam Valence in Com: Berks Esquire one of ye Groomes of ye Privy Chamber to Queene Eliz: dyed ye 12: of Feb. 1597 [1597-8] and was buried at Spine in Barks ye 7th of March. He served King H: 8: in his warrs in France & Qu: Eliz. for his faithfull service gave ye Canton Ermyne in his Armes for an augmentacon of honor. = Margarett da: and sole heire to Bartholmew Compaigne borne at Florence who was ye principall Mercht to K: H: 8: who added a rose gules in his Armes as an augmentacon of honor for his faithfull service.

│
┌──────────────┬─────────────────────────────────┐
'Valentine seconde sonne. │ Sr Francis Baptist Castelion of Benam Valence in Co Berks living 1602, made Knt at Charterhouse 1603. = Eliz: da: to Wm St John of .... in Co: Berks.

│
Barbara.   A

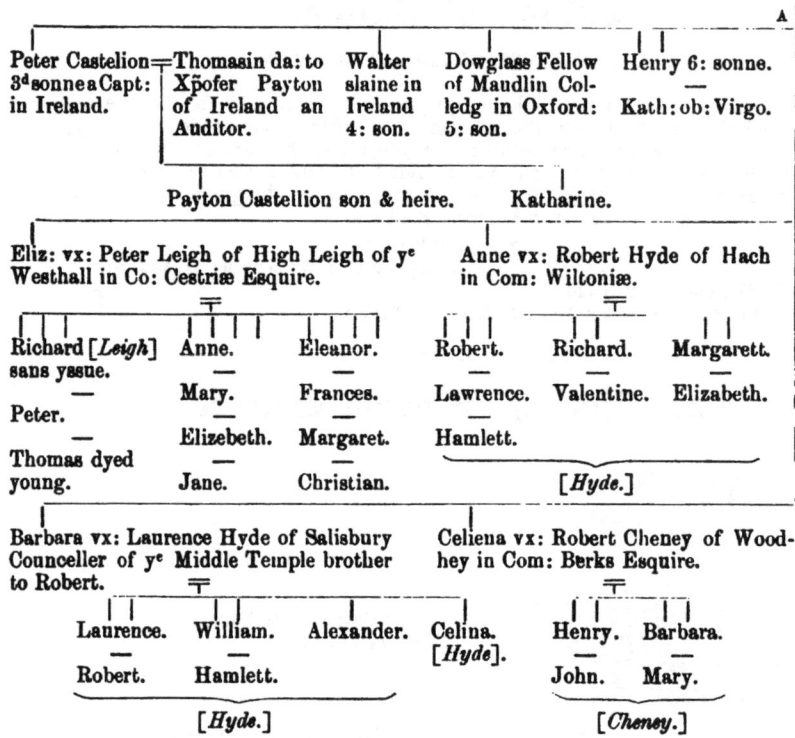

See a very full and complete pedigree of Castillion, by G. E. Cokayne, Esq., F.S.A., Clarenceux, printed in the "Genealogist," New Series, vol. xvii., pp. 73, 199, 225; also an account of Speen Church by Walter Money, Esq., F.S.A., in which the monuments are described. The Arms of Castillion are of considerable interest. The original Arms are given at the foot of the Funeral Certificate of John Baptist Castillion who died on the 12th of February 1597-8, and was buried at Speen, near Newbury, on the 17th of March following (see the facsimile, "Genealogist," vol. xvii.). It is marked, " This is the true Coate of John Baptist Castillion as it was sent from Piemont." Gules, a lion rampant Argent, in the dexter chief point a tower Or. No Crest is given.

There are two Castillion tombs at Speen, the older one to the memory of John Baptist Castillion. This fine tomb has not been improved by being removed to a corner, and then overshadowed by a painted window in the worst possible taste. It originally shewed the "true coate" as above, with the difference that it is a castle with three towers in the corner of the shield, and not a single tower. The other tomb is that of Elizabeth the first wife of Sir Francis Castillion; it was erected according to the inscription it bears in the year 1604. This tomb also originally had the "true coate."

In all the Castillion Arms on the two tombs the lion rampant is carved in relief, and in some of the shields the castle in the corner is slightly raised. At some period the

Arms have been altered in every shield, by fastening over the lower half of the lion a tower, gilding the upper half of the lion, and painting a small ermine canton over the castle in the corner. The tower has now fallen away, and the mark of it still remains; the gold castle lined out with black originally in the corner can also easily be traced.

The painted impalements recording the various marriages, reaching to 1607, may have been added at any time.

I here print three drafts of patents from MSS. in the College of Arms, the "Latin" following the originals. The first is taken from the "Genealogist" by the kind permission of Mr. Cokayne. In my opinion the first two of these were never executed; they are both by Sir Gilbert Dethick, who is said in the third draft to have issued the real patent, which agrees with neither. They were, I think, simply efforts towards granting the proposed augmentation.

The third draft is by Sir William Dethick, and appears to be an exemplification of the Arms and Crest as given in Sir Gilbert Dethick's patent.

About the year 1563, judging from the date of the two earliest drafts, it was intended to grant the augmentation. This I conclude also from the large introduction of ermine into the Arms tricked on both of Sir Gilbert Dethick's drafts.

In 1565 the manor of Benham Valance was given to John Baptist Castillion, so perhaps it might be concluded that the patent of Arms, not now extant, was granted some time between or about the years 1563 and 1565. Sir Gilbert Dethick died in October 1584.

The last of the three drafts, by William Dethick and William Camden, is dated the 13th of December 1597. Notwithstanding the "excogitavimus et assignavimus" of the "Latin" text, with regard to the Crest, it will be safer to rely on the English draft, that they "ratified & confermed this Creast or Cognizance of the Salamanders hed couppe proper (?) wth an Empresse or word of delight appropriat to the same, wth helmelt and mantle."

A docket of this patent seems to be preserved in Stowe MS. 676, fol. 140, as follows: " In Campo Rosso supra el Castillo d'argente ung medio de Leone rampante d'oro : for the Creast a Salamanders head Coupee with an impress or word appropriate to the same, with the helmet and mantells, granted by Will: Dethick Garter to Jno Baptista Castillion from Piedmont in Italy."

It will be noticed that in the two drafts by Sir Gilbert Dethick, dated the 1st of May and the 20th of August 1563, the salamander's head is given as the Crest. It now appears only once on the monuments, at the feet of the figure of J. B. Castillion, where it is represented in a different form from that usually found in the tricks. It has a kind of upper beak and a beard; the ears, as well as plaited lines of a mane, are of gold. As in the drafts of Sir Gilbert Dethick it is placed in a crown of gold.

In the draft of William Dethick, now dated 1597, it is stated that the Arms the renowned and ancient family of Castillion bore was, on a field gules a demi lion gold, rising out of a silver castle, as confirmed by Sir Gilbert Dethick. These were probably the Arms confirmed, but they were not the ancient Arms of the family. It is, however, clear, from the drafts of patents dated 1563, that Sir Gilbert Dethick had already started the idea of placing the demi lion in the tower. This change in the position of the charges may have resulted from the augmentation of the ermine canton.

In the draft by William Dethick the Crest is simply described as a salamander's head proper, couped on a wreath of his colours; the crown is not mentioned. It is, however, quite clear that this draft of 1597 ratified and confirmed the Arms and Crest, as they had been before ratified and confirmed by Sir Gilbert Dethick.

Ashmole refers in the annexed pedigree to the ermine canton given by Queen Elizabeth to Castillion as well as to the rose added to the Arms of Compaigne by Henry the VIIIth.

The Arms of Castillion and Compaigne impaled are represented in the facsimile of the Funeral Certificate given with Mr. Cokayne's article in the " Genealogist," as also the Salamander's head Crest in a crown. The trick at the head of Ashmole's pedigree gives the same Arms quartered and the same Crest.

J. B. Castillion died on the 12th of February 1597-8 and was buried on the 17th of March following. This exemplification by William Dethick seems to be dated the 13th of December 1597. It is difficult to see the purpose of it, a little more than two months before Castillion died, unless the previous patent of Sir Gilbert Dethick could not be found.

The idea of course at once occurs, considering the narrowness of the dates, that it was made because it would be required for the proper marshalling of the funeral.

It is puzzling to know at what time the alterations were made in the Arms; it may have been done by J. B. Castillion on his receiving the augmentation, if some portions of the tombs at Speen were prepared before his death in 1598. The later tomb is unfortunately like the older one, neither in its original position nor condition, but the Arms upon it are those of Sir Francis Castillion and Dorothy (St. John) his wife impaled. If their marriage took place, as stated, in the year 1597, the impaled Arms must have been placed on the base in or after that year, and possibly the figure and inscription were not added until 1604. Or it may be suggested that after the funeral of J. B. Castillion, Camden and Thompson, the Heralds, ordered the alteration mentioned above, and made the Arms on both the tombs agree with those exemplified by William Dethick, and with those given on the funeral certificate.

Benham Valance was sold in or after 1630, and notwithstanding the patent of Sir Gilbert Dethick, confirmed in the exemplification of the Arms and Crest by his son Sir William Dethick, Francis Castillion, as pointed out by Mr. Cokayne, was able to prove to the satisfaction of Chitting and Philipott, who acted for Camden at the Visitation of 1623, that the Arms he was entitled to bear were the true Arms as received from Piedmont, quartering Compaigne with the rose granted by Henry the VIIIth (see Vol. I., p. 79).

The same Arms with a different Crest are found on the tomb of the Rev. John Castillion, D.D., Dean of Rochester, buried 1688 (" Genealogist," xvii., p. 204).

Draft of a patent to John Baptist Castillion by Gilbert Dethick, Garter, dated the 1st of May 1563 (printed in the "Genealogist," New Series, vol. xvii.).

Gilbertus Dethick aïs Garter principalis Rex Armorum &c : Sapientium oīum Consensu palam est nihil esse Reipub : tam salutare quam ut neque benefactis desint præmia, neque prave factis penæ ; Quippe cum illis ad præclaræ de Rep : merendum, atq, ad omnem virtutem Excitentur generosi animi, hisce afflagitijs absteneantur improbi honore atq, laude nullum esse decentius virtutis præmium neque magis proprium quam cum animo reputemus essentq, perspecta nobis Ornatissimi viri Johannis Baptistæ Castilioni patria pedemontam Insignia virtutum Merita & mores undiquaq, intigerimi tum vero Emerita Magna cū Laude Stipendia sub serenissimo felicis Memoriæ Rege : H : 8. atq, admodum diuturna eiusdem servitus apud sereniss Elizabetham nunc Angliæ Franciæ et Hiberniæ Reginam fidei defensatricem suma fide atq, sedulitate prestita : qui demum iam inde ab ipsius Regni initio in Eius intimorum cubiculariorum (generosos privatæ Cameræ appelatos) numerum Coaptatus fuit hæc igitur cum Nobis essent ob oculos, ut et ipsius Johannis Baptistæ posteri Ex eius Meritorum illustrarentur splendore, et inde tam idem posteri, tum alij ad similium laudum decus accederentur : putavimus nri esse muneris tot tantaq, Merita aliquo condecorare ornamento : Itaq, dicti Regis Officij Armorum, Autoritate

& potestate nobis Concessa et l̃ris patentibus sub magno Sigillum Regni Expressa qua fungimur Predictum Joħem Baptistam et Eius filios ac posteros Ex eo legitime descendentes in numerum dignitatem et statum veterum Regni Angliæ Nobilium evehimus atq̃ adscissimur eumq̃ et eos omnibus honoribus, dignitatibus privilegijs preheminentijs im̃unitatibus ac Ornamentis Insignimus, quibus alij veteres regni Angliæ Nobiles utuntur ac fruuntur prætereaq̃ in Eiusmodi Nobilitatis ornamentum hæc illi decernimus et largimur Armorũ Insignia vizt : In Argenteo Scuto nigris notis deorsim mediantibus insignito ceruleum Castrum cum aureo Leone media anteriore parte ex eo eminente, et in sinistrum latus verso insuper Militaris autem galeæ aurea Corona insignito insertum viridi Colore Salamandiæ Caput argenteis rubeisq̃ lacinijs hinc inde flamitantibus ut melius hic pictura Expressa conspicitur: Que quidem Insignia tam ipsi quam Eius legitimis posteris gestandi in Armis Militaribus vexillis vestibus, eisq̃ utandi in sigillis, Monumentis, vasibus et quibuscunq̃ utensilibus & ad omnes alios usus, quibus alij veteres Nobiles suis Insignibus uti Consueverunt aut uti possunt plenam ac liberam potestatem facimus. In Cuius rei Testimonium hasce fieri Mandavimus ac ñri manus subscripcõe & dicti officij ñri sigillo Com̃univimus Datam Londini I° die Maij : An° dñi 1563 Anno 5to Elizabethæ.

Draft of a patent to John Baptist Castillion by Gilbert Dethick, Garter, dated the 20th of August, 5th Eliz. 1563.

Omnibus et Singulis proteribus preclaris et Nobilibus ad quos presentes l̃re parvenerint, Gilbertus Dethicke als Garter principalis Rex Armorum Salutem cum debita com̃endacione nobilitate vr̃e constare non dubito quomodo ratio exegit et equitas dictat̃ vt homines vertũosi Laudabilis, disposicionis et vite honorabilis, fuit ppter eorũ fama et condigna merita honorati et remunerati, non solum in eorũ pprijs personis, dum hac caduca vita frumit̃ (que Licet quam brevis sit) memoriam tamen ipsius propter preclara gesta qui longam efficere par est, virũ etiam alij ex eorũ corporibus procreati su[nt] in quolibet loco honoris signorũ et exemplor̃ virtutis et etiam nobilitatis Demonstratione pre ceteris exaltandi et honorandi, e . . intentione, vt per eorũ exempla eorum posteri et allij magis conent̃. vitam su . . . in validissimorum, armorũ, actibus operibusque clarissimis exercere Et tum dominus Joħnes Baptiste, castilio . . . . Italios et in nobili principatu pedemontis sub ditione Ducis sabandie et in burgi gassim oriundus diu in virtute clarint a quam fidelissime Serenissime et illustr[i]ssime Principe Elizabeth dei grati[a] Anglie franncce et hibernie Regine fidei Defenso etc. diu insermerit, vnde propter eius confirmatū servitiū in v ... generosum private Camere dicte domine Regine merito &c acceptus et admissus fuit, Igitur ego p̄dict̄ Garter Rex armorum vt supra perpendens, aioq̨, revoluens, eiusdem Joh̄i Baptiste preclara gesta variasq̨, eius animi et corporis Dotis merito Duxi eū numerari admitti et recepi in numerū et consortū aliorū veterū et illustuū virorū quapropter per auctoritate et potestatem michi garterio Rege armorę officioq̨, meo p̄ verba in īras patentes ordinavi et assignaui sub mangno Sigillo anglie spāl'r expressa concessas ordinaui et assignaui eidem Joh Baptiste Scutum cum insingnijs honorijs Sicut hic galice declarabitur, viz. Dargent deux flanches herminis vng chastnau Dasur yssuant Du de hors vng demi Lion dor tenant en sa patte vng panse du propre collour le porte du Lion poir so [n] timbre sur vng coroue dor, la teste demy Salamande in son naturell mantelle genls doble dargent, vt latius in Scuto hic depicto apparet habendum et tenendum eidem Joh̄ne Baptiste et heredibus suis de corpore suo legitime pereatis et vt ipse in his ornati sint ad eorum honorem imppetium In cuius rei testimoniū ego p̄fatus garter Rex armorum vt supra Sigillum meū ad arma una cū Sigillo officij meij Regis armorū presentibus apposui ac manu mea ppi ... Subscripsi dat̄ Londonij xxº die mensis Augusti Anno dom milesimo quingentesimo trigesimo tertio ac Anno Regni Regine Ellizabeth dei grā anglie france et hibernie Regine fidei defensore etc., Quinto.*

Draft of Exemplification of arms and crest and an augmentation to John Baptist Castillion by William Dethick Garter, and William Camden, Clarenceux, dated the 13th of December 1597.

[*Vniu*]ersis & singulis tam nobilibus & Generosis quàm cæteris cuiuscunq̨, loci aut conditionis hæc pervenerint Guil: Dethik Garterius Principalis Rex Armoȓ et Gulielmus Camden Clarenceux Rex Armorū Salutem, Cùm ab heroicis usq̨, temporibus viris rebus gestis, excellenti animi magnitudine æclaris, prudentia, fide in Principem cæterisq̨, vertutibusq̨, conspicuis varia honoris ornamenta, gloriæ monumenta & .... idis insignia laudatissimo maiorum instituto conferri soleāt ; & inter ea Insignia et Clypeis, quæ vulgò Arma vocantur ... t vsatissima cùmq̨, ad nos authoritate à Regia Maiestate delata, inter alia, imprimis spectet non solùm eiusmodi insignia .... edem verùm etiam confirmare posteritati testari, & quasi consecrare. Vobis & omnium seculorum si fieri possi .... ritati notum facimus, declaramus & attestamur (quod Gilbert[9] Dethik miles Garterius principalis Rex Armorum .... ante fecit) nos grauibus firmis & fide dignis testimonijs accepisse quod Johannis Baptista Castillion de Benham Valence in Commitatu Berks Armiger in regione Pedemontana Italiæ juxta Turinum Petro Castillione patre prognatus sit ex .... celebri & antiqua castilionum familia, qui in clypeo gentilitio rubro medium Leonem aureum ex argenteo castello exilientum gesserunt. Qui quidem Johannes Baptista Castillion stipendia fecit primùm in expeditione .... esiana posteà in expugnatione Boloniæ, & præsidio Caletano sub signis fœlicissimæ memoriæ Principis Henrici VIII .... Angliæ Frāciæ &c. Qui demum ab operam fortiter nauatam iure & libertate subditoȓ regni Angliæ donauit simulq̨, Serenissimæ eius filiæ Dominæ Elizabethæ et .... ularetur, commendauit cui singulari fide, & summa diligentia quinquaginta tres annos inseruiuit Mariaq̨, ... conante ob hanc fidem dominæ præstitam totos quatuor annos in carcerē erat conclusus. Tandem Verò serenissima Elizabetha ad regiam dignitatem Dei prouidentia euecta illum ob singulares virtutes, probitatem, moderationem, industriam, ... spectatam in aduersis fidem non solùm in vallettorum sacri cubiculi numerum asciuit, verùm etiam iussit vt insignia eius auita Cantone ex Erminis adaugerentur, ita vt ipse & eius liberis Quos ex Margarita filia & hærede Bartholomæi Compaigne nobilis perspicuus ciuis Florentini suscepit quorumq̨, nomina & nuptiæ in tabulas officij

---

* *The 20th of August, 5th Eliz., was 1563.*

OF BERKSHIRE. 97

Armorum sunt selata jam inde in Clypeo gestent In campo rosso sopra el castello di Argento medio d'Leone rampante d'Oro con el cantone d'Ermine, Tumq autem Cristæ in Italia minime sunt in vsu rogauitq vt antiquis his armis Cristam pro more regni Angliæ optaremus nos ne quid tanti viri dignitati deesse videretur excogitauimus & assignauimus vt pro Crista vtatur Salamandræ capite dissecto super Tortile ex suis coloribus cum chlamide rubra argento duplicata. Quæ arma vnà cum crista et singulis eorum partibus vt in margine depinguntur eidem Johanne Baptistæ, ejusq liberis legitimis vt habeant erant accutantur, ratificamus & confirmamus perinde vt Gilb. Dethik Garterius Principalis Rex Armorum superioribus annis raticauit & confirmauit. In cuius rei testimonium sub scriptionem nostram & sigillam urā apposuimus Anno regni Reginæ Elizabethæ 40 Dat quinto* die Decembris xiij° 1597.

Catcher, of Binfield.

Visitation of London, 1634-5, *Harl. Soc.*, Vol. XV., p. 145.

Vintry Ward, May the 5, 1634.

Octavo die Julij anno Domini 1634. Bee it knowne unto all men by these presents that I John Catcher of Binfield in the County Berks Knight do acknowledge and confesse myself to come of a younger brother and that Richard Catcher D^r of Phisick and one of the colledge of Physitians in London cometh of the elder Brother, wherefore I am content to beare my coate with a distinction.

JOHN CATCHER.

I Thomas Catcher sonn and heyre of the abovenamed Sr John Catcher ackowledg the like.

THOMAS CATCHER.

[*John Catcher was Knighted Aug. 27, 1619. He and his son Thomas Catcher Esq. were buried in Binfield Church.*]

The Armes & Creast confirmed by Robert Cooke Clar. in 1587 [*to John Catcher Sheriff of London, a Clothworker, buried at St. Peter the Poor*].

Vpon an auntient monument in Hackney Church wheron are the Pictures of a man and a woman in brass with 12 children vidz^t 5 sonnes and 7 daughters with this inscription soe worne as it can hardly be read.

Hic jacet Joh'is Cacher Katina et Agnes vxor' eius qui quidam Joh'is obijt ix die mensis Maij a° Dni Milessimo ccccIxxxiiij. Amen.

John Cacher died the 9th Maij 1484=Agnes.

Thomas Catcher marchant of the=Matild da. of W^m and Katherine
Staple in the Towne of Callis. | Toppesfeild.

Thomas Catcher of Hackney in co. Middlesex.=
A

---

* *The word* quinto *should have been struck out when the date was altered from* quinto die Januarij *to the 13th of December 1597.*

VOL. II. O

NOTES : VISITATIONS

```
                                                 ▲
        ┌────────────────────────────┬────────────────────────────┐
        Thomas Catcher of Hackney  = Sabina da. of Francis Eastfeild of
        dyed in Tottenham.           Walthamstow in com. Essex.
        │
    Richard Catcher of London Doctor in Phisick = Elizabeth da. & coheire of Tho.
    lineing aº 1634 [died 1 June 1651].          Godman of Letherhed com. Surry.
        │
    Thomas Catcher eldest sonn.
```

RICHARD CATCHER.

Cater, of Letcombe Regis.

Confirmation of the Arms of John Cater, of Letcombe Regis, to Margery Cater his daughter, wife of William Hyde, of South Denchworth, by William Harvy, Clarenceux, dated 20th of April, 1559. MS. Ashm. 840, pp. 412-13 (see " Genealogist," ii. 355).

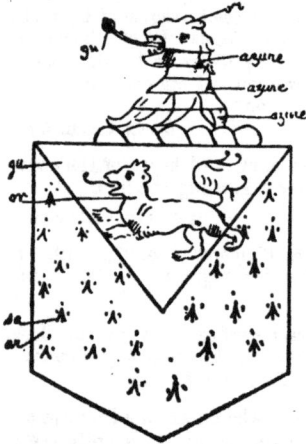

To all and singuler aswell Kinges heraldes and Officers of Armes, as Nobles gentilmen and others which these presentes shall see or here, William Hervye Esquyre otherwise called Clarencieulx Principall heralde and Kinge of Armes of the Sowthe Easte and Weast parties of England sendith due commendaçõns and greetinges, fforasmoche as auncientlie from the begynnynge the Valeaunte and vertuous actes of excellent parsons have ben comendid to the worlde with svndrye monuments and remembraunces of their good desertę Emonges the which one of the chefiest and most vsuall hath ben the bearing of signes and tokens in shildes called Armes, the which are none other thinges then evidences and demonstraçõns of prowes and valoure diverslie distributed according to the Quallities and deserttes of the parsons that such signes and tokens of the Diligent faithfull and Cowragious myght apeare before the negligent cowarde and ignorant and be an efficient cawse to move stire and kindle the harttes of menn to the imytaçõn of vertue and noblenes, Even so hath the same ben and yet ys contynuallie observid to thintent that suche as have don cõmendable service to their Prince or Contrey eyther in Ware or Peace, maye both receyve due honor in their lyves and also deryve the same successively to their posteritie after them   And being reqnyred of Margerye Cater doughter and heire of John Cater of Letcom Regis in the Countie of Berkshire gentilman to make searche in the Registers and recordes of myne Office for the Armes and Creast belonginge to the saide John Cater her Father and his auncestors and I fownde the same accordinglie   And so consideringe the antiquitie thereof coulde not alter nor change the same nor no parte nor percell thereof but to the great prejudice of the said Margerye.   In consideraçõn whereof I the saide Clarencieulx Kynge of Armes by powere and auctoritie to myne Office annexed and graunted by Lrēs Pattents vnder the greate Seale of England have ratefyed and confyrmed vnto the saide Margerye Doughter to the saide John

OF BERKSHIRE.

Cater and now wyfe to William Hyde of South Denchworth yn the Countie of Berkshire Esquyre the sayde Armes with thappurtenaunces hereafter followinge. That is to saye Ermyns on a Pyle gules a Lyon passant golde The Creaste vpon the heaulme a Lyons head razid barrey of six peces golde and azure on a wreathe gold and gules mantelled gules doubled argent as more playnly appeareth depicted yn this margent. To have and to houlde the said Armes and Creaste vnto the saide Margerye Cater gentlewoman Daughter to the foresaide John Cater and vnto all the Posteritie of the saide John Cater for evermore and therin to be revested to theyr wourshippes at their libertie and pleasure without ympediment lett or interrupcōn of anye pson or psons. In witnes wherof I the said Clarencieulx Kinge of Armes have signed these presentss with my hande and set therevnto the seale of myne offyce and the seale of myne Armes. yeven at Londou the xxth daye of Apryll in the yeare of owre Lorde god a thousand fyve hundrid fiftie and nyne, and in the firste yeare of the reigne of owre most dread sovereigne Ladye Elizabeth by the grace of Godd Queene of England ffraunce and Ireland deffendor of the faithe &c.

W HERUY alias Clarencieulx
King of Armes.

Champion, of Reading.

[*MS. Ashmole* 852, p. 34.]

1. *CHAMPION.*
2. *OYRE.*
3. *GAMBO.*
4. *RAMPIER.*
5. *DALISON.*
6. *DREW.*
7. . . . .
8. *SANCHETT.*
Inescutcheon . . . .

Townsend's MS. says, "A Ped^{ee} 11 gen[eration]^s higher in C. 2, 267," but does not give them. The following pedigree contains eleven generations higher than Townsend's first entry.

The pedigree so far as John Champion who married Isabell Sanchet appears to be taken from (C. 2, College of Arms) Visitation of Surrey, 1623.

The children of John, the second son of Arnold Champion, are omitted by Ashmole, as well as the descent from Thomas Champion of Horsham, second son of John by his wife Isabell Sanchett. These I have added to Ashmole's pedigree from a MS. copy of the Visitation of Surrey, 1623.

Peter Le Neve, who formerly owned this copy, perhaps justly expresses the opinion that it "was transcribed by a very ignorant fellow who ever he was."

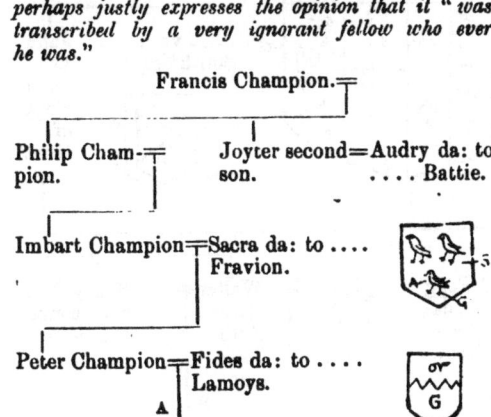

Francis Champion.=

Philip Champion. = | Joyter second son. = Audry da: to .... Battie.

Imbart Champion = Sacra da: to .... Fravion.

Peter Champion = Fides da: to .... Lamoys.

100 • NOTES: VISITATIONS

▲

Geffery [2 sonne] marryed Mary Dallalione.

Peter Champion son & heire.=Blanch da: & heire of .... Oyre.

Philip 3ᵈ son mar: Thebis Gasprian.

John slayne agᵗ yᵉ Turks.

2 daūrs.

Leopard Champion [*fil et hæres*].=Isabell da: and heire of .... Gambo.

Philip slayn in Spayn.

Blanch vx: John Amson [*Amersom*].

Henry Champion son & heire.=Joyce da: & heire of .... Rampier.

Lathanell vx: John Pooley.

Anne vx: Wᵐ Gaswine [*Gascoigne*].

Peter Champion [*filius et heres*].=Edith da: & heire of .... Dalison.

Leopard dyed at Paris marryed .... da: to .... Mortimer of Attilburgh [*Alesburow in Co: Norfolk*].

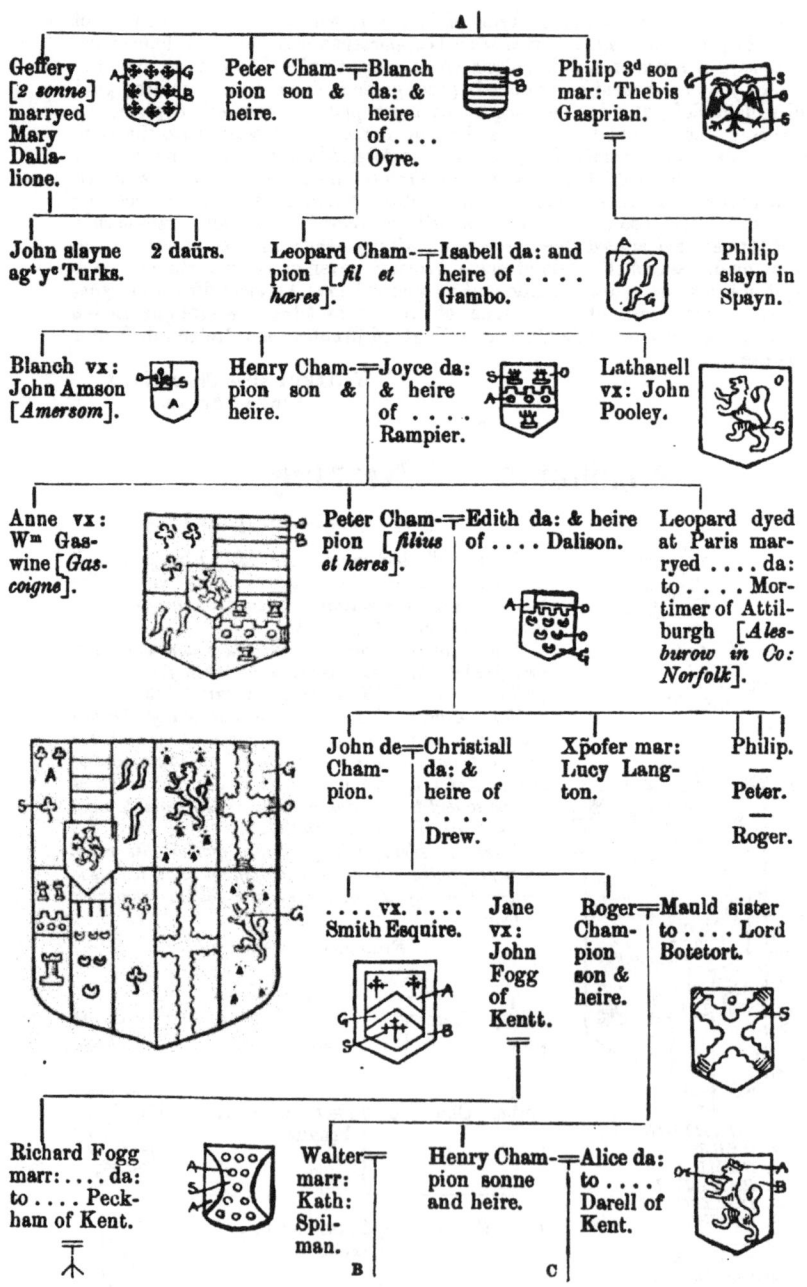

John de Champion.=Christiall da: & heire of .... Drew.

Xp̄ofer mar: Lucy Langton.

Philip.
—
Peter.
—
Roger.

.... vx: .... Smith Esquire.

Jane vx: John Fogg of Kentt.

Roger Champion son & heire.=Mauld sister to .... Lord Botetort.

Richard Fogg marr: .... da: to .... Peckham of Kent.

Walter marr: Kath: Spilman.

Henry Champion sonne and heire.=Alice da: to .... Darell of Kent.

B   C

OF BERKSHIRE.

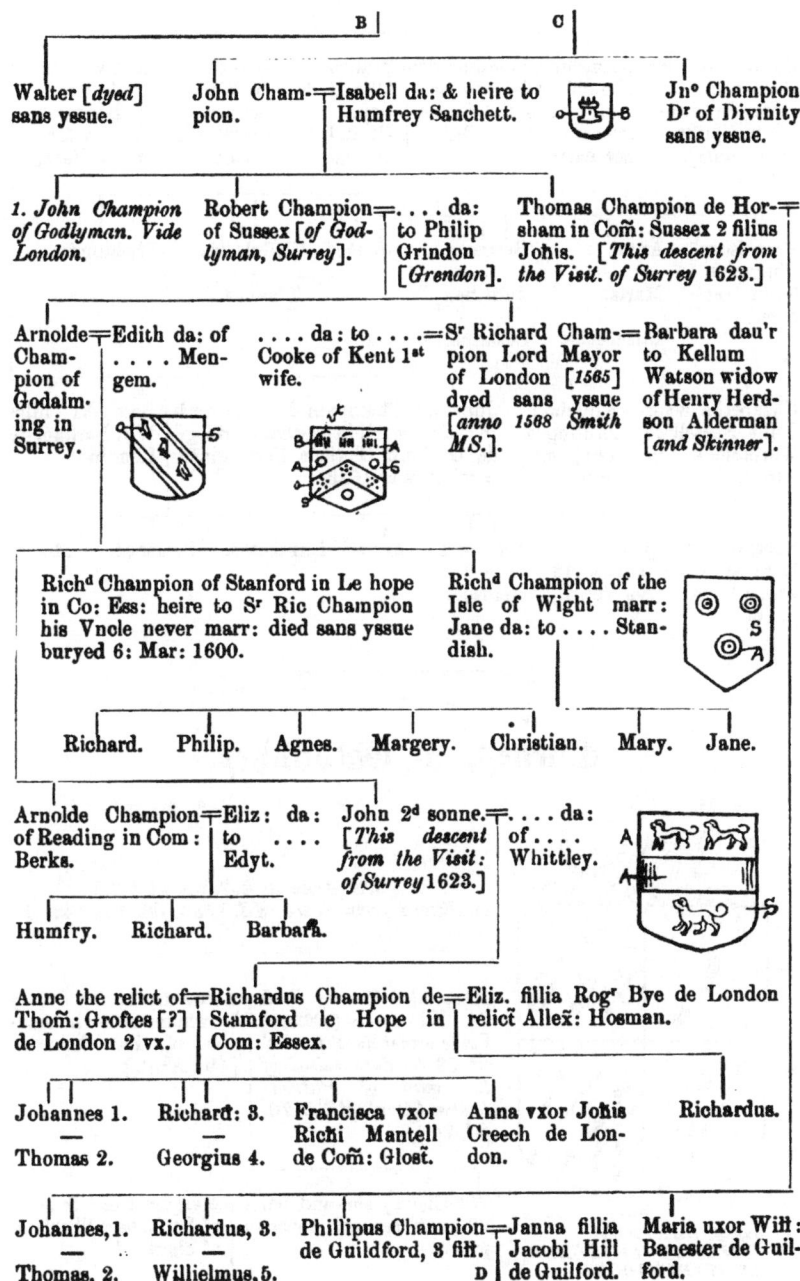

B | C |

Walter [dyed] sans yssue. — John Champion. =Isabell da: & heire to Humfrey Sanchett. — Jn° Champion Dr of Divinity sans yssue.

1. *John Champion of Godlyman. Vide London.* — Robert Champion of Sussex [*of Godlyman, Surrey*]. = ... da: to Philip Grindon [*Grendon*]. — Thomas Champion de Horsham in Com: Sussex 2 filius Johis. [*This descent from the Visit. of Surrey 1623.*]

Arnolde=Edith da: of Champion of ... Mengem. Godalming in Surrey. — .... da: to .... Cooke of Kent 1st wife. =Sr Richard Champion Lord Mayor of London [1565] dyed sans yssue [*anno 1568 Smith MS.*]. =Barbara dau'r to Kellum Watson widow of Henry Herdson Alderman [*and Skinner*].

Richd Champion of Stanford in Le hope in Co: Ess: heire to Sr Ric Champion his Vncle never marr: died sans yssue buryed 6: Mar: 1600. — Richd Champion of the Isle of Wight marr: Jane da: to .... Standish.

Richard. Philip. Agnes. Margery. Christian. Mary. Jane.

Arnolde Champion=Eliz: da: of Reading in Com: to .... Berks. Edyt. — John 2d sonne.=.... da: of .... [*This descent from the Visit: of Surrey 1623.*] Whittley.

Humfry. Richard. Barbara.

Anne the relict of=Richardus Champion de=Eliz. fillia Rogr Bye de London Thom: Groftes [?] Stamford le Hope in relict Allex: Hosman. de London 2 vx. Com: Essex.

Johannes 1. — Thomas 2. | Richard: 3. — Georgius 4. | Francisca vxor Richi Mantell de Com: Glost. | Anna vxor Johis Creech de London. | Richardus.

Johannes, 1. — Thomas, 2. | Richardus, 3. — Willielmus, 5. | Phillipus Champion=Janna fillia de Guilford, 3 fill. Jacobi Hill D | de Guilford. | Maria uxor Will: Banester de Guilford.

NOTES: VISITATIONS

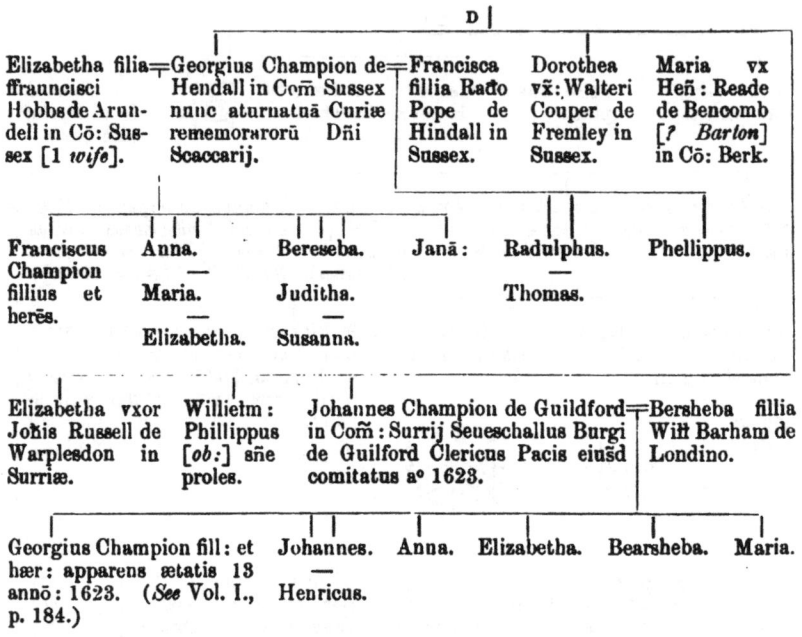

| Elizabetha filia ffrauncisci Hobbs de Arundell in Cō: Sussex [1 *wife*]. | = | Georgius Champion de Hendall in Cōm Sussex nunc aturnatuā Curiæ rememoraroru Dñi Scaccarij. | = | Francisca fillia Rađo Pope de Hindall in Sussex. | Dorothea vx̄: Walteri Couper de Fremley in Sussex. | Maria vx Heñ: Reade de Bencomb [? *Barton*] in Cō: Berk. |

| Franciscus Champion fillius et herēs. | Anna. — Maria. — Elizabetha. | Beresheba. — Juditha. — Susanna. | Janā: | Radulphus. — Thomas. | Phellippus. |

| Elizabetha vxor Johis Russell de Warplesdon in Surriæ. | Willielm: Phillippus [*ob:*] sñe proles. | Johannes Champion de Guildford in Cōm: Surrij Seueschallus Burgi de Guilford Clericus Pacis eiusd comitatus aº 1623. | = | Bersheba fillia Wiłł Barham de Londino. |

| Georgius Champion fill: et hær: apparens ætatis 13 annō: 1623. (*See* Vol. I., p. 184.) | Johannes. — Henricus. | Anna. | Elizabetha. | Bearsheba. | Maria. |

𝕮𝖍𝖊𝖓𝖊𝖕, of 𝖂𝖔𝖔𝖉𝖍𝖊𝖕.

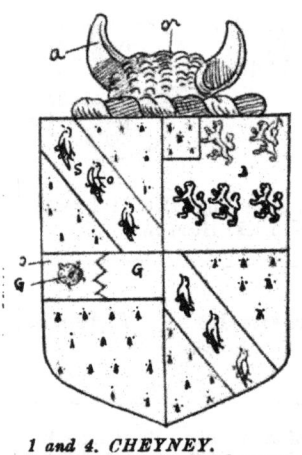

1 and 4. *CHEYNEY.*
2. *CHEYNEY (SHIRLAND).*
3. *SHOTTESBROOKE.*

[*MS. Ashmole* 852, pp. 44-5-6.]
Additions from Harl. MS. 1532, *fol.* 131-132, &c.

| Alexander Cheney dyed 24 Edw: I. [*1295-96*] [*vide escaet de aº predcō nº 26 he dyed seised of the man' of Patricsbourne* (*Harl. MS.* 6173, *fol.* 24ᵇ)]. | = | Agnes da: of Wᵐ de Say by whome came the mannor of Patricksborne. [*Co: Kent.*] |

| Wᵐ Cheney son and heire 22 annorᵉ ad mortem patris. | = | Margarett da: & heire of Sʳ Robert Sherland of Sherland. |

OF BERKSHIRE.   103

▲

1. Wm Cheney son and heire dyed anno 8 E. 3 [*1334-5*] aged 58, s.p.

2. Sr Robert Cheney *of Sherland in y^e Ile of Sheppey in Com. Kent* brother & heire 30: yeares old ob: 38: Ed: 3 [*1364-5*].

1. Sr Richard Cheney *of* Sherland K^t 10 yeares old 36: Edw: 3 [*1362-3*] = Margery da: & coheire of Robert Crall *of Crall in Com. Sussex* & Margarett his wife da: & h: of Symon Peplasham.

2. Roger Cheney 6 yeares olde 36: Edw: 3 [*1362-3*]

Eliz: 1st marr: John Wilcotts of Oxfordshire 2^{ly} to Sr Rich: Walksted Kn^t *of whome com hales.*

Isabel vx: John Pimp, *of whome comes Scott of Kent.*

Symon Cheney 2^d son of Richd Cheney & of Margery his wife *of whome comes Cheney of Crall in Sussex. Vide Sussex.* = Elianor da: and heire of John Nottingham.

Alexander Cheney.

Richard Cheney.

Robert Cheney of Crall & Higham. = Anne da: of Richd Lovelace.

Wm Cheney de Warbleton in Hinck Cheyney de Sussex qui nunc est. = Margarett da: of .... Righley.

John Cheyney de Sittingborne.

Humfrey Cheyney of Higham in Milsted. [*See Visitation of Kent*, 1619, p. 43.] = Alice da: of Sr Nich: Wootton of Boughton malherb.

Jno Cheney 3^d sonne.

Roger Cheney.

John Cheney of Crall. = Agnes da: & heire of Jno Farby.

Wm Cheney. = Malyn Fincham.

Margrett vx: Rich: Oxenbrige.

Parnell vx: Ric: Belingham.

Eliz: vx: Henry Darrell. — Joane.

Thomas Cheyney 2^d sonn. = Constance da: of Rich: Seras.

Wm Cheyney = Margarett da: to .... Palmer.

Tho: Cheyney = ... da: & heir of .... Hinxsted of Winchelsey.

John Cheyney = Eliz: da: to John Palmer Sister to Sr Anthony Palmer Kn^t of the Bath.

Eliz: da: & heire wife to Sr Tho: Colpepper of Grenway Court in Kent.

Wm Cheney of Sherland Esquire eldest sonne. = Elianor da: of John Salerne of Iden in Com: Sussex. B

Alice wife to John Cobham of Belancte [*Beland*].

Margery marr: Jacob Donet [*James dannett*] 2: to John Salerne of Iden, *of whom comes St Leger.*

Joane vx: Tho: Atrown *Towne, of whome com. Somes.*

NOTES : VISITATIONS

B |

Sʳ John Shotesbrook Knt. 12. E. 1 [1283-84]=

John Shotesbrooke lord of pebeworth [co: Glouc:]= & Ordeston in Com' Berks, 34 E. 1 [1305-6].

Robert Standon in= Com. Stafford.

Sʳ Gilbert Shotesbrooke 1. E. 2 [1307-8].=

Sʳ Vivian Standon knt.=

Agnes vx. Sʳ John lassells knt.

Sʳ Gilbert Shotsbrooke= Elizabeth d. & coheire.
knt.

Sʳ Robert= Edith or Elizabeth d. of John lord Stourton.= Sʳ John Beauchamp of
Shottes- [Sir John Stourton, Kᵗ, and Widow to Sʳ powick 1 husband.
brooke   John Beauchamp, Kᵗ, Mother to Margarett
knt.   Dutchess of Somerset. Ashm: Berks: iii. 301.]

Margerett duches of Somerset.

Sʳ John Cheney of Sherland in yᵉ= Elenor da: & coheire to Sʳ Robert Shotesbrooke
Isle of Shepey in Kent Knight.   [in Com. Berks (Harl. MS. 6173)].

1. Isabell da: to Sʳ Geffrey Bullen= Wᵐ Cheney Esquire= 2. Margaret Younge.
Kt Mayor of London.   of Sherland.

Sʳ Francis= .... [Wer- Friswith da: &= Sʳ Tho: Cheney= Anne da: & co-
Cheney [Con- burga] d.   coheire to Sʳ Knᵗ of yᵉ Garter heire to Sʳ Jnᵒ
stable of Quin- of .... Tho: Frowike   Lord Warden of   Broughton of
borough] dyed [Brierton] [the] Justice. yᵉ Cinque Ports Tuddington in
s. prole.   [Harl. MS. First Wife.   dyed 1558.   Co: Bedford 2ᵈ
             6173].   wife.

Henry Lord Cheney of Tuddington= Jone da: to Tho: Lord Wentworth.
dyed s.p. 1587.   of Nettlested in Com. Suffolk.

John Cheney= Margrett da: Kath: vx: Sʳ   Francis vx: Nich: Anne vx:
slaine at Mon- to George   Tho: Kempe   Cripps son & heire Sʳ John
trell in Picardy, Nevill Lord of Olentigh to Sʳ Hen: Cripps Parrott
s: prole.   Burgeny.   in Kent.   sine prole.   [Perrott].

Sʳ Tho: Parrott= Dorothy da: of Walter Deuereus E. of Essex.

Penelope [Parrott].

C

OF BERKSHIRE.

3. Sr John Cheney Knt of yᵉ Garter. | Edmund Cheney ob young [eldest son]. | Edward [Cheney] of Sarum [1486—1502] [4th son]. | Deane | Sr Robert sine prole [5th son].

Sr Roger Cheney of w: Woodhey Com' Berks [6th son]. = Anne da: to Ric Stanley of Pipe [co. Lanc.]. | Sr Alexander Cheney [7th son]. | Humfry Cheney ob. young. | Edith vx: Sr Wᵐ Sandes mother to Wᵐ Lord Sandes.

Joane sister of John lord williams of Thame, renupt. Edward Harvey of Thirley in Com. Bedford. [See Visit. 1532, Vol. I., p. 4.] = Jnᵒ Cheney of Woodhey in Co: Berks. *Esq. to* yᵉ body of H. 8. = Jane da: to Sr Wᵐ Norrys of Yattendon in Co: Berks. knᵗ. 1 wife. | Julian.

John Cheney of Bamsted [*of hampsted*] 3ᵈ sonne. = Elizabeth Tydder. | Many daūrs as in Wiltshire appeareth. [*Visit.* 1565.]

Tho: Cheney living 1589 = Eliz: da: to .... Stoughton.

William Cheney.

John Cheney of West Woodhey in Co: Berks Esqʳ. = Dorothy da: to Jnᵒ Yate of Charney Esqʳ. | 2. Humffrey ob. s.p. | Edw: Cheney of Vphaven in Wiltsh: 2ᵈ son. *Vide idem.* = Margery yᵉ relict of Tho: King.

1. Mary da: of Tho: Roberts of Glastenbury in Com: Kent. = Tho: Cheney of Woodhey. | 2. Anne da: to Edward Scott of yᵉ mote in Com. Sussex Esqʳ.

Tho: Cheney of *West Wood*hay, living 1587 [? 1589]. = *Elizabeth da: to* .... Ruffin. | Margaret. | Robert Cheney of *West*woodhay. = Celina da: to Jnᵒ Baptist Castelion of Benham Vallens in Com. Berks. | Henry Cheney = ... d. of Sr George Philpott.

henrey of Cir. 15 yeres of age. | dorathie sister & heire vx. Thomas polden. | Henry Cheney. | John Cheney. | Barbara [Cheney].
Mary [Cheney].

Choke, of Abington, co. Berks.

Confirmation of Arms and grant of a Crest to Richard Choke of Avington by Robert Cooke, Clarenceux, dated the 4th of July 1576.

No Arms tricked, MS. Ashmole's 858, pp. 216—218, so I have added the Arms given in G. 13, fol. 26, Coll. of Arms.

1. CHOKKE.   2. WITHERIGE.   1 and 4. CHOKKE.   2. GETON.
3. CHOKKE.   4. GETON.   3. WITHERIGE.

To all and singuler as well Nobles and Gentills as others to whome these p'sents shall come, Robert Cooke Esquire alias Clarencieulx Principal Herehault and Kinge of Armes of the Sowth, East, and Weast partes of this Realme of England from the Ryver of Trent sowthwardes sendith greeting in our Lord God Everlasting. Whereas aunciently from the beginning the valiant and vertuous Actes of worthy psons have bin commended to the Worlde in all ages with sondry Monum[ts] and Remembrances of their good deserte Emongst the which the chiefest and most vsuall hath ben the bearing of Signes and tokens in Shildes called Armes which are evident demonstracōns of Prowes and valour diversly distributed according to the Qualities and deserts of the psons, w[ch] Order as it was most prudently devised in the beginning to stirre and kindle the hearts of men to the Imitacon of Vertue and noblenes even so hath the same ben and yet is continually observed to th'ende that such as have don commendable service to their prince or Country either in Warre or peace may both receive due honor in their Lyves, and also derive the same successively to their Posterity for ever And being required of Richard Choke of Avington in the County of Berks Esquire, second sonne to Alexander Choke, and brother and heire to S[r] John Choke Kn[t] son and heire to John Choke, son and heire to S[r] Richard Choke of Long Asheton in the County of Somersett Kn[t], one of the Justices of the Common Pleas at Westme[n]ster to make sarche in the Registers and Records of my Office for the aunciect Armes belonging to that name and ffamily wherof he is descended, I have at his request made search accordingly,

And finding the same in the Records of myne Office, I coulde not without his great Prejudice assigne vnto him any other Armes then those which are lawfully to him descended from his Auncestors, And in Consideracōn therof I have confirmed assigned and graunted vnto and for the sayd Rich: Choke Esquire the oulde auncient Armes of his Auncestors as followeth That is to saye he beareth quarterly in the firste for Choke Gules thre barres wavey argent, in the second for Witherige Argent a Cheveron sables betweene thre Lyons cowshant gules, in the third for Geton argent thre flower de Lucis semy Crosse Crosseletts azure, the last as the first. And for as much as I finde no Creast vnto the same as commonly to all auncient Armes there belongeth none, I have given vnto him by Way of Encrease for his Creast & Cognizance on a Wreath argent and gules a Cranes head between two Winges Argent in a Crowne Golde, manteled gules dobled argent as more plainly apperith depicted in this Margent, which Armes and Creast I the sayd Clarencieulx Kinge of Armes, by the power and aucthoritie to myne Office annexed and granted by Lrēs Patents vnder the great Seale of England have ratifyed, confirmed assigned and granted vnto and for the sayd Rich: Choke Esquire and to his posterity with their due differences the same to vse beare and shewe for evermore in Shilde Cote Armour or otherwise, and therein to be revested at his and their Liberty and pleasure without Impedim^t Lett or Interrupcōn of any pson or persons. In witnes wherof I have sett herevnto my hande and Seale of Office the fourth day of July in An° Dñi 1576: and in the Eighteenth Yeare of the Raigne of our Soveraigne Lady Quene Elizabeth &c:

ROB: COOKE Alias Clarencieulx
Roy Darmes.

Chock, of Abington.

In the copy of the Visitation of Berkshire made in 1566 ; *MS. No.* 531, *in the Library of Gonville and Caius College, Cambridge, the pedigree of Chock is headed by the following :—*

Memorand' quod tempore Regis Edw. 2. et longe ante usque ad et post An. 10 eiusdem Regis [*1316-1317*] Malherbe erat dominus manerii de Standewick cuis [*sic*] nominis quidem Johannes Maleherbe vendidit manerium predictum cuidem Johanni Clevidon mil' qui quidem Johannes Clevedon per Cartam datam 43 Ed. 3. [*1369-1370*] dedit manerium predict' cuidam Matheo de Clivedon et al'qui quidem Matheus de Clivedon et ceteri per Cartam suam datam 44. Ed. 3. [*1370-1371*] dederunt dictum Manerium Johanni de Sutland mil' qui quidem Johannes de Sutland vx' capiens fil' predicti Johannis de Clevedon exit' habuit Alexander et Elizabeth et predict Alexander eum supervixit, qui quidem Alexander seit' existen' de dicto Manerio in dominico suo vt de feod' obiit infra etatem, post cuius mortem predict' Maner' discendebat vt de iure hereditaris sorori sue dict' Elizabeth, que quidem Elizabeth nupta fuit Willelmo Botreaux mil' per quem habuit exit' fil' et hered' willelmum dominum Botreaux cui post matris mortem dict' Maner' descendebat qui quidem willelmus dominus Botreux per cartam suam geren' datum Anno 2. Ed. 4. [*1462-1463*] Vendidit dictum manerium Ricardo Chock mil' vn' Justic' dicti Regis de Com' Banco Et idem Ricardus Recuperauit Manerium predict' versus predict' dominum Guilielmum per breve de Rect' (Cuius breve dat' est ij Maii 2. Ed. 4.) et habuit versus ipsum iudicium final' Qui quidem Ricardus Chock dedit et ffeoffauit dict' Manerium cuidam Spencer et al' et qui quidem Spencer et reliqui per cartam suam dat' 1. H. 7. [*1485-1486*] dederunt predictum Manerium cuidam Ricardo Chock filio secundo dicti Richardi Mil' in feod' talliato cuius hered' Mascul' dict' Maner' contin' vsque ad ffranciscum Chock de Avington nuper defunct' qui illud dedit' Ricardo Chock defunct' patri Alexandri Chock defunct' Avunculo Alexandri Chock iam tenen'. Qui qui lem Ricardus Chock de Avington descendebat de Johanni Chock mil' fil" et hered' primo dicti Ricardi Chock mil' vt patet per le pedigree.

Clarke, of Ardington.

MS. Ashmole 852, p. 47.

Granted by Wm Dethick Garter & William Camden Clarenc: 22 Oct: 1600 p Edw: Clarke de Ardington in Com̃ Berke geñ [*added by Ashmole*].

CLARKE quartering CHAMPENEY.

John Clarke of Basledon=Eliz: da: & heire of
in Com: Bark.   . . . . Champney.

Augustin Clarke of Basledon=. . . .

John Clarke [*of*=[*Alicia daur: and heir of . . . . Pikeman of
Ardington*].   *Basledon in Com: Berks.*]

Henry   John Clarke [*of*=[*Dorothy dau: of Richard Smith of Nether*   Richard
Clarke.   *Ardington*].   *Winchingdon in com Bucks. 1st wife.*]   Clarke.

Edward Clarke of Ardington in Com:=   John Clarke.
Berks gent: living 1600.

In the begining of the reigne of K^g Charles the first, he was knighted ; vizt : when he was high Sheriff of Berke [*in Ashmole's handwriting*].

Clavile.

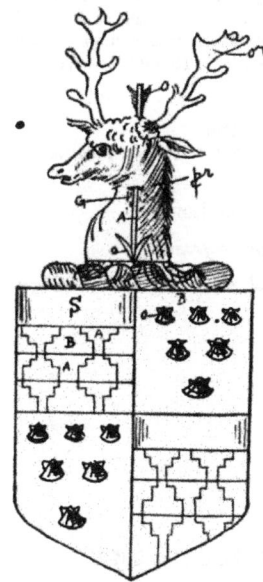

CLAVILE *quartering* ESTOCK.

MS. Ashmole 852, p. 35.

John Clavile of Barneston=
in the Isle of Purkike
[*Purbeck*] [*and Countie of
Berks*] in Co: Berks. (*Harl.
MS.* 1139, *f.* 118 *b, where
the name is written Clanvile*).

Collins, of Betterton.

MS. Rawlinson D. 865, *fol.* 121.

Sr

Mr Champion informs me yt you expect to hear from me, and had e're this time, had I not lately purchased land, which renders me incapable at present for another purchase, soe yt I fear together with the misfortunes of the times yt I shall not be able to defray easily soe great fees till another year, Besides Sr I am in hope to clear a title to yt coat by the name of Collins Vert a Gryphon segreant Or, And the reason besides the carelessness of mens keeping of antient writings may be this, why we are ignorant of our descent yt since the first of Henry the Seventh there have been seven lineall descents all of one name which I can manifest soe yt the son was never old enough to receiv anything by tradition of the father, whereby alsoe we have been consened of our Estate there being severall famylys Extant at this day raised out of it. But Sr you were pleased to say yt you would confirme the same coate to me only with some addition, now if the addition of a Crest be a sufficient distinction I would indevour to pay the ffees by the next returne. Only I desire you to favour me with a line or two, and whether my descent as far as I can produce by writings may not be inserted If your Occasions call you any more into this country you shall be welcom to my house, Still I remain a lover & honourer of y^r pson & studys

Whilest.

Betterton nigh Wantage
June the 16th 1666.

Jo: COLLINS
per virtutem nobilitas

[*Addressed*] To Elias Ashmole Esq, att the Middle Temple London

[*There is a small seal of Arms bearing a griffin segreant.*]

John Collins of Betterton, entered his pedigree without Arms at the Visitation 1665-6, see Vol. I., p. 187.]

Grant of Arms to John Collins of Betterton, Co. Berks, 6 May 1672.
Coll. of Arms. O. 2, 18 (extract.)

Grant of Arms and Crest by Sr Edward Bysshe Knight Clarenceux Principall Herald and King of Armes to John Collins of Betterton co. Barks gent & the heirs of his body lawfully begotten to be borne in Seale Shield Penon Coat armor or otherwise accordinge to the law of Armes for ever. The Armes;—Vert a griffon passant Or a chief Ermyn, and for his Crest :— On a Helmet and wreath of his coullers a griffons head erased Vert Crowned Or Mantled Gules doubled Argent, as in the margent is more liuely depicted. Dated the sixt day of May An° Dom. 1672.

EDWARD BYSSHE Clarenceux
King of Armes.

Curteys, of Enborne.

Confirmation of Arms and Grant of a Crest to Griffyne Curteys of Enborne in the County of Berks, Esquire, by Sir Gilbert Dethick, Knt., Garter, dated the 2nd of June 1559. (MS. Coll. of Arms, Grants, vol. i., p. 182.)

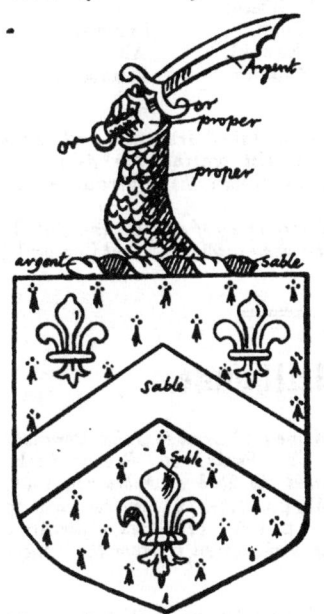

To all and Singular as well Nobles & Gentellmen as others to whome these p^rsents shall Come I Gilbert Dethicke Knight at̃s Garter principall Kinge of Armes send Greetinge: Forasmuche as auncyently from the Beginninge the Valiaunte & Verteous Actes of Excellent Parsons have been Cõmended to the Worlde & posteritie with sondry Monuments & Remembrances of their good deseartes amonge the whiche the cheifest and moste usuall have beene the Bearing of Signes in Sheildes called Armes wch are Evident demonstracõns and Tokens of Prowes & Valour div'sely distributed according to the Qualities of Each Person demeritinge the same: And whereas theire fore Griffyne Curteys of East-Enborne in the County of Barkshire Esqr hath of long tyme ben one of the Bearers of theise auncyent Armes Viz^t Ermin a cheveron betweene three flower de Luces sable And yet knowing Certayne of noe Creast duly apperteyning thereunto hath requestede me the sayd Garter to assigne to his sayd auncyente Coate Armo^r such Creaste as he may lawfully Beare. In Consideratione wheirof & for a further declaratione of the worthines of the sayd Griffin, I the sayd Garter have given & graunted him this Creaste or Cognisance following: to wit: On a Wreath argent & sable a Sarasins Arme Cooped & armed in Mayll the hand proper houldinge an arming Sworde argent Hilt & pomell or: Mantled argent, doubled gules, As more playnely in this Margent depicted apperethe. Which sayd Armes & Creaste I the sayd Garter doe Ratefie Conferme & Allowe unto the foresayd Gryffin & to his posteritie foreuer: And he & they, to have hold use beare & enioye the same w^thout the lett impedim^t or Interrupcõn of any other Parson or Parsons whatsoev^r. In Witness whereof I have signed theise p^rsents wth myne hand, & sett thereunto the Seales of my Office & Armes. Dated the second of June in the second yere of the Raigne of our most gratious Soveraigne Ladye, Elizabethe by the Grace of God, Queene of Englande France & Ireland, Defendor of the fayth the Anno Domini 1559.

Dalby, of Reading.

MS. Rawl. D. 865, fol. 98. Not in Ashmole's hand. Original paper.

Exhibited at the Beare in Reading Cõm Berks. Marcij 11° 1664.

The Pedigree.

Edward Dalby of the Inner Templa London Esqr sonne of Thomas Dalby (by Amy his wife) Cittizen, and Marchant of London deceased, sonne of Thomas Dalby, being one of the younger brothers of the Family of Dalby's of Brookhampton in the County of Warrwick.

NOTES: VISITATIONS

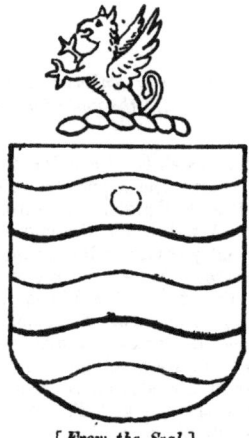

The Marriage & Issue of the said Edw. Dalby.
} The sayd Edward Dalby, by Frances his wife being the second daughter of Charles Holloway of Oxoñ s'jeant at Law, hath issue

John.　　　　Frances.
Edward.　　　Alice.
Charles.　　　Elizabeth.

The Paternall Coate, Crest, and difference, given by the sayd Edw: Dalby.
} [*A small seal of Arms here with helmet and mantlet bearing the Arms and Crest as above: the difference is not clear.*

Barry wavy of six [*Or and Gules*]; *Crest a demi griffin segreant* [*proper*].]

[*From the Seal.*]

Dancastle, of Wellhouse.

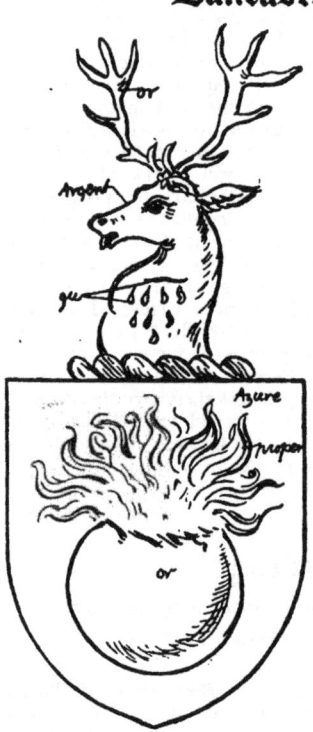

Patent of Arms and Crest to John Dancastle of Wellhouse, Co: Berks, by Robert Cooke, Clarenceux, dated the 25th of February, 1586. MS. Ashm. 858, pp. 211-212; another copy in MS. Ashm. 840, p. 409. (No trick of the Arms in either. The Trick given is from the College of Arms.)

To all and singular as well Nobles and Gentils as others to whome these Presents shall come be seene heard read or vnderstood Robert Cooke Esquire alias Clarenceux Kinge of Armes and Principall Herald of the East West and South Partes of this Realme of England Sendeth greeting in oʳ Lord God Everlasting. Aunciently from the beginning the verteous Actes of worthy persons have beene commended to the World with sundry Monuments and Remembrances of their good deserts, amongst the wᶜʰ the cheifest and most vsuall hath beene the bearing of Signes and Tokens in Sheilde called Armes &c: And being requyred by John Dancastle of Wellhouse in the County of Berks Gentleman to make searche in the Registers, and Recorde of my Office, for suche Armes and Creast, as he may lawfully beare, wherevpon I have made searche accordingly and doe finde that he may rightfully beare these Armes and Crest hereafter followinge. That is to say, the ffield azure, a Balle of Wildfire gold, and to his Crest vpon the Helme, on a Wreath Gold and azure, a Staggs head coupee silver, wounded gules, the hornes Golde, Mantled gules, dubled silver as more plainely appeareth

OF BERKSHIRE.

depicted in the Margent hereof. Which Armes and Creast & every parte and parcell thereof, I the sayd Clarencieux King of Armes doe by these p'sente ratifie, confirme, give, grant and allow vnto the sayd John Dancastle Gentleman and to his Posterity with their due difference to vse beare enjoy and shew forth at all tymes and for ever hereafter according to the aunciept Lawes of Armes, without the Impedim[t] Lett or Interrupcoñ of any person or persons. In wittnesse whereof &c: the 25th day of ffebruary in the Yeare of o[r] Lord God 1586, and in the 29: Yeare of the Raigne &c: Queene Elizabeth.

Day, of Windsor.

Exemplification of Arms to William Day, S.T.B., Provost of Eton College, and Dean of Windsor, by William Flower, Norroy, dated 28th October 1582. MS. Ashmole 834, f. 55; another copy, MS. Ashmole 858, p. 44, for the Deane of Windesore.

Omnibus et singulis tam regibus ad Arma siue Heraldis, quam Nobilibus cæterisque hoc scriptum visuris, lecturis, vel auditoris, Gulielmus Flower Armiger, aliter dictus Norroy, Rex Armorum, et principalis Heraldus partium regni Angliæ Orientalium Occidentalium, et borealium vltra ripam fluuij de Trent, Salutem in Domino sempiternam. QVVM venerabilis vir Gulielmus Daije sacræ Theologiæ Bacchalaurus, Præpositus Etonensis Collegij, et Decanus Windesoriensis, ex generosa Cambrensium familia oriundus, filius scilicet iunior Ricardi Daije, qui fuit filius Nicholai Daije fiilij Johannis Dee aliter ab Anglis cognominati Daye, filij Morgani Dee fratris iunioris Ricardi Dee Cambrobritanni: multisque alijs nominibus clarus, me præfatum Norroy Regem Armorum obnixè rogauerit, vt antiqua generis sui Arma siue insignia gentilitia, iuxta veram Heraldicè artis disciplinam ei significarem verbisque conceptis describerem: Ego quidem non solùm quod est officij mei execuutus sum, sed etiam viro virtute et eruditione claro, deque Principe et patria optimè merito gratificari cupiens, antiqua et autentica Officij mei Registra scriniaque sacra diligenter perlustraui, in quibus avita ac propria generis sui Arma siue insignia à maioribus suis hactenus visitata, inueni. Et ne rei tam memoria dignæ cognitio diutius delitesceret, ne ve temporis iniuria seu alia quavis occasione, noue inquisitionis materia denuò præbeatur Arma siue insignia prædicta antiqua in forma quæ sequitur descripsi, et pro pleniori notitia in margine præsentium magis ad viuum suis metallis atque coloribus delineanda, illuminanda, depingendaque curavi, videlicet in Scuto aureo et asorio similiter admodum tigni sive signi capitalis æqualiter diuiso, tres maculæ siue molettæ triangulariter positæ, quarum superiores duæ asoriæ sunt, infima tota est aurea. Pro Crista verò galeæ cui appendit clypeus, supereminent manus duæ alatæ inuicem coniunctæ: quarum alarum extensarum prima aurea, maculam præ se fert ceruleam, secunda asoria, auream ostentat maculam; supra Torquem ex auro et asorio contextum pulcherimè situatæ. Quibus appendent Mantellæ rubræ, argento intrinsecus duplicatæ et condecoratæ. Quæ quidem insignia clypei antiqua vnà cum apice seu Christa galeæ imposita cæterisque appendicibus ac ornamentis, Ego piænominatus Norroy rex Armorum virtute et authoritate functionis et officij mei à Reginea Majestate mihi in hac parte concessæ dicto venerabili viro Gulielmo Daije posterisque suis addixi tradidi et inperpetuum confirmavi per præsentes. Habenda vtenda gerenda et ostendenda honoris gratia quibuscunque loco et tempore pro eorum arbitrio, aliquo impedimento, contradictione, aut prohibitione id vt ne fieri possit, non obstantibus. In quorum omnium fidem et testimonium, ego Norroy rex Armorum prædictus hijs præsentibus nomen meum manu mea propria subscripsi, et appensione sigilli officij mei, præsens meum diploma corroboraui. Datum Windesori 28 die Octobris, Anno ab incarnatione Domini ac Redemptoris nostri Jesu Christi MDLXXXIj. Regni verò Serenissimæ Reginæ Elizabethæ vicesimo quarto.

Deane, of Wallingford.

No Arms given.

Visitation of Hampshire, 1622-34, College of Arms, C. 19, fol. 67ᵇ. The pedigree is not signed. It seems possible that it is a later addition to the MS.

In *Camden's Guifts and Grants*, vol. iii., page 7, *College of Arms*, is the following:—Of Mattingley in Co: South. Deane. Vᵗ on chevron bet 3 Griffons heads erased or beaked g. 5 molletts sa.

Creast, a Griffons head erased Or beaked .... wᵗʰ a collar Vᵗ betw: 2 wings Vᵗ.

[*Confirmed by Camden 1623 (Burke)*] *to John Deane of Mattingley, in the Isle of Wight. They were previously of Wallingford. There appears to have been another Berkshire family of Dene or Deane, who bore, argent two bars Sable, within a bordure Gules. Add. MS. 14283, p. 60.*

William Deane de Wallingford in Com: Berks.=
[*William à Dene, senʳ and junʳ, were Aldermen of Wallingford in 1523.*]*

Johes Deane de Wallingford.=Margareta filia Edmunds.

Johes Deane modo superstes apud=Alicea filia et hæres Hugonis Kanion
Mattingley, in Com. South.   de Garton in Com. Lancast.

* [*For some early members of this family 1308, 1317, 1383, etc., see Wallingford, by J. Kirby Hedges.*]

OF BERKSHIRE.

Vincent's *Hampshire, College of Arms, Vinc:* 130, *folios* 85*b*, 86, *gives a brother of the second John, Nich'us Deane Philisarius Com: Suffolciæ s.p., and adds the children of John Deane and Alicia.*

Thomas Deane=Phœbe filia Johis Hancok Johannes, 1. Henricus, 3.
fil. 2.   de Co. Cantabr.

Alicia modo infans.

Denton, of Witham.

From Le Neve's copy of the Visitation of Oxford, 1574-5. (*Coll. of Arms, G.* 3.) *See a pedigree in the Visitations of Oxfordshire, Harl. Soc.,* Vol. V., *p.* 228. *Le Neve's trick of the Arms gives no colours, and the 7th quarter is blank.*

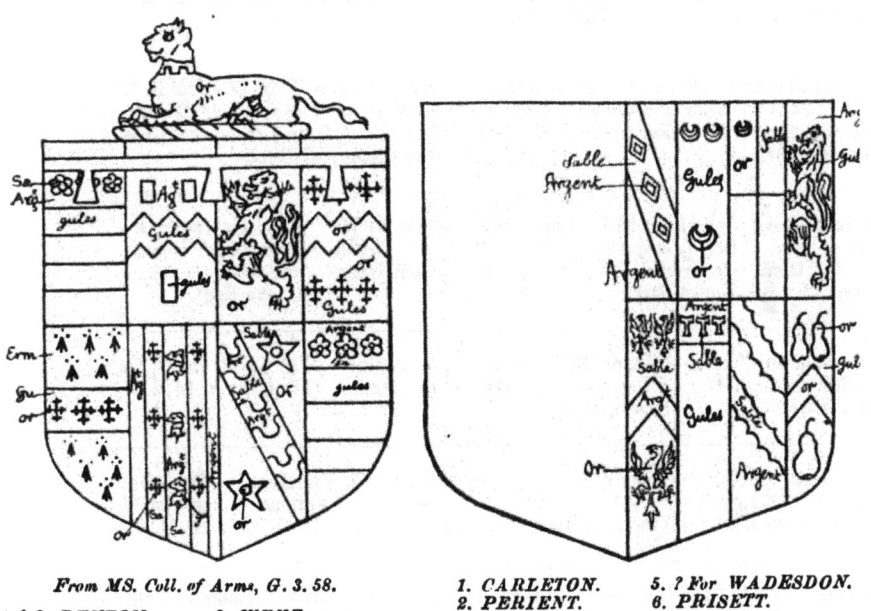

From MS. Coll. of Arms, G. 3. 58.

1 & 8. DENTON.   5. WYKE.
2. DE LA LAUNDE. 6. GRYMSTEDD.
3.   7.
4. ? LONGUEVILLE.

1. CARLETON.   5. ? For WADESDON.
2. PERIENT.   6. PRISETT.
3. DREWELL.   7. EMPSON.
4.   8. ABBOT.

Thomas Denton of Appleton and Eaton in Com. Berks.=

John Denton of y*e* same place esq*r* sone & heire.=

NOTES: VISITATIONS

A |

Thomas Denton of yͤ same place=.... daur. of Sir John Wike of Wike Esqʳ sone & heire. [Visit. Oxon., p. 228].

John Denton of Fysfeild [*Fyffeild*] in Coṁ=Johanne sister and coheire to Sʳ Berks: Esqʳ sone and heire. Thomas De la launde Knight.

Thomas Denton of Fysfeild Esqʳ=Agnes da to Wᵐ Baldington of Sheptoʳ sone & heire. [*Shipton*] in Coṁ Oxon Esqʳ.

Thomas Denton of Fysfeild=Alice *one of the* da: & h: *of Willm Dauncey first marr*: [*in Com. Oxon. 3ᵈ Husband*] *to Wm. Browninge* [*and secondly*] to Rich: Wighton sone and heire. *of Barkly*, juxta Oxford Esqʳ.

John Denton of Wight-=Issabell wid: to Phillip Purifoy of Shalsone in Coṁ. ham in Coṁ Berks: Buck: Esqʳ da to John Browne of Badesley in Coṁ Esqʳ son & h: Warw: Esqʳ.

Thomas Denton of Oauersfeild in=Jane da: [*& coh:*] to John Webb of Cardiffe Esqʳ Coṁ Buck. Esqʳ sone & heire [*of* gent to K. Edw. yᵉ 4ᵗʰ [*widdowe of Cheney of Appleton, Co. Berks. Visit. North-* Chesham Boyes (Visit. Oxon.) Harl. Soc.*] Sister ampton. 1564*]. to Eliz: wife to Cheney of Buck:

| Susan a Close Nun at Studley in Coṁ Oxon. | Jane mar: to Jo: Langest [*Langeston*] of Cauerfeild in Coṁ Bucks Esqʳ. | Anne mar. to Wᵐ Ann of Northaston Coṁ Oxon: Esqʳ. | Eliz: mar. to Edw: Grenfeild of Wooton undʳwood Coṁ Bucks Esqʳ. |

John Denton of Am-=Magdalin da: to Sʳ John Brome Thomas 2ᵈ sone [*See* bresden in Coṁ Ox: [*Browne*] *of Halton in Com'.* Visit. Oxon. 1634*]. Son: & h: *Oxon. Knt.*

| Jane mar to Tho: Heath of Shelleswell in Coṁ Oxon Esqʳ. | Georg 6. son. — Xtopher 5 sone. | Wᵐ 4 sõ. s.p. — Anne mar. to .... | Bridget unmaried 1575. | Dorothy unmaried Aᵒ 1575. |

| Thomas 3ᵈ s.p. | [1] Jo: Denton mar Theodorus da: & one of yᵉ heires to Jo: Blundell of Barton Coṁ Oxon: Esqʳ. | Edward Denton=Joyce da: to Anthoney Carlston of Hampton of Baldwyn Brightwell Coṁ Poyle in Coṁ Oxon Esqʳ & of Ann his wife one Oxon: Son: & of yᵉ da: of Tho: perient of heire. Digoswnell Coṁ. Hertf. Esqʳ. |

Dorothy 1575. Jane 1575.

OF BERKSHIRE.   117

Draper, of Sunninghill.

MS. Rawl. D. 865, fol. 149.

Sʳ
  I am sorry I cannot to day giue you the attendance wᶜʰ my respects dictate to your worth, being preuented by some seruice his Maᵗⁱᵉ hath comaunded mee: but I shall not be wanting to giue you satisfaction in London the next Terme, and to that purpose I shall desyre Mʳ Leigh to waite upon you: in the mean tyme I hope for to be excus'd, wᶜʰ shall gratefully be acknowledg'd by

Sʳ
Yoʳ humble seruant
Tʜᴏ. Dʀᴀᴘᴇʀ.

From Sunninghill Park
March the 30ᵗʰ 1665.

[*Addressed*]   To my much honour'd Elias Ashmole
          Esq. at Windsor Berks p̃sent this.

[*Sealed with a Crest only : on a wreath a stag's head couped and collared.*]
  In the list Sir Thomas Draper of Sunninghill Park, Justice of the Peace, *is adjourned. See the Complete Baronetage*, iii., p. 35.

Visitation of London 1634-5, *Harl. Soc.*, Vol. XV., p. 240.

Castle Baynard.

Vide the Booke of Certificates, i. 23, 62.

Thomas Draper of Lin-=Sarah da. of Roger=Sir Nicholas Kempe
colnes Inn gent.   James of Holland.   second husband.

1. Thomas   2. Robert Draper [*of Remenham*   3. Roger Draper of london,
s.p.   *co. Berks*].   marchantaylor 1634.

ROGER DRAPER.

Funeral Certificate of Thomas Draper, of Islington, Gent. 1631. MS. College of Arms, I. 23, p. 62ᵇ.

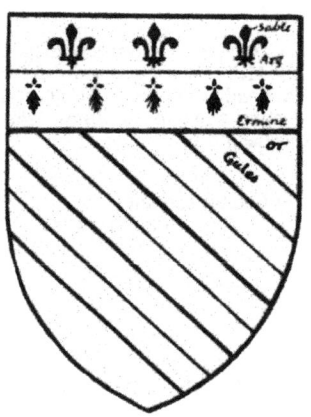

Thomas Draper of Islington neare London Gentᵗ: sonne and heire of Thomas Draper of Lincolnes Inn, Gentᵗ. and of Sarah his Wife daughter of Roger James of London Gent: (which Sarah was afterwards married to Sir Nicholas Kempe of Islington, Knight), Departed this mortall life at Islington aforesaid, yᵉ .... day of .... 1631 and was interred at Islington. He was never maried. He made Mʳ Robert Draper his 2ᵈ Brother his sole Executor. This Certificate was taken by us Thomas Preston Portcullis and George Owen Rougecroix to be recorded in yᵉ Office of Armes.

[*Signed*] ROBERT DRAPER.

I certify the above to be correctly copied from the Records (I. 23. p. 62ᵇ) in the College of Arms London.

[*Signed*] EVERARD GREEN,
Rouge Dragon.

MS. College of Arms, Grants, vol. ii., pp. 592, *etc. The trick from Camden's Guifts and Grants,* ii., 26ᵇ.

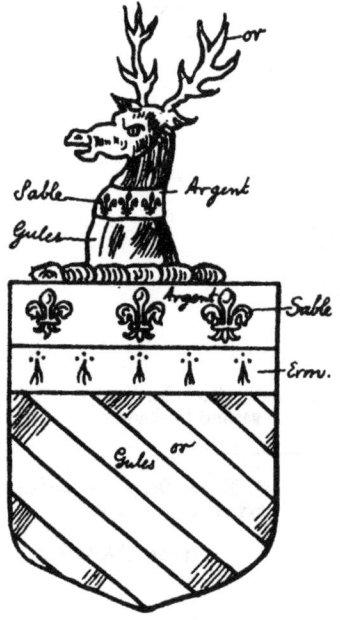

To all and singular as well nobles & gentlemen & others to whom these presents shall come .... I William Camden Clarenceux King of Arms .... sendeth greeting in our Lord God Everlasting.... Wheares Thomas Draper of Stroud Green in the County of Middlesex sonne of John Draper descended of a family which hath ancyently borne armes has desired me to exemplefy and emblazon the arms of the said family in such manner as he may not prejudice any other of that family .... I thought it reasonable to complie to his request herein considering his wise desire good parts and that Godshelp enabled him to mayntayne the reputation of Armes and do find that he may beare in a field or four bends gules, a chief ermine, with three fleurs-de-lis sable in a surchief argent, and for his crest upon a helme & wreath of his colours a stags head couped gules attired or with three fleurs-de-lis sable in a collar argent, mantled gules doubled silver as more playnly appearith, which I William Camden Clarenceux King of Arms by virtue & authoretie annexed to my office under the great seale of England do ratify allow & confirm to the said Thomas Draper and his posterity to use bear & shew forth with the due differences according to the law of Armes & the lawdable custome of England & I have hereunto set my hand & seal of office this second day of August 1612, 20 James.

This Patent was not passed at the time but was granted in Feb. 1613-14 to his son Thomas Draper (see Camden's Grants, i.e. Dockets, vol. i., p. 20b, and vol. ii., p. 26b).

[Signed] EVERARD GREEN,
Rouge Dragon.

Heralds' College, March 1908.

The reason for the delay appears to have been that Thomas Draper, the original grantee, died on the 23rd of October 1612.

MS. Rawl. B. 74, fol. 174b.

Roger Draper of Dodington Oxōn with in two miles of Aynho had issue in E. 2d Alice wife to Edmond Brudenell by her of Dodington, Godington [sic].

Christopher Draper son of John Drap of Melton Mowbray Leic. Ironmongr & lord M. of London 1566. [*Alderman of Cordwainers' Ward: had three sons-in-law Lord Mayors. For this family of Draper, see Visit. London 1568, Harl. Soc. I., p. 4, and the edition printed by the Lond. and Midd. Arch. Soc., vol. iii., appendix, pp. 18-19, with Notes by Dr. Jackson Howard.*]

Christopher Draper L[ord] M[ayor of] L[ondon] 1566 [*—1567*] Ironmonger. [*Kntd at Westminster, Sunday 16 Feb: 1566 i.e. 1566-7, when Lord Mayor.*]

Robert Draper Esq. of Remenham Berkes frō London b[rewer] maryed Elizabeth da: of .... Morgan of Henly Oxoñ & had issue

Bendy of 8 G. & O. on a cheiffe p fesse ·⋏· & A. 3 Delisses S. in the ·⋏· for Draper, Camdens gift ffeb: 1613, eadem cum ffarmer alias Draper de Merlowe.

1°. Sr Thomas Draper of Sonning hill knt baronett 1660 maryed ... da. of Sr Tho: Allen of ffynchley Midsex & hath issue.

2. Roger.
—
3. Edmond.

Sarah wife of Sr Purbecke Temple [*of Croydon Surrey, Kntd 3 Sep. 1660*].

Elizabeth wife of Edmond Partridge Esq:

This pedigree gives the correct parentage of Sir Thomas Draper, but I have found no proof that his wife Mary was one of the daughters of Sir Thomas Allen of Finchley.

NOTES : VISITATIONS

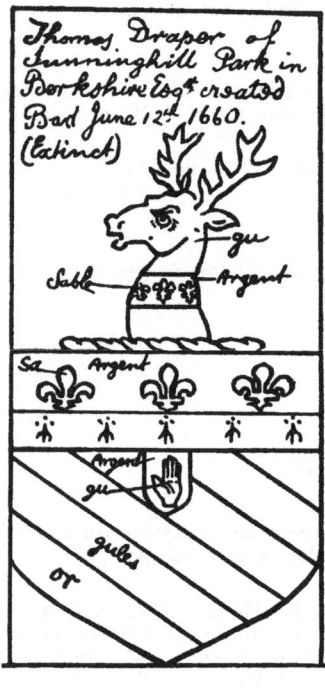

From a MS. Collection of Baronets' Arms in the Coll. of Arms, part ij., fol. 41. The Coat is wrongly tricked (see page 118).

Musgrave's "Obituary" (Harl. Soc.) gives a Sir Thomas Draper, Baronet [who died in?] 1660; the reference is Wotton's Baronetage. The date 1660 refers to the year in which he was made a Baronet, not to his death (see Wotton, ed. 1741, vol. iv., p. 275).

This is not the place to print a laboured pedigree of the Draper family, but I shall publish one elsewhere.

𝕮𝖉𝖒𝖆𝖓𝖉𝖘, of 𝕴𝖓𝖐𝖕𝖊𝖓.

MS. Rawl. D. 865, folio 78. Prepared for the Visitation 1665-6, in Ashmole's handwriting, not included. No Arms.

Kintbury hund.

```
Disclaimed        Thomas Edmande of New-=....da: to....
after entry.      bury [in Co. Berks].    | Browne.
                              |
           John Edmande of Newbury=Christian da: to....
           obijt aº 1654.          | Pinfall of Newbury.
                              |
           John Edmande of Inkpen in Com Berke=Eliz: da: to Tho: Brickenden
           æt: 38 annorum 23 Mar: 1664.         | of Inkpen Esqr.
                              |
   ┌──────────────────────────┼──────────────┬──────────┐
John son & heire æt: 16 ann: 23 Mar: 1664.  2. Joseph.  3. Thomas.
```

JO: EDMANDS [*Original*].

Englefield, of Englefield.

MS. Rawl. D. 865, *fol.* 124.

Sʳ
   I receiued yʳ sommons, and intended most reddely to haue obayd yʳ cōmands, but that I receiued a letter from London, that my sonne, and only sonne, is very dangerously il, soe that my wife and I are necessitated to goe and see him, wᶜʰ I am sorry for the occasion to craue yʳ pardon. For my coate, it is barry of 6, geules and argent, in a Cheefe ore, a Lyon passant azure, arm'd and Langu'd of the first, a martlet for the distinction of a fourth brother.

   Now Sʳ I conceiue that beinge a younger brother, my Nephew Sʳ Francis beinge the cheefe of our famely should giue an account of his bearinge, and by that wee are all involued, but be not liuinge in this county, perhaps may be out of your virge, or sōmons, how euer my brother Anthony Englefyld of White Knights beinge my elder brother, his account will giue you satisfaction, wᶜʰ I doubt not but that he will appeare; And I am sorry I cānot waight on you accordinge to my desier, wᶜʰ was extreamely coueted, by

       Sʳ
      Yʳ most faithfull humble seruant
         HENRY ENGLEFYLDE.

from Englefyld the 20ᵗʰ
 of March 1664 [*1664-65*].

The crest, a spread Eagle.

[*Addressed*] These for Elias Ashmole Esqʳ present.

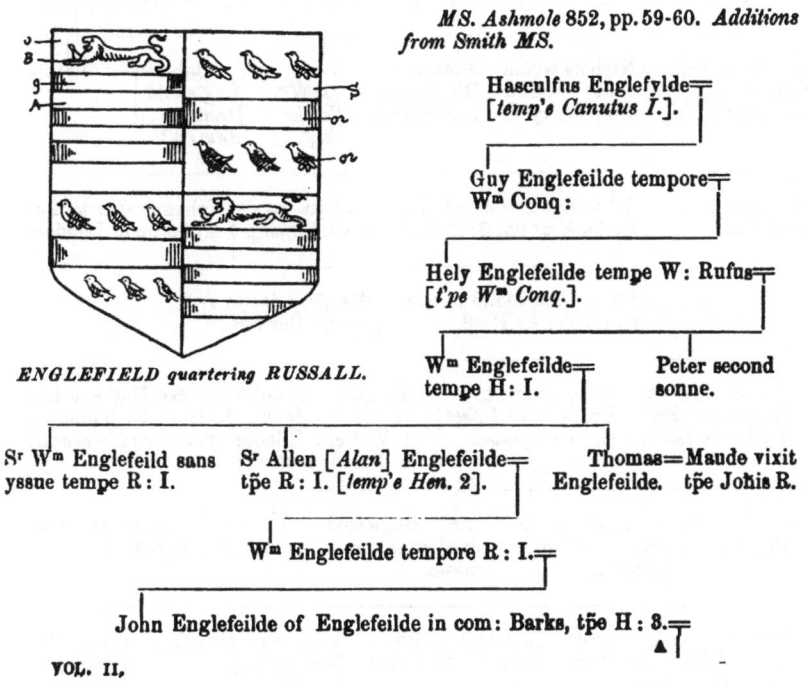

ENGLEFIELD *quartering* RUSSALL.

MS. Ashmole 852, pp. 59-60. *Additions from Smith MS.*

Hasculfus Englefylde=
[*temp'e Canutus I.*].

Guy Englefeilde tempore=
Wᵐ Conq:

Hely Englefeilde tempe W: Rufus=
[*t'pe Wᵐ Conq.*].

Wᵐ Englefeilde= Peter second
tempe H: I.   sonne.

Sʳ Wᵐ Englefeild sans Sʳ Allen [*Alan*] Englefeilde= Thomas=Maude vixit
yssue tempe R: I. tp̄e R: I. [*temp'e Hen.* 2]. Englefeilde. tp̄e Joñis R.

Wᵐ Englefeilde tempore R: I.=

John Englefeilde of Englefeilde in com: Barks, tp̄e H: 3.=

NOTES : VISITATIONS

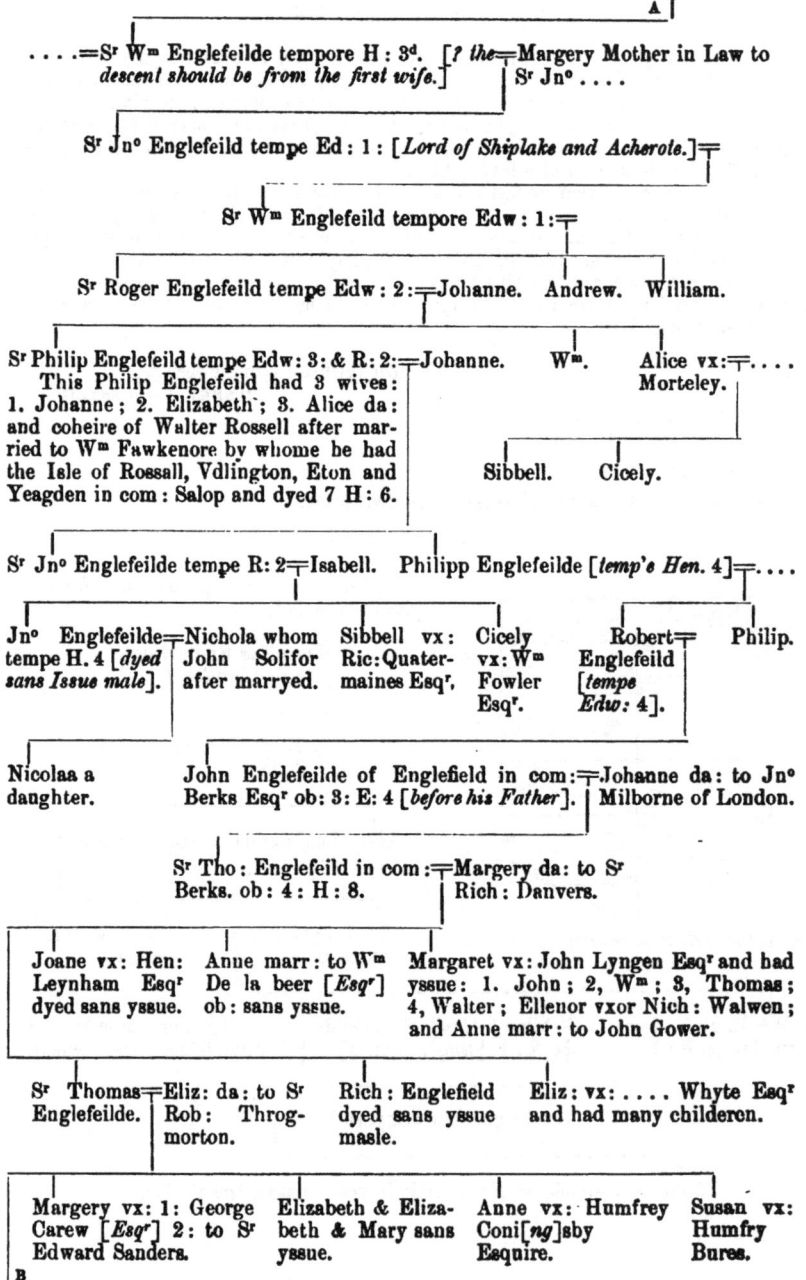

Pedigree (Englefeilde):

....=Sʳ Wᵐ Englefeilde tempore H: 3ᵈ. [? *the* descent should be from the first wife.]=Margery Mother in Law to Sʳ Jnᵒ ....

Sʳ Jnᵒ Englefeild tempe Ed: 1: [*Lord of Shiplake and Acherote.*]=

Sʳ Wᵐ Englefeild tempore Edw: 1:=

Sʳ Roger Englefeild tempe Edw: 2:=Johanne. Andrew. William.

Sʳ Philip Englefeild tempe Edw: 3: & R: 2:=Johanne. Wᵐ. Alice vx:=.... Morteley.
This Philip Englefeild had 3 wives:
1. Johanne; 2. Elizabeth; 3. Alice da:
and coheire of Walter Rossell after married to Wᵐ Fawkenore by whome he had the Isle of Rossall, Vdlington, Eton and Yeagden in com: Salop and dyed 7 H: 6.

Sibbell. Cicely.

Sʳ Jnᵒ Englefeilde tempe R: 2=Isabell. Philipp Englefeilde [*temp's Hen. 4*]=....

Jnᵒ Englefeilde tempe H. 4 [*dyed sans Issue male*].=Nichola whom John Solifor after marryed. | Sibbell vx: Ric: Quatermaines Esqʳ. | Cicely vx: Wᵐ Fowler Esqʳ. | Robert Englefeild [*tempe Edw: 4*].= | Philip.

Nicolaa a daughter.

John Englefeilde of Englefield in com:=Johanne da: to Jnᵒ Berks Esqʳ ob: 3: E: 4 [*before his Father*]. Milborne of London.

Sʳ Tho: Englefeild in com:=Margery da: to Sʳ Berks. ob: 4: H: 8. Rich: Danvers.

Joane vx: Hen: Leynham Esqʳ dyed sans yssue. | Anne marr: to Wᵐ De la beer [*Esqʳ*] ob: sans yssue. | Margaret vx: John Lyngen Esqʳ and had yssue: 1. John; 2, Wᵐ; 3, Thomas; 4, Walter; Ellenor vxor Nich: Walwen; and Anne marr: to John Gower.

Sʳ Thomas Englefeilde.=Eliz: da: to Sʳ Rob: Throgmorton. | Rich: Englefield dyed sans yssue masle. | Eliz: vx: .... Whyte Esqʳ and had many childeren.

Margery vx: 1: George Carew [*Esqʳ*] 2: to Sʳ Edward Sanders. | Elizabeth & Elizabeth & Mary sans yssue. | Anne vx: Humfrey Coni[ng]sby Esquire. | Susan vx: Humfry Bures.

OF BERKSHIRE.

B				
Thomas sine prole.	Sr Francis Englefeild of Englefeild Kn^t in co: Berks sans yssue 1571.	=Kath: da: and coheire to Sr Tho: Fettiplace.	John Englefeild second sonne.	=Margaret da: to Sr Edward Fitton of Gosworth. [Com Cestr. Kn^t.]

Francis Englefield heire to Sr Francis his Vnckle=Jane sister to Anthony dyed 26: Octob: 1631, buryed at Englefeild | Browne Viscount Baronet. | Mounacute.

Tho: 2^d sonn marr: Mary da: of Wm Williscott of Shinfeild in co: Berks [3^d son].	1 [*Thomas Eldest*] sonne and two daughters obijt sine prole.	Mary vx: .... Morgan. — Margaret.	*John Englefield 4th son dyed without Issue.*

[*Sr Charles Englefield of Englefield Bar^t son of Thomas, and cousin and heir to Sr Francis.*]

3. [5] Anthony (see PEDIGREE A. — 4. W^m. 5. Henry.	2. Sr Francis Englefeild of Wootton Bassett in Co: Wilts Kn^t & B^t [2^d son and heir].	=Winifrid da: and coheire of Wm Brookesby of Shoulby in co: Leic: Esqr.

Sr Francis Englefield Baronet son and heir to Sr Francis, dy'd sans Issue.	*Charles Englefeilde son & heire [not in Smith. MS.].*	*Mary wife to Christopher Roper Baron of Tenham.*	*Hellen married to .... Waldegrave of .... in Com' .... by whom she had Issue Henry Lord Waldegrave, Father of James Lord Waldegrave a° 1708.*

PEDIGREE A.

From Anthony, 5th son of Sr Francis Englefield, and Jane Browne his wife, Smith MS. continues as follows:—

5. *Anthony Englefield of White Knights in com' Berks Gent 5th son*=....

Anthony Englefield of White Knights aforesaid=*Alice dau'r of Thomas Stokes.*

1. Anthony dyed young.	2. Martha wife of Lister Blount of Maple Durham in com' Oxon Esqr.	7. Susan dyed unmarried at 17 years of age.	8. Henry Englefield of .... in Com' .... gent. 4th son but 8th child, now living a° 1708.	=Catherine dau'r of .... Pool of ....
	Michael Blount æt. circa 12 annor' a° 1708.	Two daughters.	Henry Englefield son and heir to Henry aged .... years a° 1708.	.... a Daughter.

124 NOTES: VISITATIONS

14. *Dorothy Englefield a Nun a° 1708.*
15. *William Englefield dyed sans issue.*
16. *Winifrid Englefield a Nun a° 1708.*
17. *Marke Englefield dyed a Schollar beyond Sea.*

9. *Guy Englefield living unmarr⁴ anno 1708.*
10. *John Englefield living and travelling beyond sea a° 1708.*
11. *Anthony Englefield dyed at 7 years of Age.*
12. *Hellen Englefield a Nun a° 1708.*
13. *Alice Englefield a Nun anno 1708.*

3. *Elizabeth first married to . . . . Doddington of . . . . and after to Edw⁴ Armstrong gent.*
4. *Thomas dyed without Issue.*
5. *Mary wife of S⁺ Wm Swinburn Bar⁺ Eldest Son of S⁺ John Swinburn of Caple-Eaton in Com' Northumberland Bar⁺.*
6. *Francis Englefield dyed a Religious man.*

1. *John Swinburn Esqr Eldest Son a° 1708.*
2. *Mathew Swinburn 2⁴ Son a° 1708.*
Thomas Swinburn 3⁴ Son a° 1708.

Essex, of Lamborne.

MS. Ashmole 852, pp. 62-63.

[*The inscriptions added by Ashmole.*]

In Kensington Church neere London :—
   Hic iacet Thomas Essex ar. filius & hæres Gulielmi Essex armigeri Rememeratoris Dnī Regis Edwardi quarti in Scaccario ac in Thesaurarij Angliæ qui obijt primo die Novembris An° Dnī 1500 cuius animæ ppitietur Deus Amen.
   Vnder his feete a Hound.

In Lamborne Church :—
   Here lyeth the body of Sr Thomas Essex Knight, who deceased the 29th of August Anno 1558, & Dame Margaret his wife.

1 and 6. ESSEX. 2. BABTHORPE. 3. ROGERS.
4. SHOTTESBROKE [*COCKBURNE* or *MARKAUNTE*].
5. BROWNE [*SHOTTESBROKE*].
Names in Ashmole's handwriting.

[*A portion of the motto, De tiel En mieulz, under the Arms in a riband (see Vol. I., p. 24), has been cut away by the binder.*]

OF BERKSHIRE.

Wm Essex of Wandowne greene in Co: Middx: Esqr vnder Treasurer of England. = Edith da: to *William* Marrow of Stepney in Co: Midd: Esquire. [*Harl. MS.* 4108, 87b.]

Tho: Essex of Wandown-greene in Com: Midd: dyed jo Novemb: 1500. = Eliz: da: & heire to Wm Babthorpe of Elstone in Co: Leic: Esqr.   Anne.   Elizabeth.

Sr Wm Essex of Lamborne in Com: Berks Esquire. = Eliz: da: & sole heire to Tho: Rogers of Benam [*in com. Berks*] heire to John Shottesbrooke of Beckett Esquire.   Kath: vx: John Hulcott [*of Bercot*] in Com Berks Esquire.   Anne vx: Jno Estbury Esquire.

Sr Tho: Essex of Lamborne in Berks dyed ye 29th of Aug: 1558. = Margarett 2d da: to Sr Wm Lord Sandes Lord Chamberlaine to Ks Henry 8.   Winifrid vx: Richd Edgercombe [*of Cornwall*] Esquire.

[2]. Alice vx: Wm Hyde of South Denchworth [*in Com. Berks*].   [3]. Mary vx: Edw̃ Fettiplace of Pusey [*in com. Berks*].   [4]. Anne vx: Edward Butts.   [5]. Margery vx: Anth: Disney of Lincolnshr.

[4]. Humfry [*Essex of Lambourne*]. = Lucy da: to Rob: Browne of Walcott in Northton Esquire.   [5]. George.   [1]. Eliz: vx: Edward Darrell of Littlecott [*in com. Wilts*].

Humfry.   William.   Lucy.   Elizabeth.   Bridgett.

[1]. Wm dyed before his Father sans yssue *eldest son*.   [2]. Tho. Essex of Lamborne in Co: Berks Esqr 1566. = Jane da: to Robert Browne of Walcott in Com: Northton Esquire.   [3]. Edmund Essex of Lamborne in Berks 3d sonne [*1566*]. = Dorothy da: to Edward Powell of Sandford in Com: Oxon [*Essex*].

Edmund.   Thomas.

[2]. Scipio.

[3]. [*Sir*] Edward [*Kt.*].

[4]. William.   [1]. Tho: Essex Esquire [*1566*]. = Jone da: to Tho: Harison of Bramford [*Brentford and London*].   [5]. Rob: marr: Mary da: to Tho: Blenhasset [*of Suffolk*].   [1]. Isabell.

[2.] Jane.   [3]. Alice vx: Sr George Gill of Widgell in Com: Hertford.

Humfry [*Essex*].   Wm Essex of Lamborne Esqr. = Jane eldest da: to Sr Walter Harcourt of Stanton Harcourt [*Kt.*].   Jane Vx: Tho: Sherley of Preston in Sussex.   Joane.

William [*Essex*].   Charles [*Essex*].   Richard [*Essex*].

Everard.

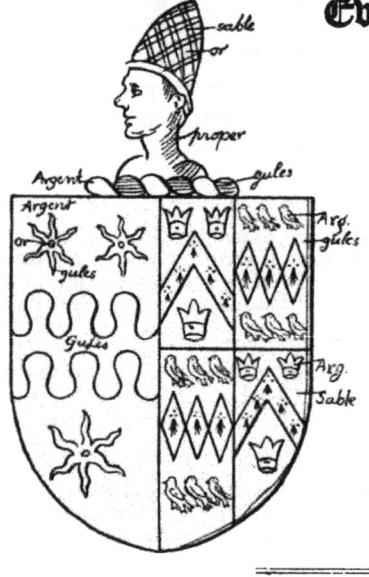

MS. Coll. of Arms, Misc. Grants, I. 130^b.

Under Robert Cooke's hand.

I did see Robert Cookes hand at this: Everard and Wiseman impaled as you see.

Allowed by Robert Cooke, Clarenceux, about the year 1564.

Confirmed under the hand of Will'm Harvey als Clarenceux King of Armes and Clarenceux Cooke. (See Visit: Essex, vol. i., 193, 395. Harl. Soc., Vol. XIII.)

Ferrers, of Cookham.

Visitation of London 1634-5, Vol. XV., p. 272, Harl. Soc.

1. FERRERS; 2. HEUER. By Pattent vnder the hand and seale of Clarenceux Tong dated 6 Nov. 1534, a° 26 H. 8 to Thomas [and] Richard Heuer of Cookfeild com. Sussex.

William fferrers of Toplow Court co. Berks. = Sibell da. of Thomas Doyley of Chiselhampton co. Oxon Esqr.

Thomas fferrers of Cookham Lowabrooke co. Berks. = Mary da. of .... Kember and Christian da. of .... Blackmore.

John fferrers of Cookham Lowabrooke co. Berks. = Mary da. and heire of Thomas Hever of Cookfeild, co. Sussex.

Samuel fferrers sonne and heire now liuing a^c 1633. = Susanna da. of Giles ffleming of Warly in com. Essex Esqr.

Benjamin fferrers sonne & heire.   2. John.   Susanna.

SAMUEL FFERRERS.

Fetiplace, of Buckland.

MS. Rawl. D. 865, fol. 114.   Original paper for the Visitation 1665-6. Not included.

S{r}

I vnderstand that S{r} Charles Yate did tell you the cause whie I did not wait on you at Farringdon, and you would bee informed of my pedigree, my Grandfather his name was Robert who married with Hamson of . . . . by her he had 6 sones and 3 Daughters, Thomas, John, Bartholomewe, Peter, Rowland, and Hulcott, Elizabeth, Martha, and Bridgett, Rowland was my Father, who tooke to wife Sarah, only daughter to Robert Davis of Longworth in Berks, by her he had 5 Children 4 Daughters, and one sone, my selfe, my sisters names was Susana, Hanah, Jane and Elizabeth. I haue had 2 wives my first was Eliza: Daughter to Mathewe Teversham of Balsome in Cambridgsheire by her I had 3 Daughters only, Sarah, Ann and Frances, by this woman I have nowe 3 Children, Rowland, Mary and Charles, she was Daughter to Richard Janinges of Fauler in Berks, S{r} I am of Buckland howe longe our Famelie haue been there is better knowne to you then my selfe, I would gladlie haue wated on you, but owinge money to Rowndheads Durst not and if you sit in Oxfordsheire, if I may knowe when and where I will wait on you, S{r} I humbly take my leaue and rest as becometh me, S{r}

I am your humble servant
JO: FETIPLACE.

Duxford, this 21º of March 1664.

[*near Hinton Waldrist, co. Berks.   See present* Vol., p. 21.]

[*Addressed*] For the honourable Harauld at Armes sittinge at the Beare in Wantinge humbley p{r}sent.

Fettiplace, of Lambourne.

MS. Ashm. 836, p. 687.   Original paper sent in for the Visitation of 1665-6.

Berckes.   The 21 of March 1664 [*1664-65*].

The Pedegree of Charles Fettiplace of Lambourne Gent. or Esqui{r} soe styled by the kinges Maiestyes Comission for the Peace videlicet.

Thomas Fettiplace of Shifford Parua Esq{r} had for his Eldest* sonn John Fettiplace of the same place Esq{r} & John his Eldest sonn was Richard Fettiplace of Bezells Lee frō whom are descended the Fettiplaces of the famyly of Bezells Lee.

The sayd John of Shifford had also Anthony Fettiplace of Swinbrooke for his second sonn Esqui{r} of the body to kinge Henry the 7{th}.

From this Anthony are descended the Fettiplaces of Chiley [*Childrey*] Barkes. Alexander Fettiplace of Chil[*dr*]ey was the Eldest sonn of Anthony aforesayd. William Fettiplace of Chil[*dr*]ey† was the Eldest sō of Alexand{r} aforesayd, Sir Edmond Fettiplace of Chil[*dr*]ey was the Eldest sonn of Will aforesayd, Charles Fettiplace of Lambourne was the 5{th} sonn of Sir Edmond Fettiplace of Chil[*dr*]ey but may be reckoned for the second sonn of S{r} Edmond because only Edward had Issue male & all the rest being 10 sonns deceassed w{th}out Issue.

Charles Fettiplace the 5{th} sonn of Sir Edmond or rather the second sonn because the others had noe Issue, Married w{th} Anne Garrard daughter of Roger Garrard of Lambourne Gent: the s{d} Charles now liuinge hath Issue by the s{d} Anne

---

* *Over Eldest, Ashmole has written third.*
† *Over Chiley, Ashmole has written Swinbroh.*

Roger Fettiplace his Eldest sonn & Charles Fettiplace his second sonn & 5 daughters wherof Anne the Eldest daughter is married vnto M{r} John Collins of Betterton.

His coate of Armes is thus Blazoned videlicet he beareth Gules 2 Cheurons Argent w{th} the difference of a halfe moone as decended from Anthony the second sonn of John of Shifford as is aboue expressed & this Charles beareth a halfe moone w{th} in a halfe moone as a difference or distinctiō beinge the second sonn of a second sonn. The crest is a Griphons head erased.

CHARLES FETTIPLACE.

I cannot clayme the tytle of Esq{r} beinge the 5{th} sonn for there can be but I Esq{r} in a famyly nor can I transfer it to my sō: Roger Fettiplace.

My name hath been twice registred both in my fathers time in my my [*sic*] broth{r} Jo: Fettiplace time.

Flegg, of Bray.

Harl. MS. 1532, fol. 139, gives the arms in trick. Per pale Argent and Or, a chevron per pale Sable and Azure, on the chevron a martlet Or.

Burke gives the arms, Per pale Or and Sable a chevron counterchanged. Crest, two lions' gambs in saltire Sable enfiled with two laurel branches in orle Vert.

Fuller or Fulwar, of Chamberhouse.

Le Neve's Knts., Harl. Soc., Vol. VIII., p. 176.

See J. 19, fol. 79. Arg. 3 bars & a canton Gules, certificate. See C. 19, fol. 68{b}, Hants Visit.*

Harl. MS. 1483, p. 22{b}, *gives the same Arms, with a tower Or, in the canton; quartering MEUX, paly of six Or, and Azure, and on a chief Gules three crosses pattée Argent on the fess point a crescent for difference, Crest out of a ducal coronet Or a dexter arm embowed in armour Sable, holding in the gauntlet a sword Argent, with the note [Peter] Fuller alyas Fulwer, [of Shellers] the Isle of Wight in Hampsh. by Robert Cooke Claren'. The Crest of Fuller for co: Berks is given (Add. MS. 14283, fol. 107.) a beacon Argent fired proper.*

[Thomas Fuller of Neates Hall in the Isle of Sheppy, Kent.]
    |
[Nicholas Fuller, younger son, of the City of London, Merchant.]
    |

Nicholas Fuller of Chamberhouse Berks dyed there 23 Febr. 1619 & buried in Thatcham Church in the South Ile belonging to Chamberhouse Mannor [*purchased Chamberhouse in 1583*],	=	Sara d{r} of Nicolas Backhouse Alderman of London. [*Sheriff* 1577-8,]

A

---

* *J. 19, fol. 79, is the Funeral Certificate of Nicholas Fuller, 1619, printed in Mr. Parfield's Thatcham, vol. ii., p. 256, C. 19, fol. 68b is the following pedigree of Dowse of Morecourt, Hampshire.*

OF BERKSHIRE. 129

Sʳ Nicolas Fuller Kᵗ=Maria dʳ of George Dowse of Morecourt Hants esqʳ. See 28 yʳˢ old at his father's death. | visit. Hants 69. remar. to Tho. son of Tho. son & heir of Sʳ Tho. Lee of Moreton bucks Kᵗ.

Douze Fuller 2 yʳˢ old 1619=

Richard Fuller of Chamberhouse=.... dʳ of Sʳ Thomas Jervice of Heryot Hants Kᵗ.

Sʳ Dowse Fuller of Chamberhouse Knighted as above=
(Kted 6 Octob 1663 at Whitehall, Douse fuller esqʳ.)

This last descent is doubted by Mʳ S. Barfield (Thatcham, Berks, and its Manors, vol. ii., p. 269) in a note to his pedigree of Fuller. It is clear that there is an error from the following fragment of the long pedigree registered in the College of Arms (7. D. 14, pp. 153-154). Dowse (and not Richard) Fuller of Chamberhouse, son of Nicholas, married Anne daughter of Sʳ Thomas Jervoise, and Sir Dowse Fuller was one of their sons. Ashmole says that Sir Dowse married the only daughter of Sir Thomas Allen of London (see p. 35). He married in 1663, Elizabeth daughter of Sir Thomas Alleyn, Knt. and Baronet, Lord Mayor of London, in 1659-60, son of William Allen of Hatfield Peverel, co. Essex. (Barfield's Thatcham, vol. i., 306 n., and ii., 269.)

Portion of pedigree from 7 D. 14, pp. 153-154, College of Arms.

Frances, da. of .... second wife, living 1654. =Sir Thomas Jervoise of Herriard, Co. South-ampton & Chelmarsh, Co. Salop, Kᵗ Representatives in several Parliaments for the Co. of Southampton, born at Britford, Co. Wilts, 11 June 1587. By his Will dat. 19 Oct. & proved by his son Thomas, Executor, 5 Dec: 1654 he directs to be buried in the Church of Herriard near his deceased wife Dame Lucy. =Lucy, eldest dau: & co-heir of Sir Richard Pawlet of Herriard, Kᵗ, by Anne his wife dau. of Sir Henry Wallop of Farley Walton Kᵗ marr: in 1613, died before 1654, & was buried at Herriard 1 wife.

Thomas Jervoise 1654.
—
Bernard Jervoise 1654.

Richard Jervoise of Herriard son & heir æt. 7, 1623. =
2 daughters.

Henry Jervoise 2 son 1654. ob. s.p.

Thomas Jervoise of Herriard 3 son. =Mary dau. of George Purefoy of Wadley, Co. Berks, marr. 1687 at Farringdon.
Jervoise of Herriard.

Lucy 1623, not in her father's Will 1654 died young.

Winifred unmarr: 1654, afterwards wife of Richard Chandler Esq., Alderman of London.

Anne, not in her father's Will 1654, married to Dowse Fulwer of Chamberhouse Co: Berks Esqʳᵉ.

Mary, 1654 died unmarrᵈ.

VOL. II.

DOWSE OF MORECOURT.

Visitation of Hampshire, 1622-23,
C. 19, p. 68ᵇ. *MS. College of Arms.*

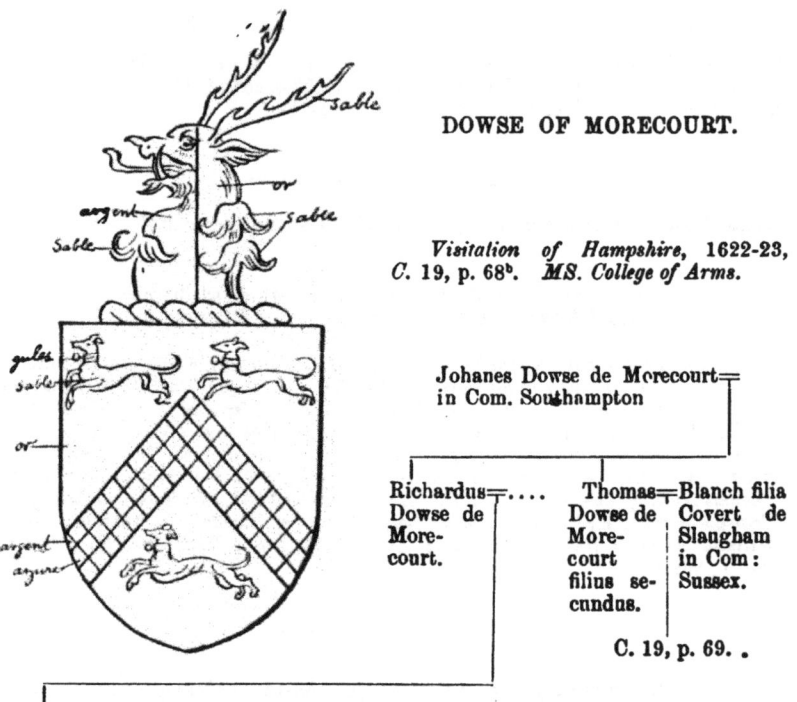

Johanes Dowse de Morecourt= in Com. Southampton

Richardus=.... Dowse de Morecourt.

Thomas=Blanch filia Dowse de Covert de Morecourt Slaugham filius se- in Com: cundus. Sussex.

C. 19, p. 69.

Georgius Dowce de Morecourt=Elizabetha filia Johis Clovell de Barnstone in Com Armiger Modo Superstes 1623. | Dorsett Arg. soror hodieni Wˡ Clovell militis.

Nicholaus Fuller=Maria Unica=Thomas Lee filius Thomæ Lee Johanes Douce
de Chamberhouse filia et Hæres filii et Hæredis aparentis Tho- unicus filius
in Com : Berks aparens. Bis mas Lee de Moreton in Com. obijt sine prole.
Miles vir primus. nupta. Buks militis maritus secundus.

Douceus Fuller unicus filius.

[*Signed*] GEORGE DOWCE.

I hereby certify that the above is correctly copied from the Records (C. 19, p. 68ᵇ) in the Heralds' College. Witness my hand this 26ᵗʰ day of June, 1907.

[*Signed*] EVERARD GREEN,
Rouge Dragon.

Gardiner, of White Waltham.

Harl: MS. 1532, fol. 147, gives the Arms in trick. Azure on a chevron embattled Argent between three griffins' heads erased silver, beaked Or, three martlets Sable.
Crest, (added in Pencil) a griffin's head erased Argent, murally [?] gorged Or.
p. Sr RICHARD St GEORGE, Clarenceulx King at Armes. [*Claren.* 1623 *to* 1635.]

These Arms were entered to Roger Gardner of London, descended from Roger Gardner of Forton, co. Lanc., in the Visitation of London, 1684-5. (Harl. Soc., XV., p. 300.)

Garrard, of Newbury.

MS. Rawl. D. 865, *fol.* 92, *in Ashmole's handwriting. Prepared for the Visitation* 1665-6; *not included. No Arms given. Marked,* Fee suspended.

Kintb: hund.

John Garrard of Inkpen [*in Co. Berks*, 2nd *son of William*, Vol. I., p. 210]. =Margery da: & Coheire to Robt Blount of Standen Hussey in Com̄ Wilt$_e$.

William Garrard of Inkpen. =Susan da: to .... Fisher of Liddington in Com̄ Wilt$_e$.

Edward Garrard of Inkpen. =Katherine da: to Walter Foldervey of the Citty of Oxford 3^d wife.

Joseph Garrard of Newbury æt: 38 an: 23 Mar: 1664. =Joane da: to John Knight of Kingscleare in com̄ Southton & Relict of Robt Blount of Newbury.

Joseph son & heire a q^{r}ter old.

JOS: GARRARD [*original*].

Gaulton, of Ashampsted.

Harl. MS. 1532, fol. 138, gives the Arms in trick: Quarterly, 1. Sable, a chevron engrailed between three talbots statant argent; 2. Gules, a chevron between three crescents argent [? *intended for* GODDARD (*modern*) *gules, a chevron vair between three crescents Argent, on each an ermine spot Sable*]; 3. [*Azure*] five lozenges conjoined in fesse between three falcons' heads erased [*Or*] [GODDARD (*ancient*)].

Geffe, or Jeffe of Enborne, Berks.

Patent of Arms to Nicholas Geffe of Enborne, co. Berks, by Robert Cooke, Clarenceux, dated April 21 Eliz. 1579. MS. Coll. of Arms, Misc. Grants, i., 65b.

Nicholas Geffe of Enborne in the Countye of Berks, 4th sonne of Andrew Geff of Nasing in the Countie of Essex: the son of Thomas Geff of Broxborne in the Countie of Hertford. A Patent by Robert Cooke, under his hand and seale bearing date the first of Aprill An° 1579, the 21 of Q. E[lizabeth].

Goodyer, of New Windsor.

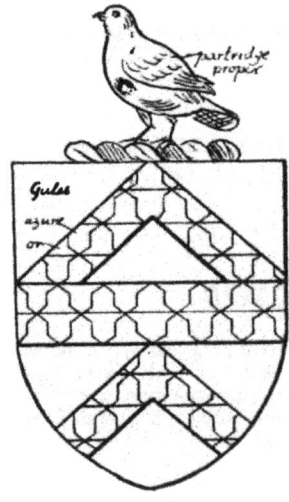

Grant to Thomas Goodyer of New Windsor, Berks, by Robert Cooke, dated 19th October 1579. MS. Coll. of Arms, Vincent 161, 2.

Thomas Goodier of Newe Windsor in barksh. p. Rō Cooke, Claṝ October 19, 1579.

Gules, a fesse between two chevrons vair. Crest, a partridge proper.
In some of the tricks the bird is called a goldfinch, and holds in his beak an ear of corn, or.

Gosson, of Binfield.

MS. Rawl. D. 865, *fol.* 118.
March the 29th, 1666.

S^r

It hath pleased God by a long time of sicknesse and extreame fitts of the Gout, to take away the vse of all my Lymbs, in soe much that all they that know mee, are able to testifie, that for aboue these seauen yeares I haue not beene able to goe into or out of my Bedd, but as two haue lifted mee in and two haue lifted mee out, soe that it is impossible for mee to waite vppon you. But I desire to present thus much vnto you concerning the businesse in hand, That I Robert Gosson of Binfeild in the County of Barks, sonne and heire of Richard Gosson, Cytizen and gentleman of London, ought to beare or vse these armes following at my pleasure. Namely, Azure a fece battaillee ermyne betweene three Goates heads coped d'or, And to the badge or Creast, out of a Crowne Murall d'or a Goates head coped argente, gorged with a garland of ynie proper, manteled gules dubled argent.

These armes I had entered or recorded in the office or Court of Heralds in London after the death of my father.

I haue neither sonne nor brother Only one daughter Elizabeth who is married to William Angell the sonne and heire of John Angell of Crowhurst in the County of Surrey, Esq.

This with my respects presented to you, I rest

Your seruant
ROBERT GOSSON.

[*Addressed*] For Elias Ashmole Esq., Windsor-Herald, these p̃sent.
[*Black wax seal, bearing a human head.*]
Ashmole marks in the List Robert Gosson, Esq., mort.

From Camden's Guifts and Grants, MS. College of Arms, Camden, iii., 11. *No date given.*

[*Granted or confirmed to Robert Gosson* 1 *November* 1608.]

Gossen, B. a fess embatt: ⋏· betw. 3 Goates heads Coupé or. Creast a Goates head cope Ar: wth a Garland v^t in a crowne Murall or.

NOTES: VISITATIONS

Gwynne, of Windsor.

1. GWYN.   2. TALKE.

Visitation of London, 1634-35, (I. 338).
Harl. Soc., Vol. XV., *additions from Harl.
MS.,* 1532, p. 64.

Criplegate Without.

Enter this descent and Armes in the Visitation booke of Berkshire.

Mathew Gwyn borne in Montgomerieshire in Wales died seised of landes in Windsour and Cluer that he purchased, and of other landes in Montgomeryshire that were Patrimoniall.

Edward Gwyn son of Mathew. = Elizabeth d. of Thayre.

William Gwyn son of Mathew Gwyn died seised of lands in New Windsore com. Berks.

Jane ux. Thomas personn of London. vide London.

3. Edmond Gwyn.

Mathew Gwyn of London Doctor of Phisick was son of Edward. = ... = Sara d. of duncombe.

Roger Gwyn of London Grocer. vide London.

John Gwyn.

Richard Gwyn now liueing at Windsore 1621 son of William Gwyn. = Suzan dau'r and heir of James Talke of Apuldercombe in the Isle of Wight descended of that Auntient ffamelie of the Talkes of Sussex and Hampshire.

William Gwyn one of his Maties Auditors eldest son. = Anne dau'r of Henry Ward of Norfolk descended out of Suffolke.

2. Thomas Gwyn s.p.

1. Eme wife of John Wagstaff.

2. Blanch.
—
3. Suzan Gwyn.

Richard Gwyn died young.   1. Anne Gwyn.   2. Suzan.

WM. GWYNNE.

Gyles, of Windsor.

MS. Ashmole 852, p. 77.

[*No Arms tricked.*]

Nathanyell Gyles of New Windsore Doctor in Musique Mr of the Chappell of St George [*Queen Eliz: K. James and K. Charles*] [*& Mr of ye Chappell Royall ob: 24 January 1633, aged 75 years (Harl. MS. 1532, p. 144)*]. [*Born in or near Worcester.*] = Anne, eldest da: of John Stayner of .... in Com: Worc: by whome he had issue 4: sonns 5 daũrs.

| Eliza-beth 2d: da: | = Ric: Braham of Wandsworth in Com: Surr: [*See* Vol. I., p. 179.] | Susan first daughter. — John Gyles 2: son. | Robert Gyles 3d sonne. — Nathanyell Gyles eldest sonne [*living* 1634.] | Henry Gyles 4: sonne. — Anne 3d daughter. | Frances 4 daughter. — Susan 5 daughter. |

Hallsted, of Sonning.

Visitation of London, 1634-35, *Harl. Soc.*, Vol. XV., p. 343.

Faringdon Without.

Graunted by Sr William Segar Garter to Lawrence Hallsted of Sunninge in com. Berk, by Patent dated 20 of Nouemb. 4 of Kinge Charles 1628.

Oliuer Hallsted of Rowley in the Countie of Lanc.

John Hallsted of Rowley in the countie aforesaid. = Mary da. of .... Seller of .... in com. Lanc.

```
                                    ┌─────────┴─────────┐
                                              A
┌──────────────┬──────────────────────────┬──────────────────────┬──────────┐
John Hall-   2. Lawrence Hallsted of Sun-═Hester da. of Abraham  3. George
sted of Row-   ninge in com. Berk. Esq. a │ Chambrelan of London   3 sonne.
ley eldest     marchant of London liuing  │ marchant.
sonne.         1634.
                                          │
┌──────────────────────┬──────────┬──────┬──────────┬──────┬──────────┐
Laurance Hallsted eldest sonne 12   2. Abraham.   4. Oliuer.   6. Mathias.
yeares old 1634.                    ─────────     ─────────   ──────────
                                    3. John.     5. James.    7. William.
```

LAW. HALSTEED.

Exemplification of Arms and Grant of Crest to Laurence Halstedd of Sonning, from MS. College of Arms, R. 22, p. 321.

MS. *College of Arms, Segar's Grants*, 144, *gives a trick of the Arms and Crest; the blazon in English, Latin, and French, and the date:*—

G., an Eagle dispd ⋅𝝠⋅ a chief chequy O. & B.

In Campo miniato Aquilam argenteam expansam maculis Armenii Muris respersam, et summitatiam Scutariam tessalarum ductibus ex auro et cæruleo distinctam.

De Gueles à l'Aigle exploie, d'Hermines au chef echequité d'or & Azure.

Crest: Viz., out of a Murall Crown B. a demi Eagle despl. ⋅𝝠⋅ beaked O.

Nov. xx Anº Regni Car: 1, iv. Anº Dom: 1628.

To all and singular psons, as well Nobles, as others to whome theis pñts shall Come, Sʳ Wᵐ Segar Kᵗ Garter principall King of Armes sendeth his due salutacons & greeting. Knowe yee that whereas anciently from the begyning, yᵗ hath byn a custome in all countryes & comon welthes well governed, that the bearing of certeyne marcks in sheilds (comonly called Arms) have byn & are the only signes & demonstracons either of prowesse & valoure atchyved in tymes of warre or of good life & Civill conversacon used in tymes of peace, according to the qualityes of the psons demeriting the same, Among the wᶜʰ number I fynde Lawrence Halstedd, now of Soñing in the County of Berks esquire, inhabiting in the mansion howse of that Manor & is Lord of the same, albeit a second sonne of that surname & familye in the County of Lancaster, and beareth for his ancient Coat Armor, gules an egle displayed ermyn. A cheif checkey or & Asure, And wanting further for an ornament unto his said Coat, a coutrement Creast or Cognisance fytt to be borne hath requested mee the said garter to appoint hym suche a one as hee maye lawfully beare wᵗʰoute wronge doing or preiudise to any pson or psons whatsoeū, wᶜʰ according to his request I have accomplished & granted in manner & forme followg vidlt On a healme forth of a Crowne murall Asure a demy Eagle ermine.

Hanson, of Blewbury.

Visitation of London, 1664, MS. College of Arms, D 12, p. 1. Additions, printed in italics, from Le Neve's Knights, Harl. Soc., VIII., p. 202, where the sons by the first wife are 1. *Berkley,* 2. *William, and by the second wife* 3. *Robert,* 4. *William.*

The certificate below, of course, only refers to the portion printed in ordinary type.

Thomas Hanson = Mary da: of .... [*Aston of*] Aston Hall in Com Chester.
of Blewberry in Com. Berks.

John Hanson of Blew- = Isabell da: of William berry and Cittizen of Lee of Abington in London. Com: Berks.

Kath: da: of Edw: Jones of = Robert Hanson Ar: alderman = Barbara da: of Geo: Wrexam in Com: Denbigh & heire to Edw: Jones and to Hugh Jones her grandfather by y^e mothers side [*bur. in St Mary at Hill church by her husband*].
of y^e Citty of London 1664 [*Sheriff* 1665, *Lord Mayor* 1678, *was by trade a* [*Grocer*] *lived in bow lane in Aldermary p'sh in Lond. buried in St Mary at hill Church London K^ted.* 1 *Feb.* 1665.
Norton of Great Chart in Com. Kent [*Grocer*] 1 wife [*buried in Aldermary Churchyard in London*].

Edw: Will. Kath: | Berkley sonne and heire æt: 16 An° 1664. | 2. Robert. Elizabeth.

[*Signed*] ROBERT HANSON.

I hereby certify that the above is correctly copied from the Records (D. 19, p. 1) in the Heralds' College. Witness my hand this 26th day of June 1907.

EVERARD GREEN,

Rouge Dragon.

𝕳𝖆𝖗𝖊𝖈𝖔𝖚𝖗𝖙, of 𝖂𝖎𝖙𝖍𝖆𝖒.

HARECOURT quartering
ST. CLERE.

Harl. MS. 1532, p. 135.

willm harecourte=of witham in Com. Berks.
|
Anne eldest d. vx John Anne of north Aston in Com. Northton [*see Harl. Soc.*, Vol. V., *Oxfordshire*, p. 191, *and Northampton*, 1564, p. 2].
|
harecourte a third brother=

|—Richard harecourte=.... d. of ob. s.p.   .... haule.
|—ffrancis hareCourte of Wytham in Com Berks marid .... d. of S\`r\` John Radley.

   |—Robert hareCourte dyed wthout yssue.
   |—Elizabeth d & heire vx Roger Snapp of Sunlake in Com Oxon. vide Oxon. [*Harl. Soc.*, Vol. V., p. 135.]

𝕳𝖆𝖗𝖗𝖎𝖘, of 𝕹𝖊𝖜 𝖂𝖎𝖓𝖉𝖘𝖔𝖗.

Harl. MS. 1532, pp. 142ᵇ, 143.

The Arms of Harris, of Windsor, given in Add. MS. 14283, fol. 108, are, *Ermine, on a bend Azure three hedgehogs passant Or.*
Crest, a demi pegasus rampant Gules, wings endorsed Or.
In Harl. MS. 1532 the Arms are, *Quarterly*, 1 and 4, HARRIS, *as above*; 2, HODELEY (?) *Gules, on a chevron Argent, between three birds silver, beaked and legged Or, a martlet Sable for difference*; 3, ELLIOTT, *Argent, on a fesse Gules between two bars gemelles wavy Azure three martlets Or.*
Crest, as above, over the Arms is written henry harris of windsor Clarke of ye lands to the Colledg of Eton ye 2 ffirst & [*below the shield*] Edward Harris of ye temple as it is.

Rowland Harris of .... in Com.=Joyce d. of george holberk Yorke.   vt 5 escallops or.
|
Thomas Harris of .... in=Ursula d. of John Rodney, A, 13 eglett s displayed g. Com Lincoln.   within a border B.

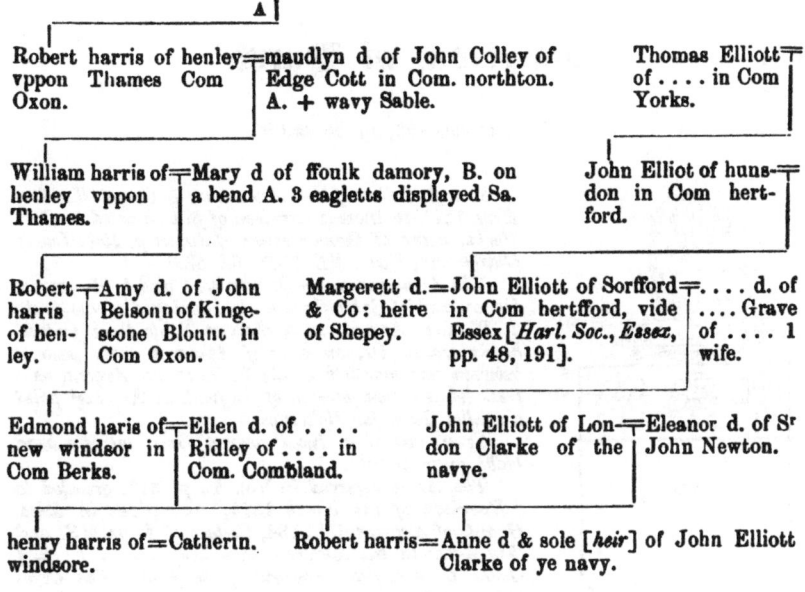

Harison, of Beech Hill.

[*MS. Rawl. D.* 865, *fol.* 131.]

S^r

I receved a sumons from yo̊urself for my personall appearance before your self this day att Reding, and I offer for my excuse that I am in ye 80th year of my age, and soe lately vnder the obedience of a violent Ague wch hath for the p̊sent soe mortified my old bones that I am not yet in Condicon to travell.

I am well knowen to Sr Edward Bishe one of you office and shall not fayle to wayte on you both this next terme if it please God to bless mee wth life & health and will in ye interim remaine willing to deserve well of you.

Jo. HARISON ye eldest.

From Beachill
    25 mātij 1665.

[*Addressed*]   For my worthy friend Elias Ashmole
                Esq. at Reding.

[*His pedigree was entered in the Visitation*, 1665-6. *See* Vol. I., p. 220.]

Harrison, of Hurst.

MS. Ashmole 852, pp. 96 and 97.

A confirmation of thes Ancl. Coat & Creast the 4 of May 1574 to thomas harrison of ffinchamsted in Com. Berks, sonne of thomas sonne of James p. Rob: Cooke, Clarenceux, Harl. MS. 1532, fol. 53.

The Arms given are Quarterly, 1 and 4, HARRISON, Or, on a chief Sable three eagles displayed of the first; 2, WARDE, Argent, on a chevron Sable three wolves' heads erased Or, on a chief Azure a cross patonce between two martlets Gold; 3, GARRARD, Argent, on a fesse Sable a lion passant of the field, in the chief point a mullet Gules for difference.

Crest, out of a ducal coronet Or a talbot's head Gold, guttè de poix.

The Arms referred in Vol. I., p. 219, granted to "Harrison of the North 1574," are given in Misc. Grants of Arms, vol. i., 134, College of Arms MS., and they differ in the colours; they are, Or, on a chief Gules three eagles displayed of the field. The Crest is the same.

James Harrison of Cumberland.=

James Harrison of =Alice da: to ....
Southampton.   Phetiplace.

Thomas Harrison of Finchampsted=Elizabeth da: to Jn° Slitherhurst
in Com: Berks.   of Tenterden in Wales.

1 *wife* Alice da:=Tho: Harrison of Finchamsted in=2 *wife* Kath:=Tho: Anton
to Rich: Warde | Com: Berks Surveyor of the Staple | da: to James | of Stratfield
of Hurst in Co: | to Qu: Eliz: marryed to his 3ᵈ wife | Chamberleine | Sey in Com:
Berks Esqʳ Cof- | Eliz: da: to Henry Becher [*Alder-* | of Spersholt | Hampt: first
ferer to Qu: | *man of London (Smith MS.)*] relict | in Com: | husband.
Eliz: | of Clement Kelk: living 1574: ob: | Berks.
                | 25: of February 1602.

Thomas   John   Tho. Spyer of Huntercombe=Kath: marr: after to George
2 sonn. 3 son. in Com: Oxon son & heire | Carleton of Brightwell in
                of Ralph. | Oxon.

Ralph Spyer son & heire.

OF BERKSHIRE.   141

A						B
Richd Harrison obijt vivo patre.	=Eliz: da: to Tho: Anton Renupta Robert [George] Marsh de London.	Thomas Anton marr: in Ireland.	....da:= to .... Tailer of Lincon first wife.	George Anton Recorder of Lincolne.	=....da: to ....Fitzwilliams of Mablethorpe 2^d wife.	James Anton.
Thomas sans yssue.	Richard *of Hurst, co. Berks* son and heire [*died* 1656] marr: Frances da: & coheir of George Gerrard of London 2^d son to Sr Wm Gerrard Lord Mayor of London. [*See Pedigree of Harrison of Hurst* 1664-66.]					John [*Harrison of Beechill Visit.*1664-6.]

Children of Richard: Richard. John. Elizabeth. Frances.

Harrison, of Reading.

Visitation of London, 1634-5, *Harl. Soc.,* Vol. XV., p. 352.

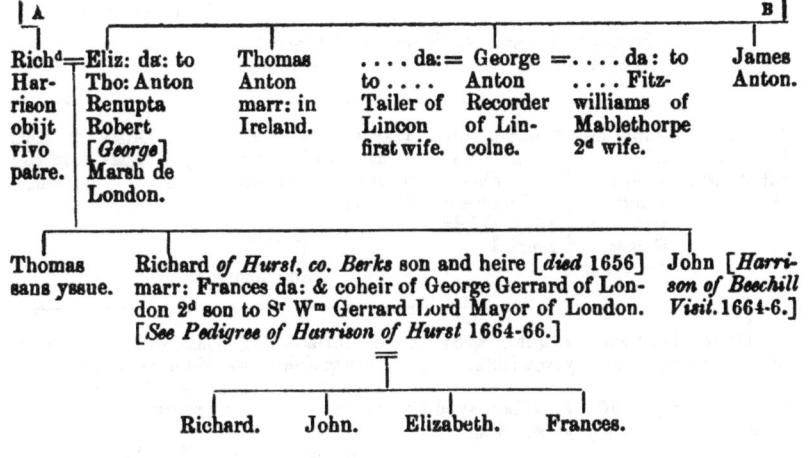

These Armes and Creast are exemplified vnder the hand and seale of Sr William Segar K^t Garter principall King of Armes by patent dated the 17 day of July 1633 a° 9th King Charles, granted to Gilbert Haryson alias Hardegson descended of a family of that surname in the Dutchy of Brunswick.

GRAFTON and WOOD.

Vnder the hand of Sr Wm Segar Knight Garter.

NOTES: VISITATIONS

Tower Street Ward.

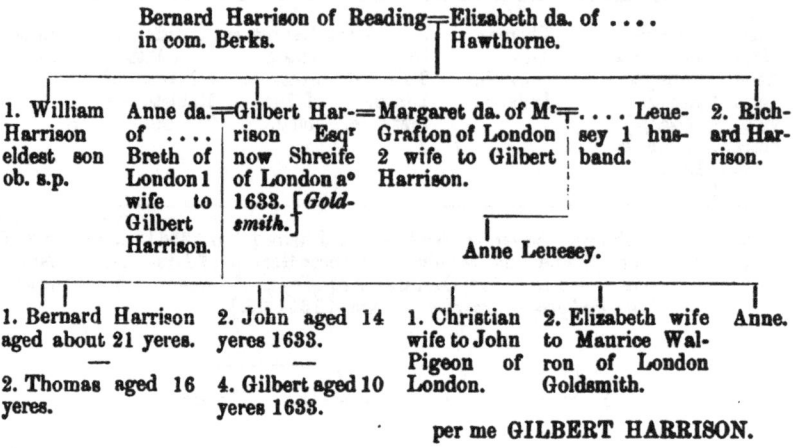

per me GILBERT HARRISON.

Hatt, of Leckampsted.

Visit. Lond. 1634-35, Harl. Soc., Vol. XV., p. 364.
Additions from the Visit. of Essex 1664-1668, ed. by Dr. J. J. Howard, p. 45.

Criplegate Within.

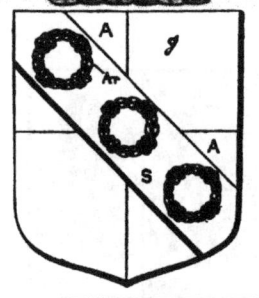

Hayes, of Windsor.

MS. Coll. of Arms, Misc. Grants, ii., 162, *and Bysshe's Grants, fol.* 3.

Sir Edward Bysshe Knight, Clarenceux. . . . . Wheras Thomas Hayes of Windsor in the County of Barkes senior and James Hayes his brother Cittizen and Letherseller of London sons of Alexander Hayes of Windsor aforesaid deceased have desired me to assigne unto them such Armes as they and their posterity may Lawfully beare ; Know yee therefore that I have thought fitt to assigne unto them the Armes hereafter Mentioned (that is to say) Argent a Chaveron betweene Three Tygers heads sable erased and langued Gules, and for his Crest on a helmet and wreath of his Culleres ; a Tiger's head (betweene two dragons wings displayed sable) Langued Gules, Mantled Gules doubled Argent as in the margent hereof are more lively depicted. All w[ch] Armes and Crest I the said Clarenceux King of Arms by power and authority of my Office to me granted und[r] the Great Seale of England do give and grant unto the foresaid Thomas Hayes and James Hayes his brother & to the severall issues begotten observing their due differences according to the Laws of Armes for ever. In witness wherof I have unto theis p[r]sents affixed the seale of my office & subscribed my name: dated 13 day of May An° Dni. 1661.

Haynes, of Reading.

Exemplification of Arms and Crest to Nicholas Haynes of Hackney, co. Middlesex (from Berkshire), by Robert Cooke Clarenceux, 1578. MS. Ashm. 840, p. 399.

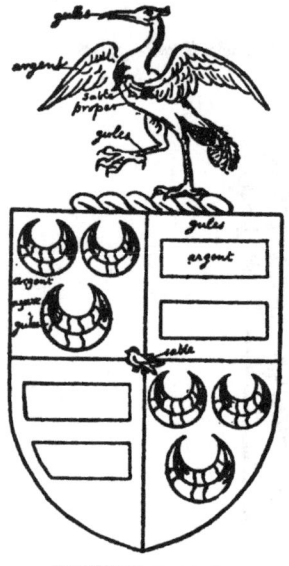

HAYNES *quartering* FOXLEY. *MS. Coll. of Arms, E.D.N.I. 35.**

To all and singuler as well Nobells and Gentiles as others to whome these presents shall come Robert Cooke Esquire alias Clarencieux princepall heraulte Kinge of Armes of the Sowth East and West partes of this Realme of England from the River of Trent Sowthwardes sendeth greeting in our Lord God Everlastinge whereas antiently from the beginninge the valiant & vertuous actes of excellent psons have bene comended vnto yᵉ worlde with sundrye monumentes and remembrances of thire good deseartes amongest the which the cheifest and most vsuall hathe bene the bearinge of Signes in shildes called Armes which are none other then demonstracōns of prowes aud valour diversly distributed accordinge to the quallities & deseartes of the parsons That such signes and Tokens of the dilligent faythfull & coragious might appeare before yᵉ Neegligent Coward and iguorant and bee a sufficient cause to move stire and kindle the hartes of men toe the imitacōn of vertue and Nobellnesse even so hathe some bene and yet is continually observed to the entent yᵗ such as have done comendable servise to theire Prince or Contrye eather in warr or peace maye both receave due honor in theire Lives and alsoe derive the same successively to theire posterritie after them And beinge required of Nicholas Haynes of Hackney in Midlesex fowrth son of Richard Haynes of Redinge in the County of Barkeshire gentilman and of Thomasen his wife daughter and coheire of John ffoxley of .... gentilman in yᵉ County of Barkshire to make serche in yᵉ Registers and Recordes of my Office for the auntient Armes and Creast belonging to yᵗ name and famyly wheareof he is desended Whearevppon I have made searche accordingely and doe fynde yᵗ he maye lawfully beare as his Auncestors heretofore have borne thes Armes and Creast heareafter followeing That is to say yᵉ first for Haynes Argent three Cressants vnde azure and gules, the second for ffoxley gules twoo bares humite silver and so quarterlly and to his Creast vppon the healme on a wreathe silver and gules a Heron volant the boddye in proper couller wynges si[l]ver Legged and beaked goulde houldinge vp one of his ffeete Mantelled gules doubled silver as more playnly is depicted in yᵉ Margent, The which Armes & Creast and every parte and parcell thereof I the said Clarencieulx Kinge of Armes by power and auctoritie anexed vnto me comitted by Lrēs Patents vnder the great Seale of England do ratiffy confirme give and graunte vnto the said Nicholas Haynes gent. and to his posterity with their due differences and he & thay the same to vse beare and shew forth at his and theire liberty & pleasure withoute impediment lett or interupcōn of any pson or persons. I witnes whereof I the said Clarencieulx Kinge of Armes, have signed these presents with my hand and sett herevnto the seale of my Office año Dñi 1578, and in the xxᵗʰ yeare of the Raigne of oure Soveraigne La[d]y Queene Elizabeth &c.

ROBERT COOKE alias
Clarencieulx Roy Darme[s].

* *The trick of Arms in MS. Ashm. 840 is lightly drawn, so I have substituted the above.*

Henn or Hene, of Winkfield.

MS. Coll. of Arms, Misc. Grants, vol. ii., 133 (*abstract*). *These Arms appear in some of the MSS. Compare the trick given with the pedigree,* Vol. I., p. 222.

Sir John Borough Knight Garter .... credibly informed that the Auncesters of Sir Henry Henn ats Hene of Wingfeild in the County of Berks : Knight & Baronett, were originally native of South Wales from whence his grandfather transplanting himself into the County of Surrey dyed there, leaving Wm Henn alias Hene his sonn father of Sr Henry aforesaid very young by reason whereof the perfect knowledge of his descent is for the present left uncertyne. And although it appeareth that the Hennes in South Wales were gentlemen of good noate and of Coate Armour from whom it may probably be supposed the said Sr Henry Henn alias Hene to bee discended. Yet hee being no ways willing to encroach upon the Armes and kindred of a family from whom he cannot demonstratively derive himself (wch not withstanding he hopeth may be herafter claired) hath made earnest request unto mee, that I would in the meane tyme decleare & assigne unto him such Armes as hee and his posterity may lawfully beare, without doing wronge or injury to any other person whatsoever, Know yee therefore that I having seriously considered the premises, as also the quality & worth of the said Sr Henry Henn alias Hene, have thought fitt to declare and assigne unto him the Armes here under mentioned. Videlicet. Vert a cheveron or, in Cheife three Lyons rampant of the Second armed gules, And for his Creast, on a healme mantled gules doubled argent, & a torce of his colours, a demy Leopard proper holding in his right paw a battle Axe Argent, As in the margent mor lively is depicted, which Armes (as before expressed) the said Sr John Borough K^t Garter principal King of Armes of Englishmen, by the authority annexed unto the office of Garter, by the statutes of the Most Noble Order of the Garter continued practice, and the Letters Pattents of my said Office, made unto me under the Great Seale of England, do by theis presents declare assigne give grant & confirme unto the aforesaid Sr Henry Henn alias Hen[e] & to the heirs of his body Lawfully begotten, to be by thē, & every of them borne with their due differences according to the Laws of Arms for ever. In witness wherof I have unto theis presents affixed the seale of my office & subscribed my name. Dated ye eight & Twentith day of December In ye eighteenth yeare of the raigne of our dread soveraigne Lord Charles by the greace of God King of Great Brittaine and Ireland. Defend^r of the faith etc., 1642.

[*Signed*]   John Borough Garter Principall
King of Armes of Englishmen.

𝕳𝖊𝖗𝖇𝖊𝖗𝖙, 𝖔𝖋 𝕬𝖗𝖇𝖔𝖗𝖋𝖎𝖊𝖑𝖉.

MS. Rawl. D. 865, *fol.* 123.

S^r

  I am now bounde for London to wayte vpon the Kinge, it beinge my waytinge quarter, so that I cannot come to Reddinge to shew you my Coate and my Crest, which you will finde in yor booke : my Father was Sr Arnold Herbert, and giues the three white Lyons rampant for the Coate, and the White Lyon rampant for ye Crest. I shall satisfy you more when I see you at Court till which tyme I shall remaine

            Yo^r servant
              EDWARD HERBERT.

Arborfeild, ye 11th
 March 1664.

[*Addressed*] These For Elias Ashmole, Esq., at
     the Beare at Reddinge psent.

In the List Ashmole makes this note to the name of Edward Herbert, Esqr. : *Vide l're, son to Sr Arnold Herbert a gent.-Pensioner.*

Sir Arnold Herbert, Knt., and his wife were buried at Warfield. The tombstone has been destroyed [*Berks Arch. Soc.*, 1879-80, p. 66]. *The stones had neither names nor dates.*

𝕳𝖎𝖑𝖑.

Exemplification of Arms to James Hill by Sir William Segar, Garter, dated the 2 September, the 16th of James the 1st (1618), *in Ashmole's handwriting.* (*MS. Ashm.* 840, *pp.* 415-16.) *No Trick of Arms.*

  Vniuersis et singulis cuiuscunque loci, statur, gradus, ordinis ac condicionis ad quos presentes peruenerint, Guilielmus Segarus Eques auratus et principalis Rex Armorum Anglicorum, Salutem in Domino sempiternam. Cum omnium omnino sit veritatem tueri, et ad eandem asserendam testimonium perhibere, tum mea inprimis interest qui Rex Armorum florentissimi Regni Angliæ sum iuratus, et regia authoritate ad hoc munitus, vt Genealogias virorum nobilium hujus Regni vnacum Armis siue Clypeis gentilitijs in Officio Armorum fideliter conseruem, et de eisdem quoties rogatus fuerim attester. Ego itaque predictus Rex Armorum notum testatumque facio, et hoc presenti scripto declaro, quod Jacobus Hill Anglus, iam ex Almania, et alijs transmarinis partibus reuersurus, natus erat ex antiqua, et nobili familia eiusdem nominis in Comitatu Suffolciæ in Anglia, prout in libris memorandum nobilium Anglicorum videre licet, et Arma istius portat, gallice sic describenda D'Asur troix barres d'Argent, vn Griphe d'or, sergreant sur tout armee de gules ; Et pour son Tymbre sur vn torce de se couleurs, vn bras, et main dextre armèe, avançant vne Lance en charge rompu ; sicut latius in margine depingunter Qui quidem Jacobus Hill Præfectus Equitum, Pedetumque propter singularem, eximiamque eius scientiam, et experientiam, tam in rebus bellicis, quàm civilibus obeundis, gerendisque dexteritatem, ante aliquot annos in legationibus ad exteros Principes, Imperatores, et Reges missus, famam sibi, generique suo dignam acquisiuit ; Cum verò hoc mihi haud obscure pateat, testimonium eiusmodi hisce literis meis confirmandum opere pretium duxi. Quæ omnia Arma et Christam Ego prædictus Garterius principalis Rex Armorum Anglicorum confirmo prædicto illi Jacobo, eiusque posteris, ad vtendum, gerendum, et ferendum in Clypeis, Vexillis, Armatura, sigillis, fenestris, ædificijs, monumentis, aut alia quacunque ratione, omnibus temporibus et locis singulis, prout sibi et illis libitum et placitum fuerit, iuxta ius feciale. In cuius rei testimonium huic presenti scripto, manum meum proprium apposui, et sigillum officij mei affixi. Datum Londini in Officio Armorum secundo die Septembris, Anno regni Domini nostri Jacobi dei gratia Angliæ, Franciæ, et Hiberniæ, regis fidei defensoris decimo sexto, Scotiæ verò Quinquegesimo tertio.

GUIL: SEGARUS Garterius.

Hoby, of Bisham.

MS. Rawl. D. 865, *fol.* 127.

Bishame, Aprel 27 [16]65:

Honored Sir

Mr Hoby hauing a greate Cold att prenent [*sic*] apointed me to let you know y^t hee receued yours of ye 26: Instant but last night (being ye 26) he returnes you thankes for it and for your Ciuility to him, and also lets you know y^t hee did receue a Sumonds to appeare before you March 28da [16]65: but being to goe from home beefore y^t day, and my selfe and most of our family, and not to returne tell after, hee not knowing you, nor wher you liued, and being well a quainted with Sir Edward Bisshe, Mr Hoby sent to a freind to desier him to let Sir Ed: know y^t hee was to goe frome home, and so desired him y^t hee might be excused for not appering then, and also Mr Hoby desired his freind to goe to you to let you know y^t hee was to goe from home and y^t you would excuse his not appering then, and y^t what Fees were to be paied to you and any other should be truely paied, and Mr Hoby receued a letter from his freind that hee had benn with you, and y^t as Mr Hoby vnderstood you were satisfied, and therfore hee hauing no busness att london this tearme thought hee might defer it tell the next sitting of Parlament and so hee desiers hee may, and hee hauing such a Cold cannot well come this tearme, and he desires hee may know from you what fees are due, and so with his serues and mine I rest

Sir,
Your freind and seruant
KAT. HOBY.

[*Addressed*] These For her honored freind Elias Ashmole Esqr att his Chamber in the Middle Temple ouer against Hall Court London.

This letter was in reply to that of Ashmole, dated 20 April 1665, of which the draft copy is here printed under the name Touchet.

Part of the seal remains. It may be a lion or a unicorn rampant; perhaps the crest referred to in the letter dated the 16th of October 1667, or that granted in 1570.

MS. Rawl. D. 865, *fol.* 220ᵇ.

Honourd Sʳ

Had I knowne you had tooke care to excuse yʳ appance at Maidenhead, I had not troubled you wᵗʰ my l're, but that Excuse came to my knowledge but 2 dayes since. As I am most ready to show all respect to the gentry of yoʳ Country, so in pticular am most willˢ to comply wᵗʰ what you desire: & shall therefore respit the entrying of yoʳ descent, till yoʳ owne conveniency will better pmit, wᶜʰ when it falls out, if you please to give me notice I shall most readily serve you & in the meane tyme rem̄

[E. A.]

To Peregrine Hobbey
   Esqʳ at Bysham.

This is a reply to the letter of Mrs. Hoby, dated 27 April 1665, just printed.

MS. Rawl. D. 865, *fol.* 225.
26 May 1666.

Madam,

I recᵈ a l̄re from you of the 22ᵈ instant, but am not willing to receiue any Fee, before I haue done my duty & deserved it: In case therefore that Mʳ Hoby come not to Towne next Tearme, yet if you be pleased to send any one to me (to my Chamber in the Midle Temple) with an Account of his Descent, Matches & Issue, as also the Matches and Issues of his Brothers, Sisters, or other Colaterall lynes, I shall make entry thereof, & of his Arms, & that being done, will then gladly receiue the accustomed Fee.

I must beg your excuse for not answering your Questions concerning Precedency in writing, that being a thing properly to be done by the Officers of Arms in Chapter, & I ought not to take vpon me the giving my owne opinion singly in cases of such Concernemᵗ: Nor is it vsuall for them to make Certificate of things in this nature, vnles it first come to them by Comand from the Lords Comʳˢ for the Office of Earle Marshall. Nevertheles I will not refuse to discourse my Opinion to you (or other Person desiring it) if there happen an opertunity to doe it verbally: But to send it by way of Letter, & vnder my hand, I hold it not convenient for many Reasons. In what I may, I wilbe serviceable to Mʳ Hoby & your selfe, of wᶜʰ I beg you will be pleased to receiue the assurance, from

                                  Madam
                          Yoʳ most humble servant
To Mʳˢ Hoby at Bysham neere Maidenhead   E. A[*shmole*].
        These

MS. Rawl. D. 865, *fol.* 227.
Bishame yᵉ 16 October 1667.

Sir,

You cannot but wonder you haue not hard from Mʳ Hoby or from mee before this but I thought wee should haue benn in London before this, but my husband and my sonn both haue benn ill, my sonn was so ill yᵗ it put us in greate feare wᵗ the Euent would bee, yᵉ small pox wee fered, but I thanke god it was not and both Mʳ Hoby and my sonn are resnable well and Mʳ Hoby gonn to London yesterday, but I supose hee may forgett to speake wᵗʰ you therfore I thought good to let you know yᵗ formerly Mʳ Hoby did send mee to Mʳ Rylie I thinke his name was, Rielye (or Reyly), and he told me yᵗ Mʳ Hoby might giue Sir Edward Hobys Armes wᵗʰ a barr, wᶜʰ out any charge or leaue from your office, if so then Mʳ Hoby doth hope yᵗ Sir Edward Bish will not Aske much for to lett him giue it yᵗ way wᶜʰ you spake offe, wᶜʰ is yᵉ better way. So I doe desier to know of you this, whether Mr Hoby may giue Sir Edward Hoby his Fathers armes wth ye Barr without any Charge or leaue from your office, and next what Sir Edward Bish and ye office must haue, to haue leaue to giue thes Armes as you mentioned, wch is ye best way. Sir Edward did giue a very fine Crest wch I beliue hee did purchace,* for formerly I finde they gaue an uother, and Mr Hoby hath ye patten for ye new Crest now in ye hous, wch I doe Intend to bring to london yer long, but you told me sumthing must be donn now before the tearme, but if it could hansomly be deferred tell I could come to london wch will be aboue a fortnight hence then I could know Mr Hobys minde and let you know it, but if y^t cannot be pray let me know as soone as you can whether Mr Hoby may give the Hobys armes without leaue from your office (and also our Children) or whether it must be purchased, and if so w^t the charge will bee, y^t so wee may know what to doe and giue you an Ansur directly. Sir, This is all att present from

Your freind and seruant
Kat. Hoby.

Exemplification of Arms and Grant of a Crest to Edward Hoby by Sir Gilbert Dethick, Knt. Garter, dated the 10th of June 1570. (MS. Ashm. 858, pp. 230—232.)

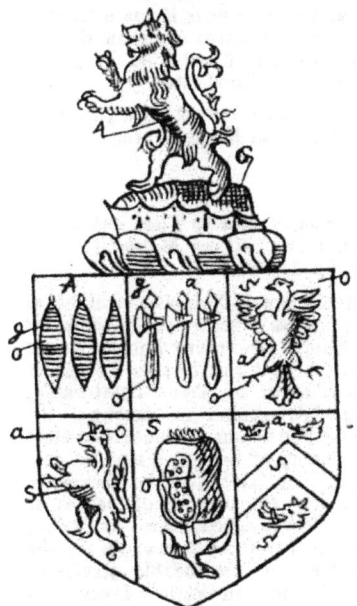

1. HOBY (BADLOND).
2. BYLMORE.
3. LLEWELLYN AP GREGEUR.
4. RHYS AP TUDOR.
5. MEREDITH GETH.
6. PHILIP DOILLIE.

Omnibus Christi Fidelibus ad quos præsentes literæ pervenerint Gilbertus Dethyck Miles alias Garterus Principalis Rex Armorum Angliæ salutem. Quoniam brevis hæc hominum vita varijs subjicitur fortunæ casibus, ejusque memoria sæpissimè perpetua oblivione deletur: Quapropter ardenti affectu clari nominis Generosos et Magnanimos indies augendi et proficiscendi (sola virtus) infinita cogit tentare et perficere qua gradus honoris scandere ad culmen peruenire et inter mortales perpetuò vivere conceditur. Vnde alij eorum exemplis ad virtutis exercendi studium alliciuntur, et incitantur. Et quia inter alia per multa præclari nominis præmia antiquus hic armorum sive iusigniorum in Parmis Clipeisque deliniandorum mos dignitatis famæ, honoris prosapiæ et virtutis indicat testimonium de quibus nos fæciales autoritate regia commemoratores dignissimi judicamur. Ego prædictus Gilbertus Dethick Miles alias Garterus Principalis Rex Armorum Angliæ ad hoc rogatus ex certa scientia et fide dignorum testimonijs veraciter instructus et informatus. Quod illustrissimus Edwardus Hoby tam animæ, corporis quam fortunæ dotibus insignis: filius primogenitus Domini Thomæ Hoby Equitis, dum Legati ad Regem Gallorum in celtica pro patria fungeretur officio nuper defuncti. Cujus Edwardi prosapiam progeniemvé vna cum alijs monumentis inspeximus his Armis,

---

* *Possibly during the period 1646 to 1660, when Sir Edward Bysshe intruded into the office of Garter for the Parliament. He was reduced to his proper office of Clarenceux at the Restoration.*

insignibusque antiquissimis legittimè sit decoratus: Ego tamen vt nunquam de ijsdem imposterum dubitetur, nec aliqua racione impugnentur, eadem sicut apparent depicta Literis meis pateutibus exemplificavi. Et vt ad omnes vsus militares tam belli quam pacis fulgentia quædam certa et genuina insignia Clypeis galeis alijsque rebus quibuscunque (nominis et honoris sui designandi gratia) demonstrare valeat, eidem vlterius Cristam hanc assignavi, videlicet, In Pileum honoris rubeum duplicatum Armeniaco Tygridem salientem de argento. Chlamide rubea duplicata item Argento. Quemadmodum hic magis delucidè depicta apparet. Habendum et tenendum præfato Edwardo Hoby et hæredibus suis imperpetuum quibus illis et illorum singulis ab hijs legittime descendentibus tam in Clypeis, Scutis, armis, Castris, tentorijs, Vexillis cæterisque belli apparatibus, quam in sigillis, annulis, fenestris, sculpturis, monumentis, sepulturis, omnique suppellectili: (modestè vt decet virtutis observantia (consuetis differentijs) vti posse aut velle permittitur: Denique vt ipsi et ipsorum singuli omnes rei militaris exercitationes, hastiludia, torniamenta, duella, aut hujusmodi belli præludia, ingredi aut exercere, et ad honoris gradus pervenire valeant absque molestatione aut perturbatione quacunque. Quamobrem vt præmissarum memoria pervulgata permanere reique certitudo apparere possit quoscunque de ijs in posterium legittimè descendentes, devotionibus et dilectionibns vestris benevole et gratiose commendamus. Et vt præheminentijs privilegijs et liberatibus Nobilium in omnibus secundetis et frui sinatis. In cujus rei testimonium has Literas meas patentes fieri feci, manu propriâ subscripsi, et Sigillo meo nec non Sigillo Officij mei vulgo Garteri Principalis Regis Armorum Angliæ consignavi. Datum Londini ex Officio et Collegio nostro Armorum decimo die Junij Anno Domini 1570. Anno Regni Augustissimæ Elizabethæ dei gratia Angliæ Franciæ et Hiberniæ Reginæ fidei Defensoris &c: Duodecimo.

       per me G. DETHICK alias garter
        principall Kinge of armes.

Draft of a Grant of Arms to Peregrine Hoby, of Bisham, sent by Elias Ashmole to Sir Edward Bysshe, Knight Clarenceux, dated the 17th of November, 1664. In Ashmole's handwriting. MS. Ashm. 840, pp. 433-34.

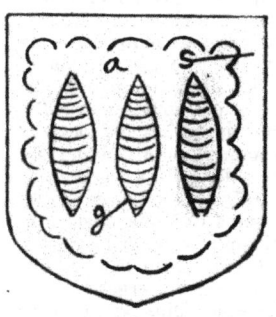

To all & singular, aswell Nobles as Gentiles, as others to whome these p̃sentẹ shall come, Sʳ Edward Bysshe Knight Clarenceux King of Armes of the South East & west ptẹ of this Realme of England from the River of Trent Southwardẹ, sendeth greeting. Forasmuch as amongst the sundry Monumᵗˢ devised by our prudent Auncestors to comend the memory of deserving men to succeeding ages, it is observable that the cheifest & most vsuall haue been the bearing of markes or signes in Sheilds comonly called Armes, as evident demonstracōns of their vertues & rewards for the same, And that for their comendable service to their Prince and Country, in Warr or Peace they might in their lyfe tyme receiue due honor & afterwardẹ transmitt the same to their successive posterity. In which respect whereas Peregrine Hoby of Bysham in the County of Berkẹ Esqʳ naturall son to Sʳ Edward Hoby of Bysham aforesᵈ Knight is generally knowne to be a person well deserving not only for his good conversacoñ & discreet demeanour, but also for a prudent discharge of his duty to his Country having been a Burgess of Parliamᵗ for the Towne of Merlow in Com̃ Buk: both in the reigne of King Charles the first of blessed memory & of King Charles the 2ᵈ now hapily reigning, as also a Justice of Peace in the sᵈ County of Berkẹ for many yeares past.

Know yee therefore that I the said Clarenceux for the consideracōns aforesaid, haue by power also of my Office, vnder the greate Seale of England, at the instant request of him the s^d Peregrine Hoby, given granted assigned and confirmed, and by these p^rsente doe giue grant assigne & confirme vnto him the s^d Peregrine a Border engraled sable, vpon the Escotcheon of his Armes, as in the margent of these p^rsente is more fully to be seene, as a fitt and noted distinccoñ in his said Armes* or Ensignes of Honour from any other of y^t name or family. So that he the said Peregrine Hoby and his descend^{ts} may at all tymes & vpon all occasions, beare & shew forth the same Armes in sheld Coate Armour or otherwise wth their due differences, accord^g to the law of Armes & laudable cus[t]ome of this realme wthout the inpediment let or interrupcoñ of any pson or psons whatsoever. In wittnes whereof I the said Clarenceux haue herevnto subscribed my name, & affixed the seale of my Office the 17th day of November in the 16th yeare of the reigne of our 'Soueraigne lord Charles the 2^d by the grace of God, of England Scotland france & Ireland King defendor of the faith, And in the yeare of o^r Ld God 1664.

Pray Sr Correct & mend this as you think fitt, & retorne it so as you would have me Engross it.

Yo^r most humble serv^t
E: A.

[*Addressed*] For my honourd freind Sr Edward Bysshe
Knight at Mr Goddarde house in St Johns close.

[*Sealed, but the seal not clear.*]

Grant of Arms (MS. Coll. of Arms, Bysshe's Grants, p. 20).

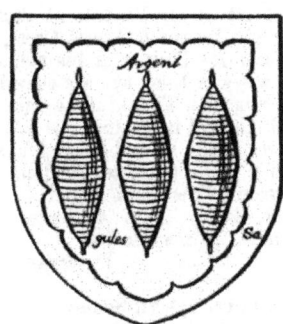

To Peregrin Hoby of Bysham, natural son of Sir Edward Hoby of Bysham in com. Berks, K^t, 17 Nov. 1664.

Argent three bottommes gules threaded or, a bordure engrailed sable.

* *Peregrine Hoby had no Arms; the Arms confirmed or granted to him, with the addition of the bordure engrailed, were the Arms of Badlond assumed by Hoby on account of the marriage with the heiress of that family, discarding their more appropriate bearing (see "Miscel. Geneal. et Herald.," i., 141-2). Also an exemplification of these Arms to Sir Thomas Posthumous Hoby, Knt., brother to Sir Edward Hoby, Knt., by William Dethick Garter, and William Camden Clarenceux, dated the 10th of July, 1598. A pedigree is also given to the same date. Cf. also "Miscel. Geneal. et Herald.," 2nd Series, iii., 351.*

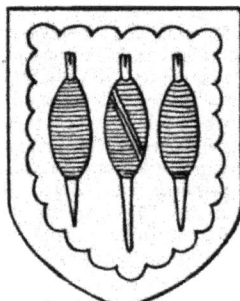

Mrs. Hoby, when she wrote to Ashmole on the 16th of October 1667 (as above), can hardly refer to the Crest granted to Sir Edward Hoby by Dethick on the 10th of June 1570. She says, "Sir Edward [Bysshe] did giue a very fine Crest wch I beliue he [Peregrine Hoby] did purchace, for formerly I finde they gaue an other, and M^r [Peregrine] Hoby hath ye patten for ye new Crest now in ye hous, wch I doe Intend to bring to london yer long." Of this crest granted by Sir Edward Bysshe I can find no record. Possibly it was one of the grants cancelled at the Restoration, given by Bysshe during the years 1646 to 1660, when he intruded into the office of Garter for the Parliament.

At the same time Mrs. Hoby seems to have been labouring under some misconception when she wrote about the arms. They had been granted as above on the 17th of November 1664, and were allowed by Ashmole at the Visitation of 1665-66.

The bottoms or weavers' spindles wound with thread (literally balls of thread) seem to be better tricked in Harl. MS. 1483, fol. 139^b.

Holloway, of Sunningwell.

MS. Rawl. D. 865, fol. 119.

Sir,
I receiv'd a sumons, left at my Tenants at Suningwell, my owne dwelling being in Oxford, to shew y^w my discent & Armes, Crest, &c. This is no more then what I shewd to y^r Predecessor Mr Philpot at his visitacōn held at Oxford about 1640-41, or therabouts, all wch was then by mee shewd & entred with him, vpon his then Record: for wch I was then Thankfull to him. I am now & shalbe till my going to the terme much Ingagd in busines, soe as I shall desire y^w to dispence with my attendance: however if any thing be due I shall be ready to satisfy y^w at my chamber In serieants Inne In fleet-streete London. Mean while y^w will finde my Coate to bee A fess between 3 Cresceants Argent In a field gules with a Canton Ermin In the dexter point, & my Crest A Goates head Coupee Collard with 3 Cresceants gules, as I take it. I doe remaine

Y^r servant & freind
CHARLES HOLLOWAY.

From my howse in Oxford over ag^t All-Soules
in Oxford : March 15, 1664 [*1664-65*].

[*Addressed*] To my worthy freind Elias Ashmole Esqr Windsor herauld at Armes, at the New Inne In Abingdon.

Leaue this lre with Mr Edward hart there To be deliverd with Care as is directed.

[*Red wax seal bearing the above Arms without colours but the canton ermine, and no crest.*]

OF BERKSHIRE.

Charles Holloway, Serjant-at-Law, entered the following pedigree :—

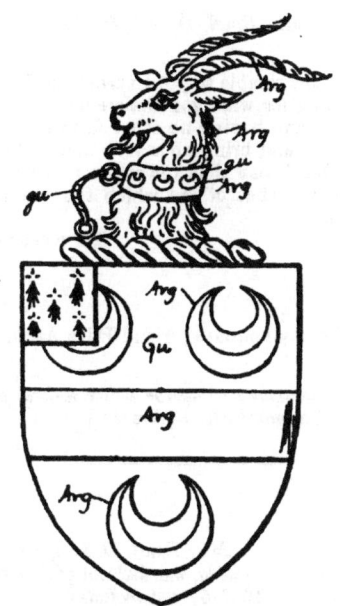

Visitation of Oxford 1634, from MS. College of Arms, C. 29, 111ᵇ.

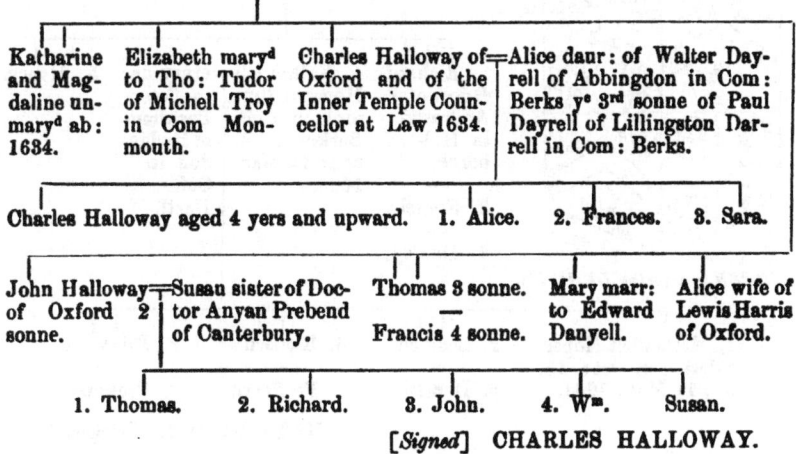

[Signed] CHARLES HALLOWAY.

𝔥𝔬𝔭𝔢𝔯, 𝔬𝔣 𝔖𝔬𝔫𝔫𝔦𝔫𝔤.

MS. Rawl. D. 865, fol. 126.

Sʳ,

Were my estate answerable to yoʳ Expectacõn I should not have putt you to the trouble of weighting for what you Claime as yoʳ fee: But being a younger Brother, as you well know, and having no other fortune but a bare inconsiderable Annuitye for to mainteyne and bring up a Wife and eight small Children, I looke upon you, as so much a Gentleman that you will rather behold me as an object fitt for Compassion, then require that of me which the weaknesse of my estate is not able to satisfye: Sir I am

Yoʳ most humble servant

NAT. HOPER.

28 March 1665.

[*Addressed*] These For my honoured friend Elias Ashmole Esq; at yᵉ Beare in Reading present.

[*The small seal bears the arms: a chevron between three pomegranates stalked and leaved; in the middle chief, a martlet for difference.*]

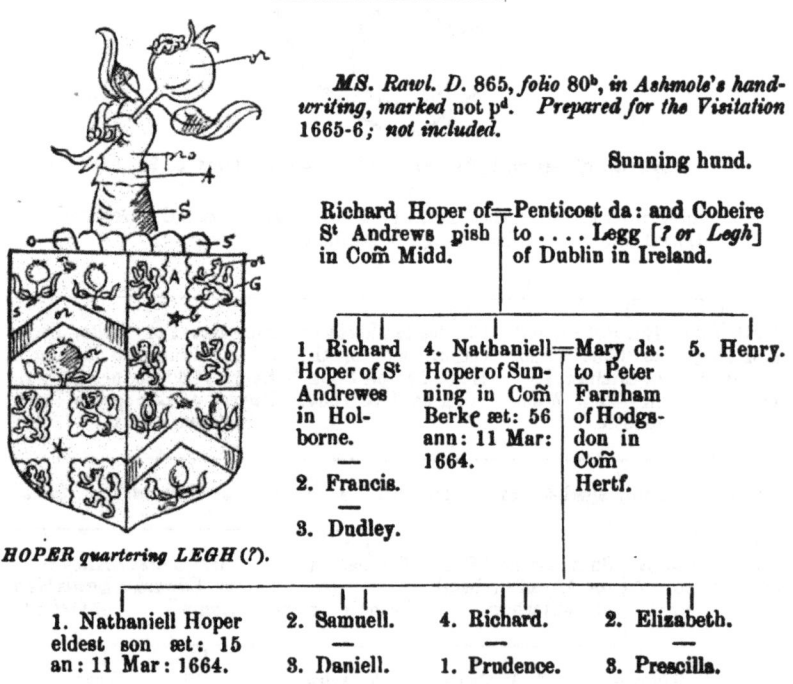

HOPER quartering LEGH (?).

MS. Rawl. D. 865, folio 80ᵇ, in Ashmole's handwriting, marked not pᵈ. *Prepared for the Visitation 1665-6; not included.*

Sunning hund.

Richard Hoper of Sᵗ Andrews pish in Coɱ Midd. =Penticost da: and Cobeire to .... Legg [? or *Legh*] of Dublin in Ireland.

1. Richard Hoper of Sᵗ Andrewes in Holborne.
—
2. Francis.
—
3. Dudley.

4. Nathaniell Hoper of Sunning in Coɱ Berkₑ æt: 56 ann: 11 Mar: 1664. =Mary da: to Peter Farnham of Hodgsdon in Coɱ Hertf.

5. Henry.

1. Nathaniell Hoper eldest son æt: 15 an: 11 Mar: 1664.

2. Samuell.
—
3. Daniell.

4. Richard.
—
1. Prudence.

2. Elizabeth.
—
3. Prescilla.

NAT: HOPER. [*Original.*]

OF BERKSHIRE. 155

Horde, of Shilton.

[*MS. Rawl. D.* 865, *fol.* 132.]

S^r,
 I haue receaued a sūmons from you to appeare before you ye 18th day of this month att Farrington. I haue not liued in ye County of Berkes this two yeares but during that time I haue been resident in ye County of Oxō, where I expect ye like sumōns vpon the same occasion, and shall with ye rest of my Neighbo^{rs} and Countreymen giue my attendance there, if required : in ye interim I am
             S^r
            Yo^r servant
From Coat in Oxoñsheire ye 7th of   THO: HORDE.
 March: 64 [*1664-65*].

[*Addressed*] These are For Elias Ashmole Esq, att y^e Crowne
        in Faringdon, Berkes.

[*The red wax seal bears the crest only, On a wreath a horse's head.*]

The following is the pedigree entered :—

Visitation of Oxfordshire, 1634, *from MS. College of Arms, C.* 29, *fol.* 72^b.

1. HORDE.   4. STAPLETON.   7. MASSY.
2. PALMER.   5. MATHEWE.   8. KINGSTON.
3. PERRELL or PERLE. 6. VEALE or VEELE. 9. VYELL.

Allan Hord of Hord Park in Com Salop =.... daughter of
son of Alan Hord. | .... Blount.
             A

Dorothey marr: to Geo: Rowe of Kingston House in ye parish of Staverto: in Com. Devon.	Sr Tho: Hord of Coate in Com: Oxon. Kt 1634.=Frances daur of Sr Tho: Gardner.

| Barbara 1. | Frances 2. | Dorothey 3. | John 3 son. | Thomas Hord eldest sonne. | Allan 2 son. | Willm 4 sonne. |

[Signed] THO: HORD.

Hungerford, of Buscott.

MS. Ashmole 836, p. 681. *Original paper sent in for the Visitation* 1665-66.

Walter Hungerford Dr of Divinitie & Rector of Buscot in the County of Berks, married Mrs Cicelie Dearinge widowe, & hath noe child, she was the Daughtr of Mr William Younge of Ogborne [*co. Wilts*].

Wch Waltr was the Soñe of John Hungerford of Cadnam in the County of Wilts Esqr, who married Mrs Elizabeth Escourt, Sister to Sr Thomas Escourt of Lashborough in the County of Gloucester.

Wch sd John Hungerford was the Soñe of Walter Hungerford of Cadnam, who married one Mrs Cocke or Mrs .... Peverell (as I thinke)* Lady of Honour to Queene Elizabeth.

Wch John Hungerford & Waltr & Robert Hungerford of Cadnam & many others were descended from the Lord Robert Hungerford of Downe Amney in the County of Gloucester.

[*Red wax seal bearing the Arms, with helm and mantlet* (Sable), *two bars* (Argent), *in chief three roundels* (plates). *Crest, in a ducal coronet* (Or) *a pepper garb* (Gold), *between two sickles erect* (proper).]

Hyde, of South Denchworth.

Confirmation of a Crest to George Hyde of South Denchworth by William Camden, Clarenceux, dated the 22 *of November,* 1600. *MS. Ashm.* 840, p. 411. (*See* "*Miscel. G. et H.*," *New Series,* iii., p. 53.)

To all and singuler to whome theis presents shall come to be sene, read, or heard William Camden Esquire, alias Clarenceux Principall Herald and King of Armes of the East West and South Partes of England from the river of Trent Southward sendeth due Commendacõns in or Lord god everlasting. Forasmuche as it is evedently and plainely appeareth by divers and sundry aunctient evidences dated the fieft yeare of King Edward the third: That the Ancestors of George Hyde of South-denchworth in the County of Berks Esquier have heretofore in their Seales vsed for their devise or Cognizaunce, a Lance or Horsemans staff, with a flagge or cornet thereat &c. And being required by the said George Hyde Esquier to ratefie and confirme vnto him the said devise, empresse or cognizance have at

---

* Sr *Walter Lord Hungerfford, Knt. of* ye *Order of the Garter and Lord Threasurer of England, married Catherin d. and* coh-ire *of* Sr *Thom. Peverell, Knt.* (*Visit. Gloucester* 1623, *Harl. Soc.,* Vol. XXI., p. 87). *Walter Hungerfford of Cadnam,* 1565, *married Frances d. of Richard Cock of Broxborne in com. Hertfford* (*Ibid.,* p. 88).

his request, ratefied and confirmed, and by theis presentes doe ratefie and confirme vnto the said George Hyde Esquier and to his Posteritie that is to say, On a wreath Argent and Gules, a Lance or Horsemans staffe silver with a flagge or Cornett gules fringed argent, as more plainly appeareth depicted in the margent; Which Creast or Cognizaunce, I the said Clarencieulx King of Armes by power and authoritie vnto my Office attributed and annexed, doe by theis presentes confirme and warrant to the said George Hyde Esquier and to his posteritie with their due differences and he or they the same to vse, beare or shew forth, at his or their libertie and pleasure for evermore without any contradiccōn or controllment of any pson or psons whatsoever In witnes whereof I the King of Armes aforesaide have herevnto sett my hand and Seale of Office. Dated the Twoe and Twentieth day of November in the Three and ffortith yeare of the raigne of our Soveraigne Lady Elizabeth by the grace of God Quene of England ffraunce and Ireland defender of the ffayth &c: 1600.

WILL'M CAMDEN Clarenceux
Kinge of Armes.

Hyde, atte Hyde, of Denchworth.

MS. Rawl. D. 865, *fol.* 74.

Fragments in Ashmole's handwriting. Abstracts of the documents from which they are taken, with others, are printed in Clarke's Hundred of Wanting, pp. 97—103.
Some very early references to members of the family of Hyde of Denchworth will be found in the Berks Arch. Journ., vol. vii., 1901-2, p. 61.

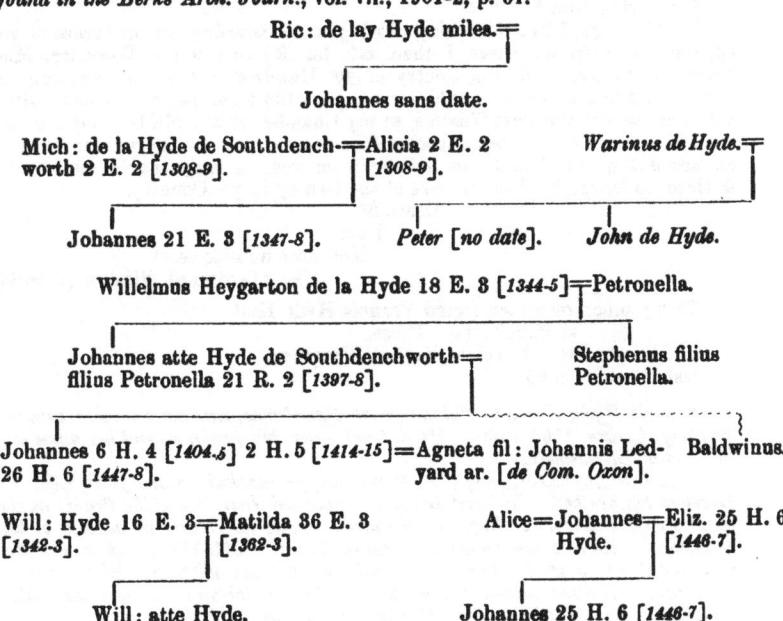

Hyde, of Kingston Lisle.

[*MS. Rawl. D. 865, fol. 148.*]

S^r

I doe not remember that I entred my Sister to you at Wantinge the 21th of this Moneth: Her name was Dorothy, shee maryed Henry Neuill of Bath-weeke in the County of Somerset (the Sonne of Henry the yongest brother to the Lord Abergaueny) by whome shee hath 3 Sonnes & 3 daughters: Henry, Edward, nowe a Barister of Graies-Inn; & Ralfe; & the Father & Mother are both dead.

Your reddy seruant
HUM: HYDE.

Kingston-Lisley:
    March: 23th 1664.

[*Addressed*] For Elyas Ashmole Esq.

Hyde, of Pangborn.

[*MS. Rawl. D. 865, fol. 221^b. Draft of Letter.*]

Swallowfield. 27 Mar. 1665.

My worthy freind

Although I heard nothing from you on Saterday last, in excuse of yor non appance at Redding, where I then sat, for Registring the Descente, Matches, Issues, & Armes, of all the Gentry of yor Hundred, yet being vnwilling that so auncient an acquaintance should want any civility I can pay him, I haue adjourned yor appance till the next Tearme, at my Chamber in the Midle Temple ou ag^t the Hall Court; where I shall expect either to see you, or otherwise to receiue such an account of yor Family, in writing from you, as may enable me to doe you & them no less right then the rest of the Gentry in yor Country.

Deare S^r
    I am
        Yo^r most humble serv^t
            E. A[SHMOLE] Windsor [*Herald*].

To my much respected freind Francis Hyde Esqr
    at Pangborne These.
The like to Rich: Lovelace Esqr at Wargrave.
Dat. 20 Apr: 1665.

Francis Hyde, Esqr., of Sulham, near Pangborne, was among those summoned to Reading Assizes, 1665-1666. He did not enter his pedigree, and his name is not in the List of Disclaimers.

RICHARD LOVELACE, Esqr, of Wargrave, is marked in the first List, Francis Lovelace his brother. Richard Lovelace is marked Just:[ice of the Peace] in the final list. Francis Lovelace, Esq., of Wargrave, made no return in answer to the first Summons. He was summoned to Reading Assises, 1665-1666, and in the final list is marked B^r to ye L. Lovelace, dwells at Kilham with Mr Rich: Lovelace at Wargrave. Neither names appear among the Disclaimers, nor did they enter their pedigree. John, Lord Lovelace, Hurley, appears in the first list, and drops out.

OF BERKSHIRE.

Hyde, of Wallingford.

Visitation of London, 1634-35, Harl. Soc., XV., p. 410. These Arms are evidently based on those of Hyde of Norbury, co. Chester. See Visit. 1580, Harl. Soc Vol. XVIII., p. 131.

Langborne.

John Hyde of Wallingford.=

| John Hyde of London descended from Wallingford co. Berks. | =Hellen da. of Thomas Sanderson of London Vintener. | =Sr James Altham one of the Barons of the Exchecqr 2 husband. |

| 1. John Hyde Grocer. | 2. Beniamyn & 3. Nathaniell Twynes. | Andrew Hyde of London Draper, aº 1633. | Margaret wife to Thomas Bancroft. | Elizabeth. — Jane. | Julian. — Sarah. |

ANDREW HYDE.

Joanes, of Welford.

MS. Ashmole 852, p. 101.

See Lord Mayors and Sheriffs of London 1601-1625, by G. E. Cokayne, Esq., 1897, p. 90, and N. & Q., 1901, vol. viii.

John Joanes of Ludstone, in the= Parish of Claverley in Com: Salop.

John Joanes of Claverley in Com: Salop.=

| Sr Francis Joanes [Alderman of Aldgate, Haberdashers' Company, purchased an estate at Welford], [Sheriff 1610-11], Lord Maior of London aº [1620-21]. | =Ellen, da: of .... bur. at St. Andrew's Undershaft 11 November 1606. |

See Jhones of Welford, Vol. I., p. 234.

Justice, of Reading.

Grant of Arms to MARY JUSTICE *of Reading, co. Berks, wife of John Yate of Lyford, gent.,* 20 *February* 1551, *by Thomas Hawley, Clarenceux. Extract from MS. College of Arms,* 2 H. 5, 84.

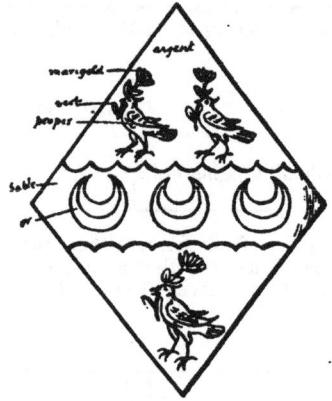

Mary Justice.

The Armes of Mary dowghter & heyer of William Justyce of Reding in the Counẽ of Barkẹ gentillwoman and at this p̄nte tyme wif to John Yates, gentleman of Lyvorde in the saide Counẽ. she bereth a lozenge silv̄ on a fesse engrailed sable thre Cressaunts golde betwene thre Turtle Doves in theire prop couler beked & membred geules holding in every beke a Marygolde stalked & leved vert as more plainly appereth here depicted. Yeven & graunted by me Thomas Hawley al̄s Clarenceux King of Armes the xx^t daye of februarye in the vth yere of the Reigne of o^r sov^{r}eyne Lorde Kinge Edward the vjth [*1551*].

Grant of Arms to MARIE JUSTICE *of Reading, wife of John Yate,* 1574, *by Robert Cooke, Clarenceux. MS. College of Arms, Vincent,* 161, 2.

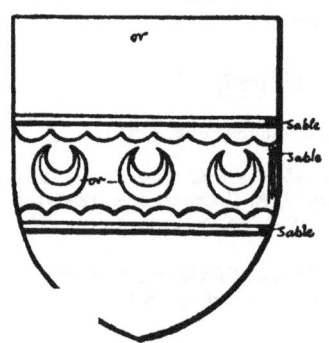

Marie d. & heire of Wm Justice of Readinge in barkshere, p Cõ [*Robert Cooke*] Clar̄ 1574, wyf to John Yate [*of Buckland*] [*See* Vol. I., pp. 60, 149].

Harl. MS. 1532, *fol.* 55, *gives these Arms with the note: Thomas Justice of Reading Clarke of the law,* 1526.

Kete or Keate.

MS. Ashm. 846, *fol.* 48. *Not in Ashmole's handwriting, but he has made some corrections. The dates are from Clarke's Hundred of Wanting.*

Willelmus Kete de Est Ilesley in Com : Berks duxit Mariam⹀ filiam .... condidit Testamentum 18° Aprilis 1524.

OF BERKSHIRE.

▲

Johannes Kete filius primogenitus obijt sine prole.

Willelmus Kete de Hagborne in Com :⊤....
Berks duxit filiam .... Angers.

Johannes Kete de⊤Franc: filia   Agneta nupta   Radulphus Kete⊤Anna filia
Checkington in | Petty ....   Edwardo Wal-   de Whaddon | ....
Com: Berks filius| de Com: dron de Al-   juxta Sarum in| Clarke de
et hæres [? Chet-| Oxon. de   borne in Com: Com: Wilts 2: | Ardington
kendon, Co. Oxon].| Tetsworth. Wilts: ob: sine   filius. | in Com:
                               prole. | Berks.

Johannes Kete filius et hæres duxit fil: Owini⊤
Oglethorp de Com: Oxon: Militis.

Leonardus=.... Filia et hæres Ricardi Moore   Johannes Kete 2 fil: duxit
Kete Filius   Militis et Magistri Cancellariæ. filiam .... Robartes de
et hæres.   Com: Essex.

Johannes Kete de Enedor in Co: Cornub:⊤   Willelmus Kete de Heldrop⊤
3: filius duxit fil .... Colquite de Com: | in Co: Wiltɛ: 2: filius.
Cornubiæ.

Willielmus filius primogenitus   Georgius 2ª Filius 20:   Edw: Kete Fil: et
æt: 22: annorum 1627.   annorum [1627].   hæres ætat 19:
                                                           annorum 1627.

Sepheronia fil⊤Radulphus Kete=Anna fil: Willelmi   Gilbertus Kete 4 filius⊤
.... Colman, | de Sᵗ Cullombe Arscott de Holles- duxit Johannam fil
Relicta Petri | in Co: Cornub: worthy in Co: Devon: [Nicholas Turbervile]
Bere vx: 2ª. | fil: primogeni- et Juliana fil: Wil- de Kirton [Crediton]
              | tus.   lelmi Hender vx: 1ª. in Com: Devon:

Gilbertus Kete 4: Fil: æt: Willelmus Kete filius   Susanna æt:
10 annorum 1627. [See   et hæres æt: 14   15, 1627.
Visit. Essex 1664—68.]   [1627].

Rebecca vxor   Elizabetha   Johannes Kete   Willelmus Kete   Radulphus Kete,
Georgij Bere   fil: 2ª.   2 filius, ætatis   Filius et hæres   3 Filius, ætat:
fil Petri Bere —   24: annorum   æt: 27: annorum   15: annorum
de E[rvin] in Anna   1627.   1627.   1627.
Com: Cornub: 3 filia.

Georgius   Hugo Kete de⊤   Edward Kete de Lock-⊤Johanna filia Johannis
Kete 4:   Hagborne in   aige [Lockinge] in Com: Doe de Com: Berks et
filius obijt Com: Berks   Berks 3 filius [b. 1539, Cohe: de Lockaige [Lock-
sine prole. 5 filius.   d. 1624].   inge] [mar. 1565: d.
                  B   C   1624].

VOL. II.

NOTES : VISITATIONS

B

- [*George Keate of Hagborne* (see p. 14)].
  — Hugo Kete filius et hæres.
- Joana Filia prima vxor Ricardi Southby postea nupta Tho: Pollington de Parva Stoke in Com: Oxoñ:
- Agneta 2: Filia nupta Thomæ Dolman de Childeray in Com: Berks.
- Christiana 3: fil: vx: Rob: Brent de Thrup in Com: Oxon: 2: vx: Tho: Chamberlaine de Odington Glouc:

C

- Elianora 4 fil: nupta Johanni Ascotte de Kings.. ire [? *Kingsclere*] in Com: South[t] [*Ascotte added by Ashmole*].

- Maria 5: Filia innupta.
  — Dorothea 6 filia vxor Capitani Hawkins.
- Edwardus Kete filius primogenitus et cœlebs 1627 [*born 1570*].
- Franciscus Kete 3 fil:=Francisca filia de Lockaige [*Lockinge*] in Com: Berks & Jurisperitus de Medio Templo 1627 [*d. 1649*].
- Francisca filia Johannis Hungerforde de Cadnam in Co: Wilte Armiger.
- Willelmus Kete 2: fil: ob sine prole [*born 1575*].

- Franciscus Kete filius 2[dus] [*died in France*].
- Edw: Kete filius primogenitus æt: 7: annorum 1627.
- 1. Elizabetha.
  — 2. Francisca.

Keate, of Hagborne.

Visitation of London 1633-35, Vol. XVII., p. 24, *Harl. Soc.*

Vide the Visitation of Berks.

Tower Street Ward.

William Keate of Hagborne=.... da. of
Com. Berks. |.... Angors.

- 1. John Keate of Chetington Co. Berks son & heire [*Checkendon in Com. Oxon?*].
- 2. Rafe Keate=Anne da. of of Whaddon John Clarke nigh Sarum of Arlington Co. Wilts. [*Ardinglon*] Com. Berks.
- 3. Edward Keate of Locking [*Co. Berks. See* Vol. I, p. 235].
- 4. George Keate [*obijt sine prole*].
  — 5. Hugh Keate of Hagborne.

OF BERKSHIRE.   163

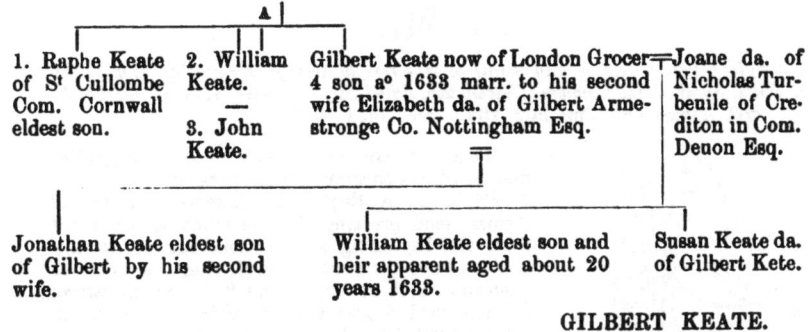

1. Raphe Keate of St Cullombe Com. Cornwall eldest son.

2. William Keate. —

3. John Keate.

Gilbert Keate now of London Grocer 4 son a° 1633 marr. to his second wife Elizabeth da. of Gilbert Armestronge Co. Nottingham Esq. = Joane da. of Nicholas Turbeuile of Crediton in Com. Deuon Esq.

Jonathan Keate eldest son of Gilbert by his second wife.

William Keate eldest son and heir apparent aged about 20 years 1633.

Susan Keate da. of Gilbert Kete.

GILBERT KEATE.

Keate, of Cholsey.

MS. Rawl. D. 865, *fol.* 116.

Sir,

My indispotion of body at p^rsent is such That I dare not take such a Jorney to waite on you, neither haue I bin soe farr from my habitation This 12 Months, The winter of old age haueing seissed on me being of 80: yeares & accompanied wth diuers Infirmities That make me altogeather vnfitt for trauile or to indure winter stormes. Notwthstanding I shall in some measure giue you an account of what Armes & Crest I beare, who am a younger Brother of the Eldest house of our family or name, yet cannot write my selfe of any place haueing neither land in this County nor house in other Besides I am all the male That are in being of my family & howe soone it may be extinct none knows, will you Therefore thinke it fitt as ye case stands for me to blase my Armes or seeke for any addition thereto, giue me leaue Thus farr only to informe you, That I Married into the family of The Roberte as may by my Seale hereto sett appeare to you Thus much from him That is

S^r

Your most reall freind & Seruant

To his power euer To serue you

Choulsey this 24 of March 1664.

JOHN KEATE.

If the weather be any thing milde I shalbe in London this Tearme & we shall further debate this busines.

[*Addressed*]   These ffor the Wor^{pll} Elias Ashmole Esqr
   att the vpper Shipp in Readinge p^rsent.

[*The seal is too worn to be made out. Ashmole has added the following in red ink:—*]

= John Keate. = This John Keate is son to John Keate of West Locking who disclaimed a° 1623.

Thomas Waller of Beoconsfield = Anne sole da: & heire.

Kemble.

Exemplification of Arms and grant of a Crest to George Kemble of Wydell in Com. Wilts, by William Camden, Clarenceux, dated 21 November 45th of Elizabeth, 1602. MS. Ashmole 858, pp. 202, 203. See Vol. I., p. 236.

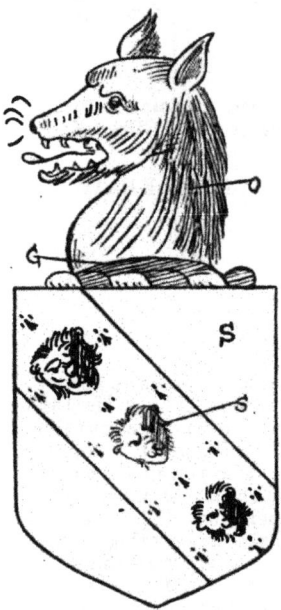

To all and singuler, as well Nobles and gentlemen as others to whome these presents shall come I Wm Camden Esqr alias Clarenceux King of Armes, send greeting, For as much as anciently from the beginning the virtuous acts of worthy persons have bene commended vnto the world & posterity, with sundry monum^{ts} & remembrances of their good deserts amonge which the chifest & most vsuall have been the bearing of signes in shields, called Armes, being evident demonstraĉons & tokens of prowes & valour diversly distributed according to Qualitees of the psons demeriting the same & whereas George Kemble of wydell in the County of wilts gentleman having of long tyme been one of the bearers of the auncient Armes, vizt sable on a bend Ermyne three Leopards heads of the first, and beying desirous to alter his former Creast, hath requested mee the saide Clarenceux King of Armes to assigne vnto him such a Creast as he may lawfully beare, In consideraĉon whereof & for the further declaraĉon of the worthinesse of the said George Kemble, I the s^d Clarenceux have given & granted him this Creast or Cognizance following vid: on a wreath of his Colours, a wolves head, trunked & imbrued or mantled Gules doubled Argent as more plainly in [*the*] Margent depicted appeares, which sayd Armes & Creast with every part & pcell thereof, I the said Clarenceux King of Armes do ratifie confirme & allow vnto the said George Kemble and to his posteritye for ever to have & to holde vse beare & enjoy without the lett impedim^t or interrupĉon of any pson or psons whatsoever, In witnesse whereof I have signed these p'sents with my hand & sett therevnto the seale of my Office dated the one and twentyeth day of Nov: in the 5. & 40: yeare of the reigne of o^r most gracious so^v Lady Eliz by the grace of God of England ffrance & Irland Queene Defender of the faith:

Anno salutis 1602.

Ex^d.

Kent, of Abington.

MS. Rawl. D. 865, folio 79^b. Ashmole's handwriting, prepared for the Visitation 1665-6, not included. No Arms. Marked not p^d.

{ Kintbury hund.

John Kent of the Devises in Com̃ Wiltẹ=.... da: to ....

Thomas Kent of the Devises=Margery da: to Tho: Hunt of Longstreet in
obijt a° 1656.   ▲ | the pish of Enford in Com̃ Wiltẹ.

OF BERKSHIRE.

```
                              ▲
2. William   1. Thomas Kent of Aving-══Alice da: to Alexan-   Anne wife to
   Kent.       ton in Coṁ Berkę æt: 39   der Cheeve of Bluns-   George Clementę
               annorum 23 Mar. 1664.     don in Coṁ Wiltę.      of Salisbury.

               1. John son & heire      2. Thomas.    1. Margery.
                  æt: 10 annorum 23       —
                  Mar: 1664.            3. William.   2. Frances.
```

THO: KENT. [*Original.*]

MS. Rawl. D. 865, *fol.* 224. *Draft of Letter.*

Mr Kent

I have made Search in the Office of Armes for that Coate wch you produced to me at Newbury & p̃tend to beare; but cannot find that you may lawfully beare either it or any Armes at all: And therefore I doe hereby giue you notice that if you do not sometyme in the next Tearme, come or send to me to my Chamber in the Midle Temple, & there make better proofe for the Coate of Armes you assume, I must in pursuance of the K^s Coṁ & duty of my place, ranke you with those who vsurpe Armes wthout iust title thereto, & at the next assises for the County of Berkę pclaime as well as record you to be noe Gentleman. In expectacōn therefore of hear^g frō you at the tyme aboues^d I rest

Yo^r humble servant
E. ASHMOLE, Windsor Herald.

Midle Temple, 28 May 1666.
To Mr Tho: Kent of Avington
    These.

The note in Ashmole's final List is: Intr: will pay 23 Mar: but did not. Mr Maior of Newbury & Mr Sand^{rs} can p'us his p'mise. Thomas Kent of Avington, is in the List of Disclaimers.

The Arms given to Kent in Harl. MS. 5189, *fol.* 51, *marked "ye coat & Crest Wiltsh," are, Azure a lion passant guardant Or, a chief ermine (marked "quere if not erminoise"). Crest: A lion's head erased, erminois, collared and lined and ringed Azure.*

Burke enters these Arms to Kent of Thatcham, and again to Berks and other counties, and states that it was granted by Richard St. George.

𝕶irton.

In the notes by Robert Dale, Richmond Herald, of Wiltshire Arms and descents the following occurs (*Wilts Arch. Soc.,* vol. ix., pp. 223, *etc.*):—

[*From*] Berkshire, 84, Kirton of Woton or Wooton, a younger brother from .... Arg., a fess and in chief a chevron gules. London [1568] 116, vide Middlesex.

Knight, of Reading, parish of St. Laurence.

MS. Rawl. D. 865, fol. 146.

Sir,
    I haue bynne severall tymes att yor chamber to have weited on you accordinge to my pmise but it was not my good fortune to finde you within. I shall bee ready to weite vpon [*you*] when & wher you please to appointe wth my Coate of armes & yor Fee wch I shall be readye to paye whensoever you please to command it & therfore I desire that I maye not bee recorded amongest the number of defalters. Soe wth my service psented I rest
                                            Yo^r servant to Com^d
                                                    W^A. KNIGHT.
22 Junij 1665
   Staple Inne.
[*Addressed*] To my honored freind Elias Ashmole Esqr theis psent.

In the List Walter Knight of the Parish of St. Laurence, Reading, is adj^d.
He did not enter his pedigree, and is not in the list of Disclaimers.
The pedigree of Knight in Harl. MS. 1139, p. 116^b, is of two generations, as below, from the Visitation of Hampshire 1634.
The Arms given are: Quarterly 1 and 4, Or, on a chief Sable three griffins segreant of the field; 2 and 3, per saltire Argent and checky Or and Sable [? intended for Bedwell]. Crest: on a ducal coronet Gules an eagle displayed Or.

John Knight of Newberie = Elizabeth da. of william Jackman ma: 2 Robt.
in Barkshire 1 husband. | Parys, & 3 S^r ffrancis dawtrey K^t.

John Knight 2 son of S^t [? Dennis]   Richard = Constance da: of John Mitchell of
in the Co. of Southam' gent.   Knight   Stammerham [co. Sussex].
                                         1 son.

Knight, of Ruscombe.

Argent, three palets Gules on a canton of the second, a spur, rowel downwards leathered Or, all within a bordure engrailed Sable [? *Azure*].

These Arms were confirmed to Richard Knight of St. Dennis In Hampshire in 1583, by Robert Cooke, Clarenceux (?), with the quarterings 2. Or, on a chief three griffins segreant of the field, [Knight]; 3. per saltire Ermine and checky, Or and Sable [? Bedwell]. Crest: on a ducal coronet Gules an eagle displayed Or. (Book of Grants, p. 2) (Le Neve's Knights, p. 214).
Confirmed (?) to Sir John Knight of Bristol, by Sir Edward Bysshe . . . . 1668. See Bysshe's Grants, fol. 21 [Coll. of Arms]. (Le Neve's Knights, pp. 175, 363.)

OF BERKSHIRE. 167

Langley, of York.

Visitation of Co. York, 1666, C. 40, p. 150, College of Arms.

He referreth himselfe to the visitation of Berkshire for proofe of these Armes.

Yorke Citty.   *Yorke, 19 Martij,* 1665.

Henry Langley of Hill end=.... in Com. Berks.
|
Thomas Langley of Clifton in Com. Oxon=....
|
William Langley of Aking-=.... daughter of John ton in com. Berks, died in Carryer of .... in aº ....   Com.....

Anne, daughter of=William Langley, M^r of Arts, some-=Priscilla, daughter of
Henry Langley of times of Pembroke Colledge in Ox- Henry Ayscough of y^e
Hill-end in Com. ford now residing in the City of Citty of Yorke 2^d wife.
Berks.1 Wife, obijt Yorke, ætatis 57 ann. 19º Martij,
sine prole.   Aº Domini 1665.

Certified by WILL^m LANGLEY.

I hereby certify that the above is correctly copied from the Records (C. 40, p. 150) in the Heralds' College. Witness my hand this 26th day of June, 1907.

EVERARD GREEN,
Rouge Dragon.

Langton, of Staneswick.

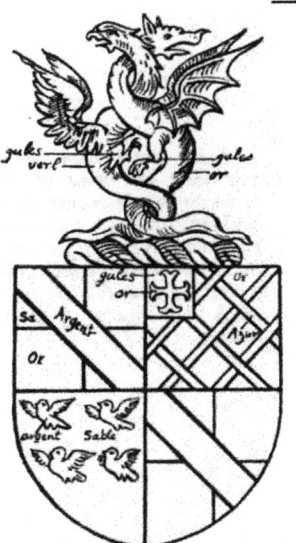

See Vol. I., p. 238, *William Langton is entered under Shrivenham. Stainswick is marked in the map of Berkshire in Camden's Britannia, by Gough,* 1806 (i., p. 213), *as a hamlet a little south of Shrivenham.*

The annexed trick of the Arms is from the Visitation of Lincolnshire, 1634, *MS. College of Arms, C.* 23. *The Crest may be compared with that given in the Visitation of Berks.*

1 and 4. *LANGTON.* 2. *MUMBY.*
3. *MEWTER.*

NOTES: VISITATIONS

Lawrence, of Chilton.

MS. Rawl. D. 865, folio 77, in Ashmole's handwriting. Original paper for the Visitation 1665-66, but not included. No Arms. Marked gratis.

Compton hund.

Gyles Laurence Chanon of Christchurch in=Katherine da: to
Oxford & Greeke pfessor there 40 yeares. | .... Parsons.

Eliz: da: to .... Berry=Thomas Laurence fellow of=Blanch da: to Roger Parry
of Culham first wife. | Madgelen Coll: in Oxford. | of Poston in Coṁ Heref:

1. Gyles.   3. Edward.   Thomas Lawrence Rector of=Alice da: to Robert Hut-
— | Chilton in Coṁ Berkẹ æt: 48 | chins of West hendred
2. John. | an: 14 Mar: 1664. | in Coṁ Berkẹ.

1. Thomas æt: 4 annorum 14 Mar: 1664.   Edward.   Alice.

THOMAS LAWRENCE. [*Original.*]

Leder.

These Arms have found their way into some of the Armories as belonging to a Berkshire family. I have not found any authority for this: the Arms appear in MS. Coll. of Arms, L. 10, fol. 99, from which the annexed trick is taken.

Lenthall, of Bessils Leigh.

MS. Rawl. D. 865, fol. 220. Draft of Letter.

Sr

When yor servt came to me to Abingdon (in March last) to enter yor descent & Armes, he could not sufficiently informe me of yor Mothers name & family, or how I might be iustified if I should enter you by the Tytle of an Esqr & being loath to omitt the entry of any thing in the Visitacōn Booke that may tend to the honor of you or any othr gent: of the Country, I desire you will please to satisfie me in both these pticulars, sometyme the next Tearme, before the Booke be deliued in the Office of Armes: Besides I then acquainted yor servt wth a fee due to me for such entry, wch I haue not yet recd but desire you'll please to send it to Mr Harte at the new Inn at Abingdon, & he will safely convey it to me.

     Sr
   I am
    Yor most humble servt
     E. A[shmole], W[indsor] Herald.

Midle Temple 6 May 1665.
To John Lenthall Esq at Besselsleigh in Berke.

Lenthall, of Bessels Leigh.

MS. Rawl. D. 865, folio 90, in Ashmole's handwriting. Prepared for the Visitation 1665-6. Not included. No Arms given. Marked not pd.

Hormer Hund.

Mary da: & one of the Coheires to Sr William Ashcombe of Alscott im Cōm Oxon first wife.	John Lenthall of Besselsleigh.	Mary da: to James Blewet of Greenham in Cōm Somrst the relict of Sr James Stoñehouse Kt second wife.
William dyed young.	William son & heire æt: 4 annorum 16 Mar: 1664.	Elizabeth æt: 2 annorum 16 Mar. 1664.

SIMON BRIDGES for my Mr JOHN LENTHALL. [*Original.*]

Lenthall, of Besselsleigh.

MS. Rawl. D. 866, fol. 75. In the writing of Peter le Neve. Some additions from Le Neve's Knights, Harl. Soc., Vol. VIII., p. 324.

William Lenthall of Lachford in the County of Oxford. = Frances daughter of Thomas Southwell of St Faiths in Norfolk, esqr.

A

3. Thomas =Anne dr of | Sr John Lenthall=Bridget dr | William Lent-=Elizabeth
Lenthall of | George | Kt of Creslow *and* | of Sr Tho: | hall of Lin- | dr of Am-
London | Molle of | Blechington & | Temple of | colns Inne & | brose
merchant | Culworth | Hasley in Oxford- | Stow in | of Burford in | Evans of
see C: 24 | in North- | shire Knight, | Bucking- | Oxfordshire | Loding-
fo: 28 B. | tonshire. | *Keeper of Kings* | hamshire | esqr of the | ton in
lived AD | | *Bench prison: he* | Kt and | house of | North-
1634. | | *dyed in his house* | Bart *and* | Comons in the | tonshire
| | *in Southwark* 20 | *sister to* Sr | late times, | esqr dyed
Anne mar. to .... faunt | *day of Octob:* 1668 | *Peter Tem-* | dyed 3d of Sep- | 19 of
of Woodford in Essex. | *buried at* .... | *ple.* | tember 1662, | Aprill
| *Oxon.* | | buried at Bur- | 1661
William Lenthall lived | | | ford. | [? 1662]
at Woodford in Essex. | | | | bur. at
| | | | burford.

James=2. Kath. | Sr John Lenthall of=Mary dr of .... | 2. William
Hamil- | (qre Cath.) | Besiles Ley in Berk- | Blewet *of Holcombe,* | Lenthall.
ton | dr of Sr | shire Kted 10 of | *Devon* relict of Sr | —
Lord | Jo. Lent- | March 1677, dyed | *James* Stonehouse | 1. Frances.
Pays- | hall. | there & bur 9 Nov: | of *Ambersden hall* | —
ley of | | 1681 [*æt.* 9 annor' | *in Essex & buried at* | 2. Katerine.
Scotld. | | 1634 *Visit. of Oxford-* | *Besils Lee.* |
| | *shire*]. | |

Catherine dr of James Hamilton=William Lenthall *of Besiles Lee aforesd* esqr
Lord Paysley .... remared to   dyed at Burford & buried there *by his grand-*
Charles Earle of Abercorne.   *father* 5 Sept. 1686, *aged* 27.

John Lenthall esqr liveing 1701.   2. *James Lenthall.*

Will Moor of=3. .... | .... mar. to ....= | .... mar. to Lytcotte who=
.... in Sur- | dr .... | Wyld bore by whom | was captain in Scotland in
rey esqr. | | .... Wyld[*bore*]. | the troublesome times q.

John [*Wildbore*].   q. Sr John Lytcotte in france.=
                                                          人

William Lenthall esqr | Henry Gilborne (husband=Anne [*erased and* Elizt. 1 w.
of Hasley &c. and of | of Anne) of Woolwich in | *written over*] sister of Wiltm
the Kings bench in | Kent esqr called Collonell | Lenthall died .. day of ....
Surry, dyed vnmaried | Gilborne dyed at Chisel- | AD .... buried at 2d
.... day of .... AD | hurst in Kent buried .... | wife Anne dr of John Polley of
.... buried at .... | day of .... in St Georges | Shoreham & Preston, Kent, no
| Church Southwark. | child.

B

OF BERKSHIRE. 171

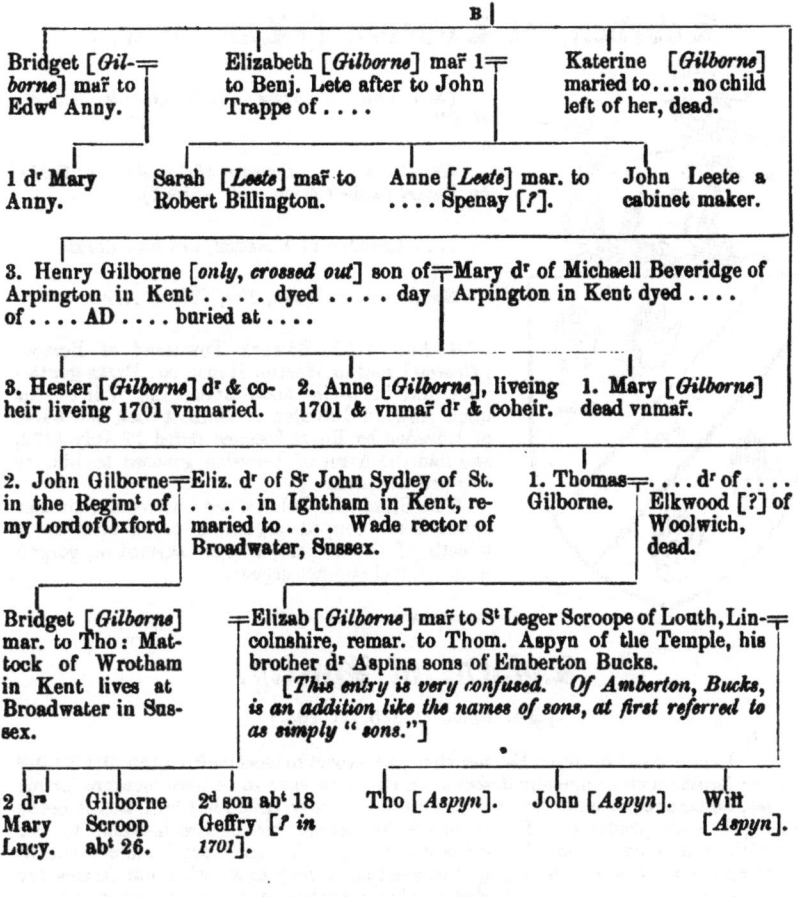

Loveday.

MS. Rawl. D. 865, *fol.* 74. *In Ashmole's handwriting.*

Johannes Loveday.=....

Johannes Loveday 1 E. 3 [*1327-8*].=Sarah 5 Ed. 3 vidua [*1331-2*].

Johannes Shelford 6. R. 2=Eliz: fil. & heres 6 R. 2   Johannes Loveday 23 E. 3
[*1382-3*].   [*1382-3*].   [*1349-50*].

Loveden, of Loveden [? Lamborne.]

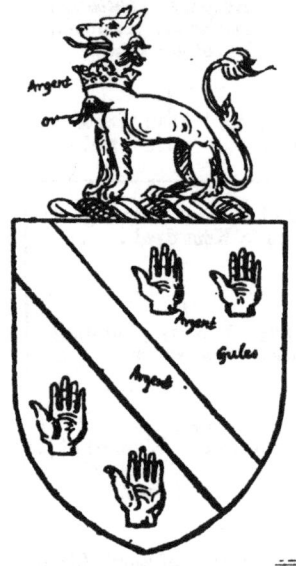

(*MS. Coll. of Arms, Cook's Grants, E.D.N., B.* 82b.)

Granted to .... Loveden of Loveden, co. Berks, by Robert Cooke Clarenceux, (1589 ?).

.... Loveden of Loveden, in Com. Berks.

See *Grants*, vol. xii., 209, *Coll. of Arms.*

1 Aug. 1772, Edward Townsend of Burscot [*Buscott*], and of Weston House, co: Berks gentleman and his heirs male under the Will of his uncle Edward Loveden of Burscot took the name of Loveden by Royal Licence dated 17 July 1772, and had the Arms of Loveden granted to him as Edward Loveden.

The Blazon is, Gules, a bend between 4 sinister hands erect couped argent, & for a crest on a wreath of the colours, a tyger sejeant or, gorged with a ducal coronet argent.

Lyford, of Hurley.

.[*MS. Rawl. D.* 865, *fol.* 108.]

Sir
    I vnderstand by John Heynes that you expect to receaue from mee 01^l 07^s 06^d for my Brothers enteringe our descent, which I conceaue to be hard measure for me to pay, he beinge the elder Brother and had the larger estate left him, had it beene managed with prudence. If his estate be lessned his charge is small to bee maintein'd in comparison of mine which is eight for one: but I am content to beare an equall sheare with him in this, soe that I may know what our Armes are which is vnknowne to mee at psent: this I shalbe ready to pay when, and to whome, you shall appoint, which will (I hope) giue you satisfaction, from him, who is
                Sir
          Your frend and Seruant to cõmand
Rushdeanes   JOHN LYFORD.
June the 12th 65.

[*Addressed*] These For the Hon^{red} Elias Ashmole,
             Esqr.

[*MS. Rawl. D.* 865, *fol.* 107.]

S^r
    I haueing so conuenient a Messinger to send by as the bareor hereof Richard Collebery wch has bine formerly my saruant for many yeares I made bould to send to yo^w for the 13^s 9^d wch I humbly thanke yo^w for the gayneinge of it from my brother John Lyford, but I forgot to aske yo^w what I must say to my brother Lyford which yo^w had of mee, & if he should aske mee that question when I goe ouer to them, & if he should aske me what Armes we doe giue yo^w cannott for

the p̃sent resolue vs because that for the p̃sent yo͏ͧʷ cannott finde any : I haue heare sent yo͏ͧʷ the greatest Light that I canne for the p̃sent find ought w͏ᶜʰ M͏ʳ Wilkeson did giue mee w͏ᶜʰ I forgott to showe yo͏ͧʷ att my house ; if yo͏ͧʷ canne by this, or any other meanes finde ought what Armes wee doe giue, or wheather wee maye giue any : I knowe that my brother John Lyford will bee willinge to Joyne with mee to pay yo͏ͧʷ for itt : if yo͏ͧʷ canne doe vs any good hearin if yo͏ͧʷ will be pleased to send at any time by Richard Seward my Carrier & directe it for M͏ʳ Thomas Lyford the Elder of Knowlehill to be Left at one William Kildalls for mee, where Seward Leaues me a booke euery weecke of newes I shall haue it safe & I shall euer Remayne

S͏ʳ yo͏ͧʳ most obleadged sarnant to Command

THOMAS : LYFORD senio͏ʳ.

Knowlehill in p̃ish of Hurley 7° March [16]65.

[*Addressed*]   For his Much honored Freind Elias Ashmole Esquire
at the Vpper Shippe in Readinge this present.

[*The red wax seal bears a lion rampant, within an eight-sided border line.*]

MS. Rawl. D. 865, *fol.* 105. *Fol.* 104 *is a short account of the pedigree. All the additions it contains are here given in italics ; those from fol.* 106, *another account, are printed in italics within square brackets.*

Thomas Lyford o͏ʳ Great Grandfather had 6 sonnes : hee Liued in his latter dayes in Stanford Dingely p̃ish at the farme but hee had the Mannour of Peasemo͏ʳ & Aduouson [*of Peasemore*] of Catmer & sume Meanes in p̃ish of Buckelbury.

1. Was John our grãdfather And then Richard, Thomas, William, Leonard, and Sebastion.

1. Johns first wife was Joane Winchcombe, by hir he had but one dafter, w͏ᶜʰ one Littelfeild Married.

2. His second wife was Anne Sladd [*Sledd*] by whome hee had John, Thomas, Richard, Daniell, and Nathaniell.

3. His third wife was the Widdow Hopkins, by hur he had : Franncis, Aurthur, William, & John these ware all the sonnes.

Richard [*w͏ᶜʰ Liued at Rushdeanes,*] the Third sonne of John had three Sonnes : *1.* Richard [*my Elder Brother w͏ᶜʰ Liues now at Rushdeanes*], *2.* Thomas [*w͏ᶜʰ is my selfe*], and *3.* John, w͏ᶜʰ is our descent : the other before dyed Childelesse [*and theare are 2 Daughters Lieuinge, Anne & Margreat*].

2. Richard Sonne of Thomas the̲lder had Richard, Thomas, John, William, Sebastion, & Samuell.

3. Thomas sonne of Thomas the̲lder had one sonne Thomas w͏ᶜʰ was o͏ʳ Cozen Clarke father.

4. William, sonne of Thomas the̲lder had William, Edward, Bernhard, & Richard.

Richard Lyford my father Married w͏ᵗʰ one Joane Sheperey dafter of Robert Sheprue, Late of East Hanney & had three sonnes & 2 dafters : Anne, Richard, Thomas, Margreatt & John.

1. [*My Elder Brother*] Richard the eldest sonne Married w͏ᵗʰ one Mary Castell dafter of Thomas Castell of Hendred, And he had but one dafter, Mary, w͏ᶜʰ is now Married to one M͏ʳ Thomas Coward *parson of Buckelbury Parish in Berks* [*w͏ᶜʰ was S͏ʳ Henrey Winchcombes Tutor*].

2. Thomas the second sonne of Richard Married w͏ᵗʰ one Mary Jacobb dafter of William Jacobb of Readinge & had one sonne & one dafter, Thomas, and Mary.

3. John the Third sonne of Richard, Married w͏ᵗʰ one Mary Allworth dafter of Gyles Allworth of Wroton [*Wroughton*] in the County of Wilks : he had 4 sonnes 4 dafters John, Gyles, Henrey, & Richard : Anne, Mary, Susane, & . . . .

1. Anne o^r sister Married wth one Thomas Whistler & had one dafter, hir Name is Anne.
2. Margarett o^r sister Married wth one Adam Jourdin of Poughefely & has 3 sonnes, & one dafter Elizabeth.

Folio 106 contains the following at the end :—

Mr Thomas Wilkeson the Minister of Lawrence Waltham has giuen mee this accounte heare vnder written & hee had it att Coronall Rich: Neuells at Billingebeare in Dr Tho: Fullers Booke wch is theare wch giues the accounte of Many Moore gen^t in our sheire besides o^r famely that was then psented to the Kinge: as Mr Tho: Wilkeson haue toulde mee since yo^w ware at my house a Munday Last : & that those armes wch I shew'd vnto yo^w at Maydenhead are the Lyfords:

Dr Thomas Fuller in his Booke saith that Thomas Lyford in the year 1433 : In Henry the 6 time Was Signifyed to the Kinge a gentleman amongest Many others in the County of Berks :*

Lytcott.

College of Arms, K. 9, fol. 237 ; Visitation of London, 1687—1700 ; with the additions in italics, this pedigree contains all the information given in MS. Ashm., Lydcott of Rushcombe (852, p. 109).

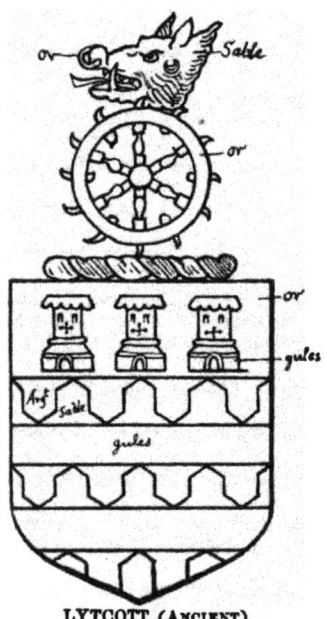

LYTCOTT (ANCIENT).

[*MS. Ashm.* 852, p. 109, *gives these Arms quartering Burley: Antiqua.*]

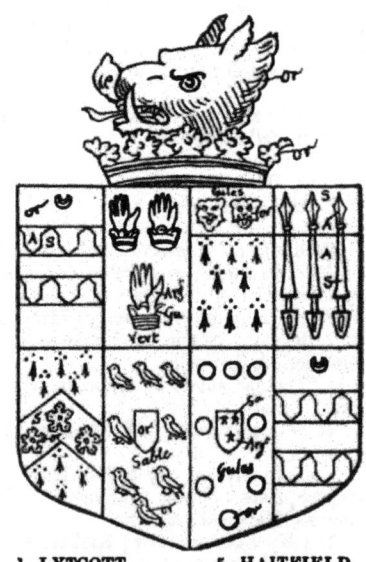

1. LYTCOTT.
2. WOLVERTON.
3. FIFIELD.
4. BURLEY.
5. HAITFIELD.
6. GENNEY.
7. HUNKES.
8. LYTCOTT.

[*MS. Ashm.* 852, p. 109, *gives these Arms, omitting Hunckes.*]

* In the list of the names of gentry of this County, returned by the Commissioners in the twelfth year of King Henry the Sixth, 1433 (*Fuller's Worthies of England*, ed. 1811, by John Nichols, F.A.S., vol. i., p. 96).

OF BERKSHIRE.

William Lytcott of Lytcott in Com. Bucks=Elizabeth daūr and Coheir
Esq[r] Grandson and heir of John Lytcott | of Nicholas Wolverton
of Lytcott Esq[r]. | Esq[r].

John Lytcott of Lytcott aforesaid Esq[r]=Agnes daughter of Henry
son and heir. | Rouse of . . . .

William Lytcott of Lytcott Esq[r] son=Bridget daughter and sole heir of William
and heir of John. | Fifeild Esq[r].

John Lytcott of Ruscomb and=Alice daughter and sole heir of Henry Burley of
Twyford in Comit. Berks Esq[r]. | Wokingham in Com̄ Berks Esq[r].

Roger Lytcott of Ruscoomb and Twyford=Julian daughter of John | Anne wife
Esq[r] Marshall of the Hall to King | Barker of Sunning in | of Robert
Hen: 7th. | Com̄ Berks Esq[r]. | Vaughan.

Christopher Lytcott Esq[r] gent. Pensioner=Catherine daūr of | 2. John Lytcott
to King Hen. 8th and Train Bearer to | S[r] Robert Cheney | 2[d] son.
Queen Anne Bullen Dyed 6 Dec: 1554 | of Chesham Boys | —
Buried at Swallowfeild. [*Of Ruscombe,* | in Com̄ Bucks | 3. William Lytcott
in Com. Berks, esquire. MS. *Ashm.* 852, | Kn̄t. | 3[d] son.
p. 109.]

Jane widow of=S[r] Christopher Lytcott Kn̄t 3[d] son,=Catherine daughter of Wil-
Thomas Essex | twice High Sheriff of Berkshire | liam Barker of Sunning in
of Becket | Knighted in the Camp before Roan | Com̄ Berks Esq[r] widow of
House in Com̄ | by King Hen. 4th of France 16 | William Young of Bastle-
Berks Esq[r]. | Nov: 1591, he died without Issue | don Esqr she dyed 17 Jan:
1. wife. | at Bastledon 25 April A[o] 1599 | 1630 æt. 70 ann:
| buried at Hanny. |

1. John Lytcott=Ursula daūr | 2. Leonard Lyt-=Frances daūr | Dorothy wife
Esq[r] son and heir | and heir of | cott of Checken- | of John Petty | of S[r] Christo-
gentleman Pen- | John Hunkes | don in Com̄ Oxon. | of Tetsworth | pher Edmonds
sioner to Qu: Eli- | of Rodbroke | 2[d] son gent Pen- | in Com̄ Oxen | of Lewknor in
zabeth [*of Rus-* | Esq[r] [*John* | sioner to Queen | Esq[r]. | Com̄ Oxōn,
combe in Com. | *Dunch. MS.* | Elizabeth [*1574*]. | | Kn̄t.
Berks Esquire. | *Ashm.* 852, | | |
MS. Ashm. 852, | p. 109]. | | |
p. 109].

4. Richard Lytcott of=Judith daur. | Mary wife | Mary daughter and sole
Woodburcot in Com̄ | of Anthony | of Richard | heir wife of Robert Writhe
Northton 4th son A[o] | Gate of . . . . | Barker of | [*vz: Rob[t] Rich Esquire.*
1618 had issue 4 sons. | Oxfordshire. | Anstey in | *MS. Ashm.* 852, p. 109.]
| | Com̄ Warf. |

NOTES: VISITATIONS

| A |

2. [Sʳ] John Lytcott of Moul-═**Mary daūr of Sʳ** | **1. Christopher** [*of Ruscombe in com. Berks, Esqʳ. MS. Ashm. 852, p. 109*]. | **3. Jerome** dyed without issue.
sey in Com̃ Surrey Kñt 2ᵈ son | Nicholas and
Gentⁿ Pensioner to King James | sister of Sʳ Thomas Overbury
the First. | Kñt.

1. Robert Lytcott Esqʳ eldest son married Eleanor daughter of .... of Staffordshire. ═

2. John Lytcott 2ᵈ son dyed a Batchellor.

3. Nicholas Lytcott 3ᵈ son married .... daughter & heir of Sʳ Henry Hunkes Kñt sometime Governour of Antigua but dyed sans issue.

John Lytcott of Wrinehill in Com: Staff.═.... daūr of ....
Esqʳ only surviving son.

Severall other children all dead sans issue.

Charles Lytcott Esqʳ only child living Aº 1694-5.

4. Thomas.
—
5. Richard.
—
6. Thomas.
—
7. Charles.
—
8. Christopher.
all dyed unmarried.

9. Gyles Lytcott, Esqʳ 9ᵗʰ and youngest═**Sarah** daughter and heir of Richard Culling of the City of Exōn merchant of the family of Cullings of Woodland in Com̃ Devon, she is yet living Aº 1694-5.
son was the First Comptroller General of the Customs by Patent under the Great Seal dated 6 Nov: Aº 23 Car. 2. and confirmed by another Patᵗ from K. James 2. dated 17 Aug. Aº 1 Jac. 2. as likewise by another Pat. dated 31 May Aº I. Gul. et Mariæ. He is living Aº 1694-5.

1. Giles Lytcott eldest son dyed in the East Indies unmarried.

3. Richard and
4. Culling died infants.

5. Richard Lytcott 5ᵗʰ and youngest son now living Aº 1694-5.

2. John Lytcott 2ᵈ son now Commander of his Maᵗⁱᵉˢ Ship the Saphire Aº 1694-5, cœlebs.

1. Mary married to Laurence Peacock son of .... Peacock of Battersea in Com̃ Surrey.

2. Elizabeth married to George Turvile Gent. of the Family of the Turvills of Thurleston in Com̃ Leicester.

3. Sarah married to Major Nathaniel Long descended by his Fathers side from the Longs of Draycot and by his Mothers side from the Longs of Wraxal both in Com̃ Wilts.

1. Dorothy married to John Offley of Madeley in Com̃ Staff: Esq.

2. Mary married to Thomas Lamb merchᵗ of London mother of Dʳ John Lamb Dean of Ely.

3. Anne married to John Thurloe Esqʳ Secretary to Oliver Cromwell.

4. Jane married to John Upton Esqʳ one of the Comʳˢ of the Customes.

5. Ursula first married to George Clarke of London Esqʳ afterwards to John Upton of Lupton in Com̃ Devon, Esqʳ.

[Signed] G. LYTCOTT.

OF BERKSHIRE.

Lyttell, of Bray.

Harl. MS. 1532, 138^b, gives the Arms, Per chevron Argent and Sable, in chief two fleurs-de-lis, and in base a tower triple towered, all counterchanged.
Crest, "a pigorgs hed" erased Sable bearded Or, maned Argent and Gold, ducally gorged Silver.

THOMAS LYTTELL of Bray p. Clarenceux Garter.

These Arms are found on the Brass of Thomas Lyttell of Bray, who died in 1567.

Marshall, of Blewbury.

Add. MS. 14,283, fol. 72, gives the arms: Or, four bars Sable, in chief a chess-rook between two mullets of the last.
Burke describes the arms as two bars gemelles, and adds: Crest, a griffin's head erased Or, charged on the neck with a chess-rook between two mullets Sable.

Maryett, of Remenham.

Harl. MS. 1172, *fol.* 7.

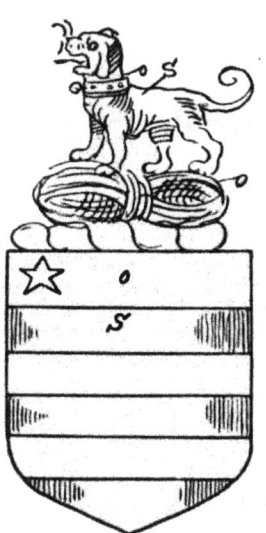

Exemplification of Arms and Grant of a Crest to Thomas Maryet of Remenham by Robert Cooke, Clarenceux, 16th of June 1586.
The Crest is wrongly drawn, the hound being collared and lined, the single line under his feet. I have therefore substituted the trick from a MS. collection of Arms.

To all and singular aswell Nobles and gentilz as others to whome these presents shall come be seene heard, read or Vnderstood Robert Cooke Esqr alias Clarencieulx King of Armes and principall Heralde of the East, West and South ptes of this Realme of England sendith greeting in o^r Lord god eurlasting. Whereas aunciently from the beginning the Vertuous acts of worthey persons haue been commended to ye world with sondry monumentes and rememberances of there good deseartes. Emongest the which the chiefest and most vsuall hath ben the bearing of signes and tokens in sheldes called Armes being euident demonstracõns and testimonies of prowes and Valoir diuersly distributed according to the qualities and deseartes of the persons meritinge the same, Which Order as it was prudiently deuised to stirre vp and enflame the hartes of men to the imitation of Vertue, Euen soe hathe the same ben continued from tyme to tyme and yett is continually obserued to the entent that such as haue done comendable seruice to thejr Prince or Contrey either in Warre or peace may therfore receaue due honor in their lyues and alsoe deriue the same successiuely to their posterity for euer And being required of Thomas Maryet of Remneham in the County of Berks Esquire to make search in the Regester and Recordes of myne Office for the Aunctent Armes belonging vnto that name and famely whereof the Records of myne Office do proue he is descended. I haue att his request made search accordingly and finding the same in yᵉ auncient Recordes of myne Office I could not without great Iniurye assigne vnto him any other Armes then those wᶜʰ are lawfully vnto him descended from his Auncestorˢ, That is to say Barrey of sixe Golde and Sables, And for asmuch as I finde noe Creast vnto the same (as comonly to all auncient Armes there belongith none) I haue giuen and allowed vnto him by way of encrease for his Creast or Cognizance vpon yᵉ healme on a wreath Gold and Sables, a Hound Sables standing on a Lyme & his Coller gold, mantled Gules doubled Argent, as more plainely appeareth depicted in yᵉ margent heereof, Which Armes and Creast I the said Clarencieulx Kinge of Armes by power and auctoretie to myne Office annexed and graunted by Letters Patentes vnder the great seale of England haue ratefied, confirmed assigned, giuen and graunted vnto yᵉ said Thomas Maryett Esquire & to all his posterety with their dewe differences, the same to vse, beare, enioy and shewe forthe att all times and for euer hereafter according to yᵉ auncient Lawes of Armes without yᵉ impedimᵗ lett or interrupčon of any pson or psons, In witnesse whereof, I the saide Clarencieulx Kinge of Armes haue hereunto subscribed my name and thereto putt the Seale of myne Office, the xviᵗʰ day of June in the yere of our Lord god 1586 and in the xxviijᵗʰ yere of yᵉ raigne of our most gracious soueraigne Lady Queene Elizabeth &c.

Robᵗ Cooke Alias Clarencieulx
Roy Darmes.

Mayott, of Abingdon.

MS. Rawl. D. 865, fol. 220 ; Draft of Letter.

Mʳ Mayott

You pmised before seu]all of yoʳ neighbours to send me my fee for entring of yoʳ descent the morning before I went from Abingdon, but you were not so good as yoʳ word: nor have I heard from you since. Pray let me not be put to the trouble of writˢ againe about it, lest any Inconvenience arise from yoʳ refusall.

Yoʳ lovᵉ freind
E. A[shmole] W[indsor] H[erald].

Midle Temple 6 May [16]65.
To Mʳ John Mayott at Abingdon.

The Fee was no doubt paid, as the pedigree is included in the Visitation.

There was another family of Mayott of Abingdon: they bore for Arms, Barry of six, in chief a lion passant guardant.

Michell, of Old Windsor.

Exemplification of Arms, and Grant of a Crest to Humfrey Michell of Old Windsor, Co. Berks, by William Flower Norroy, dated the 7th of April, 1581. MS. College of Arms.

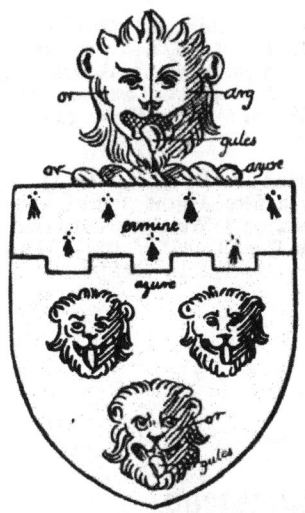

To all and singuler etc. Willm fflower Esquire ais Norroy principall herald and Kinge of Armes of the East West and North partes of this realme of England from the ryver of Trent Northward Sendeth greeting etc. Wheras ancyently from the beginninge etc. Amongest the which nomber Humfrey Michell of Old Wyndesore in Berkshire Esquire, being descended from the family of his surname in the countie of Yorke which of longe tyme have ben berars of those tokens of honō. and yet not knowenge any Creast or Cognoysance properly to belonge unto the auncyent Armes (as unto meny ancyent Armes ther be none) have requyred me the sayd Norroy Kinge of Armes to assigne unto his said ancyent Armes a Cognoysance meete and lawfull to be boren without preiudice or offence to any other person. In consyderation whereof, for a further declaration of the worthynesse of the sayd Humfrey Michell and at his request, I the sayd Norroy Kinge of Armes by power and authoritie to me comitted by letters patentes undr the greate seale of England, have assigned gyven and graunted unto the sayd Humfrey Michell to the ancyent Armes of his family and surname beinge Azure three leopardes heddes caboched gold langued gules, a chief embateled ermyn : and for the Creast upon the healme on a Torce gold and asure, a leopardes hedde caboched party per pale gold and argent : mantelled azure doubled Argent : as more playnly appereth depicted in the margine herof. Which Armes and Creast etc. He & they the same to have hold etc. In witnesse wherof I the said Norroy Kinge of Armes have herunto subscrybed my name and sette to the seale of myne Office the vii[th] day of Aprill In the yere of our lord god 1581, and in the xxiii[th] Yere of the reigne of our most gracious soueigne Lady queene Elizabeth etc.

The Abstracts of the Patents to this Humfrey Michell granting the offices of Clerk of the Constable or of the Works of Windsor Castle, and of Steward 16th of May 11 Eliz. [1569], are found in MS. Ashmole 1115, fol. 33, &c.

In N. & Q., IXth Series, 1901, vol. vii., p. 145, it is stated that the above Arms were in substitution of the ancient arms of his family (three escallops) borne by Sir John Michell of Yorkshire and Berkshire (1424), his immediate ancestor.

Mills, of Knightington.

Books of Grants, also Add. MS. 4961, p. 94ᵇ. Patent of Arms by Robert Cooke, Clarenceux, to Richard Mylls of Knightington in Barkshire p Rougecross 1588. [? *Knighton, Compton Beauchamp.* Some *MSS.* give the place *Kenstington.*]

Ermine, a Millrind [*Sable*] a Chief Or, Q'ring .... (viz.) vᵗ on a ffess Argent 3 dex: hands appalm'd G. Crest, on a Wreath a Lion rampᵗ Or in his Mouth a Hand Gules [*cf. Mylles, Visit. London* 1568, *Harl. Soc.,* Vol. I., p. 11].

Morland, of Sulhamstead.

Visitation of London, 1687—1700, *College of Arms,* K. 9, *fol.* 261.

Mr Martin Morland nephew to Sr Samˡ exhibited the Arms here described, graved on a Silver Tobacco Box, wᶜʰ Arms were given to his Father as his Coat by Sr Samˡ Morland his brother, as he alledged. See the Vis: of Middlesex Aº 1663, per Riley and Dethick, fo. 56, 57. As to the Ped: he referred to Berks and Middx. but no Entry to be found in those Counties besides the Augmentation granted to his Uncle Sr Samˡ Morland entered in ye forementioned County of Middx.

[*The Grant of the Augmentation in French by Sir Edward Walker Garter to Sir Samuel Morland (alias Morley), Knt. and Bart., and one of the Gentlemen in Ordinary of the Privy Chamber,* 12 *Aug.,* 1661, *is given at length in* D. 17, *Visit. of Middlesex,* 1623. *In the dexter chief point, a lion passant guardant Or; his paternal Arms borne by the Ancient Family of Morley, Sable a leopard's head jessant dé lis Or. Crest: a like leopard's head between two wings Argent.*]

OF BERKSHIRE. 181

[Rev. Thomas] Morland [B.A. Camb., Rector of Bright Waltham 1615, and 1625 Rector of] Minister of Sullamstead in Com. Berks.

Sr Samuel Morland Knt and Baronet eldest son. [See "Complete Baronetage," vol. iii., p. 89.]

Martin Morland of Sullamstead aforesaid and late of Hackney in Com. Middx. ob. 13º Junij. 1685 ætat 60 anº. = Lidia dar of Samuel Lee Citizen and Haberdasher of London.

Benjamin Morland of Hitchin in Com. Hertford, ætat 30 añ 1687. = Elizabeth dar of .... Crettenden of Hackney.

Martin Morland Citizen and Haberdashr of London ætat. 27 añ. Cœlebs.

Samuel ætat 21, añ Cœlebs. — Joseph ætat 18 añ 1687.

Lidia ætat 15 añ. 1687.

Sarah ætat 2 añ 1687.   Lidya ætat 2 mens.

[Signed] MARTIN MORLAND.

Nevill, of Billingbere.

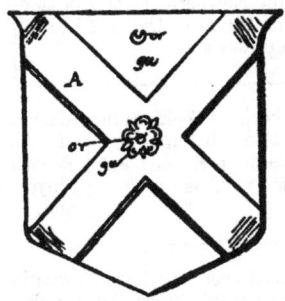

MS. Ashmole 852, p. 135.

George Nevill Lord Aburgeney obijt 1492. = Margarett da: and heire to Sr Hugh Fenne Vnder Treasurer of England, ob: 1485.

George Nevill Lord Aburgeney.

Sr Rich: Nevill Knt of the Rhodes.

Sr Edward Nevill Knt beheaded aº 1538. = Ellenor da: to Andrew Lord Windsore widow to Ralph Lord Scrope of Vpsall.

Sr Tho: Nevill of the Privy Counsell to Kg Henry 8. = Katherne widow to .... Lorde Fitzhugh.

Henry Nevill Lord Aburgaveney.

1. Edward Nevill Vocat: Sards [called Deafe Neuill]. = ... Sister to Sr Christopher Brome.

2. Sr Henry Nevill of [Billingbere]. [See Miscel. G. et H., New Series, i., 436.] = Eliz: da: & heire to Sr John Gresham. [See Miscel. G. et H., ii., 317.]

Frances vx: .... Walgrave. — .... vx: .... Haynes de Com: York.

Margaret mar: to Sr Robt Southwell Mr of the Rolls.

Mary. — Lady Jane.

Edward Nevill who claimeth to be Lord of Burgeney 1601.

Sr Henry Nevill Knt Embassador Leger in France aº 1599 [Nevill of Billingbere. See Visit. 1665-66, i., p. 250]. = Ann da: to Sr Henry Killegreve of Cornwall.

𝔑ewbery, of 𝔚olfines (𝔚olly 𝔉ynes or 𝔚olveley, a manor in the parish of 𝔚hite 𝔚altham).

MS. Coll. of Arms, K. 4, 30-31. Visitation of Worcestershire, 1682-3.

Mr Newberie exhibited these as his Arms but he must make better proof before they can be allow'd to him.

Ralph Newberie Master of the printᵉ House to Queen Eliz: & King James.
┬

Francis Newberie of Wolfines in = Mary eldest dau. Com. Berks Esq: ob^t circa an: | of Sir Henry 1651 ap^d Wolfines & sep: ap^d | Rowe Knt. Lord Whit Waltham in Com: præd. | Mayor of London.

James Newberie died at Shaclewell in Middx. unmarr^d.

Thomas Newberie went over into the Low Countries mar^d there but died s.p.

Richard Newberie of Southwark by Lond^n mar^d but died 1665, s.p.

Ralph New- = Anne d. berie of Bray | of.... in Berks ob: | Clarke. circa 1673.

Eliz: daũ of = John Newberie of = Lucie dau. of Mich: Richd Elley | Twyford in Cõ | Cobb de le Grange of Wonton in | Hants born 2 Aug. | Com: Hants 2 wife Com: Hants. | 1602 obiit circa | sup̱stes 1682. 1st wife. | 1676 s.p.

Ralphe æt: circa 20.

Anne obiit cœlebs.

Eliz: wife of John Leigh of Hatfield in Hampsh.

Henry Newberie of Wol- = Frances dau. of Dr Thofines in Berks ob. circa | mas Wilson Dean of anno 1670 æt. 76. | Worcester.

Francis died unmarried 1676 æt. 36.

John Newberie B.D. Rector of Severn = Dorothy dau. of William Stoke in co: Worc. æt. 42 et ampl̃: | Rogers of Horton near 1682, hath as yet no issue. | Leek in Com̃ Stafford.

Henry Newberie a Surveyor of the Customs in the Port of London ob: ult: Aug. 1679, æt: 38.	=	Cecelie daur. of Sir Will. Morton Kn[t] one of the Justices of the Kings Bench.	Sarah wife of John Mundy of Henley upon Thames in Com Oxon.	Susan wife of Rich. Mallet of .... in Com. Somerset. Illa Vivit 1682.
Henry Newberie only son, æt. 2 ann̄ et ampl̄. 1682.		1. Cicelie æt. 7.	2. Eliz: æt: 5.	

Certified by JOHN NEWBERY.

Newman.

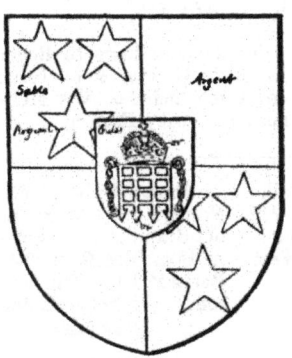

MS. Coll. of Arms, Misc. Grants, vol. vi., 117[b], 118. *Add. MS.* 14,283, *fol.* 103[b], *give these Arms, without the inescutcheon: with the Crest, a swallow volant proper, and Motto,* "Lux mea Christus," *as belonging to Newman of Berks. The Arms and Crest are also tricked in Harl. MS.* 4108, *fol.* 4[b].

Sir Edward Walker, K[t] Garter .... Whear as our Soverigne Lord King Charles the second taking into his princly consideration & very well remembering the many great and eminant Services don unto him & his Late Royall father of Ever blessed and gloriouse memory by many of their loyall subjects from the begining of the Late unhappy divisions in all his Maj[tys] dominions untill the tyme of his Maj[s] most happy restauration and being desireouse to testify unto posterity by some markes and Characters of honour the vallue and Esteeme he hath of the persons who have wth Courage, constancy & fidelity performed the same to w[h] end his Maj[y] hath bin gratiously pleased to authorize me to give grant & assigne unto such persons or any of them such Augmentations out of some of his Royall badges as may bee properly boarne for the honour of them and their posterity and where as it apeareth unto me by a Certificate under the hand and seale of Humphry Newman of Wincanton in the County of Sumersett Gent. that Richard Newman of fifehead Magdelan in County of Dorset is son & Heyre of Thomas Newman grandchild of another thomas Newman, and great grandchild of Richard Newman Gent unto whome & unto Christion his wife, Robert and Richard their sones William Abbott of S[t] Augustines in Bristoll by this deed datted the 20th Novemb. 23 H. 8 devised the site and .... of the said mannor of fifehead for their Respective Lives unto which Robert Newman also paull bush bishopp of Bristoll did by his deed dated ultimo July 4 to Edw: 6, make Another Lease of the mannās of Fifehead Magdalen Aforesaid for the terme of fowerscore yeares during which Lease and eversince the sayd Robert and his descendants have possessed the said mannor as Lessees theirof and that it is al in the possetion of Richard Newman of Duerreeth parish in the County of Summersett Esq[r] and farther being sofficiently sattisfied that the sayd Richard Newman of Fifehead Magdalen Aforesaid is A person that hath faithfully and Constantly adhered to the Interest of the Crowne during the Late tymes of distraction and hath bin a great sufferer for the same and whereas the sayed

Richard Newman beareth for the paternall Coate of his famely quarterly sable and Argent in the first and last quarters three mulletts argent Know yee theirefore that I the .... doe hereby give grant and assigne unto him the sayed Richard Newman [by way of Augmention] In an Inescocheon gules: a portcullis Crowned or as is hereafter more lively depicted with Augmentation Etc. in witness where of I have hereunto etc. the second day of Aprill in the 16th yeare of the Raigne of our Soveraigne Lord Charles the Second etc. annoq. Domi 1664.

[Signed]   EDW: WALKER, Garter.

Norris.

MS. Ashmole 852, pp. 130-131.

This is two pedigrees, Norris of Fyfield and Norris of Yattenden, joined. They are given as separate pedigrees in the Smith MS.

Sr Henry Norris=Alice da: and heire to Roger of Speake in Com: Lancast: Anno 9: H: 5. | Erneis of Chester & of Joane da: & sole heire to Wm Molineux of Crosby Esquire.

Wm Norreys of Speake in cō: Lanc: Esquire. =Percyvall, da: to Jno Huntington of Westley Com: Lanc: Esquire.

John Norreys of Bray in Com: Berks 2d sonn. =Millicent da: & heire to .... Ravenscroft of Cotton End nere Northampton Esquire.

Tho: Norreys of Speake in Com: Lanc: Esquire. =Lettice da: & sole heire to Tho: Norreys of Darby in Com: Lanc: gent.

Thomas Norreys ob: s.p.

Roger Norreys of Bray in Com: Berks Esquire.

1. *NORRIS.*
2. *ERNEYS.*
3. *MOLINEUX.*
4. *HARRINGTON.*
5. *SWINNERTON?*
6. *BALDERSTON.*
7. *FOWLER.*
8. *STAVERTON.*

Sr Wm Norreys of Speake in Com: Lanc: whose descent appeareth in the Visitacōn of Lanc. [*1567: printed by the Chetham Soc.,* vol. 81, pp. 83—86].

Edmond Norreys of Fyfeild in co: Berks 2d sonne. =Alice da: & sole heire to John Fuller of Fyfeild in Com: Berks.

John Norreys of Fyfeild in Com: Berks=Mary da: & coheire to Henry Stafferton of Bray in Com: Berks Esquire.
gent: Vshr of the black rodd.

A   B

OF BERKSHIRE.

A | B

Wm Norreys of Fyfeild =T= Mary da: to S^r   [2.] .... Nor- =T= .... da: of ....
in Co: Berks, Esquire. | Adrian Fortescue   reys of ....   Andrewes.
                        | [*by his 2^d wife*].

Sr J^{no} Norreys of Fifeild in Com: Berks made Kn^t =T= Mary da: to George Basford
at Reading a^o 1601 [*of Woodway in Com' Hertf^d*   of London Widow to Roger
Knight (*Smith MS.*, p. 84)].   Colte of Hartfordshire.

Wm Norreys son & heire   Eliz: vx: .... Webb & after to
[*of Fifield*].   Sr Edw: Norreys [*see next page*].

1. Christian d: & heire to W^m =T= Wm Norreys of Bray =T= 2. Anne da: to .... Dela-
Strech of Ruscombe [*in com.* | in Co: Berks.   viver [*Delamere*].
Berks].

Sr John Norris of Yatten- =T= Alice da: and   Wm Norreys of   Roger Norreys of
den [*in Co. Berks*] Kn^t | heire to Rich: Wingfield [*in   Cookham in Com:
Bannerett. | Merbrook of   com. Berks*]   Berks 3^d sonne.
                                  | Yattenden.   2^d sonne.

Tho: Norris of Wingfeild =T= Jane da: to .... De la Hay Widow to J^{no} Dannett.

Wm Norris marr: Alice da: to Thom: =T=   Richard a schollar in Oxford ob:
Temnes of Kidlington.   sans yssue.

Tho: Norrys Messenger of the Chamber dyed in September 1597;
marr: Margery da: to Edw: Lineall of Brandley in Worc: Widow
to Roger Ponder Physiciom.

3 sonns & a daūr before y^e Wedding.

1. .... da: & coh to =T= Sr Wm Norreys of Yattenden marr: to his =T= 2. Jane da: to
John Nevill Marques | 3: wife Anne da: to John Horne Alderman | J^{no} Vere E. of
Mountacute. | of London & Widow to Sr J^{no} Harcourt. | Oxford.

A son dyed in y^e cradle.

Lyonell   Kath: vx: Sr John   Anne vx: Thomas   Eliz: vx: W^m   Jane vx John
sans   Longford.   Wroughton.   Farmer, s.p.   Cheney [*see
yssue.   Vol. I., p. 5*].

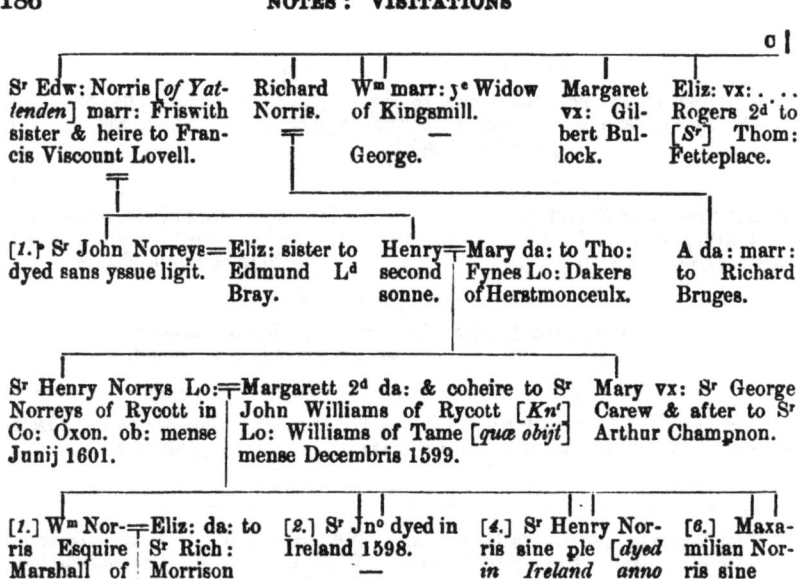

Sʳ Edw: Norris [*of Yattenden*] marr: Friswith sister & heire to Francis Viscount Lovell.

Richard Norris.

Wᵐ marr: yᵉ Widow of Kingsmill. — George.

Margaret vx: Gilbert Bullock.

Eliz: vx: .... Rogers 2ᵈ· to [Sʳ] Thom: Fetteplace.

[*1.*] Sʳ John Norreys dyed sans yssue ligit.

Eliz: sister to Edmund Lᵈ Bray.

Henry second sonne.

Mary da: to Tho: Fynes Lo: Dakers of Herstmonceulx.

A da: marr: to Richard Bruges.

Sʳ Henry Norrys Lo: Norreys of Rycott in Co: Oxon. ob: mense Junij 1601.

Margarett 2ᵈ da: & coheire to Sʳ John Williams of Rycott [*Knᵗ*] Lo: Williams of Tame [*quæ obijt*] mense Decembris 1599.

Mary vx: Sʳ George Carew & after to Sʳ Arthur Champnon.

[*1.*] Wᵐ Norris Esquire Marshall of Barwike, dyed in Ireland [*vita patris*].

Eliz: da: to Sʳ Rich: Morrison after married to Hen: Earle of Linc.

[*2.*] Sʳ Jnᵒ dyed in Ireland 1598. — [*3.*] Sʳ Edw: marr: Eliz: da: to Sʳ John Norreys of Fyfeild Widow to .... Webb.

[*4.*] Sʳ Henry Norris sine ple [*dyed in Ireland anno 1598*]. — [*5.*] Sʳ Tho: Norris marr: Bridgitt da: to Sʳ Wᵐ Kingsmill.

[*6.*] Maxamilian Norris sine prole. — Kath: vx: Sʳ Anthony Pawlett.

Francis Lo: Norris of Rycott in Co: Oxon: now living 1602.

Bridgit da: to Edw: Vere Earle of Oxon. [*Lord Great Chamberlain of England*].

𝔒rp𝔴oo𝔡, of 𝔄bingdon.

MS. Ashm. 852, p. 140.

Arms p. Wm. Camden 18 *Oct.* 1600 (*Harl. MS.* 1532, *fol.* 75) *to Thomas, son of Paul, son of Thomas, all of Abingdon.*

Tho: Orpwood Mayor of Abington in Com: Berks gent. [*Thomas Orpwood was Mayor in* 1562, 1569, *and* 1575.]

Eliz: da: to .... Pullen de Com: Wilts.

Paule Orpwood Mayor of Abingdon in Com: Berks gent: 1566. [*Paul Orpwood was Mayor of Abingdon in* 1585 *and* 1593.]

Mary da: to Richard Mayott of Abingdon. [*Richard Mayott was Mayor of Abingdon in* 1556, 1568, *and died during his Mayoralty in* 1578.]

OF BERKSHIRE. 187

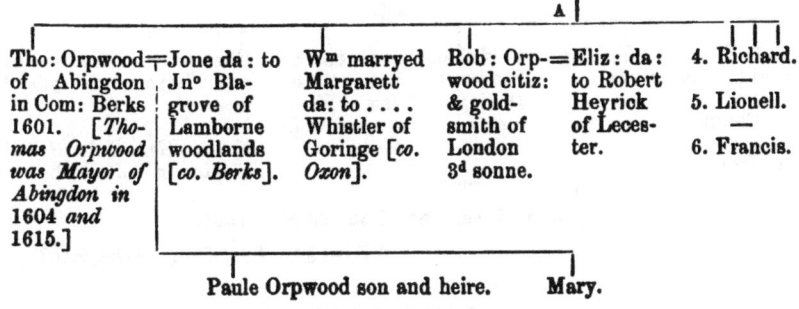

Orpwood, of Apleford.

MS. Rawl. D. 865, *folio* 89, *in Ashmole's handwriting. Original paper for Visitation* 1665-6, *not included. No Arms. Marked* he refused to subscribe [*i.e.* sign] or pay the fee.
Arms confirmed to Thomas Orpwood of Abingdon, 18 October, 1600, by William Camden. Vert three crosses formies Ar: on a chief Ar: 3 Boars heads couped Sable. Crest: a boar passant, quarterly ermine and ermines armed, bristled and hoofed Or.

Ocke hund.

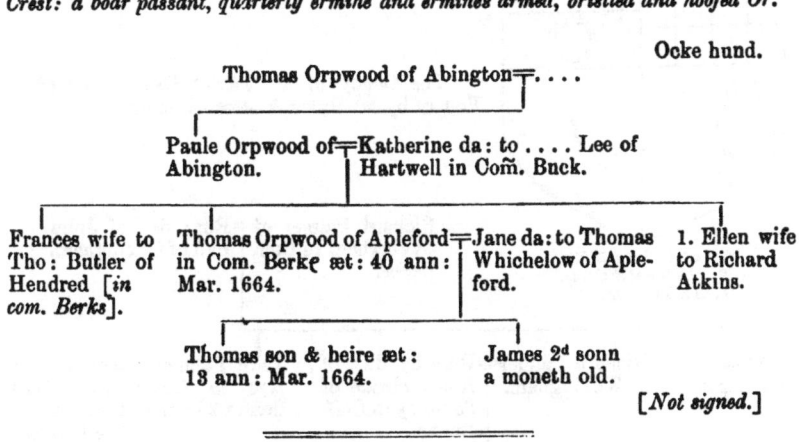

[*Not signed.*]

Packer, of Donington.

MS. Rawl. D. 865, *fol.* 76. *Original Paper for the Visitation*, 1665-6. *No Arms. In Ashmole's handwriting. Marked* refused to pay, *but he was included in the Visitation pedigree*, 1665—6, *see* Vol. I., p. 254.

Faircross hund.

John Packer one of the Clearkes⊤Philippa da: to . . . , Mills of
of the Privy Seale. | Bitterne in Com Hante.

Ro̅b̅t Packer of Shellingford [in com. Berks].
2. Philipp.
3. John.

4. William = Jane da: to Tho: Saunders of Woolston in Com̅ Berk͜e.
Packer of Donington.

Eliz: wife to John Browne now Clerke of the pliam͏ͭ men.

Kath: wife to John Gell of Hopton in Com̅ Der̅b.

John son & heire æt: 7 an: 23 Mar. 1664.

WILLIAM PACKER. [*Original.*]

Palmer, of Wokingham.

MS. Rawl. D. 865, *fol.* 57, 57ᵇ. *In Ashmole's handwriting.*

The Coppy of Mʳ Palmʳˢ Descent entred in Vellom by Mʳ Ryley & attested vt infra.

1 and 4. *PALMER*.
2. *UNDERWOOD*.
3. *SYMONDS*.

Richard Palmer of = Eliz: da: of John Ball of Ockingham.
Ockingham in Com̅ Berk͜e.

Francis ob: s: ple.

Richard Palmer of Wokingham. = Dorothy da: of Rich: Meade of Soulbery in Com̅ Buck͜e.

John Palmer of Rye in Com: Sussex 2ᵈ sonne. = Eliz: da: of .... Cary nere Lewis in Sussex.

2. John.
3. Robᵗ.

4. Thomas.
Anne.

1. Richard Palmer of Ockingham. = Mary da: of Oliver Fish of Bigleswade in Com̅ Bedd. gen̅.

Richard ætatis 8, 1655. Mary. Martha.

Thomas Palmer of Rye. = Sarah da: of .... Isham in Com̅ Berk͜e [? *Bucks*].

2. Richard. 3. Marke.

OF BERKSHIRE.   189

Genealogiam et Insignia, prout superius depicta & delineata existant, cùm Evidentijs præscriptis, fideliter examinavi & veritati esse consona adiudicavi.
Ita testor
GULIELMUS RYLEY, Lancaster.

The Title to Mr Palmers Pedigree drawne by Mr Ryley. An Exact & pfect Collection of the deedes & Evidences of Richard Palmer of Wokyngham in the County of Berke Gent. who is lineally descended from Richard Palmer son & heire of John Palmer (otherwise called Vnderwode) late of Wokingham who descended from Robt Palmer that married Agnes da: & heire of John Vnderwode of Wokingham, who married Agnes the da: & heire of John Symonde of Woodcrich in the pish of Wokingham afores^d, as by the Evidences vnder written may app.

Persons menčoned in the Evidences coppied out by Mr Ryley & placed aboue Mr Palmers descent entred as afores^d.

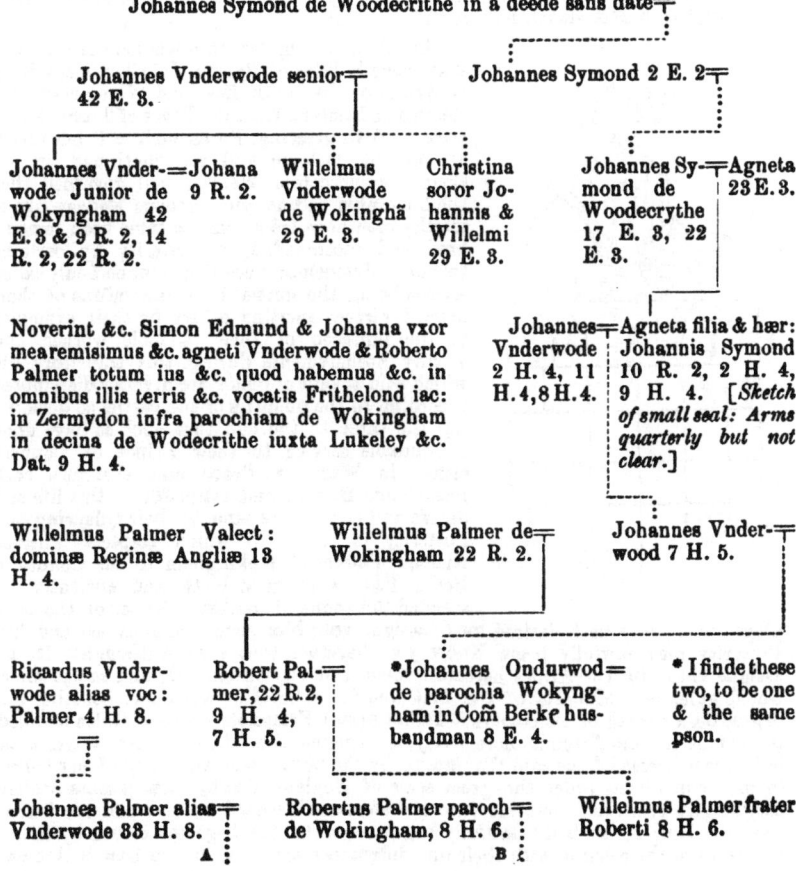

```
         A                                    B
Ricardus Palmer      *Johannes Palmer alias    Sciant &c quod Ego Willelmus
alias Vnderwode      dict: Johannes Vnder-     Mathew de Wokyngham dedi
de Wokyngham         wode nuper de Wokyng-     &c Johanni Symond de Wode-
4 E. 5 & 3 Mar:      ham 1. H. 7.              cryth et Agneti vxori suæ
                                               vnam Moram vocatam Gode-
                                               wyke &c dat. 20 Dec. 28 E. 3.
         Ricardus filius & hæres 1 H. 7.       [*Sketch of Seal: bearing a kind
                                               of possenet, and on a chief two
                                               estoiles.*]
```

Grant of Arms to Richard Palmer of Wokingham, by Sir Edward Bysshe, Clarenceux, dated the 20th of February, 1664 (1664-5). MS. Ashm. 840, p. 429; another copy is in MS. Ashm. 858, p. 212.

To all and singular vnto whome these p'sents shall come Sr Edward Bysshe Knt Clarenceux King of Armes of the South East and West pts of this Realme of England from the River of Trent Southward sendeth greeting, Forasmuch as it hath been an antient custome and soe continued in all Countries and comon Wealths well governed that the honorable acc͡ons and vertuous Endeavours of worthy men have from tyme to tyme been remembred and recom͡ended to Posterity by certaine tokens and remembrances of honour com͡only called Armes being the outward demonstrac͡ons of their inward Virtues inciting others by their examples to the imitac͡on of their laudable workes and worthy Atcheivments during this transitory life which said tokens of honor are diversly distributed according to the qualities of the parties so demeriting the same to the end that such as have done com͡endable service to their Prince or Country either in Warr or Peace may therefore both receive due Honour and estimac͡on in this life and derive and convey the same to their Offspring and Posterity for ever, In which respects whereas Richard Palmer of Wokingham in the County of Berks Esqr is of good birth and antiently descended the sonne of Richard Palmer of the same place and County hath desired me to assigne vnto him such Armes as hee and his Posterity may lawfully beare Know yee therefore that I have thought fitt to assigne vnto him the Armes hereafter menc͡oned viz. Checkey Or and sables on a Cheife gules two Mulletts of the first and for a Crest on a helmett befitting his degree on a wreath of his colours a Talbot sejant Ermynois mantled Gules doubled Argent as in the Margent more lively is depicted the which Armes & Crest as before is expressed I the said Clarenceux by the power and authority of my Office to mee committed vnder the great seale of England doe by these p'sents declare assigne give grant and confirme vnto the aforesaid Richard Palmer and his heires and to ye issue of his body Lawfully begotten or to bee begotten to bee by them and every of them borne with their due differences according to the Law of Armes,

OF BERKSHIRE. 191

In witnesse whereof I have vnto these presents affixed the seale of my Office and subscribed my name this twentieth of February in the sixteenth yeare of the Reigne of o^r Sovereigne Lord Charles the second by the grace of God King of England Scotland France & Ireland Defender of the ffaith Annoque Domini 1664.

EDWARD BYSSHE
Clarenceux King of Armes.

Parry, of Hampstead Marshall.

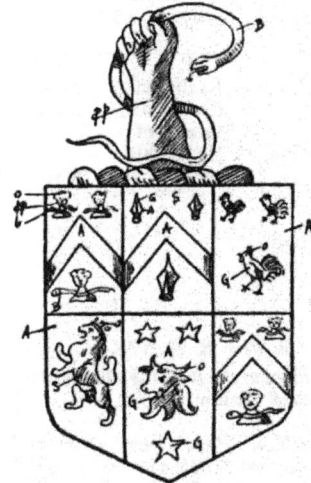

1 and 6. *VAUGHAN*.
2. *WATKYN* or *GAM*.
3. *GAM*.
4. *GAM* or *WATKYN*.
5. ? *HAVARD*.

MS. Ashmole 852, p. 150.

Henry Vaughan Esquire.=⊤

Sr Tho: ap harry (alias)=Anne da: to Sr Wm Parry Kn^t Treasurer of Reade of Borestall the Qu: house house [*sic*] widow to Sr Gyles ob: 1560: sepult: apud Grevell, and Sr Adrian Westminst. Fortescue quæ ob: 1585.

Sr Tho: Parry of=Dorothy da: Edward Hamsted marshall to .... 2^d sonne. in Com: Berks K^t Brooke of 1601. Bristowe.

Muriell vx: Sr Tho: Knevett of Ash- | Anne vx: Griffin | Frances vx: John
welthorp in Com: Norff: [*see Le Neve's* | Hamden de Com: | Abrahall of Here-
Knts., *Harl. Soc.*, Vol. VIII., p. 22]. | Buckingham. | forde.

John Abrahall son and heire.

Paul, of Bray.

Le Neve's Knights, p. 249, *Harl. Soc.*, Vol. VIII.

William Paul Bishop of Oxon. born in east cheap London Rector of=
Baldwin brightwell Oxon enstalled 1663 dyed at Chinnor 24 May
1665 buried at Brightwell Oxon. where ....
A

NOTES: VISITATIONS

			A		
2. James Paule=.... dʳ of Sʳ of Lond. Linen Tho. Duppa Draper in Sᵗ Gent. Vsher Michaells Cornhill Lond.	of the black rod remarried to .... Aspin.	1. Sʳ William Paule=.... of Bray in Berks dʳ of Kted as above he .... dyed without issue. (Knighted at Windsor 6 July 1671. See Wood's Athenæ Oxon., vol. 2, fol. 666.)		.... mar. to Sʳ fairmedow Peniston bart. Sir Fairmedow Peniston, bart., married 2ndly Mary, 1st dau: of John Powney of Old Windsor, co. Berks, and widow of Sir William Paul of Bray. (Complete Baronetage, i., 88.)	

2. James Paul dyed vnmaried.	1. William=Kat. dʳ of Sʳ Paule of Vere Vane Bray Wyke Earle of berks esqʳ. Westmʳland.	3. Xtofer Paule dyed vnmaried. — 4. Thomas Paule liveing.	Rachel mar. to .... Clitherow of Maidenhith berks.	Martha mar. .... — Mary.

Paul.

MS. Coll. of Arms, Walker's Grants, i. 7; ii. 87; *R.* 23, 174.

The following draft in the handwriting of Sir Edward Walker, Garter.

Dʳ *William Paul was afterwards Bishop of Oxford* (1663-4); *his daughter Judith was the wife of Alban Pigot* (V⁺ I., p. 260).

Sir Edward Walker, Kᵗ Garter Principall King of Armes of Englishmen .... whereas the Reverend Dʳ William Paule was many years Chaplaine in ordinary unto the late Kg Charles the first of ever glorious and blessed memory and in the late unhappy time of Distraction faithfully and actively assisted the .... of his Cause & likewise at present Chaplaine in ordinary unto his Maᵗⁱᵉ and by him in the 2d year of his Reigne made Deane of the Cathedrall Church of Lichfield wᶜʰ he now worthyly injoyeth Hee doeth therefore justly meritt some perticular marke of Distinction to evidence the same to all posterity Know yee therefore that I the said Sir Edw. Walker Kᵗ Garter .... have given granted and assigned unto him the sayd Dʳ William Paule and to his heirs and Descendants for ever the Coate of Armes and Creast hereafter mentioned, Vizᵗ Argent opon a Crosse ingrayled sable five stares wavy of

OF BERKSHIRE.

the first, and for his Creast upon a helmet proper mantled gules doubled argent a stare wavy or between 2 winges out of a Crowne per pale argent and sable counterchanged as in the Margent more lively is depicted the w[ch] Armes and Creast there due and proper differences may shall lawfully use beare and set forth at all times and upon all occasions according unto the Law and practise of Armes without the Lett or molestation of any person whatsoever. In witness whereof I have hereunder subscribed my name and affixed the seale of my office the eighteenth day of ffeb. in the thirteenth yeare of the Reigne of our Soveraigne L[d] Charles the 2d of that name by the Grace of God King of Eng[d] Scotland ffrance and Ireland Defender of the faith et Ann. Dni. 1660.

Peck, of Remenham.

Visitation of London, 1633-35, Harl. Soc., Vol. XVII., p. 148.

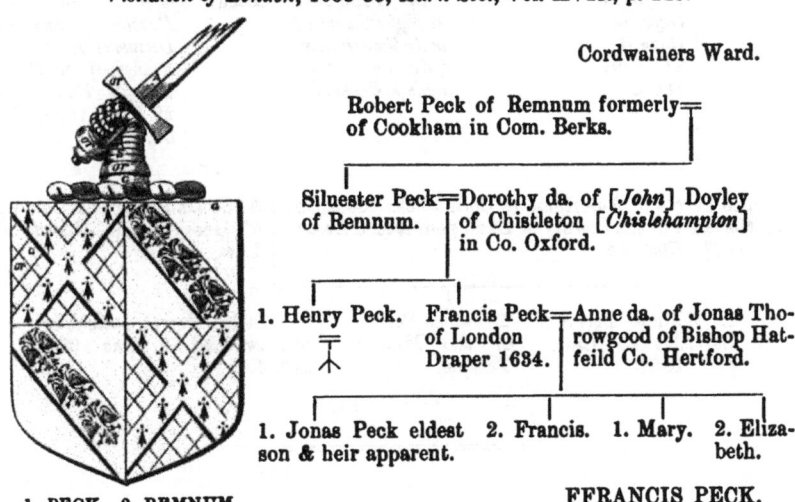

Cordwainers Ward.

Robert Peck of Remnum formerly of Cookham in Com. Berks.

Siluester Peck = Dorothy da. of [John] Doyley of Remnum. of Chistleton [Chislehampton] in Co. Oxford.

1. Henry Peck.   Francis Peck = Anne da. of Jonas Thorowgood of Bishop Hatfeild Co. Hertford. of London Draper 1634.

1. Jonas Peck eldest son & heir apparent.   2. Francis.   1. Mary.   2. Elizabeth.

1. PECK.   2. REMNUM.   FFRANCIS PECK.

Perrot.

MS. Ashm. 846, fol. 45[b]. See a pedigree, Ashm. Berks, iii., p. 323, and Visitation of Oxfordshire, 1634, Harl. Soc., V., p. 245. The Chancel of this Church [Fyfield] belongs to the family of Perrott of North Leigh in Oxfordshire, an antient and genteel Family, who are obliged to keep it in constant Repair (Ashm. Antiq. of Berks, i., p. 97). The Perrot family buried at Fyfield, and used the Arms described in the Patent (4 January 1550), printed in the Miscel. Geneal. et Her., 3rd Series, iii., p. 1: Geules, three peares gold on a chief argent a demy lyon [issuant] rampant sable, and for his Creast, on a wreath argent and geules a Parrot proper armed geules houlding in the right pawe a peare gold.

William White of Reading, Gent. = ...
A

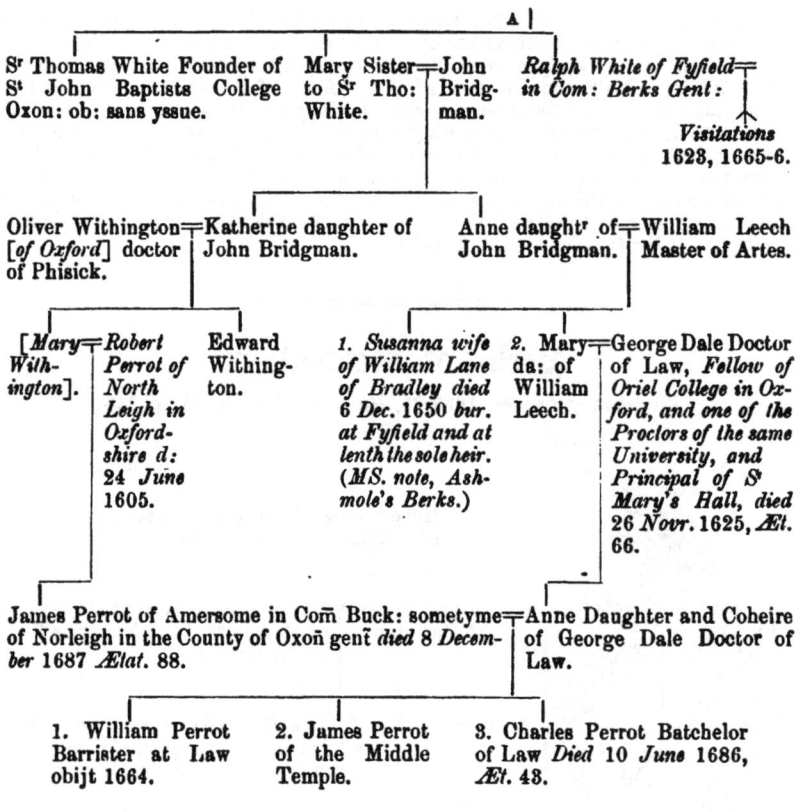

Phelipes, of Hurst.

In the copy of the Visitation of 1566, made by William Smith, Rouge Dragon 1602, and enlarged by John Withy 1628 (Harl. MS. 1081, fol. 59[b]*) the following Arms are given, in trick: Per pale Gules and Sable, semée of crosses crosslet Arge a lion rampant Or. Crest: On a wreath, two dolphins back to back Or, banded w a riband Gules. They are described as the Arms of* Henry Phelypes, *of* Hur *Clarke of the Kechyin to* Q: Eliz. *I have not found any authority for these Arms.*

OF BERKSHIRE.

Phipps, of Reading.

MS. Rawl. D. 865, fol. 86, in Ashmole's handwriting. Original paper for the Visitation, 1665-6. Marked Gratis, *but not included.*

[*Sable, a trefoil slipped between eight mullets Argent. Crest: A lion's gamb erect and erased Sable, holding erect a trefoil as in the Arms.*]

From the impression of a small seal, with helm and mantlet, preserved with the pedigree.

Reading Towne.

Robert Phipps of Nottingham.=

2. Anthony.	George Phipps of Walton hall neere Nottinghā.	=Anne da: to .... Elliot & relict of John Power.
3. William.		

2. Caleb Phipps dyed wᵗʰout yssue.	1. Francis Phipps of Reading in Coṁ Berkᵉ æt: 54 annorum 11 Mar: 1664.	=Anne da: of .... Sharpe of Cirencester in Coṁ Glouc.	1. Anne. 2. Judith.

1. Francis son & heire now of Kings Colledge in Cambridge ætatis 19 annorum 11 Mar. 1664.	2. George. 3. Thomas.	4. James. 5. Constantine.	1. Mary. 2. Anna.

FFRA: PHIPPS. [*Original.*]

Picton, of Wyvill Court.

MS. Ashm. 852, p. 149.

Add. *MS.* 14,283, *fol.* 75, *gives the Arms*: *Sable guttée d'or, a lion rampant of the second. Crest: A demi-lion rampant gules.* "*The Armes confirmed to* Jo: Picton p' T. Holme al's Clarenceux K. of Armes 1486, *The mantle purple, the insyde & the outside Sa: set all with gouttes or.*"

Leonard Picton of Wyuill Court in Com: Berks [? *Wyfield, in the parish of Boxford*].=

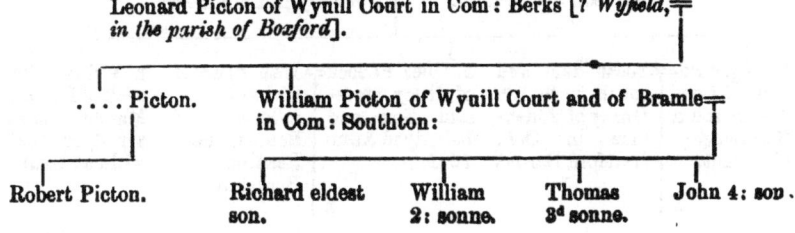

.... Picton.	William Picton of Wyuill Court and of Bramle= in Com: Southton:			
Robert Picton.	Richard eldest son.	William 2: sonne.	Thomas 3ᵈ sonne.	John 4: son.

Pleydell, of Shrivenham.

MS. Rawl. D. 865, fol. 59ᵇ, not in Ashmole's handwriting. Original paper for the Visitation of 1665-6. There is a rough trick of the Arms of Reason, Gules, a lion rampant Or, between four crosses patonce " varry," with the note, Arma concessa Tho. Playdell de Colshill in 21 H. 7, 1505, p' Tho. Writh alias Wriothsley Regem Armorum.

John Pleydell late of Shryuenhā had foure sonns, & one daughter by Anne his wife, who was the daughter of Oliuer Ayshcombe of Lyford in this County of Berks: three of the said sons, to wit, Thomas, William & John dyed & were neuer marryed, the daughter was named Martha, & she was giuen in marriage to Thomas Saunders of Wolston in the said County. Oliver Pleydell who liues now at Shryuenham is the onely suruiuing sonne of the aboue named John Pleydell. The said Oliuer Pleydell married Martha Brennd the daughter of Nicholas Brennd the sonne of John Brennd of Wanborrough in the County of Wilts: And the said Oliuer hath issue by the said Martha, 2 sonns, Thomas & Oliuer, & foure daughters, to wit, Anne, Martha, Mary & Elizabeth; Anne the eldest daughter was giuen in marriage to Samuell Ashe of Langlee in the County of Wilts, all the other children both sons & daughters are yet vnmarried.

Pocock, of Chieveley.

Extra pedigree in a copy of the Visitation of Berks, 1566, transcribed and augmented by William Smith, al's Rouge dragon, anno 1600.

This Family of Pocock have rais'd themselves by the Clothing Trade (having been considerable clothiers) but never pretended to Armes or Gentility, for the Father of Roger, Giles and William Disclaimed Armes in the Visitation of Berkshire made Anno 1664, Mark'd G. 12. Yet Roger Pocock bore for his Armes Argᵗ 3 mullets sa. on a chief gu: 3 Cinqfoils Or. and Mʳ King Rougedragon Painted them into Sʳ Thomas Travels Pedigree anno 1684 for the Armes of Elizabeth Lady Travel daūr of the said Roger, and the same were Used in a Funeral Hatchment and Scotcheons upon her death Anno 1686, but neither She nor her Father nor any of this Family have a Right to bear the said Armes, or any other.

Ita Testor Samˡ Stebbing, Somerset.

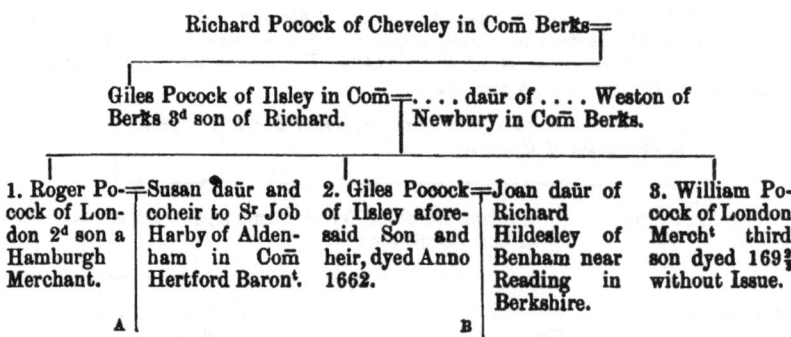

OF BERKSHIRE.

```
A |                              B |
    |─────────────────────────────|──────────────────────|
    Sʳ Thomas Travel of London Knight = Elizabeth daūr and sole
    married to his First Wife.         heir to Roger Pocock.
    |────────────────────────|─────────────────────────|
1. Giles Pocock eldest son of   2. Richard Po-=....    3. Roger Pocock a=....
   Giles was a Merchant of         cock of London daūr    Merchant of Ham-  daūr
   Hamburgh, and dyed Un-          Merchant 2ᵈ son  of    burgh 3ᵈ son Marrᵈ of
   married Anno 1693.              married.        ....   and hath Issue.   ....
```

Pocock.

Grant of Arms, 1761. *College of Arms, Grants,* x., 274.

Grant of Arms and Crest by Stephen Martin Leake Esqʳᵉ Garter Principal King of Arms and Charles Townley Esqʳᵉ Clarenceux King of Arms, to George Pocock of the Parish of Sᵗ Margaret Westminster co. Middx. Esqʳ Representative in the present Parliament for the Borough of Plymouth co. Devon, a Vice Admiral of the Red Squadron of His Majesty's Fleet, & his descendants & the descendants of his father Thomas Pocock late of Pembroke College, Oxford, A.M. Rector of Danbury and Lashington co. Essex, Chaplain to George late Viscount Torrington & to the Royal Hospital at Greenwich, deceased whose ancestors were the ancient family of Pocock of Cheveley co. Berks.

Arms, Checky Argent and Gules a Lyon rampant guardant Or.

Crest, On a wreath of the Colours An Antelopes Head proper attired Or, issuant out of a Naval Crown Gold.

Motto, Regi Regnoque Fidelis.

S. Martin Leake Garter   Charles Townley
Principal King of Arms.   Clarenceux King of Arms.

Earl Marshal's Warrant dated 5 Jan.

Grant dated 23 Jan. 1761.

Pococke.

MS. Rawl. D. 865, fol. 129.

Much honoʳed Sʳ,

I had sent to me a summons which was sent to Childrey from you, to warne me to appear before you at Wantage for such reasons as were therin specified. I have not pretended hitherto to bear armes ; but had thoughts to enquire whither any pertained to oʳ family, and if I had not found out any, to have procured some. And if I had been in the country, or at present in a condition fit for travelling, I should have willingly waited on you, and presumed to aske yoʳ advice therin, though I have not had the happines of farther acquaintance with you then to be sometimes in your company with my worthy Friend and yoʳ reall honoʳer, while he lived, Dʳ Langbain, but yoʳ known candoʳ & civility would have given me that boldnes.

Sʳ I take leave
Yoʳ humble servᵗ
EDW: POCOCKE.

Oxon Xᵗ Church
March 13, 1664.

[*Addressed*] For the worthily Honoʳed Elias Ashmole, Esquire, Windsore-Herald at Armes, these at the signe of the Bear in Wantage.

[*The seal, not armorial, bears a tree. This was the celebrated Dr. Edward Pocock, Rector of Childrey, Berks, Canon of Christ Church, Oxford. He brought from the East the Cedars and other trees in the garden at Childrey.*]

Powle.

Grant of Arms and Crest to Thomas Powle of London, Esquire, by Sir Gilbert Dethick, Knight, Garter, Robert Cooke, Clarenceux, William Flower, Norroy, dated the 7th of May 1569. (MS. Coll. of Arms, Dethick's Giftes.)

To all and singular as well nobles and gentilmen as others to whom these presentes shall come be seene hearde read or understood We Sʳ Gilbert Dethicke Knight als Garter principall Kinge of Armes, Robert Cooke Esquyer als Clarenceux Kinge of Armes of the Southe partes and Willm Flower Esquyer als Norroy Kinge of Armes of the north partes of England sendith greetinge in the Lord God Everlastinge. For as much as aunciently from the beginninge of the valiant and Vertouse actes of excellent personnes have been commendid to the world and posteritie with soundry monuments and remembrances of their good desertes Amongst the which the chiefest and most usuall hath been the bearinge of figures in shyldes called Armes beinge none other thing than demonstrations, or tokens, of prowisse & valour diuersely distributed according to the quallities of the personnes meriting the same. To thintent that such as by their vertues do adde to the advancemēt of the common weale the shyne of their good lyfe and so conversacon in dayly practyse of thynga worthy and commendable being the very true and pfecte tokens of a right noble dysposition may therefore receive dewe honor in their lyves and also desyre &

continue the same successively in their posteritie for ever. Amongst the which number Thomas Powle of London Escuyer Clerke of Croune to the Queen's Majesty's Court of Chancerye one of the six clerkes and comptroller of the hanaper in the same Court and also steward of her ma^ties forest of Waltham in the County of Essex beinge one of the bearers of these tokens of honor to witte of Armes with healme mantles torce and creast to him assigned by William Harvy late Clarenceux Kinge of Armes of the South partes of England by letters patentes bearinge date the xxiij of June 1559, These Armes and creast withstandinge beinge not so well & belyked of for some respects of the officers of Armes well known to the sayd Thomas Powle hath required us the Kings of Armes to showe him favor and to gratifye him in the alteration & changinge & amendinge of his sayd owld Armes & Creast. In Consideracion wherof and at his instant request and for a further proof of our good affection . . . . him we the sayd Kinges of Armes by power and authority to us committed by letters patentes under the great seale of England have assigned given & grannted unto the same Thomas Powle in lieu and place of his sayd old armes and creast these armes and creast following viz. azure a fese ermyne between three lyons passant gold, uppon his healme on a torce silver and goules an unicorne passant azure mained bearded flashed ungled & horned gold about the neck a croune silver mantled geules doubled silver as more playnly appeareth depicted in the margent which arms & creast and every part & parcell therof we the said Kinges of Armes do by these presentes certifie confirme and graunt to the said Thomas Powle and to his posteritie for ever and he and they the same armes to have hold beare enioy and shew forth with their due differences in shyld, cote, Armour, seale, or otherwyse at all tymes and for ever hereafter at his or their lybertes and pleasures without the impediment loss or interruption of any personn or psonnes. In witness whereof we the Kinges of armes aforesayd have assigned these pnts with o^r handes and sett therunto o^r severall seales of Armes the VIIth of May 1569.

The original of this Grant was exhibited at the Society of Antiquaries on the 1st of April 1897. It is signed by the three Kings of Arms. The seals of Garter and Norroy remain, that of Clarenceux is lost. The Grant has a curious painted border with Tudor badges and flowers, and in the initial a figure of Garter pointing to the arms depicted in the margin. A docket, together with the above description, is printed in the Proceedings (Second Series, xvi., p. 351).

There is a docket of this Grant in Ashmole's handwriting (MS. Ashm. 858, p. 215).

𝔓oynant.

Grant of Arms to Mighell Poynant of London, 1508. *MS. Ashm.* 840, pp. 377, 378 (*see Allen of Streatley,* Vol. I., p. 156).

To all cristeñ people thies present letters heryng seyng or redyng I Cristofer Carlyle otherwise callid Norrey principall herawld & Kyng of Armes of the North parties of this Realme of Englond sende due & humble recomendacoñ in oure Lorde God everlasting. And where equytie willeth & also reason ordeyneth that men of Lawdable & vertuous conversacoñ & lyvyng be hadd in a perpetuall memory & whereas noblesse is oonys in a blood it may not be lost without to long continuance in slouth & vices Gayus fflamyneus seyth y^t honest poverty taketh away no p^t of noblesse & ye Doctor Bartilmew in his Tretie of Tokens of Arms seyth y^t if y^e

Armes be first ours they no maner of wise may be taken from vs & sith it is so yᵗ by the aunciēt & lawdable custome of Armes noon may bere yᵉ hole Armes without difference savȳrg yᵉ oldest & chieff of the house or stoke of a kyndred without preiudice of the other therefore forasmuch as Mighell Poynant Gentilman resseant in London & oon of the Clerks of the Kings Chancery is comen & descended of the house & stoke of the Hichendens sometyme of the County of Buk aunciēnt noblemen he not willing to use or beare any Armes in preiudice of any of them or other of his blood but with a due difference hath required me the fore- said King of Armes & to order his said Armes & to assigne vnto him such due difference as may stonde wᵗ right, To whom I yᵉ said Kynge of Armes by the auctoritie of myn̄ office knowing his virtue & substaunce wᵗ sufficient habilitie to maynteyne the said armes have assigned & devysed vnto the said Mighell for his armes in maner & forme as herafter foloweth yᵗ is to say Azur a fece Dauncey gold three flours de lices in ye chieff billittee of the same in yᵉ poynte of the feld an harts hedd cowpey of the fece vpon yᵉ same a skalopp̄ azur for his difference as in the Mergene of thies pʳsents more pleynly doth appere, To have & to holde to the said Mighell Poynant and to his posteritie & blood and he & they from hensforth to enioye the said Armes to theym & to sett the same in all plac̄s con- venyent at their pleasur forevermore. In wittness wherof I the said Kyng of Armes have signed thies presents with myn̄ owne hand & sett therunto the seale of myn̄ office, yoven̄ at London xiiij day of March. In yᵉ yere of oure Lord Jh̄u crist A thousand fyve hundreth & eight And of the reigne of oure moost dred & redoubted Sovereigne Lord Kynge Henry the seventh the xxiiijᵗʰ yere.

                                                                                    p me Norroy &c.

Pusey, of Pusey.

MS. Ashm. 836, p. 689. Original paper for Visitation, 1665-6.

Hugh Pusey aliàs Pesey; had sonnes,

    Richard.
    Thomas; dead; left 2 sons, Thomas & Anthony; & 2 daughters; at Marcham.
    Jonas; dead; left one sonne, now a prentise in London.
    Hugh; yet liuing, vnmarried.

Jane Shury of Marchā: his last wife: by whom all these children; saue onely Elizabeth; by a former wife.

    —— daughters
    Elizabeth, yet liuing, married to one Cox of Chilton.
    Jane, married to John Huet of Duxford in the parish of Hinton.
    Katharine, an aunciēnt mayd yet liuing.
    A 4ᵗʰ daughter, married to one Horneby in London.

OF BERKSHIRE.

Richard Pusey; aliàs Pesey; had & hath sons,

His wife, Martha Alder of Wantinge.
- Richard.
- William.
- Thomas.
- Martha.
- Mary, married to one Mr Alder, a tradesman in London.
- Margaret.

——daughters,

Richard, the eldest sonne, deceased Augt ye 2de A.D. 1655; left by his wife Mary Blagraue of Wantinge:

sons
Richard, 14 yeeres old.
Edward, 10 y^{rs} old,
and one daughter Mary, 12 yeeres old.

Mr Wm Pusey, a merchant liuing on great-Tower-Hill, in Colchester street neere Crouched Friers, can tell you How & where you may speak with his father, and see ye Horne and Armes.

[*Note by Ashmole.*] This pap was deliued into me at Farringdon 18 March, 1664, by Mr Joseph Hill, minister of Hinton, & sent from Mrs Martha Pusey grandmoth^r to Richard the youngest of the three Richards.

Quarles.

Grant of a Crest to John Quarles, by Robert Cooke, Clarenceux, dated the 15th of February 1577. (*MS. Ashm.* 858, pp. 218, 219, *in Ashmole's handwriting. See Dolman of Shaw,* Vol. I., p. 193.)

To all & singular as well nobles as gentils &c: Robert Cooke Esqr alias Clarenceux principall Herald, &c: Whereas anciently from the begining the valiant & vertuous acts of excellent psons &c: Among the which nomber John Quarles Esquier eldest son of John Quarles Esquire late Citizen & Drap of London deceased, being one of the bearers of those tokens of Honour by iust descent & p'rogatiue of birth from his ancestors, & yet not knowing of any Crest or Cognizance pply to belong to his ancient Armes &c: In consideracōn whereof for a farther declaracōn of the worthynes of the said John Quarles & at his request, I the said Clarenceux &c: Haue assigned given & granted vnto the said John Quarles for his Crest or Cognizance vpon the Healme, on a Torce or wreath argent & sable a demy Eagle displaied vert, with a Coronet about the neck gold, Mantled gules doubled argent, as more plainely may app depicted in the margent hereof together with his said ancient Armes. Which Crest or Cognizance & eu'y pte & pcell thereof I the said Clarenceux King of Armes doe by these presents ratifie confirme giue & grant vnto the the [sic] said John Quarles the son, & to all the ofspring & posterity of the before named John Quarles the Father for ever. He & they the same to haue hold vse beare enioy & shew forth at all tymes for eū hereafter, with their due differences, according to the law of Armes at his & their liberty & pleasure; without the impediment lett or interrupcōn of any pson & psons. In wittnes whereof I the said Clarenceux haue herevnto subscribed my name & set to the seale of myne Office the 15th day of February in the yeare of o' Lord God 1577 annoque Eliz: Reg: 20º.

ROB: COOKE Clarenceulx
Roy d'Armes.

Reade, of Barton.

MS. Coll. of Arms, Misc. Grants, vol. i., 134.
Camden's Grants, vol. iii., 22b.

[*Confirmed ? 1597, to Thomas Reade of Barton, son of Thomas Reade of Barton.*]

Thō Reade of Barton in com Barksh: g. a saltire bet. 4 Garbes or. Crista, a Sparrow-hauke Rowsant on a stock pp: the Jests g. the bells or.

Reade, of Pumney.

MS. Rawl. D. 865, folio 84. In Ashmole's handwriting. Original Paper for the Visitation, 1665-6, not included. No Arms. Marked fee vnpᵈ.

In the list of non-appearances the name of Alexander Read is marked, Entr: but voyd (see p. 11). He is called of Thrup, in Hormer Hundred. Pumney Farm is marked in Greenwood's Map 1829, a little south of Radley.

Hormer hund.

Reade of Barton in Cōm Berke Esqʳ═

| 2. John ob. s. prole. | 1. Sʳ Thomas Reade of Barton in Cōm Berke Knight. | 3. Richard Read of Danes-tew in Com. Oxon obijt aº 1659. | Ellen da: to Sʳ Alexander Cave of Rotherby in Cōm Leic: Kᵗ. |

A

OF BERKSHIRE. 203

A

Alexander Read of Pumney in = Mary da: to Tho: | Charles Reade = Katherine.
Coḿ Berkę æt: 44 ann: Mar. | Rufin of litle Ayot | of White friers
1664. | in Coḿ Hertf: | in London.

1. Alexauder son & 2. Charles.   1. Mary.   4. Jane.
heire ætatis 10 an: —   —
Mar: 1664.   3. Russell. 3. Elizabeth.

ALEX: READE. [*Original.*]

Reade, of Barton.

MS. Ashmole 852, pp. 156, 157. *Additions from Smith MS.*, p. 87.

Robert Lo: Hoo = Anne da: to
ob: 26: Octob: | Jnᵒ Lord
1000, buried at | Griffith of
Lewton. | Wales.

Tho: Lo: Hoo ob = Agnes da: to Sʳ Wᵐ
1042: buryed in yᵉ | Wawton ob: 19:
Grey Fryers of Bed- | Octob 1048: buryed
foy [*Bedford*]. | at Lewton.

Rob: Lo: Hoo = Wilmott da: to John Mal-
ob: 28: Febr: | maynes of Normandy ob:
1129. | 24: Jan: 1148.

Rob: Lo: Hoo ob: 1: = Rosamond da: to Tho: Lord Chelron,
August 1166. | obijt 1191.

Alexander Lord Hoo = Darnell da: to Alexander King of Scotts.

Rob: Lo: Hoo =
A

A]

Rob: Lo: Hoo ob: 9 May = Beatrix da: to Alexander Lo: of Andevill in Normandy ob: 28 May 1314.
1310.

Rob: Lo: Hoo ob 1° Novembris 1811. = Hauice da: to Foulke Lo: Fitz Warren ob: 2: Septemb 1344.

Tho: Lo: Hoo ob: 28 Sept: 1380. = Eliz: da: & heire to Sr Jno St Leger ob: 22° July 1393.

Wm Lo: Hoo ob: 22: Nov: 1410. = Alice da: and heire to Tho: St Omer ob: 10: Octob: 1456.

Eliz: da: and heire to Wm Wichingham *William de Echingham. 2d wife.* = Tho: Lo: Hoo ob 23 Aug: 1420. = Ellenor da: to Thomas Felton. *First wife.*

Tho: Lo: Hoo & Hastings ob: 11: Febr: 1454. [*Smith MS. makes these descend from Eleanor 1st wife.*] = Ellenor da: to Lyonell Lord Welles.   Tho: Hoo ob: 1480. = ... da: and heire of .... Norwood.

Anne *dau'r and heir* vx: Sr Geffrey Bullen Lord Mayor of London [*1457-58*]. =   Tho: Hoo of Hoo in co: Hartford Esquire ob: 20: Mar: 1516. = Maude da: to Edmond Bardolph Esquire.

Sr Wm Bullen K.B. =   Thomas Hoo of Hoo Esqr ob: 11: June 1551. = ... da: and coheire of John Newman [*Newnham*] of Hatfeilde.

Sir Tho: Bullen K.G. Earle of Wiltshire. =   Tho: Hoo Esquire marr: Lucy Sister to Sr Jno Brockett. =   ¶ Tho Reade of Barton neere Abington in co: Berks Esqr ob: 1575. = Anne da: to Tho: Hoo of Hoo Esquire [*in com. Hartf.*].   Dorothy vx: Wm Cater of Vffington in co: Berks. gent.   Margarett vx: Nicholas Brockett.

Queene Anne Vx: K: H: 8:   *Mary wife of William Cary.*   Thomas. — Nicholas.   Margret vx: George Asden.   Grace vx: Francis Markham.   Jane. — Thomasin.

B]

OF BERKSHIRE.

Tho: Reade of Barton in com: Berks Esquire.	=Mary da: to George Stonehouse of Little Peckham in Kent Esq' Clarke of the greene cloth to Q: Mary.	Kath: vx: Tho: Vachell son & heire to Tho: Vachell of Ip[s]den co: Oxon.	Eliz: vx: Rich: Beke of white Knightes in com: Berks.	Mary vx: .... Ward of Hurst and after to Edw: Martin of Shinfeilde in com: Berks Esq'.
S' Tho: Reade of Barton neere Abington Esquire & of Brockett hall in com: Hartford.	=Mary da: & co-heire to S' Jn° Brockett of Brockett hall in com: Hartford Kn'.	John. — Richard.	Mary vx: .... Boulstred.	Ann dau'r and heir to Edward Martin, wife of William Wollascott of Tidmarsh in Berkshire Esq'.

𝕽𝖊𝖞𝖓𝖆𝖑𝖉𝖘.

In the notes by Robert Dale, Richmond Herald, occurs the following. (*Wilts. Arch. Soc.*, ix. 223, *etc.*)

[*From*] Berkshire 168, Reynalds of Trowbridge, Az. on a fess or, 3 cross crosslets fitché gules.

𝕽𝖞𝖉𝖊𝖗, 𝖔𝖋 𝕹𝖊𝖜𝖇𝖚𝖗𝖞.

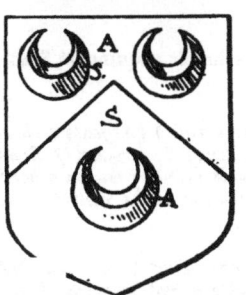

Patent of Arms and Crest to Anthony and John Ryder of Newbury, by S' Edward Walker, Knt., Garter, dated 10th of July, 1662. (*Add. MS.* 14,293, *fol.* 31.) *No Arms tricked. The Trick is taken from a copy of the Grant in the Coll. of Arms.*

To all and singuler vnto whom these presents shall come S' Edward Walker K' Garter principle King of Armes sendeth greeting, Whereas it hath been an Ancient custom in all well gouerned Kingdoms & Common welths to distinguish the conditions & degrees of men by markes & signes of Honour called Armes, such being outward demōstrations of the Inward worth of the bearers Acheived either by their valour in time of war or by their virtueous Indeavours in times of peace; In which respect whereas Anthony Ryder son of John Ryder of Newbry in ye County Berks, Physition did with great Industry & fidelity serve his late Ma'tie King Charles the first of ever blessed memory dureing ye late Rebellion & allso attended his Ma'tie that is now is [*sic*] in forregne parts, And whereas John Ryder of Newbery afores'd Physition [Eldest Brother of the said Anthony Ryder] is a person who hath allways lived in good esteeme & reputation, so that they may deserve to have such Armes Assigned them as they may lawfully beare for the Honour of them & there posterity, Know ye therefore that I the s'd S' Edward

Walker Garter principall King of Armes by the power & Authority Annexed vnto my office by the statutes of ye most noble order of the Garter & confirmed vnto me by Letters patents vnder the great Seale of England doe by these p^rsents give grant & assigne vnto them the said Anthony & John Ryder & to the Heires & dependants [*sic*] of there & either of their Bodyes for ever the coat of Armes & crest hereafter mentioned [vizt] per cheveron Argent & sable three cressants counterchanged and for their crest vpon an Helmett proper mantled gules dubled Argent & wreath of their colours A cresant sable between two wings Argent as hereafter is more lively depicted the which Armes & crest the said Anthony & John Ryder & ye Heires & descendants of their & every of theire Bodyes, lawfully begotten for ever [bearing there true & proper difference] may & shall lawfully at all times & vpon all occasions vse bear & sett forth in Sheild, coat Armour, Seale or otherwise [according to the Law & practice of Armes] without the lett or Interuption of any person whatsoever. In wittness whereof I have herevnto subscribed my name & Affixed the seale of my office this Tenth of July in the 14th yeare of the Raigne of our Soueraigne Lord King Charles the second by the grace of God King of England Scottland ffrance & Ireland, defender of the faith Annoq̃ Dom̃ 1662.

Sambourne, of Aston Tirrold.

MS. Rawl. D. 865, fol. 133.

Sir:

I haue receiued a warrant from yo^w wherein I am to appeare before yo^w this day in Wallingford to shew my descent wth the Arms and Crest I beare, and since I receiued yor warrant I haue made search for y^t and can by noe meanes as yet finde it, wherefore my humble suit is vnto yo^w that yo^w would be pleased to doe me that fauour that I may waite vppon yo^w at London (where yo^w shall appoint) the next terme where I doubt not, but to giue yo^w sattisfaccõn according to yor desire. I would haue waited vppon yo^u to day but by reason I am not freed of my troubles I am something Cautious of com̃eing into the Towne wch I hope yo^w will consider of, from him that is:

Yo^r freind and servant
HENRY SAMBOURNE.

Aston this 14: of
March 1664 [*1664-5*].

[*Addressed*] Theis: For his honored Freind Elias Ashmole Esquire att Wallingford wth trust / present.

[*The broken red wax seal bears a quartered Arms: 1 and 4 (Argent) a chevron (Sable) between three mullets (Gules pierced Or)* SAMBOURNE; *2, perished (? Ermine, a lion passant Gules),* DREW; *3, (Argent) a pale dancettée (Gules) within a bordure (Azure bezantée) for* LUSHILL. *The same arms were allowed at the Visitation made in 1623, see Vol. I., p. 125.*]

Ashmole notes in the list of those adjourned till Lady Day 1655 : that Henry Sambourne app'ed, but being he is entred in the last Visit: & not married, & consequently no addicc'on to the family I dismist him.

OF BERKSHIRE.

Sampson, of Binfield.

MS. Ashmole, 852, p. 173.

Anne da: to .... Chatterton of Chester. == Robert Sampson of Kersay hall in com: Suff: Esquire. == .... da: to .... Felton of Suff: Esqr [2. *wife*].

John Mallett son to Wm Mallett of Ereby in Linc: Esqr. == Anne da: to .... Booth of Chester.

Richard Sampson of Kersay hall in Suffolke Esqr.

Robert Sampson of Bynfeld in co: Berks clarke of ye Counsell to Ks H: 7: & K: H: 8. == Katharine da: to John Mallett of Ereby in Lincolñ Esquire.

Tho: Sampson of Bynfeld in com: Berks Esquire [1589]. == Anne da: to Rich: Staverton.

Simon Sampson. == Jane da: to Nic: Denton of Cardut in Cumb: Esquire [*Cardus*].

Eliz: vx: John Saundes [*Sanders*] Esquire.

Grace vx: John Lovelace of Hurley in com: Berks Esquire [*died* 12 *Nov.* 1579, *bur. at Hurley*].

Turner [? *Thomas*] Sampson of Bynfeld in com: Berks Esqr 1589: first marr: Julyan da: to Jno Redish of Bynfeld in com: Berks. == .... da: to John Yonge of Bynfeld 2: wife.

Robert Sampson a Petitõner for ye roome of a Poore Knt at Windsore. ==

Richard [*Sampson*].

John 5. Joseph 6. Robert 7. William 8. *Ellenor*. Anthony. Symon.

Tho: Sampson second sonne. == Mary da: of .... Doncastle.

George [*eldest son*]. 3. Christopher. 4. Richard.

Frances wife to James Waltham of Denham in com: Buck.

Mary. Katharine.

Scowles, of Charleton in Wantage.

MS. Segar's Grants, College of Arms.
(*See* Vol. I., p. 143.)

A Patent given of these Coat and Creast to Jasper Scowles of chantan in the Parish of Wanting in Barkeshire by William Segar, Garter, the 10 of July An° Domini 1613.

[Signed]   WILLIAM SEGAR, Garter.

Smith, of Abingdon.

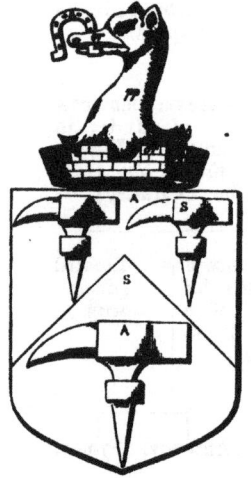

Visitation of London, 1634-35, *Harl. Soc.,*
Vol. XVII., 246.

Richard Smith of Abingdon in Com. Berks═╗
gentl. Vsher to Queen Elizabeth.

Richard Smith of Abingdon═Barbara da. of ·. . . .
sonne & heire.   Jawtherell [*Jawdrell*]
                                            of Derbysheir.

Richard Smith═Martha da. of Pawle Dayrell	Thomas Smith 2 sonne.	3. Edward Smith of the Middle Temple.
of Abingdon of Lillingston Dayrell in		
sonne & heir. Com. Buck. Esq.		
▲		

OF BERKSHIRE. 209

A

Richard Smith = Eliza. da. | Thomas 2. | Anthony. | Walter = Anne da. of Tho-
[of Abingdon | of George | — | — | Smith | mas Edwards D^r
and] of London | Deane of | Edward. | Michaell. | of Lon- | of the Ciuill Law
[gen.] sonne & | Stepney | | | don. | & Chancellor of
heir [living A°] | [in Co̅ | | | | London.
1634. | Midd"]. | | | |

John sonne   2. Thomas.   1. Martha.   2. Anne.   1. Elizabeth.   2. Anne.
& heire.

RIC. SMYTH.

Visitation of London, 1687—1700 (Rothwell), College of Arms, K. 9, fol. 226.

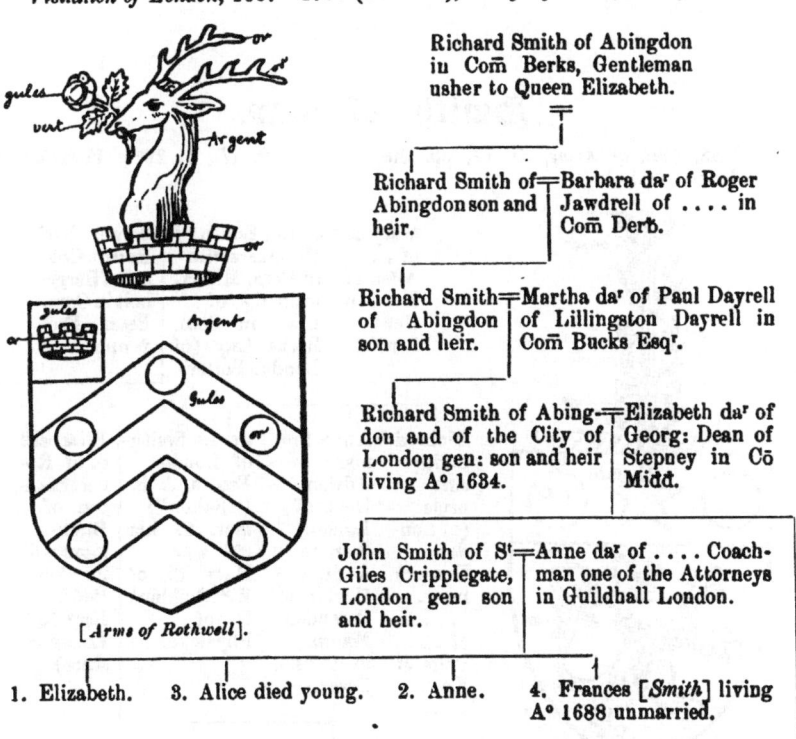

[Arms of Rothwell].

Richard Smith of Abingdon iu Com̅ Berks, Gentleman usher to Queen Elizabeth.

Richard Smith of Abingdon son and heir. = Barbara da^r of Roger Jawdrell of .... in Com̅ Derb.

Richard Smith of Abingdon son and heir. = Martha da^r of Paul Dayrell of Lillingston Dayrell in Com̅ Bucks Esqr.

Richard Smith of Abingdon and of the City of London gen: son and heir living A° 1634. = Elizabeth da^r of Georg: Dean of Stepney in Co̅ Midd.

John Smith of St Giles Cripplegate, London gen. son and heir. = Anne da^r of .... Coachman one of the Attorneys in Guildhall London.

1. Elizabeth.   3. Alice died young.   2. Anne.   4. Frances [Smith] living A° 1688 unmarried.

William Hacker gen. Citizen and Merch^t of London murthered beyond sea. = Martha, eldest da^r of Richard Smith of the City of London gen.   Thomas 2^d son died a child.   Anne 2^d da^r mar. to Jeffry Fleetwood of Holland in Com̅ Palat. Lanc.

A   B

210 NOTES: VISITATIONS

A |
B |

James Rothwell Esq. = Elizabeth eldest da^r and Coheir of William Hacker gen. | Anne [*Hacker*] 2^d da^r and coheir mar^d to Major John Mutlow of Chislehurst in Com Cantij.

1. Richard. — 2. Geffry. — 3. William. — 4. Thomas.

1. Elizabeth. — 2. Anne. — 3. Cecilia.

Martha only da^r born 8th and bapt. the 25th of Dec: 1679.

James Rothwell son and heir born the 21th of March 168⁴/₅, and bapt. the 30th of the same month.

Thomas second son born the 5th and bapt. the 20th of Jan. 1684-5.

[Signed] JA. ROTHWELL.

𝔖mith, of 𝔅ray.

MSS. Coll. of Arms, D. 17, pp. 30^b, 31; *E. D. N.,* I. 29^b; *Visitation of Middlesex,* 1663.

Mary d. of .... Allen of London Gent. 1 wife. = James Smith of Hammersmith in Com. Middx. formerly of Bray in Com. Berks Esqr (of London Salter). = Sarah, d. of Robert Cotton of Bargeholt in Com. Essex Esqr 2 wife.

Richard Smith sine prole (of London Draper) marr. .... d. of .... Colfe of Kew.

Anne first mar: to Adrian Dent of London then to Andrew Harbin of Parenden Magna in Com. Essex.

James Smith of London Esqr s. & h. ("Salter") mar. to his 2nd wife Mary d: of Wm Goddard D^r of Physicke. = Elizabeth d. of Robert Stanton of Birchmorehall in Com. Bedf. Esqr (of Leicestershire).

Mary, aged 15 years 1663.

Sarah wife of Bud Wase of Datchett in Com. Bucks Gent. 1 dau.

Thomas Smith 2 son.

Philip Smith 3 son.

Charles Smith 4 son.

Eliz: wife of Henry Street of London Gent. 2^d daur.

A

OF BERKSHIRE. 211

| Mary wife of Abraham Otgar of London Marchant 3 daur. | Susan 4 daur. — Sarah 5 daur. | Jane dau: of Captain Robert Deane of London 2 wife. | =John Smyth of London Esqr. | =Anne d: of Wm Wase of Windsor in Com. Berks Gent. |

John Smith aged 1 year 1663.   James Smith only sonne aged 8 years 1663.
               [Signed] JOHN SMITH for my father
                                  JAMES SMITH Esqr.

EVERARD GREEN,
    Rouge Dragon, 1908.

Smith, of Cookham and Bray.

MS. Coll. of Arms, D. 19, 121ᵇ, 122 ; Visitation of London, 1664, by Bysshe. Additions from Le Neve's Knights, Harl. Soc., Vol. VIII.

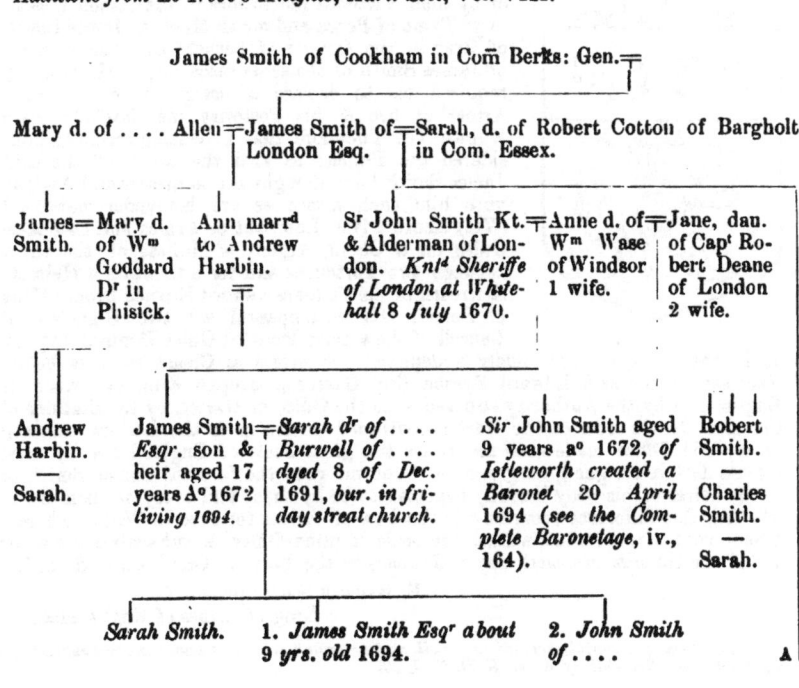

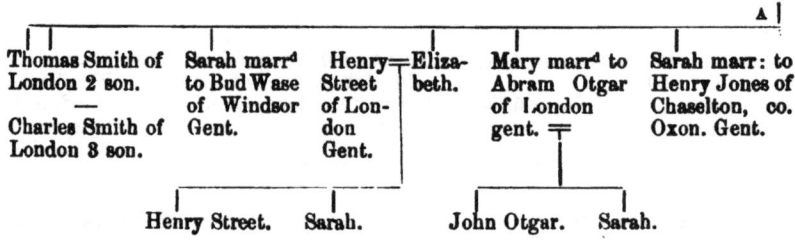

| Thomas Smith of London 2 son. — Charles Smith of London 3 son. | Sarah marr^d to Bud Wase of Windsor Gent. | Henry Street of London Gent. | = | Eliza-beth. | Mary marr^d to Abram Otgar of London gent. $\top$ | Sarah marr: to Henry Jones of Chaselton, co. Oxon. Gent. |

Henry Street.   Sarah.   John Otgar.   Sarah.

Grant of Arms to James Smith of Bray, co. Berks, 23 *January,* 1653 [1653-4]. *MS. Rawl. D.* 865, *fol.* 231.*   *Also MS. Coll. of Arms, E. D. N.,* I. 30.

To all and singuler vnto whom these presents shall come Edward Bysche Esqr Garter principall King of Armes of Englishmen sendeth greeting whereas antiently it hath been a custome & to this day is continued that all Estates & degrees of men haue been & are distinguished each from other by sundry Markes or signes cōmonly called Armes being no otherwise then outward demonstrations & remembrances of the inward worth of the bearers Atcheived either by their Valoure in the feild in tyme of Warre or by their Virtuous indeavours in the Cōmon Wealth in ye Tyme of Peace and for as Much as James Smith of Bray in the County of Berksh^r Esqr Son & heire of James Smith of the same place Esqr hath instantly required me to declare & assigne vnto him such Armes as hee & his Posterity may lawfully beare Knowe Yee Therefore that I haueing seriously Considered the P^{r}mises as also the worth of the said James Smith haue thought fitt to declare and Assigne vnto him such armes as are herevnder menoōned (Viz) Azure a lyon Rampant or Armed and Lampasse Gules on a Cheiff Argent a Mullett of the third between two Torteuxes and for a Crest on a Helmett & wreath of his Collours a sword Erected proper Hilts & Pomell OR encompassed wth two Branches of Laurell of the second Mantled Gules Doubled Argent, as in the Margent more linely is depicted wch Armes & Creast as it is before Expressed I the said Edward Bysche Esqr Garter princepall King of Armes of Englishmen by the Authority annexed vnto the Office of Garter, by the Statutes of the most Noble order of the Garter continued practized & the Letters pattent$_e$ of my said Office made vnto me vnder the great Seale of England doe by these p^{r}sents declare assigne giue graunt & Confirme vnto the foresaid James Smith & to the heires of his body lawfully begotten to be by them and every of them borne wth their due difference according to the Law of Armes for ever In Witnes whereof I haue vnto these presents affixed the seale of mine Office & subscribed my name Dated the three & twentieth day of January in the Yeare of Our Lord God 1653.

E. BYSSHE Garter principall
King of Armes of Englishmen.

* *The Arms are roughly tricked in pencil, and are much rubbed. I have therefore substituted the trick from MS. Coll. of Arms, E. D. N., I. 30.*

Smith, of Old Windsor.

MS. Rawl. D. 865, *fol.* 142.

Sʳ

    I am drawne away this day by an extraordinary occasion soe yᵗ I canne not giue my attendance wᵗʰ yᵘ, but (God willing) will not faile to wait on yᵘ at yᵘʳ chamber in Middle Temple in behalfe of my brother Mʳ Wᵐ Smith and my selfe, there to make yᵉ same entry as is already made wᵗʰ Sʳ Edward Bish. Sʳ, I remaine

Yʳ humble servant
JAMES SMITH.

30ᵗʰ March [16]65
Old Windsor.

[*Addressed*]   For my honored friend Elias Ashmole Esqʳ this.

Black seal with Arms, helmet, and mantlet, three birds. Crest: On a wreath, a bird. Probably the seal mentioned in the patent given below.

Ashmole's Note in the Final List is: Has entred wᵗʰ Sʳ Edw: Byssh—he has not. There is no pedigree in Surrey 1662-68. He did not enter his pedigree, and is not in the list of Disclaimers.

Harl. MS. 1172, 49.

Exemplification of Arms and Crest to the sons of Christopher Smith, late of Windsor, dated the 21st of April, 1671.

Whereas Willm Smith of Old Windsor in the County of Berks, Christopher Smith of Buckhurst in the County of Sussex and James Smith of New Windsor in the County of Berks aforesaide & Simon Smith of Westminster in the County of Midsx. sons of Christopher Smith late of Windsor afore saide, haue desired me to assigne them such Collers as they may lawfully beare vnto a Coate that they haue A very Just & resonable pretense vnto, having A seale of there Grand fathers Walter Smith father to the late named Christopher Smith theire father and severall auntient deeds and Evidenses sealed with the same many of which I haue seene and pervsed & being willing to gratefie so many Worthey persons in theire so Just a Request, by the Authority Committed to me vnder the great seale of England I doe Assigne vnto the said Willm Christopher James & Simon & euery of them borne with theire due diffrenses according to the Law of Armes, thease Collers following viz. in a feild or. 3 Martletts purpure, vntill vpon dilligent serch they shall find what were the Originall Collers of the said Coate of Armes & seale they doe pretend vnto & I doe like wise assigne then, for A Crest, on A Wreethe of theire Collers A Martlett purpure. Witnesse my hand yᵉ 21ˢᵗ day of Aprill 1671.

Snowball, of Old Windsor.

Visitation of Northamptonshire, 1564, H. 4, p. 16, College of Arms.

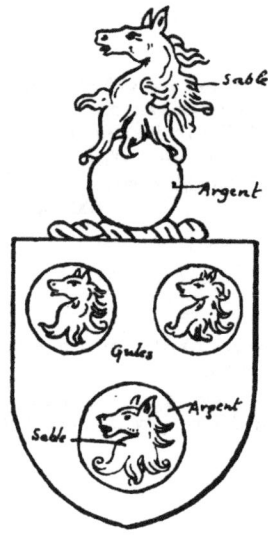

William Snowball of Oulde Wyndesore in Com. Barkes gent maryed Margaret daughter of .... Cranolde of Stoke in Com Bucks gent and by her had yssue Wyllm Snowball his eldest sonne and heir Richard second sonne Katheryn maryed to Wyllm Stasey of Wyndsore in Com Barks gent Margaret maryed to Richard Whyght of London Cittizen Ciscelly maryed to Thomas Leonard of Whyttilburye in Com Northampton.

William Snowball of Potterspurye Parke in Com Northampton gent eldest sonne and heir to Wyllm maryd Eleanore daughter of Robart Colles of London Citizen.

I hereby certify that the above is correctly copied from the Records (H. 4, p. 16) in the Heralds' College. Witness my hand this 26th day of June 1907.

EVERARD GREEN,
Rouge Dragon.

Southby, of Careswell.

Exemplification of Arms and Crest to John Southby of Careswell, by Sir William Segar, Knight, Garter, dated the 10th of February 1631. MS. Ashm. 840, p. 406.

Scutum Gentilitium, sive Paludamentum et Christa Johannis Southby de Careswell in Comitatu Berks Generosi, filij et hæredis Ricardi Southby filij Johannis Southby. Exemplificata singula sibique hæredibus, posteriaque suis confirmata inperpetuum, vna cum propria eorundem descripcione per me Guilielmum Segar Militem, Garterum Principalem Regem Armorum, Dat. sub manû mea et sigillo Officij mei decimo die Mensis Februarij Anno Regni Regis Caroli septimo Annoque Domini 1631.

Je port d'Or, vn Cheveron entre trois Pommes de Gueles et pour son Tymbre sur vn Heaulme et Tortillon de ses couleurs, vn demy Lion rampant d'Or, tenant en son patte vne Pomme de Gueles, Le Manteau rouge doublée d'Argent.

Par moy Guillaume Segar Jartier
  premier Roy d'Armes des Anglois

Southby of Abingdon *a crescent.*
Southby of Appleton *a mullet.*

sigillum officij Garterij principalis regis Armorum [*added by Ashmole*].

Stafford, of Bradfield.

1. STAFFORD.
2. LANGFORD.
3. NORRIS.
4. HORNE.

MS. Ashmole 852, p. 161.
Additions from Smith MS.

Sʳ Wᵐ Norris=Anne da: and heire to Wᵐ Horne Alderman of London 1476 & Maior 1488: third wife.

Sʳ John=Katha-Langford. rine Norris *dau'r & coheir.*

Anne *dau'r & coheir* vx: Thomæ Wroughton Esquire.

Jane *dau'r & coheir* vx: John Cheney of West Woodbey in Berks.

Eliz: *dau'r & coheir* Vx: Wᵐ Farmer of Somerton in Oxon: Esquire sans yssue.

Wᵐ Stafford de=Anne da: and Brodfelde *Esqʳ* heire to Sʳ Jnᵒ in Com. Berks. Langford Kᵗ.

Sʳ William Wroughton of Wiltshire.

John Che-=Dorothy ney. Yate.

Thomas Staf-=Anne daūr to ford *Esqʳ*. .... Best of London.

Thomas=Mary *dau'r and* Wrough- *heir to John Bar-* ton. *wick.*

Thomas Cheney of West Woodhey.

Sʳ Read Staf-=Mabell da: to Rich: ford of Brod- Staverton of Warfeld feild in com: widow to *Francis* Berks made *Waferer and also to* Knᵗ 1601. Nicholas Williams of Burfeld, *Esqʳ*.

Anne vx: .... Fabian.
—
Eliz: Vxor Thomas [*John*] Berry *Esqʳ*.
—
Ellenor vx: Frances Wellesborne.

Edward married [*Anne*] da: to .... Dockwray.
—
Sʳ Frances stafford made Knᵗ 1599 [? 1591].
—
Edward [*Edmund*] sans yssue.

Stampe, of Moulsford.

Patent of Arms, ? 1586, by Robert Cooke, Clarenceux, to Thomas Stampe of Moulford in co: Barks. (*MS. Coll. of Arms, Misc. Grants,* iv. 134.)

Sable a ffess ermine bet: 3 Horses p^t Argent, Q^ring . . . . (*viz*) *Gules ffrette A. & a Chief Argent.*

Crest: *on a wreath a deme Horse saliant Argent.*

[*The horses are generally represented in full course, making the Arms more allusive.*]

Stonhouse, of Radley.

MS. Rawl. D. 865, fol. 220^b. Draft of Letter.

Honourd S^r

There is a fee due to me for entring yor Armes & descent when I was at Abingdon & wch yor Son vndertook to send me to Wantage: but hav^e not yet rec^d it, or since heard from you, I thought good to acquaint yor [*self*] therewith: & if you please to send it to Mr Harte at the new Inn in Abingdon it will suffice, & save you the trouble of conveying it thither.

      Honord S^r
       I am
        Yo^r most humble serv^t
         E. A[*shmole*] W[*indsor*] Herald.

To the right woll Sr Geo: Stonehouse
 Bar^t at Radley in Berke.

[*The Fee was not paid, therefore the pedigree was not included in the Visitation; see the next page.*]

OF BERKSHIRE. 217

Stonhouse.

MS. Ashmole 852, p. 174.

[*See The Complete Baronetage, by G. E. C., vol. ii., p. 36.*]

1. [*Wife*]=George Stone-=2. [*Wife*] Eliz: da: to
Eliz: da   house of Little   Davy Woodroff Alder-
to ....   Peckham in   man of Lond: [*and*
Gibson of Kent Esquire   *sometime*, 1554-5,
Kentt   [*and of Radley,* *Sheriff of London*]
gentle-   *co. Berks*] one   Sister to Sr Nic: Wood-
man.   of the Clarkes   roff widow to Walter
           of the greene   Lewson & 3ly mar: to
           cloth to Qu: Rich: Kingsmill Esqr
           Elizabeth ob: Surveyor to the Court
           1572.   of Wardes.

Edward.	Rose vx:	Mary vx: Tho:	William	Nicholas.	Dionisia a daughter
—	Robt	Read of Barton	[*of Rad-*	—	married to Sr Ed-
Thomas.	Tailor	neere Abington	*ley. See*	Walter.	ward Hext of Ham
	one of the	in Berks Esqr.	*Visit.*	—	in com: Somerset
	Tellors.		1623].	James.	Knight.

Stonhouse, of Radley.

Original paper for the Visitation, 1665-6. Not included.   *MS. Rawl. D. 865,*
fol. 93, in Ashmole's handwriting. No arms. Marked not pd.

Hormer hund.

The Armes were granted to George Stonehouse Grandfather to Wm Stonehouse, herevnder named by Sr Gilbert Dethick Garter the 5 Feb: ao 2 & 3 Ph. & Mar.

Sr William Stonehouse of Radley=Eliz: da: & sole heire of Jo:
in Com Berke Baronet. | Powell in Com Heref:

1. Sr John	2. Sr George=Margaret	3. William=.... da:	Eliz: wife to Edward
Stone-	Stonehouse da: to	Stone- to	Parrot of Huike in
house Knt	of Radley Rich: Ld	house. Creswell	Com Berke.
obijt s:	Barrt æt: 61 Love-	Sergeant	
prole.	ann: 16 Mar: lace.	at Law.	Mary wife of Will:
	1664.		Langton Dr in Di-
			vinity.

1. George son and heire æt: 2. John.   Elizabeth wife to Sr Richard Stiddolfe
28 annorum 16 Mar: 1664.   —   of Norbury in Com Surr.
                               3. James.

JOHN STONHOUSE for my Father
Sr GEORGE STONHOUSE. [*Original.*]

Stonhouse, of Radley.

Arms and Crest assigned to George Stonehouse of Little Peckham, Co. Kent, by Sir Gilbert Dethick, Knight, Garter, dated the 5th of February, 2 and 3 of Philip and Mary [1556]. *MS. Ashm.* 858, p. 195; *another copy MS. Ashm.* 840, p. 387.

S[r] Gilbert Dethick Garter 5: Febr 2 & 3: Ph: & Mary assignes to George Stonehouse of letle Peckham in Cōm Kent Gentleman silver on a Fesse sable a Lyons head Cabocke betweene two mollets Gold, betweene 3 Faulcons volant asure beaked membred the Gestes gold, vpon a helme on a Torse gold & azure a spanyells hedd copped silver, holding in his mouth a pertryge in his pp colour about his neck vpon a collar sable 3 Besantes rynged & porfled gold mantled Gū: doubled selver.
Sealed both with his seale of Armes & of his Office.
Ex.

Syms or Sims.

In some Books of Grants these Arms are entered under Berks and Somerset.]

Granted to William Syms of Charde, co. Somersett, by Robert Cooke, Clarenceux, 6 August, 1591.

MS. College of Arms, Misc. Grants, E. D. N., B. 55.

William Syms of Charde in Com: Somersett.

Azure five crosses crosslet in saltire Or. Crest: a demi greyhound erased Or.

(*Burke describes the crest as a demi leopard proper.*)

OF BERKSHIRE.

Thorold, of Binfield.

MS. Rawl. D. 865, fol. 82; in Ashmole's handwriting. Original paper for the Visitation, 1665-6. Not in the Visitation. No Arms given.

Cookham hund.

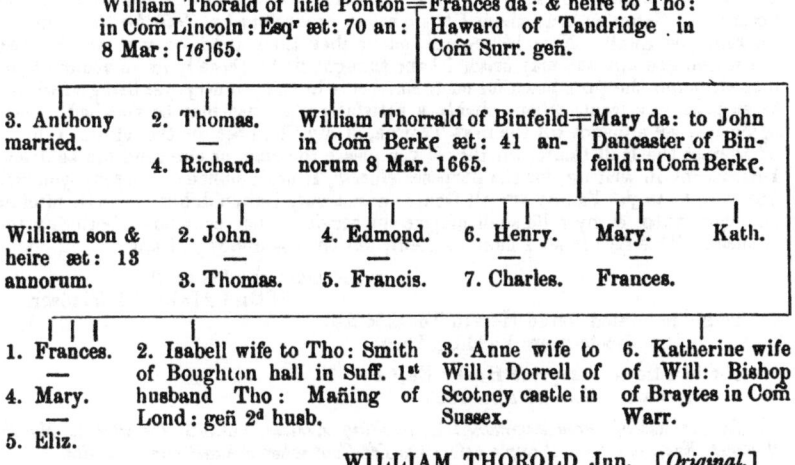

William Thorald of litle Ponton=Frances da: & heire to Tho:
in Com̃ Lincoln: Esqr æt: 70 an: Haward of Tandridge in
8 Mar: [16]65. Com̃ Surr. gen̄.

3. Anthony married. 2. Thomas. 4. Richard. | William Thorrald of Binfeild=Mary da: to John Dancaster of Binfeild in Com̃ Berke.
in Com̃ Berke æt: 41 annorum 8 Mar. 1665.

William son & heire æt: 13 annorum. | 2. John. 3. Thomas. | 4. Edmond. 5. Francis. | 6. Henry. 7. Charles. | Mary. Frances. | Kath.

1. Frances. 4. Mary. 5. Eliz. | 2. Isabell wife to Tho: Smith of Boughton hall in Suff. 1st husband Tho: Mañing of Lond: gen̄ 2^d husb. | 3. Anne wife to Will: Dorrell of Scotney castle in Sussex. | 6. Katherine wife of Will: Bishop of Braytes in Com̃ Warr.

WILLIAM THOROLD Jun. [*Original.*]

Thorne, of Sonning.

Visitation of Surrey, 1572. College of Arms, G. 17, p. 88. No arms given.

Nicholaus Thorne de Sunning in com: Berks.=

Nicholaus Thorne=Alicia, filia Robti Burnam
de Sunning. relicta Johis Knight.

Nicholaus=Margeria filia | Thomas Thorne of=Agnes filia .... Cattell*
Thorne. .... Lygins. | Apscourt in Surrey. relicta William Leigh.

Walterus Thorne.

---

* *This pedigree is copied into Vincent's Surrey, p. 288, where this name appears as Agnes filia S.... Conell. Cottell, Visitations of Surrey, Harl. Soc., XLIII., p. 41.*

Touchet, of Southcott.

MS. Rawl. D. 865, *fol.* 221.

S[r]

Swallowfield 27 Mar. 1665.

In pursuance of his Ma[ties] Com vnder the greate Seale of England, for Registring the descente, Matches, Issues, & Armes, of all the Gentry w[th]in this County, the high Constable of Theale hundred hath retorned you sumoned to Redding on Saterday last, where I there sat in execucōn of y[t] Com for the Hundred wherein you dwell. Now in regard you neither then appd, or sent any Excuse, to the end noe mistake may arise, I haue thought fit by these lynes to acquaint you that although the pper place for such Entries is in the Country, yet being vnwilling to surprise any Gent: where pbably a satisfactory excuse may be vouched, I haue adjourned yo[r] appance till the next Tearme, at my Chamber in the Midle Temple, ou against the Hall Court, whether if you please to come, or else send me sufficient Instruccōns in writing, for the purposes aforesd, It shall suffice: & hereby you will doe y[t] right to yo[r] Family w[ch] all Gent: are not only inioyn'd, but count themselues obleidged vnto: & my selfe shall pforme the service I am comanded, both for you & them. This (S[r]) is all I haue at psent, but the assurance y[t] I am

Yo[r] most humble serv[t]

E[*lias*] A[*shmole*] Windsor.

To my honoured freind Mervin Touchet Esq[r]
at Southcote neere Redding These.

The like tre to Peregrine Hobby Esq[r] at
Bysham. Dat. 20 Apr. 1665.

In the list of those summoned to Reading Assizes, 1665-6, the note to Mervin Tutchet, Esq., is: *he will app'e before the L[ds] Con[s] when I shall summon him.*

Trumbull, of East Hampstead.

Grant of Arms and Crest to William Trumbull of East Hampstead, by S[r] Edward Walker, Knight, Garter, dated the 10th of October, 1662. *MS. Ashm.* 858, pp. 189-190.

To all and singular vnto whom these presents shall come S[r] Edward Walker Kn[t] Garter Principall King of Armes of Englishmen sendeth greeting. Whereas it hath been an antient Custome and to this day continued, that all estates and degrees of men have been and are distinguished each from other by markes or Signes called Armes being outward demonstracōns of the inward worth of the Bearers. And whereas William Trumbull of Easthampstead in the County of Berks Esquire one of the Clerks of the Signet in Ordinary, Sonne of William Trumbull Agent for his late Ma[tie] of ever blessed memory at Bruxells in Flanders, and one of the Clerkes of his Ma[ties] most hon[ble] Privy Councell who deriveth his descent from y[e] antient Family of Trumbulls in y[e] Kingdome of

OF BERKSHIRE.   221

Scotland hath requested me to assigne and confirme vnto him such Armes as he
may lawfully beare for the honour of himselfe and his Posterity. Know yee
therefore, that I the s^d Sr Edward Walker Kn^t Garter Principall King of Armes,
by the Power and authority annexed to my Office by the Statutes of the most
Noble Order of the Garter, and confirmed vnto me by Letters Patents vnder the great
Seale of England, doe hereby give grant assigne and confirme vnto him the said
William Trumbull, and to the heires & descend^ts of his body for ever ye Coate of
Armes and Creast hereafter mencōned vizt Argent three Buffells heads erased
Sable, Armed azure, each of them breathing fire; And for his Creast, vpon an
Helmet proper, Mantled Gules doubled Argent, and Wreath of his colours, A
Buffells head Erased Sable, Armed azure, breathing Fire, as in the Margent hereof
more lively is depicted. The which Armes and Creast he the said William
Trumbull, and the heires and Descendants of his Body lawfully begotten for ever
(bearing their due & proper differences) may and shall lawfully at all tymes, and
vpon all occasions, vse, beare, and set forth in Sheild, Coat Armour, Pennon, Seale,
or [o]therwise, without the lett, interrupcōn, dispute, or contradiccōn of any person
whatsoever. In Witnes whereof I have herevnto subscribed my name, and affixed
the Seale of my Office this tenth day of October, in the fowerteenth yeare of the
reigne of our Soveraigne Lord Charles the second by y^e grace of God King of England, Scotland, France and Ireland Defender of the faith &c: Annoque Domini 1662.

                                                              EDW: WALKER Garter.

Unton, of Wadley.

1 and 4. UNTON.
2. FETEPLACE.
3. YOUNGE.

The Arms were granted to Sir Thomas Unton in
the reign of Henry VIII., by Barker, Garter.

MS. Ashm. 852, p. 182. Additions from "The
Unton Inventories."

Hugh Vmpton=Sibbell da: and sole heire to W^m
alias Vmton | Fetiplace of Stoken Church in
Esquire. | com: Oxon: Esquire.

Sr Thomas=Eliz: da: and heire of [William] Younge
Vmton of | [Elizabeth da' & heire of John [Oliver]
Wadley in | Hide of Denchworth in Abington (Harl.
com: Berks| MS. 1153, fol. 30, and 1139, p. 114)].
Knight.

NOTES: VISITATIONS

A

Thomas Unton of Letrombe Regis co: Berks. ? d. s.p. = **Anne dau:** of John Cottesmore of Brightwell in Co: Oxon she mar: for her 2d husband Thomas [John] Tyghall of .... in Com: Berks. (*Visit. Oxon, Harl. Soc.*, p. 196.)

[*Edyth*], Vx. Sr John Russell [*of Strensham*] de Com: Vigorn.

— [Sr Thomas Russell.]

Anne Unton wife of John Vampage Esq: of Wollashull co: Worcester.

Mary Bourchier elder dau: & coh: of John Lord Berners died s.p. = **Sr Alexander Vnton** of Wadley in com: Berks gent. Knight died 16 Decr. 1547. ⊤ **Cicely** da: to Edward Boulstrell Bulstrode of Bradbury [Bradborough] co: Bedford, Esqr. She afterwards mar: [Sir Robert] Kelloway of Minster Lovell in Com: Oxford (*Visit. Bucks* 1634).

Alice Kelloway only dau. & heire mar: John Lord Harrington.

Sr Edward Vnton of Wadley in co: Berks made Kn^t of the Bath anno primo Regis Elizabeth 1556: obijt 1588 [1583]. = **Anne da:** to Edw: Seamer Duke of Somerset Earle of Hartford and Viscount Beauchamp widow to John Dudley Earle of Warwick.

Eliz: vx: [Sir] John Crooke [Croke] of Chilton in Com Berks Esquire [*Bucks, Visit. Bucks*, 1634].

Henry Unton (*Visit. Bucks:* 1634).

Thomas Umton died s.p. and 4 other sons ? died s.p.

[*Dorothy*] [*Richard*] da: to Knightly of Fawsley in Northamptonshire Kn^t 1 wife. = [1.] **Colonel Edward Vnton** of Wadley Esqr sans yssue. = **Kath:** elder da: to Sir George Hastings of Gopsal, co. Leic: Kn^t. She mar: 2 Sir Walter Chetwynd of Ingestre, co. Stafford Knt.

[2.] **Sr Henry Vnton** of Wadley in co: Barks, made Kn^t by y^e Earle of Leic: in Holland 1586 Ambassador to France ob: in France 1596 s.p. = **Dorothy da:** to Sr Thomas Wroughton of Broadhinton of Co: Wilts mar. 2 George Shirley Esq. of Staunton Harold co: Leic.

Alexander. — **Francis.** — **Edmund.** All sans ysue [*in the lifetime of their father*].

[1.] **Anne vx:** Sr Valentine Knightley de Fawsley co: Northton Kn^t of Woodlech in Com: Buck Son & heire of Rich. (*Visit. Bucks*, 1634).

[2.] **Cicely vx:** John Wentworth of Gosfield in Essex and 2 to Sir Edward Hoby of Bisham Co: Berks Kn^t.

OF BERKSHIRE.

Wake, of Windsor.

Le Neve's Copy of the Visitation of Bucks, 1634, *fol.* 56. *See Foster's Alumni Oxon.*

[*No arms tricked*]. *Arms from MS. Coll. of Arms,* 2 *C.* 26, *fol.* 20[b]. *Visitation of Bucks,* 1634. *Vincent,* 114, 19.

John Wake of Hartwell, co: Northampton. =⊤= Elizabeth dau: of Sir Edward Gorges Knt.

Arthur Wake *Clerk* [*of Oxford*] 3rd Son, Rector of Great Billing, Northampton.

S[r] Isaack Wake, his Ma[ts] Resident Embasodor died [*July* 1632] Sans Isue att Paris & was Brought into England & buried at Douer [*Castle*] in Kent [*second son*].

Abram Wake now liueing at Winsore in Com Berks.

Eliz: mar: to ....   Mary.

Wattys.

MS. College of Arms, Oxford Grants, i., 45.

A confirmation of Arms & Crest, by [? *Roger Machado*] Richemont otherwise Clarencieux Principall Herauld and Kinge of Armes to Robert Wattys and John Wattys, gentlemen, whose auncestors were most inhabiten in the countie of Barkeshire, & theire posterite for evermore thus : Quarterly, firste quarter Siluer a fece synople on the fece three crosses sarselley siluer betwixt three Rauenys hedes rased sable. Second quarter : Goylys a dragon golde volaunt armyd siluer a chief siluer a labell wth three poinctes armyn. Crest : Vpon the healme a rauens hede sett in a wrethe sinople and siluer manteld and lyned of the same.

Youen at London xxvj[ti] day of Septembre 1503.

No trick of the Arms or Crest.

Wellesborne, of Hanney.

MS. Ashmole 852, p. 191.

Partly published in the book called Ashmole's Antiquities of Berkshire.

Thomas Welles-=[*Margery Daughter to
borne of Wick-   Thomas Powre, of Blech-
ham in com :   ingdon in Oxfordshire
Buck, Esquire. (Ashm. Berks, iii., 299).*]

Sʳ John Wellesborne of | [*Lucy, Wife of* .... | Arthur | [*Margery, Wife of Ro-
Fulwell in com : Oxon. | *Hyde of Stokelyne in* | sine | *bert à Wood (Ashm.
                       | *Oxfordshire (Ashm.* | prole. | *Berks, iii., 299).*]
                       | *Berks, iii., 299).*] | |

John Wellesborne [*Esqʳ now living (Smith MS.,* p. 86)].

Joane [*Joyce*]=Oliver Wellesborne of West han-=Jane da: to Jnᵒ Yate of Lyford
da: to .... | ney in Com: Berks Gent. | in com: Berks. 2ᵈ *wife.*
Humfreys of
Abendon [*Com'*
Berks. First
Wife].

                Dorothy vx: Jnᵒ Latton   .... vx: ....
                [*Esqʳ*].   Blomer.

Alice da: to .... Mar-=Francis Wellesborn=Elenor da: to Tho- | Friswith vx:
tin of Evelton widow of Westhanny in com: | mas Stafford of | Ric: Hynton
to Hen: Barton. [*First* | Berks, 1589 [*died* | Brodfeld in com: | [*of Bourton*
Wife, died s.p.] | 6 *Dec.* 1602, æt. 76]. | Berks. [2ᵈ *wife.*] | *co : Berks*].

Frances da: & coheire vx: Paule   Katharine   Anne [2 *da. and Coheire.*
Ambrosi Crooke Esquire.   [*d. young*]. *Harl. MS.* 1139, p. 135].

[*John Wells-* | [*Dorothy, Wife of* | [*Margery*] | .... vx: | [.... *first married to*
bourne (Ashm. | *John Latton of* | vx: Jnᵒ | .... | .... *Eiston of* ....
Berks, iii., | *Kingeston Bake-* | Ashcombe | Coxshed | 2ᵈˡʸ *to* .... *Hewet and*
299.] | *puze (Ashm. Berks,* | of Lyford. | of Genge | 3ʳᵈˡʸ *to* .... *Fournes*
                | iii., 299).] | | [*co :* | *de Com' Oxon.*]
                | | | *Berks*]. |

White, of Wokingham.

MS. Rawl. D. 865, fol. 69, original paper. Arms on fol. 68, White of Fyfield.

My grand fathers name was William White borne at East Hendred in Comitat. Berks, hee had 5 sonns, first John, hee died without jssue, the seconds name William, he had 4 sonns John, Richard, Thomas, and John. His 3^d sonn John he had 3 sons, William, Richard and Bartholomew, his 4th sons name John, hee died without jssue. His 5 sonn was Ralph, he had 3 sonns Thomas, William, and John, his sonn Thomas had one sonn his name Thomas, William has 2 sonns William and George.

My grand father had 3 sonns named John, I doe not knowe my great grand fathers name, my grand father liued in Henry the eights tyme, queene Maryes tyme and died in queene Elizabeths Reigne.

My great grandfather had noe more sonns but my grandfather.

[*fol.* 101.]   [*No Signature.*]

S^r My Childrenes Names are William and Winnefred.

                             JOHN WHITE of Southwarmborw in Hamsheere.

And in Ashmole's handwriting:—

Sr John White   Mr John White of Okingham
was his brother.   Son to Sr John White [*of*] Warnborow.
Fee paid.

Whitlock, of Wokingham.

MS. Rawl. D. 865, fol. 112.

                                               London the 6 March 1664.

S^r

Aboute 3 : yeares past : I liuing Att Clapham in Surry : Receued A Summones to Apeare In Southwarke : before the Heralds Att Armes : where I did Appeare & my Descent & Armes ware Entred And the Fees paid Accordingly : which I thought good to Certyfy : who Am

                               Your Servante
                                             RO : WHITLOCK.

For Elias Ashmole
Esquire These.

[*This letter is written on the back of the printed summons, ordering Robert Whitlock to appear before Elias Ashmole, Windsor-Herald at Arms, on Saturday, March 11 next* [1664-65], *at the Sign of the Bear in Reading, there to enter his descent and Arms. In the margin is written—Wokingham Parish. A note by Ashmole in the Summons List says that he lives in London.*]

The following is the pedigree entered :—

Visitation of Surrey, 1662—1668, from MS. College of Arms, D. 15, fol. 96^b.

                 John Whitlock of Wokingham in Com. Berks.

Richard Whitlock of London Merch^t═Katherine da : of John Burchett of Kent.

226   NOTES: VISITATIONS

▲

[2.] Robert Whitlock of Clapham = Mary da: of Ralph Maddison of
in Com. Surry Merch‴. | Newcastle upon Tyne Ar:

Richard son and heire Katherine. Elizabeth. Mary. Apolina. Anne.
æt. 10 An° 1662.

[Signed] ROBERT WHITLOCK.

From the Visitation of London, 1633-4-5, Harl. Soc., XVII., p. 347.

Whitlock, qua'rtly 1 and 4, bl[ue], a chevron indent betwn 3 falcons or; 2 & 3, vair, [a] lab[el] of 3 [points] sa.

Crest, a tower vair, on the summit a falcon perched with wings retro extensis gold.

Confirmed to Richard Whitlock, gent., son of Rich. Whitlock, gent., by W. D[ethick], G[arter], 20 April 1592 (*Stowe MS.* 676, pp. 87ᵇ and 99ᵇ).

Broad Street Ward.

John Whitlock = Anne daūr of   Richard Whitlock =
of Ockingham | John Plumer   second son of Lon-
in Com. Berks.| of Ockingham.   don Mʳchant.

Richard Whit- = Catherin daūr   Sʳ James Whittlock
lock of London of David Bur-   Knight one of the
Mʳchant aº   chet of Wy in   Judges of the King's
1633.   Kent.   Bench.

1. Richard.   2. Robert.   3. John.   Katherin.

RICHARD WHITLOCK.

WHITLOCK quartering DE LA BECHE.

From Le Neve's copy of the Visitation of Buckingham, 1634, fol. 55 (*see Fam. Minor. Gent.*, vol. iii., p. 1124, Harl. Soc., Vol. XXXIX.). *No Arms tricked.*

Roger. =   factū sine dat.

Wᵐ Delabech 1231. =   15 of H. 3 [*1230-1*] & 31 of H: 3ᵈ [*1246-7*].

Galfridus Delabech. =   in deeds 2 Ed: 1ˢᵗ [*1273-4*].
▲

OF BERKSHIRE.   227

A

Rogerum Delabech.=⊤   in deeds 19 Ed: 2ᵈ [1325-6].

Galfrid⁹ Delabech.=⊤   in deeds 31 Ed: 2ᵈ [? 13ᵗʰ 1319-20]

Johannes Delabech.=⊤   in deeds 19 Ed: 2ᵈ [1325-6] 13 Ed: 3ᵈ
                         [1339-40] 22 Ed: 3ᵈ [1348-9].

Tho: Delabech.=⊤   in deeds 26 Ed. 3ᵈ [1352-3] 45 of Ed: 3ᵈ
                         [1371-2].

Richardus Delabech.=⊤   in deeds 10 Rich. 2ᵈ [1386-7] 21 of Rich. 2ᵈ
                         [1397-8] 15 of H. 4ᵗʰ [1413?].

Robert Delabech.=⊤   in deeds 4 of H. 5 [1416-7] 9 H. 5 [1421-2]
                         17 H. 6 [1439].

John Whitlocke mar.=Agnes Delabech   32 H. 6 circa   intaled by Agnes De-
to his wife Agnes De-| mar. & had issue Aᵒ Domⁿ 1454. labech 31 of H: 6
labech about 32 y. | to Jo: Whit-   Before yᵉ mariage.
of H: 6 [1453-4]. | locke.

       William Whitlock.=⊤   10: H: 7 [1494-5] 1: H: 8 [1509-10].

       Rich: Whitlock.=⊤   2: H: 8 [1510-11] 3: H. 8 [1511-12].

John Whitlocke [of Ocking-=⊤   [2.] Richard Whitelocke=⊤   Jeromie=⊤
ham in com. Berks].   [of London Merchant].   Whitelocke.

Dela- | Wᵐ Whitlocke now=⊤   Edmⁿ   Jacobus=⊤Eliz: filia Edri   Wᵐ=⊤
bech | Lord of yᵉ Mannʳ of White- White- | Bulstrode de   White-
Whit- | Beche nere Oken-   locke   locke | Hedgeley: Bul-   locke.
locke. | ham Comⁿ Berks: of   a Capt. miles | strode in Com.
        | Becheslands & Whit- of .... Justici-| Buck: Armi-
        | church in Comⁿ.   s.p.   arius in| ger.
        | Oxonⁿ.   Banco:
                                       Domini   Willmⁿ White-
                                       Regi.   locke.

        William Whitelocke.

Eliz: ux: Tho: Moston   Bulstrode White-=Rebecca da: of   Cicely ux: Edri
de Motton [Moston] in   lock of fauley   .... Bennet   Dixon de folden
Walles Kᵗ.   Court in Comⁿ   Aldʳmⁿ of Lond. in Tunbridge in
                        Buck.   Comⁿ Kent.

𝔚ickham, of Abingdon.

From Harl. MS. 1557, *fol.* 51ᵇ. *The Visitation of the County of Oxfford made by John Phillipott Somerset herald & William Ryley Blewmantelle purseuant of Armes in* Aº 1634. *In the handwriting of Richard Mundy, with additions by him.*

To all Christian people to whome this present wrighting shall Come. I Richard Wickham of SwayCliffe in the Countie of Ooxon esqr aged eightie yeares & vpwards doe by these presents Certiffie publish & deClare that William Wickham of Abingdon in Com Berks sonn of John Wickham of Rotherffeld in the Countie of Sussex is my kinsman in Blood & descended ffrom the house of the Wickhams of SwaCliff Insomuch that me selfe haueing no yssue at all & neither of my brothers ffor along time haueing any yssue male I intended for many yeares together (notwithstanding one of my brothers had many daughters), to settle the mannor of Swacliff where my predecessors haue continued aboue 3. hundred years vppon my kinsman Willm Wickham of Abingdon & his heires male wch I would not haue done but that I was long since ffully asured by my ffather that John Wickham of Rotherffeld afforesaid was the nearest kinsman of my Blood & name Witnes my hand & seale Dated the twoo & twenty day of may in the Eleuenth of our soueraigne lord King Charles Anno q, dm̃. 1635.

                RICHARD WICKHAM.

published acknowledged
& declared in the spreence of vs
Thomas Meriett humphery Wickham
fferdenand Wickham Timothey Crayker
Thomas Burden his mark Thomas harper.

Thomas Burden maketh oth that hee was present as a witnes when the aboue named Richard Wickham did publish seale & subscribe this present wrighting in the presence of the parties aboue named who then subscribed there names a witnes thereunto.

            Jur. 4º Junij, 1635.

                 Ro RICHE.

𝔚ilkinson, of Laurence 𝔚altham.

MS. Ashm. 836, p. 679. *Original notes for Visitation,* 1665-66 (Vol. I., p. 810).

Roger Wilkinson of Barnesley Yorkeshire bare Geules a fesse vaire an vnicorne cursant in cheife Or, yᵉ Creast was giuen by W: Flower Norroy 13 Sept: 1563, maryd . . . . & had issue

John Wilkinson of Barnesley Yorkeshire maryed Elizabeth da: of John Snell of Rotheram yorkeshire & had issue Will & Robert.

Williā Wilkinson of Ealand yorkesh: maryd . . . . da: of . . . . & had

| William Wilkinson of Bolton on Dearne maryed Bridgett da: of Will Sacheuerell of Hemshall Derbish: & had Francis, Patrick, John & Ellen. A | Robert Wilkinson of Ealand Yorkeshire maryed Margarett da: of John Smith & had issue Tho: Robert, John, Williā Jeffry & Isabell. B | Christopher Wilkinson, maryed & had issue Isabell wife to Thomas Wilkinson of Ealand. | Robert Wilkinson of Ealand Yorkesh eldest brother to Christopher had issue C |

OF BERKSHIRE.   229

A |

1º. Francis Wilkinson of Bolton on Deane &c.

3º. John Wilkinson of Ealand Yorkeshire had issue onely Frances wife to .... Smith & Elizabeth wife to ....Crowther.

B |

1º. Thomas Wilkinson of Ealand Yorkesh: dyed 1603, maryed Isabell da: of Christopher Wilkinson his onely child. G. a fess vaire an vnicorne cursant in cheife Or, within a bordure engrailed of the last egressed, & had issue

C |

William Wilkinson of Ealand maryed Jennett da: of Henry Sauill Esq: & sister of Sᵣ Henry Sauill prouost of Eaton Colledge Bucks & Warden of Merton College Oxō. & had

Gabriel Wilkinson of Vpper Winchingdon & [*Vicar of*] Bishops Wooburne Buckes. borne 1576 dyed 17ᵗʰ Dec: 1658, maryed Margery da: of Robert .... of Vxbridge in Com: Midsex gent: & had Tho: Will: John Margᵗ Mary John Arthur Richᵈ Matthewe Gabriell & Robert.

1º. John Wilkinson D.D. principall of Magdalen Hall in Oxoñ who dyed issueless & left all to Henry Wilkinson D.D. & principall of Magdalen hall Oxoñ also.

2º. William Wilkinson maryed Mary da: of Henry Postlethwaite of Ormethorpe & had issue

1º. Thomas Wilkinson of Laurance [*Waltham*] Berkes Clarke maryed Hester da: of Will Hauteyn & hath Elizabeth born 20ᵗʰ of July 1659, & Thomas borne 13ᵗʰ of Jan. 1661. [*There are astrological signs to these dates.*]

1º. Henry [*Wilkinson*] D.D. who maryed Elizabeth da: of Anthony Gifford & hath John & Henry &c.

𝔚illiams, of 𝔅urfield.

MS. Ashm. 852, p. 188, *gives the quarterings and Crest :—*

1 *and* 4. WILLIAMS, *Azure, two organ-pipes in saltire, the sinister surmounted by the dexter, between four crosses pattée Argent.*

2. MORE, *Argent, a moor-cock* (?) *Sable.*

3. FOX, [*Gules*] *a chevron ermine between three lions' heads erased Or, on a chief barry nebulée Argent and Vert, a pale* [*Sable*] *charged with a pelican Or, all within a bordure of the same charged with ten hurts.*

Crest, a fish weir.

Wilmott, of Letcombe Regis.

(Vol. I., p. 142.)

Exemplification of Arms and Crest to George Wilmott of Letcombe Regis, by Sir William Segar, Knight, Garter, dated the 10th of February, 1627. MS. Ashm. 858, p. 193, etc. Another copy in MS. Ashm. 840, p. 419.

To all & singular as well Nobles and Gentlemen as others to whome these presents shall come, William Segar Kn[t] Garter principall King of Armes of Englishmen, sendeth greeting in our Lord God everlasting whereas aunciently from the beginning the valiant and vertuous actes of worthy psons have bene cõmended to the world with sundry monuments & remembrances of their good deserts: Amongst which the cheifest & most vsuall hath bene the bearing of signes & tokens in sheilds cõmonly called Armes which are evident demonstraõns of Prowes & valour diversly distributed according to the Qualities & deserts of the psons meryting the same: which Order as it was most prudently devised in the beginning to stir & kindle the heartes of men to the imytaõn of virtue and Nobleness even so hath the same bene & yet is contynually observed to the end that such as have done cõmendable se[r]vice to the Prince or Country either in warr or peace, might receave due hono[r] in their Lyves & also derive the same successively to their posteritie after their deathes forever & to register & record them in the Office of Armes that vpon all occasions the Kinges & Heraldes of Armes who were instituted for the preservaçõn of the Nobilitie & Gentry of this Kingedome might make such exemplificaçõn of them as should be requyred. In which respect George Wilmote of Letcombe in the County of Berks Esq, being touched with a care for the preservaçõn of the memory of his auncestors hath had conference with me & by good & venerable proofe hath made it appeere that divers monuments of his predecessors have suffred by the iniquitie of tyme, The brasse being so pulled away, as it is not extant what armes were insculped to demonstrate with whome they maryed, yet hath sufficiently manyfested himselfe descended from very good auncestors: which vpon his request I have recorded in the Registers of my Office. And further he hath desired me to exemplifye vnto him his Armes and Creast with that difference that he & his postiritie may lawfully beare them without offence to the Lawes of Armes or any other of his name or kindred which accordingly I have done & in such mañer as they are heere depicted in the margent soe are they heere described with the apt & pp termes of Blazon vizt In a sheild Argent a fesse gules charged with an vnicorne seiant and twoe flower deluces Or betwene three Egles heades erazed sable And for his Creast vpon a Helme and wreath of his Collours Argent and gules a demy ounce proper houlding a battaile Axe or, with mantells of gules doubled Argent which Armes & Creast & every part & pcell thereof I the King of Armes afores[d] by vertue of my Office of principall King of Armes of

Englishmen according as by the Originall institucon thereof appeereth Doe by these p'sents approve exemplifye ratifye and confirme vnto the said George Wilmote and his posteritie vsing due differences for ever, And that he & they the Same may vse beare and shew forth in sheeld signett Hatchment pennon Coat Armor Trumpett banners & also vpon Jewells plate Glasse or any other way according to the Lawes of Armes or Lawdable customes of this Realme of England at his or their liberty and pleasure without the lett impediment or interupcon of any pson or psons whatsoever In witnes whereof I have here vnto sett my hand & seale the tenth day of February Anno Domini 1627.

WILLM SEGAR Garter.

Ex.

Winch, of Fifield.

MS. Rawl. D. 865, fol. 223. Draft of Letter. The pedigree was entered, but no Arms (see Vol. I., p. 312).

Sr

This follow^g Tearme I am to deliu in to the Office of Armes the Heraldicall Visitaco I lately tooke of the County of Berke & in regard I cannot (vpon search) finde you haue right to those Armes you pduced to me when I sat at Maidenhead I may not enter them wthout further satisfaccon from you. Besides you have entred yor Grandmother Eleanor as a daughter & heire to Robert Loggs (& consequently would draw in the q^rtering of the Armes of Loggins Stafferton & Haddock) when by the form Visitacons it is manifest she was no heire, there being seuall heires male continued downe from Robt Logins who married Eleanor d: & heire to Humfr. Staulton.*

I therefore desire to rec: some further & more satisfactory account from you touch^g these pticulars else I cannot doe you that service I willingly would. You may finde me any morning early at my Chamb in the Midle Temple, wch Mr Turvile can readily direct you too.

In expectacon therefore to heare from you by the begining of the Tearme at furthest (but sooner if you can) I rem

Yo^r humble servant & ready friend
E. A[shmole], Windsor Herald.

7 Oct. 1667.

For my very loving friend Mr Symon
  Winch of fifield in Bray These.

It seems clear that if Simon Winch of Fyfield had been able to prove his right to the quarterings he claimed, they would have been tricked in the Visitation. These quarterings are found in some of the MS. copies mentioned above (see Vol. I., p. 312). They were not allowed by the Heralds.

---

* See Vol. I., p. 107.

Winchcombe, of Newbury.

Grant of Arms and Crest to John Wy[n]chcombe of Newbury, co. Berks, by Sir Christopher Barker, Kn^t, Garter, dated the 26th of October 1549.

MS. Ashm. 858, p. 72. A copy of this Grant was printed (pp. 149-50) in the History of Newbury and its Environs, 1839.

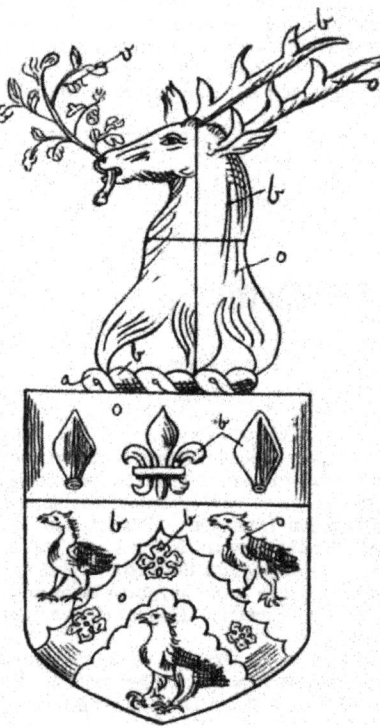

To all present and to come which these present Letters shall see, rede or here, Syr Xp̄ofer Barker Knyght ats Garter principall King of Armes of Englesshmen Sendethe due & humble recōmendacion of gretinge, Equite Willethe and reason ordeyneth that men vertuous & of commendable disposicion & lyvenge, be by theire merytes and good renoamne rewarded & had in ꝑpetuall memory for theire good name, and to be in all places of honoure and Worshipp, amonges other noble parsons accepted and reputed, by shewing of certein Insignes and tokens of Vertue, honoure & gentelnes that is to wytt Armes and Crestes, To thentente, that by theire Insaumple other shulde the more perseverauntly Inforce themselves to vse theire tyme in suche honourable wourkes & vertuous dedes, whereby they myght also purchase and gett the renoume of auntient Noblesse in their Ligne & Posteritee. And therefore I the foresaid Syr Xp̄ofer Barker Knyght ats Garter principall Kinge of Armes as abovesayd, which not alonely by the comen vulgar fame, but also by myne owen knowlege and by the reporte of divers auncient gentlemen and other credable parsons, am truly Informed & advertysed that John Wychecome of Newbury in the County of Barkeshere, hathe longe contynued in vertue, and in all his actes and other his Demeaninge, hath discretly and wourss shipfully guyded and governed hymselfe, so that he hath deserved and ys well wourthy from henseforthe to be in all places of honure and wourss shipp, amonges other noble Parsons accepted and reputed into the noumber and company of auncient gentell and noblemen, And for the Remembraunce and consideracon of the same his vertue habillitee and gentlenes, and also by vertue power and auctoritee to myne Office of principall Kinge of Armes annexed and attributed by the Kinge our Soverain Lorde: I have devised, ordained and assigned vnto and for the said John Wychecome the Armes and Crest withe thappurtenn̄cs hereafter followinge, that is to wytt, Asure a cheueron in gralled betwene iij. closse Egletts golde vpon the cheueron iij. Cynkfolles of the felde perceyd of second, A Cheffe of the same a flordellis betwene ij. Spereshedes of the feld appon his Crest a Roo buckes hed Rassed quarterly golde & asure holdynge in his Mouthe a brery vert, set apon a torche argent & asure, the mantelletts guels lyned argent bottoned gold, as more plainly apperethe depicted in this Margent. To have & to holde vnto the said John Wechecome and his

OF BERKSHIRE.

posteritee, with theire due differaunce therein to be revested to his honoure for evermore. In wittnes whereof I the said Garter principall King of Armes as abovesaid have signed these presents withe myne owne hande and therevnto have sett the Seale of myne Office, & also the Seale of myne armes. Yeven at London the xxvj: daye of October in the yere of our Lord God M^t.V^c.XL.IX and of the Reigne of our Sovereigne Lord King Edwarde syxt by the grace of God King of Englande Fraunce & Irelande Defendor of the ffayth & in earthe of the Churche of Englande & also of Irelande the supreme hed, the thyrde yere.

 als gartier principall
Kyng of Armes of Englishmen.

MS. Ashm. 852, p. 184.

Notes on the Winchcombe pedigree will be found in the Journ. Arch. Assoc., vol. xvi., p. 233; *The History of Newbury, by Walter Money, F.S.A.; Thatcham and its Manors, by the late Samuel Barfield,* vol. ii., p. 304, *and notes.*

John Wynchcombe=Eliz: da: of ....
of Newbury in Co: | Hyde of Hamp-
Berks. | shire.

John Wynchcombe=Jane da: of ....
[or] Wychcombe. | Careage.

John=Aleyne [*Helena*] | Henry=Agnes da: of | Thomas=Dorothy | Anne.
Wynch- | da: of Thomas | Wynch- | Thom: Hurte | Wynch- | da: to
combe | St Lowe [*Tho-* | combe. | [*Horton of* | combe. | John
second | *mas Taylor*]. | | *Iford, co:* | | Vampage.
sonne. | | | *Wilts (Visit.* | |
 | | | *Wilts,* 1565, | |
 | | | p. 24)]. | |

Jane [? *John*] | Francis Winchcombe= | Anne Winch- | Agnes Wynch-
Wynchcombe. | died 3 *January* 1619. | combe. | combe.

Henry Winchcombe, begins the Pedigree, Visit. 1665-6, Vol. I., p. 313.

Wintersell, of Sutton, co. Berks.

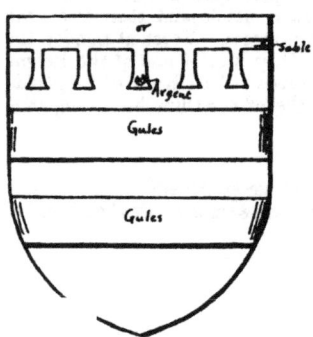

Coll. of Arms G. 8, fol. 14. *Visitation of Wiltshire*, 1565.

Henrye Wintersell of Wyntershull in the countie of Sutherye gent. maryed Jone doughter to William Sandys of Buckinghamshire and by her had yssue Rycharde Wintersell his eldiste sonne and heire, Edwarde seconde sonne and John thirde sonne, Jane & Jane Elizabeth Alyce & Anne. Rycharde Wyntersell of Sutton in the countie of Berkshire gent., eldiste sonne and heire to Henrye maryed Jone doughter of .... Humfrey of .... and by her had yssue Rycharde Wyntersell his eldiste sonne & heire, Thomas Wyntersell seconde sonne, Elizabeth maryed to Thomas Coxe of Hanney in com̄ Berks gent.

Thomas Wyntersell of Radborne Cheyney in the countie of Wiltes gent. seconde sonne to Rycharde Wyntersell aforesaide maryed Anne doughter to Arthure Pulley, wydow to Thomas Webbe and by her hath yssue Thomas Wyntersell his eldiste sonne and heir aparante, Roger seconde sonne.

Heralds' Coll., 19 Aug. 1907.

EVERARD GREEN,
Rouge Dragon.

Yate, of Buckland.

MS. Ashm. 840, p. 379, *all in Ashmole's handwriting. See* Vol. I., p. 149.

C. 19, p. 27 Hantę [*1622*]. This 3ᵈ Quartering is q'rtered by Goddard of Est Woodhey in Hantę who giue the Cressantę ⋏ &c. not by yᵗ family of the Goddardę whose d: & h: Yates married.

Sʳ John Yates Barᵗ 17 yearę old 1623.

Visum agnitum et in monumentis Collegij Heraldorum relatum tempore visitacionis Com: Berkę 1623 virtute Comiss: Willelmi Cambden alias Clarenceux Regis Armorum a me Jo: Philpot Rouge Dragon Deputato suo in Com: prædicto.

1. YATE. 2. GODDARD. 3. GODDARD (*ancient*) *granted to William Goddard of co. Middlesex, by Christopher Barker. Garter, 3 December* 1536, *Azure, five fusils in fesse between three ger-falcons' heads erased Or.* 4. JUSTICE, *inescutcheon* PACKINGTON *of Chaddesley Corbett, co. Worc.* (see Vol. I., p. 318).

John Yate of Charney married for his first wife Joan, da. and heir to Richard Goddard of Upham in Com: Wilts (Vol. I., p. 148). *In the notes by Robert Dale, Richmond Herald* (*Wilts Arch. Soc.*, ix., p. 223, *etc.*), *on Wiltshire Arms and Descents, under Goddard of Upham* (*from Berkshire*), *the quarterings 2 and 3 are given:* "2 *coats*, 1st *the modern, gules, a chevron vairé between* 3 *crescents arg., on each an ermine spot sable;* 2, *Az.,* 5 *lozenges* (or *fusils*) *in fess between* 3 *falcons' heads erased or.*"

OF BERKSHIRE.

Yonge de Basildon, Barksh.

From the Visitation of Northumberland, MS. Coll. of Arms, C. 41.

College of Arms, Camden's Grifts, iii., 30.

Ar on a chevron b. 3 roundles or, in a cheife g. 2 cinquefoils or. Crista, a Goates head Or attired Or in a Crowne murall g.

The Visitation of Northumberland, 1666 (Foster, p. 128), under Young of Newcastle-on-Tyne, the above arms are given without the colours, and the following notes appear: See the Visitation of London for proof of these Arms and the colours; Vide Mr. Hare's booke, fol. 80° for ye colors; see also Anne Yonge of Basilden, Berks, granted 1607.

The first two references occur in C. 41, part 3, folio 9, MS. College of Arms. Mr. Hare may have been John Hare, who was successively Rouge Dragon and Richmond Herald. He died on the 14th of May 1720, aged 52.

The arms are not to be found in any of the Visitations of London. The note about the Grant having been made to Anne Yonge is an addition not given in C. 41, and I have been unable to verify it.

This crest occurs in MS. Coll. of Arms, Vincent, 161, 19, as that of Yonge, Bark.

Yong.

The following occur in Harl. MS. 1532, fol. 55 :—

YONG of Basendon [*Basildon*], Argent, a chevron Azure, and chief Gules.

YONG of Wittenham, Lozengy, Argent and Vert, on a chevron Azure three bezants: on a chief gules a goat's head erased between two cinquefoils Or. [? *Granted temp. Henry VIII.*]

CORRIGENDA.

Vol. II., p. 54.—Pedigree drop should be over Anne, dau. & h. of John Purye, *not* over William Danvers her husband.

INDEX NOMINUM.

Pedigrees are printed in SMALL CAPITALS; Arms in *italics*.

Abbot, 115.
Abbot (Abbott), William, 183.
Abdy, Mary, 78; Roger, 78.
Abercorne, Catherine, Countess of, 170; Charles, Earl of, 170.
Abergavenny (Aburgaveney, Aburgenny), Edward Nevill, Lord, 181; George Nevill, Lord, 104, 181 (2); Henry Nevill, Lord, 181; Margaret Nevill, Lady, 181; — Nevill, Lord, 158.
Abrahall, Frances, 191; John, 79, 191 (2); Margaret, 79.
Acres, Gregory, 5.
Adams, Rev. Peter, 20.
Aden, Thomas, 6.
À Dene, *see* Deane.
Ager, Simon, 41.
Albery, 48.
Albery, Thomas, 48.
Aldem, Joan, 69; —, 69.
Alden, Robert, 19.
Alder, Rev. Bryan, 32; Martha, 201; Mary, 201; Richard, 5; Mr., 201.
ALDRIDGE, 48, 49.
Aldridge, Anne, 49; Elizabeth, 48 (2), 49; Hanna, 48; Henry, 49; John, 48 (2); Katherine, 49; Mary, 48 (3); Ralph, 49; Robert, 45, 48 (5); Samuel, 48 (2); Thomas, 19, 35, 48, 49 (2).
ALDWORTH, 49, 50.
Aldworth, 49, 49 n., 50.
Aldworth, Alice, 50; Amy, 50; Anne, 50 (2); George, 50; Henry, 50; John, 50 (2); Margaret, 50 (2); Richard, 4, 17 (2), 39, 49, 50 (3); Robert, 50; Thomas, 19, 50 (2); William, 50 (2); Family of, 49.
Alexander, King of Scotts, 203.
Alexander, Dorothy, 83; Paul, 83.
Alexander *alias* Zinzan, *see* Zinzan.
Allen (Allin), Elizabeth, 78, 129; Henry, 15; John, 2 (2), 5, 15 (2), 23; Mary, 119 n., 210, 211; Sir Thomas, Bart., 129; Sir Thomas, 35, 119, 119 n., 129; William, 78, 129; —, 35, 119, 129, 210, 211.
Allworth, Gyles, 173; Mary, 173.
Alnewick, Christopher, 2, 15.
Altham, Hellen, 159; Sir James, 159.
Ambrose, Lawrence, 21.
Amerson, *see* Amson.
AMORE, 51.
Amore, Agnes, 51; Christian, 51; Elizabeth, 51 (2); Ellenor, 51; Henry, 51; Joan, 51 (3); John, 51 (3); Margaret, 51 (3); Maude, 51 (2); Nicholas, 51; Richard, 51; Thomas, 51; William, 51 (2); —, 51 (3).
Amson (Amerson), 100.
Amson (Amerson), Blanch, 100; John, 100.
Anderton, Rev. James, 28, 31.
Andevill, Alexander, Lord of, 204; Beatrix, dau. to Alexander, Lord of, 204.
Andrewes (Andrews), Margaret, 82; —, 82, 185 (2).
Andrewes *alias* Taylour, Richard, 14.
ANGELL, 51.
Angell seal, 51.
Angell, Elizabeth, 52 (4), 133; Frances, 52; James, 52; Joan, 52; John, 51, 52 (4), 133; Justinian, 52; Mary, 52; Robert, 52; Thomas, 51, 52; Thomasine, 52; William, 42, 51, 52 (3), 133; —, 51, 52.
Anger (Aunger), John, 4, 39.
Angers (Angors), —, 161, 162 (2).
Ann (Anne), Anne, 116, 138; John, 138; William, 116.
Anny, Bridget, 171; Edward, 171; Mary, 171.
Ansley (Anslow), Edmund, 41; James, 16 Mr., 41.
Anton, Katherine, 140; Thomas, 140.
Anyan, Susan. 153; Rev. Dr., 153.
Arden, —, widow, 22.
Ardway, Joane, 56; —, 56.
Armorer, 52. 53.
Armorer, Sir William, 4, 32, 52 (2), 53 (4).
Armstrong (Armestrong), Edward, 124; Elizabeth, 124, 163; Gilbert, 163; Richard, 14; Capt., 33.
Arnold, Richard, 22.
Arscott, Ann, 161; Juliana, 161; William, 161.
Artwick, Christopher, 15.
Ascotte, Eleanor, 162; John, 162.
Ashoombe (Ayshoombe), Anne, 196; Johan, 18; John, 18, 224; Margery, 224; Mary, 169; Oliver, 196; Sir William, 169; —, 18.
Ashe, Anne, 196; Samuel, 196.
Ashmole, Elias, Windsor Herald, 2, 9, 51, 65, 66, 73, 91, 110, 117, 121, 133, 139, 146, 147, 148, 150, 152 (3), 154, 155, 158 (2), 163, 165, 166, 169, 172, 173, 178, 187, 198, 206, 213, 216, 220, 225, 231; Mr., 64.
Aspin (Aspyn), Elizabeth, 171; John, 171; Thomas, 171 (2); William, 171; —, 192 (2).
Aston, Alice, 78; Mary, 137; Sir Thomas, 18; —, 78, 137.
Atfield, Francis, 31.
Atkins, Ellen, 187; Richard, 187.

Atkinson, Francis, 29.
ATMORE, 53.
Atmore, 53.
Atmore, Alice, 54; Ellenor, 54; Isabell, 54; Jennett, 54; Joan, 54 (2); John, 53 (2), 54 (3); Mathew, 54; Maud, 54 (3); Nicholas, 53, 54; Stephen, 54; Thomas, 54; William, 54 (2); —, 53 (3), 54 (3).
Atrown, Joan, 103; Thomas, 103.
Audley, Elizabeth, 75; Hugh, Lord, 75.
Aunger, *see* Anger.
AVELYNE, 54.
Avelyne, 54.
Avelyne, Agnes, 55 (2); Christopher, 55, 55 *n*.; Edith, 55; Edward, 55; Elizabeth, 55; Hugh, 55; Isabell, 55: John, 55 (2); Joyce, 55, 55 *n*.; Julyan, 55; Mary, 55; Richard, 55; Robert, 55 (2); Thomas, 55; Ursulah, 55.
Avery, Henry, 11.
À Wood, *see* Wood.
Ayes, *see* Cyes.
Ayleffe, Peter, 14.
Ayleworth, Andrew, 20; Anthony, 20.
Aylioyn, Thomas, 3.
Aylmer, Elizabeth, 88; Theophilus, 88; —, 88.
Ayscough, Henry, 167; Priscilla, 167.
Ayshcombe, *see* Ashcombe.
Ayston, *see* Eyston.

B.

BABHAM, 56.
Babham, 56.
Babham, Dorothy, 56 *n*.; Eleanor, 56; Elizabeth, 56; Hellyn, 56 *n*.; Henry, 56 (2); Joan, 56; John, 56 (2), 56 *n*.; Joyce, 56 (2); Richard, 56; Thomas, 56 *n*.
Babthorpe, 124.
Babthorpe, Elizabeth, 125; William, 125.
Backhouse, 57, 58.
Backhouse, Ellen, 58; Nicholas, 57 (6), 58 (2), 128; Sara, 128; Thomas, 57, 58; Sir William, Bart., 41; Sir W., Bart., 4.
Badcock, Jonas, 10; Richard, 18.
Badlond, 149, 151.
Baggs, William, 22; —, 22.
Bagley (Baglyes), Richard, 46; Thomas, 40; Mr., 46.
Baker, 59, 60, 61.
Baker, Alexander, 47; Christopher, 60 (2); George, 59 (3), 60 (4); John, 47, 60; Richard, 7; Symond, 60; Thomas, 46; William, 26, 47, 61 (3).
Balam, Charles, 90; Susanna, 90.
Balderston, 184.
Baldington, Agnes, 116; William, 116.
Baldwyn, Mary, 48; —, 48.
Baley, *see* Bayly.
BALL, 62.
Ball, 62.
Ball, Agnes, 62 (2); Ale, 62 (2); Blanch, 62; Dorothy, 62; Edward, 62; Elizabeth, 62 (3), 188; George, 62; Joane, 62 (2); John, 62 (2), 188; Mary, 62; Rachel, 62 (2); Richard, 62 (2); Robert, 62 (2); Samuel, 62; Suzan, 62; Thomas, 62 (2); William, 62 (5); —, 4.
Balle, Edward, 21.
Bamfield, 63.
Bamfield (Bamfeilde, Barnfield), Sir Amyas, 63; Robert, 63.

Bancroft, Margaret, 159; Thomas, 159.
Banet, *see* Barret.
Banister (Banester), Maria, 101; Samuel, 41; William, 101.
Bankes, Richard, 39; Mr., 47.
Bardolph, Edmond, 204; Maude, 204.
Barely, Richard, 5.
Barfield, Samuel, 233.
Barham, Bathsheba, 102; William, 102.
BARKER, 63, 64.
Barker, 64.
Barker, Ambrose, 64; Anne, 64 (6); Sir Anthony, 64; Anthony, 5, 8, 39, 64 (2); Catherine, 175; Sir Christopher (Garter), 56, 63, 64, 221, 232 (4), 233, 234; Frances, 64; Francis, 64; Capt. Henry, 38; Henry, 4, 64; Hugh, M.D., 30, 63, 64; Jane, 64 (2); Joan, 63; John, 64 (2), 175; Julian, 175; Katherine, 64, 82; Lawrence, 64; Lettice, 64; Margaret, 64; Marie, 63; Mary, 64 (3), 175; Nathaniel, 64; Richard, 63, 64, 175; Robert, 63 (2), 64; Thomas, 4, 46, 64 (2); William, 4, 39, 63, 64 (7), 82, 175; Dr., 63; —, 63 (2), 64 (3).
Barley, Thomas, 22.
Barnard, Alexander, 40; Constantine, 10; Francis, 33, 42; Solomon, 33.
BARNES, 65.
Barnes, Elizabeth, 65 (3); Hanna, 65 (2); Jane, 65; Joseph, 65 (3); Richard, 44, 65 (4); Roger, 43; Mr., 65.
Barnfeld, *see* Bamfield.
Baron (*Barrey*, *Barrery*), 66.
Baron (Barrey, Barrery), Hargill, 47; John, 45, 66 *n*.; William, 66, 66 *n*.
Barr, William, 19.
Barret (Banet), Thomas, 28.
Barrey (Barrery), *see* Baron.
Bartlet, William, 17.
Barton, Alice, 224; Henry, 224.
Barwick, John, 215; Mary, 215.
Basford, George, 185; Mary, 185.
BASKERVILLE, 66.
Baskerville, 66.
Baskerville, Agnes, 77; Alice, 66; Anne, 66; Arnold, 66; Constance, 66; George, 66; Gertrude, 66; Haniball, 11 (2), 66 (2); Henry, 66 (2); Sir James, 66; John, 66 (3); Mary, 66 (2); Capt. Nicholas, 66 (2); Nicholas, 66; Philip, 66; Randall, 77; Robert, 66; Sybill, 66; Sir Thomas, 66 (2); Thomas, 66; Sir Walter, 66; William, 66.
Basset, Jane, 82; Thomas, M.D., 82; Thomas 2, 16.
Bateman, Katherine, 49; —, 49.
Bathurst, Samuel, 5, 19.
Battie, Audry, 99; —, 99.
Battin, Adam, 24; —, 24.
Bayly (Baley), George, 10; Richard, D.D., 36, 47.
Beard, Anne, 85; John, 85.
Beasley, *see* Beisley.
Beauchamp, Edith, 104; Edward Seamer, Viscount, 222; Elizabeth, 104; Sir John, 104 (2); Margaret, 104.
Becher, Elizabeth, 140; Henry, 140.
Beckington, Roger, 29.
Beckley, Humphrey, 44, 48; Mary, 48; Symon, 3, 44.
Bedford, John, 5.
Bedwell, 166 (2).

INDEX NOMINUM. 239

Beisley (Beasley, Byseley, Byseleye), Alexander, 10, 67 ; Hugh, 67 (2) ; Thomas, 67.
Beke, Elizabeth, 205 ; Isabella, 55 ; Richard, 205 ; —, 55.
Bell, 67.
Bell, Angell, 4, 38.
Bellamy, 68, 72.
Bellamy (Belamy, Bellame), Joane, 70 ; Richard, 68 ; Thomas, 68 (3) ; William, 68, 70.
Bellenger, Rev. Edward, 15.
BELLINGHAM, 69.
Bellingham, 69.
Bellingham, Dorothy, 69 ; Henry, 69 (2) ; Joan, 69 ; John, 69 (5) ; Parnell, 103 ; Richard, 103 ; Sir Roger, 69 ; —, 69.
Belson, Amy, 139 ; John, 139 ; —, 88.
Bennet, Jacob, 14 ; John, 47 ; Leonard, 47 ; Rebecca, 227 ; Robert, 43 ; —, 227.
Bere, George, 161 ; Peter, 161 (2) ; Rebecca, 161 ; Sepheronia, 161.
Bereff, Maude, 51 ; Thomas, 51.
Berks, —, Earl of, 8.
Berners, John Bourchier, Lord, 222.
Berry, Elizabeth, 168, 215 ; John, 215 ; Thomas, 215 ; Mrs., 12 ; —, 168.
Berwick, Elizabeth, 20.
BESSELLS, 69.
Bessells, Alice, 70 ; Eleanor, 70 ; Elizabeth, 69. 70 ; Geoffrey, 70 ; Marie, 70 ; Mathew, 69 ; Peter, 70 ; Sir Thomas, 70 ; Thomas, 70 ; William, 70 (2) ; —. 70.
Best, Anne, 215 ; —, 215.
Beveridge, Mary, 171 ; Michaell, 171.
Biddolph, Anthony, 87 ; Mary, 87.
Bigg, Richard, 39.
Billingsley, John, 10.
Billington, Robert, 171 ; Sarah, 171.
Bingley, Rev. Giles, 20.
Binte, William, 5.
Bishop (Byshop), Katherine, 219 ; Thomas, 16 ; William, 219.
Bisset, James, 31.
Bitterley, Robert, 55 ; Ursulah, 55.
Blackmore, Christian, 126 ; —, 126.
Blacknall, Jane. 71 ; John, 71.
Black Prince, 75.
BLAGRAVE, 70, 72.
Blagrave, 72.
Blagrave (Blagrove), Alexander, 36, 71, 72 (2), 84 ; Alice, 74 ; Allan, 71 ; Anne, 70 (2), 71 (2), 72, 84 ; Anthony, 70, 71 (4) ; Charles, 25 ; Cheyney, 71 ; Daniel, 72 (2) ; Dorothy, 71 (3) ; Drew, 71 ; Edward, 71 (4) ; Elizabeth, 70, 71 (2), 73 (2) ; Frances, 72 ; George, 39 ; Giles, 3, 31 ; Henry, 3, 32 ; Jane, 71 (3) ; Jeremiah, 72 ; Joan, 70, 187 ; Sir John, 71 ; John, 5, 26, 39, 70 (2), 71 (2), 72, 187 ; Joseph, 72 ; Joshua, 72 ; Judith, 72 ; Magdalen, 71 ; Margaret, 71 (2), 72 (2) ; Martha, 71 ; Mary, 70, 71 (3), 201 ; Nathaniel. 72 ; Obadiah, 73 (2) ; Oliver, 71 ; Ralph, 70 ; Richard, 70, 71 (2), 72 : Robert, 70, 71 ; Dame Rose, 36 ; Ruth, 73 ; Susan, 71 ; Susannah, 73 ; Rev. Thomas, 27, 37 ; Thomas, 22, 70, 71 (3) ; Walter, 34, 72 ; Zephaniah, 73 ; —, 68, 70 (3), 71 (3), 72 (2).
Blake, Anne, 49 ; John, 34, 73, 73 *n*. ; Richard, 2, 14 ; —, 49.
Blanch, John, 36.
Blandy, Adam, 3, 27 ; Elizabeth, 27 ; John, 3, 27, 28.

Blany, Thomas, 33.
Blenerhasset, Mary, 125 ; Thomas, 125.
Blew, John, 46.
Blewet, James, 169 ; Mary, 169, 170 ; —, 170.
Blomer, —, 224 (2).
Blount, Joan, 131 ; Lister, 123 ; Margaret, 77 ; Margery, 131 ; Martha, 123 ; Michael, 123 ; Richard, 77 ; Robert, 131 (2) ; —, 123, 155 (2).
Blower, Christopher, 11, 39 ; Robert, 11, 39 (2) ; Thomas, 33.
Blundell, Elizabeth, 85 ; John, 116 ; Theodorus, 116.
Blundeville, 76.
Blundeville, Randolph, 76.
Blunt, William, 37.
Bodkin, William, 41.
BOND, 74.
Bond, 74.
Bond, Alice, 74 ; Dorothy, 74 ; Elizabeth, 74 ; James, 74 ; Joan, 74 ; John. 74 (3) ; Mabell, 74 ; Roger, 74 ; Thomas, 74 ; William, 12, 74 ; —, 74 (5).
Booth (Booths), Anne, 207 ; John, 38, 40 ; Richard, 1 ; —, 207.
Borlacy, Jane, 71 ; Sir John, 71.
Borough, Sir John (Garter), 145 (3).
Boseley, Henry, 14.
BOSTOCK, 74, 76.
Bostock, 76.
Bostock, Sir Adam, 75 (7), 76 ; Agnes, 77 ; Alice 77 (2), 78 (2) ; Amy, 78 (2) ; Anne. 77, 78 (2), 79 (2) ; Anthony, 79 ; Barbara, 77 ; Brigitt, 79 ; David, 75 ; Edith, 77 ; Sir Edward, 75 ; Edward, 77, 79 ; Eleanor, 75 ; Elizabeth, 75 (2), 76, 77, 78, 79 ; Ellen, 77 ; Felice, 77 ; Frances, 77 ; George, 77, 78 (4) ; Sir Gilbert, 75 ; Hanna, 65 ; Hawise, 75 ; Sir Henry, 75 ; Henry, 75 ; Hugh, 74, 75 (2), 77 ; Humfry, 77 (2) ; Ida, 77 ; Isabel, 75 ; James, 79 ; Jane, 77 ; Jenet, 75 ; Joan, 77 (5), 78 (2) ; John, 65, 77 (2), 78 (2) ; Katherine, 77 (2) ; Lionell, 77 (2) ; Margaret, 75, 77 (2), 78 ; Margery, 75, 77 (3), 79 ; Mary, 78 ; Maud, 78 ; Nicholas, 77 ; Sir Osmer, 74 ; Sir Ralph, 75 (3), 77 ; Ralph, 75, 77, 78 ; Randall, 77 ; Ranulph, 75 ; Richard, 74, 77 (2), 79 ; Rev. Roger, 78 ; Roger, 74, 77, 78 ; Thomas, 77 (2), 78 (2), 79 (3) ; Sir Warren, 75 ; Sir William, 75 (3) ; William, 10, 11, 77 (3), 78 (2), 79 ; —, 74 (4), 75 (5), 77 (2).
Boswell, Edward, 12.
Botetort, Mauld, 100 ; Lord, 100.
Botreaux, Elizabeth, 107 ; William, Lord, 107 (3) ; Sir William, 107.
Bottendon, Thomas, 10.
BOULSTRODE, 79.
Boulstrode (Bolstrode, Boulstred, Boulstrell, Bulstred, Bulstrode), Agnes, 79 (4), 79 *n*. ; Alice, 79 (2), 80 ; Anne, 80 (2) ; Brigit, 80 ; Cicely, 222 ; Edmund, 79, 80 ; Edward, 80, 222, 227 ; Elizabeth, 80, 227 ; Ellen, 80 ; George, 79 ; Henry, 4, 42, 79 ; Jane, 79 ; Joan, 80 ; John, 79 (3), 79 *n*., 80 ; Lettice, 80 ; Margaret, 79 (3). 80 ; Margery, 80 ; Mary, 80, 205 ; Richard, 79 (2), 79 *n*. ; Robert, 79 (3), 80 (2) ; Roger, 79 ; Thomas, 79, 80 (2) ; William, 79 ; —, 205.
Boult, Henry, 40 ; John, 41.
Bourchier, John, Lord Berners, 222 ; Mary, 222.
Bovill, *see* de Bovill.
Bowler, John, 33.

THE VISITATIONS OF BERKSHIRE.

Bowles, John, 18; William, 46, 47.
Bowlis, Edward, 20; John. 18.
Bowyer, John, 34 (2).
Boylett, John, 44.
Boys, 68.
Brackston, William, 34.
Bradgate, Abigail, 88; Christopher, 88.
BRADLEY, 80.
Bradley, 80.
Bradley, Abell, 80; Barbara, 80, 81; Frances, 80; Francis, 81; Henry, 80 (2); John, 80 (2); Richard, 80; Savile, 81; Susan, 80; Thomas, D.D., 80, 81; Thomas, 81; William, 12, 51; —, 38, 51, 80.
Bradshaw, Sir Henry, 75; Jenet, 75.
Braham, 81.
Braham, Elizabeth, 135; Sir Richard, Bart., 4, 47; Sir Richard, 81 (3), 82; Richard, 135.
Bramley, Richard, 31.
Branch, Barbara, 78; William, 78.
Braxton. William, 7 (2).
Bray, Edmund, Lord, 186; Elizabeth, 186; Reynold, 23.
BRAYBROOKE, 82. 83.
Braybrooke, 82. 83.
Braybrooke, Christian, 83; Dorothy, 83; Edward. 83; Elizabeth, 82, 83 (2); James, 82 (2), 83; Jane, 82; Katherine, 82, 83; Lucie, 83; Margaret. 82, 83 (3); Margery, 82; Marie, 83; Martha, 82, 83 (3); Mary, 83; Richard. 83 (3); Robert, 83 (2); Thomas, 82; William, 82, 83 (3).
Brayton, Henry, 36.
Breach, —, 5.
Bredon, Rev. —, 14.
Brennd, John, 196; Martha, 196; Nicholas, 196.
Brent, Christiana, 162; Robert, 162.
Brereton, —, 75 (2).
Breth, Anne, 142; —, 142.
Brett, George, 90; Joyce, 90.
Brewer, Richard, 38.
Brian, Bridget. 85; Robert, 85.
Brice, Rev. John, 46; John, 45; Nicholas, 43.
Brickenden. Elizabeth, 120; Thomas, 28, 120.
Bridges, Alice, 66; John, 66; Simon. 169.
Bridgman, Anne, 194; John, 194 (3); Katherine, 194; Mary, 194.
Bridon, Anne, 64; —, 64.
Brierton, Werburga, 104; —, 104.
Bright, Alice, 78; Rev. Thomas, 41; —, 78.
BRIGHTWELL, 84.
Brightwell, Anna, 84; Anne, 72, 84 (2); Loftus, 84; Mary, 84; Samuel. 37, 84 (2); Susanna, 84 (2); Thomas, 72, 84 (2); —, 37.
BRINCKHURST, 84.
Brinckhurst, 84.
Brinckhurst, Charles, 85 (2); Elizabeth, 85 (2); George, 85; Jane, 85; John, 84, 85 (4); Mary, 85 (3); Richard, 85; Robert, 85; Rupert, 85; Susan, 85; —, 84.
Bristow, Rev. Robert, 13.
Broad, Rev. William, 31.
Brockes, *see* Brookes.
Brockett, Sir John, 204, 205; Lucy, 204; Margaret. 204; Mary. 205; Nicholas, 204.
Broderwick, Richard, 22.
Brome, Sir Christopher, 181; Sir John, 116; Magdalin, 116; —, 181.
Brooke, Dorothy, 191; Reynold, 1; —, 191.

Brookes (Brockes), Randolph, 32; Richard, 19, 33; William. 37.
Brookesby, William, 123; Winifred, 123.
Broughton, Anne, 104; Francis, 46; Humfry, 38, 46; Sir John. 104; Thomas, 10.
Broune, Anne, 79; John, 79.
Brounker, Elizabeth, 82; Henry, 82.
Browne, 124.
Browne, Anthony, Viscount Mounacute, 123; Elizabeth, 188; Sir George, K.B., 25, 26; Isabel, 116; Jane, 123 (2), 125; Sir John, 116; John, 116, 188; Lucy, 125; Magdalin, 116; Robert, 125 (2); Thomas, 36; William, 34; —, 120 (2).
BROWNE *alias* MOSES, 85.
Browne alias *Moses*, 85.
Browne *alias* Moses, Anne, 85 (2); Bridget, 85; John. 85 (3); Richard, 85 (4); —, 85.
Browninge, Alice, 116; William, 116.
Brudenell (Brudnell), Agnes, 79, 79 *n*.; Alice, 119; Edmond, 56 (2). 119; Edward, 79; Elizabeth, 56; Joyce, 56; William, 79. 79 *n*.
Bruges. Frances, 78; Richard. 186; William, Lord Chandos, 78; —, 186.
Bryant, William, 22.
Buckingham, Duke of, 32.
Buckland, *see* De Buckland.
Buckridge (Buckeridge). Thomas, 2, 15.
Bullen, Queen Anne, 204; Anne, 204; Sir Geffrey, 104, 204; Isabel, 104; Mary, 204; Sir Thomas, K.G., Earl of Wiltshire, 204; Sir William, K.B., 204.
BULLOCK, 86.
Bullock, Alice, 86; Anne, 86; Gilbert, 86 (2), 186; John, 13; Margaret. 86, 186; Richard, 86; Robert, 86 (4); Thomas, 42, 86.
Bunce, Henry, 14; John, 11; Rev. Thomas, 25; William, 19.
Burch, Anthony, 21.
Burchett (Burchet), Catherine, 226; David, 226; John, 225; Katherine, 225.
Burden, Thomas, 228.
Burdet, Henry, 27; Robert, 29.
Bures, Humfry, 122; Susan, 122.
BURLEY, 86.
Burley, 174.
Burley (Burghley), Alice, 86 (2), 175; Anne, 64, 86 (2); Elizabeth, 86; Ellenor, 86; Henry, 86 (3), 175; Margaret, 86; Raphe, 86; Richard, 86; Thomas, 86; William, 64, 86 (2).
Burnam, Alice, 219; Robert, 219.
Burnishead, 69.
BURREN, 87.
Burren, 87.
Burren, Anne, 87 (2); Anthony, 87 (2); Avice, 87; Mary, 87 (2); Richard, 87 (3); Mr., 87; Mrs., 87; —, 87 (2).
Burwell, Sarah, 211; —, 211.
Bury, Mrs., 12.
Busfield, William, 12.
Bush, Paul, Bishop of Bristol, 183; Walter, 22.
Butcher, Richard, 20, 28.
Butler, Frances, 187; Thomas, 187; Coll., 20.
Button, William, 40.
Butts, Anne, 125; Edward, 125.
Bye, Elizabeth, 101; Roger, 101.
Bylmore, 149.
Byseley, *see* Beisley.
Byshop, *see* Bishop.

INDEX NOMINUM.

Bysshe (Bish), Sir Edward (Clarencieux), 2, 8 n., 42, 45, 51 (2), 61 (4), 110 (2), 139, 143, 147, 148, 149 (2), 149 n., 150, 151, 152 (3), 166, 190 (2), 191, 212 (3), 213 (2).

C

CALCOTT (CALDECOTT), 87.
Calcott (Caldecott), 89.
Calcott (Caldecott), Abigail, 88 (2); Agnes, 88; Alexander, 88; Anne, 88; Dorothy, 88; Edward, 88; Elizabeth, 88 (2); George, 88; Henry, 88; Isabella, 88; Johanna, 88 (2); John, 88 (2); Mary, 88 (4); Matilda, 88; Rev. Dr. Randolph, 89 (2); Thomas, 87 (3), 88 (5), 89; Walter, 88; William, 88 (2); —, 87 (2), 88.
CALTON, 90.
Calton, 90.
Calton, Bridget, 90; Jane, 90; Joyce, 90 (2); Mary, 90 (2); Paul, 17, 90 (3), 91; Robert, 90 (2); Susanna, 90 (2).
Calverley (Calverly), Charles, 33; Hugh, 33.
Calvert, Thomas, 33.
Camden, William (Clarenceux), 63, 68 (3), 69 (2), 93, 94 (2), 96 (2), 108, 118 (2), 151 n., 156 (2), 157 (3), 164 (5), 186. 187, 234.
Cant, Elizabeth, 65; John. 65.
Cantrell, Humphrey, 38 (2); Jane, 31.
Cantwell, William, 12.
Careage, Jane, 233; —, 233.
Carew, Sir George, 186; George, 122; Margery, 122; Mary, 186.
Carey, *see* Cary.
Carleton, 115.
Carleton, Sir Dudley, 90; George, 140; Joyce, 90; Katherine, 140.
Carliel, *see* Carlyle.
Carlston, Anne, 116; Anthony, 116; Joyce, 116.
Carlyle, 200.
Carlyle (Carliel), Christopher (Norroy), 199; Francis, 10.
Carrant, Mr., 24.
Carryer, John, 167; —, 167.
Carter, Margaret, 64; Richard, 16; Thomas, 64.
Carwarden, George, 30.
Carwood, Thomas, 17.
Cary (Carey), Elizabeth, 188; Mary, 204; William, 7, 46, 204; —, 188.
Castell, *see* Castle.
CASTELLION, 91.
Castellion, 91, 92, 93, 94, 95, 96, 97.
Castellion (Castelion, Castilian), Anne, 92; Barbara, 91, 92; Celiena, 92, 105; Dorothy, 94; Dowglass, 92; Elizabeth, 29, 91, 92 (2); Sir Francis, 92, 94; Sir Francis Baptist, 91; Francis, 94; Henry, 92; John, D.D., Dean of Rochester, 94; John Baptist, 91, 92 (3), 93 (4), 94 (4), 95, 96 (6), 97, 105; Katherine, 92 (2); Margaret, 91; Payton, 92; Capt. Peter, 92; Peter, 91; Thomasin, 92; Valentine, 91; Walter, 92.
Castle (Castell), George, M.D., 16; Lawrence, 19; Mary, 173; Richard, 17; Thomas, 1, 173; Dr., 16.
CATCHER, 97.
Catcher, 97.
Catcher, Agnes, 97 (2); Elizabeth, 98; Sir John, 97 (3); John, 97 (5); Katina, 97; Matilda, 97; Richard, M.D., 97, 98; Sabina, 98; Thomas, 97 (5), 98 (2); —, 97.
Cater, 98.
Cater, Dorothy, 204; John, 98 (4), 99 (2); Margery, 98 (4), 99; William, 204.
Cattell, Agnes, 219, 219 n.; —, 219.
Causlade (Cawslade), *see* Cowslade.
Cave, Sir Alexander, 202; Ellen, 202.
Cawslade, *see* Cowslade.
Chadsey, Jeremy, 29.
Chamberlaine (Chamberleine, Chambrelan), Abraham, 136; Christiana, 162; Hester, 136; James, 140; Katherine, 140; Thomas, 162.
Champeney, 108.
Champeney (Champney), Elizabeth, 108; —, 108.
CHAMPION, 99.
Champion, 99.
Champion, Agnes, 101; Alice, 100; Anna, 101, 102 (2); Anne, 100, 101; Arnold, 99, 101 (2); Sir Arthur, 186; Audry, 99; Barbara, 101 (2); Bethsheba, 102 (3); Blanch, 100 (2); Christiall, 100; Christian, 101; Christopher, 100; Dorothy, 102; Edith, 100, 101; Elizabeth, 101 (2), 102 (4); Fides, 99; Frances, 101, 102; Francis, 99, 102; Geffery, 100; George, 19, 101, 102 (2); Henry, 100 (2), 102; Hugh, 39; Humphrey, 101; Imbart, 99; Isabel, 99 (2), 100, 101; Jane, 100, 101 (3), 102; Rev. Dr. John, 101; John, 99 (3), 100 (2), 101 (6). 102 (2); Joyce, 100; Joyter, 99; Judith, 102; Katherine, 100; Lathanell, 100; Leopard, 100 (2); Lucy, 100; Margery, 101; Maria, 101, 102 (3); Mary, 100, 101, 186; Mauld, 100; Peter, 99, 100 (3); Philip, 99, 100 (3), 101 (2), 102; Ralph, 102; Sir Richard, 101 (2); Richard, 101 (8); Robert, 101; Roger, 100 (2); Sacra, 99; Susanna, 102; Thomas, 99, 101 (3), 102; Walter, 100, 101; William, 101; William Philip, 102; Mr., 109; —, 99, 100 (3), 101 (4).
Chancellor, William, 13.
Chandler, Richard, 129; Winifred, 129.
Chandos (Shandos), William Bruges, Lord, 78.
Chaney, *see* Cheney.
Charles I., King of England, 52 (2), 53, 72, 82, 108, 135, 141, 205.
Charles II., King of England, 52.
Charles V. of Germany, 85.
Chatterton, Anne, 207; —, 207.
Cheeve, Alexander, 165; Alice, 165.
Chelron, Rosamond, 203; Thomas, Lord, 203.
CHENEY, 102.
Cheney, 102.
Cheney (Cheyney, Chaney), Agnes, 102, 103; Sir Alexander, 105; Alexander, 102, 103; Alice, 103 (2); Anne, 103, 104 (2), 105 (2); Barbara, 92, 105; Catherine, 175; Celiena, 92, 105; Constance, 103; Dorothy, 105 (2), 215; Edith, 105; Edmund, 105; Edward, Dean of Sarum, 105; Edward, 105; Eleanor, 56, 103 (2), 104; Elizabeth, 71, 103 (4), 105 (3), 116; Frances, 104; Sir Francis, 104; Friswith, 104; Henry, Lord, 104; Henry, 92, 105 (3); Humphrey, 82, 83, 103, 105 (2); Isabel, 103, 104; Jane, 105, 116, 185, 215; Jennett, 54; Joane, 103 (2), 104, 105; Sir John, K.G., 105; Sir John, 104; John, 56, 92, 103 (4), 104, 105 (4), 185, 215 (2); Julian, 105; Katherine, 104; Malyn, 103; Margaret,

102, 103 (3), 104 (2), 105; Margery, 103 (3), 105; Martha, 82, 83; Mary, 92, 105 (2); Parnell, 103; Sir Richard, 103; Richard, 103 (2); Sir Robert, 103, 105, 175; Robert, 92, 103, 105; Sir Roger, 105; Roger, 103 (2); Symon, 103; Sir Thomas, K.G., 104; Thomas, 3, 29, 103 (2), 105 (3), 215; Werburga, 104; William, 10, 13, 43, 45, 102, 103 (5), 104, 105; —, 54, 71, 103, 105, 116 (2).
Cherry, John, 7 (3); William, 43, 45.
Chesington, John, 14.
Chester and Lincoln, Randulph, 3rd Earl of, 75.
Chetwynd, Katherine, 222; Sir Walter, 222.
Childley, Rev. William, 27.
Chitting, — (Herald), 94.
CHOKE, 107.
Choke (Chokke), 106 (2), 107.
Choke (Chokke, Chock), Alexander, 31, 37, 106, 107 (2); Sir Francis, 37; Francis, 28, 107; Sir John, 106, 107; John, 106; Sir Richard, 106 (4); Richard, 106 (2), 107 (5).
Choone, Henry, 7.
Christmas, —, 45.
Church, John, 7; Richard, 7.
Cisu *alias* Sawoer. *see* Sawoer *alias* Cisu.
Clanvile, *see* Clavile.
Clargis, Sir Thomas, Bart., 33.
CLARKE, 108.
Clarke, 108.
Clarke (Clearke), Alicia, 108; Ann, 161, 162, 182; Augustin, 108; Dorothy, 108; Edward, 108 (2); Elizabeth, 108; George, 176; Henry, 108; Joan, 74; Rev. John, 20, 29; John, 20, 49, 108 (4), 162; Katherine, 49; Richard, 108; Thomas, 25, 30; Ursula, 176; Rev. William, 43; William, 20, 40; —, 40, 74, 108, 161, 173, 182.
Clarkson, Samuel, 29.
Clarvox, Margaret, 71; Thomas, 71.
Claver, Anne, 88; Marmaduke, 88.
Clavile, 109.
Clavile (Clanvile) John, 109.
Claydon, William, 34.
Clayton, Rev. Richard, 21.
Clearke, *see* Clarke.
Cleaver, Anne, 84, 87; Richard, 84; —, 87.
Clement, Robert, 5 (2); —, 70 (2).
Clements, Anne, 165; George, 165.
Clerke, Ferdinando, 5, 30; Philip, 22.
Cleve, Alexander, 22; Edward, 3, 12.
Clevedon (Clevidon, Clivedon), Alexander, 107 (3); Elizabeth, 107 (3); Sir John, 107 (3); Mathew, 107 (2); —, 107.
Clifford, Richard, 29.
Clitherow, Rachel, 192; —, 192.
Clobbert, Ellinor, 54; John, 54; —, 54.
Clopton, Nicholas, 79.
Cloudes, Nicholas, 30.
Clovell, Elizabeth, 130; John, 130; Sir William, 130.
Clyderow, 58.
Coachman, Anne, 209; —, 209.
Cobb, Lucie, 182; Michael, 182.
Cobham, Alice, 103; John, 103.
Cockburne, 124.
Cocke (Cock), Frances, 156 *n.*; Richard, 156 *n.*; Mrs., 156.
Coolough (Coldclough), Sir Cæsar, Bart., 4, 30.
Cokayne, G. E. (Clarenceux), 92, 159; Mr., 93 (2), 94.
Cokswell, —, 78 (2).

Coldclough, *see* Coclough.
Cole (Coles), George, 40; John, 3, 25, 40.
Colfe, —, 210 (2).
Collebery, Richard, 172.
Colles, Eleanore, 214; Robert, 214.
Colley, 139.
Colley, John, 139; Maudlyn, 139.
Collier, Philip, 22.
Collins, 109, 110.
Collins, Anne, 128; John, 3, 5, 20, 110 (4), 128; Nathaniel, 30; Richard, 14; Thomas, 18.
Colman, Sepheronia, 161; —, 161.
Colpepper, Elizabeth, 103; Sir Thomas, 103.
Colquite, —. 161 (2).
Colte, Mary, 185; Roger, 185.
Comen, Peter, Marques, 47.
Compaigne, 91.
Compaigne, Bartholomew, 91; Margaret, 91.
Comyn, —, 34.
Conell, Agnes, 219 *n.*; S...., 219 *n.*
Coningsby, Anne, 122; Humfrey, 122.
Constantine, Judith, 72; —, 72.
Cooke, 101.
Cooke, Augustine, 19; Richard, 45; Robert (Clarencieux), 48, 57 (5), 59 (5), 60 (6), 68, 97, 106 (2), 107 (2), 112 (2), 113, 126 (3), 128, 132 (4), 140, 144 (5), 160 (2), 166, 172. 177 (2), 178, 180, 198 (2), 201 (4), 202 (2), 216, 218; William, 2, 16; —, 101 (2).
Cooper (Couper), Dorothy, 102; John, 37; Walter, 102.
Copley, Mary, 22.
Corderay, Henry, 14.
Cornish, Rev. George, 11.
Coteel, Magdalen, 71; Thomas, 71.
Cotes, Thomas, 7.
Cotrill, *see* Cottrell.
Cottell, —, 219 *n.*
Cotten, *see* Cotton.
Cottesmore, Anne, 222; John, 222.
Cotton (Cotten), Edward, 38; Robert, 210, 211; Sarah, 210, 211; Thomas, 42.
Cottrell, John, 5, 38.
Couldrey, Moses, 5.
Couper, *see* Cooper.
Coverley, Charles, 42; Hugh, 42.
Covert, Blanch, 130; —, 130.
Coward, Mary, 173; Rev. Thomas, 35, 173.
Cowdray, John, 33.
Cowley, John, 7.
Cowslade, George, 3, 6, 30; Thomas, 3, 6, 30.
Cowslip, Edward, 16.
Cox (Coxe), Edward, 26; Elizabeth, 200, 234; Gabriell, 6, 30; James, 35; John, 3, 20, 25; Richard, 31; Thomas, 20, 47, 234; —, 200.
Coxhead (Coxhed), Francis, 3, 30; —, 224 (2).
Coxiter, George, 11.
Crall, Margaret, 103; Margery, 103; Robert, 103.
Cranolde, Margaret, 214; —, 214.
Craven, Lord, 6.
Crawley, Rev. Francis, 43.
Crayker, Timothy, 228.
Creech, Anna, 101; John, 101.
Creede, Robert, 7.
Cressell, Richard, 14.
Creswell, —, 217 (2).
Cretenden, Elizabeth, 181; —, 181.
Cripps, Francis, 104; Sir Henry, 104; Nicholas, 104.
Crofts, Edward, 73; Elizabeth, 73.

INDEX NOMINUM.

Croker, John, 63 ; —, 63.
Cromwell, Oliver, 176.
Crooke, Elizabeth, 222 ; Frances, 224 ; Sir John, 222 ; Paule Ambrosi, 224.
Croswell, William, 11.
Crowch, Stoner, 16.
Crowther, Elizabeth, 229 ; —, 229.
Culling, Richard, 176 ; Sarah, 176.
Culvar, John, 46.
Curr, John, 3, 28 (2) ; —, 29.
Curteys, 111.
Curteys, Griffyne, 111 (4).
Curtin, James, 10.
Curtis, John, 17, 34 (2) ; Robert, 44 ; Thomas, 14, 32.
Cyes, Richard, 1.

D

Dacres, Thomas Fynes, Lord, 186.
DALBY, 111.
Dalby, 112.
Dalby, Alice, 112 ; Amy, 111 ; Charles, 112 ; Edward, 5, 7, 32, 111, 112 (4) ; Elizabeth, 112 ; Frances, 112 (2) ; John, 112 ; Thomas, 111 (2).
Dale, Anne, 194 ; George, 194 (2) ; Mary, 194 ; Robert (Richmond Herald), 165, 205, 234.
Dalison, 99, 100.
Dalison, Edith, 100 ; —, 100.
Dallalione, 100.
Dallalione, Mary, 100.
Damory, 139.
Damory, Foulk, 139 ; Mary, 139.
Damsell, Eleanor, 70 ; William, 70.
Danby, Henry, Earl of, 63.
Dancaster (Doncaster), John, 219 ; Mary, 219 ; Mr., 43 ; —, 43.
Dancastle, 112.
Dancastle, John, 32, 112 (2), 113.
Dancer, Rev. —, 37.
Dannett (Donet), Jacob. 103 ; James, 103 ; Jane, 185 ; John, 185 ; Margery, 103.
Danvers (Davers), Anne, 54 ; Henry, Earl of Danby, 63 ; Sir John, 63 ; John, 54 ; Margery, 122 ; Marie, 63 ; Sir Richard, 122 ; William, 54, 63.
Danyell, Edward, 153 ; Mary, 153.
Darell, 100.
Darell (Darrell, Dayrell), Alice, 100, 153 ; Dame Ann, 28 ; Edward, 125 ; Elizabeth, 103, 125 ; Henry, 103 ; Martha, 78, 208, 209 ; Paul, 78, 153, 208, 209 ; Walter, 153 ; —, 100.
Dauncey, Alice, 116 ; William, 116.
Davers, *see* Danvers.
Davies, Edward, 26 ; William, 13.
Davis (Davys), Sir John, 4, 34 ; Robert, 127 ; Sarah, 127.
Dawkes, Robert, 42.
Dawtrey (Dawtry), Elizabeth, 166 ; Sir Francis, 166 ; Henry, 24.
DAY, 113.
Day, 113.
Day (Dee), Francis, 6, 8, 16 ; John, 113 ; Morgan, 113 ; Nicholas, 113 ; Ralph, 43 ; Richard, 113 (2) ; William, S.T.B., Dean of Windsor, 113 (2) ; William, 21, 22 ; Dr., Bishop of Winchester and Deane of Windsor, 16 ; Rev. Mr., 27.
Dayrell, *see* Darell.

Deacon, John, 21.
Deakins, Ambrose, 10.
DEANE, 114.
Deane, 114.
Deane (Dene, à Dene), Alice, 114, 115 (2) ; Elizabeth, 209 (2) ; George, 209 (2) ; Henry, 115 ; Jane, 211 ; John, 114 (3), 115 (3) ; Margaret, 50, 114 ; Nicholas, 115 ; Phœbe, 115 ; Capt. Robert, 211 ; Thomas, 50, 115 ; William, 114 (2).
Dearinge, Cicelie, 156.
De Averingis, Elizabeth, 69 ; John, 69 (2) ; Maud, 69 ; William, 69.
De Bostock, *see* Bostock.
De Bovill, Avis, 69 ; John, 69.
De Buckland, Avis, 69 ; Joan, 69 ; Maud, 69 ; William, 69.
Dee, *see* Day.
De Echingham, *see* Wichingham.
De Ferrars, *see* Ferrars.
De la Beche, 226.
De la Beche (Delabech), Agnes, 227 (3) ; Geoffrey, 226, 227 ; John, 227 ; Richard, 227 ; Robert, 227 ; Roger, 226, 227 ; Thomas, 227 ; William, 226.
De la Beer, Anne, 122 ; William, 122.
De la Hay, Jane, 185 ; —, 185.
De la Hyde, *see* Hyde.
De la Launde, 115.
De la Launde, Johanne, 116 ; Thomas, 116.
Delaviver (Delamere), Anne, 185 ; —, 185.
De Leygh, *see* Leygh.
Del Heath, 76.
Del Heath, John, 77 ; Jone, 77.
Denham, John, M.D., 46.
Dennington, William, 29.
Dent, Adrian, 210 ; Anne, 210.
DENTON, 115.
Denton, 115.
Denton, Agnes, 116 ; Alice, 116 ; Anne, 116 (2) ; Bridget, 116 ; Christopher, 116 ; Dorothy, 116 (2) ; Edward, 116 ; Elizabeth, 116 ; George, 116 ; Isabel, 116 ; Jane, 116 (4), 207 ; Johanne, 116 ; John, 115, 116 (4) ; Joyce, 116 ; Magdalin, 116 ; Nicholas, 207 ; Susan, 116 ; Theodorus, 116 ; Thomas, 115, 116 (6) ; William, 116 ; —, 115 (2), 116.
De Quinci, Hawise, Countess of Lincoln, 75 ; Robert, Earl of Lincoln, 75.
De Say, *see* Say.
De Sutland, Sir John, 107 ; —, 107.
Dethick, Sir Gilbert (Garter), 58 (3), 93 (9), 94 (4), 95 (2), 97, 111 (2), 149 (3), 150, 151, 198 (2), 217, 218 (2) ; Sir William (Garter), 74, 93 (5), 94 (3), 96 (3), 108, 226.
Devereux, Dorothy, 104 ; Sybil, 66 ; Walter, Lord Ferrers, 66 ; Walter, Earl of Essex, 104.
De Vernon, *see* Vernon.
Dew, Henry, 19 ; John, 10, 13, 21.
De Wyke, *see* Wyke.
Dicy, Thomas, 39.
Disney, Anthony, 125 ; Margery, 125.
Dixon, Cicely, 227 ; Edward, 227.
Dockwray, Anne, 215 ; —, 215.
Doddington, Elizabeth, 124 ; —, 124.
Dodson, John, 43.
Dodwell, Richard, 18.
Doe, Joan, 161 ; John, 3, 20, 161 ; Thomas, 16.
Doillie, *see* Doyley.

Dolman (Doleman), Agnes, 162; Dorothy, 71; John, 23; Robert, 72; Sir Thomas, 4, 31; Thomas, 1, 70, 71, 162; —, 70, 72.
Doncaster, *see* Dancaster.
Doncastle (Doncastell), Francis, 31; John, 42; Mary, 207; Mr., 31; —, 207.
Donet, *see* Dannett.
Dormer, William, 5.
Dorrell, Anne, 219; William, 219.
Downes, George, 46.
DOWSE, 130.
Dowse, 130.
Dowse, Blanch, 130; Elizabeth, 130; George, 129, 130 (2); John, 130 (2); Maria, 129, 130; Richard, 130; Thomas, 130; —, 128 n., 130 (2).
Doyley (Doillie), 149.
Doyley (Doillie), Dorothy, 193; John, 193; Philip, 149; Sibell, 126; Thomas, 126.
Drake, Rev. Humfry, 36.
DRAPER, 117.
Draper, 117, 118 (2), 119, 120.
Draper, Alice, 119; Christopher, 119 (2); Edmond, 119; Elizabeth, 119 (2); John, 118, 119; Mary, 119 n.; Robert, 117, 118 (2), 119; Roger, 5, 117 (2), 119 (2); Sarah, 117, 118, 119; Sir Thomas, Bart., 4, 42, 119, 119 n., 120 (2); Sir Thomas, 117; Thomas, 117 (3), 118 (5), 119 (2); —, 119.
Drew, 99, 100, 206.
Drew, Christiall, 100; —, 71 (2), 100.
Drewell, 115.
Dudley, Anne, Countess of Warwick, 222; John, Earl of Warwick, 222.
Dudson, Edward, 12.
Dunch, Edmund, 17; John, 21 (2), 175.
Duncombe, Sara, 134; —, 134.
Dunridge, Anne, 55; Elizabeth, 55; John, 55 (2); Mary, 55; Robert, 55.
Dunsdon, Thomas, 20.
Duppa, Sir Thomas, 192: —, 192.
Dutton, Alice, 77; Sir Thomas, 77.
Dyer, William, 29.

E

Eastfeild, Francis, 98; Sabina, 98.
Eaton, Lewis, 77; Margery, 77.
Edgercombe, Richard, 125; Winifred, 125.
Edkins, John, 33.
Edling, John, 15.
Edlyn, Peter, 5.
EDMANDS, 120.
Edmands (Edmonde, Edmonds, Edmund, Edmunds), Christian, 120; Sir Christopher, 175; Dorothy, 175; Elizabeth, 120; Johanna, 189; John, 3, 6, 27, 30, 120 (4); Joseph, 120; Margaret, 114; Simon, 189; Thomas, 120 (2); —, 114, 120.
Edmondson, Rev. Richard, 19.
Edolfe, Elizabeth, 52; Sir Robert, 52.
Edward I., King of England, 75.
Edward III., King of England, 75.
Edward IV., King of England, 77.
Edwards, Anne, 209; Thomas, D.C.L., 209; —, 39.
Edyngton, Isabell, 54; John, 54.
Edyt, Elizabeth, 101; —, 101.
Eiston, *see* Eyston.

Eldridge, Griffin, 33; Thomas, 8, 16.
Elkes, Rev. William, 31.
Elkwood, —, 171 (2).
Elles, —, 33.
Elley, Elizabeth, 182; Richard, 182.
Elliott, 138.
Elliott (Elliot), Anne, 139, 195; Eleanor, 139; John, 139 (4); Margaret, 139; Thomas, 139; William, 16; —, 139 (3), 195.
Ellrick, *see* Ettrick.
Elmes, William, 15.
Elston, *see* Eyston.
Elton, —, 32.
Elvington, Edward, 64; Jane, 64.
Elwaies, Francis, 28.
Elwes, John, 5, 28.
Ely, Richard, 10; Thomas, 16.
Eman, Timothy, 47.
Empson, 115.
Enewright, Peter, 16.
ENGLEFIELD, 121.
Englefield, 121.
Englefield (Englefylde), Alice, 122 (2), 123, 124; Sir Allen, 121; Andrew, 122; Anne, 122 (2); Anthony, 26, 36, 41 (2), 121, 123 (5), 124; Catherine, 123; Sir Charles, Bart., 123; Charles, 123; Cicely, 122 (2); Dorothy, 124; Elizabeth, 122 (5), 124; Sir Francis, Bart., 123 (6); Sir Francis, 121, 123 (2); Francis, 124; Guy, 121, 124; Hasculfus, 121; Hellen, 123, 124; Hely, 121; Henry, 36, 121, 123 (4); Isabel, 122; Jane, 123 (2); Joan, 122; Johanne, 122 (3); Sir John, 122 (2); John, 121, 122 (2), 123 (2), 124; Katherine, 123; Margaret, 122, 123 (2); Margery, 122 (3); Marke, 124; Martha, 123; Mary, 122, 123 (3), 124; Maud, 121; Nichola, 122 (2); Peter, 121; Sir Philip, 122; Philip, 122 (2); Richard, 122; Robert, 122; Sir Roger, 122; Sibbell, 122 (2); Susan, 122, 123; Sir Thomas, 35, 122 (2); Thomas, 121, 123 (4), 124; Sir William, 121, 122 (2); William, 121 (2), 122 (2), 123, 124; Winifred, 123, 124; Mr., 41; —, 35, 121 (5), 122 (4), 123 (2).
Erneys, 184.
Erneys (Erneis), Alice, 184; Joane, 184; Roger, 184.
Escourt, Elizabeth, 156; Sir Thomas, 156.
ESSEX, 124.
Essex, 124.
Essex, Alice, 125 (2); Anne, 125 (3); Bridget, 125; Charles, 125; Dorothy, 125; Edith, 125; Edmund, 125 (2); Sir Edward, 125; Elizabeth, 125 (5); George, 125; Humfry, 125 (3); Isabell, 125; Jane, 125 (4); Jone, 125 (2); Katherine, 125; Lucy, 125 (2); Dame Margaret, 124, 125; Margery, 125; Mary, 125 (2); Richard, 125; Robert, 125; Scipio, 125; Sir Thomas, 124, 125; Thomas, 124, 125 (4), 175; Sir William, 125; William, 124, 125 (6); Winifred, 125.
Estbury, Anne, 125; John, 125.
Estock, 109.
Ettrick, Anthony, 28.
Evans, Ambrose, 170; Charles, 36; Elizabeth, 170; Katherine, 17; Matilda, 88; —, 88.
Everard, 126.
Eyes, *see* Oyes.
Eyston (Eiston, Eston, Ayston, Elston), John, 15, 24, 35; Katherine, 83; Martyn, 41; William, 20, 35, 83; —, 224 (2).

INDEX NOMINUM. 245

F

Fabian, Anne, 215 ; —, 215.
Fairbeard, Anthony, 26.
Falbrooke, William, 26.
Falham, *see* Fulham.
Falwer, *see* Fuller.
Fane, George, 15 ; —, K.B., 15.
Fanner (Farnour), Richard, 3, 29.
Farby, Agnes, 103 ; John, 103.
Farmer, Rev. Edward, 27 ; Elizabeth, 185, 215 ; John, 24 ; Thomas, 19 ; William, 185, 215.
- Farmer *alias* Draper, *see* Draper *alias* Farmer.
Farnham, Mary, 154 ; Peter, 154.
Farnnour, *see* Fanner.
Farr, Laurence, 3.
Faukner, Widow, 35.
Faunt, Anne, 170 ; —, 170.
Fawkenore, Alice, 122 ; William, 122.
Fawrer, Barton, 83 ; Christian, 83.
Fayrer, James, 37.
Feilder, John, 80 ; Susan, 80.
Fellowes, Richard, 7.
Felton, Ellenor, 204 ; Thomas, 204 ; —, 207 (2).
Fenever, *see* Jenivor.
Fenn (Fenne), Sir Hugh, 181 ; Margaret, 181 ; Robert, 40.
Fenwick, John, 43.
Ferebe, Rev. John, 25.
FERRERS, 126.
Ferrers, 126.
Ferrers (Ferrers, de Ferrars), Benjamin, 126 ; Joane, 69 ; John, 43, 126 (2) ; Mary, 126 (2) ; Robert, 69 ; Samuel, 126 (2) ; Sibell, 126 ; Susanna, 126 (2) ; Thomas, 126 ; William, 126.
Ferriman, Hugh, 39.
Ferry, Rev. Stephen, 41.
FETIPLACE, 127 (2).
Fetiplace, 128, 221.
Fettiplace (Feteplace, Phetiplace), Alexander, 26, 27, 127 ; Alice, 140 ; Amy, 78 ; Anne, 127 (3), 128 ; Anthony, 127 (4), 128 ; Bartholomew, 127 ; Bessels, 77 ; Bridgett, 127 ; Charles, 5, 24, 127 (5), 128 (3) ; Edith, 77 ; Sir Edmond, 127 (4) ; Edmund, 26 ; Edward, 125, 127 ; Elizabeth, 70, 127 (3), 186 ; Frances, 127 ; Hanah, 127 ; Hulcott, 127 ; Ida, 77 ; Jane, 127 ; Sir John, 4, 19, 41 ; John, 21, 82, 127 (5), 128 (2) ; Katherine, 123 ; Margaret, 82 ; Martha, 127 ; Mary, 22, 125, 127 ; Peter, 127 ; Sir Richard, 77 ; Richard, 70, 127 ; Robert, 127 ; Roger, 128 (2) ; Rowland, 127 (3) ; Sarah, 127 (2) ; Sibbell, 221 ; Susanna, 127 ; Sir Thomas, 123, 186 ; Thomas, 5, 26, 78, 127 (2) ; William, 127 (2), 221 ; —, 70, 140.
Fewin, John, 17.
Field, Thomas, 14.
Fifield, 174.
Fifield, Bridget, 175 ; William, 175.
Finch, John, 47, 84 ; Mary, 85 ; William, 41.
Fincham, Malyn, 103.
Fincher, Major, 46.
Finmore (Fynmore), John, 2, 10 ; William, 1 (2), 2, 13.
Fish, Mary, 188 ; Oliver, 188.
Fishbourne, Richard, 47.
Fisher, James, 19 ; Susan, 131 ; —, 131.
Fitton, Sir Edward, 123 ; Margaret, 123.
Fitzhugh, Katherine, Lady, 181 ; Lord, 181.
FitzWarren, Foulke, Lord, 204 ; Hauice, 204.
Fleetwood, Anne, 209, 210 ; Cecilia, 210 ; Elizabeth, 210 ; Jeffry, 209, 210 ; Richard, 210 ; Thomas, 210 ; William, 210.
Flegg, 128.
Fleming, Giles, 126 ; Robert, 73 ; Ruth, 73 ; Susanna, 126.
Fletcher, John, 10.
Flood, Joseph, 45.
Flower, William (Norroy), 113 (2), 179 (5), 198 (2), 228.
Fogg, Jane, 100 ; John, 100 ; Richard, 100 ; —, 100.
Foldervey, Katherine, 131 ; Walter, 131.
Foote, Sir Thomas, 42.
Ford, John, 15.
Forrest, John, 43.
Forster, Sir Humfrey, Bart., 37 ; William, 10 ; —, Bart., 37.
Fortescue, Sir Adrian, 185, 191 ; Anne, 191 ; Mary, 185.
Fortie, John, 13.
Foster, Edmund, 78 ; Margaret, 78.
Fountaine, —, 10.
Fournes, —, 224 (2).
Fowler, 184.
Fowler, Alice, 55 ; Rev. Christopher, 33 ; Cicely, 122 ; John, 55 ; Rev. Thomas, 22 ; William, 122.
Fox, 229.
Fox, Samuel, 14 ; William, 10.
Foxley, 144.
Foxley, John, 144 ; Thomasen, 144.
Franklyn, Edmond, 10 ; Richard, 25, 44 ; William, M.D., 47.
Fravion, 99.
Fravion, Sacra, 99 ; —, 99.
Freare, Margery, 78 ; —, 78.
Freeman, John, 16.
Frowike, Friswith, 104 ; Sir Thomas, 104.
Fulham (Falham), Rev. Dr. Edward, 44 ; Dr., 23 (2).
FULLER (FULWAR), 128.
Fuller (Fulwar), 128.
Fuller (Fulwar), Alice, 184 ; Anne, 129 (2) ; Bostock, 77 ; Sir Dowse, 35, 129 (3) ; Dowse (Douze), 129 (3), 130 ; Elizabeth, 129 ; John, 181 ; Katherine, 77 ; Maria, 129, 130 ; Sir Nicholas, 129 ; Nicholas, 128 (2), 128 n., 129, 130 ; Peter, 128 ; Richard, 77, 129 (2) ; Sara, 128 ; Dr. Thomas, 174 (2) ; Thomas, 128 ; —, 128 (2), 129 (3).
Fynes, Mary, 186 ; Thomas, Lord Dacres, 186.
Fynmore, *see* Finmore.

G

Galland, William, 6 (2).
Gallant, Mr., 39.
Gam, 191 (3).
Gambo, 99, 100.
Gambo, Isabel, 100 ; —, 100.
Garbrand *alias* Harkes, Tobias, M.D., 10.
Gardiner, 131.
Gardiner (Gardner), Frances, 156 ; Roger, 131 (2) ; Sir Thomas, 156 ; Thomas, 13.
Garnam, William, 2, 23 ; Mr., 2.
Garr, Martha, 83 ; Otho, 83.
GARRARD, 131.
Garrard, 140.
Garrard, Anne, 127 ; Charles, 24 ; Edward, 131 ; Elizabeth, 24 ; Gilbert, 41 ; Joan, 131 ;

John, 131; Joseph, 6, 30, 131 (3); Katherine, 131; Margery, 131; Philip, 24 (2); Richard, 31; Robert, 6 (2), 29, 30, 35; Roger, 24 (2), 127; Susan, 131; Thomas, 5, 24; William, 131 (2); Mr., 24.
Garret, —, 37.
Gascoigne, 100.
Gascoigne, Anne, 100; William, 100.
Gasprian, 100.
Gasprian, Thebis, 100.
Gate, Anthony, 175; Judith, 175.
Gattaker, Elizabeth, 77; John, 77.
Gaulton, 131.
Geale, Richard, 39; Samuel, 39.
Gearing (Geering, Geringe, Gery), Gregory, 4, 19, 26.
GEFFE (JEFFE), 132.
Geffe (Jeffe), 132.
Geffe (Geff, Jeffe), Andrew, 132; Nicholas, 132 (2); Thomas, 132.
Gell, John, 188; Katherine, 188.
Genney, 174.
Genny, Margaret, 86; Thomas, 86.
George, James, 20; Thomas, 27.
Geringe, *see* Gearing.
Gerrard, Frances, 141; George, 141; Sir William, 141.
Geth, Meredith, 149.
Geton, 106 (2), 107.
Gibson, John, 46.
Gibson, Elizabeth, 217; —, 217.
Gifford, Anthony, 229; Elizabeth, 229; John, 24.
Gilborne, Anne, 170, 171; Bridget, 171 (2); Elisabeth, 171 (3); Col. Henry, 170; Henry, 171; Hester, 171; John, 171; Katerine, 171; Mary, 171 (2); Thomas, 171; —, 171.
Giles, *see* Gyles.
Gill, Alice, 125; Sir George, 125.
Glass, Thomas, 27.
Glover, John, 12.
Goddard, 131, 234.
Goddard, Daniel, 38; Edward, 63; Elizabeth, 71; George, 1; Joan, 63, 234; John, 29; Mary, 210, 211; Richard, 234; Thomas, 29; Vincent, 1. 38; William, M.D., 210, 211; William, 234; Mr., 151; —, 71.
Godfrey, Barbara, 81; Charles, 81; Daniel, 81 (2); Thomas, 1; William, 12.
Godman, Elizabeth, 98; Thomas, 98.
Godwin, William, 6.
Goldborne, William, 30.
Goldier, Norris, 35.
Good, Rev. Martin, 37.
Goodall, Anne, 78; Richard, 21; —, 78.
Goodday, Richard, 14.
Gooding, John 38.
Goodlack, 68.
Goodlake, Thomas, 27.
Goodwyn, William, 30.
Goodyer, 132.
Goodyer, Thomas, 132 (2).
Gorges, Sir Edward, 223; Elizabeth, 223.
Gosling, Maud, 78; William, 78.
Gosson, 133.
Gosson, Angell, 42; Elizabeth, 52, 133; Richard, 52, 133; Robert, 42 (2), 51, 133 (4); —, 42, 51.
Gough, Rev. William, 28.
Gower, Anne, 122; John, 122.
Grafton, 141.

Grafton, Margaret, 142; Mr., 142.
Grave, —, 139.
Gray, Anne, 74; Henry, 74; —, Earl of Kent 74.
Greay, Adam, 84; —, 84.
Green (Greene), Edmond, 12; Everard (Rouge Dragon), 53, 69, 81, 89, 119, 130, 137, 167, 211, 214, 234; William, 5.
Greenaway, Katherine, 13; Robert, 11.
Greetham, Rev. Henry, 27.
Gregory, Edmund, 25; Frances, 72; John, 14, 16; Thomas, 72.
Grendon (Grindon), Philip, 101; —, 101.
Grenfield (Grinfield), Edward, 116; Elizabeth, 116; Thomas, 31.
Gresham, Elizabeth, 181; Sir John, 181.
Grevell, Anne, 191; Sir Gyles, 191.
Griffith, Anne. 203; John, Lord, 203.
Grigson, Roger, 15.
Grindon, *see* Grendon.
Grinfield, *see* Grenfield.
Groftes, Anne, 101; Thomas, 101.
Grove, Elizabeth. 48; Rev. Francis, 22; Henry, 19; John, 5, 42, 48; Thomas, 40; William, 4, 5, 19; —, 22.
Grymstedd, 115.
Gunter. Ferdinando, 28; Nicholas, 34; Mr., 28 (2).
Gwilliams, John, 142; Mary, 142.
GWYNNE, 134.
Gwynne, 134.
Gwynne (Gwyn), Anne, 134 (2); Blanch, 134; Edmond. 134; Edward, 134 (2); Elizabeth, 134; Eme. 134; Jane, 134; John, 134; Mathew, M.D., 134; Mathew, 134 (3); Richard, 134 (2); Roger, 134; Sara, 134; Susan, 134 (3); Thomas, 134; William, 134 (4); —, 134 (3).
GYLES, 135.
Gyles (Giles), Anne, 135 (2); Elizabeth, 135; Frances, 135; Henry, 135; John, 6, 135; Nathaniel, 135 (2); Robert, 135; Susan, 135 (2); Dr., 45.

H

Hacker, Anne, 210; Elizabeth, 210; Martha, 209; William, 209, 210.
Haddock, —, 231.
Hagthorne, Nathaniel, 1.
Haitfield, 174.
Haitfield, Anne, 86; Pierce, 86.
Hales, Samuel, 47; —, 103.
Hall, Richard, 3; William, 5.
Halloway, *see* Holloway.
HALLSTED, 135.
Hallsted, 135.
Hallsted (Halsted), Abraham, 136; George, 136; Hester, 136; James, 136; John, 135, 136 (2); Laurence, 39, 135, 136 (5); Mary, 135; Mathias, 136; Oliver, 135, 136; William, 136.
Hamden, Anne, 191; Griffen, 191.
Hamilton, Catherine, 170; James, Lord Paysley, 170 (2); Katherine, Lady Paysley, 170.
Hamson, —, 127.
Hancock (Hancok), John, 115; Phœbe, 115; Thomas, 42.
Hand, Jeremiah, 3, 30.
Hanford, John, 85; Mary, 85.

INDEX NOMINUM. 247

HANSON, 137.
Hanson, 137.
Hanson, Barbara, 137; Berkley, 137 (2); Edward, 137; Elizabeth, 137; Isabell, 137; John, 10, 137; Katherine, 137 (2); Mary, 137; Robert, 137 (4); Thomas, 137; William, 137 (3).
Harbin, Andrew, 210, 211 (2); Anne, 210. 211; Sarah, 211.
Harby, Sir Job, Bart., 196; Susan, 196.
Harcourt, *see* Harecourt.
Harding, John, 4, 25; Rev. —, 40.
Hardward, John, 52; Mary, 52.
Hare, John (Rouge Dragon and Richmond Herald), 235; Mr., 235 (2).
HARECOURT, 138.
Harecourt, 138.
Harecourt (Harcourt), Alice, 70; Anne, 138, 185; Elizabeth, 138; Francis, 138; Jane, 125; Sir John, 185; Sir Richard, 70; Richard, 138; Robert, 138; Sir Walter, 125; William, 138; —, 138 (3).
Harington, *see* Harrington.
Harison, *see* Harrison.
Harkes *alias* Garbrand, *see* Garbrand *alias* Harkes.
Harmor, —, 45.
Harper, Thomas, 228 (2).
Harrington, 184.
Harrington (Harington), Alice, Lady, 222; John, Lord, 222; John, 86; Margaret, 86.
HARRIS, 138.
Harris, 138.
Harris, Alice, 153; Amy, 139; Catherine, 139; Edward, 138; Ellen, 139; Francis, 46; Henry, 138, 139; Joyce, 138; Lewis, 153; Mary, 139; Maudlyn, 139; Capt. Nathaniel, 47; Robert, 47, 139 (3); Rowland, 138; Thomas, 138; Ursula, 138; Rev. William, 23; William, 139.
HARRISON, 139, 140, 141.
Harrison, 140, 141.
Harrison (Harison), Alice, 140 (2); Anne, 142 (2); Bernard, 142 (2); Christian, 142; Elizabeth, 36, 140 (2), 141 (2), 142 (2); Frances, 141 (2); Gilbert, 141, 142 (5); James, 143; John, 5, 33, 36 (2), 37, 139, 140, 141 (2), 142; Jone, 125; Katherine, 140 (2); Margaret, 142; Richard, 4, 40, 141 (3), 142; Thomas, 33, 125, 140 (5), 141, 142; William, 142; Mr., 37; —, 140.
Hart (Harte), Edward, 9, 152; Thomas, 11; Mr., 17, 21, 91 (2), 169, 216.
Hartford, Edward Seamer, Earl of, 222.
Harvey (Harvy, Hervye), Anthony, 15; Edward, 105; Joane, 105; William (Clarencieux), 98 (3), 99 (2), 126, 199.
Harward, Thomas, 14.
Harwell, John, 13.
Haryson *alias* Hardegson, *see* Harrison.
Hasler, Peter, 10.
Hassall, John, 35.
Hastings, Sir George, 222; Katherine, 222.
Hatch, Emanuel, 42.
Hathaway, Rev. Francis, 21.
HATT, 142.
Hatt, 142.
Hatt, Adam, 32; Dorothy, 142 (3); Elizabeth, 142; Giles, 142; John, 142 (2); Mary, 142 (2); Richard, 32, 142 (3); Col., 31; —, 142.
Hatton, Margery, 77; Peter, 77.

Haule, —, 138 (2).
Hauteyn, Hester, 229; William, 229.
Havard, 191.
Havell, John, 15.
Haward, Frances, 219; Thomas, 219.
Hawes, Jonathan, 10; Marie, 70; Thomas, 40; —, 70.
Hawker, Thomas, 6.
Hawkins, Dorothea, 162; John, 5, 18, 35; Simon. 10; Capt., 162.
Hawley, Thomas (Clarencieux), 160 (2).
Hawthorne, Elizabeth, 142; —, 142.
Hayes, 143.
Hayes, Alexander, 45, 143; James, 143 (2); Thomas, 46, 143 (2).
Haylor, James, 47.
Haynes, 144.
Haynes (Heynes), Daniel, 28 (2); John, 34, 72; Nicholas, 144 (3); Richard, 33, 144; Thomasen, 144; —, 62.
Hayte, John, 51; Margaret, 51.
Hazell, Rev. Richard, 23.
Head, Adam, 3, 27 (2); Edward, 23; John, 2, 23.
Headland, Thomas, 37.
Heath, Jane, 116; Thomas, 116.
Heaton, Felice, 77; John, 77.
Hedges, John, 6, 29; William, 5.
Hender, Juliana, 161; William, 161.
Henn *alias* Hene, Sir Henry, Bart., 46, 145 (5); William, 145; —, 145.
Henry IV., King of England, 54, 75.
Henry V., King of England, 75.
Henry VI., King of England, 75.
Henry VII., King of England, 82, 109, 127, 175, 207.
Henry VIII., King of England, 80, 91 (3), 93, 94, 175, 181, 204, 208.
Henton, Felice, 77; John, 77.
Henwood, Thomas, 37.
Herbert, Sir Arnold, 38, 146 (3); Edward, 38, 146 (2); James, 29; Rev. John, 11.
Herbye, —, 51 (2).
Hercy, John, 46.
Herdson, Barbara, 101; Henry, 101.
Heredge, Thomas, 15.
Heron, James, 11; Margaret, 28.
Hervye, *see* Harvey.
Hewer, 126.
Heuer, Mary, 126; Richard, 126; Thomas, 126 (2).
Hewet, —, 224 (2).
Hext, Dionisia, 217; Sir Edward, 217.
Heygarton, William, 157.
Heynes, *see* Haynes.
Heyrick, Elizabeth, 187; Robert, 187.
Hicks, Simon, 45.
Hide, *see* Hyde.
Higginson, Margery, 77; —, 77.
Higgs, Richard, 37.
Hignill, Robert, 23.
Hildesley, Francis, 23; Joan, 196; Richard, 35, 196; William, 38.
Hill, 146.
Hill, Dorothy, 78; Jacob, 101; James, 146 (3), 147; Jane, 101; John, 46; Rev. Joseph, 21, 201; Richard, 29; —, 78.
Hillary, Rev. Edward, 26.
Hinckley, Rev. John, 25.
Hinton (Hynton), Friswith, 224; Richard, 224; Thomas, 25, 26; William, 5.

Hinxsted, —, 103 (2).
Hissey, John, 18.
Hoare. John, 43.
Hobbs, Bennet, 20 (2); Elizabeth. 102; Francis, 102; Margaret, 27; Martin, 34; Richard, 20.
Hoby, 149. 151.
Hoby (Hobby, Hobbey, Hooby), Cicely, 222; Sir Edward, 148, 149, 150. 151. 151 *n.*, 152; Edward, 5. 149 (3). 150. 222; Eustace, 41; Katherine. 147. 149; Peregrine. 4. 40. 148, 150 (2). 151 (4). 151 *n.*, 152 (2). 220; Sir Thomas. 149; Sir Thomas Posthumous. 151 *n.*; Mr., 147 (5), 148 (6), 149 (4); Mrs., 148 (2), 152 (2); —, 151.
Hockley, William, 44.
Hodelry, 138.
Hodges, Rev. Anthony, 12; George, 38; Henry, 25.
Hodgeson. Henry. 17.
Holberk. 138.
Holberk. George. 138; Joyce. 138.
Holford, Thomas, 47.
Holland. 76.
Holland. Rev. Bryan. 17.
Holliday. William. 10.
Hollier, John. 5.
HOLLOWAY. 153.
Holloway, 153.
Holloway (Halloway), Agnes, 62; Alice, 153 (4); Charles. 11. 112, 152. 153 (4); Elizabeth, 153; Frances, 112, 153; Francis, 153; John, 153 (3); Katharine. 153; Magdaline, 153; Mary, 153; Richard. 62, 153; Sara, 153; Susan. 153 (2); Thomas. 153 (2); William, 153.
Holmes (Holme), Alice, 78; Thomas, 23; T. (Clarencieux), 195; —. 78.
Holt, Sir Edward, 77; Jane, 77; Thomas, 5, 10.
Hoo, 203.
Hoo, Agnes, Lady. 203; Alexander, Lord. 203; Alice, Lady, 204; Anne, Lady, 203; Anne, 204 (2); Beatrix, Lady, 204; Darnell, Lady, 203; Dorothy, 204; Elizabeth, Lady, 204 (2); Ellenor. Lady, 204 (3); Grace, 204; Hauice, Lady, 204; Jane, 204; Lucy, 204; Margaret, 204 (2); Maud. 204; Nicholas, 204; Robert, Lord, 203 (4). 204 (2); Rosamond, Lady, 203; Thomas. Lord, 203, 204 (3); Thomas, 204 (6); Thomasin, 204; William, Lord, 204; Wilmott, Lady, 203; —, 204 (2).
Hooby, *see* Hoby.
Hooke, —, 41.
HOPER, 154.
Hoper, 154.
Hoper (Hopper), Daniel, 154; Dudley, 154; Elizabeth, 154; Francis, 154; Henry, 154; Mary. 154; Nathaniel, 39, 154 (4); Penticost, 154; Priscilla, 154; Prudence, 154; Richard, 154 (3); Samuel, 154.
Hopkins, Widow, 173.
Hopper, *see* Hoper.
HORDE. 155.
Horde, 155.
Horde, Allan, 155 (2), 156; Barbara, 156; Dorothy, 156 (2); Frances, 156 (2); John, 156; Sir Thomas, 156; Thomas, 22, 155, 156 (2); William, 152; —, 155.
Horne, 215.
Horne, Anne, 185, 215; Joan, 54, 78; John, 54, 78, 185; William, 215.

Horneby, —, 200 (2).
Horsford. Isaack, 16; Thomas, 16.
Horton, Agnes, 233; Thomas, 233.
Hosman, Alexander, 101; Elizabeth, 101.
House, *see* Howes.
Howard, Dr. Jackson, 119; Thomas, 18; William, 18.
Howes (Howe, Howse, House), Agnes, 87, 88; John, 30, 32; Jonathan, 6, 10; Richard, 22, 34, 88; William, 32.
Hucotta, Thomas, 10.
Huet. Jane, 200; John, 200.
Huggeford, Abigail, 88; John, 88.
Hughson. Rev. William, 41.
Hulcott, John, 125; Katherine, 125.
Hulet, Rev. Robert, 15.
Humes. Robert, 43.
Humfrey (Humfry), Jone, 234; Richard, 42; —, 234.
Humfreys (Humfries), Joane, 224; Joyce, 224; Thomas, 14; —, 224.
HUNGERFORD, 156.
Hungerford, 156.
Hungerford, Anne, 70; Sir Anthony, 70; Catherine, 156; Cicelie, 156; Edward, 90; Elizabeth, 156; Frances, 156, 162; Francis, M.D., 33; John, 156 (3). 162; Mary, 90; Lord Robert, 156; Robert, 156; Sir Walter, Lord, 156 *n.*; Rev. Dr. Walter, 25, 156 (4); Walter, 156.
Hunkes, 174.
Hunkes, Sir Henry, 176; John, 175; Ursula, 175; —, 176.
Hunt, Margery, 164; Thomas, 164.
Huntington, John, 184; Percyvall, 184.
Hurdman, Thomas, 19.
Hurlock, Francis, 1; —, 1.
Hurte, Agnes, 233; Thomas, 233.
Hutch, Mr., 35.
Hutt. Henry, 12.
HYDE, 157, 159.
Hyde, 159, (crest) 156.
Hyde (Hide, de la Hyde, atte Hyde), Agnes, 157; Alexander, 92; Alice, 125, 157 (2); Andrew, 159 (2); Anne, 92; Baldwin, 157; Barbara. 92; Benjamin, 159; Celina, 92; Dorothy, 158; Edward, 20; Elizabeth, 92, 157, 159. 221, 233; Francis, 36, 158 (2); George. 156 (3). 157 (2); Hamlett, 92 (2); Hellen, 159; Humfry, 4, 26, 158; Jane, 159; John, 12, 41, 157 (7), 159 (3), 221; Julian, 159; Lawrence. 92 (3); Lucy, 224; Margaret, 92, 159; Margery, 98, 99; Matilda, 157; Michael, 157; Nathaniel, 159; Oliver, 221; Peter, 157; Petronella, 157 (3); Sir Richard. 12, 157; Richard, 12. 41, 92; Robert, 2, 4, 6, 13 (2), 14 (2), 92 (4); Sarah, 159; Stephen, 157; Valentine, 92; Warin, 157; William, 92, 98, 99, 125, 157 (3); —, 157, 159, 224, 233.
Hyne, Rev. George, 17.
Hynton, *see* Hinton.

Inglefield, *see* Englefield.
Ingram, Rev. Peter, 21.
Ireland, —, 16.
Isham, Sarah, 188; —, 188.

INDEX NOMINUM. 249

J

Jackman, Elizabeth, 166; William, 166.
Jacobb, Mary, 173; William, 173.
James, Ann, 36; Benjamin, 34; Rev. John, 23; Richard, 40; Roger, 117, 118; Sarah, 117, 118; Walter, M.D., 30; William, 5, 28, 30, 36.
James I., King of England, 52, 53, 135, 147, 176, 182.
Janinges, *see* Jennings.
Jawdrell (Jawtherell), *see* Jodrell.
Jeffe, *see* Geffe.
Jemett, Samuel, 33.
Jenivor, Amy, 78; William, 78.
Jennings (Jenings, Janinges), Alice, 78; Barbara, 78; Edward, 4, 13, 14; James, 4, 17; John, 13, 19; Jone, 78 (2); Richard, 78, 127; Robert, 2, 14; Thomas, 78 (2); William, 78 (2); —, 17, 78, 127.
Jerman, Mr., 35.
Jervoise (Jervice), Anne, 129 (2); Bernard, 129; Frances, 129; Henry, 129; Lucy, 129 (3); Mary, 129 (2); Richard, 129; Sir Thomas, 129 (3); Thomas, 129 (3); Winifred, 129; —, 129 (3).
JOANES, 159.
Joanes, 159.
Joanes, Ellen, 159; Sir Francis, 159; John, 159 (2); —, 159 (2).
Jodrell, Barbara, 78, 208, 209; Roger, 209; —, 208.
Johnson (Johnston), Edward, 7, 33; Nicholas, 33; Richard, 33; —, 33, 44.
Jones, Edward, 137 (2); Elizabeth, 73; Hugh, 137; John, 21, 73; Katherine, 137; Mary, 32 (2); Richard, 31, 32; Walter, D.D., 11; Mr., 31, 32.
Jordan, Dorothy, 142; Richard, 142; William, 21.
Jourdin, Adam, 174; Elizabeth, 174; Margaret, 174; —, 174.
Joyner, Richard, 5; Thomas, 25.
Justice, 160 (2), 234.
Justice, Edward, 35; John, 34; Mary, 160 (5); Thomas, 17, 35, 160; William, 160 (2).

K

Kanion, *see* Kenyon.
KEATE (KETE), 161.
Keate (Kete), Agnes, 161, 162; Ann, 161 (3), 162, 163; Christiana, 162; Dorothy, 162; Edward, 5, 20, 161 (2), 162 (3); Eleanor, 162; Elizabeth, 161, 162, 163; Frances, 161, 162 (2); Francis, 162 (2); George, 14, 161 (2), 162 (2); Gilbert, 161 (2), 163 (4); Hugh, 1, 14, 161, 162 (2); Joan, 161 (2), 162, 163; Rev. John, 19; John, 1, 34, 161 (6), 162, 163 (5); Jonathan, 163; Leonard, 161; Mary, 160, 162; Ralph, 161 (3), 162, 163; Rebecca, 161; Sepheronia, 161; Susan, 163; Susanna, 161; William, 160, 161 (5), 162 (2), 163 (2); —, 161 (3), 162.
Kelk, Clement, 140; Elizabeth, 140.
Kelloway, Alice, 222; Cicely, 222; Sir Robert, 222.
Kember, Christian, 126; Mary, 126; —, 126.
Kemble, 164.
Kemble (Kemball), George, 164 (4); John, 24; Thomas, 44.

Kempe, Katherine, 104; Sir Nicholas, 117, 118; Sarah, 117, 118; Sir Thomas, 104.
Kendall, —, 51 (2).
Kendrick (Kenrick), William, 34 (2).
Kent, Alice, 165; Anne, 165; Frances, 165; John, 164, 165; Margery, 164, 165; Thomas, 4, 28, 164, 165 (5); William, 165 (2); —, Earl of, 74; Mr., 165; —, 164.
Kenton, John, 34; Thomas, 6, 7, 34.
Kenyon, Alice, 114; Hugh, 114.
Kerfoote, John, 14; Nicholas, 15.
Kete, *see* Keate.
Kevelioc, 76.
Kevilioc, Hugh, 76.
Keys (Keyes, Kys), Richard, 1 (2).
Kidgell, Francis, 32.
Kidwell, Nevill, 7, 43; —, 43.
Kildalls, William, 173.
Killegreve, Ann, 181; Sir Henry, 181.
King, Margery, 105; Thomas, 105; William, 22; Mr. (Rouge Dragon), 196.
King Alexander of Scotland, 203.
King Charles I. of England, 52 (2), 53, 72, 82, 108, 135, 141, 205.
King Charles II. of England, 52.
King Charles V. of Germany, 85.
King Edward I. of England, 75.
King Edward III. of England, 75.
King Edward IV. of England, 77.
King Henry IV. of England, 54, 75.
King Henry V. of England, 75.
King Henry VI. of England, 75.
King Henry VII. of England, 82, 109, 127, 175, 207.
King Henry VIII. of England, 80, 91 (2), 93, 94, 125, 175, 181, 204, 208.
King Richard II. of England, 75.
Kingsley *alias* Whetnall, *see* Whetnall *alias* Kingsley.
Kingsmill, Bridget, 186; Elizabeth, 217; John, 30; Richard, 217; Sir William, 186; —, 186.
Kingston, 155.
Kirby, George, 29; Richard, 2, 16; William, 44.
Kirkeby, Eleanor, 86; William, 86.
Kirton, 165.
Knapp (Knap), Francis, 5, 22; George, 4, 23; Henry, 16; John, 2, 12.
Knevett, Muriel, 191; Sir Thomas, 191.
Kniffe (Knyffe), Alice, 79; Margaret, 79; Richard, 79; Thomas, 79.
KNIGHT, 166.
Knight, 166 (2).
Knight, Alice, 219; Bostock, 77; Constance, 166; Elizabeth, 166; John, 131, 166 (2), 219; Sir John, 166; Jone, 77, 131; Richard, 166 (2); Roger, 4, 19, 30; Walter, 33, 166 (2); William, 77.
Knightly, Anne, 222; Dorothy, 222; Richard, 222 (2); Sir Valentine, 222.
Knyffe, *see* Kniffe.
Kys, *see* Keys.

L

Lake, Joyce, 56; William, 56.
Lamb, Dr. John, Dean of Ely, 176; Mary, 176; Thomas, 176.
Lamoys, 99.
Lamoys, Fides, 99; —, 99.
Lane, Barbara, 80; John, 2, 18; Josiah, M.D., 16; Susanna, 194; Walter, 80; William, 1, 8, 16, 194; Mrs., 12.

Langbain, Dr., 198.
Langeston (Langest), Jane, 116 ; John, 116.
Langford, 215.
Langford, Anne, 215 ; Edward, 32 ; Sir John, 215 (2) ; Rev. John, 12 ; Katherine, 215 ; Thomas, 4, 26.
LANGLEY, 167.
Langley, 167.
Langley, Anne, 167 ; Henry, D.D., 18 ; Henry, 167 (2) ; Priscilla, 167 ; Thomas, 167 ; Rev. William, 167 ; William, 167 (2) ; —, 167.
Langton, 167.
Langton, Christopher, 100 ; Lucy, 100 ; Mary, 25, 217 ; William, D.D., 217 ; William, 25, 167.
Lapetch, William, 29.
Lapworth, Thomas, 11.
Larkin, Francis, 5.
Latham. Luke, 27.
Latton (Latten), Dorothy, 224 (2) ; John, 224 (2) ; Thomas, 17.
LAWRENCE, 168.
Lawrence, Alice, 168 (2) ; Blanch, 168 ; Edward, 168 (2) ; Elizabeth, 168 ; Gyles, 168 (2) ; John, 168 ; Katherine, 168 ; Rev. Thomas, 23, 168 ; Thomas, 168 (3) ; William, 36.
Lawton, 76.
Lawton, Isabel, 75 ; William, 75.
Lay, George, 46.
Leake, Stephen Martin (Garter), 197 (2).
Leaver, *see* Lever.
Leaving. Richard, 12.
Leder, 168.
Leder, Olyver, 168.
Ledyard, Agnes, 157 ; John, 157.
Lee, Isabel, 137 ; Katherine, 187 ; Lidia, 181 ; Maria, 129, 130 ; Robert, 42 ; Samuel, 181 ; Sir Thomas. 35, 129, 130 ; Thomas, 129 (2), 130 (2) ; William, 42, 137 ; Mr., 43 ; —, 43, 187.
Leech, Anne, 194 ; Mary, 194 ; Susanna, 194 ; Rev. William, 194 (2).
Legatt, Walter, 22.
Legh (*Legg*), 154.
Legh (Legg), Penticost, 154 ; —, 154.
Leicester, Earl of, 222.
Leigh (Leygh, de Leygh), Agnes, 219 ; Alice, 153 ; Anne, 92 ; Christian. 92 ; Eleanor, 92 ; Elizabeth, 92 (2), 182 ; Frances, 92 ; Jane, 92 ; John, 70, 182 ; Katherine, 70 ; Margaret, 92 ; Mary, 92 ; Miles, 153 ; Peter. 92 (2) ; Richard, 92 ; Thomas, 70, 92 ; William, 70, 219 ; Mr., 42, 117.
Le Neve, Peter, 99, 169.
LENTHALL, 169 (2).
Lenthall, Anne, 170 (4) ; Bridget, 170 ; Catherine, 170 ; Elizabeth, 169, 170 (2) ; Frances, 169, 170 ; James, 170 ; Sir John, 170 (3) ; John, 11, 169 (3), 170 ; Katherine, 170 (2) ; Mary, 169 (2), 170 ; Thomas, 170 ; William, 169 (3), 170 (6) ; —, 170 (3).
Lenton, —, 55.
Leonard, Ciscelly, 214 ; Thomas, 214.
Lete, Anne, 171 ; Benjamin, 171 ; Elizabeth, 171 ; John, 171 ; Sarah, 171.
Lever (Leaver, Levar), Anthony, 8, 14, 16 ; Francis, 45 ; Hanna, 48 ; John, 2, 14, 48 ; Thomas, 2, 14 ; William, 2 (2), 14 (3).
Levesey, Anne, 142 ; Margaret, 142 ; —, 142.
Leveston, —, 36.
Lewenden, Lawrence, 14.

Lewkenor, Dorothy, 69 ; —, 69.
Lewson, Elizabeth, 217 ; Walter, 217.
Leygh (de Leygh), *see* Leigh.
Leynham, Henry, 122 ; Joan, 122.
Libb (Lybb), Anne, 71 ; Anthony, 15 ; Jone, 71 ; Richard, 36, 71.
Lidcott, *see* Lytcotte.
Linch, Henry, 30.
Lincoln, Elizabeth, Countess of, 186 ; Hawice de Quinci, Countess of, 75 ; Henry, Earl of, 186 ; Robert de Quinci, Earl of, 75.
Lindsey, Earl of, 12.
Lineall, Edward, 185 ; Margery, 185.
Litcott, *see* Lytcotte.
Litleton, George, 47.
Littelfeild, —, 173.
Llewellyn ap Gregeur, 149.
Lloyd, William, 73.
Lock, Richard, 46.
Loder (Loader, Lother), John, 3 (3), 13, 20, 21 (2), 28 (2) ; Richard, 41 ; Robert, 13 ; William, 8. 16 (2) ; Mr., 28.
Lodge, Anne, 70 ; Blagrave, 70 ; Honor, 70 ; John, 70 ; Mary, 70 (2) ; Richard, 39 ; Sir Thomas, 70 ; William, 70.
Loftus, Joshua, 84 ; Susanna, 84.
Loggins (Logins), Alice, 74 ; Eleanor, 231 (2) ; Robert, 231 (2) ; Simon. 74.
Long, Major Nathaniel, 176 ; Sarah, 176.
Longford, Sir John, 185 ; Katherine, 185.
Longuerille, 115.
Lord, John, 24.
Lorymer, Agnes, 55 (2) ; Anne, 55 (2) ; Christian, 55 ; John, 55 (2) ; Thomas, 55 (2).
Lother, *see* Loder.
Louch, William, 4, 31.
LOVEDAY, 171.
Loveday, Christopher, 25 ; Edward, 25 ; Elizabeth, 171 ; John, 31, 171 (4) ; Sarah, 171 ; —, 171.
Loreden, 172.
Loveden, Edward, 172 (2) ; —, 172 (2).
Lovelace, Anne, 103 ; Francis, 39, 42, 158 (2) ; Grace, 207 ; John, Lord, 39, 158 ; John, 4, 207 ; Margaret, 217 ; Richard, Lord, 217 ; Richard, 39, 42, 103, 158 (4) ; Lord, 4, 39, 42, 158.
Lovell, Francis, Viscount, 186 ; Friswith, 186.
Lovelock, Edward, 37 ; Thomas, 28.
Lowth, Rev. Simon, 34.
Lucas, Timothy, 3, 29.
Lupus, 76.
Lupus, Hugh. 76.
Lushill, 206.
Lutton, Alice, 86 ; —, 86.
Lybb, *see* Libb.
Lydall, Robert, 13.
Lydcott, *see* Lytcotte.
LYFORD, 172.
Lyford, Anne, 173 (4), 174 ; Arthur, 173 ; Bernhard, 173 ; Daniel, 173 ; Edward, 173 ; Francis, 173 ; Gyles, 173 ; Henry, 173 ; Joan. 173 (2) ; John, 39, 172 (2), 173 (11) ; Leonard, 173 ; Margaret, 173 (2), 174 ; Mary, 173 (6) ; Nathaniel, 173 ; Richard, 173 (13) ; Samuel, 173 ; Sebastian, 173 (2) ; Susan, 173 ; Thomas, 30 (2), 39, 173 (15), 174 ; William, 44, 173 (5).
Lygins, Margery, 219 ; —, 219.
Lyngen, Anne, 122 ; Ellenor, 122 ; John, 122 (2) ; Margaret, 122 ; Thomas, 122 ; Walter, 122 ; William, 122.

INDEX NOMINUM.

LYTCOTTE, 174.
Lytcotte, 174 (2).
Lytcotte (Lidcott, Litcott, Lydcott, Lytcott),
Agnes, 175 ; Alice, 86, 175 ; Anne, 175, 176 ;
Bridget, 175 ; Catherine, 175 (2) ; Charles,
176 (2) ; Sir Christopher, 175 ; Christopher,
175, 176 (2) ; Culling, 176 ; Dorothy, 175,
176 ; Eleanor, 176 ; Elizabeth, 175, 176 ;
Frances, 175 ; Giles, 176 (2) ; G., 176 ; Jane,
175, 176 ; Jerome, 176 ; Sir John, 170, 176 ;
Comr. John, 176 ; John, 64, 86, 175 (6), 176
(2) ; Judith, 175 ; Julian, 175 ; Leonard, 175 ;
Mary, 64, 175 (2), 176 (3) ; Nicholas, 176 ;
Richard, 175, 176 (3) ; Robert, 176 ; Roger,
175 ; Sarah, 176 (2) ; Thomas, 176 (2) ;
Ursula, 175, 176 ; William, 175 (3) ; Capt.,
170 ; —, 170, 176 (2).
Lyttell, 177.
Lyttell, Thomas, 177 (2).

M

Machado, Roger (Clarenceux), 82, 223.
Machin, Bridget, 90 ; John, 90.
Maddison, Mary, 226 ; Ralph, 226.
Maior, Mr., 28.
Malbank, 76.
Maleherbe, John, 107.
Mallet (Mallett), Anne, 207 ; John, 207 (2) ;
Katherine, 207 ; Michael, 17 ; Richard, 183 ;
Susan, 183 ; William, 207 ; Judge, 17 ; Mr.,
17.
Malmaynes, John, 203 ; Wilmott, 203.
Malorough, Widow, 15.
Malpas, 76 (2).
Maltis (Malthus), Austin, M.A., 33 ; Stephen,
36.
Mandefeld, Frances, 64 ; Henry, 64.
Maning, Isabell, 219 ; Thomas, 219.
Mansfield, Thomas, 7, 46.
Mantell, Frances, 101 ; Richard, 101.
Marden, John, 42.
Markaunte, 124.
Markham, Francis, 204 ; Grace, 204 ; William,
2, 23.
Marlow, Clement, 3, 32 ; William, 38.
Marriott, Richard, 52 ; Thomazine, 52.
Marrow, Edith, 125 ; William, 125.
Marry, John, 41.
Marshall, 177.
Marten (Martin), Alice, 224 ; Ann, 21, 205 ;
Edward, 64, 205 (2) ; Henry, 21 (2) ; Katherine, 64 ; Mary, 205 ; Robert, 43 ; Thomas,
2, 38, 40 ; Coll., 21 ; —, 224.
Maryett, 177, 178.
Maryett, Thomas, 177, 178.
Mashing, Thomas, 24.
Masmore, William, 19.
Mason, Ann, 71 ; Humfry, 3 ; Robert, 36 ; Thomas, 71.
Massy, 155.
Mathewe, 155.
Mathewe (Mathew), Griffin, 18 ; Isaack, 15 ;
Richard, 3, 30 ; William, 190.
Mathews, James, 38.
Mattock, Bridget, 171 ; Thomas, 171.
May, Anne, 50 ; Richard, 46. 50.
Mayland, William, 25.
Maynard, James, 3, 32 ; Moses, 4, 39.
Mayne, John, 14.

Maynwaring, Arthur, 36.
Mayott, 178.
Mayott, John, 10 (2), 178 ; Mary, 186 ; Richard, 186 (2) ; Robert, 10 ; Mr., 178.
Mayres, William, 27.
Meade, Dorothy, 188 ; Richard, 188.
Meales, Henry, 10.
Medcalfe, Anthony, M.D., 33.
Meere, William, 3.
Meller, William, 5.
Mellish, —, 52 (2).
Melward, Anthony, 32.
Mengem, 101.
Mengem, Edith, 101 ; —, 101.
Merbrook, Alice, 185 ; Richard, 185.
Meredith Geth, 149.
Meriett, Thomas, 228.
Merriman (Merryman), John, 3, 30.
Merwyn, Thomas, 7.
Meux, 128.
Meux, Anne, 84 ; Henry, 84.
Mewes, —, D.D., 33.
Mewter, 167.
Michell, 179.
Michell (Mitchell), Constance, 166 ; Humfrey,
45, 179 (5) ; Sir John, 179 ; John, 166.
Micklam, Thomas, 44.
Micklen, John, 40.
Midlemore (Midelmore), Margaret, 83 (2) ;
Richard, 83 (2).
Mihill, Samuel, 7.
Milborne, Johanne, 122 ; John, 122.
Miller, George, 72 ; Jane, 90 ; Sir John, 90 ;
Margaret, 72 ; Thomas, 2, 38.
Mills, 180.
Mills, Edward, 29 ; John, 33 ; Philippa, 187 ;
Richard, 180 ; Robert, 5 ; William, 2 ; —,
187.
Milson, Richard, 34.
Mitchell, *see* Michell.
Mobberley, 76.
Moburley, Katherine, 77 ; Sir William, 77.
Molineux, 184.
Molineux, Joane, 184 ; William, 184.
Molle, Anne, 170 ; George, 170.
Money, Walter, F.S.A., 92, 233.
Montague, *see* Mountague.
Moore, 229.
Moore (Moor, More), Dame Elizabeth, 24 ; Sir
Francis, 27 ; Sir Henry, Bart., 4, 27 (2) ; Sir
Henry, 24 (2) ; Humfry, 34 ; Sir Richard,
161 ; Sir St. John, 30 ; Thomas, 27 ; William,
170 ; Rev. —, 30 ; —, 161, 170.
Mordant, John, Viscount, 6.
Morgan, Elizabeth, 119 ; John, 66 ; Mary, 66,
123 ; —, 119, 123.
MORLAND, 180.
Morland, 180.
Morland (Morland *alias* Morley), Benjamin,
181 ; Elizabeth, 181 ; Joseph, 181 ; Lidia,
181 (3) ; Martin, 180, 181 (3) ; Sir Samuel,
Bart., 180 (4), 181 ; Samuel, 181 ; Sarah, 181 ;
Rev. Thomas, 181.
Morrice, Francis, 22.
Morrison, Elizabeth, 186 ; Sir Richard, 186.
Morry, John, 41.
Morteley, Alice, 122 ; —, 122.
Mortimer, Bartholomew, 35 ; —, 100 (2).
Morton, Cecelie, 183 ; Sir William, 183.
Mose, Thomas, 33.
Moston, Elizabeth, 227 ; Thomas, 227.

Mottram, Alice, 77 ; —, 77.
Moulder, John, 20.
Mountacute, Anthony Browne, Viscount, 123 ; John Nevill, Marques, 185.
Mountague (Montague), Bartholomew, 46, 47 ; Henry, 38.
Mountes, John, 54 ; Maud, 54 ; Rev. William, 54 ; William, 54.
Mountforth, Hugh, 79 ; Margaret, 79.
Mullens, —, Esq., 15.
Mumby, 167.
Munday (Mundy), Rev. Dr. Francis, 32 ; Major John, 6 ; John, 6, 29, 30, 183 ; Richard, 74 *n.* (2), 228 ; Robert, 42 ; Sarah, 183 ; Mr., 28 (3), 30, 32.
Mutlow, Anne, 210 ; Major John, 210.
Mylam, Andrew, 46.

N

Narraway, Jonas, 6 ; Thomas, 35.
Nash, John, 7, 46 ; Richard, 7, 46.
Neale, Mary, 90 ; Sir Paul, 40 ; Sir Thomas, 90.
Neirford, Elizabeth, 86 ; John, 86.
Nelson, Jone, 71 ; Samuel, 43 ; William, 5, 18, 27, 71.
NEVILL, 181.
Nevill, 181.
Nevill (Nevil, Nevell), Anne, 86, 181 ; Dorothy, 158 ; Edward, Lord of Burgeny, 181 ; Sir Edward, 181 ; Edward, 158, 181 ; Elizabeth, 181 ; Ellenor, 181 ; Frances, 181 ; George, Lord Abergavenny, 104, 181 (2) ; Henry, Lord Abergavenny, 181 ; Sir Henry, 181 (2) ; Henry, 158 (3) ; Lady Jane, 181 ; John, Marques Montacute, 185 ; Katherine, 181 ; Margaret, Lady, 181 ; Margaret, 104, 181 ; Mary, 181 ; Ralfe, 158 ; Sir Richard, 181 ; Richard, 4, 42, 174 ; Sir Thomas, 181 ; Thomas, 5, 86 ; —, Lord Abergavenny, 158 ; —, 181 (2), 185.
NEWBERY, 182.
Newbery, 182.
Newbery (Newberie, Newberry), Anne, 182 (2) ; Cecelie, 183 (2) ; Dorothy, 182 ; Elizabeth, 182 (2), 183 ; Frances, 182 ; Francis, 182 (2) ; Henry, 182, 183 (2) ; James, 182 ; Rev. John, B.D., 182 ; John, 182, 183 ; Lucie, 182 ; Mary, 85, 182 ; Ralph, 182 (3) ; Richard, 182 ; Sarah, 183 ; Susan, 183 ; Thomas, 182 ; William, 85 ; Mr., 182.
Newman, 183, 184.
Newman (Newnham), Christian, 183 ; Humphry, 183 ; John, 204 ; Richard, 183 (5), 184 (2) ; Robert, 183 (3) ; Thomas, 183 (2) ; —, 204.
Newton, Eleanor, 139 ; Sir John, 139.
Nixon, Rev. Joseph, 26 ; Rev. Richard, 31.
Noble, George, 13.
NORRIS, 184.
Norris, 184, 215.
Norris (Norreis, Norreys, Norrys), Agnes, 79 ; Alice, 55, 184 (2), 185 (2) ; Anne, 185 (3), 215 (2) ; Bridgit, Lady, 186 ; Bridgit, 186 ; Christian, 185 ; Edmond, 184 ; Sir Edward, 186 (2) ; Edward, 55 ; Elizabeth, 185 (2), 186 (4), 215 ; Francis, Lord, 186 ; Friswith, 186 ; George, 186 ; Sir Henry, Lord, 186 ; Sir Henry, 184, 186 ; Henry, 186 ; Jane, 105, 185 (3), 215 ; Sir John, 185 (2), 186 (2) ; John,

55 (2), 55 *n.*, 184 (2), 186 ; Joyce, 55 ; Katherine, 185, 186, 215 ; Lettice, 54, 184 ; Lyonell, 185 ; Margaret, Lady, 186 ; Margaret, 186 ; Margery, 185 ; Mary, 55, 184, 185 (2), 186 (2) ; Maximilian, 186 ; Millicent, 184 ; Percyvall, 184 ; Richard, 185, 186 ; Rev. Robert, 20 ; Roger, 184, 185 ; Sir Thomas, 186 ; Thomas, 55, 184 (3), 185 (2) ; Sir William, 105, 184, 185, 215 ; William, 79, 184, 185 (5), 186 (2) ; —, 185 (3).
North, John, 23 ; Robert, 24 ; Thomas, 11 ; Lady, 39.
Norton, Barbara, 137 ; George, 137 ; Paul, 13 ; Thomas, 2, 13 (2), 16.
Norwood, —, 204 (2).
Nott, Charles, 21.
Nottingham, Eleanor, 103 ; John, 103.
Noyes, Peter, 37, 41.
Nye, Philip, 33.
Nye, 68.

O

Ockham, Elizabeth, 70 ; —, 70.
Odey, William, 22.
Offley, Dorothy, 176 ; John, 176 ; William, 39.
Oglethorp, Sir Owen, 161 ; —, 161.
Onley, Samuel, 46.
ORPWOOD, 186, 187.
Orpwood, 186, 187.
Orpwood, Elizabeth, 186, 187 ; Ellen, 187 ; Frances, 187 ; Francis, 187 ; James, 187 ; Jane, 187 ; Jone, 187 ; Katherine, 187 ; Lionell, 187 ; Margaret, 187 ; Mary, 186, 187 ; Paul, 186 (3), 187 (2) ; Richard, 187 ; Robert, 187 ; Thomas, 17, 186 (4), 187 (6) ; William, 187 ; —, 187.
Osborne, Edward, 28 ; Rev. John, 28 ; Thomas, 28 ; William, 41.
Otgar, Abraham, 211, 212 ; John, 212 ; Mary, 211, 212 ; Sarah, 212.
Overbury, Mary, 176 ; Sir Nicholas, 176 ; Sir Thomas, 176.
Owen, George (Rouge Croix), 118.
Oxenbrige, Margaret, 103 ; Richard, 103.
Oxford, Edward Vere, Earl of, 186 ; John Vere, Earl of, 185.
Oyre, 99, 100.
Oyre, Blanch, 100 ; —, 100.

PACKER, 187.
Packer, 187.
Packer, Elizabeth, 188 ; Jane, 188 ; John, 187, 188 (2) ; Katherine, 188 ; Philip, 188 ; Philippa, 187 ; Robert, 5, 21, 188 ; William, 32, 188 (2).
Packington, 234.
Page, John, 1 ; Simon, 44, 46 ; Thomas, 44 ; — D.D., 20.
Paice, John, 33.
Paine, *see* Payne.
PALMER, 188.
Palmer, 155, 188, 190.
Palmer (Palmer *alias* Underwood), Agnes, 189 ; Anne, 188 ; Sir Anthony, 103 ; Christopher, 37 ; Dorothy, 188 ; Elizabeth, 103, 188 (2) ; Francis, 188 ; John, 103, 188 (2), 189 (2), 190 ; Mark, 188 ; Martha, 188 ; Mary, 188

INDEX NOMINUM. 253

(2); Richard, 5, 38, 40, 188 (5), 189 (3), 190 (6); Robert, 188, 189 (5); Sarah, 188; Thomas, 21, 188 (2); William, 189 (3); Mr., 188, 189 (2).
Panton, Edward, 13.
Parfitt, Frances, 5.
Paris (Parys), Rev. Edward. 36; Elizabeth, 166; Robert, 166.
Parker, Ellen, 58; John, 32; Richard, 58.
Parrott, *see* Perrott.
PARRY, 191.
Parry, 191.
Parry, Anne, 191 (2); Blanch, 168; Dorothy, 191; Edward, 191; Frances, 191; Muriell, 191; Roger, 168; Sir Thomas, 191 (2).
Parsons, 49.
Parsons (Personn, Persons), Amy, 50; Jane, 134; Katherine, 168; Thomas, 50, 134; —, 168.
Partridge (Parteridge), Edmond, 119; Sir Edward, 40; Elizabeth, 119; Henry, 44.
Parys, *see* Paris.
Paty, Edward, 30.
PAUL, 191.
Paul, 192.
Paul, Christopher, 192; James, 192 (2); Judith, 192; Katherine, 192; Martha, 192; Mary, 192 (2); Rachel, 192; Thomas, 192; Dr. William, Bishop of Oxford, 191, 192 (3), 193; Sir William, 192 (2); William, 192; —, 191, 192 (3).
Pawlet (Pawlett), Anne, 129; Sir Anthony, 186; Henry, Lord, 37; Katherine, 186; Lucy, 129; Sir Richard, 129.
Paxton, Edmund, 3.
Payne (Paine), Francis, 10; Henry, 33; Rev. John, 22; Richard, 16; Robert, 3, 10; William, 14; —, 24.
Paynell, Anne, 86; Sir Lewes, 86.
Paysley, James Hamilton, Lord, 170; Katherine Hamilton, Lady, 170.
Payton, Christopher, 92; Thomasin, 92.
Peacock, Francis, 12; John, 12, 19; Lawrence, 176; Mary, 176; —, 176.
Peade, Henry, 5, 18.
Pearce (Pearse, Pierce), Charles, 37 (2); Francis, 3, 24; Rev. Henry, 31; Joseph. 2, 5, 13; Thomas, 4, 24, 26, 30; William, 3, 6, 30.
Peareman, Edward, 29.
Pearse, *see* Pearce.
Pearson, Robert, 16.
PECK, 193.
Peck, 193.
Peck, Anne, 193; Dorothy, 193; Elizabeth, 193; Francis, 193; Henry, 193; Capt. John, 10; John, 4, 18; Jonas, 193; Mary, 193; Robert, 193; Silvester, 193.
Peckham, —, 100 (2).
Pembroke, —, Earl of, 29.
Peneman, John, 43.
Peniston, Sir Fairmeadow, Bart., 192 (2); Mary, 192; —, 192.
Pennington, George, 47.
Peplasham, Margaret, 103; Symon, 103.
Perient, 115.
Perient, Ann, 116; Thomas, 116.
Perkins, Francis, 35, 37; Richard, 35; —, 35.
Perrell or *Perle*, 155.
PERROT, 193, 194.
Perrot, 193.
Perrot (Parrott, Perrott), Anne, 104, 194;
Charles, 194; Dorothy, 104; Edward, 217; Elizabeth, 217; James, 194 (2); Sir John, 104; Mary, 194; Penelope, 104; Robert, 194; Sir Thomas, 104; William, 194.
Persons, *see* Parsons.
Petifer (Pettifer), Mathew, 5, 44; Richard, 19.
Petit, Elizabeth, 142; Thomas, 142.
Petty, Frances, 161, 175; John, 175; —, 28, 161.
Peverell, Catherine, 156 n.; Sir Thomas, 156 n.; Mrs., 156.
Phelipes (Phelypes), 194.
Phelipes (Phelypes), Henry, 194; *see also* Philips.
Phelpe, John, 4, 41.
Philip, Anthony, 87; Avice, 87.
Philipott, *see* Philpott.
Philips (Phillips, Phillipps), Joane, 51; Robert, 1; Thomas, 10; William, 25; —, 51; *see also* Phelipes.
Philipson (Phillipson), George, 15; Robert, 1; William, 12; —, 15.
Philpott (Philpot, Phillipott), Sir George, 105; John (Somerset Herald), 49, 94, 152, 228, 234; —, 105.
PHIPPS, 195.
Phipps, 195.
Phipps (Phips), Ann, 195 (3); Anna, 195; Anthony, 195; Caleb, 195; Constantine, 195; Francis, 33, 42, 195 (3); George, 195 (2); James. 195; Judith, 195; Mary, 195; Robert, 195; Thomas, 195; William, 195.
PICTON, 195.
Picton, 195.
Picton, John, 195 (2); Leonard, 195; Richard 195; Robert, 195; Thomas, 195; William, 195 (2); —, 195 (3).
Pierce, *see* Pearce.
Pigeon, Christian, 142; John, 142.
Pigott (Pigot, Piggot, Piggott), Alban, 27, 192; Dorothy, 142; Francis, 5, 17, 27; Judith, 192; Ralph, 27; Richard, 142.
Pike (Pyke), Anne, 70; Thomas, 70; —, 70.
Pikeman, Alicia, 108; —, 108.
Pile, Gabriell, 27; Sir Seamor, 27.
Pimp, Isabel, 103; John, 103.
Pinfall, Christian, 120; Joseph, 6, 29; —, 120.
Piper, Lawrence, 23.
Planer (Planner), John, 38; Pearce, 38.
Platt, Edmund, 14.
PLEYDELL, 196.
Pleydell. Anne, 196 (3); Elizabeth, 196; John, 196 (3); Martha, 196 (4); Mary, 196; Oliver, 25. 196 (4); Robert, 31; Thomas, 196 (3); William, 196.
Plumer (Plummer), Anne, 226; John, 47, 226; —, 43.
Plumpton, Andrew, 47.
POCOCK, 196, 197.
Pocock, 196, 197, 198.
Pocock, Edward. D.D., 19, 198; Edward, 198; Elizabeth, 196, 197; Vice-Admiral George, 197; Giles, 31, 33, 196 (3), 197 (2); Joan, 196; John, 2, 3, 5, 23, 27, 43; Dr. Richard, 30; Richard, 3, 6, 31, 196, 197; Roger, 196 (4), 197 (2); Susan, 196; Rev. Thomas, 197; William, 23, 196 (2); Rev. Zachary, 31; —, 196, 197.
Polden, Dorothy, 105; Thomas, 105.
Polley, Anne, 170; John, 170.
Pollington, Joan, 162; Thomas, 162.
Pomfrey, John, 20; Thomas, 23.

Pool (Poole), Catherine, 123; Eleanor, 75; William, 7, 46; —, 75, 123.
Pooley, John, 100; Lathanell, 100.
Pope, Frances, 102; Ralph, 102; Robert, 5.
Pordage, Dr. John, 36.
Porter, Henry, 5; William, 11.
Postlethwaite, Henry, 229; Mary, 229.
Pottinger (Potinger), Mary, 36; Nicholas, 32; Richard, 1, 2, 23, 37.
Pouder, Margery, 185; Roger, 185.
Poulton, Elizabeth, 85; Francis, 85.
Pount, Henry, 14.
Pouten, Edward, 43.
Povey, Joan, 52; —, 52.
Powell (*Powle*). 198, 199.
Powell (Powle), Dorothy, 125; Edward, 125; Elizabeth, 217; Francis, 4, 35; John, 217; Sir Richard, K.B.. 4, 40; Thomas, 4, 35. 198, 199 (4); William, 45.
Power (Powre), Anne, 74, 195; Elizabeth, 74; John, 195; Margery, 224; Richard, 74; Thomas, 224.
Powle, *see* Powell.
Powlton, Francis, 45.
Powney, John, 45, 192; Mary, 192; Richard, 3, 44; Robert, 3.
Powning, Richard, 1.
Powre, *see* Power.
Poynant, 199, 200.
Poynant, Mighell, 199, 200 (3).
Pratt, Sir George, Bart., 4, 25.
Prescot, Alexander, 88; Mary, 88.
Preston, Thomas (Portcullis), 118.
Pretty, Oliver, 46.
Price, Rev. Bartholomew, 23; Thomas, 11; William. 2, 23.
Prince, John, 10.
Prisett, 115.
Proctor, Henry. 45.
Pullen, Elizabeth, 186; William, 5; —, 186.
Pulley, Anne, 234; Arthur, 234.
Punt, Henry, 14.
Purefoy (Purifoy), George, 5, 25, 129; Isabel, 116; Mary, 129; Philip, 116; Mr., 25.
Pury, Ann, 54; Elizabeth, 54; Isabell, 54; John, 54 (2); Marjery, 54; Maud, 54; Thomas, 54.
PUSEY, 200.
Pusey (Pesey), Anthony, 200; Edward, 201; Elizabeth, 200 (2); Hugh, 200 (2); Jane, 200 (2); Jonas, 200; Katherine, 200; Margaret, 201; Martha, 201 (3); Mary, 21, 201 (3); Richard, 200, 201 (6); Thomas, 200 (2), 201; William. 201 (2); —, 21, 200, 201.
Pye, Sir Robert, 4, 22.
Pyke, *see* Pike.

Quarles, 201.
Quarles, John, 201 (5), 202 (2).
Quartermain (Quartermaines, Quarterman), Daniel, 46; Richard, 122; Sibbell, 122; Thomas, 1.
Queen Anne Bullen, 175, 204.
Queen Elizabeth, 57, 60, 69, 78, 91 (2), 93, 107, 135, 140 (2), 144, 156, 175, 182, 208, 209.
Queen Mary, 205.
Quelch, John, 17.
Quinci, *see* de Quinci.

R

Radley, Sir John, 138; —, 138.
Rampirr, 99, 100.
Rampier, Joyce, 100; —, 100.
Ranckell (Ranckle), Henry, 2; Peter, 2, 13.
Randall, John, 7.
Ravenscroft, Millicent, 184; —, 184.
Ravisburrow, Capt. Edward, 47.
Ray, John, 5.
Rayner, Rev. Samuel, 39.
READE, 202, 203.
Reade, 202, 203.
Reade, Alexander, 11, 202, 203 (3); Anne, 191, 204; Charles, 203; Elizabeth, 203, 205; Ellen, 202; Henry, 102; Hugh, 42; Jane, 203; Rev. John, 17; John. 202, 205; Katherine. 203, 205; Maria, 102; Mary, 203 (2), 205 (4), 217; Mathew, 40; Richard, 202, 205; Russell, 203; Sir Thomas, 11, 202, 205; Thomas, 17, 202 (3), 204, 205, 217; Sir William, 191; —, 202.
Reading, Michael, 7.
Reason, 196.
Reddall, Ralph, 2.
Reddit, Ralph, 34.
Redford, Edward, 25.
Redish, John, 207; Julyan, 207.
Reeves, William, 41; Mr., 27.
Remnum, 193.
Reynalds, 205.
Reynolds, Thomas, 20.
Rhys ap Tudor. 149.
Rich, Mary, 175; Robert, 175; Sir Thomas, Bart.. 4. 39.
Richard II., King of England, 75.
Richards, John, 38; Samuel, 41 (2); Thomas, 4, 41; —, 42.
Richardson, Thomas, 16.
Rider, *see* Ryder.
Ridley, Ellen, 139; Francis, 6, 46; John, 25; —, 139.
Righley, Margaret, 103; —, 103.
Ring, Thomas, 3.
Rivers, Crane, 22.
Robartes, —, 161 (2).
Roberts, Mary, 105; Thomas, 105.
Robinson, Richard, 7, 43.
Rod, Hugh, 42.
Rodney, 138.
Rodney, John, 138; Ursula, 138.
Rogers. 124.
Rogers, Dorothy, 182; Elizabeth, 125, 186; Nathan. 42; Thomas, 125; William, 182; —, 186.
Roper, Christopher, 123; Mary, 123.
Russell, 121.
Rossell (Russall), Alice, 122; Walter, 122; *see also* Russell.
Rothwell, 209.
Rothwell, Elizabeth, 210; James, 210 (3); Martha. 210; Thomas, 210.
Rouse. Agnes, 175; Henry, 175; James, 38.
Row (Rowe), Dorothy, 156; George, 156; Sir Henry, 182; Mary, 182; William, 7.
Rowland, Thomas, 5.
Ruddyerd, Benjamin, 28; Sarah, 28.
Ruffin (Rufin), Elizabeth, 105; Henry, 13; Mary, 203; Thomas, 203; —, 105.
Rufford, Anne, 66; John, 66.
Rugman, Widow, 44.

INDEX NOMINUM. 255

Rusden, John, 2, 16.
Russell, Edyth, 222; Elizabeth, 102; Sir John, 222; John, 102; Sir Thomas, 222; Thomas, 7; William, 5; —, 87; *see also* Rossell.
Ryder, 205, 206.
Ryder (Rider), Anthony, 205 (3), 206 (2); John, 6, 30, 63, 205 (3), 206 (2); Mr., 30, 64.
Ryley (Rylie, Reyly, Rielye), William (Lancaster Herald), 148, 188, 189 (2), 228.

S

Sacheverell, Bridget, 228; William, 228.
St. Clere, 138.
St. George, Sir Richard (Clarenceux), 131, 165.
St. John, Dorothy, 94; Elizabeth, 91; William, 91.
St. Leger, Elizabeth, 204; Sir John, 204; —, 103.
St. Lowe, Aleyne, 233; Thomas, 233.
St. Omer, Alice, 204; Thomas. 204.
Salerne, Eleanor, 103; John, 103 (2); Margery, 103.
Salter, John, 40, 44; Robert, 44.
Samborne, 206.
Samborne, Henry, 15, 206 (2); Richard, 34; —, 15.
SAMPSON, 207.
Sampson, 207.
Sampson, Agnes, 79; Anne, 207 (2); Anthony, 207; Christopher, 207; Elizabeth, 207; Ellenor, 207; Frances, 207; George, 207; Grace, 207; Jane, 207; John, 38, 207; Joseph, 207; Julian, 207; Katherine, 207 (2); Mary, 207 (2); Richard, 207 (3); Robert, 207 (4); Simon, 207 (2); Thomas, 207 (3); Turner, 207; William, 207; —, 79, 207 (2).
Sanchett, 99, 101.
Sanchett, Humphrey, 101; Isabel, 99, 101.
Sanders (Saundes), Sir Edward, 122; Elizabeth, 207; George, 3, 37; John, 207; Margery, 122; Thomas, 5; Mr., 28; *see also* Saunders.
Sanderson, Hellen, 159; Thomas, 159.
Sandes, Edith, 105; Margaret, 125; Sir William, Lord, 105, 125; Sir William, 105.
Sandys, Jone, 234; William, 234.
Sare, Joseph, 5.
Saunders, Jane, 188; John, 3, 26, 27; Martha, 196; Mary, 64; Thomas, 3, 26, 27, 188, 196; —, 64; *see also* Sanders.
Savage, Anne, 77; Sir Edmund, 40; Sir John, 77.
Savile (Savill), Frances, 80; Sir Henry, 229; Henry, 229; Jennett, 229; John, Lord, 80.
Savory, Thomas, 32.
Sawcer *alias* Cisu and Sesdio, Richard, 1.
Sawyer, Sir Edmund, 40; Edward, 2, 13; Rev. Joseph, 30; Rev. —, 42; —, 34.
Saxon, Samuel. 19.
Say (De Say), Agnes, 102; George, 7; William, 102.
Sayer, Sir Edward, 4; Rev. John. 13; Jonathan, 2, 14; Rev. Joseph, 30 (2); Robert, 2, 14.
Scholes, *see* Scowles.
Scott, Anne, 105; Edward, 105; Joan, 54; —, 54, 103.
Scowles, 208.
Scowles (Scholes), Jasper, 28, 208.
Scrope (Scroope, Scroop), Elizabeth, 171; Ellenor, Lady, 181; Geffry, 171; Gilborne, 171; Lucy, 171; Mary, 171; Ralph, Lord, 181; St. Leger, 171.
Seakes, Thomas, 7, 34.
Seamour, *see* Seymour.
Seaward, *see* Seward.
Seely, John. 29.
Segar, Sir William (Garter), 135, 136, 141 (2), 146 (2), 147 (2), 208 (2), 214 (3), 230 (3), 231.
Seller, Mary. 135; —, 135.
Sellwood, Richard, 18.
Senton, —, 55.
Seras, Constance, 103; Richard, 103.
Sesdio *alias* Sawcer, Richard. 1.
Seward (Seaward, Seyward), James, 3, 44; . Richard, 173 (2); Thomas, 5.
Seymour (Seymor, Seamour, Seamer), Anne, 222; Edward, Duke of Somerset, etc., 222; Elizabeth, 24; John, 5; Richard, 16; Thomas, 24 (2).
Seyward, *see* Seward.
Sharpe, Anne, 195; Henry, 3; —, 195.
Shaw, Richard, 6.
Shepard, Widow, 22.
Sheperey (Sheprue), Joan, 173; Robert. 173.
Shepey, Margaret, 139; —, 139.
Sherland, *see* Shirland.
Sherley, *see* Shirley.
Sherwood, Charles, 11; John, 20 (2); Ralph, 14; —, 32.
Shewrey. *see* Shury.
Shirland, 102.
Shirland (Sherland), Margaret, 102; Sir Robert, 102.
Shirley (Sherley), Dorothy, 222; George, 222; Jane, 125; Thomas, 32, 125.
Shottesbrooke, 102, 124.
Shottesbrooke, Agnes, 104; Edith, 104; Eleanor, 104; Elizabeth, 104 (2); Sir Gilbert, 104 (2); Sir John, 104; John, 104, 125; Sir Robert, 104 (2).
Shurtley, *see* Sturteley.
Shury (Shewrey), Francis, 2, 18; Jane, 200; Thomas. 1.
Siggenham, Christian, 55; William, 55.
Silverwood, John, 3.
Silvester, William, 7, 45.
Sims, *see* Syms.
Singleton, Thomas, 32; Rev. —, 15; —, 5 (2).
Skermer, Richard, 23.
Skinner, Constantine, 35, 36; Richard, 8, 16.
Sladd (Sledd), Anne, 173.
Slade, Rev. Francis, 19; Henry, 14; Leonard, 15; Moses, 2, 16.
Slitherhurst. Elizabeth. 140; John, 140.
Smalbone, Henry, 16, 24; John, 16, 24; Richard, 16.
Smart, William, 6, 30.
Smeaton, Robert, 35 (2).
SMITH, 208, 209, 210, 211.
Smith, 100, 208, 210, 212, 213.
Smith, Alice, 78 (2), 209; Anne, 209 (6), 210, 211 (8); Anthony, 209; Barbara, 78. 208, 209; Bartholomew, 37; Charles, 210, 211, 212; Christopher, 213 (5); Dorothy, 108; Edward, 78 (2), 208, 209; Eleanor, 78; Elizabeth, 79, 209 (4), 210 (2), 212; Frances, 78, 209, 229; Francisca, 78; George, 25; Isabel, 219; James, 45 (2), 210 (2), 211 (7), 212 (5), 213 (3); Jane, 211 (2); Joan, 78; Sir John, Bart.,

256   THE VISITATIONS OF BERKSHIRE.

211 ; Sir John, 211 ; John, 11, 23, 43, 78, 209 (2), 211 (4), 228 ; Levy, 6 ; Margaret, 228 ; Martha, 78, 208, 209 (3) ; Mary, 210 (3), 211 (3), 212 ; Michaell, 209 ; Philip, 210 ; Ralph, 79 ; Capt. Richard, 78 ; Richard, 5, 38, 73, 78 (4), 108, 208 (3), 209 (6), 210 ; Robert, 211 ; Rev. Samuel, 30 ; Sarah, 210 (2), 211 (5), 212 (2) ; Simon, 213 (2) ; Susan, 211 ; Susannah, 73 ; Sir Thomas, 78 ; Thomas, 26, 27, 45, 78 (3), 208, 209 (3) ; 210, 212, 219 ; Walter, 209, 213 ; William (Rouge Dragon), 194, 196 ; William, 3, 29, 42, 45, 78, 213 (3) ; —, 39, 100 (2), 208, 229.
Snapp, Elizabeth, 138 ; Roger, 138.
Snell, Elizabeth, 228 ; John, 228.
Snow, John, 30.
SNOWBALL, 214.
Snowball, 214.
Snowball, Ciscelly, 214 ; Eleanor, 214 ; Katherine, 214 ; Margaret, 214 (2) ; Richard, 214 ; William, 214 (4).
Snyff, Alice, 79 ; Richard, 79.
Solifor, John, 122 ; Nichola, 122.
Somerset, Edward Seamer, Duke of, 222 ; Margaret, Duchess of, 104 (2).
Somes, —, 103.
Sondly, Elizabeth, 73 ; William, 73.
Sothwick, Maud, 54 ; —, 54.
Southby, 214.
Southby (Sowthby), Joan, 162 ; John, 5, 21 (2), 214 (3) ; Richard, 162, 214 ; Robert, 4, 18 (2), 25 ; Thomas, 10, 20 ; Justice, 22 ; —, 24.
Southcoote, Sir John, 16.
Southwell, Frances, 169 ; Margaret, 181 ; Sir Robert, 181 ; Thomas, 169.
Southwood, —, 45.
Sowthby, *see* Southby.
Sparke, Peter, 41.
Sparkes, Thomas, 10.
Spenay, Anne, 171 ; —, 171.
Spencer, Elizabeth, 65 ; Mary, 87 ; Richard, 47 ; Thomas, 87 ; —, 65, 107.
Spene, John, 13.
Spicer, Giles, 3, 24, 32.
Spier (Spire, Spyer). Anthony, 38 ; Katherine, 140 ; Ralph, 140 (2) ; Richard, 38, 42 ; Thomas, 140.
Spilman, 100.
Spilman, Katherine, 100 ; Walter, 100.
Spire, *see* Spier.
Spooner, Abraham, 39.
Spratley, James, 7.
Springet, Bartholomew, 35.
Spyer, *see* Spier.
Squibb, Robert, 33.
Stafferton, *see* Staverton.
STAFFORD, 215.
Stafford, 215.
Stafford, Anne, 215 (4) ; Charles, 36 ; Edmund, 215 ; Edward, 215 (2) ; Eleanor, 215, 224 ; Elizabeth, 215 ; Sir Francis, 215 ; Humfrey, 168 ; Mabel, 215 ; Sir Read, 215 ; Thomas, 215, 224 ; William, 215.
Stampe, 216.
Stampe, John, 41 ; Thomas, 31, 33, 216.
Standen, *see* Standon.
Standish, 101.
Standish, Jane, 101 ; —, 101.
Standon (Standen), Elizabeth, 104 ; Robert, 104 ; Sir Vivian, 104 ; William, 38.
Stanley, Anne, 105 ; Richard, 105.

Stanton, Elizabeth, 210 ; Robert, 210.
Stany, Francis, 12.
Staples, Alexander, 37, 45 ; Thomas, 7, 45.
Stapleton, 155.
Starkey, George, 47.
Stasey, Katherine, 214 ; William, 214.
Staveley, Rev. Ambrose, 34.
Staverton, 184.
Staverton (Stafferton), Anne, 64, 207 ; Elizabeth, 55 ; Henry, 38, 55 (2), 184 ; Humphrey, 231 ; Mabel, 215 ; Mary, 55, 184 ; Ralph, 64 ; Richard, 207, 215 ; William, 64 ; —, 55 (2), 231.
Stayner, Anne, 135 ; John, 135.
Stebbing, Samuel (Somerset Herald), 196.
Steele, Anne, 79 ; Thomas, 79.
Stephens, *see* Stevens.
Sterling, Henry, Lord, 43.
Stevens (Stephens), Alice, 16 ; Jacob, 18 ; Joell, 33, 37 ; Peter, 3, 18 ; Thomas, 1, 22 ; Rev. Timothy, 27 (2).
Stevenson. John, 11 ; William, 10.
Stibbs, Richard, 12.
Stiddolfe, Elizabeth, 217 ; Sir Richard, 217.
Stiles, Clement, 2.
Stilman, —, 78 (2).
Stoakes, *see* Stokes.
Stockwell, Abraham, 6.
Stokes (Stoakes), Rev. Alexander, 38, 40 ; Alice, 123 ; Major John, 26 ; John, 41 ; Thomas, 123.
Stone, Robert, 17.
STONEHOUSE, 217 (2).
Stonehouse, 217, 218.
Stonehouse (Stonhouse), Dionisia, 217 ; Edward, 217 ; Elizabeth, 217 (5) ; Sir George, Bart. 11, 216, 217 (2) ; George, 205, 217 (3), 218 (2) ; Sir Ger., Bart., 4 ; Sir James, 169, 170 ; James, 217 (2) ; Sir John, 217 ; John, 217 (2) ; Margaret, 217 ; Mary, 169, 170, 205, 217 (2) ; Nicholas, 217 ; Rose, 217 ; Thomas, 217 ; Walter, 217 ; Sir William, Bart., 217 ; William, 217 (3) ; —, 217.
Stoughton, Elizabeth, 105 ; —, 105.
Stourton, Edith, 104 ; Elizabeth, 104 ; John, Lord, 104 ; Sir John, 104.
Strand, John, 26.
Strangles, Edward, 79 ; Jane, 79.
Stratton, Jane, 25 ; Thomas, 4, 25.
Strech, Christian, 185 ; William, 185.
Street, Elizabeth, 210, 212 ; Henry, 210, 212 (2) ; Sarah, 212.
Stroud (Stroude, Strowde), Edward, 5 ; John, 3, 26 ; William, 4, 39.
Stroughill, John, 40.
Stroughton, Anne, 64 ; Laurence, 64.
Sturteley (Shurtley), Agnes, 55 ; Robert, 55 ; Thomas, 55 (2).
Styles, Clement, 14 ; Robert, 42.
Sunnibanks, Johan, 47.
Swift, Alice, 79 ; Richard, 79.
Swinburne (Swinburn), Sir John, Bart., 124 ; John, 73, 124 ; Mary, 124 ; Mathew, 124 ; Ruth, 73 ; Thomas, 124 ; Sir William, Bart., 124.
Swinnerton, 184.
Sydley, Elizabeth, 171 ; Sir John, 171.
Symonds, 188.
Symonds (Symond), Agnes, 189 (2), 190 ; John, 189 (5), 190 ; Solomon, 22.
Symons, Thomas, 5 ; —, 72 (2).

INDEX NOMINUM.

Syms (Sims), 218.
Syms (Sims), William, 218 (2).
Sysley, Elizabeth, 54 ; Sir John, 54.

Taim, *see* Tame.
Talke, 134.
Talke, James, 134 ; Suzan, 134.
Tame (Taim, Taine, Tanne, Tavie), Alexander, 3, 19, 22 ; —, 22.
Tarrant, William, 5.
Tatnall, William, 33.
Tavie, *see* Tame.
Taylor (Taylour, Tailor, Tayleur), Helena, 233 ; Henry, 12 ; Richard, 3, 40 ; Robert, 73, 217 ; Rose, 217 ; Susannah, 73 ; Thomas, 233 ; William, 46.
Taylour *alias* Andrewes, *see* Andrewes *alias* Taylour.
Temnes, Alice, 185 ; Thomas, 185.
Temple, Bridget, 170 ; Sir Peter, 170 ; Sir Purbecke, 119 ; Sarah, 119 ; Sir Thomas, Bart., 170.
Terrent, Rev. Jeremy, 46.
Terrill, Robert, 34.
Terrold, Robert, 7.
Terry, Rev. Stephen, 41.
Tettershall, George, 41.
Teversham, Elizabeth, 127 ; Mathew, 127.
Thatcher, John, 11 (2).
Thayre, Elizabeth, 134 ; —, 134.
Thomas, William, 13.
Thompson, Samuel (Portcullis), 94.
THORNE, 219.
Thorne, Agnes, 219 ; Alice, 54, 219 ; George, 7, 33 ; John, 54 ; Margery, 219 ; Nicholas, 219 (3) ; Thomas, 219 ; Walter, 219.
THOROLD, 219.
Thorold (Thorald), Anne, 219 ; Anthony, 219 ; Charles, 219 ; Edmond, 219 ; Elizabeth, 219 ; Frances, 219 (3) ; Francis, 219 ; Henry, 219 ; Isabell, 219 ; John, 219 ; Katherine, 219 (2) ; Mary, 219 (3) ; Richard, 219 ; Thomas, 219 (2) ; William, 43 (2), 219 (4).
Thorowgood, Anne, 193 ; Jonas, 193.
Throgmorton, Anne, 64 ; Elizabeth, 122 ; Mary, 66 ; Sir Robert, 122 ; Sir Thomas, 66 ; —, 64.
Thurloe, Anne, 176 ; John, 176.
Tilliard, Thomas, 7.
Tinder, John, 26.
Tipping, Bartholomew, 28.
Tirrold, John, 14 ; Richard, 15 ; Robert, 16.
Tomlins, Francis, 11.
Tong, Thomas (Clarenceux), 126.
Topham, John, 47.
Toppesfeild, Katherine, 97 ; Matilda, 97 ; William, 97.
Torrington, George, Viscount, 197.
Touchet (Tutchet), Mervin, 36, 220 (2) ; —, 147.
Towes, Christopher, 44.
Towne, Joane, 103 ; Thomas, 103.
Townley, Charles (Clarenceux), 197 (2).
Townsend, Edward, 172.
Trapham, Thomas, 10.
Trappe, Elizabeth, 171 ; John, 171.
Travel, Elizabeth, Lady, 196, 197 ; Sir Thomas, 196, 197.
Trevor, Thomas, 33.
Trumbull, 220, 221.

Trumbull (Trumball), William, 5, 46, 220 (3), 221 (2).
Tubb, James, 18 ; John, 26.
Tucker, Charles, 1, 10 ; Gabriell, 22.
Tuckwell, Thomas, 17, 21.
Tudor, Elizabeth, 153 ; Thomas, 153.
Tull, Jethro, 29 (2) ; John, 27.
Tunstall, Robert, 69 ; —, 69.
Turbervile (Turbervill), Anthony, 43 ; Joan, 161, 163 ; Nicholas, 161, 163 ; Mr., 43, 45 (2)
Turfory, Anthony, 22 ; Thomas, 22.
Turner, John, 5, 22 ; Thomas, 1.
Turvile, Elizabeth, 176 ; George, 176 ; Mr. 231.
Tutball, —, 1.
Tutchet, *see* Touchet.
Twyford, Henry, 55 (2) ; Sybbell, 55 (2).
Tydder, Elizabeth, 105.
Tyghall, Anne, 222 ; John, 222 ; Thomas, 222.
Tyle, John, 40.
Tyler, Joseph, 45.

U

Underwood, 188.
Underwood (Ondurwod, Underwode, Undyrwoode), Agnes, 189 (4) ; Christian, 189 ; Johanna, 189 ; John, 189 (7) ; Richard, 189 William, 189 (2).
Underwood *alias* Palmer, *see* Palmer.
UNTON, 221.
Unton, 221.
Unton (Umpton, Umton), Sir Alexander, 222 ; Alexander, 222 ; Anne, 222 (4) ; Cicely, 222 (2) ; Dorothy, 222 (2) ; Edith, 222 ; Edmund, 222 ; Sir Edward, K.B., 222 ; Colonel Edward, 222 ; Elizabeth, 221, 222 ; Francis, 222 ; Sir Henry, 222 ; Henry, 222 ; Hugh, 221 ; Katherine, 222 ; Mary, 222 ; Sibell, 221 ; Sir Thomas, 221 (2), 222.
Upton, Jane, 176 ; John, 176 (2) ; Ursula, 176.
Utkins, Richard, 5.

V

Vachell, Katherine, 205 ; Dame Lettice, 33 ; Thomas, 47, 205 (2).
Vampage, Anne, 222 ; Dorothy, 233 ; John, 222, 233.
Vane, Katherine, 192 ; Sir Vere, Earl of Westmorland, 192.
Vantare, Cecill, 51 ; Elizabeth, 51 (2) ; Florence, 51 ; Flower, 51 ; Jane, 51 ; John, 51 ; Maud, 51 ; William, 51 (2).
Vaughan, 191.
Vaughan, Anne, 175 ; Henry, 191 ; Robert, 175.
Veale or *Veele*, 155.
Venables, 76.
Venables, Elizabeth, 75, 76 ; Hugh, 75, 76.
Vere, Bridgit, 186 ; Edward, Earl of Oxford, 186 ; Jane, 185 ; John, Earl of Oxford, 185.
Verney, Edmund, 2, 38.
Vernon, 76 (2).
Vernon (De Vernon), John, 16 ; Margaret, 75 ; Warren, 75.
Vinar, William, 12.
Vines, John, 25.
Vintner, Rev. Robert, 37.
Vyell, 155.

W

Wade, Elizabeth, 171; Nathaniel, 40; Robert, 40; Rev. —, 171.
Wadeson, 115.
Waferer, Francis, 215; Mabel, 215.
Wagstaff, Eme, 134; John, 134.
WAKE, 223.
Wake, 223.
Wake, Abram, 223; Rev. Arthur, 223; Elizabeth, 223 (2); Sir Isaac, 223; John, 223; Mary, 223.
Wakeman, Jone, 69; —, 69.
Waldegrave (Walgrave), Frances, 181; Hellen, 123; Henry, Lord, 123; James, Lord, 123; —, 123, 181.
Waldron (Walron), Agnes, 161; Edward, 161; Elizabeth, 142; Maurice, 142.
Walgrave, *see* Waldegrave.
Walker, Barbara, 77; Sir Edward (Garter), 30, 52 (2), 81 (3), 82, 180, 183, 184, 192 (3), 205 (3), 206, 220 (2), 221 (2).
Walksted, Elizabeth, 103; Sir Richard, 103.
Waller, Anne, 163; Thomas, 163; —, 35.
Wallington, Francis, 27.
Wallop, Anne, 129; Sir Henry, 129.
Walron, *see* Waldron.
Waltham. Als, 62; Frances, 207; James, 207; Richard, 62.
Walwen, Eleanor, 122; Nicholas, 122.
Warde, 140.
Warde (Ward), Alice, 140; Anne, 134; Henry, 134; Mary, 205; Richard, 140; —, 205.
Warneford, Henry, 21.
Warner, Thomas, 34.
Warwick, Anne, Countess of, 222; John Dudley, Earl of, 222; Thomas, 3, 23.
Wase, Anne, 211; Bud, 210, 212; Sarah, 210, 212; William, 211.
Waterman, John, 28.
Watkyn, 191 (2).
Watson, Barbara, 101; Kellum, 101.
Watte, James, 6.
Watts, Henry, 32; John, 3, 32; Richard, 29.
Wattys, 223.
Wattys, John, 223; Robert, 223.
Wawne, Isabel, 54; —, 54.
Wawton, Agnes, 203; Sir William, 203.
Webb, Anne, 234; Anthony, 19; David, 32; Elizabeth, 62, 116, 185; Henry, 4, 28; Jane, 116; John, 116; Richard, 39, 46; Thomas, 62, 234; —, 185, 186.
Webster, Christopher, 14.
Weekes, Anthony, 25.
Weke, *see* Wyke.
Welbeck, Leonard, 33, 35.
Weldon (Welden), Edith, 55; Edward, 55; George, 40, 45; Isabella, 55; William, 43; —, 40, 45.
Welles (Wells), Eleanor, 204; Lyonell, Lord, 204; Thomas, 19; William, 10.
WELLESBORNE, 224.
Wellesborne, 224.
Wellesborne, Alice, 224; Anne, 224; Arthur, 224; Dorothy, 224 (2); Eleanor, 215, 224; Frances, 215, 224; Francis, 224; Friswith, 224; Jane, 224; Joan, 224; Sir John, 224; John, 224 (2); Joyce, 224; Katherine, 224; Lucy, 224; Margery, 224 (3); Oliver, 224; Thomas, 224; —, 224 (3).
Wender, Samuel, 44.

Wentworth, Cicely, 222; Joan, 104; John, 222; Thomas, Lord, 104.
West, John, 5; Richard, 10, 19, 43; Robert, 7.
Westhrop, Thomas, 46.
Westmoreland, Sir Vere Vane, Earl of, 192.
Weston, Edward, 11; John, 40; Philip, 6, 30; William, 10; —, 196 (2).
Wettenhall, 76.
Wettenhall (Whetnall) alias *Kingsley*, 76.
Wettenhall (Whetnall) *alias* Kingsley, John, 75; Margery, 75.
Wharton, George, 36.
Wheeler, Alice, 74; Paul, 5 (2), 8, 29; Thomas, 74.
Whetnall *alias* Kingsley, *see* Wettenhall.
Whichelow (Wichelow, Whithilowe), Jane, 17, 187; John, 11, 14, 34; Thomas, 187.
Whightwick, *see* Whitwick.
Whistler (Whisler), Anne, 174 (2); Elizabeth, 83 (2); Ellen, 23; John, 15, 23 (3), 83 (2); Lawrence, 4, 15 (2); Margaret, 187; Margets, 23; Ralph, 2, 14; Thomas, 174; —, 15, 37, 187.
Whitchcock, Christopher, 47.
WHITE, 225.
White (Whyte, Whyght, Wight), Bartholomew, 225; Charles, 17 (2); Daniel, 37; Elizabeth, 122; George, 225; Sir John, 225 (2); John, 15, 38, 225 (9); Margaret, 214; Mary, 30, 194; Ralph, 194, 225; Sir Richard, 38; Richard, 1, 16, 214, 225 (2); Sir Thomas, 194 (2); Rev. Thomas, 20; Thomas, 3, 25, 225 (4); William, 193, 225 (7); Winnefred, 225; —, 17, 122.
Whiteaker (Whittacre), Charles, 47; Read, 37.
Whitfield, John, 40, 44, 45.
Whithilowe, *see* Whichelow.
WHITLOCK, 225.
Whitlock, 226.
Whitlock (Whelocks). Anne, 226 (2); Apolina, 226; Sir Bulstrode, 26; Bulstrode, 227; Catherine, 226; Cicely, 227; Delabech, 227; Edmund, 227; Elizabeth, 226, 227 (2); Sir James, 226, 227; Jeromie, 227; John, 225, 226 (2), 227 (3); Katherine, 225, 226 (2); Mary, 226; Rebecca, 227; Richard, 225, 226 (7), 227 (2); Robert, 38, 225 (2), 226 (3); William, 227 (5).
Whitney, Margaret, 77; William, 77.
Whittacre, *see* Whiteacre.
Whittley, 101.
Whittley, —, 101 (2).
Whitwick (Whightwick, Wightwick), John, 31; Rev. Thomas, 28; Walter, 2, 18.
Whyght (Whyte), *see* White.
Wibbley, Henry, 17.
Wichelow, *see* Whichelow.
Wichingham (de Echingham), Elizabeth; William, 204.
Wicker, Henry, 35. 204;
WICKHAM, 228.
Wickham, Ferdinand, 228; Humphry, John, 228 (2); Richard, 228 (3); Rob. 228; William, 228 (2); William of, 63.
Wight, *see* White.
Wighton, Alice, 116; William, 116.
Wightwick, *see* Whitwick.
Wigmore, —, 45.
Wike, *see* Wyke.
Wilcotts, Elizabeth, 103; John, 103.
Wilcox (Wilcocks), Peregrine, 44.
Wildbore (Wyldbore), John, 170; —, 170 (3).

Wilder, John, 34 ; Richard, 34 (2) ; William, 3, 33 ; Farmer, 22.
Wildman, Major John, 25 (2), 26.
Wilkes, Simon, 46.
Wilkins, John, 14.
WILKINSON, 228.
Wilkinson, 228, 229.
Wilkinson (Wilkeson), Arthur, 229 ; Bridget, 228 ; Christopher, 228 (2), 229 ; Elizabeth, 228, 229 (3) ; Ellen, 228 ; Frances, 229 ; Francis, 228, 229 ; Rev. Gabriel, 229 ; Gabriel, 229 ; Henry, D.D., 229 (2) ; Henry, 229 ; Hester, 229 ; Isabel, 228 (2), 229 ; Jeffry, 228 ; Jennett, 229 ; John, DD., 229 ; John, 228 (3), 229 (4) ; Margaret, 228, 229 ; Margery, 229 ; Mary, 229 (2) ; Matthew, 229 ; Patrick, 228 ; Richard, 229 ; Robert, 228 (4), 229 ; Roger, 228 ; Rev. Thomas, 42, 174 (2) ; Thomas, 228 (2), 229 (4) ; William, 228 (4), 229 (3) ; Mr., 173 ; —, 228.
Willgoose, Thomas, 12.
Williams, 229.
Williams, Jane, 65 ; Joan, 105 ; John, Lord, 105, 186 ; John, 1 ; Mabell, 215 ; Margaret, 186 ; Nicholas, 215 ; —, 65.
Willis, John, 12.
Williscott, *see* Wollascott.
Willmot, *see* Wilmot.
Willps, John, 13.
Wilmer, William, 33, 34.
Wilmot, 230.
Wilmot (Willmot, Willmott), Sir George, 19, 24 ; George, 50, 230 (2), 231 ; Margaret, 50 ; William, 10, 24.
Wilson, Edmund, 47 ; Frances, 182 ; Dr. Thomas, Dean of Worcester, 182 ; Thomas, 6, 30.
Wiltshire, Sir Thomas Bullen, K.G., Earl of, 204.
Winch, James, 1, 7 ; Richard, 43, 46 ; Simon, 44. 231 (2) ; William, 43.
WINCHCOMBE, 233.
Winchcombe, 232, 233.
Winchcoombe (Wechecome, Wychcombe, Wynchcombe), Agnes, 233 (2) ; Aleyne, 233 ; Anne, 233 (2) ; Dorothy, 233 ; Elizabeth, 233 ; Francis, 233 ; Helena, 233 ; Sir Henry, Bart., 36 (2) ; Sir Henry, 173 ; Henry, 233 (2) ; Jane, 233 ; Joan, 173 ; John, 35, 232 (4), 233 (4) ; Thomas, 233.
Winder, Samuel, 4, 46.
Windsore, Andrew, Lord, 181 ; Eleanor, 181.
Wingfield, William, 5, 36.
Wingrove, Thomas, 44.
Winnington, 76.
▬nington, Sir Richard, 75 ; —, 75.
Tomltterborne, Thomas, 19.
Tong, TERSELL, 234.
Tophatersell, 234.
Toppatersell (Winterahell), Alice, 234 ; Anne, list34 (2) ; Edward, 234 ; Elizabeth, 234 (2) ; Tor Henry, 234 (2) ; Jane, 234 (2) ; Joan, 234 To (2) ; John, 234 ; Richard, 234 (4) ; Roger, T, 234 ; Thomas. 234 (3) ; —, 45.
T Wise, John, 27.
" *Wiseman*, 126.
Wiseman, Sir Charles, 20, 71 ; Edmund, 19, 20 ; Mary, 71.
Witherige, 106 (2), 107.
Withers, Brigitt, 79 ; John, 79.
Withington, Edward, 194 ; Katherine, 194 ; Mary, 194 ; Oliver, M.D., 194.
Withy, John, 194.

Wixstede, Amy, 78 ; —, 78.
Wodwell, Alice, 79 ; William, 79.
Wollascott (Williscott), Ann, 205 ; Martin, 36 ; Mary, 123 ; Thomas, 17 ; William, 123, 205.
Wolley, Joan, 77 ; Thomas, 77.
Wollgar (Woulger), Arthur, 3, 35.
Wolverton, 174.
Wolverton, Elizabeth, 175 ; Nicholas, 175.
Wood, 141.
Wood (à Wood), Margery, 224 ; Robert, 224.
Woodbridge, Rev. Benjamin, 30 ; John, 21.
Woodcock. Margery, 82 ; Samuel, 41 (2) ; —, 82.
Woodford, Jane, 85.
Woodier, *see* Woodyer.
Woodroff, Davy, 217 ; Elizabeth, 217 ; Sir Nicholas, 217.
Woodson, John, 47 (2).
Woodward, Amy, 78 ; Dorothy, 78 ; Lionell, 78 (2) ; Dame Margaret, 30 ; Rev. Samuel, 23 ; Thomas, 78.
Woodyer (Woodyerre, Woodier), Michael, 1 ; Richard, 43.
Wootton, Alice, 103 ; Sir Nicholas, 103.
Worrall. Rev. Thomas, 31 ; Mr., 31.
Worthien, Richard, 22.
Woulger, *see* Wollgar.
Wrigglesworth, Francis, 18 ; John, 18 ; William, 18 ; —, 18.
Wright, Rev. Joseph, 21 ; Rev. Richard, 36 ; Thomas, 13.
Wring, *see* Ring.
Writh *alias* Wriothsley, Thomas, 196.
Writhe, Mary, 175 ; Robert, 175.
Wroughton, Anne, 185, 215 ; Dorothy, 222 ; Mary, 215 ; Sir Thomas, 222 ; Thomas, 185, 215 (2) ; Sir William, 215.
Wrytt, 72.
Wrytt, Joane, 70 ; —, 70.
Wyke, 115.
Wyke (Wike, de Wyke, de Weke), Henry, 55 (2) ; Sir John, 116 ; Julyan, 55 ; Sybell, 55 ; —, 116.
Wyldbore, *see* Wildbore.

Yate, 234.
Yate (Yates, Yeate, Yeates), Bartholomew, 22 ; Sir Charles, Bart., 21 (3) ; Sir Charles, 127 ; Dorothy, 105, 215 ; Jane, 224 ; Joan. 234 ; Sir John, Bart., 234 ; John, 18, 20, 82, 83, 105, 160 (4). 224, 234 ; Martha, 82, 83 ; Mary, 160 (4) ; Peter, 18 ; William, 20.
Yateman, Francis, 17 ; John, 11.
Yates, *see* Yate.
Yeading. Alice, 86.
Yeate, *see* Yate.
Yeldesley, *see* Hildesley.
Yong (Yonge), *see* Young.
Yorke, Duke of, 12.
Young (*Yonge*), 221, 235.
Young (Younge, Yong, Yonge), Anne, 235 (2) ; Catherine, 175 ; Cicelie, 156 ; Elizabeth, 221 ; Francis, 28 ; Gabriell, 43 ; John, 207 ; Lovell, 42 ; Margaret, 104 ; Richard, 6, 29 ; William, 3, 27, 156, 175, 221 ; —, 207.

Z

Zigher, Marke, 20.
Zinzan *alias* Alexander, Henry, 34.

INDEX LOCORUM.

VOLS. I. AND II.

* This denotes that the place occurs more than once on a page.

Abingdon (Abbingdon, Abbington, Abinton), I., 13,* 37,* 56, 63,* 71,* 98, 100,* 124, 135,* 141, 142, 152, 153,* 172,* 177, 178,* 224, 229,* 245,* 246,* 257, 271, 285,* 294*; II., 1*, 2, 3, 4,* 5, 6, 8, 9, 10, 11,* 14, 23, 67, 71, 77, 78,* 79,* 82, 87,* 91, 137, 152, 153, 178,* 186,* 187,* 204, 205, 208,* 209,* 214, 216, 217, 221, 224, 228.*
Abingdon, Abbey of, I., 1.*
Abingdon, Christ's Hospital, I., 153.
Abingdon, New Inn, I., 9, 152, 216.
Abingdon, St. Helen's, I., 246.
Abstreete, II., 35.
Acherote, II., 122.
Ackworth, Yorkshire, II., 80.
Acton, I., 69.
Adderbury (Aderburye), Oxon, I., 21, 227.
Adderley, Salop, I., 222.
Adlington, Cheshire, II., 153.
Agincourt, II., 75.
Agmondesbury, see Almondsbury.
Agmondisham, see Amersham.
Akington, II., 167.
Albrighton, I., 147.
Aldborough (Alesburow), Norfolk, II., 100.
Aldbourne (Alborne, Auborne), Wilts, I., 221; II., 161.
Aldbourne Chase, 1., 52.
Aldenham, Hertford, II., 196.
Alder, I., 159.
Aldermaston (Aldermarston, Aldermanston), I., 8, 9, 29,* 86, 193, 207, 208,* 224, 245, 266, 288; II., 31, 37.
Aldersbroke, Essex, I., 203.
Aldersfield, Worcestershire, I., 113.
Aldsworth (Alsworth), Gloucestershire, I., 265.
Aldworth, II., 23, 49.*
Alford, I., 65.
Allerton (Alerton), North, Yorkshire, I., 281.
Almondsbury (Agmondesbury), Gloucestershire, I., 160.
Alton (Awlton, Awlton Estbroke), Hants, I., 55.*
Alton-Barnes or Berners (Alton), Wilts, I., 21.
Alvescott (Alscott), Oxon, I., 67; II., 169.
Ambersden Hall, Essex, II., 170.
Amberton, Bucks, II., 171.
Ambrosden (Ambresden), Oxon, II., 116.
Amerden Hall, Kent, I., 238.
Amerdenarshe, Bucks, I., 8, 27.

Amerdon in Taplow, Bucks, I., 275.
Amersham (Amersome, Agmundesham), Bucks, II., 79, 194.
Amesbury (Amesburye), I., 28, 37, 38.
Andevill, Normandy, II., 204.
Andover (Andeva, Andevor), Hants, I., 54, 95, 165,* 252,* 302.
Annesley, Nottinghamshire, I., 15.
Anstey, Warwickshire, II., 175.
Antwerp, II., 137.
Appleford (Apleford), I., 271, 272, 279; II., 17, 187.*
Appleton (Apleton), I., 195, 283, 285*; II., 2,* 3, 18,* 115, 116, 214.
Appulderoomb (Apulderoombe, Apledoroombe), Isle of Wight, I., 250; II., 134.
Apscourt, Surrey, II., 219.
Arborfield (Abberfelde, Arberfield), I., 4,* 16, 18, 19,* 20, 25, 46, 160, 176,* 177, 309; II., 38, 40,* 43, 86, 146.*
Arde in Picardy, I., 82.
Ardington (Arlington), I., 49, 81,* 123, 169,* 185,* 200, 227,* 278, 279, 314, 315, 316; II., 3, 20, 49, 108,* 161, 162.
Ardingtonwicke, I., 186, 279.*
Ardley, Oxon, L, 257.
Arnecrofte, Derbyshire, I., 17.
Arneton (? Ardington, Berks), I., 242.
Arundel, Sussex, II., 102.
Ash, Durham, I., 202.
Ashampstead (Ashampsted, Ashamstead), II., 15, 131.
Ashbury (Aishbury, Ashbery, Ashburye), I., 108*; II., 3,* 4, 25.
Ashford Bowdlers (Ashford Bowdler), I., 146.
Ashton, Long (Astun, Long, Asheton, Long Somerset, I., 6,* 22,* 184; II., 106.
Ashwell, Herts, I., 70.
Ashwelthorpe, Norfolk, II., 191.
Aston, Berks, I., 126.
Aston Clinton, Bucks, II., 56n.
Aston Hall, Cheshire, II., 137.
Aston-le-Walls (Aston in the Walles), Northants, I., 50.
Aston, Northants, I., 121, 260.
Aston, North, Northants, II., 138.
Aston, North (Northaston), Oxon, L, 132; II., 116.

INDEX LOCORUM.   261

Aston Tirrold (Aston Terold, Aston Thorald, Aston Torrolde, Aston Turrolde), I., 25,* 60, 149; II., 2, 15, 206.*
Aston Upthorpe (Aston Upthorpp), II., 15.
Audston, I., 189.
Avebury (Abebery, Abery), Wilts, I., 88.*
Avington (Avynton), I., 6,* 22,* 23,* 82, 138, 184, 185,* 276; II., 4, 28, 106,* 107.* 164, 165.*
Aylesbury (Alesbury), Bucks, II., 88.
Aynho (Aynhoe), Northants, II., 119.
Ayott, Little (Ayot, Little), Herts, II., 203.

Babington, I., 158.
Baconsthorpe (Baconthorpe), Norfolk, I., 250.
Baddesley, Warwickshire, II., 116.
Baddesley, North, Hants, I., 196.
Baghurst, *see* Baughurst.
Bagnor, II., 32.
Bagsholt, II., 29.
Bagshot, I., 114*; II., 29.
Baintunes, I., 12.
Baldock, I., 70.
Baldwyn-Brightwell, Oxon, II., 116, 191.
Balking, *see* Baulking.
Balsam Park, *see* Balston Park.
Balsham (Balsome), Cambridgeshire, II., 127.
Balston Park (Balsam Park), I., 241*; II., 13, 28.*
Bampton, *see* Baunton.
Banbury, Oxon, I., 227, 240, 303.
Banester, I., 9.
Barbadoes, I., 251.*
Barfield, II., 32.
Barkham, I., 18, 176, 177,* 225, 290, 291*; II., 38, 40, 62.*
Barkly juxta Oxford, II., 116.
Barnet, II., 77.
Barnsley, Yorkshire, II., 228.*
Barnstaple (Barnstable), I., 260.
Barnstone (Barneston, Barstone), Dorset, I., 9; II., 109, 130.
Barrington, II., 23.
Barrow, Rutlandshire, II., 88.
Barrow, Surrey, I., 173.
Barstone, *see* Barnstone.
Barton, I., 2, 124*; II., 5, 11, 102, 202,* 203, 204, 205,* 217, 271.
Barton Court, Berks, I., 198,* 236.
Barton, Oxon, II., 116.
Barton, Wilts, I., 138.*
Barwick (Barwicke), I., 78*; II., 186.
Basildon (Baselden, Basledon, Basselden, Bassendon, Bastledon), I., 33, 54, 81, 292; II., 2, 15. 108,* 175,* 235.*
Basing, Hants, I., 252; II., 31.
Basingstoke (Bassingstoke), Hants, I., 217, 226.
Bassingham (Basingham), Lincolnshire, I., 148.
Batchford, *see* Batsford.
Bath, I., 281; II., 138.
Bathwick (Bathweeke), Somerset, I., 233; II., 158.
Batley House, Ebor., I., 199.
Batsford (Batchford, Batisford, Battesford, Battisford), Gloucestershire, I., 166, 180, 267, 270; II., 63.*
Battersea, Surrey, II., 176.
Batterton, *see* Betterton.
Battlefield (Batlefield), College of, Salop, I., 147.

Baucombe, Essex, *see* Beauchamp Roding.
Baughurst (Baghurst), Hants, I., 297.
Baulking (Balking, Bawlkinge), I., 50, 183, 184; II., 26.
Baunton (Bampton), Gloucestershire, I., 230.
Baxwell, *see* Boxwell.
Bayworth. I., 68,* 168; II., 66.*
Beach Hill, *see* Beechhill.
Beachampton (Beachampton alias Beckington, Bechehampton), Bucks, I., 61.*
Beaconsfield (Becconsfield, Beconsfield, Bekensfield), Bucks, I., 106, 177, 240; II., 38, 56, 163.
Beauchamp Roding (Baucombe), Essex, I., 184.
Beche, Manor of, near Okenham (Wokingham), II., 227.
Becheslands. Oxon, II., 227.
Beck Hill, *see* Beechhill.
Beckett (Beckott), I., 24, 27, 91; II., 25, 125.
Beckett House, II., 175.
Beckington (Bekington), Somerset, I., 80.
Bedford, Grey Friars, II., 203.
Bedsbury, Kent, I., 112.
Beech Hall (Birch Hall), Essex, I., 163; II., 64.
Beechhill (Beach Hill, Beck Hill), Berks, I., 220,* 245,* 259; II., 5, 36, 37, 139,* 141.
Beedon (Bedon, Beeden, Bydden), I., 52; II., 31.
Beenham Valence, *see* Benham.
Bekesborne, Kent, I., 170, 218,* 262.
Beland, II., 103.
Bellhows, Essex, I., 10.
Beltring, Kent, I., 296.
Benenden (Bennendon), Kent, I., 171.*
Benham Valence (Beenham, Benam, Benham, Bena', Benham Vallens), I., 7, 24, 37,* 38, 79,* 80, 224,* 249, 287; II., 1,* 29,* 35, 91,* 93, 94, 96, 105, 125, 196.
Bensington *or* Benson, Oxon, I., 52; II., 90.
Bentley, Hants, I., 174; II., 72.
Bere Court by Pangbourne, I., 191.*
Bergholt (Bargeholt), Essex, II., 210, 211.
Berry, II., 40.
Bessesleigh (Besiles Ley, Besiles Lee, Bessilles Lye, Bessils Leigh, Bezells Lee), I., 28,* 92, 180, 204*; II., 11, 26, 69, 70, 127, 169,* 170.*
Bethersden (Betersden), Kent, I., 221.
Betterton (Batterton), I., 187,* 206, 243; II., 3, 20, 109, 110,* 128.
Beverley, II., 54.
Beynhurst, Hundred of, I., 228, 244, 265, 275, 304; II., 5, 8, 9, 30, 39, 40, 42, 44.
Bicester (Bisiter), Oxon, I., 282.
Biddesdone (Bidesden), Wilts, I., 248.*
Biggleswade (Bigleswade), Bedfordshire, I., 256; II., 188.
Billing, Great, Northants, II., 223.
Billingbeare (Billingebeare), I., 249, 250,* 250 n.; II., 4, 174, 181.*
Binfield (Bingfield, Bynfelde), I., 19, 50, 106,* 194, 240,* 241, 249, 317; II., 32, 42,* 43,* 51,* 52,* 97,* 133,* 207,* 219.*
Birch Hall, Essex, *see* Beech Hall.
Bircham, ? Norfolk, I., 78.*
Birchmorehall, Bedfordshire, II., 210.
Birdsplace, Herts, I., 179.
Bisham (Bysham), I., 228*; II., 4, 40, 84,* 85,* 147, 148,* 150,* 151, 220, 222.
Bishop's Cannings, *see* Cannings, Bishop's.
Bishop's-Hatfield. Herts, II., 193.
Bishop's Stortford (Sartford), Herts, II., 139.
Bishopston (Bishopton), Wilts, II., 89.

Bishopstone (Byshopston), Herefordshire, I., 274.
Bishops Wooburne, see Wooburne.
Bisiter, see Bicester.
Bisley All Saints (Beisley, Byseley All Saints), Gloucestershire, II., 67.*
Bitterne, Hants, II., 187.
Blackbourton or Burton-Abbots (Blackborton), Oxon, I., 296.
Blagrave House, II., 12,* 24.
Blagrove (Blackgrove), I., 100.
Bledlow (Bledlowe), Bucks, I., 56.
Bletchingley (Blechinglye. Bleckinglegh), Surrey, II., 77.
Bletchington (Blechingdon). Oxon, II., 170, 224.
Blewbury (Blewberry, Blewberye), I., 29,* 32, 51, 105, 111,* 217, 280; II., 35, 137,* 177.
Blore Heath, II., 75,* 76.
Bloxwich (Blockswich), Staffordshire, I., 274.
Blunsdon, Wilts. I., 260, 277*; II., 22, 165.
Boarstall (Borestall, Bostall, Burstall), Bucks, I., 118, 133; II., 191.
Bobbing, Kent, I., 268.
Bockhampton (Bockington), I., 93,* 126,* 138, 211, 280*; II., 24.
Bockleton, Worcestershire, I., 272.
Bockmore, Bucks, II., 71.
Bollingham (Bellingham, ? Bolingford), Herefordshire, I., 45.
Bolney, Sussex, I., 72, 73.*
Bolton on Dearne (Bolton on Deane), Yorkshire, II., 228, 229.
Bolton, Little (Boulton, Little), Lancashire, I., 234.
Bonds Castell, Northumberland, II., 74.
Boningale (Buntingdall), Salop, I., 33.
Boothby Pagnell (Boothby Painell), Lincolnshire, I., 268.
Borestall, see Boarstall.
Boscombe, Wilts, I., 186, 187.
Bostal, see Boarstall.
Bostock, II., 75, 76, 77.
Botley, ? Hants, II., 2,* 13.
Botreux Castle, Cornwall, I., 188.
Bottomsted, II., 32.
Boughton Hall, Suffolk, II., 219.
Boughton Malherbe, Kent, II., 103.
Boughton Monchelsea, Kent, I., 115.
Bouldthrop, see Burethrope.
Boulogne, France, II., 80.
Bourton (Borton), Berks, I., 38, 39,* 226,* 227,* 236; II., 4, 25,* 224.
Bourton (Bowrton), Oxon, I., 62.
Boveney, Bucks, I., 23.
Bowden, Cheshire, I., 163.
Bowlney (Bowlnehaye, Boulney, Bowney), Oxon, I., 30, 129, 208, 286.
Boxford, II., 28, 31, 195.
Boxwell (Baxwell), Gloucestershire, I., 68, 168.
Bradborough (Bradbury), Bedfordshire, II., 222.
Bradfield (Brodfilde), I., 11, 21, 52,* 208, 263,* 288,* 289, 297; II., 17, 36, 215.*
Bradford, Wilts, I., 130, 290.
Bradley, I., 298, 299,* 309; II., 194.
Bradway, see Broadway.
Bradwell, Oxon, I., 48.
Brailes (Braytes), Warwickshire, II., 219.
Braintree (Brayntree), Essex, I., 44.
Bramhall, Suffolk, I., 74.
Bramley (Branley), Hants, I., 157; II., 195.
Brampton, Hunts, I., 265.

Brasted, Kent, I., 105, 239.
Braudley, Worcestershire, II., 185.
Bray, I., 4, 19, 20, 23,* 30,* 40.* 46,* 83,* 107,* 130, 131, 134, 135, 139, 251, 254,* 255, 275, 297, 298,* 309, 312,* 317; II., 4, 43,* 44,* 45, 46,* 48, 53,* 65,* 74, 79, 128, 177,* 182, 184,* 185, 191, 192,* 210,* 211, 212,* 231.
Bray, Hundred of, I., 251, 254, 298, 309, 312; II., 5, 8, 9. 43, 44, 45, 65.
Bray-wick, II., 44.
Breamore, Hants, I., 228.
Bremhill (Bremble), Wilts, I., 18.
Brentford (Brainford), Middlesex, I., 267; II. 125.
Brereton, ? Staffordshire, II., 75.
Bretforton, Worcestershire, I., 268.
Bridde, Dorset, II., 90.
Brightwalton (Bright Walton), II., 31, 82,* 83,* 181.
Brightwell, I., 51, 55, 216; II., 2,* 3, 14, 140, 222.
Brill, I., 240; II., 88.
Brimpton (Brympton), I., 24,* 38,* 85,* 192,* 215, 241, 242; II., 1, 31.
Bristol, II., 166.
Bristol, St. Augustine's, II., 183.
Bristowe (Brystowe), I., 6,* 22, 138, 169, 300*; II., 191.
Britford, Wilts, II., 129.
Britwell (Bretwell), Oxon, I., 9.
Brize-Norton (Brise Norton), Oxon, I., 195.
Broadfield (Brodfield), Herts, I., 105, 126; II., 224.
Broad-Hinton (Brodehenton), Wilts, I., 22*; II., 222.
Broadwater, Sussex, II., 171.*
Broadway (Bradwey), ? Gloucestershire, I., 204, 219.
Brocket Hall, Herts, I., 124, 271; II., 205.
Brocton, II., 78.
Bromley, Kent, I., 207.
Bromley, Lincolnshire, I., 160.
Brookhampton, Warwickshire, II., 111.
Broughton, Wilts, I., 39.
Broughton, Staffordshire, I., 75, 131.
Broxbourne (Bloxburne), Herts, I., 70, 170; II., 132, 156 n.
Brussels, I., 295, 296 : II., 220.
Buckhurst. Sussex, II., 213.
Buckland (Buklande), I., 8, 25, 27, 47, 60,* 61,* 104, 121, 126, 148, 149,* 283, 302,* 318*; II., 21, 127,* 160, 234.
Bucklebury (Buckhilbury, Burghlebury, Burghulbury), I., 147, 225, 241,* 244, 259, 308, 313*; II., 3, 35. 173.*
Bulmarsh (Bulmersh), I., 86, 173,* 174, 314; II., 39, 71.*
Bulmarsh (Bulnash) Court, I., 16; II., 70.
Buntingdall, see Boningale.
Burches, Suffolk, I . 222.
Burcott (Bercott, Barcott, Beckoot), Oxon, I., 7,* 24, 61; II., 125.
Burethrope (Burdorp, Bouldthorp), Wilts, I., 44, 117, 150.
Burford, Oxon, I., 26, 53, 189, 195, 282; II., 170.*
Burford, Salop, I., 271,* 272.
Burghclere (Burclere), Hants, I., 248, 264.
Burghfield (Burfield, Burfelde), I., 52, 58,* 263, 264, 288; II., 1,* 37, 38, 215, 229.
Burley, Northants, I., 217.
Burneside, Westmorland, II., 69.

INDEX LOCORUM. 263

Burnham, Bucks, I., 69, 73, 83.
Burrough Court, Hants, I., 134.
Burstall, *see* Boarstall.
Burton, Bucks, I., 12, 57; II., 85.
Burton-on-Trent, I., 253.
Bury St. Edmunds, I., 78.
Buscot (Burscoot, Burscourt), I., 108,* 216,* 231,* 242,* 281,* 282*; II., 25, 156,* 172.
Bushey (Busshie), Herts, I., 57.
Buttermere (Battermere), Wilts, I., 309.
Bydden, *see* Beedon.
Bynolde, Wilts, I., 38.
Bysham, *see* Bisham.

C

Cadenham (Cadnam), Wilts. I., 231,* 235, 311; II., 156,* 156 *n*., 162.
Cadmore (Cadmer), Oxon, I., 89.
Calais (Callis), II., 97.
Caldecote. Warwickshire, I., 267, 268.
Caldicot (Caldicut, Calicut), Monmouthshire, I., 264.
Caldicott, Cheshire, II., 89.
Calne (Colne, Cawne). Wilts, I., 125, 249.
Cambridge, I., 46,* 223.
Cambridge, King's Coll., I., 46; II., 195.
Camells, Surrey, I., 131.
Cannings, Bishop's (Bysshoppes Cannynge), Wilts, I., 35, 72.
Canterbury, I., 142.
Canwick, Lincolnshire (? Kenwick, Norfolk). I., 111.
Caple-Eaton, Northumberland, 124.
Carbrooke (Carbroke), Norfolk, I., 218.
Cardut, Cumberland, II., 207.
Carswell (Careswell), I., 145, 234, 282, 283,* 284. 285, 285 *n*.; II., 5, 21, 214.*
Catesby, Northants, I., 253.
Catmore (Catmer, Catmere). I., 88, 119, 244, 259; II., 2, 23, 83, 173.
Catthorpe (Catthorp), Leicestershire, II., 88,* 89.
Caughton, II., 64.
Caversfield, Bucks, ? Oxon, II., 116.*
Caversham, Oxon, II., 41.
Cawne, *see* Calne, Wilts.
Cerne, Dorset (? Sene, Wilts), I., 215.
Chaddesley Corbett, Worcestershire, I., 318; II., 234.
Chaddleworth, I., 114, 115,* 116,* 247, 248, 248 *n*., 249,* 261*; II., 3, 5, 18, 27, 71, 142.
Chalfont St. Peter's, Bucks, II., 79.
Chalgrove, Oxon (Chaugraue, Bucks). I., 243.
Challow (Chalow, Chawlow), I., 9, 256.
Challow, East (Challowe, East), I., 59, 143, 296*; II., 27.
Challow, West (Chaley, West), I., 260; II., 27.
Chalvey, Bucks, II., 79.
Chamberhouse (Camberhouse, Chamb'house), I., 125, 160, 288; II., 35,* 54,* 128,* 129,* 130.
Chard, Somerset, II., 218.*
Charlton (Charleton), I., 59,* 97,* 99, 100, 115, 143,* 168, 169,* 180, 311*; II., 19, 49,* 208.*
Charlton, Hundred of, I., 160, 200, 215, 219, 231, 286, 291, 292; II., 5, 8,* 36, 40, 41.
Charlton in Andover, Hants, I., 302.
Charlynch (Charling), Somerset, I., 290.
Charney (Chernet, Cherney), I., 8, 27. 60,* 61,* 90,* 91, 148,* 149, 150; II., 21, 105, 234.
Chartley, II., 66.

Chastleton (Chaselton), Oxon, II., 212.
Chaugraue, Bucks, *see* Chalgrove, Oxon.
Chawley, I., 257*; II., 12.
Chawley, West, I., 260.
Chawton, Hants, I., 164.
Chechurst, Oxon, I., 165.
Checkendon (Checkington, Chetington, Chetkendon), Oxon, I., 229; II., 161, 162, 175.
Cheldswell (Chelsewell), I., 257; II., 1, 13.
Chelmarsh, Salop, II., 129.
Chelmsford, Essex, I, 108, 214.
Cheltenham (Keltnam), Gloucestershire, I., 48., 122, 195.
Cherington, Salop, II., 78.*
Cherney (Chernet), *see* Charney.
Chertsey (Chersey), Surrey, I., 57.
Chesham, Surrey, ? Bucks, I., 222.
Chesham-Bois (Chesham Boyes, Chesham Boyse), Bucks, I., 44, 91, 106; II., 116, 175.
Chester, I., 291; II., 184, 207.*
Chesterton, I., 257.
Chieveley (Chevele, Chevely, Cheively, Chively), I., 72,* 229, 241, 290; II., 3, 31, 196,* 197.
Chignal, Essex, II., 64.
Childrey (Childeray), I., 8, 205, 206,* 207,* 302; II., 4.* 19, 41, 127,* 162, 198.*
Child's Ercall (Childs Arcoll), Salop, II., 78.*
Chilton, Berks, I., 2, 60, 104, 105, 129, 133, 149, 261, 278; II., 4, 23, 168,* 200, 222.
Chilton, ? Foliat, Wilts, I., 319.
Chinnor, Oxon, I., 111; II., 191.
Chiping, II., 5.
Chiping Lamborne, II., 24.
Chipping Farringdon (Cheppinge Farrington), I., 47, 60, 149.
Chiseworth, Derbyshire, I., 17.*
Chislehampton (Chistlehampton, Chistleton), Oxon, II., 126, 193.
Chislehurst (Chiselhurst), Kent, II., 170. 210.
Chislington, Oxon, II., 88.
Cholsey (Choulsey, Chowlseye), I., 16, 29, 37,* 51,* 52, 53, 276,* 279, 297; II., 34, 163.*
Christchurch, Hants, I., 304.
Church Aston, Salop, I., 260.
Church Speen, *see* Speen.
Churton, II., 75.
Churton Heath, Cheshire, II., 77.
Chute, Wilts, I., 127,* 128.*
Cirencester, Gloucestershire. I., 165, 266, 298*; II., 195.
Clanfield (Glanvill), Hants, I., 55,* 230.
Clanfield (Glanvile, Glavylde), Oxon, I., 49, 123, 247.
Clapcott (Clapkott), I., 112*; II., 15.
Clapham, Surrey, II., 38, 225, 226.
Clare, I., 135.
Claverley, Salop, II., 159.*
Clevedon, Somerset, I., 22.
Clewer (Cluer, Cleworthe), I., 30,* 300,* 317*; II., 5, 45, 46, 134.
Clifton, Oxon, II., 167.
Coakewood, II, 29.
Coate (Cote), Oxon, II., 22, 156.
Coates, Gloucestershire, I., 65, 265.
Coberley (Cubberlye), Gloucestershire, I., 3.
Cobham, Surrey, I., 20.
Codrington, Wilts, ? Gloucestershire, I., 259.
Cogges (Coggs), Oxon, I., 26.
Colbrook, II., 44.
Coldrake, II., 35.
Colerne (Collen), Wilts, II., 78.

Coleshill (Colshill, Collishill, Cowlshull), I.,
  47,* 48,* 122, 189,* 208, 236, 266, 295 ; II.,
  25, 196.
Colewich (Collwick), Bucks, I., 121, 256.
Colley (Colle, Coley), I., 12,* 56,* 136,* 292, 301.
Collingbourne, Wilts, I., 114, 138.
Coln St. Aldwyn (Colnallens), Gloucestershire,
  I., 265.
Colts Hall, Suffolk, I., 291.
Combe (Comb), Hants, I., 59, 143.
Comner, see Cumnor.
Compton, Berks, I., 52, 196, 279 ; II., 2,* 23, 26.
Compton, East, II., 23.
Compton, Hundred of, I., 209, 225 ; II., 5, 8,*
  23, 35, 168.
Compton, Hants, I., 88.
Compton Beauchamp, I., 261*; II., 180.
Cookfeild, Sussex, I., 203 ; II., 126.*
Cookham (Cokeham, Cowkham), I., 30, 31, 44,*
  139,* 208, 273,* 275, 292, 298,* 299,* 304,
  305,* 310, 312 ; II., 1,* 42, 43, 45,* 54, 56,*
  56n., 126, 185, 193, 211.*
Cookham, Hundred of, I., 194, 203, 240,* 299 ;
  II., 5, 8, 9, 42, 43, 219.
Cookham Lowabrooke, I., 203*; II., 126.*
Copdmore, Cardiganshire, I., 219.
Corfe Castle (Crofte Castle), Dorset, I., 47. 48.
Cornburgh, Yorkshire, I., 305.
Cornbury, Oxon, I., 3.
Coscott (Coscutt), II., 2, 14.
Cosforde, Bucks, I., 35, 100.
Cote, see Coat.
Cothorp (Cowthrop), Oxon, II., 54.
Cottells, Wilts, I., 283, 284.
Cotton End, Northants, II., 184.
Coulshill, Suffolk, I., 222.
Coventry, Warwickshire, I., 34, 268.
Cowley, Gloucestershire, I., 195.*
Coxham (Coocksham), Oxon, I., 195, 216,* 281.
Coxwell (Coswell, Kokeswell), I., 45,* 142,
  247,* 294.
Coxwell, Great, I., 21, 25 ; II., 22.
Coxwell, Little, II., 22.
Coyty (Coyte), Glamorganshire, II., 43.
Crall, Sussex, II., 103.*
Cranbrook, Kent, I., 179.
Craven, Yorkshire, I., 296.
Crawley, Bedfordshire, I., 305.
Crediton (Kirton), Devon, I., 236 ; II., 161, 163.
Crendon (Grendon), Bucks, I., 41,* 108.
Creslow, Oxon, ? Bucks, II., 170.
Cressage (Cressedge), Salop, I., 44.
Creswell, I., 309*; II., 44, 65.
Cricklade (Crekelade), Wilts, I., 122.
Crickley, Gloucestershire, I., 172.
Crondall (Crundwell), Hants, I., 169.
Crosby, II., 184.
Crowell, Oxon, I., 229.
Crowhurst, Surrey, II., 51, 52, 133.
Crowmarsh, Preston, Oxon, I., 209.
Croxall, Derbyshire, I., 160.
Croydon, Surrey, II., 119.
Cruchfield (Crutchfield), I., 97,* 223.*
Cuckfield, Sussex, I., 162.
Cufand (Cuffold), Hants, I., 281.
Culham (Culnaham, Chulham), Oxon, I., 20,*
  21, 37, 52, 53, 100, 105, 255, 312 ; II., 12, 168.
Culworth, Northants, I., 166 ; II., 63, 170.
Cumnor (Cumner, Comner, Combner), I., 58,
  180, 195, 229, 257 ; II., 1,* 3, 12.
Cunyside, Lancashire, I., 160.

D

Dale, I., 146.
Danbury, Essex, II., 197.
Dance-tew, Oxon, see Dunstew.
Darby, Lancashire, II., 184.
Dartford, Kent, I., 196.
Dartmouth Castle, Devon, I., 179.
Datchet (Dotchet), Bucks, I., 241 ; II., 68,*
  210.
Dauntsey (Dawncey), Wilts, I., 28.
Deane (Dene), Hants, I., 282.
Deddington (Dedington), Oxon, I., 48.
Dedworth, II., 46.
Delverne, Staffordshire, I., 79, 182.
Denardiston (Dennerdiston), Suffolk, I., 305.
Denchworth, I., 21, 25, 37, 89,* 90, 98, 204, 205 ;
  II., 12. 19, 157 (2), 221.
Denchworth, North, I., 8,* 27,* 90,* 91,* 123.
Denchworth, South, I., 35,* 60, 98,* 99,* 100,*
  148, 241 ; II., 4, 98, 99, 125, 156,* 157.*
Denford, I., 138,* 173, 233, 234, 283 ; II., 5, 36.
Denham, Bucks, II., 207.
Denham Hall, Suffolk, II., 250.
Denington, I., 101, 254, 277 ; II., 5.
Deptford (Detford), Kent, I., 242 ; II., 49.
Derby, I., 44.
Deusworth, Sussex, I., 116.
Devizes (Devises), Wilts, II., 164.*
Dicklestone (Dicleston), Gloucestershire, I., 28.
Didcot (Dudcott), I., 243 ; II., 2,* 13, 14.
Digswell (Digsonwell), Herts, II., 116.
Doddershall (Dodersall), Bucks, I., 121.
Dodington, Oxon, II., 119.*
Donhead (Dunnet), Wilts, I., 278.
Donnington, I., 101 ; II., 32, 187, 188.
Donnington Castle by Newbury, I., 80.*
Dorchester, II., 90.
Dorchester, Oxon, I., 120.
Dorking (Darking), Surrey, I., 54, 222 ; II., 74.
Dorney (Dornaye), Bucks, I., 23, 30.
Dorton (Dourton), Bucks, I., 118, 124.
Dover Castle, I., 289 ; II., 223.
Down Ampney (Downe Amney), Gloucestershire,
  I., 16, 28,* 30, 174, 186, 208 ; II., 70, 156, 197.
Draycoot, Wilts, II., 176.
Draycott, Oxon, ? Wilts, I., 133,* 265.
Draycott Moore, II., 18.
Drayton, Berks, I., 59, 143, 279 ; II., 16.
Drayton, Leicestershire, I., 267.*
Drayton, Oxon, I., 120, 220, 287.
Drayton Beauchamp, II., 56.
Driffield, Gloucestershire, II., 73.
Dublin, Ireland, I., 116 ; II., 154.
Ducklington (Duckelton), Oxon, I., 157.
Dudcote (Dudcot), I., 187, 243.
Duerreeth, Somerset, II., 183.
Dunstew (Dance-tew), Oxon, II., 202.
Durham, I., 36.
Durley, Hants, I., 58.
Dutton, Cheshire, II., 77.
Duxford, II., 21, 200.
Dymock (Dymmok), Gloucestershire, I., 3.

E

Earley (Early), II., 36, 41.
Earl's Court (Earlescourt), I., 114.
Easthampstead (Esthampsted, East Hamsted),
  I., 99, 181, 295, 296* ; II., 4, 5, 46, 220.*

INDEX LOCORUM. 265

Eastleach Turnstile (Eastlech-Turvill), Gloucestershire, I., 180.
Eastmeon (Eastmeane, Estmayne), Hants, I., 28, 55.*
Easton, II., 32.
Eaton, Berks, I., 195; II., 115.
Eaton, Salop, II., 122.
Eaton Hastings, Berks, I., 189*; II., 26.
Edenbridge (Eatonbridge), Kent, II., 65.
Edgarley, Cheshire, II., 77.
Edgbaston, Warwickshire, II., 83.*
Edgcote (Edge Cott), Northants, II., 139.
Edgeworth, Gloucestershire, I., 172.
Edgmond, Salop, II., 63.
Edington, II., 29.
Egham, Surrey; I., 46, 115, 162; II., 55, 74.
Elford, ? Elsfield, Oxon, I., 92.
Eling (Elling, Elyng), I., 123, 224*, II., 32.
Elland (Eland, Ealand), Yorkshire, I., 310*; II., 228,* 229.*
Ellistown (Ellston, Elston), Leicestershire, I., 7, 24; II., 125.
Elmley, Worcestershire, I., 92.
Elmstone (Elmeston), Kent, I., 209.
Eltham, Kent, I., 148.
Elton, I., 214, 230; II., 32.
Ely, Isle of, I., 208; II., 90.
Emeley, Ireland, I., 318.
Emmington (Elmyngton), Oxon, I., 35, 37.
Enborne (Enboren), I., 35, 100; II., 3, 27, 111,* 132.*
Enborne, East. II., 111.
Enford, Wilts, II., 164.
Englefield (Inggilfelde), I., 7; II., 36, 121,* 122, 123.*
Euglisham, I., 282; II., 22.
Enmore, Somerset, I., 307.
Ercall, High (High Arcoll), Salop, I., 265.
Eresby (Ereby), Lincolnshire, II., 207.*
Erleston, Hants, II., 28.
Ermington (Armington), Devon, I., 188.
Ervin, *see* St. Ervan.
Estcotte (Escot), Wilts, I., 38, 227.
Eton, Bucks, I., 69,* 84.*
Eton College, Bucks, II., 229.
Evelton, II., 224.
Eversley, Hants, I., 287.
Everton, Bedfordshire, I., 23.
Ewhurst (Yowhurste), Surrey, I., 54.
Excheccares in Stokenchurch, Oxon, I., 11.
Exeter, Devon, I., 294, 295*; II., 176.

F

Faccombe (Fackombe), Hants, I., 32.
Faire Cross, Hundred of, I., 190, 192, 193, 213, 230, 235, 241, 289, 308; II., 5, 8, 9, 30, 31, 32, 187.
Faringdon (Farington), Berks, I., 47, 189,* 211, 218, 267, 270,* 278, 294,* 295, 319*; II., 3, 22, 127, 129, 201.
Faringdon, The Crown, II., 9, 155.
Faringdon, Great, II., 22.
Faringdon, Hospital Liberty in, II., 22.
Faringdon, Hundred of, I., 180, 247; II., 5, 8, 9, 22, 23.
Faringdon, Little, I., 35, 100; II., 3, 23.
Faringdon (Ferrington), Hants, I., 9.
Farington Popham, Hants, I., 29.
Farley, II., 4.

Farley Walton, II., 129.
Farnborough (Farnburow, Farnebarow), I., 59, 143, 209*; II., 2, 23.
Farnham, Surrey, I., 183, 225.
Farnham Royal, Bucks, I., 312.
Faversham (Feversham), Kent, I., 179; II., 60.
Fawler (Fauler), Oxon, II., 26, 127.
Fawler Court, I., 17,* 73.*
Fawley, I., 65, 246, 261; II., 24.
Fawley Court, Bucks, II., 227.
Fawley, North, II., 27.
Fawley, South, I., 246,* 247; II., 27.
Fawsley (Fawlesley), Northants, I., 20; II., 222.*
Feckenham, Worcestershire, I., 273.
Feens, *see* Fins.
Felhouse, I., 259.
Fernham, I., 91, 92, 203, 204,* 302, 319; II., 26.
Fifehead Magdalen, Dorsetshire, II., 183.*
Finchampstead (Finchamsted, Fynchampsted), I., 57, 88, 89, 194, 286, 292*; II., 41, 62, 69,* 140.*
Finchingfield (Finchfield), Essex, I., 78.
Finchley (Fynchley), Middlesex, II., 119.*
Fins (Feens), II., 40.
Fitz harris in Abingdon, II., 77.*
Flamstead, Herts, I., 195.
Flitwick (Fleetwick, Fleetwood), Bedfordshire, I., 216.
Florence, Italy, I., 79; II., 91.
Flushing. II., 66.
Folden, Kent, II., 227.
Ford Abbey. Devon, I., 191.*
Ford House in Wargrave, I., 274.*
Fordwich, Kent, I., 142.
Forton, Lancashire, II., 131.
Foxley, I., 31.
Frankmarsh, near Barnstaple, I., 260.
Freefolk (Frefolk), Hants, I., 66.
Fremley, *see* Frimley.
Frilford, I., 260; II., 18.
Frilsham, II., 30.
Frimley, Surrey (Fremley, Sussex), I., 183; II., 102.
Frithelond, II., 189.
Frogmore, II., 54, 55.*
Frome Selwood, Somerset, I., 47.
Fulham, Middlesex, I., 232.
Fullpluck, Oxon, I., 310.
Fulscot, I., 157.
Fulwell, Oxon, II., 224.
Furle, Sussex, I., 318.
Fyfield (Fysfeild, Fifield), I., 41,* 108, 131, 140,* 141,* 306,* 307, 312, 315; II., 3,* 17, 44, 55, 116,* 184,* 185,* 186, 193,* 194,* 231.*

G

Gainfield (Ganfield), Hundred of, I., 196, 254, 256, 269, 283, 284, 302, 318; II., 5, 8, 9, 10, 13, 20, 21.
Garford, II., 18.
Garsington (Gatington, Gazington), Oxon, I., 156, 241. 303.
Garston, East, I., 156, 169*; II., 24.
Garston, Lancashire, II., 114.
Gatehampton, *see* Yattendon.
Gawsworth (Gosworth), Cheshire, II., 123.
Gayer, Cornwall, I., 31.
Gayton, I., 301.
Gifford's Hall, Suffolk, I., 96.
Ginge (Genge), I., 187; II., 224.

Ginge, East, II., 20.
Ginge, West, II., 20.
Glanvile, *see* Clanfield.
Glastenbury, Kent, II., 105.
Glemham, Suffolk, I., 137.
Gloucester, I., 273.
Glynne, Northants, II., 51.
Godalming (Godlyman), Surrey, I., 183; II., 100.*
Goldingfeild (Goldingafield), I., 39,* 101.
Golton, Yorks, I., 281.*
Good-Rest. Warwickshire, I., 68, 168.
Goosey, II., 18.
Gopsal, Leicestershire, II., 222.
Goring, Oxon, I., 157*; II., 23, 90, 187.
Gosfield, Essex, II., 222.
Goudhurst (Goodhurst), Kent, II., 65.
Grafton, I., 127.
Grampole (Grampound), I., 224*; II., 11.
Grange, The, Berks, I., 184, 190.*
Grange, The, Hants, II., 182.
Grange, The, Oxon, I., 51.
Gravesend, I., 209.
Grays, I., 103.
Grazeley (Greasly), II., 36.
Greenham (Grenham), I., 127,* 128, 229, 230*; II., 30, 32, 83.
Greenham, Somerset, II., 169.
Greenwich, Kent, I., 234.
Greenwich, Royal Hospital, II., 197.
Grenway Court, Kent, II., 103.
Greystock, I., 251.
Greywell (Grewell), Hants, I., 40, 130.
Grimstead, West (Grunstede, West), Wilts, I., 9.
Groombridge, Kent, I., 254.
Grove, Berks, I., 50, 290; II., 4, 19.
Grove, Notts, I., 97.
Grovehurst, Kent, II., 85.
Guildford (Guilford, Gylforde), Surrey, I., 183*; II., 69, 101,* 102.
Guynney, I., 233.
Gwernevit, Brecknockshire, I., 309.

H

Haccombe (Haycome), Devon, I., 5.
Hackney, Middlesex, I., 131, 162; II., 97,* 98, 144,* 181.*
Haddenham (Hadenham, Hadnam), Bucks, I., 2,* 139, 293.
Hadham, Herts, I., 111.
Haddon, Oxon, I., 28.
Hadley, I., 211, 212; II., 24.*
Hagbourne (Hagborne), I., 235, 287; II, 1, 161,* 162.*
Hagbourne, East, II., 2, 13, 14.
Hagbourne, West, II., 14.
Haines Hill in Hurst, I., 171.*
Hall Place in Hurley, I., 65*; II., 40; *see also* Hurley.
Halton, Oxon, ? Bucks. I., 272, 302; II., 116.
Ham, Somerset, II., 217.
Hambledon (Hamilton), Bucks, I., 71.
Hamburg, II., 196, 197.*
Hammersmith, Middlesex, II., 210.
Hampden, Bucks, I., 270.
Hampnet, Sussex, I., 173.
Hampstead, II., 105.
Hampstead Marshall (Hampsted, Hamsted), I., 50,* 105, 210; II., 6, 27, 191.*

Hampstead Norreys (Norris), I., 187; II., 3, 30, 32.
Hampton Court, I., 162.
Hampton, East (Estum'ton), I., 9.
Hampton Poyle, Oxon, I., 20; II., 116.
Hanford, Dorset, I., 287.
Hanley Castle, Worcestershire, I., 71.
Hanney, I., 52, 53, 89, 184, 225; II., 175, 224, 234.
Hanney, East (East Hanny), I., 11, 244, 280; II., 18, 19, 173.
Hanney, West, I., 26, 39, 60, 105, 157,* 158, 201; II., 20, 224.*
Hannington, Wilts, I., 236.
Hansaker Hall, Staffordshire, I., 320.
Hanslope (Hemsloppe), Bucks, I., 53.
Harden, I., 128.
Hardwick, Oxfordshire, I., 118, 229, 249, 292, 296; II., 15, 71.
Hare Court, I , 52.
Harpeden (Harpden, Harpeden), Oxon, I., 9, 29.
Harrold (Harald), Bedfordshire, I., 162.
Harrow, ? Berks, I., 243.
Harrow on the Hill, Middlesex, I., 70, 170, 262; II.. 68.
Hartland, Devon, I., 188.
Hartley Dummer, II., 37.
Hartley Wespall (Hartley Westfield), Hants, I., 160.
Hartridge, *see* Headington.
Hartwell, Bucks, I., 191; II., 187.
Hartwell, Northants, II., 223.
Harwell, I., 59, 143, 187, 241,* 280, 293; II., 3, 4,* 13, 14,* 26.
Haseley (Hasle, Hasley), Oxon, I., 9; II., 23, 170.*
Haseley, Worcestershire, I., 207.
Hassall, Cheshire, I., 221, 221n.
Hatch (Hach), Wilts, I., 80; II., 92.
Hatfield, II., 204.
Hatfield, Hants, II., 182.
Hatfield Peverel, Essex, II., 129.
Hatford (Hattford), I., 120, 121,* 256,* 260*; II., 13, 21.
Hatherley, Gloucestershire, II., 90.
Hawthorne in Bray, II., 3.
Hawton, *see* Horton.
Hawtrey, ? Heavitree, Devon, I., 188.
Haycome, *see* Haccombe, Devon.
Hayes, Middlesex, I., 267.
Haynes Hill, II., 39.
Headington (Hartridge Hedington), Oxon, I., 52.
Heath Lane, II., 78.
Heathly Hall in Warfield, I., 250; *see also* Warfield.
Heckfield, ? Hants. II., 43.
Hedgerley Bulstrode. Bucks, II., 227.
Heldrop, Wilts, I., 161.
Hemingstone, Suffolk, I., 78.*
Hempstead. Essex, I., 96.
Hemshall, Derbyshire, *see* Hensall, Yorks.
Hendall (Hindall), Sussex, II., 102.
Hendred, I., 319; II., 173.
Hendred, East (Esthenrethe). I., 26,* 53, 60,* 88, 148, 150. 201,* 202,* 244, 278,* 279, 281 ; II., 1, 20, 35,* 187, 225.
Hendred, West, I., 186, 306, 314; II., 20, 168.
Henley, I., 177, 243, 293; II., 77.
Henley-on-Thames, Oxon, II., 85, 119, 139,* 182.

INDEX LOCORUM.

Hensall, Yorks, ? (Hemshall, Derbyshire), II., 228.
Henstridge (Hounstred), Somerset, I., 261.
Hentland, Pembrokeshire, ? Herefordshire, I., 295.
Henwick, Berks, II., 35.
Henwick in Thatcham, I., 281.*
Henwood Hall, Warwickshire, II., 88.
Henwood, Warwickshire, I., 92, 204.
Hereford, I., 68, 167, 271; II., 66, 191.
Hereford, East, I., 16.
Herriard (Heryard, Heryot), Hants, I., 268; II., 129.*
Hewthwait, see Husthwaite, Yorks.
Heywood, II., 40.
Hide End, I., 259.
Hiden, II., 29.
Higham, Kent, II., 103.*
High Leigh, Cheshire, I., 80; II., 92.
Highworth, Wilts, I., 32, 95, 180,
Hildesley, see Ilsley.
Hill End, II., 13, 167.*
Hillesdon, Bucks, I., 28.
Hinck Cheyney, Sussex, II., 103.
Hinksey (Hinxe), I., 132.
Hinksey, North, II., 2, 13.
Hinksey, South, II., 2, 13.
Hinton (Hynton), I., 60, 149; II., 21, 200.
Hinton, Cambridge, I., 318.
Hinton Parva, Wilts, I., 91, 205, 231.
Hinton, St. George, Somerset, I., 311.
Hinton Waldrist, II., 127.
Hinxsill, Kent, II., 52.
Hitchin, Herts, II., 181.
Hitchingfield, Herefordshire, II., 79.
Hodcott, I., 51, 52.
Hoddesdon (Hodgsdon), Hertfordshire, II., 154.
Hodson, Wilts, I., 319.
Holcombe, Devon, II., 170.
Holcombe Grange, Oxon, I., 286, 287.
Holland, Lancashire, II., 209.
Holme, Cumberland, I., 160.*
Holsworthy (Hollesworthy), Devon, II., 161.
Holt Castle, I., 65.
Holt in Kintbury, I., 302.*
Holt, Leicestershire, I., 160.
Holy Port in Bray, II., 44.
Hoo (Hooe), Herts, I. 21, 124; II., 204.*
Hook (Hooke), Hants, I., 193; II., 41.
Hopton, Derbyshire, I., 254; II., 188.
Hord Park, Salop, II., 155.
Horley, ? Oxon, I., 46.
Hormer Hundred, I., 167, 195, 224, 257; II., 5, 8, 9, 10, 11, 12, 13, 39, 169, 202,* 217.
Horsham, Sussex, I., 144, 183; II., 99, 101.
Horsleydown, Surrey, I., 139.
Horsmonden, Kent, I., 142.
Horton Kirby, Kent, I., 168, 169.
Horton, Northamptonshire, I., 136.
Horton (Hawton), Staffordshire, I., 117; II., 182.
Horwood, Great, Bucks, I., 166; II., 63.
Hounstred, see Henstridge.
Howbery, Oxon, II., 16.
Huckeslegrene, Cheshire, I., 33.
Huike, Berks, II., 217.
Hulcote, Bucks, I., 106.
Hulse, The, Chester, I., 34.
Humfreston, Salop, I., 34.
Hungerford, Wilts, I., 32, 37, 82, 95, 212, 234, 282; II., 3, 29.
Hungerford Park, I., 169.

Hunsdon, Herts, II., 139.
Huntercombe, Oxon, I., 129,* 220; II., 140.
Hunton Hall, Lancashire, I., 11.
Hurley, I., 57, 65,* 244, 304; II., 3, 4, 30, 39, 40, 42, 79, 172, 173, 207*; see also Hall Place in Hurley.
Hursley (Hurstley), Hants, I., 196.
Hurst, Berks, I., 12, 20, 57,* 66,* 98, 99.* 113,* 134, 164, 165,* 171,* 182, 215, 219,* 253, 265, 293; II., 1, 4, 11, 38, 39,* 40, 64, 140,* 141, 194,* 205.
Hurst, Wilts, I., 79.
Hurstbourne (Hushbourne), Hants, I., 128.
Hurstmonceaux (Hurstmonceulx), II., 186.
Hurtlo, Cumberland, I., 160.
Husthwaite (Hewthwait), Yorks, I., 281.*

I

Ichell, Hants, I., 149.
Ichington, Warwickshire, I., 58.
Ichington, Long, Warwickshire, I., 35.
Iden, Sussex, II., 103.*
Idson (Idstone), II., 24.
Ightfield, Salop, I., 245.*
Ightham (Igtham), Kent, II., 171.
Ilford, Essex, II., 70.
Ilford, Wilts, II., 233.
Ilsley (Hildsley, Ildsley, Ilesley), I., 73, 225*; II., 196.*
Ilsley, East (Hildsley), II., 2, 23,* 160.
Ilsley, West, I., 296; II., 2, 23.
Ingestre, Staffordshire, II., 222.
Ingleton, Staffordshire, I., 308.
Inglewood, I., 95; II., 3.
Inkpen (Inckpen), I., 93, 24, 179,* 210*; II., 3, 28, 120,* 131.*
Ipsden (Ipston), Oxon, I., 157; II., 88, 205, 272.
Ipswich (Gipw.), Suffolk, I., 105, 164, 179, 298.
Isbury, II., 24.
Isham, Berks or Bucks, II., 188.
Isledon, Middlesex, I., 142.
Isleworth (Istleworth), II., 211.
Islington, Middlesex, II., 118.*
Ispahan, Persia, I., 251.
Iver, Bucks, I., 58.

J

Jedsly, West (Ildsley), I., 296.

K

Keele, Montgomeryshire, I., 175.*
Keltnam, see Cheltenham.
Kemble, Wilts, I., 270.
Kempsford, Gloucestershire, I., 32.
Kempshot, Hants, I., 189.
Kencot (Kempscot, Kencotte), Oxon, I., 48, 60 n., 214.
Kennington, II., 1, 11.
Kenoe, Bedfordshire, II., 246.
Kensington, Middlesex, II., 124.
Kenstington, II., 180.
Kentwood, I., 29, 87, 196.
Kenwick, see Canwick.
Kersey Hall, Suffolk, II., 207.*
Kettleby, Lincolnshire, ? Leicestershire, I., 76.

Kew, Surrey, II., 210.
Keynsham, Somerset, I., 42.
Kidlington (Adlington), Oxon, I., 240; II., 185.
Kilham, II., 39, 158.
Kinderton, II., 75, 76.
Kingsclere (Kingscleare), I., 37, 85, 192; II., 131, 162.
King's Lynn, Norfolk, I., 300.
Kingston, Berks, I., 48; II., 4, 41, 43.
Kingston Bagpuize (Bagpuze), Berks, I., 104, 105,* 110, 239*; II., 17, 224.
Kingston Blount, Oxon. II., 139.
Kingston Lisle (Lysley), I., 100, 205, 232, 233,* 296; II., 26, 41, 158.*
Kingston Marleward, Dorset, I., 268.
Kingston upon Thames. Surrey, I., 320.*
Kintbury (Kyntbury, Kinbury, Kynbury). I., 29, 32, 82, 94, 95.* 198, 217,* 218,* 234, 241, 283, 296, 302*; II., 13, 28.
Kintbury, Hundred of. I., 179, 185, 186, 198, 210, 215, 217, 221, 241, 246, 248, 261, 275, 293, 296; II., 5, 8, 9, 18, 25, 36, 120, 131, 164.
Kintbury-Amesbury, II., 4, 28.
Kintbury Eagle, Hundred of, I., 297; II., 26, 27, 28, 29.
Kintbury Eaton, I., 186, 187, 221,* 293*; II., 3, 28.*
Kirkbiehat, Lincolnshire, I., 95.
Kirstibirches, Cheshire, II., 77.
Knap, Oxon, I., 272.
Knaresborough, Yorks, I., 31.*
Knightington, II., 180.*
Knighton, Berks, II., 4, 26,* 180.
Knighton (Nighton), Isle of Wight, I., 317.
Knowl-Hill, II., 173.*
Knowlton, Kent, I., 218.
Kynkborne, Yorks, I., 58.

L

Lachford, Oxon, II., 169.
Lagham, Surrey, I., 283, 284.
Lambeth, Surrey, I., 103.
Lambourn (Lamborne, Lamburn), I., 7, 8, 24,* 25,* 27, 35, 41,* 89, 90, 92, 93,* 95, 100, 108,* 116,* 117,* 142, 210,* 211,* 212, 213,* 214, 230, 280; II., 24,* 124,* 125,* 127,* 172.
Lambourn, Hundred of, I., 169. 206, 211, 214, 236, 277, 280; II., 5, 8, 9, 24.
Lambourn, Upper, I., 187, 205, 206,* 213, 236*; II., 24.
Lambourn Woodlands, I., 201, 213, 242, 277*; II., 187.
Langford, Berks, I., 180,* 256, 267; II., 22.
Langford, Salop, I., 318.
Langford, Wilts, I., 9.
Langham, Dorset, I., 179.
Langley, I., 79.
Langley (Longley), Wilts, I., 138; II., 196.
Langley, Bucks, II., 47, 79.
Langridge (Langrage), Somerset, I., 230.
Langton, Lincolnshire, I., 238.*
Larden, Salop, I., 44.*
Lasborough (Lashborough), Gloucestershire, I., 231; II., 156.
Latchingdon (Lashington). Essex, II., 197.
Laverstoke (Laverstocke), Hants, I., 53, 289.
Lavington, East, Wilts, I., 36.
Layer Breton (Larre Britten), Essex, I., 149.
Lechlade, Gloucestershire, I., 205.

Leckhampstead (Lackhampsted, Lackhamsted), I., 52; II., 3,* 32, 142.*
Leek, Staffordshire, II., 182.
Leicester, II., 187.
Leigh (Le), Somerset, I., 9.
Leigh Farm near Lambourn, I., 89.
Leith, Scotland, I., 320.
Letcombe. I., 35, 36,* 91,* 98, 100,* 159, 311; II., 50.
Letcombe Basset, I., 296; II., 3,* 27.
Letcombe Regis, I., 21,* 62, 142,* 143, 204, 205, 215,* 306, 315; II., 27, 98,* 222, 230.*
Letherhead, Surrey, II., 98.
Leverton, I., 29.
Lewes, Sussex, I., 255; II., 188.
Lewknor (Lewkner), Oxon, I., 165, 309; II., 175.
Lewton, II., 203.*
Liddington, Wilts, I., 210; II., 131.
Liddingtonwick, Wilts, I., 302.
Lilleshall (Lilshull), Salop. II., 78.
Lillingstone Dayrell (Darrell), Bucks, I., 77; II., 78, 153, 208, 209.
Lincoln (Lincon), II., 141.*
Linstead (Linstede), Suffolk, I., 145, 314.
Linton (Lynton), Kent, I., 149.
Liss, Hants, II., 40.
Littlecote (Lyttlecott), Wilts, I., 3, 23, 25, 82*; II., 125.
Littleworth (Litleworth), II., 25.
Llanarth Court, Monmouthshire, I., 259.
Llanfoist, Monmouthshire, I., 291.
Llanfrynach, Glamorganshire, I., 309.
Llantrithyd, Glamorganshire, I., 291.
Llanvaches. Monmouthshire, I., 274.*
Lockinge, I., 49, 73, 187, 206, 235, 283, 284, 285; II., 1, 5, 161,* 162.*
Lockinge, East, I., 235.* 236; II., 3,* 20.
Lockinge, West, I., 17, 50; II., 20, 163.
Loddington (Lodington), Northants, II., 170.
London, I., 3, 8, 16, 20,* 27, 44.* 54, 56, 58, 60, 61, 65. 70, 74, 78,* 79, 86, 87,* 91,* 93,* 95,* 96, 101,* 102, 103, 106, 109, 110, 113,* 121, 130, 131,* 132, 134, 135,* 137,* 140, 141, 142, 145,* 147,* 148,* 149, 157, 159, 160,* 161, 163,* 168, 171,* 175, 176,* 182, 183, 188, 189,* 190, 191, 192, 193, 198,* 199,* 200, 206, 209, 217, 219,* 221,* 226, 227, 229,* 231, 232,* 234, 235,* 239, 240,* 241,* 242, 243, 247, 248, 251,* 252,* 253,* 254, 255, 256, 257, 258, 260,* 262,* 263,* 266.* 269, 272, 273, 278,* 279, 282,* 283, 288,* 291, 300,* 309, 311, 314, 316, 317, 320; II., 11,* 16, 17, 18,* 20, 22, 28, 29, 30,* 31, 33, 35,* 36,* 38,* 39, 40, 42,* 43, 44, 45,* 46,* 47,* 50,* 52, 55, 56 n., 57,* 58.* 59, 60, 62, 70, 71, 72,* 73,* 78, 79,* 84, 85,* 87,* 88,* 97, 101,* 102, 111, 117. 118, 122, 125, 128,* 129,* 131, 133, 134,* 136,* 139, 141,* 142,* 143, 147,* 148, 149,* 150, 152,* 159,* 163,* 170, 176,* 181, 182, 183, 185,* 187, 192, 193, 196,* 197,* 198, 199. 200,* 201,* 209,* 210,* 211,* 212,* 214,* 215,* 217. 219, 223, 225,* 226,* 227,* 233.
London, Aldermary, II., 137.
  Aldersgate Street, I., 300.
  Aldgate, II., 159.
  Billingsgate, I., 65.
  Bow Lane, Aldermary, II., 137.
  Brick Court, Middle Temple, II., 45.
  Broad Street Ward, II., 226.
  Castle Baynard Ward, II., 117.
  Chapel Royal, II., 71, 135.
  Clement's Inn, I., 52, 53.

INDEX LOCORUM. 269

London—*continued*.
Clerkenwell, II., 46, 70.
Cordwainer's Ward, II., 193.
Covent Garden, I., 227.
Cripplegate Within, Ward of, II., 142.
Cripplegate Without, Ward of, II., 134.
Eastcheap, II , 191.
Farringdon Without. Ward of, II., 85, 135.
Friday Street Church, II., 211.
Gray's Inn, I., 139, 180, 205, 234. 262, 272 ; II., 47, 158.
Hall Court, II., 147.
Hatton Gardens, II., 21.
Holborn Conduit, II., 28.
Holborn, The Black Swan, II., 35.
Inner Temple, I., 53, 189, 208, 232, 245, 246, 252, 266 ; II., 111, 153.
Langborne Ward, II.. 159.
Lincoln's Inn, I., 52, 53, 135, 206 ; II., 37, 38. 44, 62, 84, 117, 118, 170.
Middle Temple, I., 28, 52, 71, 106, 178, 208, 235, 307 ; II., 45, 46, 65, 92, 110, 147, 148, 162, 165,* 169, 178, 194, 208, 213, 220, 231.
New Fish Street, I., 9.
New Inne, I., 30.
St. Andrew, Holborn, II., 154.
St. Andrew Undershaft. II , 159.
St. Botolph, Bishopsgate, I., 65.
St. Clements Danes, I., 162.
St. Giles, Cripplegate, II., 209.
St. Giles in the Fields, I., 171.
St. John. Clerkenwell, I., 250.
St. Margaret, Lothbury, I., 91.
St. Martin in the Fields, I., 309.
St. Mary, Aldermanbury. II., 50.
St. Mary at Hill, II., 137.*
St. Michael, Cornhill, II., 192.
St. Paul's, I., 168.
St. Peter-le-Poer, II., 97.
St. Swithun, I., 262.
Salutacon Tavern, II., 44.
Sergeant's Inn, Fleet St., II., 152.
Shoe Lane, II., 44.
The Temple, I., 23 ; II , 37, 44.
The Tower, I., 250 ; II., 210.
Tower Hill, II.. 201.
Tower Street Ward, II., 142. 162.
Vintry Ward, II , 97.
White Friars, II.. 203.
Long Ashton, *see* Ashton.
Longcot, II., 26.
Longley, *see* Langley.
Longmore near Reading, I., 280.
Longstreet, Enford, Wilts, II., 164.
Longworth, I., 60, 61,* 149, 178 ; II., 21, 78, 127.
Loseley, Surrey, I., 245.
Lostock, Lancashire, I., 299.
Loughborough (Loughborow), Leicestershire, I., 176.
Louth, Lincolnshire, II., 171.
Lovedaye, Oxon, I.. 35, 37, 100.
Loveden, II., 172.*
Lovington (Lavington), Wilts, I., 278.
Lowbrooks, I., 40 n.
Ludstone, Salop. II., 159.
Lukeley, II., 189.
Lupton, Devon, II., 176.
Lutterworth, Leicestershire, II., 88.
Lydd (Lidd), Kent, I., 291.*

Lydiard Millicent (Lidiard Millisent), Wilts, I., 73, 190.
Lydiard-Tregoz (Lydyarde-Tregose), Wilts, I., 47, 48, 125.
Lyford, I., 26, 33. 34, 35, 38, 39, 43, 60,* 61, 62, 67.* 71, 88, 89. 90, 100, 105,* 121, 122. 148,* 158.* 159,* 201,* 202, 226, 292, 319 ; II., 18,* 20, 82, 83, 150,* 160.* 196, 224.*
Lynn Regis, *see* King's Lynn.
Lytcott, Bucks, II., 175.*

M

Mablethorpe. Lincolnshire, II., 141.
Mackney, I., 112.*
Maddington (Madington), Wilts, I., 135.*
Madeley, Staffordshire, II., 176.
Madenburgh, I., 137.
Maidenhead (Maydenhead), I.. 15.* 32, 39. 64,* 101, 139, 220 ; II., I. 7, 40, 43,* 45, 65, 148,* 174, 192, 231.
Maidenhead. The Sign of the Bear, II., 9.
Maidstone, Kent, I., 205, 253.
Malmesbury, Wilts, I., 27.
Malpas, Northants, II., 85.
Malsanger (Waltsanger), Hants, I., 45.
Malston, Berks, II., 83.
Mansell, Somerset, I., 195.
Mantua, Italy, I., 79.
Manydowne, Hants, I., 264.
Mapledurham (Maple Dereham), Oxon, I., 52,* 76, 242 ; II., 123.
Marcham (Marsham), I., 60, 120, 121, 123, 142, 148, 157,* 260,* 272* ; II., 1, 2, 5, 17, 18, 27, 200.*
Marlborough (Marlborow), Wilts, I., 24, 35, 50, 85, 95, 138,* 204, 217, 227, 283, 286 ; II., 29.
Marleston (Marlstone), I., 308, 309 ; II., 4, 31.
Marlow (Merlow, Merelow), Bucks, I., 20, 160,* 228 ; II., 119. 150.
Marlow, Great, Bucks, II., 85.
Marlow, Little, Bucks, I., 133.
Marshwood (Marswoode). Dorset, I., 37.
Marston. Oxon, I., 51, 272.
Marston. South, Wilts, I., 212.
Martin. Norfolk, ? Lincolnshire, I., 218.
Marylebone (Maribone), Middlesex, I., 298.
Mattingley, Isle of Wight, II., 114.*
Maudesley (Mawdisley), Lancashire, I., 114,* 115.
Maydencote (Maydencotte), I., 8, 27, 29.*
Maydenhatche, I.. 32,* 33.*
Mayfield, Sussex, I., 250.
Meare (Meere), Wilts, I., 166.*
Medbury, Bedfordshire, I., 179.
Medmenham (Meidenham) Abbey, Bucks, I., 78.
Meend, The, Herefordshire, I., 270.
Melbury (Milbury), Dorset, I., 291.
Melksham (Mellisham), Wilts, II., 82.
Melton Mowbray, Leicestershire, II., 119.
Membris, II., 29.
Merton, Derbyshire, I., 114.
Merton, Oxon, I., 133,* 293.
Meux, Yorkshire, I., 65.*
Michel-Troy, Monmouthshire, II., 153.
Mickleton, Gloucestershire, I., 207.*
Midgham (Midgiam, Mygham), I., 56, 186, 212, 213,* 218, 264, 297 ; II., 31.
Milstead (Milsted), Kent, II., 103.
Milton, Berks, I., 77*; II., 17, 90,* 91.

Milton, Northants, I., 101.
Milton, Wilts, I., 32, 95,* 217.
Milton, Great, Oxon, I., 155 ; II., 50.
Minster Lovell, Oxon, I., 257 ; II., 222.
Missenden (Musindon), Bucks, I., 121.
Missenden, Great, Bucks, I., 228, 240.
Missenden, Little, Bucks, I., 228.
Mobberley (Modburley), Cheshire, I., 33*; II., 77.*
Moccas (Mookas), Herefordshire, I., 262.
Moche Stoughton, *see* Stoughton.
Molesey (Moulsey), I., 320 ; II., 176.
Mongewell (Mungwell, Mundswell, Monjoywell), Oxon, I., 34, 126, 157, 157 n., 280 ; II., 5.
Monktonmill (Mouncton Myll), I., 49, 123.
Monmouth, I., 265.
Monnington's Court, Herefordshire, I., 308.
Montacute (Montague), Somerset, I., 270.
Montrell in Picardy, II., 104.
Morecourt, Hants, II., 128 n., 129, 130.*
Moreton (Morton), Hundred of, I., 156, 201, 209, 243, 265 ; II., 5, 8,* 13, 14, 15, 16.
Moreton, Bucks, II., 129, 130.
Moreton, North, II., 2, 14.
Moreton, South, I., 230, 264, 265*; II., 2, 14.
Moreton-Say (Mortensey), Salop, II., 77.
Morgan, Glamorganshire, I., 299.
Mostyn (Moston), Wales, II., 227.
Mote, ye, Sussex, II., 105.
Moulsford (Mowlsforde, Molsford), I., 51, 52, 125, 126,* 134, 276, 293 ; II., 4, 15, 216.*
Moulton, II., 75.
Mountain Up Wimborne, Dorset, I., 277.

Napton-on-the-Hill, Warwickshire, I., 53.
Nash, Kent, I., 225, 317.
Nazaret, Spain, II., 75.
Nazing, Essex, II., 132.
Neates Hall, Isle of Sheppy, II., 128.
Nethercoat, Oxon, I., 219.
Netherhaven, Wilts, I., 80.
Nettlestead, Suffolk, II., 104.
Newark in Gloucester, I., 185, 261.
Newbottle, Northamptonshire, I., 121.
Newbury, Hundred of, II., 9.
Newbury (Newbery, Newberie), I., 24, 42,* 51, 64, 80,* 85, 86,* 118, 151,* 165, 179, 193, 209, 210, 211,* 221,* 230,* 248,* 278, 313 ; II., 3,* 6,* 8, 18, 28,* 29,* 30, 31, 35, 63,* 120,* 131,* 165,* 166, 196, 205,* 232,* 233.*
Newbury, Sign of the Mairemaid, II., 9.
Newcastle-on-Tyne, I., 256 ; II., 226, 235.
Newington, Oxon, I., 65.
Newland, II., 39.
Newnham Murren (Morrin), Oxon, I., 51, 52, 53, 121.*
Norbury, Cheshire, I., 34 ; II., 41, 159.
Norbury, Surrey, II., 217.
Norcot (Norcott), I., 98, 233 II., 11.
Northampton, II., 88.*
Northleigh (Northly, Norleigh), Oxon, I., 243 ; II., 193, 194.*
Northwood, Isle of Wight, II., 71.
Norton, Cheshire. I., 250.
Norton, Cornwall, I., 180.
Norton, Herts, II., 84,* 87.

Norton Bavante, Wilts, I., 43.
Norwey, Gloucestershire, I., 232.
Norwich, I., 78 ; II., 71.
Nottingham, I., 206 ; II., 195.*
Nuffield, Oxon, II., 81.

O

Ockeley, East, in Bray, II., 44.*
Oddington (Odington), Gloucestershire, II., 162.
Odiham (Odyham), Hants, I., 43.
Odson, II., 25.
Offeley, Hunts, I., 46, 251.
Ogbourne (Ogborn). Wilts, I., 231 ; II., 156.
Oke (Ocke, Ock), Hundred of, I., 197, 239, 260, 271, 279, 280, 285, 306, 315 ; II., 5, 8, 9, 16, 17, 18, 187.
Okemarch (Oakmarch) in Chaddleworth, I., 247, 261.*
Okingham, *see* Wokingham.
Olantigh (Olentigh), Kent. II., 104.
Onslow, Salop, I., 227.
Ordeston, II., 104.
Ormethorpe, II., 229.
Orpington (Arpington), Kent, II., 171.*
Orsett, Essex, II., 142.
Orston, St. George, Wilts, II., 69.
Orton, I., 296.
Ostenhanger, Kent, I., 250.
Otford (Oatford), Kent, I., 204.
Overton, Hants. I., 52 ; II., 54.
Oving, Bucks, II., 88.
Oxenwood, Wilts, I., 214, 291.
Oxford, I., 61, 114, 120, 136, 157, 200, 224, 246 ; II., 11,* 16, 23, 112, 131, 152,* 153,* 185, 194, 223.
Oxford, All Souls' Coll., I., 157 ; II., 152.
  Christ Church, II., 168, 198.*
  Magdalen Coll.. I.. 80, 132 ; II., 81, 92, 168.
  Magdalen Hall. II., 33, 229.*
  Merton Coll., II., 229.
  New Coll., II., 63.
  Oriel Coll., I., 135, 180 ; II., 194.
  Pembroke Coll., II., 167, 197.
  St. John's Coll., I., 140 ; II., 194.
  St. Mary's Hall, II., 194.
  Trinity College, I., 230.

Padua, I., 157.
Padworth, II., 37, 72, 84.*
Pangbourne (Pangborne), I., 36,* 73, 139, 191, 264 ; II., 34, 158.*
Paris, I., 318 ; II., 223.
Parndon, Great (Parenden Magna), Essex, II., 210.
Parson's Green, Middlesex, II., 71.
Patrixbourne (Patricsbourne), Kent, II., 102.*
Paulton (Powlton), Wilts, I., 138.
Peakirk, Northants, II., 51.
Peasemore (Pesemere, Pessmore), I., 53, 72, 244,* 289, 290* ; II., 32, 88, 173.*
Peasmarsh, Sussex, I., 291.
Pebworth, Gloucestershire, II., 104.
Peckham, Little, Kent, I., 124, 132* ; II., 205, 217, 218.*
Peckleton, Leicestershire, I., 136.
Pedell, *see* Piddle.

INDEX LOCORUM.   271

Pembridge, Herefordshire, I., 300.
Pengethley (Pengeshley), Herefordshire, I., 132.
Penistone (Penison), Yorks, I., 248.
Penlline (Penllyne), Glamorganshire, I., 299.
Penn (Pen), Bucks, I., 275.*
Penshurst, Kent, II., 65.
Penwartham, Lancashire, I., 268.
Peover, Cheshire, I., 245.
Perchley, Northants, II., 79.
Pertwood. Wilts, I., 166.
Peterlee, Bucks, I., 202.
Petherton, North (Northfetherton), Somerset, I., 195.
Philberds Manor in Bray, II., 55.
Picardy, II., 66.
Picthorne, I., 106.
Piddle (Pedell), Dorset, I , 9.
Piedmont, Italy, II., 91, 92, 93, 94, 96.
Pinner, Herts, I., 180.
Pipe (Pype), Lancashire, I., 4 ; II., 105.
Plymouth, Devon, II., 197.
Pocklington, Yorks, I., 281.
Poffley, see Poughley.
Poltimore (Poultemore), Devon, II., 63.
Pontefract (Pomfret), Yorkshire, II., 80.
Ponton, Little, Lincolnshire, II., 219.
Popham, Farington, see Farington Popham.
Popham, Hants, I., 9, 192.
Portsea, Hants, I., 179.
Portsmouth, Hants, I., 179.
Portwood, Cheshire, I., 49.
Poston, Herefordshire, II., 168.
Poswick, Yorks, I., 57.
Potterspury Park, Northants, II., 214.
Poughley (Poughefely, Paufley, Poffley), I., 156 ; II., 27, 174.
Prestbury, Gloucestershire, I., 159, 306.
Presthawes (Presthause), Sussex, I., 89, 201, 202.
Preston, Kent, II., 170.
Preston, Sussex, II., 125.
Preston Crowmarsh, see Crowmarsh.
Priesthill, I., 251.*
Prior's Hold (Pryor's Hold) in Wantage, I., 143, 144 ; II., 19.
Priour's Court, I., 52.
Pryory, II., 15.
Pumney, II., 11, 202,* 203.
Purley, I., 249 ; II., 1, 26, 27, 37.
Purton (Pirton), Wilts, I., 125.
Pusey (Pyssey), I., 25, 29, 49,* 60, 91,* 123,* 149, 196,* 261, 268, 269,* 315 ; II., 21,* 125, 200.
Putney, Surrey, I., 253.*

Q

Quarley (Quarle). Hants, I., 196, 212.
Quarrendon (Quaringdon, Quadrington), Bucks, I , 106.*
Queen Camel, Somerset, I., 214.

R

Radbourne, see Rodbourne.
Radley (Radney), I., 132,* 238 ; II., 11, 202, 216,* 217,* 218.
Reading, I., 12, 13, 14,* 16,* 18,* 19, 20,* 25, 39, 43, 52, 53, 54,* 56,* 56 n., 60, 64, 71, 95,* 101, 102,* 103.* 108, 131, 136,* 140, 142, 149, 152,* 155, 157, 173, 174,* 175,* 176,* 178, 189,* 208, 216, 217,* 229. 230,* 231,* 237,* 244, 246,* 264, 279. 280, 287,* 288, 301, 303,* 312, 320 ; II.. 1, 2,* 3.* 4,* 5,* 6, 7, 8 n., 19, 23,* 25, 26,* 27,* 28,* 29,* 30,* 31,* 32,* 33, 34, 35,* 36,* 37,* 38,* 39.* 40, 41,* 42,* 43,* 44, 45,* 46,* 47,* 50,* 52, 54, 66, 70, 72, 73,* 80, 87,* 99, 101. 111, 139,* 141, 142, 144,* 146,* 158,* 160,* 173, 185, 193, 195,* 196, 220.
Reading. Abbey of, I , 1.
The Bear, II., 111, 154, 225.
Hundred of, I., 191, 220, 221, 229, 237, 245, 276, 281, 313, 320 ; II., 5, 8,* 9, 32, 33, 34, 35, 36.
St. Giles, II., 34.*
St. Lawrence, II., 33, 166.*
St. Mary. II., 33, 70, 71.
The Upper Ship. II., 9, 163, 173.
Redish, Lancashire, I , 49.*
Reedly, I., 6.
Reigate, Surrey, II., 6.
Remenham (Remnham, Remnam), I., 105, 110,* 275* ; II., 40, 44, 117, 119, 177,* 178, 193.*
Richmond, Surrey, I., 251 ; II., 80.
Ridge (Rudge), Staffordshire, I., 39, 101.
Ripplesmore (Ripplesmere), Hundred of, I., 222, 223, 226, 296, 300 ; II., 5, 8, 9, 45, 46, 47.
Risley, Derbyshire, I., 268.
Rodbourne Cheney (Radborne Cheyney), Wilts, I., 125,* 281 ; II., 234.
Rodbroke, II., 175.
Rodwell, Yorks, I., 128.
Rootham, Kent, I., 175.
Rossall (Rossale), Salop, I., 145. 147 ; II., 122.
Rotherby, Leicestershire, II., 202.
Rotherfield, I.. 142.
Rotherfield, Oxon, I., 103.
Rotherfield, Sussex, II., 228.*
Rotherham (Rotheram), Yorks, II.. 228.
Rotherhithe (Redriff), Surrey, I., 162.
Rougham, Norfolk, I., 96.
Roundwood House. II., 37.
Rowley, Lancashire, ? Yorks, II., 135,* 136.
Ruddington (Rodington), Notts., I., 15.*
Rudge, see Ridge.
Ruscombe (Rushcombe), I., 155* ; II., 4,* 39,* 50,* 62, 86, 166, 174, 175,* 176, 185.
Rushdeanes, II., 172, 173.*
Russall, Norfolk, I., 78.
Ruxford, Devon, I., 188.
Rycote (Rycott), II., 186.*
Rye, Sussex, I., 255* ; II., 188.*

S

Saddington (Sadington), Worcestershire, I., 200.
St. Alban's, Herts, I., 320.*
St. Andrew's, Middlesex, II., 154.
St. Buryan (Buriam), Cornwall, I., 252.
St. Columb (St. Cullombe), Cornwall, II., 161, 163.
St. Dennis, Hampshire, II., 166.
St. Enoder (Enedor), Cornwall, II., 161.
St. Ervan (Ervin), Cornwall, II., 161.
St. Faith's, Norfolk, II., 169.
St. Margarett's, Wilts, I., 35, 142, 283.
Salisbury (Salysburye), Wilts, I., 39, 230, 233, 248 ; II., 92, 165.

Sandall, Hants, I., 100.
Sandenfee, II., 29.
Sanderstead, Surrey, II., 52.
Sandford, Berks,*II., 11.
Sandford, Oxon, I., 25 ; II., 125.
Sandhurst, I., 165 ; II., 39.
Sandleford, I.. 128 ; II., 30.
Sapperton (Saberton), Gloucestershire, I., 204.
Satwell (Sotwell), II., 15.
Sawlowferrye, Derbyshire, I., 18.*
Scarletts, near Wargrave, I., 129.*
Scotney (Scoteney), Sussex, I., 9.
Scotney Castle. Sussex. II., 219.
Scotter, Lincolnshire, I.. 257.
Sea Court, II., 12.
Seale, Leicestershire, I., 273.
Seas. Surrey. I., 245.
Semington (Sennington), Wilts, I., 180.
Sene, *see* Cerne.
Sevenhampton (Stevenhampton), Wilts, I., 41, 60, 108, 148, 302.
Severn-Stoke, Worcestershire, II.. 182.
Shabbington (Shabington), Bucks, I., 293.
Shacklewell (Shaclewell). Middlesex, II., 182.
Shadlestone (Shadeston), Bucks, I., 267.
Shaftesbroke. I., 139.
Shaftesbury, Dorset. I., 291.
Shalbourne (Shaborne, Shawborne), I., 114, 187, 297* ; II., 3,* 29.*
Shalford. I., 146.
Shalstone (Shaldeston, Shalsone), Bucks, I., 28, 268 ; II., 116.
Shaw, I., 86,* 173, 190,* 193* ; II., 31, 70, 71.
Shefford (Sheford, Shifford), I., 3, 76,* 82, 90, 218.
Shefford, Great or West, I., 218 ; II., 3, 4. 25, 26.
Shefford Parva or East, I., 28,* 60 ; II., 26, 70, 127.*
Shellers, Isle of Wight, II., 128.
Shelleswell, Oxon, II., 116.
Shellingford, I., 254* ; II., 3, 21, 188.
Shepton Mallet, Somerset, I., 242.
Sherborne, Gloucestershire, I., 295.
Sherfield (Shirvilde, Shurford), Hants, I., 35, 45, 93, 100.
Sherland, Isle of Sheppey, II., 102, 103,* 104.*
Shersforde, I., 61.
Shilton (Shulton), Oxon, I., 45, 60, 149 ; II., 22, 155.
Shinfield (Chinfield, Shenfield, Shynfelde, Shynyngfelde), I., 3, 18, 19,* 35, 44,* 93, 95, 100, 146, 164, 176, 214, 215,* 217, 231, 232,* 252,* 315,* 316* ; II., 4,* 38, 41, 64, 82, 123, 205.
Shipbrook (Shipbroke), Cheshire, II., 75.
Shiplake (Shipplacke), Oxon, I., 40 ; II., 122.
Shippon, I., 178 ; II., 11.*
Shipton, Oxon, I., 26, 119, 178, 272 ; II., 116.
Shirburn (Shirborne), Oxon, I., 80.*
Shobington (Shobingston), Bucks, I., 133.*
Shobrooke (Shoebrook), Devon, I., 188.
Sholey (Sholeby, Shoulby), Leicestershire, I., 200 ; II., 123.
Shoreham, Kent, II., 170.
Shotover, Oxon, I., 228.
Shottesbrooke (Shatsbroke), I., 46,* 139, 140, 223, 265,* 287, 303, 304* ; II., 40.*
Shrewsbury, I., 39, 101.
Shrewton (Shruton), Wilts, I., 135.
Shrivenham (Shryveham, Shrevenham), I., 48,* 60, 122,* 149, 216, 227, 231, 277 ; II., 4, 25. 167,* 196.*
Shrivenham, Hundred of, I., 189, 204, 205, 226, 233, 238, 242, 266, 267, 277, 281 ; II., 5, 8, 9, 24, 25, 26, 41.
Siddington Langley (Syddington), Gloucestershire, I., 28.
Silchester (Sylchester), Hants. I., 37, 38.
Silemstede, I., 9 ; *see also* Sulhampstead.
Singley Rayles (Simley Rayles), II., 46.
Sinsham Green, II., 39.
Sintcley, Worcestershire, I., 317.
Sissinghurst, Kent, I.. 149, 318.
Sittingbourne, Kent, II., 103.
Skeres, Hants, I., 24, 85.
Slaugham (Shaugham), Sussex, I., 28, 204 ; II., 130.
Smarden, Kent, I., 36.
Sodbury (Soddbury), Gloucestershire, I., 254.
Somerford, Wilts, I.. 283.
Somerton, Oxon, II.. 215.
Sonning (Sonnynge, Sunning, Sunnyng), I., 2, 16, 71, 78,* 84, 109,* 125, 126, 145. 163,* 164,* 165, 173, 182, 200,* 223. 230, 243, 253, 273,* 276,* 307 ; II., 4, 5, 39, 64,* 135,* 136,* 154,* 175,* 219.*
Sonning, Hundred of, I., 173, 176, 181, 182, 188, 224, 253. 255, 273 ; II., 5, 8,* 38, 39, 40. 154.
Sotwell, II., 15.
Soulbury (Soulbery, Sulbury), Bucks, I., 58, 255 ; II., 188.
Southampton, I., 95, 254, 314.
Southampton, St. Denys, II., 166.*
Southcott (Southcoat. Suthcot), I., 173, 174,* 214, 291 ; II., 5. 36, 39, 71,* 72,* 84, 220.*
Southwark, II., 170, 182, 225.
Southwark, St. George, II., 170.
Sparham, ? Norfolk, I.. 78.
Sparsholt (Spersholt), I., 48,* 51, 52, 60 n. ; II., 1, 3, 19, 22. 82, 140.
Sparsholts Court, I., 186, 196, 306, 314, 315 ; II., 20.
Sparsole (Sparsall), I., 9, 80 ; *see also* Sparsholt.
Speen (Church Speene, Spine), I., 79 ; II., 29, 79, 91. 92,* 94.
Speenhamland, I., 289, 290 ; II., 31.
Speke (Speake), Lancashire, II., 184.*
Staaksley, *see* Stokesley.
Staines (Stanes), Middlesex, I., 38, 46 ; II., 47.
Stainswick (Staneswick), I., 238* ; II., 167.*
Stamersham (Stammerham), Sussex, II., 166.
Stamford (Staumford), Northants, I., 46,* 217, 251.*
Stanclere, Wilts, I., 127.*
Standen. I., 127, 187.
Standen Hussey, Wilts, I., 28, 210 ; II., 131.
Standewick, II., 107.
Standish, Lancashire, I., 53.
Standlake (Stanlake, Sunlake), Oxon, I., 34, 60, 148 ; II., 18, 138.
Stanford (Stanforde), I., 62,* 96, 103,* 283, 314 ; II., 3, 10, 20, 21.
Stanford Dingley, I., 208, 244 ; II., 30, 39, 173.
Stanford in the Vale, I., 236, 284.*
Stanford-le-Hope, Essex, II., 101.*
Stansfield, Suffolk, I., 305.
Stanton Harcourt, Oxon, I., 9, 10 ; II., 125.
Stanwardine, I.. 146.*
Stanway, Gloucestershire, I., 295.
Stanwell, Middlesex, I., 312.
Stapleford, Wilts, I., 292.
Staunton Harold, Leicestershire, II.. 222.
Staverton, I., 40,* 107,* 108, 130* ; II., 74.
Staverton, Devon, Kingston House, II., 156,

INDEX LOCORUM. 273

Stepney (Stepboneheathe), Middlesex, I., 24; II., 125, 209.*
Sterley, Notts., I., 320.
Stevenage (Stevenache), Herts, I., 51.
Stevenhampton, *see* Sevenhampton.
Steventon, I., 51, 81, 126,* 144, 145,* 148, 185, 187, 215, 224, 227, 279,* 280,* 283,* 314*; II., 1, 16, 71.
Stipe, Wilts, II., 9.
Stoke, Bucks, I., 273*; II., 214.
Stoke, Wilts, I., 60, 148.
Stoke Bery, Herefordshire, I., 70.
Stoke, Little, Oxon, I., 225, 313; II., 23, 162.
Stoke-Lyne, Oxon, II., 224.
Stoke Mandeville, Bucks, II., 56.*
Stoke, South, Oxon, I., 316; II., 83.
Stoke Talmage (Falmage), Oxon, I., 164.
Stokenchurch (Stokin Churche), Oxon, I., 11, 293*; II., 221.
Stokes Farme, near Okingham, I., 276.
Stokesley (Staaksley, Stoaksley), Yorks, I., 166; II., 63.
Ston Easton (Stony Aston), Somerset, I., 117.
Stone, Kent, II., 65.
Stone, Staffordshire, I., 195.
Stonehow (? Stannow), Norfolk, I., 78.
Stoner, Oxon, I., 29.
Stoughton (Moche Stoughton), Hunts, ? Leicestershire, II., 168.
Stourbridge (Sturbridg), Worcestershire, I., 303.
Stowe, Bucks, I., 81; II., 170.
Stowe, Oxon, I., 185.
Stowmarket, Suffolk, I., 209.
Strand in Bray, II., 44.
Stratfield Mortimer, I., 20,* 258; II., 37, 45.
Stratfieldsaye (Stratfield Sey), Hants, I., 220; II., 140.
Stratford Bow, I., 137.
Stratford, Herts, I., 44.
Stratton, Salop, I., 45.
Stratton, St. Margaret, Wilts, I., 236.*
Streatley (Stretley), I., 16,* 67, 88, 89, 140, 156,* 157,* 158, 201,* 202, 272, 304; II., 5, 15, 24, 35,* 199.
Strensham, Worcestershire, I., 11; II., 222.
Strodehall, I., 130.*
Stroud in Bray, I., 312; II., 12.
Stroud Green, Middlesex, II., 118.
Studley, Oxon, II., 116.
Studley (Stodley), Wilts, I., 277.
Sulham, II., 36, 158.
Sulhampstead Banister (Sullamsted Banister), I., 9; II., 3, 37, 180, 181.*
Sunlake, *see* Standlake.
Sunninghill (Sonninghill), II., 42, 117, 119.
Sunninghill Park, II., 117,* 120.
Sunningwell, I., 167, 168; II., 11, 39, 66, 152.*
Surat, East Indies, I., 251.
Suston, Herefordshire, I., 52.
Sutton, I., 51, 60, 133, 146, 148, 218; II., 82, 234.*
Sutton, Somerset, I., 22, 185.
Sutton Courtney, I., 33, 34,* 120,* 241, 315,* 316, 317; II., 17.
Sutton, East, I., 168.
Sutton Wick, II., 17.
Swalcliffe (Sway Cliffe), Oxon, II., 228.*
Swallowfield, I., 159, 160, 313; II., 41, 64, 72, 158, 175.

VOL. II.

Swansea (Swansey), Glamorganshire, I., 299.
Swinbrook (Swinbroke), Oxon, I., 91, 206; II., 19, 127.
Swindon, Wilts, I., 212, 237.*
Swinford in Cumnor, II., 2, 12.
Swyncombe (Swincombe, Swancombe), Oxon, I., 194, 315.
Sydmonton (Sidmonton), Hants, I., 208.
Syon, I., 28, 60, 149.

T

Tame, *see* Thame.
Tamworth, Warwickshire, I., 100, 233.
Tamworth Castle, I., 233.
Tandridge (Tanridge), Surrey, I., 162; II., 77, 219.
Tandridge Court, II., 77.
Tangley, Hants, I., 302*; II., 38.
Taplow, Bucks, I., 165; II., 64.
Taplow (Toplow) Court, II., 126.
Tedbury, Worcestershire, I., 263.
Tedworth, *see* Tidworth.
Tenterden, ? Kent, II., 60.
Tenterden, Wales, II., 140.
Tetsworth, Oxon, II., 161, 175.
Tetworthe, Hunts, II., 23.
Tew, Oxon, I., 227.*
Tew, Somerset, I., 266.
Thame, Oxon, I., 58, 99, 284, 287,* 309; II., 105, 186.
Thanington, Kent, I., 218.
Thatcham, I., 127, 128, 221,* 281*; II., 4,* 35, 128 s., 129,* 165, 233.
Theale (Theald), Hundred of, I., 174, 208, 252, 258, 259, 263, 264, 288, 316; II., 5, 8, 9, 34,* 36, 37, 38, 84, 220.
Thistleworth (Thestleworth), Middlesex, I., 58, 257.
Thoby, Leicestershire, II., 88.
Thorneton, Warwickshire, I., 193.
Thornham, Suffolk, I., 144, 314.
Thornhambye, Yorks, I., 46.
Thorpe juxta Norwich, I., 78.
Thorpe, Surrey, II., 74.
Thorpe Mandeville (Mandeyvill), Northants, I., 88.
Throppe (Thrup, Thrupp), Berks, I., 49, 123, 242; II., 11, 25, 202.
Thrup, Oxon, II., 162.
Thurleigh (Thurley, Thirley), Bedfordshire, I., 58; II., 105.
Thurleston, Leicestershire, I., 95, 218; II., 176.
Tichborne, Hants, I., 150.
Tickleford (Fideford), Dorset, I., 191.
Tidmarsh (Tidmersh), I., 34, 146, 315*; II., 35, 36, 205.
Tidworth (Tydworth), Wilts, I., 138, 248.
Tilehurst (Tylehurst), I., 72, 73,* 126, 137,* 217, 320*; II., 34.*
Titon (Teton, Tilton), Northants, I., 89, 201.
Tortworth, Gloucestershire, I., 68.
Totforde, Hants, I., 34.
Tuttenham Court (Totnam), Middlesex, I., 186; II., 49, 98.
Touchen End (Tutchin) in Bray, II., 44.
Tretower (Tretowr), Breconshire, I., 274.
Treworgan, Herefordshire, I., 280.
Tring (Trenge), Herts, II., 56.
Trowbridge, ? Wilts, II., 205.

N N

Trunkwood (Trunkwall), I., 252*; II., 41.
Truro, Cornwall, I., 288.
Tubney, II., 18.
Tuddington, Bedfordshire, ? Middlesex, II., 104.*
Tunbridge, Kent, II., 227.
Turin (Thurin), Italy, II., 91.
Turnors Court, Oxon, I., 51.
Turvey, Bedfordshire, I., 28.
Twickenham (Twyknam), Middlesex, I., 15.
Twyford, Berks, II., 86, 175.*
Twyford, Hants, II., 182.
Tygehall in East Meon, Hants, I., 55.
Typpinge Hall, Lancashire, I., 133.
Tysoe, Warwickshire, I., 309.

U

Uckfield, ? Sussex, I., 20.*
Udlington, ? Uffington, Salop, II., 122.
Uffington (Uffinton), I., 21,* 45, 158; II., 26, 204.*
Ufton (Uffton), I., 89, 118, 119,* 192, 201, 245, 258, 259,* 292; II., 37.
Ufton Court, I., 259, 313.
Upavon (Uphaven), Wilts, II., 105.
Upham, Wilts, I., 60,* 61, 148, 149, 319; II., 234.*
Upleadon (Upladen), Gloucestershire, I., 212.
Uppenham, Wilts, I., 38, 39.
Upsall, II., 181.
Upton, I., 50, 104,* 105,* 227, 279; II., 79.*
Up Wimborne, Dorset, I., 277.
Urshant, ? Urchfont, Wilts, I., 204.
Uswelborough, Hants, I., 162.
Uttoxeter (Utoxer), Staffordshire, I., 16; II., 70.
Uxbridge, Middlesex, I., 310; II., 229.
Uxmore, Oxon, I., 243.*

V

Virginia, I., 209; II., 81.
Vyne, The, Hants, I., 30.

W

Waddell, I., 1.
Waddesdon (Wadsden, Wadesden), Bucks, I., 121,* 180, 256.
Wadley (Wadeley), I., 11, 45, 55, 267,* 268; II., 5, 25, 129, 221,* 222.*
Wainfleet (Wainflete), Lincolnshire, I., 130 n.
Walcott (Wacott), Northants, I., 25*; II., 125.*
Walden St. Paul, Herts, I., 222.
Waldridge, Bucks, I., 139, 305.
Waldron (Walderne), Sussex, II., 65.*
Walford, Herefordshire, I., 270.
Wallingford, I., 52, 53, 64, 112,* 117,* 118,* 153, 154, 156, 170, 171, 179, 209,* 216, 254; II., 2,* 5, 6, 8,* 16, 21, 114,* 159,* 206.*
Wallingford Castle, II., 16.
Wallingford Priory, II., 55 n.
Wallop (Walley), Hants, I., 260.
Walsingham, Norfolk, II., 49.
Walston, I., 122.

Waltham, Forest of, Essex, II., 199.
Waltham, St. Lawrence, I., 46,* 69,* 223, 304, 310*; II., 42, 67, 174, 228, 229.
Waltham (Walton), White, I., 18, 40, 107, 176; II., 40, 131, 182.*
Walthamstow, Essex, II., 98, 142.
Walton Hall, near Nottingham, II., 195.
Walton on Thames, Surrey, I., 320.
Waltsanger, see Malsanger.
Wanborough (Wanborow), Wilts, I., 44, 126; II., 196.
Wandowne (Waundowne) Green, Middlesex, I., 24*; II., 125.*
Wandsworth, Surrey, I., 74, 179; II., 135.
Wanstrow, Somerset, I., 260.
Wantage (Wanting), I., 51,* 52, 53,* 62, 94, 99, 100, 115,* 123, 142, 143,* 147, 156,* 158, 168, 169, 180,* 183, 184,* 186, 214, 221, 230, 247, 269,* 269 n., 280, 290, 311, 314*; II., 11, 12, 16, 22,* 49,* 110, 158, 160, 198, 201,* 208,* 216.
Wantage, The sign of the Bear, II., 9, 198.
Wantage (Wanting), Hundred of, I., 157, 168, 183, 185, 187, 202, 207, 227, 235, 278,* 311, 314; II., 5, 8, 9, 19, 20.
Wapping, Middlesex, I., 221.
Warbleton, Sussex, II., 103.
Wardour Castle, Wilts. I., 317.
Warfield (Warveylde, Warvile), I., 58, 75, 130, 131,* 223, 250, 288, 312; II., 4, 41, 42, 146, 215; see also Heathly Hall.
Wargrave (Wargrove), I., 129,* 155, 274, 286, 287; II., 38, 39, 42, 50,* 158.*
Wargrave, Hundred of, I., 250, 274, 286, 310; II., 5, 8, 9, 41, 42.
Warley (Warly), Essex, I., 10, 26; II., 126.
Warley Place, Essex, I., 203.
Warnborough, South (Southwarmborw, Southwarnborrow), Hants, I., 161, 307, 308; II., 25, 38, 225.*
Warnell (Warwell), Cumberland, I., 301.
Warnford, Hants, II., 90.
Warnidge, Wilts, I., 238.
Wasing (Wazing), I., 54*; II., 31.
Watchfield, I., 189, 210; II., 25.
Watling Street, II., 78.
Watlington, Norfolk, I., 179, 191.
Watlington (Watleton), Oxon, I., 215.
Weadon, Bucks, II., 79.
Weldon, Northants, I., 266.
Welford, I., 234, 235*; II., 31, 32,* 159.*
Welhouse, I., 190,* 194,* 292; II., 31, 32, 42, 112.*
Wellington, Salop, I., 297.
Wells, Somerset, I., 180.
Wem, Salop, II., 77.*
Weobley (Webeley), Herefordshire, I., 16.
Werttesdon, II., 55.
Westbrooke (Westbroke), I., 319*; II., 29.
Westbury, Somerset, I., 22.*
Westbury, Wilts, I., 6.
Westleigh (Westley), Lancashire, II., 184.
Westminster, I., 162, 196, 254, 296; II., 11, 16, 119, 213.
Westminster, St. Margaret, II., 197.
Weston, II., 32.
Weston sub Edge, Gloucestershire, I., 149.
Weston Turville, Bucks, II., 56.*
Wethersfield, Essex, I., 286.
Wever, II., 29.
Wexham, Bucks, I., 310.

INDEX LOCORUM. 275

Whaddon, Bucks, I., 121.
Whaddon, Cambridgeshire, II., 142.
Whaddon, Wilts, I., 161, 162.
Whatcombe, II., 3, 27.
Wheatfield, Oxon, I., 133.
Whitchurch, Glamorganshire, I., 274.
Whitchurch, Oxon, I., 36, 229; II., 227.
Whitchurch, Salop, I., 34.
Whitechapel, Middlesex, II., 61.
Whitechurch, Dorset, I., 287, 288.
Whitehorse, Vale of the, I., 284.
Whiteknights (Whit-knights, Whyte knights), I., 2,* 25, 200*; II., 55, 123,* 205.
Whitelackington (White Lagenton), Somerset, I., 15, 270.
Whitfilde, Gloucestershire, I., 28.
Whitley, I., 164, 195,* 229, 230; II., 2, 12, 34.
Whitrigge (Whitrige), Cumberland, I., 159, 160*; II., 57, 58.
Whittington, Gloucestershire, I., 134.
Whittlebury (Whyttilburye), Northants, II., 214.
Whitwell, Rutlandshire, II., 88.
Wibtoft, Warwickshire, II., 88.
Wick, Wilts, I., 319.
Wickham, Suffolk, I., 74.
Wickhambreux, Kent, I., 76.*
Wickhambrook (Wickam Broke), Suffolk, I., 96.
Widdington Hall, Essex, I., 286.*
Wightham, II., 12; *see also* Wytham.
Wightwicke, Staffordshire, I., 308.*
Wike, II., 116.
Wildmore, ? Lincolnshire, II., 77.
Wilisill, Worcestershire, I., 11.
Willesden, Middlesex, I., 98.
Wilsons Green, Bucks, II., 48.
Wilye, Sussex, I., 250.
Wimbich, Essex, I., 286.
Wincanton, Somerset, II., 183.
Winchelsea (Winchelsey), Surrey, II., 103.
Winchendon (Winchinden, Winchingdon), Nether, Bucks, I., 81; II., 108.
Winchendon, Upper, I., 310; II., 229.
Winchester, I., 95, 183, 192, 226,* 227, 278, 317.
Winchester College, II., 63.
Windrush (Windredg, Windridge, Wynryche), Gloucestershire, I., 20, 105; II., 90.
Windsor (Wyndsore), I., 18, 40, 46, 64, 66,* 70,* 74,* 84,* 135, 166, 167, 195,* 199, 218, 226, 258, 262,* 291.* 298; II., 4. 6,* 8, 46, 47, 55, 113, 117, 134,* 135,* 138,* 139, 143,* 192, 207, 211,* 212, 214, 223.*
Windsor Castle, I., 218, 292, 301; II., 6, 179.
Windsor, Chapel of St. George, I., 135.
Windsor College, I., 2.
Windsor Forest, I., 223, 226, 292.
Windsor Great Park, I., 30.
Windsor, New, I., 14.* 154,* 155, 161,* 162,* 163,* 166, 170,* 178, 179,* 199,* 206,* 218,* 253,* 262,* 301,* 305,* 306, 317*; II., 46, 47, 55,* 61,* 81, 132,* 134, 135, 138, 139, 213.
Windsor, New, Hundred of, II., 9.
Windsor, Old, I., 111; II., 45, 48,* 179,* 192, 213,* 214.*
Windsor, The Three Tuns, II., 9, 51.
Wing, Bucks, I., 71.*
Wingfield, *see* Winkfield.
Winhurst in Hurst, II., 4, 39.

Winkfield (Wynkefelde, Wingfield), I., 57, 75,* 130,* 181, 222,* 255, 304, 312; II., 46, 47, 145,* 185.*
Winterborne, II., 31.
Winterbourne Stoke, Wilts, I., 166.
Wintershall (Wyntershull), Surrey, II., 234.
Wisbich, ? Wisbech, Cambridgeshire, I., 266.
Wistley, II., 40.
Witham (Wytham), I., 9; II.. 12, 115, 138.*
Withington, Gloucestershire, I., 47,* 48.
Witney (Whitney), Oxon, I., 21 n., 100, 307, 314.
Wittenham, Little (Wittnam, Witenham), I., 87,* 196,* 197*; II., 17.
Wittenham, Long (Longwittenham, Wittnam, Witenham), I., 37.* 51, 100; II., 1,* 4, 17.
Wokefield (Wookefield), I., 258*; II., 37.
Wokingham, (Ockingham, Ockyngham, Okeingham, Okingham), I., 25, 43,* 44, 60, 64, 75,* 79, 98, 99, 113,* 149, 164, 181,* 182,* 188,* 224, 225,* 255,* 256, 276, 287, 304. 307, 308; II., 2,* 4, 5, 38,* 46, 48,* 55, 62. 64,* 80,* 85,* 86,* 175, 188,* 189,* 190,* 225,* 226,* 227.
Wokingham (Okingham), Hundred of, II., 8.
Wolascot, Salop, I., 145, 146,* 147.
Wolfines (Wolly Fynes, Wolveley) in White Waltham, II., 182.*
Wolston, ? Bucks, II., 196.
Wolveley, *see* Wolfines.
Wolverde (Wolvert), Warwickshire, I., 35, 114.
Wonston (Wonton), Hants, II., 182.
Wooburne (Bishops Wooburne), Bucks, I., 21, 310; II., 229.
Woodburcot, Northants, II., 175.
Wooderich (Wodecryth) in Wokingham, II., 189.* 190.
Woodford, Essex, I., 240,* 312; II., 170.*
Woodham Ferrers, Essex, I., 98.
Woodhay (Woodhey), East, Hants, I., 82, 166; II., 29, 63, 234.
Woodhay (Woodhey), West, Berks, I., 60, 82, 101, 148, 274, 275; II., 28, 92, 102, 105,* 215.*
Woodhouse, Hants, I., 36.
Woodland, Devon, II., 176.
Woodlands, Bucks, II., 48.
Woodlands near Marlborough, I., 204.
Woodlech, Bucks, II., 222.
Woodley, I., 77, 78, 182, 252, 253.
Woodseye, I., 80.
Wood-Speen, II., 3, 32.
Woodstock, Oxon, I., 246; II., 13.
Woodway, Herts, II., 185.
Woolhampton (Wolhampton, Wollhampton), I., 38,* 145, 313, 316, 317; II., 36.
Woollers Hall (Wollashall, Wollashull), Worcestershire, II., 85, 222.
Woolly (Wolley), I., 126, 133, 134, 249; II., 3, 27.*
Woolstone (Woolston), I., 254, 277*; II., 26, 41, 188.
Woolwich, Kent., II., 170, 171.
Woosey, I., 296.
Wootton (Wotton), II., 3, 12, 165.
Wootton Bassett, Wilts, I., 200; II., 123.
Wootton-under-Wood, Bucks, II., 116.
Worcester, II., 135.
Workfield, II., 37.
Worminghurst, Sussex, I., 302.
Wormleighton (Wormeleyton), Warwickshire, I., 53.
Wormley, Herts, I., 267.

Worplesdon (Warplesdon), Surrey, I., 183; II., 102.
Worrould, Wilts, I., 28.
Wraxall, Wilts, II., 176.
Wrexham (Wrexam), Denbighshire, II., 137.
Wrinehill, Staffordshire, II., 176.
Wrotham, Kent, I., 115; II., 171.
Wroughton (Wroton), Wilts, I., 125, 244; II., 173.
Wyarton, Kent, I., 115.
Wycombe (Wickham), Bucks, I., 44, 157; II., 224.
Wycombe, High, Bucks, I., 229, 230.
Wycombe, West, Bucks, I., 255; II., 48, 88.
Wyddial (Widiall, Widgell), Herts, I., 100; II., 125.
Wydell (Widdell), Wilts, I., 190, 236*; II., 164.*
Wye (Wy), Kent, II., 226.
Wyfield in Boxford, II., 195.
Wymering, Hants, I., 72.
Wynthey (Wynteney), Hants, I., 43.

Wytham, *see* Witham.
Wyvill Court, II., 195.*

Yale, I., 171.
Yarlington, Somerset, I., 250.
Yarnscombe (Yarnscoum), Devon, I., 12, 56 *n*.
Yateley (Yatley), Hants, I., 54.
Yattendon (Gatehampton, Yatendon), Oxon, I., 10,* 126; II., 30, 83, 105, 184, 185,* 186.
Yeadinge, Middlesex, I., 19.
Yeagden, Salop, II., 122.
York, I., 257, 273; II., 80, 167.*

Z

Zermydon in Wokingham, II., 189.

The Harleian Society.

FOUNDED 1869.   INCORPORATED 1902.

The Harleian Society.

FOUNDED 1869. INCORPORATED 1902.

INSTITUTED FOR THE

Publication of Inedited Manuscripts

RELATING TO

GENEALOGY, FAMILY HISTORY, AND HERALDRY.

Registered Office and Council Room:
140 WARDOUR STREET, W.

Council.

SIR GEORGE J. ARMYTAGE, BT., F.S.A. (*Chairman*).
C. H. ATHILL, ESQ., F.S.A., RICHMOND HERALD.
SIR THOMAS BROOKE, BT., F.S.A.
J. W. CLAY, ESQ., F.S.A.
GEORGE E. COKAYNE, ESQ., F.S.A., CLARENCEUX KING-OF-ARMS.
ROBERT HOVENDEN, ESQ., F.S.A.
WILLOUGHBY A. LITTLEDALE, ESQ., M.A., F.S.A.
SIR CHARLES H. S. RICH, BT., F.S.A.
J. PAUL RYLANDS, ESQ., F.S.A.
W. HARRY RYLANDS, ESQ., F.S.A.
F. A. CRISP, ESQ., F.S.A.
COL. JOHN W. R. PARKER, F.S.A.

Secretary and Treasurer.
*W. BRUCE BANNERMAN, ESQ., F.S.A.
The Lindens, Sydenham Road, Croydon, Surrey.

Bankers.
THE LONDON AND COUNTY BANKING COMPANY, LIMITED,
21 Lombard Street, E.C.

Auditor.
M. W. KER, ESQ.
60 Cromwell Avenue, Highgate, N.

Publishers and Agents:
MESSRS. MITCHELL HUGHES AND CLARKE, 140 Wardour Street, London, W.

---

* To whom all Communications and Subscriptions should be forwarded.

Report for the Year 1907.

The Council have to report that at and since the Annual General Meeting, held on the 14th day of February 1907, ten new Subscribers have joined the Society, of whom four are Subscribers to the Register Section, and one Subscriber to the Visitations has joined the Register Section.

During the same period the Society has lost seven Subscribers (of whom four belonged to the Register Section) by death; eleven Subscribers (six of whom belonged to the Register Section) have resigned; and one Subscriber to the Registers has resigned the Visitation Section.

The number on the Roll on the 31st of December 1907 is two hundred and eighty-five, of whom one hundred and seventy-nine are Subscribers to the Register Section.

"The Four Visitations of Berkshire, made and taken by Thomas Benolte, Clarenceux, Anno 1532; by William Harvey, Clarenceux, Anno 1566; by Henry Chitting, Chester Herald, and John Philipott, Rouge Dragon, for William Camden, Clarenceux, Anno 1623; and by Elias Ashmole, Windsor Herald, for Sir Edward Bysshe, Clarenceux, Anno 1665-66," Vol. I., edited by W. HARRY RYLANDS, Esq., F.S.A., forming the fifty-sixth volume of the Publications, has been issued to the Subscribers for 1907.

Volume III. of "The Registers of St. Paul, Covent Garden, London," containing Marriages from 1653 to 1837, edited by the Rev. W. H. HUNT, forming the thirty-fifth volume of the Registers, will be issued to the Subscribers for 1907.

Volume II. of "The Four Visitations of Berkshire," containing Additional Pedigrees and Notes, edited by W. HARRY RYLANDS, Esq., F.S.A., is in the press.

Volume IV. of "The Registers of St. Paul, Covent Garden, London," containing the *Burials*, under the editorship of the Rev. W. H. HUNT, is in the press.

"The Registers of St. Benet, Paul's Wharf," and "The Registers of St. Peter, Paul's Wharf, London," under the editorship of WILLOUGHBY A. LITTLEDALE, Esq., M.A., F.S.A., are progressing.

The Balance Sheet for the year, duly audited, is appended to the Report.

By Order of the Council,

W. BRUCE BANNERMAN,

Secretary.

The Harleian Society.

FOUNDED 1869.   INCORPORATED 1902.

ACCOUNTS FOR THE YEAR ENDING 31ST DECEMBER, 1907.

ORDINARY ACCOUNT.

Dr.

		£ s. d.	£ s. d.
Balance to 31st December, 1906			104 6 2
Subscriptions	1902 £1 1 0		
	1903 2 2 0		
	1904 3 3 0		
	1905 3 3 0		
	1906 13 2 6		
	1907 275 2 6		
	1908 7 7 0		
			305 1 0
Cash in advance for 2 Copies of Berkshire Visitations			2 2 0
Books purchased by Subscribers			30 3 0
Dividend, 3 per cent. Stock, Lancashire and Yorkshire Railway (£500)			14 5 0
Interest on Deposit (£150)			4 15 2
			£460 12 4

Cr.

		£ s. d.	£ s. d.
April 19.	Audit of Stock (1906) (M. W. Ker)		1 1 0
Aug. 20.	Miss Parker, Transcript of Bucks Visitation		9 18 6
Oct. 5.	London and Lancashire Fire Insurance		6 5 0
Dec. 28.	Messrs. Mitchell Hughes & Clarke:—		
	Berkshire Visitations, Vol. I.	237 6 11	
	General Account	16 16 7	
"	Commission on Cheques		5 5
"	Cheque Book		3 1
"	Secretary and Treasurer		40 0 0
" 31.	Balance		148 16 10
			£460 12 4

REGISTER SECTION.

Dr.			£ s. d.	Cr.		£ s. d.
Balance to 31st December, 1906			456 3 8	April 23. Mr. A. J. Jewers, on account of Transcript of Registers of St. Benet and St. Peter's, Paul Wharf		12 0 0
Subscriptions	1902	£1 1 0		July 20. " " "		17 0 0
	1903	1 1 0		Nov. 21. " " "		20 0 0
	1904	1 1 0		Balance		593 0 2
	1905	1 1 0				
	1906	4 4 0				
	1907	169 1 0				
	1908	3 3 0	180 12 0			
Books purchased by Subscribers			5 4 6			
			£642 0 2			£642 0 2

GENERAL BALANCE.

1907.	£ s. d.	1907.	£ s. d.
To Balance, Ordinary Section	148 16 10	Dec. 31. Balance in the Bank	741 17 0
" Register "	593 0 2		
	£741 17 0		£741 17 0

Examined and approved,

M. W. KER, *Auditor.*

23rd January 1908.

W. BRUCE BANNERMAN,
Secretary and Treasurer.

List of Subscribers

ON 31st DECEMBER, 1907,

WITH THE DATES OF THEIR ELECTION.

Those marked (*) are Subscribers of an extra Guinea, and are entitled to the Publications of the Register Section.

29 Apr. 1869.	*The Lord AMHERST OF HACKNEY, F.S.A., Didlington Hall, Brandon.
31 Dec. 1875.	JOHN AMPHLETT, Clent, Stourbridge.
27 Mar. 1869.	*Sir GEORGE J. ARMYTAGE, Bt., F.S.A. (*Chairman of Council*), Kirklees Park, Brighouse.
31 Jan. 1887.	*ATHENÆUM CLUB (HENRY R. TEDDER, F.S.A., Secretary), 107 Pall Mall, S.W.
6 Feb. 1886.	C. H. ATHILL, F.S.A. (*Council*), Richmond Herald, College of Arms, Queen Victoria Street, E.C.
4 Sept. 1880.	Colonel F. W. T. ATTREE, R.E., F.S.A., 32 Park Mansions, Prince of Wales Road, S.W.
21 Oct. 1887.	W. H. G. BAGSHAWE, Ford Hall, Chapel-en-le-Frith, Stockport.
21 Jan. 1882.	FRANCIS JOSEPH BAIGENT, Winchester.
30 July, 1898.	*W. BRUCE BANNERMAN, F.S.A. (*Secretary and Treasurer*), The Lindens, Sydenham Road, Croydon, Surrey.
8 Jan. 1889.	GEORGE W. G. BARNARD, 4 Surrey Street, Norwich.
18 Mar. 1892.	WILLIAM BARTLETT, St. Clare House, Sandfield Park, W. Derby.
13 Mar. 1906.	A. RIDLEY BAX, F.S.A., Ivy Bank, Hampstead, N.W. [*Register Section*].
31 Dec. 1907.	R. A. BAYFORD, K.C., Netley Hill, Botley, Hants.
5 June, 1905.	WALTER P. BELK, Holmwood, Ecclesall, Sheffield.
22 Oct. 1874.	*REGINALD STEWART BODDINGTON, 60 High Street, Worthing.
20 Jan. 1877.	*C. E. B. BOWLES, M.A., Nether House, Wirksworth, Derbyshire.

12 Sept. 1872.	Sir EDWARD W. BRABROOK, C.B., F.S.A., 178 Bedford Hill, Balham, S.W.
10 Apr. 1888.	Colonel J. A. BRADNEY, F.S.A., Tal-y-Coed Court, Monmouth.
18 May, 1870.	The Ven. Archdeacon BREE, The Rectory, Allesley, Coventry.
4 Apr. 1898.	*HENRY BRIERLEY, Thornhill, Wigan.
24 Nov. 1869.	*Sir THOMAS BROOKE, Bt., F.S.A. (*Council*), Armitage Bridge, Huddersfield.
27 May, 1904.	*The MARQUESS OF BUTE, 22A Queen Anne's Gate, S.W. (per W. DE GRAY BIRCH, F.S.A., Librarian).
31 Dec. 1907.	*WILLIAM A. CADBURY, Wast Hills, King's Norton, Worcester.
1 Jan. 1891.	FRANCIS J. CADE, Mosborough, The Park, Cheltenham.
27 Mar. 1879.	H. H. SMITH-CARINGTON, Grangethorpe, Rusholme, Manchester.
31 Dec. 1903.	PHILIP W. POOLE CARLYON-BRITTON, F.S.A., D.L., J.P., 43 Bedford Square, W.C.
30 July, 1898.	JOSEPH J. CASEY, 20 East 130th Street, New York, U.S.A. [*Register Section*].
24 Mar. 1883.	*Major TANKERVILLE J. CHAMBERLAYNE, 80th Reg. (care of Holt, Laurie, and Co., 3 Whitehall Place, S.W.).
6 June, 1887.	H. MAPLETON CHAPMAN, Saint Martin's Priory, Canterbury.
6 Oct. 1881.	*J. W. CLAY, F.S.A. (*Council*), Rastrick House, near Brighouse.
6 Feb. 1888.	*H. J. B. CLEMENTS, Killadoon, Celbridge, co. Kildare, Ireland.
23 June, 1869.	*G. E. COKAYNE, F.S.A. (*Council*), Clarenceux King-of-Arms, College of Arms, Queen Victoria Street, E.C., and Exeter House, Roehampton.
4 Dec. 1883.	*CHARLES F. COLE, Meudon Vean, Mawnan, Falmouth.
6 Feb. 1906.	*COLLEGE OF ARMS (per C. H. ATHILL, F.S.A., Richmond Herald), London, E.C.
22 Mar. 1883.	EDWARD CONDER, F.S.A., Conigree Court, Newent, Gloucestershire.
31 Dec. 1903.	*CONSTITUTIONAL CLUB, London, W.C.
22 Feb. 1900.	JOHN HAUTENVILLE COPE, F.R.Hist.S., 18 Harrington Court, Glendower Park, S.W.
31 Oct. 1900.	W. SANDFORD COTTRILL, Orr's Buildings, Pritchard Street, Johannesburg, South Africa.
31 Dec. 1907.	Major A. TUDOR CRAIG, 30 Richmond Mansions, South Kensington, S.W.
16 Aug. 1904.	Mrs. WILFRED JOSEPH CRIPPS, Cripps Mead, Cirencester.
12 Aug. 1881.	*F. A. CRISP, F.S.A. (*Council*), Broadhurst, Godalming.
26 Nov. 1887.	LEO CULLETON, 92 Piccadilly, W.
25 Nov. 1882.	*GERY MILNER-GIBSON-CULLUM, F.S.A., 4 Sterling Street, Montpelier Square, S.W.
18 May, 1875.	*Lady ELIZABETH CUST, 13 Eccleston Square, S.W.
18 Mar. 1874.	*Rev. G. H. DAVENPORT, Foxley, Hereford.
27 Dec. 1876.	*DE BERNARDY and Co., 25 Bedford Row, W.C.

31 Dec. 1878.   B. DE BERTODANO, 22 Chester Terrace, Regent's Park, N.W.
3 June, 1899.   *CHARLES DEERING, 16 Fullerton Avenue, Chicago, New York (care of Stevens and Brown, 4 Trafalgar Square, W.C.).
27 Jan. 1899.   RICHARD SIDNEY DENDY, Black Sha, Campbell Road, Bognor.
12 May, 1894.   *The EARL OF DERBY, K.G., P.C. (Rev. JOHN RICHARDSON, Librarian), Knowsley, Prescot.
24 Jan. 1891.   *WALTER DERHAM, 76 Lancaster Gate, W.
31 Dec. 1903.   GEO. F. DUCK, 602 Keystone Buildings, Pittsburg, Pa., U.S.A.
18 Aug. 1894.   W. H. DUIGNAN, F.S.A., Gorway, Walsall, Staffordshire.
1 Nov. 1882.   Rev. R. E. H. DUKE, Maltby Rectory, Alford, Lincolnshire.
7 June, 1878.   *DURHAM, THE DEAN AND CHAPTER OF, The Library, Chapter Offices, Durham.

8 July, 1889.   Rev. JOSEPH EDLESTON, M.A., LL.D., Gainford Vicarage, near Darlington.
22 June, 1870. *V. D. H. CARY ELWES, F.S.A., Billing Hall, Northampton.
5 Oct. 1895.   A. T. EVERITT, High Street, Portsmouth.

31 Dec. 1903.   W. V. R. FANE, Fulbeck Hall, Grantham.
14 May, 1890.   *T. C. COLYER-FERGUSSON, Wombwell Hall, near Gravesend.
16 Sept. 1887. Rev. W. G. DIMOCK FLETCHER, M.A., F.S.A., Oxon Vicarage, Shrewsbury.
12 Sept. 1902. *Rev. Canon C. W. FOSTER, M.A., Timberland Vicarage, Lincoln.
27 Jan. 1902.   F. APTHORP FOSTER, 15 Oxford Street, Cambridge, Mass., U.S.A.
26 Nov. 1906.   *W. H. FOX, F.S.A., 9 Austin Friars, London, E.C.
16 Jan. 1884.   *EDWIN FRESHFIELD, LL.D., F.S.A., 31 Old Jewry, E.C.

19 Nov. 1892.   Lieut.-Col. W. A. GALE, R.E., 10 Lingfield Road, Wimbledon, Surrey.
5 Feb. 1883.   CHARLES W. GEORGE, 51 Hampton Road, Bristol.
13 Feb. 1891.   *H. MARTIN GIBBS, Down Ampney House, Cricklade, Wilts.
24 Mar. 1890.   *JAMES J. GOODWIN, 11 West 54th Street, New York, U.S.A. (care of J. B. Lippincott and Co., 5 Henrietta Street, W.C.).
31 Dec. 1903.   RICHARD W. GOULDING, Welbeck, Worksop.
25 Jan. 1889.   GEORGE GRAZEBROOK, F.S.A., Odnall Cottage, Clent, near Stourbridge.
29 Dec. 1872.   J. E. A. GWYNNE, F.S.A., F.R.G.S., Folkington, Polegate, Sussex.

19 Sept. 1900. *JOSEPH S. HANSOM, 27 Alfred Place West, South Kensington, S.W.
16 Mar. 1896.   Dr. EDW. A. HARDWICKE, J.P., Havermere, Howick Falls, Natal.
Sept. 1880.   THEODORE J. HARE, Lyne Grove, Virginia Water, Surrey.

26 Nov. 1896.   *HERBERT S. HARINGTON, A.M.I.C.E., Director of Indian Railways, Kelston, Simla, Punjaub.
22 Feb. 1883.   C. ARTHUR HEAD, Hartburn Hall, Stockton-on-Tees.
12 Apr. 1890.   HENRY PLATT HIGGINS, Moorside, Heath View Gardens, Putney Heath, S.W.
22 Oct. 1906.   *ARTHUR F. HILL, F.S.A., 140 New Bond Street, London, W.
31 Dec. 1903.   *Rev. JOHN HOLDING, M.A., Stotfold Vicarage, Baldock, Herts.
31 Dec. 1907.   *H. HOLMAN, 44 Park Street, Grosvenor Square, W.
6 Apr. 1906.   *H. WILSON HOLMAN, F.S.A., 4 Lloyds Avenue, E.C.
16 June, 1872. *ROBERT HOVENDEN, F.S.A. (*Council*), Heathcote, Park Hill Road, Croydon.
12 June, 1886. *HUGH ROBERT HUGHES, Kinmel, Abergele, North Wales.
20 Feb. 1874.   W. ESSINGTON HUGHES, F.R.Hist.S., 89 Alexandra Road, South Hampstead, N.W.
2 June, 1905.   *Rev. W. H. HUNT, The Vicarage, Burleigh Street, W.C.

20 Sept. 1892. *The Viscount IVEAGH, K.P., 5 Grosvenor Place, S.W.

31 Dec. 1907.   *A. J. JEWERS, 53 Constantine Road, Hampstead Heath, N.W.
20 Feb. 1895.   *THOMAS MORGAN JOSEPH-WATKIN, F.S.A., Portcullis Pursuivant, College of Arms, Queen Victoria Street, E.C.

31 Dec. 1907.   Rev. Canon CHARLES N. KELLY, M.A., St. Nicholas Cole Abbey, Queen Victoria Street, E.C. [*Register Section*].
11 Jan. 1892.   CHARLES EAMER KEMPE, Old Place, Lindfield, Hayward's Heath.
8 July, 1895.   WILLIAM THOMAS KNIGHT, Canok Lodge, Walton Park, Clevedon, Somerset.

12 May, 1894.   JOHN LANGHORNE, M.A., Watson Villa, Dean, Edinburgh.
4 Nov. 1870.   *THOMAS LAYTON, F.S.A., 22 Kew Bridge Road, Kew Bridge, Middlesex.
8 Nov. 1890.   J. HENRY LEA, Elmlea, South Freeport, Maine, U.S.A.
16 Dec. 1905.   *CHARLES LETTS, 8 Bartlett's Buildings, Holborn Circus, E.C.

LIBRARIES.

2 July, 1894.   *ABERDEEN UNIVERSITY LIBRARY (P. J. ANDERSON, M.A., LL.B., Librarian), Aberdeen.
31 Dec. 1903.   *ADVOCATES' LIBRARY, Edinburgh (J. T. CLARK, Keeper).
26 Feb. 1906.   *ALL SOULS' COLLEGE, OXFORD (C. W. C. OMAN, M.A., F.S.A., Librarian).
12 May, 1894.   *BATTERSEA PUBLIC LIBRARY (LAWRENCE INKSTER, Librarian), Lavender Hill, S.W.
15 July, 1899. *BERLIN ROYAL LIBRARY (per Asher and Co., 13 Bedford Street, W.C.).

12 May, 1894.	*BIRKENHEAD FREE PUBLIC LIBRARY (JOHN SHEPHERD, Librarian), Birkenhead.
24 July, 1883.	*BIRMINGHAM CENTRAL FREE LIBRARY (A. CAPEL SHAW, Librarian), Ratcliffe Place, Birmingham.
20 Jan. 1871.	*BODLEIAN LIBRARY (E. B. NICHOLSON, Librarian), Oxford.
15 Oct. 1875.	*BOSTON FREE PUBLIC LIBRARY, Boston, U.S.A. (per Kegan Paul, Trench, Trübner and Co., Dryden House, Gerrard Street, Soho).
12 May, 1894.	*BRADFORD PUBLIC FREE LIBRARY (BUTLER WOOD, Librarian), Bradford, Yorkshire.
22 July, 1893.	*BRIDGEPORT PUBLIC LIBRARY, Conn., U.S.A. (AGNES HILLS, Librarian), (care of B. F. Stevens and Brown, 4 Trafalgar Square, W.C.).
2 July, 1894.	*BRIGHTON PUBLIC LIBRARY (HENRY D. ROBERTS, Chief Librarian), Church Street, Brighton.
26 Nov. 1906.	*BRISTOL CENTRAL PUBLIC LIBRARY (E. R. N. MATHEWS, F.R.Hist.S., City Librarian), Bristol.
17 Oct. 1905.	*BRITISH MUSEUM, London, W.C. (per B. QUARITCH).
5 Oct. 1895.	*CALIFORNIA STATE LIBRARY, Sacramento, California, U.S.A. (care of B. F. Stevens and Brown, 4 Trafalgar Square, W.C.).
2 July, 1894.	*CAMBERWELL PUBLIC LIBRARIES (W. G. SNOWSILL, Librarian), Central Library, Peckham Road, S.E.
20 Nov. 1873.	*CAMBRIDGE UNIVERSITY LIBRARY (F. J. H. JENKINSON, M.A., Librarian), Cambridge.
2 July, 1894.	*CARDIFF FREE PUBLIC LIBRARIES, Cardiff.
3 Mar. 1899.	CARLISLE PUBLIC LIBRARY (ARCHIBALD SPARKE, City Librarian), Tullie House, Carlisle.
28 June, 1906.	*CARNEGIE LIBRARY, Pittsburg, Pennsylvania (per B. F. Stevens and Brown, 4 Trafalgar Square, W.C.)
12 May, 1894.	*CHELSEA PUBLIC LIBRARIES (J. HENRY QUINN, Librarian), Central Library, Manresa Road, Chelsea, S.W.
18 Oct. 1870.	*CHETHAM'S LIBRARY (WALTER T. BROWNE, Librarian), Hunt's Bank, Manchester.
22 July, 1893.	*CHICAGO PUBLIC LIBRARY (per B. F. Stevens and Brown, 4 Trafalgar Square, W.C.).
22 July, 1893.	*COLUMBIA UNIVERSITY LIBRARY, New York City, U.S.A. (G. H. BAKER, Librarian), (care of G. E. Stechert, 2 Star Yard, Carey Street, Chancery Lane, W.C.).
22 July, 1893.	*CORNELL UNIVERSITY LIBRARY, Ithaca, New York, U.S.A. (G. W. HARRIS, Librarian), (care of E. G. Allen, 14 Grape Street, Shaftesbury Avenue, W.C.).
2 July, 1894.	*CROYDON PUBLIC LIBRARIES (L. STANLEY JAST, Chief Librarian), Central Library, Croydon.
2 July, 1894.	DERBY PUBLIC FREE LIBRARY (WILLIAM CROWTHER, Secretary), Derby.
5 Nov. 1892.	*DETROIT PUBLIC LIBRARY, Michigan, U.S.A. (per B. F. Stevens and Brown, 4 Trafalgar Square, W.C.).
12 May, 1894.	DEWSBURY PUBLIC FREE LIBRARY (W. H. SMITH, Librarian), Dewsbury.

12 May, 1894.	*EDINBURGH PUBLIC LIBRARY (HEW MORRISON, Principal Librarian), George IV. Bridge, Edinburgh.
12 May, 1894.	*EXETER ROYAL ALBERT MEMORIAL PUBLIC LIBRARY (H. TAPLEY SOPER, City Librarian), Exeter.
2 July, 1894.	*GONVILLE AND CAIUS COLLEGE LIBRARY (Rev. G. A. S. SCHNEIDER, Librarian), Cambridge.
18 Mar. 1901.	*GROSVENOR PUBLIC LIBRARY, Buffalo, New York (per B. F. Stevens and Brown, 4 Trafalgar Square, W C.).
9 May. 1873.	*GUILDHALL LIBRARY (EDWARD M. BORRAJO, Librarian), London, E.C.
28 Mar. 1906.	*HAMMERSMITH PUBLIC LIBRARIES (SAMUEL MARTIN, Chief Librarian), Hammersmith.
22 July, 1893.	*HARVARD COLLEGE LIBRARY, Cambridge, Massachusetts, U.S.A. (per Kegan Paul, Trench, Trübner and Co., Dryden House, Gerrard Street, Soho, W.).
2 July, 1894.	HEREFORD FREE PUBLIC LIBRARY (JAMES COCKCROFT, Librarian), Hereford.
19 Jan. 1895.	*HULL PUBLIC LIBRARY (WM. F. LAWTON, Librarian), Hull.
2 July, 1894.	KIDDERMINSTER FREE LIBRARY, Kidderminster.
17 Apr. 1880.	KING'S INNS LIBRARY (JAS. MACIVOR, Librarian), Dublin.
12 May, 1894.	*LAMBETH PUBLIC LIBRARIES (FRANK J. BURGOYNE, Librarian), The Tate Central Library, Brixton Oval, S.W.
11 Jan. 1892.	*LEEDS LIBRARY (D. A. CRUSE, Librarian), Commercial Street, Leeds.
18 Sept. 1890.	*LEEDS PUBLIC LIBRARY (THOMAS W. HAND, Librarian), Leeds.
3 Feb. 1897.	*LIBRARY COMPANY OF PHILADELPHIA (per E. G. Allen, 14 Grape Street, Shaftesbury Avenue, W.C.)
6 Sept. 1895.	*LINCOLN'S INN, THE HONOURABLE SOCIETY OF (A. F. ETHERIDGE, Librarian), The Library, Lincoln's Inn, W.C.
5 Oct. 1872.	THE LIVERPOOL ATHENÆUM (GEORGE T. SHAW, Librarian), Liverpool.
2 Sept. 1872.	*LIVERPOOL FREE PUBLIC LIBRARY (PETER COWELL, Librarian), William Brown Street, Liverpool.
20 Dec. 1877.	*LONDON LIBRARY (C. T. H. WRIGHT, Secretary and Librarian), 14 St. James's Square, S.W.
16 Mar. 1874.	*MANCHESTER FREE LIBRARY (CHARLES W. SUTTON, Librarian), King Street, Manchester.
22 July, 1893.	*MELBOURNE PUBLIC LIBRARY (T. F. BRIDE, Librarian), (care of Agent-General for Victoria, 142 Queen Victoria Street, E.C.).
10 Sept. 1877.	MITCHELL LIBRARY (F. T. BARRETT, Librarian), 21 Miller Street, Glasgow.
28 May, 1884.	NATIONAL LIBRARY OF IRELAND (care of Hodges, Figgis, and Co., 104 Grafton Street, Dublin).
25 Oct. 1899.	*NEWBERRY LIBRARY, Chicago, U.S.A. (care of B. F. Stevens and Brown, 4 Trafalgar Square, W.C.).
23 Dec. 1889.	*NEWCASTLE-UPON-TYNE PUBLIC LIBRARY (BASIL ANDERTON, B.A., Chief Librarian), Newcastle-upon-Tyne.
22 July, 1893.	*NEW HAMPSHIRE STATE LIBRARY (ARTHUR R. KIMBALL, Librarian), Concord, New Hampshire, U.S.A.

17 Mar. 1887.	*NEW YORK PUBLIC LIBRARY (care of B. F. Stevens and Brown, 4 Trafalgar Square, W.C.).
17 Jan. 1891.	*NEW YORK STATE LIBRARY, Albany, New York, U.S.A. (care of G. E. Stechert, 2 Star Yard, Carey Street, W.C.).
7 June, 1875.	*NOTTINGHAM FREE PUBLIC LIBRARY (J. P. BRISCOE, Librarian), Nottingham.
8 June, 1903.	*PEABODY INSTITUTE LIBRARY, Baltimore, U.S.A. (care of E. G. Allen, 14 Grape Street, Shaftesbury Avenue, W.C.).
12 May, 1894.	*PLYMOUTH FREE PUBLIC LIBRARY (W. H. K. WRIGHT, Librarian), Plymouth.
31 Dec. 1903.	*PORTLAND PUBLIC LIBRARY, Portland, Maine, U.S.A. (per Edward A. Norges, Treasurer, Portland, Maine, U.S.A.).
2 July, 1894.	*READING FREE PUBLIC LIBRARY (W. H. GREENHOUGH, Librarian), Reading.
2 July, 1894.	*RICHMOND FREE PUBLIC LIBRARY (ALBERT A. BARKAS, Librarian and Secretary), Richmond, Surrey.
14 Apr. 1880.	ROCHDALE FREE PUBLIC LIBRARY (G. HANSON, Librarian), Rochdale, Lancashire.
28 May, 1869.	ROYAL LIBRARY, Windsor Castle, Windsor.
1 Dec. 1899.	*THE JOHN RYLANDS' LIBRARY, Manchester (H. GUPPY, Librarian).
4 Feb. 1891.	*ST. MARTIN-IN-THE-FIELDS FREE PUBLIC LIBRARY, 115 St. Martin's Lane, W.C. (LISTER WASHBOURN, City Comptroller).
8 Dec. 1885.	SHEFFIELD CENTRAL FREE PUBLIC LIBRARY, Surrey Street, Sheffield.
12 May, 1894.	*SIGNET LIBRARY, Edinburgh.
29 Jan. 1878.	*SION COLLEGE LIBRARY (Rev. W. H. MILMAN, Librarian), Victoria Embankment, E.C.
2 July, 1894.	*SWANSEA PUBLIC LIBRARY (S. E. THOMPSON, Librarian), Swansea.
29 Oct. 1887.	*SYDNEY FREE PUBLIC LIBRARY (care of Truslove and Hanson, 153 Oxford Street, W.).
27 Nov. 1889.	*SYRACUSE PUBLIC LIBRARY (EZEKIEL W. MUNDY, Librarian), Syracuse, New York, U.S.A.
11 Dec. 1871.	*TEMPLE, THE HONOURABLE SOCIETY OF THE INNER, The Library, Temple, E.C.
10 Mar. 1886.	*TEMPLE, THE HONOURABLE SOCIETY OF THE MIDDLE, The Library (care of Butterworth and Co., 12 Bell Yard, Fleet Street, E.C.).
22 July, 1893.	*TORONTO PUBLIC LIBRARY (JAMES BAIN, Librarian), Canada (care of C. D. Cazenove, 26 Henrietta Street, W.C.).
2 July, 1894.	*WALSALL FREE LIBRARY (ALFRED MORGAN, Librarian), Walsall, Staffordshire.
28 Feb. 1877.	*WASHINGTON LIBRARY OF CONGRESS, Washington, U.S.A. (care of E. G. Allen, 14 Grape Street, Shaftesbury Avenue, W.C.).
2 Sept. 1872.	*WATKINSON LIBRARY, Hartford, Connecticut, U.S.A. (care of E. G. Allen, 14 Grape Street, Shaftesbury Avenue, W.C.).
2 July, 1894.	*WIGAN FREE PUBLIC LIBRARY (HENRY T. FOLKARD, Librarian), Wigan.

2 July, 1894. *WILLIAM AND MARY COLLEGE LIBRARY (LYON G. TYLER, President), Williamsburg, Virginia, U.S.A.
29 Dec. 1885. *WORCESTER FREE PUBLIC LIBRARY, Worcester, Massachusetts, U.S.A. (per Kegan Paul, Trench, Trübner and Co., Dryden House, Gerrard Street W.).

---

31 Dec. 1903. *GEORGE J. LIND, F.S.A. Scot., Rua do Golgotha, Oporto, Portugal.
1 Feb. 1895. *WILLOUGHBY A. LITTLEDALE, M.A., F.S.A. (*Council*), 26 Cranley Gardens, South Kensington, S.W.
24 June, 1881. *G. B. LONGSTAFF, M.A., M.D., F.S.A., Highlands, Putney Heath, S.W.

19 Feb. 1898. W. A. MACFARLANE-GRIEVE, M.A., S.C.L., F.S.A. Scot., J.P., Impington Park, Cambridgeshire.
28 Nov. 1870. *Rev. Canon A. R. MADDISON, M.A., F.S.A., Vicars' Court, Lincoln.
29 Nov. 1890. KINGSMILL MARRS, South Park, Saxonville, Massachusetts, U.S.A.
30 Mar. 1906. GEORGE MARSHALL, F.S.A., J.P., The Manor House, Breinton, near Hereford.
2 Apr. 1906. *ISAAC MARSHALL, Sarnesfield Court, Weobley, R.S.O.
12 Mar. 1885. *Hon. ROBERT MARSHAM-TOWNSHEND, M.A., F.S.A., 5 Chesterfield Street, Mayfair, W.
31 Dec. 1907. WILLIAM MARTIN, M.A., LL.D., F.S.A., 2 Garden Court, Temple, E.C.
3 Apr. 1900. *BURDETT MASON, Château Larondouette, Près Bayonne, Basses Pyrénées, France.
6 Apr. 1905. *MERCHANT TAYLORS COMPANY (EDWARD NASH, F.S.A., Clerk), Merchant Taylors Hall, Threadneedle Street, E.C.
7 May, 1878. *THOMAS TINDAL METHOLD, 7 Ashburn Place, Cromwell Road, South Kensington, S.W.
3 Apr. 1889. Rev. A. T. MICHELL, M.A., F.S.A., Sheriffhales Vicarage, Newport, Salop.
20 July, 1878. SAMUEL MILNE MILNE, Calverley House, near Leeds.
24 Aug. 1870. Rev. JOHN MIREHOUSE, Colsterworth Rectory, Grantham.
16 Apr. 1875. *W. MARTIAL MYDDELTON, Spencer House, St. Albans.

14 Sept. 1872. NAVAL AND MILITARY CLUB, 94 Piccadilly, W.
15 Mar. 1890. ILTYD NICHOLL, F.S.A., The Ham, Cowbridge, Glamorganshire.
22 Feb. 1900. *The DUKE OF NORTHUMBERLAND, K.G., P.C., F.S.A., Alnwick Castle, Northumberland (per J. C. HODGSON, F.S.A., Alnwick Castle).

31 Dec. 1907. A. W. OKE, 32 Denmark Villas, Hove, Brighton.
16 Nov. 1885. *V. L. OLIVER, Whitmore Lodge, Sunninghill, Berkshire.
1 Feb. 1890. *OXFORD AND CAMBRIDGE CLUB (care of Harrisons, 59 Pall Mall, S.W.).

14 Feb. 1880. *Colonel JOHN W. R. PARKER, F.S.A. (*Council*), Browsholme Hall, Clitheroe, Lancashire.
28 July, 1869. Rev. A. J. PEARMAN, The Precincts, Rochester, Kent.
20 Dec. 1906. *EDWARD S. M. PEROWNE, F.S.A., 20 Randolph Road, Maida Vale, W.
31 Dec. 1907. *WILLIAM B. PHELPS, Torrey Building, Duluth, Minnesota, U.S.A. (care of C. D. Cazenove and Sons, 26 Henrietta Street, W.C.).
30 May, 1881. W. P. W. PHILLIMORE, M.A., B.C.L., 124 Chancery Lane, W.C.
15 Feb. 1873. W. DUNCOMBE PINK, Winslade, Lowton, Newton-le-Willows, Lancashire.
16 Apr. 1892. *FRANCIS W. PIXLEY, F.S.A., 12 Southwell Gardens, South Kensington, S.W.
23 July, 1885. EDGAR POWELL, Upper Cross, Whitley, Reading.
31 Dec. 1906. JOHN GEORGE PRENTICE, 20 Chapel Street, Liverpool.
2 July, 1894. PUBLIC RECORD OFFICE, Fetter Lane, E.C. (care of Wyman and Sons, 109 Fetter Lane, E.C.).

3 Mar. 1900. *BERNARD ALFRED QUARITCH, 11 Grafton Street, New Bond Street, W.

29 Oct. 1887. JOHN RADCLIFFE, Furlane, Greenfield, viâ Oldham.
15 July, 1896. H. C. F. RANDOLPH, M.A., 303 West 85th Street, New York, U.S.A.
31 Oct. 1884. *REFORM CLUB, 104 Pall Mall, S.W.
3 Sept. 1886. *Sir CHARLES H. S. RICH, Baronet of Shirley, F.S.A. (*Council*), Devizes Castle, and the Conservative Club, S.W.
10 Feb. 1906. J. RIMELL AND SON, 53 Shaftesbury Avenue, W.C.
11 Sept. 1880. BROOKE ROBINSON, Barford House, Warwick.
1 Dec. 1896. *ARTHUR A. ROLLASON, Dixon's Green, Dudley, Worcestershire.
31 Dec. 1907. L. W. S. ROSTRON, M.A., Riverside, Beddington, Surrey.
3 Dec. 1873. J. BROOKING ROWE, F.S.A., Castle Barbican, Plympton, South Devon.
2 Jan. 1901. *ROYAL SOCIETIES CLUB (D. LEWIS POOLE, Hon. Sec., 63 St. James's Street, S.W.).
26 Feb. 1890. Lady ROYDS, Greenhill, Rochdale.
31 Dec. 1907. Marquis de RUVIGNY, Galway Cottage, Chertsey.
11 Aug. 1888. JOHN WILLIAM RYLAND, F.S.A., Rowington, near Warwick.
20 Jan. 1871. *JOHN PAUL RYLANDS, F.S.A. (*Council*), 96 Bidstone Road, Birkenhead.
21 Jan. 1901. *W. HARRY RYLANDS, F.S.A. (*Council*), South Bank Lodge, 1 Campden Hill Place, Kensington, W.

28 Feb. 1906. *MRS. COLLIS ST. HILL, East Worlington, Morchard Bishop, N. Devon.

19 Nov. 1888.	JOHN SCOTT, Jun., Croft House, Skipton-in-Craven, Yorkshire.
31 Dec. 1903.	Mrs. FANNIE J. PLATT SCOTT, 17 Thayer Street, Rochester, New York, U.S.A.
26 July, 1898.	The Lord SHERBORNE, 9 St. James's Square, S.W.
18 Feb. 1873.	*CONINGSBY C. SIBTHORP, Canwick Hall, Lincoln.
10 Nov. 1873.	*J. CHALLENOR C. SMITH, F.S.A. (care of J. K. Hemp, Probate Registry, Somerset House, W.C.).
3 Oct. 1904.	S. PERCY SMITH, F.R.G.S., Matai-moana, New Plymouth, New Zealand.
5 June, 1874.	HUBERT SMITH-STAINER, Brooklynne, Willes Road, Leamington Spa.

SOCIETIES.

8 Sept. 1874.	*BOSTON ATHENÆUM, Boston, U.S.A. (per Kegan Paul, Trench, Trübner and Co., Dryden House, Gerrard Street, W.).
27 Dec. 1879.	*HISTORICAL SOCIETY OF PENNSYLVANIA, Philadelphia, Pa. (care of B. F. Stevens and Brown, 4 Trafalgar Square, W.C.).
10 Mar. 1906.	*KENT ARCHÆOLOGICAL SOCIETY, The Museum, Maidstone (S. EVANS, Hon. Sec.).
31 Dec. 1904.	*LAW SOCIETY (WALTER M. SINCLAIR, Librarian), Chancery Lane, W.C.
24 Nov. 1883.	*LEHIGH UNIVERSITY, South Bethlehem, Pennsylvania, U.S.A. (per H. Sotheran and Co., 140 Strand, W.C.).
22 Nov. 1900.	*THE LONG ISLAND HISTORICAL SOCIETY (EMMA TOEDTEBERG, Librarian), Brooklyn, New York, U.S.A.
29 Dec. 1893.	*MARYLAND HISTORICAL SOCIETY, Baltimore, Maryland, U.S.A.
5 June, 1886.	MINNESOTA HISTORICAL SOCIETY (WARREN UPHAM, Secretary and Librarian), St. Paul, Minnesota, U.S.A.
7 Sept. 1878.	*NEW ENGLAND HISTORIC GENEALOGICAL SOCIETY, 18 Somerset Street, Boston, U.S.A. (per B. F. Stevens and Brown, 4 Trafalgar Square, W.C.).
20 Oct. 1894.	*NEW YORK GENEALOGICAL AND BIOGRAPHICAL SOCIETY (JOHN R. TOTTEN, Librarian), 226 West 58th Street, New York, U.S.A.
22 July, 1893.	*NEW YORK HISTORICAL SOCIETY (ROBERT H. KELLY, Librarian), 170 Second Avenue, New York, U.S.A.
29 Jan. 1878.	*ROYAL HISTORICAL SOCIETY, 6 and 7 South Square, Gray's Inn, W.C.
20 Jan. 1871.	ROYAL IRISH ACADEMY, 19 Dawson Street, Dublin.
22 Mar. 1871.	*SOCIETY OF ANTIQUARIES OF LONDON, Burlington House, W.
12 Nov. 1883.	SOCIETY OF ANTIQUARIES OF NEWCASTLE-UPON-TYNE, The Castle, Newcastle-upon-Tyne.
7 June, 1872.	*SOMERSETSHIRE ARCHÆOLOGICAL SOCIETY, Museum, Taunton.
21 Feb. 1906.	SURREY ARCHÆOLOGICAL SOCIETY, Castle Arch, Guildford (MONTAGUE S. GIUSEPPI, F.S.A., Hon. Sec.).
13 Mar. 1906.	*SUSSEX ARCHÆOLOGICAL SOCIETY, Lewes.
30 Jan. 1888.	*WISCONSIN STATE HISTORICAL SOCIETY, Madison, U.S.A. (per H. Sotheran and Co., 140 Strand, W.C.).

7 Oct. 1879.   *YALE UNIVERSITY, New Haven, Connecticut, U.S.A. (care of E. G. Allen, 14 Grape Street, Shaftesbury Avenue, W.C.).
12 May, 1894. *YORKSHIRE ARCHÆOLOGICAL SOCIETY (the Hon. Librarian, 10 Park Street, Leeds).

17 Apr. 1886. *Captain BELLINGHAM A. SOMERVILLE, F.S.A., Clermont, Rathnew, co. Wicklow.
7 Mar. 1898.   *Colonel HERBERT R. H. SOUTHAM, V.D., F.S.A., Innellan, Shrewsbury.
18 Oct. 1894. Colonel JOHN P. STEEL, R.E., F.R.G.S., Nenehurst, Park Road, Surbiton.
30 May, 1884. Rev. FRANCIS STERRY, Chapel Cleeve, Washford, Taunton.
10 Oct. 1884. *EDWARD STONE, F.S.A., 5 Finsbury Circus, E.C.

8 July, 1895. Rev. THOMAS TAYLOR, M.A., F.S.A., The Vicarage, St. Just in Penwith R.S.O., Penzance, Cornwall.
2 Nov. 1887.   Mrs. ARTHUR CECIL TEMPEST, Broughton Hall, Skipton-in-Craven, Yorkshire.
12 May, 1894. *CHARLES M. TENISON, M.R.I.A., F.R.S.A.I., Carisbrook Cottage, West Byfleet, Surrey.
13 Apr. 1897. *JOHN S. TILNEY, 77 Main Street, Orange, New Jersey, U.S.A.
5 Nov. 1896.   WM. ASHETON TONGE, Staneclyffe, Disley, Cheshire.
9 July, 1887. *JOHN HARVEY TREAT, Lawrence, Massachusetts, U.S.A. (books to care of Harvard College Library, U.S.A.).
8 July, 1895. TRINITY COLLEGE, DUBLIN (T. K. ABBOTT, Librarian).
16 Mar. 1871. *JOSEPH HERBERT TRITTON, 4 Lowndes Square, S.W.
30 May, 1895. Lieut.-Col. W. H. TURTON, R.E., D.S.O., Harley House, Clifton Down, Bristol.

27 Jan. 1899. ULSTER KING OF ARMS, THE OFFICE OF, The Castle, Dublin (care of E. Ponsonby, 116 Grafton Street, Dublin).

9 Jan. 1875.   H. F. J. VAUGHAN, The Rosery, near Ashburton, Devon.
28 Feb. 1896. *Major C. L. VAUGHAN-ARBUCKLE (3rd Battalion West Yorkshire Regiment), Stawell House, Richmond, Surrey.
10 June, 1869. *Sir HENRY M. VAVASOUR, Bt., F.S.A., 11 Stanhope Gardens, S.W.

18 Dec. 1874. *HENRY WAGNER, M.A., F.S.A., 13 Half Moon Street, Piccadilly, W.
31 Oct. 1900. *WALFORD BROTHERS, 6 New Oxford Street, London, W.C.

14 Mar. 1906.	*DUNCAN WARRAND, M.A., F.S.A., Caledonian Club, 30 Charles Street, St. James's, S.W.
31 Dec. 1907.	Rev. D R. WEBSTER, O.S.B., Downside Abbey, Stratton-on-the-Fosse, Somerset.
18 May, 1870.	*W. H. WELDON, C.V.O., F.S.A., Norroy King-of-Arms, College of Arms, Queen Victoria Street, E.C.
17 Mar. 1900.	FRANCIS WEBB, Callingwood Hall, Tatenhill, near Burton-on-Trent, Staffordshire.
3 Mar. 1900.	CHARLES A. WHITE, New Haven, Connecticut, U.S.A.
31 Dec. 1903.	*JOHN B. WHITE, 616 East 36th Street, Kansas City, Missouri, U.S.A.
31 Dec. 1903.	Major-General Sir FRANCIS REGINALD WINGATE, K.C.B., K.C.M.G., D.S.O., D.C.L., Sirdar and Governor-General of the Sudan, The Palace, Khartoum.
5 Nov. 1892.	PHILIP JOHN WORSLEY, Rodney Lodge, Clifton, Bristol.
22 Nov. 1895.	*YORK, THE DEAN AND CHAPTER OF, Minster Gates, York.

Annual Subscription (payable in advance and due on the 1st of January in each year): One Guinea. Ditto Register Section: One Guinea. Entrance Fee: Half-a-Guinea.

Persons whose Subscriptions are due are requested to forward them to W. BRUCE BANNERMAN, Esq., F.S.A., Treasurer, at The Lindens, Sydenham Road, Croydon, Surrey, who will also receive Subscriptions for the Register Section.

Persons wishing to join the HARLEIAN SOCIETY should apply to Mr. BANNERMAN at the above address.

The Publications of the Society which are in print can only be obtained from the Publishers, Messrs. MITCHELL HUGHES and CLARKE, 140 Wardour Street, W.

VOL.
1.—THE VISITATION OF LONDON IN 1568, BY R. COOKE. Edited by J. J. HOWARD, Esq., LL.D., F.S.A., and G. J. ARMYTAGE, Esq., F.S.A. 1869
2.—THE VISITATION OF LEICESTERSHIRE IN 1619, BY CAMDEN. Edited by J. FETHERSTON, Esq., F.S.A. 1870
3.—THE VISITATION OF RUTLAND IN 1618-19, BY CAMDEN; and other Descents of Families not in the Visitation. Edited by G. J. ARMYTAGE, Esq., F.S.A. 1870
4.—THE VISITATIONS OF NOTTINGHAMSHIRE IN 1569 AND 1614, WITH MANY OTHER DESCENTS OF THE COUNTY. Edited by GEORGE W. MARSHALL, Esq., LL.D., F.S.A. 1871
5.—THE VISITATIONS OF OXFORDSHIRE IN 1566 BY W. HARVEY, 1574 BY R. LEE, AND 1634 BY J. PHILPOTT AND W. RYLEY; WITH THE GATHERINGS OF OXFORDSHIRE, COLLECTED BY R. LEE IN 1574. Edited and Annotated by W. H. TURNER, Esq. 1871
6.—THE VISITATION OF DEVONSHIRE IN 1620. Edited by the Rev. F. T. COLBY, D.D., F.R.S. 1872
7.—THE VISITATION OF CUMBERLAND IN 1615, BY R. ST. GEORGE. Edited by J. FETHERSTON, Esq., F.S.A. 1872
8.—LE NEVE'S PEDIGREES OF THE KNIGHTS MADE BY KING CHARLES II., KING JAMES II., KING WILLIAM III., AND QUEEN MARY, WILLIAM ALONE, AND QUEEN ANNE. Edited by GEORGE W. MARSHALL, Esq., LL.D., F.S.A. 1873
9.—THE VISITATION OF CORNWALL, 1620. Edited by Colonel VIVIAN and Dr. H. H. DRAKE. [*The above are all out of Print.*
10.—THE REGISTERS OF WESTMINSTER ABBEY, 1655—1875. Edited by Colonel CHESTER, D.C.L., LL.D. 21s. 1875
11.—THE VISITATION OF SOMERSETSHIRE IN 1623. Edited by the Rev. F. T. COLBY, D.D., F.S.A. 1876
[*Out of Print.*
12.—THE VISITATION OF WARWICKSHIRE IN 1619. Edited by JOHN FETHERSTON, Esq., F.S.A. 1877
[*Out of Print.*
13.—THE VISITATIONS OF ESSEX IN 1552, 1558. 1612, AND 1634. Part I. Edited by WALTER C. METCALFE, Esq., F.S.A. 1878
[*Out of Print.*
14.—THE VISITATIONS OF ESSEX, consisting of Miscellaneous Pedigrees, and Berry's Pedigrees. Part II. With general Index. Edited by WALTER C. METCALFE, Esq., F.S.A. 21s. 1879
15.—THE VISITATION OF LONDON, 1633-4. Vol. I. Edited by J. J. HOWARD, Esq., LL.D., F.S.A., and Colonel CHESTER, D.C.L., LL.D. 21s. 1880
16.—THE VISITATION OF YORKSHIRE IN 1564. Edited by the Rev. C. B. NORCLIFFE, M.A. 21s. 1881
17.—THE VISITATION OF LONDON, 1633-4. Vol. II. Edited by J. J. HOWARD, Esq., LL.D., F.S.A. 21s. 1883
18.—THE VISITATION OF CHESHIRE IN 1580. Edited by J. PAUL RYLANDS, Esq., F.S.A. 21s. 1882
19.—THE VISITATIONS OF BEDFORDSHIRE IN 1566, 1582, AND 1634. Edited by F. A. BLAYDES, Esq. 21s. 1884
20.—THE VISITATION OF DORSETSHIRE IN 1623, BY ST. GEORGE AND LENNARD AS DEPUTIES TO CAMDEN. Edited by J. PAUL RYLANDS, Esq., F.S.A. 21s. 1885
21.—THE VISITATION OF GLOUCESTERSHIRE IN 1623, BY CHITTING AND PHILLIPOT AS DEPUTIES TO CAMDEN. Edited by Sir JOHN MACLEAN, F.S.A., and W. C. HEANE, Esq., M.R.C.S. 21s. 1885
22.—THE VISITATIONS OF HERTFORDSHIRE IN 1572 AND 1634. Edited by WALTER C. METCALFE, Esq.. F.S.A. 21s. 1886
23.—MARRIAGE LICENCES : Dean and Chapter of Westminster, 1558 to 1699; Vicar-General of the Archbishop of Canterbury, 1660 to 1679. Extracted by the late Colonel CHESTER. D.C.L. Edited by GEORGE J. ARMYTAGE, Esq., F.S.A. 21s. 1886
24.—MARRIAGE LICENCES : Faculty Office of the Archbishop of Canterbury, 1543 to 1869. 21s. 1886
25.—MARRIAGE LICENCES : Bishop of London, Vol. I., 1520 to 1610. 1887 } Sold only in a
26.—MARRIAGE LICENCES : Bishop of London, Vol. II., 1611 to 1828. 1887 } Set for £2 : 2s.
27.—THE VISITATION OF WORCESTERSHIRE IN 1569. Edited by WILLIAM P. W. PHILLIMORE, Esq., M.A., B.C.L. 21s. 1888

WORKS PUBLISHED—continued.

VOL.
28.—THE VISITATION OF SHROPSHIRE, 1623; with Additions. Part I. Edited by GEORGE GRAZEBROOK, Esq., F.S.A., and J. PAUL RYLANDS, Esq., F.S.A. 1889
29.—THE VISITATION OF SHROPSHIRE, 1623; with Additions. Part II. Edited by GEORGE GRAZEBROOK, Esq., F.S.A., and J. PAUL RYLANDS, Esq., F.S.A. 1889
(Sold only in a Set for £2:2s.)
30.—MARRIAGE LICENCES: Vicar-General of Archbishop of Canterbury, 1679 to 1687. Edited by GEORGE J. ARMYTAGE, Esq., F.S.A. 1890
31.—MARRIAGE LICENCES: Vicar-General of Archbishop of Canterbury, 1687 to 1694. 1890
(Sold only in a Set for £2:2s.)
32.—THE VISITATIONS OF NORFOLK IN 1563, 1589, AND 1613. Edited by WALTER RYE, Esq. 21s. 1891
33.—MARRIAGE LICENCES: Vicar-General of the Archbishop of Canterbury, Vol. I., 1660 to 1668. Edited by GEORGE J. ARMYTAGE, Esq., F.S.A. 1892
34.—MARRIAGE LICENCES: Vicar-General of the Archbishop of Canterbury, Vol. II, 1669 to 1679. 1892
(Sold only in a Set for £2:2s.)
[N.B. Volumes 33 and 34 contain the entries not extracted by Colonel CHESTER: see Volume 23.]
35.—HAMPSHIRE ALLEGATIONS FOR MARRIAGE LICENCES ISSUED BY THE BISHOP OF WINCHESTER, 1689—1837. Vol. I. Edited by W. J. C. MOENS, Esq., F.S.A. 1893
36.—HAMPSHIRE ALLEGATIONS FOR MARRIAGE LICENCES ISSUED BY THE BISHOP OF WINCHESTER, 1689—1837. Vol. II. 1893
(Sold only in a Set for £2:2s.)
37.—HUNTER'S FAMILIÆ MINORUM GENTIUM. Vol. I. Edited by JOHN W. CLAY, Esq., F.S.A. 1894
38.—HUNTER'S FAMILIÆ MINORUM GENTIUM. Vol. II. 1895 [*Out of Print.*]
39.—HUNTER'S FAMILIÆ MINORUM GENTIUM. Vol. III. 1895 [*Out of Print.*]
40.—HUNTER'S FAMILIÆ MINORUM GENTIUM. Vol. IV., with INDEX to the whole. 21s. 1896
41.—THE VISITATIONS OF CAMBRIDGESHIRE IN 1575 AND 1619. Edited by JOHN W. CLAY, Esq., F.S.A. 21s. 1897
42.—THE VISITATION OF KENT IN 1619. Edited by ROBERT HOVENDEN, Esq., F.S.A. 21s. 1898
43.—THE VISITATIONS OF SURREY IN 1530, 1572, AND 1623. Edited by W. BRUCE BANNERMAN, Esq., F.S.A. 21s. 1899
44.—MUSGRAVE'S GENERAL NOMENCLATOR AND OBITUARY. Edited by Sir GEORGE J. ARMYTAGE, Bt., F.S.A. Vol. I. 1899
45.—MUSGRAVE'S GENERAL NOMENCLATOR AND OBITUARY. Vol. II. 1900
46.—MUSGRAVE'S GENERAL NOMENCLATOR AND OBITUARY. Vol. III. 1900
47.—MUSGRAVE'S GENERAL NOMENCLATOR AND OBITUARY. Vol. IV. 1900
48.—MUSGRAVE'S GENERAL NOMENCLATOR AND OBITUARY. Vol. V. 1901
49.—MUSGRAVE'S GENERAL NOMENCLATOR AND OBITUARY. Vol. VI. 1901
(Sold only in a Set for £4:4s.)
50.—LINCOLNSHIRE PEDIGREES. Vol. I. Edited by the Rev. A. R. MADDISON, M.A., F.S.A. 1902
51.—LINCOLNSHIRE PEDIGREES. Vol. II. Edited by the Rev. A. R. MADDISON, M.A., F.S.A. 1903
52.—LINCOLNSHIRE PEDIGREES. Vol. III. Edited by the Rev. A. R. MADDISON, M.A., F.S.A. 1904. And 55, Vol. IV., with Index to the whole. 1906
(Sold only in a Set for £4:4s.)
53.—THE VISITATIONS OF SUSSEX IN 1530 AND 1633-4. Edited by W. BRUCE BANNERMAN, Esq., F.S.A. 21s. 1905
54.—THE VISITATION OF KENT IN 1663-1668 BY SIR EDWARD BYSSHE, KNT., CLARENCIEUX. Edited by Sir GEORGE J. ARMYTAGE, Bt., F.S.A. 21s. 1906
55.—LINCOLNSHIRE PEDIGREES. Vol. IV., with INDEX to the whole. Edited by the Rev. A. R. MADDISON, M.A., F.S.A. [Sold only in a Set with Vols. I., II., and III.] 1906
56.—THE VISITATION OF BERKSHIRE IN 1532, 1566, 1623, AND 1664-66. Edited by W. HARRY RYLANDS, Esq., F.S.A. Vol. I. 21s. 1907
57.—THE VISITATION OF BERKSHIRE. Edited by W. HARRY RYLANDS, Esq., F.S.A. Vol. II. 21s. 1908
THE VISITATION OF BUCKINGHAMSHIRE IN 1634. Edited by W. HARRY RYLANDS, Esq., F.S.A. [*In progress.*]

N.B.—Very few copies of the Publications remain.

PROSPECTIVE PUBLICATIONS.

THE VISITATIONS OF HAMPSHIRE IN 1531, 1575, AND 1622.
THE VISITATION OF GLOUCESTERSHIRE IN 1533, BY BENOLTE.
THE VISITATION OF HEREFORDSHIRE IN 1634.
THE VISITATION OF WORCESTERSHIRE IN 1634.

WORKS PUBLISHED.

REGISTER SECTION.

VOL.

1.—THE REGISTERS OF ST. PETER'S, CORNHILL, LONDON. PART I., A.D. 1538 to 1666. Edited by GRANVILLE LEVESON GOWER, Esq., F.S.A.   1877

2.—THE REGISTERS OF CANTERBURY CATHEDRAL. Edited by ROBERT HOVENDEN, Esq., F.S.A.   1878

3.—THE REGISTERS OF ST. DIONIS BACKCHURCH, LONDON. Edited by Colonel J. L. CHESTER, D.C.L., LL.D.   1878

4.—THE REGISTERS OF ST. PETER'S, CORNHILL, LONDON. PART II., A.D. 1666 to 1754. Edited by GRANVILLE LEVESON GOWER, Esq., F.S.A.   1879

5.—THE REGISTERS OF ST. MARY ALDERMARY, LONDON. Edited by Colonel J. L. CHESTER, D.C.L., LL.D.   1880

6.—THE REGISTERS OF ST. THOMAS APOSTLE, LONDON. Edited by Colonel J. L. CHESTER, D.C.L., LL.D.   1881

7.—THE REGISTERS OF ST. MICHAEL, CORNHILL, LONDON. Partly Edited by Colonel J. L. CHESTER, D.C.L., LL.D.   1882

8.—THE REGISTERS OF ST. ANTHOLIN, BUDGE ROW; AND ST. JOHN BAPTIST ON WALLBROOK, LONDON.   1883

9.—THE REGISTERS OF ST. JAMES, CLERKENWELL, LONDON. Vol. I.— CHRISTENINGS, 1551 to 1700. Edited by ROBERT HOVENDEN, Esq., F.S.A.   1884

10.—THE REGISTERS OF ST. JAMES, CLERKENWELL, LONDON. Vol. II.— CHRISTENINGS, 1701 to 1754. Edited by ROBERT HOVENDEN, Esq., F.S.A.   1885

[The above are all out of Print.

11.—*THE MARRIAGE REGISTERS OF ST. GEORGE, HANOVER SQUARE, LONDON. Vol. I., 1725 to 1787. Edited by JOHN H. CHAPMAN, Esq., M.A., F.S.A.   1886

12.—THE REGISTERS OF STOURTON, CO. WILTS, FROM 1570 TO 1800. Edited by the Rev. JOHN HENRY ELLIS, M.A.   1887
[Out of Print.

13.—THE REGISTERS OF ST. JAMES, CLERKENWELL, LONDON. Vol. III.— MARRIAGES, 1551 to 1754. Edited by ROBERT HOVENDEN, Esq., F.S.A.   1887
[Out of Print.

14.—*THE MARRIAGE REGISTERS OF ST. GEORGE, HANOVER SQUARE, LONDON. Vol. II., 1788 to 1809. Edited by JOHN H. CHAPMAN, Esq., M.A., F.S.A.   1888

15.—THE REGISTER OF BAPTISMS AND MARRIAGES AT ST. GEORGE'S CHAPEL, MAY FAIR, 1740 to 1754. Edited by GEORGE J. ARMYTAGE, Esq., F.S.A. 21s.   1889

16.—THE REGISTERS OF THE PARISH CHURCH OF KENSINGTON, 1539 to 1675. Edited by Dr. F. N. MACNAMARA and A. STORY-MASKELYNE, Esq. 21s.   1890

17.—THE REGISTERS OF ST. JAMES, CLERKENWELL, LONDON. Vol. IV.— BURIALS, 1551 to 1665. Edited by ROBERT HOVENDEN, Esq., F.S.A. 21s.   1891

18.—THE REGISTERS AND MONUMENTAL INSCRIPTIONS OF CHARTERHOUSE CHAPEL, 1670 to 1854. Edited by Dr. FRANCIS COLLINS.   1892
[Out of Print.

19.—THE REGISTERS OF ST JAMES, CLERKENWELL, LONDON. Vol. V.— BURIALS, 1666 to 1719. Edited by ROBERT HOVENDEN, Esq., F.S.A.   1893
[Out of Print.

20.—THE REGISTERS OF ST. JAMES, CLERKENWELL, LONDON. Vol. VI.— BURIALS, 1720 to 1754. Edited by ROBERT HOVENDEN, Esq., F.S.A. 21s.   1894

21.—THE REGISTERS OF CHRIST CHURCH, NEWGATE STREET, LONDON, 1538 to 1754. Edited by WILLOUGHBY A. LITTLEDALE, Esq., M.A., F.S.A. 21s.   1895

REGISTERS—*continued*.

VOL.
22.—*THE MARRIAGE REGISTERS OF ST. GEORGE, HANOVER SQUARE, 1810 to 1823. Vol. III. Edited by GEORGE J. ARMYTAGE, Esq., F.S.A. 1896
23.—THE REGISTERS OF DURHAM CATHEDRAL, 1609 to 1896. Edited by GEORGE J. ARMYTAGE, Esq., F.S.A. 21s. 1897
24.—*THE MARRIAGE REGISTERS OF ST. GEORGE, HANOVER SQUARE, 1824 to 1837. Vol. IV. Edited by GEORGE J. ARMYTAGE, Esq., F.S.A. 1897
25.—THE EARLY REGISTER OF ST. MARTIN IN THE FIELDS, 1550 to 1619. Edited by THOMAS MASON, Esq. 21s. 1898
26.—THE REGISTERS OF ST. PAUL'S CATHEDRAL. Edited by JOHN W. CLAY, Esq., F.S.A. 21s. 1899
27.—THE REGISTERS OF BATH ABBEY. Vol. I.—CHRISTENINGS and MARRIAGES, 1569 to 1800. Edited by ARTHUR J. JEWERS, Esq. 1900 } Sold only in a Set £2:2s.
28.—THE REGISTERS OF BATH ABBEY. Vol. II.—BURIALS, 1569 to 1800, with INDEX to the whole. Edited by ARTHUR J. JEWERS, Esq. 1901
29.—THE REGISTERS OF ST. VEDAST, AND ST. MICHAEL LE QUERN, FOSTER LANE. Vol. I.—CHRISTENINGS, 1558 to 1836. Edited by WILLOUGHBY A. LITTLEDALE, Esq., M.A., F.S.A. 1902 } Sold only in a Set for £2:2s.
30.—THE REGISTERS OF ST. VEDAST, AND ST. MICHAEL LE QUERN, FOSTER LANE. Vol. II.—MARRIAGES and BURIALS. Edited by WILLOUGHBY A. LITTLEDALE, Esq., M.A., F.S.A. 1903
31.—THE REGISTERS OF ST. HELEN'S, BISHOPSGATE STREET, LONDON. Edited by W. BRUCE BANNERMAN, Esq., F.S.A. 21s. 1904
32.—THE REGISTERS OF ST. MARTIN OUTWICH, THREADNEEDLE STREET, LONDON. Edited by W. BRUCE BANNERMAN, Esq., F.S.A. 21s. 1905
33.—THE REGISTERS OF ST. PAUL, COVENT GARDEN, LONDON. Vol. I. } Christenings from 1653—1837. Edited by the Rev. W. H. HUNT. 1906 } Sold only in a Set at 21s. per Vol.
34.—THE REGISTERS OF ST. PAUL, COVENT GARDEN, LONDON. Vol. II. 1906
35.—THE REGISTERS OF ST. PAUL, COVENT GARDEN, LONDON. Vol. III. MARRIAGES. 21s. 1907
36.—THE REGISTERS OF ST. PAUL, COVENT GARDEN, LONDON, Vol. IV. BURIALS. [*In progress.*]

THE REGISTERS OF ST. BENET AND ST. PETER, PAUL'S WHARF, LONDON. Edited by WILLOUGHBY A. LITTLEDALE, Esq., M.A., F.S.A.
[*In progress.*]

[* Vols. 11, 14, 22, and 24 will be sold only in a Set for £4 4s.]

N.B.—Very few copies of the Registers remain.

PROSPECTIVE PUBLICATIONS.
THE REGISTERS OF ST. SEPULCHRE, LONDON.
THE REGISTERS OF THE CHAPELS ROYAL.
THE REGISTERS OF ST. JAMES, GARLICKHITHE.

The Publications of the Register Section will be supplied to Subscribers on payment of an extra Subscription of One Guinea, and can only be obtained from the Publishers, Messrs. MITCHELL HUGHES and CLARKE, 140 Wardour Street, W., at the prices named.

Forms of Application for Membership, and all other particulars, may be obtained by applying to W. BRUCE BANNERMAN, Esq., F.S.A., The Lindens, Sydenham Road, Croydon, Surrey.